HANDBOOK
OF
AMERICAN-JEWISH
LITERATURE

HANDBOOK
OF
AMERICAN-JEWISH
LITERATURE

An Analytical Guide
to
Topics, Themes, and Sources

LEWIS FRIED
Editor-in-Chief

Gene Brown,
Jules Chametzky,
and
Louis Harap
Advisory Editors

GREENWOOD PRESS
New York • Westport, Connecticut • London

Library of Congress Cataloging-in-Publication Data

Handbook of American-Jewish literature.

  Bibliography: p.
  Includes index.
  1. Jewish literature—United States—History and
criticism. 2. American literature—Jewish authors—
History and criticism. 3. Yiddish literature—United
States—History and criticism. 4. Judaism—United
States. 5. Jews in literature. I. Fried, Lewis.
II. Brown, Gene. III. Chametzky, Jules. IV. Harap,
Louis.
PS153.J4H365 1988   810'.9'8924   87-292
ISBN 0-313-24593-2 (lib. bdg. : alk. paper)

Library of Congress Catalog Card Number: 87-292
ISBN: 0-313-24593-2

First published in 1988

Greenwood Press, Inc.
88 Post Road West, Westport, Connecticut 06881

Printed in the United States of America

The paper used in this book complies with the
Permanent Paper Standard issued by the National
Information Standards Organization (Z39.48-1984).

10 9 8 7 6 5 4 3 2 1

Copyright Acknowledgments

Grateful acknowledgment is given for permission to quote the following sources:

From *Mr. Sammler's Planet* by Saul Bellow. Copyright © 1969, 1970 by Saul Bellow. Reprinted
by permission of Viking Penguin Inc.

Reprinted with permission of Macmillan Publishing Company from *After Auschwitz* by Richard
L. Rubenstein. Copyright © 1966 by Richard L. Rubenstein.

From *The Promised Land* by Mary Antin. Copyright 1912 by Houghton Mifflin Company.
Copyright renewed 1940 by Mary Antin. Foreword: Copyright © 1969 by Oscar Handlin.
Reprinted by permission of Houghton Mifflin Company.

From *Judaism as a Civilization* by Mordecai Kaplan. Copyright 1934, given by Ira Eisenstein,
the Jewish Publication Society, the Reconstructionist Press, Philadelphia and New York. 5741/
1981.

To the memory of my father,
Abraham Isaac Fried

Contents

Acknowledgments

I could not have completed this book without the advice and encouragement of Jules Chametzky, Louis Harap, and Gene Brown. Their interest in this project and their warm, forthcoming suggestions helped make this book as informative as possible.

I am grateful for the assistance of Herbert Hochhauser, Director of Jewish Studies at Kent State University, who served as a German language and literature consultant. In addition, I want to thank Sanford Marovitz, my colleague in the English Department; Lubomyr Wynar of the School of Library Science; and Michael Cole of Interlibrary Loan for their crucial support. Rita Locke, Rachela Morrison, Laura Yeager, and Mark Moriarty served as research assistants and selflessly helped proofread many of the essays. Wilma Crawford was indispensable: her work aided every aspect of the manuscript's preparation. The encouragement provided by Dean E. Wenninger of Kent State University's Office of Research was most welcome.

Special thanks to Abraham Peck, Director of the American Jewish Archives; Fannie Zelcer, Archivist at the American Jewish Archives; Ida Cohen Selavan of Hebrew Union College's library; Jean Loeb Lettofsky of the Cleveland College of Jewish Studies' library, and Morris U. Schappes. I greatly appreciate the help of Professors Ronald Crawford, Doris Kadish, Wayne Kvam, Douglas Radcliff-Umstead, and Emil Sattler of Kent State, and Igina Tattoni of the University of Rome who answered my questions about European languages. Thanks also to Helga Kaplan of the Honors College at Kent State and to Kent State's reference librarians.

Also at Kent State, I am indebted to Barbara Brock, who helped block out the topics at the project's beginning; to Helen Daly of Ethnic Studies and Marylee Richards of the English Department who helped keep the work on track; and thanks also to Thomas and Margaret Magnani, Peter and Helen Benson, and Anne Carver who offered their help whenever needed.

Cynthia Harris, Arlene Belzer, and Marilyn Brownstein, my editors at Greenwood Press, encouraged this work from the start and made my own labors easier.

I would be remiss if I did not thank two Jewish communities, one in Israel and the other in the German Democratic Republic, for sharing with me a distinct Jewish way of being, a demonstration of Jewishness that illuminated American-Jewish life. To the people of *Maoz Chaim*, and of the *Israelitische Religionsgemeinde* of Leipzig, thank you.

HANDBOOK
OF
AMERICAN-JEWISH
LITERATURE

Introduction

Lewis Fried

The purpose of this book is twofold: to acquaint the general reader with the major subjects and themes of American-Jewish literature, and to renew the scholar's familiarity with this material and its interpretation. The focus of this book is, by and large, on the literary culture produced by Eastern-European Jewish immigrants and their children as they shaped, and were shaped in turn by, American civilization.

We are far from the time when the pioneering assessments of American-Jewish creativity in *The Menorah Journal*, the early bibliographies of American Judaica in *The American Jewish Year Book*, and Joseph Mersand's citations in *Traditions in American Literature: A Study of Jewish Characters and Authors* (1939) served as both a summary and a *summa* of modern American-Jewish literature. By necessity, contemporary inquiry is specific and specialized so that it is difficult for a reader to get a sense of the larger shape of American-Jewish literature. As a result, there is a need for a work that discusses this literary culture so that its achievements are readily made known to reader and scholar. And again, there is a need for a work that presents both traditional and modern questions asked about American-Jewish literature so that the historical continuity of criticism is preserved.

Topically, this book covers the rise of modern American-Jewish letters: literature, theology, and cultural meditation from approximately 1880 to the present. Each contributor has approached a subject from his or her perspective so that the interpretation of the work is seen to have a development of its own. For example, several contributors study literary movements and traditions that have been critically ignored or slighted. Kathryn Hellerstein writes about the making of women's Yiddish poetry. R. Barbara Gitenstein discusses the creation of American-Jewish poetry and the achievements of its women poets. Ellen Schiff examines American-Jewish drama with an eye toward the emerg-

ence of the Jewish woman as character and author. Discussing an often neglected aspect of American Zionism, Rabbi David Polish studies the impact of
Reform thinkers.

In addition, there are essays that appraise the categories and history that are
germane to discussions of American-Jewish expression, such as cultural and
literary identity; the American uses of diaspora; and reconstruction in theology.
David Martin Fine, Bonnie K. Lyons, and I write about American-Jewish fiction
from 1880 to the present—each of us focusing on a chronologically relevant
sense of the American-Jewish self and community. Hannah Berliner Fischthal
studies the range of Yiddish criticism in America. Joseph C. Landis discusses
the hopes America held for Yiddish writers. Rabbi Arnold Jacob Wolf analyzes
the major thinkers of contemporary American-Jewish theology and their meditations about a Judaism in development. Steven J. Rubin explores the creation
of the American-Jewish persona in autobiography.

Finally, there are essays about American-Jewish letters in its relationship with
and to other cultures and literatures. Dorothy S. Bilik studies American-Jewish
Holocaust fiction. Saul Friedman discusses the historiography of the Holocaust.
Asher Z. Milbauer describes the image of Russia in American-Jewish literature.
Sanford Marovitz details the image of America in American-Jewish fiction.
Gershon Shaked, in his comparative study of German-Jewish and American-
Jewish letters, is concerned with dual identities and their role in producing a
modern Jewish literature. Sepp L. Tiefenthaler charts the reception of American-
Jewish fiction in Germanic-speaking countries and in addition has provided a
guide to criticism in Western Europe and Great Britain.

The book strives to embrace as many relevant critical concerns as possible.
The contributions range from considerations of traditions—religious, linguistic,
and social—and their appropriation by various writers and groups, to essays
dealing with the capacity of Jewish theology and concepts to address a singular
culture. The text, consequently, presents American-Jewish letters as an entity,
one that has a substantial unity made possible, paradoxically, by numerous
allegiances: *Yidishkayt*, Zionism, the heritage of diaspora life, and American
promises of an egalitarian, upwardly mobile society. Moreover, the book balances historically wide inquiry with studies of particular, significant movements
so that American-Jewish culture is seen in its concrete as well as general dimensions. For example, the section on Yiddish writing moves from the development of the American Yiddish literary imagination to a women's Yiddish
poetic; a discussion of the experimental nature of Jewish theology is comple-
mented by a study of American Reform thinkers' efforts to create a practical,
intentional Jewish state. As a result, the essays do—and should—overlap, so
that American-Jewish culture is not unnecessarily partitioned and simplified, but
instead is approached as a whole, and from convergent perspectives. The essays,
though valuable independently, constitute a unity and the book is meant to be
read with this in mind.

II

Each essay in this book is built upon bibliographic material. The Bibliography appended to every piece is a listing of texts cited in short form in the Notes. A For Further Reading list, appended where necessary, cites those works that should guide the reader's study.

A note about transliterations is in order. Words and phrases in German, Yiddish, and Hebrew appear in this book. In certain instances, one writer will refer to a word in Yiddish that another writer will cite in Hebrew. Since these are legitimate and consistent practices, I have not changed them. However, I have standardized variant transliterations of the same word cited in one language in the same essay—provided it is not a direct quote.

Nonetheless, it must be kept in mind that there is no customary standard for Yiddish-English and Hebrew-English transliteration. For example, in matters of Yiddish names, there are often several legitimate variants—found in common speech, journals, books, and the Library of Congress. The spellings Iceland, Eisland, and Ayzland are different transliterations of one poet's last name. In cases like these, uniformity would not be helpful. I have preserved the uniformity of the family name within *each* essay—especially in the face of variant uses in English-language articles. However, the first mention of the last name in every essay is provided with its variant form if it appears as such in another essay.

Regarding capitalization, since Yiddish and Hebrew have no initial capitals for proper nouns, only the initial letter of the first word of a title or book has been raised unless the writer prefers otherwise; similarly, an initial capital begins a single transliterated word, unless the writer insists otherwise. Again, I have made such usage consistent for the essay. Finally, distinctions in capitalization have been kept for words that play specific theological as well as secular roles in the text such as Messiah (referring to Jewish eschatology) and messiah (indicating a representative of a salvific political movement). Another example is *Midrash* in its canonical use, as opposed to *midrash* in the modern literary sense—a running commentary on any text. Here, as in other cases of variant capitalizations, I have tried to remain faithful to the contributor's intention rather than blur understandable differences. Again, for example, I have preserved the author's decision regarding the capitalization of Orthodox and orthodox.

III

American-Jewish letters has passed from being a realistic enterprise depicting the bewildering travails of immigrant Jews in a secular city to a literature that defined and represented the crisis of modernity: the need to construct a post-Holocaust humane society. No longer could classical political notions about virtues made possible by the city be professed. As an outsider—politically, religiously, and historically—the Jewish writer who attempted to use these vantage points of marginality to maintain his identity and yet promote an ethic based on universalism gave modern letters *the* relevant human drama. The recovery of man's humanizing ethical powers concerned with creation and compassion was seen as the beginning of a new politics. By insisting upon the sanctity of community, this literature depicted the Jew's struggle as a rescue and vindication of humanity in general.

To a great extent, this labor has lost its tragic immediacy—and perhaps its significance—for a number of reasons. They range from the exhaustion of the concept of alienation as the guiding thesis of social analysis, to a generation of American-Jewish authors whose identities and lives are experienced as "open" and without constraint, to a new post-social novel and criticism unconcerned with public problems, and finally to the conviction that the State of Israel is an indubitable guarantee of the psychological security of Jews in other lands. Consequently, the contemporary American-Jewish writer must discover if the hyphenated identity that has nourished a previous generation's work can be turned to yet other uses. What kind of identity is now emerging in a nation where Jews are not routinely torn by several loyalties but sustained by them? What culture is in the making that will enhance and examine this relationship of loyalties? Will there be a unique domain of experience that can sustain the modern writer so that he can bring to bear the fullness of his heritage on the present?

These questions can only be answered by reinterpreting the order of the past, one changing and changed by the present.[1] Amidst debates over what constitutes the identity of the American-Jewish community and its literature, the binding character of the controversy remains the problem itself—as if *the* distinctive characteristic of American-Jewish cultural life were its continuous, obsessive evaluation of its commitment to the *Yidishkayt* of Eastern Europe (memory) and to the instruments of American progress (reason). This book explores the literary ways the American-Jewish past has been depicted (or invented), creating consequences for the present—consequences that are enacted within the present.

IV

In 1854, for the first issue of his newspaper, *The Israelite*, Isaac Mayer Wise printed his recent sermon dealing with the spirit of modern Judaism and the character of the American nation. In this address entitled "The Fourth of July," he contended that "Our religion and republicanism are too closely identified to be separated from each other." He added that "the principles of the constitution of the United States are copied from the words of Moses and the prophets." The relationship between the Jewish prophetic legacy and the concerns of American democracy is quickly mentioned: " 'Thou shalt love thy neighbor as thyself '—'There shall be one law for you and for the stranger who sojourns among you'—'Ye shall love the stranger for ye have been strangers in the land of Egypt.' "[2]

Delivered far from the awesome New England forests, Wise's speech to his

Cincinnati congregation also appeals to the essential relationship that the Puritans believed made them new Israelites. Wise's preaching invokes the sentiment of otherness, of being apart spiritually and physically from the centers of worldliness, yet holding fast in a mission to transform other nations. His exhortation that such estrangement nourishes a polity morally and legally could only serve to remind his audience that as America acted out its destiny, so would America enact the genius of Israel.[3]

Wise argued that the Mosaic law which recognizes no earthly power as sovereign and which prohibits the idolization of the State can be realized in America. Citizenship in a democracy expresses the divine will; Judaism animates this republican sentiment. In a column entitled "To the Reader," Wise contended that Judaism is "destined to become *the religion* emphatically of the civilized world."[4]

Elsewhere, Wise had more robustly proclaimed his faith in Judaism's ability to sustain the nation. Writing to the *Asmonean* in 1849, Wise addressed the significance of America's "great destiny." "To undermine the thrones of tyrants and cause the Goddess of Liberty to move upon the vast chaos of the overthrown monarchies, crowns, sceptres, laws, privileges, and despotism is to reorganize and regenerate the world."[5]

Judaism, Wise propounded, had a complementary obligation:

uprooting the foundations of paganism, atheism, indifferentism, and a hundred other isms, together with obliterating the darkness of prejudice . . . and then to unfurl upon the corpse of that thousand-headed hydra ignorance, the banner or [*sic*] truth and enlightenment. An American Jew . . . has a two-fold mission, to promote truth and liberty.[6]

If Wise sounds like an American philosophe owing much to Franklin and Paine and a lesser debt to the guiding sentiments of German Reform theology, it is because he enthusiastically accepted the basic premise of Enlightenment political thinking: man acts rationally by discovering the causes of law and power. Institutions must be evaluated in terms of the difference between their actual origins and present functions. Truth can be separated from rationale. Just as the Mosaic law encouraged reason by devaluing the absolutism of the secular, so did republicanism confer autonomy upon the human spirit. Reason is set free from the tyranny of archaic customs and institutions. Therefore, the spirit of modern Judaism is wed to the American radical imagination. (Ironically, Wise's "The Fourth of July" sermon missed the liberating nature of another Fourth of July meditation—*Walden*, in which the a-rational nature of experience is given its due.)

Wise's optimism about the American-Jewish situation had a darker side than that found in his rendition of the spirit of the country and the genius of the Jewish people. Practically, he admitted, there was cause for despair given the rudimentary state of Jewish knowledge; the loss of dignity due to European oppression; and the desire to assimilate because of self-revulsion.[7] Nonetheless,

Americanization would make the Jew a free man and restore his self-respect. Assimilation could be combatted by Jewish education.

Wise, of course, is only one of a number of thinkers who felt that American life affirmed the basic tendency of Jewish existence: the characteristic effort to separate truth from archaic form. A nation that, to borrow Morton White's phrase, had begun its revolt against formalism, that had made a tradition of experimentalism, and that had wed itself to what was seen as a culture of opportunity and pluralism could only quicken the Jewish community.

The Reform movement propounded the theses for a new identity. The Jews are "no longer a nation but a religious community," so the 1885 Pittsburgh Conference of the Reform wing argued. Adherence to moral laws that were "adapted to the views and habits of modern civilization" did more than erode a commitment to tradition; the "central religious truth" of Jewish life—the "God-idea"—was brought into the American present. Conversely, the Conference propounded that "the broad humanity of our age" was the home from which this universalizing, democratizing truth would now go forth to establish a "kingdom of truth, justice and peace among all men."[8] The progressive Jewish presence in America would guarantee the nation's commitments to a rational society.

The diaspora, conceived by Reform as simply a physical displacement, had a civic use. Wherever it led, it was not away from the community of Jews but rather from a conquered state. Jews had no reason to deny America their future. As the Reverend Gustav Poznanski summarized the matter at the dedication of a temple in Charleston in 1841, "This country is our Palestine, this city our Jerusalem, this house of God our temple."[9]

There is another, and differing, thesis about the Jew in America. It is best found in the lament for what America portends and Europe maintained: it can be called the Jewish judgment of a profaning America. Not surprisingly, the proponents of this argument agree with Reform thinkers that American opportunities are accessible to, and democratizing, in the main, for a new generation of Jews—this time, of Eastern-European origin—coming to America since the 1880's. Wise had stressed the importance of the Jewish prophetic tradition, of the struggle of reason to emancipate Jewish life from its conventions, of the consonance of the Jewish spirit with modern politics. The dispute over America now took into account the claim of memory: forgetting who they were, and where they were, the Jewish immigrant masses re-enacted an exile not of place but of estrangement from knowing and acting upon the idea of the sacred. In this case, the idea of the sacred is inseparable from the Covenant itself.

At the convention of the Orthodox Jewish Congregational Union of America in 1900, Rabbi Jacob David Wilowsky spoke in Yiddish about the necessary role of tradition and continuity that helped European Jewry survive as people of the Covenant. The Jews had left more than their homes. Wilowsky contended, as Moshe Davis summarizes it, that "anyone who emigrated to America was a sinner, since, in America, the Oral Law is trodden under foot. It was not only home that the Jews left behind in Europe . . . it was their Torah, their Talmud, their *yeshivot*—in a word, their *Yiddishkeit*, their entire Jewish way of life.''[10] Emigration was a passage to a world in which the diaspora was deprived of the theological, moral, and social uses that had invariably held the Jewish community together.

The identification of Europe with a continuous Jewish learning and tradition and of *Yidishkayt* with Orthodoxy was polemical but assumed as a given in this disputation. Wilowsky's thesis would be broadened and made less specific as a distinctive body of American-Jewish letters emerged. The contest between reason and memory (or tradition), between the pragmatic emphasis upon adjustment to novelty and the Jewish imperative to make the comportment of faith unyielding to the attractions of the present became a prominent, if not *the* characteristic, tension of American-Jewish culture.

Nonetheless, the battle between reason and memory was hedged. Even the major figures of American Reform (for example, Wise, David Philipson, and Kaufmann Kohler) argued that their contribution to Jewish life was part of a tradition—*the* Jewish tradition—just as the major spokesman for Orthodoxy (Joseph Soloveitchik) insists upon demarcating the limits of rational experience and faith.[11] As a result, American Judaism is experimental and centrifugal. It is a theology limited by boundary assumptions (the agreement that there is a peoplehood defined by Covenant, law, and commentary), but one whose conditions of faith and commitments are being transformed. Witness, for example, post-Auschwitz theology reconceiving the nature and limitations of God—if not His existence; the debate over whether the diaspora is a tenable concept for our day; the discussions over how venturesome and justifiable the nature of a sacramental Jewish life in America can be.[12]

In *Protestant-Catholic-Jew* (1955), Will Herberg asks, at one point, how Jewish existence reconciles itself to American life. His answer is that religiosity in America has become faith in an American destiny. Social historians have observed how Jewish institutions have not only served as a buffer between the immigrant and America but also transmitted the American values of autonomy and self-creation to the immigrant. The enactment of faith now takes place in a ''man-centered'' culture and is often translated into public-seeking activities. As a result, the major concerns in modern American-Jewish life are expressed by community life and explored by sociological and political studies.[13]

Significantly, the Jewish teaching to its community and to America—early and late—became known through letters, works of a political or literary or journalistic nature. The shift of interpretive authority from the rabbinical circle to lay discussion, from Yiddish and Hebrew to English, indicates major public redefinitions of who and what the representative teachers, methods, and contents of Jewish learning are. The impact of American autonomy, public secular education, and the need to adjust to the conditions of the American urban marketplace helped create a Jewish mass more at ease with secular, positivist explanations of life than with rabbinic judgments. Moreover, an immense secularizing American-Jewish literature gave the Jewish public access to a rendition of Judaism that could be understood without a literate, religious training. This literature, often skeptical of American promises and a parochial Judaism, came to tell the Jewish populace what it was and what problems authentically confronted it. The problems so posed often came to have a legitimacy as *the issues* pertinent to the American-Jewish community. Judaism would be given a "novelistic" dimension depriving the life of faith of a richness that eluded descriptive categories. In general, *Yidishkayt* was popularly conflated with a crisis of sentiment; the enactment of faith would be explored as a denial of a full human spirit; Jewish civilization was portrayed as "closed," as particularistic.

What can be called the literature of disaffirmation composes much of this new, secular didactic. This writing is sharpened by a disenchantment with capitalism's necessarily exploitive nature and its creation of a divisive civil society. American life, a shorthand for a modern capitalist civilization, estranges man from his powers and humanizing activity. The Jew may stand, in his particularity and estranged capacities, for all men, but he cannot overcome the conditions of his alienation. Socialism, however, continues the Jewish prophetic tradition, and can justifiably absorb its moral fervor while providing the Jew with a secular, rational, and practical program—so one argument reads.

The crisis of Jewish tradition is seen in its inability to meet the demands of universalism, and at the same time in the hopelessness of its humane ethic to confront an insuperable environment. Whether presented as a character's losing sight of his true self, a self located in the past and at a distance (Abraham Cahan's *The Rise of David Levinsky*, 1917); or described as a futile attempt to heal a protagonist's willed moral incompleteness (Jerome Weidman's *I Can Get It For You Wholesale*, 1937); or seen in a novelist's refusal to let the major figure of his work be able to explain more than a distorted Judaism (Morris Bober's eloquent though banal rendition of Jewish life in Bernard Malamud's *The Assistant*, 1957); or found in the placing of Judaism on trial to condemn the inappropriateness of *its* sorrow (the trivialization of Sol Nazerman's response to the mundane in Edward Lewis Wallant's *The Pawnbroker*, 1961), the Jewish Covenantal tradition is undone.

The literature of disaffirmation is contested by those who assert that the conditions of Jewish belief and practice can be maintained as well as renewed in America. A putative Jewish tradition and an assumed heritage are, in reality, multiple. They are hyphenated traditions of class, of depth of faith, and of historical background: each has a relevance to, and a role in, American life.

Affirmative American-Jewish literature finds the critical distance between the opportunities of a democratic, capitalist America and the social desires of the Jewish self to be small. Upward mobility and an economy creating possibilities for human development need not militate against a faith and an ethic. If this affirmative literature is not academically esteemed, it is because it shares few of the suppositions that a critical realism makes explicit and finds little enchantment with the realities of left-wing politics. This affirmative literature dismisses contentions that a protagonist's maturation is marked by his estrangement from the moral nature of his society; that particularism—whether of class or race— is a barrier to universalism; that alienation is the character of contemporary life.

Instead, American life provides the Jew with the autonomy denied him in Europe, and with a major caveat: Jewish existence is not necessarily damaged by the contradictions of civil society. Jewish life can now develop freely. In short, the Jew and the American-Jewish community can determine the kind of identity and civic life they desire. A chosen public life and "inner" development are undeniable facts. In this literature, Jewish life is not estrangement but an engagement with a willed destiny.

In its uniqueness and apartness, Jewish life enriches America by broadening it. Moreover, success in making one's way into American life is a morally neutral event. Whether in Horace Kallen's *Culture and Democracy in the United States* (1924), which saw the Jew becoming more Judaized as he became more Americanized; or in Hyman and Lester Cohen's *Aaron Traum* (1930), whose protagonist re-enacts a creative Jewish heritage made possible only in America; or in Ludwig Lewisohn's polemical *The Answer* (1939), in which the Jewish faith is seen as allied to "democratic and libertarian institutions of America"; or in Norman Podhoretz's *Making It* (1967), in which ambition and prosperity are seen as American birthrights, the affirmative tradition complements American myths of individualism. It speaks directly to the Jewish public because it affirms national myths that are the substance of public life. Yet it also speaks to a shared experience of what much of American-Jewish life is.

These traditions are heuristic, provisional interpretations since the American-Jewish experience is still unfolding. They are inquiries, as Horace Kallen argued, by a community whose answers add to and change the shape of its identity.[14] Whether the American-Jewish community accedes to the authority of these theses or prepares for a different present, it demonstrates a momentous commitment to create a new being and history.

The task of books describing American-Jewish culture is to suggest the nature of the usable past and its possible redefinition. Oscar Janowsky's *The American Jew* (1942), probably the first modern collection of essays dealing with American-Jewish culture, created a pattern for future projects.[15] During the threat of Nazism, the need to define Jewish identity was imperative. The book was, Janowsky wrote, a "weapon in the struggle for survival." The subtitle, "A Composite Portrait," and Hadassah's dedication to Louis Brandeis "whose life was a synthesis of Americanism and Zionism" pointed to the unity formed by such chapters as "Historical Background," "Judaism and the Synagogue," "The Cultural Scene," and "Current Philosophies of Jewish Life in America."

Janowsky began his essay "The Historical Background" with a methodological image that was at once biblical, Romantic, American, and contemporary: a view of Jewish life in America from the summit of a mountain. Being able to distinguish the unfolding landscape, in this case the past, the "casual observer" has a clearer view of the future. The surety of the metaphor is qualified by

Janowsky's last line: "The Jewish community of the United States is the product of an evolutionary process which is still in progress, and which is fashioning an American Jewry."[16] Judaism, as Janowsky concluded, is "conceived as the totality of Jewish life. . . . " The intimation is clear: the subject is amorphous, yet it has recognizable parts. The book's method, similarly, is a combination of professional inquiries into areas ranging from sociology to philosophy without, however, constituting an embracing science.

I cite Janowsky because of his sense of the difficulty of his task and because of the book's legacy. For one, the work is a sustained inquiry into American-Jewish life rather than a set of impressions. *The American Jew* brings its subject into the realm of widening, cooperative, scholarly discussion. Moreover, the divisions of the text indicate that American-Jewish life has an integrity of its own. The differences between the Jewish community and the American public are not in question as much as the unique culture created by the two. The studies of institutions, of culture, and of faith pointed to an identity that was basically at ease with its present.

Zionist aspirations were yet another pole of communal definition, as well as an identification with the fate of European Jewry. Whereas *The American Jew* spoke of Zionism as the politics of emergency, the book also faced the problem of national and extra-national loyalties. The American-Jewish public could boast of the integrity of its national commitments and still know that a Jewish homeland would strengthen its existence as well.

Finally, the book challenged the completeness of what were essentially reports of American-Jewish life found in memoirs, impassioned sketches, specific social studies, and popular anthologies that served as a catchment for Jewish thought.[17] *The American Jew* demonstrated the success of encyclopedic efforts. Jewish life may not be categorical, but it could be usefully categorized.

Years later, the task of reassessing American Jewry found Janowsky in *The American Jew: A Reappraisal* (1964) emphasizing his rule about the totality of Jewish life, but mindful of the need to mention experience not easily subjected to empirical analysis: "Emphasis has . . . been placed on the Jewish community and its institutions, rather than on the problems and gropings of the individual Jew, and on the inner life of the Jews rather than on minority-majority relationships."[18]

Refining and augmenting previous categories ("the division into segments of a subject like the American-Jewish community must in large measure be arbitrary") underscore the fact that American-Jewish life was still deprived of a unifying science authentically its own. How does one describe a people and a community of believers in which the two are not equal? How does one do justice to a group which does not often separate its commitments to a profane, this-worldly existence from a conviction about its suprahistorical role? Can the observations of a positivistic social science be reconciled with the claims of faith?[19]

These problems are some of the boundary markers of the American-Jewish experience; they are complementary rather than paradoxical. They are best explored for all their ambiguities, I think, in literature which commits itself to multiple perspectives, not to finally resolve these unsettled issues but to ultimately preserve them. The contributors to this book tend to agree that these problematic terms of Jewish existence in America animate American-Jewish letters; that in its own way, American-Jewish culture is based on the creative use of multiple reconciliations. Literature represents and re-enacts the demands of reason and memory often without damaging their authority or their role. As a result, American-Jewish literature has a commanding strength in expressing the interior, communitarian, and yet public nature of Jewish life. This book participates in the analysis of what the American-Jewish experience is and its strategic presentation as literature.

NOTES

1. For an approach to these questions, see Jules Chametzky's *Our Decentralized Literature*.

2. Isaac Mayer Wise, "The Fourth of July," *The Israelite*, p. 3.

3. See Sacvan Bercovitch's *The American Jeremiad* for a discussion of the promise of an American destiny; Sam Girgus's *The New Covenant* for the significance of this promise in American-Jewish literature; and Louis Harap's *The Image of the Jew in American Literature* for the Jew's perceived role in American life. Morris U. Schappes's *A Documentary History of the Jews in the United States, 1654–1875* and Jacob Marcus's *Memoirs of American Jews, 1775–1865* should also be looked at.

4. Wise, "To the Reader," op. cit., p. 4.

5. Wise, "To the Editor of the Asmonean," p. 1.

6. Ibid. p. 1.

7. See Wise's *Reminiscences*, trans. and ed. David Philipson, pp. 330–332. I am referring to the accessible second edition, published by Central Synagogue of New York, 1945.

8. David Philipson, *The Reform Movement in Judaism*, cf. pp. 491–492.

9. Ibid., p. 467.

10. I am indebted to Moshe Davis's *The Emergence of Conservative Judaism*, pp. 311–326, for an account of this meeting. The Slutsker Rav's quotation is taken from p. 318.

11. See works by Philipson and Wise already cited; Kaufmann Kohler's *Jewish Theology Systematically and Historically Considered*; Rabbi Joseph Soloveitchik's *Halakhic Man*, trans. Lawrence Kaplan. (This was originally published in Hebrew as *Ish ha-halakhah*.)

12. On post-Auschwitz theology, see Eliezer Berkovits's *Faith After the Holocaust*; Arthur A. Cohen's *The Tremendum*; Emil Fackenheim's *God's Presence in History*; Jacob Neusner's *Stranger at Home*; Richard Rubenstein's *After Auschwitz* and *The Cunning of History*. On a new Jewish theology, see, among others, Eugene Borowitz's *A New Jewish Theology in the Making*; Will Herberg's *Protestant-Catholic-Jew* and *Judaism and Modern Man*; Abraham J. Heschel's *God in Search of Man*; Horace Kallen's *Judaism at Bay*; Mordecai Kaplan's *Judaism as a Civilization*. On the redefinition of the diaspora and the evolving role of Palestine and Israel in American life, see Waldo Frank's *The Jew in Our Day*; Ben Halpern's *The American Jew: A Zionist Analysis*; Arthur Hertzberg's introductory essay to his anthology *The Zionist Idea* and his *Being Jewish in America*;

Mordecai Kaplan's above-cited text; Eugene Kohn's *The Future of Judaism in America*; Ludwig Lewisohn's *Israel*. On the nature of American-Jewish life, see Joseph Blau's *Modern Varieties of Judaism*; Arnold Eisen's *The Chosen People in America*; Nathan Glazer's *American Judaism*; Bernard Martin's *Movements and Issues in American Judaism*; Jacob Neusner's *American Judaism*; Charles Silberman's *A Certain People*.

13. See, for example, Deborah Dash Moore's *At Home in America*; Irving Howe's *World of Our Fathers*; Leon Jick's *The Americanization of the Synagogue, 1820–1870*; and Daniel Elazar's *Community and Polity*.

14. See Horace Kallen's *Secularism Is the Will of God*.

15. Works such as *Christian and Jew* (1929), edited by Isaac Landman, and *Jewish Experiences in America* (1930), edited by Bruno Lasker, are not, properly, anthologies dealing solely with the American-Jewish experience. They contain a number of essays on Jewish life but for the purpose of settling Jewish-Christian tensions.

16. Oscar Janowsky, "The Historical Background," in *The American Jew*, p. 27.

17. See, for example, Isaac Mayer Wise's *Reminiscences*; the best-known sketches of Jewish life remain Jacob A. Riis's portrayal of "Jewtown" in *How the Other Half Lives* and Hutchins Hapgood's *The Spirit of the Ghetto*; Louis Wirth's *The Ghetto* is the pioneering example of the sociological description; an anthology that is important but that appears shortly after Janowsky's book is Lewis Browne's *The Wisdom of Israel*.

18. Oscar Janowsky, "Preface," *The American Jew: A Reappraisal*, p. viii.

19. Eisen's *The Chosen People in America* is also especially good in raising these questions.

BIBLIOGRAPHY

Bercovitch, Sacvan. *The American Jeremiad*. Madison: University of Wisconsin Press, 1978.

Berkovits, Eliezer. *Faith After the Holocaust*. New York: KTAV, 1973.

Blau, Joseph. *Modern Varieties of Judaism*. New York: Columbia University Press, 1966.

Borowitz, Eugene. *A New Jewish Theology in the Making*. Philadelphia: Westminster Press, 1968.

Browne, Lewis, ed. *The Wisdom of Israel*. New York: Random House, 1945.

Chametzky, Jules. *Our Decentralized Literature: Cultural Mediations in Selected Jewish and Southern Writers*. Amherst: University of Massachusetts Press, 1986.

Cohen, Arthur A. *The Tremendum: A Theological Interpretation of the Holocaust*. New York: Crossroad, 1981.

Davis, Moshe. *The Emergence of Conservative Judaism: The Historical School in 19th Century America*. Philadelphia: Jewish Publication Society, 1963.

Eisen, Arnold. *The Chosen People in America: A Study in Jewish Religious Identity*. Bloomington: Indiana University Press, 1983.

Elazar, Daniel. *Community and Polity: The Organizational Dynamics of American Jewry*. Philadelphia: Jewish Publication Society, 1976.

Fackenheim, Emil. *God's Presence in History: Jewish Affirmations and Philosophical Reflections*. New York: New York University Press, 1970.

Frank, Waldo. *The Jew in Our Day*. New York: Duell, Sloan and Pearce, 1944.

Girgus, Sam. *The New Covenant: Jewish Writers and the American Idea*. Chapel Hill: University of North Carolina Press, 1984.

Glazer, Nathan. *American Judaism*. Chicago: University of Chicago Press, 1957.

Halpern, Ben. *The American Jew: A Zionist Analysis*. New York: Theodor Herzl Foundation, 1956.

Hapgood, Hutchins. *The Spirit of the Ghetto*. New York: Funk and Wagnalls, 1902.

Harap, Louis. *The Image of the Jew in American Literature: From Early Republic to Mass Immigration*. Philadelphia: Jewish Publication Society, 1974.

Herberg, Will. *Judaism and Modern Man*. New York: Farrar, Straus, and Young, 1951.

————. *Protestant-Catholic-Jew*. Garden City, New York: Doubleday & Co., 1955.

Hertzberg, Arthur. *Being Jewish in America*. New York: Schocken Books, 1979.

————, ed. and intro. *The Zionist Idea*. New York: Herzl Press and Doubleday, 1959.

Heschel, Abraham, J. *God in Search of Man*. New York: Farrar, Straus, & Giroux, 1955.

Howe, Irving, with Kenneth Libo. *World of Our Fathers*. New York: Harcourt Brace Jovanovich, 1976.

Janowsky, Oscar, ed. *The American Jew: A Composite Portrait*. New York: Harper and Brothers, 1942.

————, ed. *The American Jew: A Reappraisal*. Philadelphia: Jewish Publication Society, 1964.

Jick, Leon. *The Americanization of the Synagogue, 1820–1870*. Hanover, New Hampshire: Brandeis University Press, 1976.

Kallen, Horace. *Judaism at Bay*. New York: Bloch Publishing Co., 1932.

————. *Secularism Is the Will of God*. New York: Twayne, 1954.

Kaplan, Mordecai. *Judaism as a Civilization*. New York: Macmillan, 1934.

————. *A New Zionism*. New York: Theodor Herzl Foundation, 1959.

Kohler, Kaufmann. *Jewish Theology Systematically and Historically Considered*. New York: Macmillan, 1918.

Kohn,Eugene. *The Future of Judaism in America*. New Rochelle, New York: Liberal Press, 1934.

Landman, Isaac, ed. *Christian and Jew*. New York: Horace Liveright, 1929.

Lasker, Bruno, ed. *Jewish Experiences in America*. New York: The Inquiry, 1930.

Lewisohn, Ludwig. *Israel*. New York: Liveright, 1925.

Marcus, Jacob, ed. *Memoirs of American Jews, 1775–1865*. 3 vols. Philadelphia: Jewish Publication Society, 1955–1956.

Martin, Bernard, ed. *Movements and Issues in American Judaism: An Analysis and Sourcebook of Development Since 1945*. Westport, Connecticut: Greenwood Press, 1978.

Moore, Deborah Dash. *At Home in America: Second Generation New York Jews*. New York: Columbia University Press, 1981.

Neusner, Jacob. *American Judaism: Adventure in Modernity*. Englewood Cliffs, New Jersey: Prentice-Hall, 1972.

————. *Stranger at Home: "the holocaust," Zionism and American Judaism*. Chicago: University of Chicago Press, 1981.

Philipson, David. *The Reform Movement in Judaism*. New York: Macmillan Company, 1907.

Riis, Jacob A. *How the Other Half Lives*. New York: Charles Scribner's, 1890.

Rubenstein, Richard. *After Auschwitz: Radical Theology and Contemporary Judaism*. New York: Macmillan, 1966.

————. *The Cunning of History*; 1975; rpt. Introduction by William Styron. New York: Harper Colophon, 1978.

Schappes, Morris U., ed. *A Documentary History of the Jews in the United States, 1654–1875*. New York: Citadel, 1950.

Silberman, Charles E. *A Certain People: American Jews and Their Lives Today*. New York: Summit Books, 1985.

Soloveitchik, Joseph. *Halakhic Man*, trans. Lawrence Kaplan. Philadelphia: Jewish Publication Society, 1983.

Wirth, Louis. *The Ghetto*. Chicago: University of Chicago Press, 1928.

Wise, Isaac Mayer. "The Fourth of July." *The Israelite*. 1. (July 15, 1854), p. 3.

———. *Reminiscences*, trans. and ed. David Philipson. New York: Central Synagogue of New York, 1945.

———. "To the Editor of the Asmonean." *The Asmonean*. 1. (November 9, 1849), p. 1.

———. "To The Reader." *The Israelite*. 1. (July 15, 1854), p. 4.

1

In the Beginning: American-Jewish Fiction, 1880–1930

David Martin Fine

I

"America has never been easy," D. H. Lawrence wrote:

Men are free when they are living in a homeland, not when they are straying and breaking away. Men are free when they are obeying some deep, inward voice of religious belief. Obeying from within. Men are free when they belong to a living, organic, *believing* community, active in fulfilling some unfulfilled, perhaps unrealized purpose. Not when they are escaping to some wild west.[1]

The paradox Lawrence addresses rests at the center of American culture and literature and informs the work of our major writers from Nathaniel Hawthorne to Saul Bellow. In the national mythology the journey west—whether west means the New World, the forest beyond the Puritan city, or some deeper penetration of the imagination's "wild west"—is the journey from the region of oppression to one of freedom. But such freedom has remained, for the seeker, elusive—and illusive. History is not easily outreached; the obligations of the past and community are not easily escapable. The collective experience of the Eastern-European Jewish immigrant and the fiction engendered by that experience have given particular intensity to this essentially American conflict between history and desire. From the clash between the claims of a world left behind and the promise of the West, the pull of the past and the urge to the present, the American-Jewish novel in the half century between 1880 and 1930 took its first mandate.

For the two million Jews who left the *shtetlach* of Eastern Europe for the New World—fully one-third of Eastern-Europe's Jews—the Old World claim had lost much of its force. The "homeland," that "living, *believing*, organic community" Lawrence speaks of, was feeling less and less like one. Czarist-encouraged pogroms and mob violence following the assassination of Alexander II in 1881 were putting the very existence of these Jews in jeopardy. At the same time the once-strong religious ties that had bound the Jewish community were unraveling. The threat to Jewish life was coming both from within and without. The massive flight to America that began in the early 1880's was less a radical, abrupt break with a stable past than a stage in a movement that had in fact begun over a century earlier. Under the flags of Enlightenment and Emancipation, Western thought had been circulating in the *shtetlach* of the Pale since the eighteenth century, challenging orthodoxy and encouraging a receptivity to new ideas and a belief in the possibilities of a new life. That belief, charged with hope, was linked to America. In *The Rise of David Levinsky* (1917), the most important novel written by a Jewish immigrant, Abraham Cahan endows his hero with this desire to possess the West and its promise. Trained as a talmudist, but fatally exposed to currents of change reaching his Russian village, David Levinsky expresses euphorically this readiness to be reborn in America:

The United States lured me not merely as a land of milk and honey, but also, and perhaps chiefly, as one of mystery, of fantastic experience, of marvelous transformations. To leave my native place and to seek my fortune in that distant, weird world seemed to me to be just the kind of sensational adventure my heart was hankering for.[2]

Levinsky's "sensational adventure" was to become an American millionaire. Yet at the height of his dazzling success he was to feel like the same lonely, hungry, unloved Jewish boy from the village of Antomir: his life, he claims, is "devoid of significance"; his inner identity, "the same as it was thirty or forty years ago." His transformation, at root, was to be no transformation at all. The old territory, the territory of the heart, had its claim.

This is the lesson learned too by the young immigrant heroines of Anzia Yezierska's novels and stories from the 1920's. Cultural baggage cannot be checked at Ellis Island for long. Yearning for love and new identity in America, Yezierska's heroines rush from the parental home only to discover a self that has a prior claim. Before the reaction sets in, though, America is indeed the land of "sensational adventure." The very sound of America had a magic to it: "I was so grateful to mingle with the American people, to hear the music of the American language, that I never knew tiredness. I felt like Columbus finding new worlds through every new word."[3]

New worlds through new words. Yiddish, the language and culture of the Eastern-European Jew, was the link to the past; English, to the present and future. To the traditional parent figure the loss of Yiddish was something to be mourned. Yiddish meant the home and family; English, the streets of the New World. "Speak to me *momme loschen*," the mother in Samuel Ornitz's *Haunch Paunch and Jowl* (1923) tells her Americanizing son, "not that nasty gibberish of the streets."[4]

Although Yiddish survived the transplantation to the New World—in the theatre, in the press, in fiction and poetry, and as ghetto vernacular—and indeed it survives today, it was soon to be displaced by English as the literary language of the immigrant author who considered himself an American Jew. Writing fiction in English was an act of assimilation, an affirmation of one's commitment to the New World, a demonstration, as Leslie Fiedler wrote, "that there is an American Jew . . . and that he feels at home!"[5]

Having the leisure to write fiction, and write it in the language of his adopted land, meant, of course, that the immigrant author had achieved a measure of success in America, had undergone some degree of assimilation. Inevitably, the tale he told, whether or not drawn directly from his life, would be about the process of assimilation. That process could be expressed in terms either of the self-conscious attempt to shed the remnants of Old World culture and absorb the values and habits of Christian America or of the somewhat broader ideal of cultural fusion, a process of mutual accommodation that went at the time under the name of the "melting pot." But while these two versions of assimilation can be distinguished in theory, they are not always distinguishable in the rhetoric of the time or in literary practice.[6] Both promulgated the desirability of assimilation, and the line between the two approaches blurred.

The real opposition, the stance that stressed the loss incurred in the letting go of the past, appears in American-Jewish fiction significantly only after the first decade and a half of the twentieth century. Looking broadly at the fiction in the half century between 1880 and 1930 one can, in fact, discern a clear shift, or transformation, just beyond the middle of the "teen" years from novels optimistically advocating one or another form of assimilation to those more soberly assessing the dilemmas posed by absorption. At the historical moment that Jews in large numbers were beginning their exodus from the urban ghettos and the liberal press was beginning to voice the ideal of cultural pluralism as an alternative to assimilation, American-Jewish writing entered a new phase that would last through the twenties, one that would pose a challenge to assimilationist orthodoxies.

Cultural pluralism, the cosmopolitan notion that America existed as a nation of nations, a confederation of culturally distinct but harmonious national and ethnic groups rarely played a part in pre-war American-Jewish fiction, except as an option to be rejected. Offered as an antidote to Americanization, one that would preserve ethnic cultures in America, the pluralist ideal, as advocated by, among others, Randolph Bourne and Horace Kallen, had little appeal to the early immigrant author.[7] His own experience as one who had risen from the ghetto dictated a different position. Perhaps, too, the immigrant author writing during the period of intense immigration before the war felt he had a stake in defending the Jew's capacity to become a successful American against the onslaught of xenophobic tirades (those of the Boston-based Anti-Immigration League of Henry Cabot Lodge, for instance) that the Russian Jew, unlike the earlier-arriving German Jew, was unassimilable. In either case, the American-Jewish novel in the pre-war period stressed, with few exceptions, the gain and not the loss incurred in assimilation.

The transformation that occurred during the war years and the post-war twenties was in part a response to new brands of nativism engendered by the foreign crisis and the Bolshevik Revolution and in part a product of the new conditions faced by the Jew as he passed beyond the walls of the ghetto and confronted Christian American society directly. In novels dealing with Jews entering the American mainstream in these years, novels like Abraham Cahan's *The Rise of David Levinsky* (1917), Sidney Nyburg's *The Chosen People* (1917), Anzia Yezierska's *Bread Givers* (1925), and Ludwig Lewisohn's *The Island Within* (1928), the American-Jewish novel comes of age. It achieves its first cultural maturity by recoiling from the overly facile celebration of assimilation and addresses the issue of what is lost, or betrayed—as well as gained—in the process of entering American life.

II

In both versions of the early American-Jewish fable the approach to America is linked dramatically and metaphorically with the approach to intermarriage; the possession of America is joined to the sexual possession of its prized female. Leslie Fiedler has described the search for America in American-Jewish fiction as "a kind of wooing," an erotic encounter between the Jewish "Don Juan and the *shiksa*."[8] More recently, Frederick Cople Jaher has written interestingly of the quest for "the ultimate *shiksa*" as "metaphor for the problematic existence of the American Jew."[9] While the *shikse* represents the opportunity for cultural reconciliation, she evokes in the Jew both guilt and anxiety over his rejection of the past. She symbolizes, Jaher observes, the unresolved conflict between Jewish origins and assimilationist desires. As the projection of Jewish male fantasies, the *shikse* appears variously in fiction as the exotic insider (counterpart to the Jew—or Jewess—in Anglo-Saxon mythology as the exotic stranger), the diabolical femme fatale, the Christian saint, or the Jew's admission ticket to Christian America. It is almost exclusively in this latter incarnation that she makes her appearance in the early American-Jewish novel. The *shikse* as erotic or forbidden object belongs to the fiction of a later generation—that of Saul Bellow, Bernard Malamud, Philip Roth, and Joseph Heller. For the immigrant protagonist, intermarriage with the Christian female, usually portrayed as the Anglo-Saxon blue blood, serves as the emblem of the hero's acceptance in America. In a rather bizarre variation, the *shikse* appears occasionally as an immigrant herself, as the daughter of the hero's Old World betrayer. In such tales, intermarriage symbolizes New World sanctioning of a union that would have been forbidden in the Old World.

Curiously, the writer who established for American-Jewish fiction the linkage between assimilation and intermarriage was himself a non-Jew, a Connecticut-born Protestant named Henry Harland. Passing himself off as a Jew named Sidney Luska, Harland expressed in three novels (*As It Was Written*, 1885; *Mrs. Peixada*, 1886; *The Yoke of the Thorah*, 1887) both his infatuation with the spiritual quality of New York's German Jews and his impatience with their "clannishness" and their resistance to assimilation. His position hovers between philo- and anti-Semitism. Intermarriage was the solution Harland/Luska posited for Jewish marginality in America. It was a strange stance for a man whose knowledge of Jews was limited largely to the assimilated, secularized, and successful German Jews he met through Felix Adler's Ethical Culture Society. Ironically, in criticizing the German Jews' reluctance to assimilate, he anticipated the criticism these same German Jews, feeling the sting of being identified with the "new immigrants," would level at their Russian brethren a decade or so later. The rivalry between the Americanized "uptown" German Jews and the "downtown" Russian Jews of the ghetto was to become a recurring conflict in American-Jewish fiction portraying labor struggles of the early twentieth century—in, for instance, James Oppenheim's *The Nine-Tenths* (1911), Arthur Bullard's *Comrade Yetta* (1913), and Sidney Nyburg's *The Chosen People* (1917). In portraying his German Jews as exotic, picturesque aliens standing at the fringes of America, resisting assimilation, Harland was assuming a strangely anachronistic position even for the 1880's.

In the first of his Jewish novels, *As It Was Written, A Jewish Musician's Story*, he gives us a Jewish violinist, Ernest Neumann (Harland's "spiritual" Jews are usually musicians or painters), who is actually a schizophrenic personality, bound by the curse of his dead father. In a trance he murders his beloved fiancée. The past (Jewish history represented by the father) has controlled him from the grave. The absurd gothic plot points to what Harland/Luska saw as the Jew's inability to free himself from history. Neumann is the new man in name only. Another character in the novel, a Christian, expresses the author's assimilationist, or melting pot, position that the Jew, once he is willing to let go of the past, will be enriched by America, just as America will be enriched by the Jew. Intermarriage will produce "a single people of homogeneous blood" and the Jew "will give fire and flavor to the decoctation. The future Americans, thanks to the Jew in them, will have passions, enthusiasms."[10]

In *Mrs. Peixada*, his next novel, he allows his Jewish heroine, cast as the familiar suffering, dark-haired beauty, to find happiness in marriage to an Anglo-Saxon lawyer who pontificates endlessly about intermarriage as a way to build a new America. *The Yoke of the Thorah*, produced the following year, returns to the theme of Jewish bondage to the past. His "spiritual" Jew, a painter named Elias Bacharach, is engaged to the lovely Christine Redmond. Warned by his uncle, an orthodox rabbi (and throwback to a medieval Jewish stereotype), that God will not permit the union, Bacharach collapses at his wedding believing he has been struck by God (an epileptic fit, one assumes, but the reader does not rule out the hand of the uncle). He recovers to renounce his intended apostasy, marries a coarse Jewess, daughter of a commercial parvenu family, and lives to regret his choice. Haunted by the memory of his lost love, he collapses and dies in Central Park (again a seizure). Intermarriage was the chance Harland/Luska offered his protagonist to escape the "Yoke of the Thorah" but Bacharach was unable, or unwilling, to accept it.

In a number of novels written by Jews through the first decade and a half of
the twentieth century, the gift of intermarriage would not only be accepted but
celebrated as the mark of the Jewish hero's true "arrival." Only on occasion
did Harland/Luska's notion of the Jew tied inexorably, unhappily, to the yoke
of history surface. One such occasion was Ezra Brudno's *The Tether* (1908), a
novel that resurrects the Harland/Luska image of the spiritual-intellectual Jew
yearning for New World love but fleeing in terror when it is presented. After
courting a German-Jewish girl, David Sphardi falls in love with and marries
Mildred Dalton, but the marriage collapses when Sphardi is unable to reconcile
his assimilationist enthusiasm with his Jewish sensibility—awakened by the
prejudice and condescension he faces in the gentile world. The prodigal son
returns to his orthodox father but it is too late: the old man, broken-hearted at
his son's apostasy, dies, and Sphardi, unable to atone, goes mad, a victim,
Brudno tells us, of "possessing an oriental heart with an occidental brain." He
can, in other words, intellectualize about cultural fusion, but emotionally he is,
like Harland/Luska's Jews, unhappily tethered to the past.

In an earlier novel, *The Fugitive* (1904), Brudno took the exactly opposite
position. America does work its transformations. The immigrant hero of this
novel, Israel Rusakoff, is a fugitive from forms of oppression perpetrated not
only by Christians but by Jews in the Old World, where the first two-thirds of
the book takes place. Russian Judaism is rendered in its most medieval, tyrannical, and reactionary aspects. Everything is different in New York. While there
is oppression in the form of sweatshop wage slavery, there is also the possibility
of remaking oneself. But one can be remade for the better or the worse. The
shister can become a mister, but the mister can also become the *shister*. Rusakoff
becomes a successfully assimilated American, but other immigrants do not fare
as well. Brudno uses the device, conventional to the immigrant novel, of dragging
figures from the protagonist's Old World past into the present, where they appear
metamorphosed. America produces radical transformations, not always for the
better. Prominent Jews, forced to flee Russia after the Czar's assassination,
reappear as pants-makers, tyrannized by German-Jewish "sweaters"; Talmud
scholars become vulgar "allrightniks," crudely flaunting their Americanization
in broken English. The strangest transformation, though, is that of Rusakoff's
Old World betrayer, Bialnik. The man who had falsely accused Rusakoff's father
of the ritual slaughter of a Russian girl, turns up, penitent, in the New World.
Along with him is his daughter Katia, who eventually becomes Rusakoff's bride.
The marriage that would have been forbidden in Russia is approved in America.
Christian and Jew, Old World enemies, are reconciled. For better or worse
America works its changes. History, in Brudno's vision, if not irrelevant, is
escapable and erasable. Past grief, pain, alienation are shed, for the protagonist
at least, as easily as earlocks and prayer shawls. There are no yokes or tethers.

Israel Zangwill, the English author, provides a similar ending to his popular
American stage melodrama of 1908, *The Melting-Pot*: the immigrant hero weds
the daughter of the Russian officer who led the 1903 Kishinev massacre in which

the boy's parents were killed! The final scene of that play, applauded by New York audiences if not by the Jewish press, is the hero's hysterical salute to America, as he stands on a tenement rooftop with his fiancée, a Russian bullet still lodged in his shoulder:

There she lies, the great Melting-Pot. . . . There gapes her mouth—the harbour where a thousand mammoth feeders come from the ends of the world to pour their human freight. . . . Here shall they all unite to build the Republic of Man and the Kingdom of God. Ah, Vera, what is the glory of Rome and Jerusalem where all nations and races come to worship and look back, compared with the glory of America where all races and nations come to labour and look forward![11]

Edward Steiner's *The Mediator* (1907) is a similarly messianic novel dealing with a Jewish immigrant who becomes, like Zangwill's and Brudno's heroes, both a symbol of cultural reconciliation and a self-styled mediator between Jew and Christian. Steiner, a sociologist and author of several books on immigration, and a Jew who converted to Christianity, presents in the novel an idealistic protagonist, Samuel Cohen, who has abandoned orthodox Judaism and his father long before his emigration and brings with him to America a rhapsodic vision of reconciling Old and New Worlds. He allies himself with a Mr. Bruce, a wealthy Christian philanthropist and evangelist bent on saving lower East Side souls, but what Cohen preaches in contrast to Bruce (the distinction should be made although one could argue that it is not much of one) is not simply salvation through conversion but through Jewish acceptance of Christ as savior of both faiths. "I am a Jew," Cohen shouts to the hostile crowds of the ghetto. "In every fiber of my soul a Jew! But, men of Israel, I believe that Jesus is the Messiah. I believe that Jesus is the redeemer of Israel."[12] Cohen ritually confirms his self-proclaimed mediator role by marrying Bruce's beautiful, patrician daughter.

Less messianic in tone, but no less enthusiastic about the happy transforming powers of America, is Elias Tobenkin's 1916 novel *Witte Arrives*. The conflict between father and son, as in Brudno's and Steiner's novels, is the conflict not between two adjoining generations but between an orthodoxy rooted in medievalism and a secular modern spirit. As a young boy, Emile Witte (born Wittowski) immigrated to America with his father and, after attending a western university, has become a successful journalist (as was Tobenkin) while his father, rooted to the past, remains a peddler in America. Witte's career, as journalist and American success-figure, skyrockets. From a Chicago newspaper he moves to New York, where he writes two books about American life and a series of magazine articles that articulate "America's Newest Problems." The immigrant has become not only the assimilated American but the interpreter of America to Americans, another cultural mediator. Witte's metamorphosis has been so thorough that his articles, we are told, have an "Emersonian flavor," one that his readers assume comes from "a scion of one of the oldest American families."

Like the American dreamers of Steiner, Brudno, and Zangwill, Witte confirms his Americanization by marrying the *shikse*—in this case a wealthy New England girl after his Jewish wife, appropriately, dies. Once again, the old life can be laid to rest and the new, in the form of American career and Christian wife, embraced without the guilt and anxiety that would haunt later Jewish writers. Union with the Christian woman—who could be either the Anglo-Saxon blue blood (Steiner and Tobenkin) or the daughter of the Old World persecutor (Zangwill and Brudno)—provides the symbolism not only for the immigrant's successful and complete release from the past, but, more broadly, for the possibilities for cultural fusion in America. Sexual and domestic bonding with the forbidden other confers on the immigrant hero of such novels both the badge signifying passage from Russian persecution to American participation and the credential establishing his rights to serve as mediator. As the marginal man who has entered the mainstream, he becomes the true interpreter of American ideals, the new prophet of the New World Dream.

III

The publication in 1917 of both Sidney Nyburg's *The Chosen People* and Abraham Cahan's *The Rise of David Levinsky* a year after Tobenkin's novel marks the shift in American-Jewish fiction away from the glib and sometimes shrill assimilationist novels one encounters in the pre-war decades. Nyburg's novel is particularly interesting in signaling this transformation because it too deals with a self-styled mediator. Philip Graetz, American-born rabbi of a Baltimore Reform synagogue, conceives his divinely appointed task to reconcile the affluent, assimilated German Jews of his congregation, the capitalist class, with the downtown Russian Jews, the proletariat. He fails miserably because he underestimates, by a long way, the chasm—economic, political, religious—that lies between the two groups of Jews in America. What he discovers is that German and Russian Jews cannot be united so long as one is the exploiter of the other.

The conflict between German and Russian Jew was not new to American-Jewish fiction in 1917. What is new is the extended use Nyburg, in this undeservedly neglected novel, makes of it as metaphor for the ambivalent position of Jews in America. Earlier novels present the clash more melodramatically: the German Jew as petty sweatshop tyrant. In Brudno's *The Fugitive* and Steiner's *The Mediator* the crude German-Jewish boss is a stock villain figure. In Edward King's *Joseph Zalmonah* (1893), a sympathetic if sentimental account of the pioneer Russian-Jewish labor leader Joseph Barondess and one of the first novels to take account of the sweatshop, the exploiters of the Russian Jews are German Jews who own the clothing firms and control the contractors, who in turn "sweat" the Russian Jews. Baumeister, the German Jew against whom Zalmonah struggles, is a caricature, in the Shylock-Fagin mold, of Jewish greed—physically deformed, ruthlessly driven, and self-destructively crazed with bitterness. One would have to look to Zerkow, the Polish Jew in Frank Norris's *McTeague* for an equally unsavory Jew in the period's fiction.

In other, later novels of Jewish labor struggles, works like James Oppenheim's *The Nine-Tenths* (1911) and Arthur Bullard's *Comrade Yetta* (1913), both based in part on the 1909 "Uprising of the 20,000" immigrant working women in the garment trades, the one novel by a Jew, the other by a non-Jew, the German boss is depicted with somewhat more complexity both as exploiter and victim of contract labor. Albert Lissner in Oppenheim's novel and Jake Goldfogle in Bullard's are small operators ruined by the walkout, themselves sacrifices to the system they helped perpetuate in order to survive. Whatever criticism such novels level at immigrant labor conditions, however, they end characteristically on an optimistic note, with an expression of worker solidarity and cooperation—and with it the prospect of a better American future. The conversion of the immigrant from exploited wage slave to committed fighter for justice in the labor arena carries with it the message—implicit or explicit—of America's redemptive promise, a promise delayed, not betrayed.

Nyburg's novel offers no such promise. Not only is Rabbi Graetz singularly unfit for his mission as mediator, but the mission itself is revealed to be beyond attainment in a competitive, capitalistic society. What America needs, the Rabbi learns, is not the rabbinical plea for more justice please, but the shrewd pragmatic bargainer—the tough-minded realist who can win one, then another, concession from the ruling class. Graetz's opposite in the novel is a tough, cynical Russian-Jewish labor attorney, David Gordon, who knows how to win such concessions from the industrialists in Graetz's congregation by exploiting their own self-interests. In the strike that serves as the symbolic focus for the uptown-downtown clash, the workers win a favorable settlement not because Graetz has aroused the conscience of his congregation, but because Gordon has marshaled an army of workers willing to challenge the Jewish plutocracy.

Gordon knows that the fight will continue so long as American Jews inhabit opposite poles in a capitalistic society. His own position is Zionism. Jewish survival depends, he argues, on defining an identity outside the competitive society of America. Only the building of their own society will bind Jews cooperatively. His position, which obviously had considerable support among American Jews in 1917, stands diametrically opposed to that of the newly affluent and assimilated members of Graetz's congregation, who fear only that their position as Americans could be undermined by identification with the "foreign" downtown Jews. It was one thing to use their labor, another to be confused with them. In the center, ambiguously between Gordon's cultural separatism and the guarded Americanization of Graetz's congregation, stands the rabbi himself. One of the ironies of the novel is that the assimilated rabbi, unable to find a solid place to stand, becomes the marginal man.

Graetz's crisis of conscience, his first recoil from the values of his congregation, comes early in the novel in a very effective, and affecting, scene. He is called out in the middle of the night to Johns Hopkins Hospital to minister to a

Russian Jew who has been struck by a car. He rushes to the bedside of the dying man, only to find that he cannot understand the man's Yiddish last words. The old man hurls the defiant "*Goy*" at him, meaning that the rabbi is no Jew at all. The scene establishes the central theme of the communication failure between German and Russian Jew. It is more than a language failure. As Gordon explains to the perplexed rabbi, "It wasn't only the Yiddish! You and the Russian could never have understood one another anyhow."[13] Graetz embarks on one, then another, act of ritual atonement (the novel begins on *Yom Kippur*, the Day of Atonement), each a disaster. He preaches a sermon on the obligation of Jew to Jew, incorporating his hospital failure, but his congregants let him know his self-flagellation is ridiculous and degrading. He hires a Russian-Jewish student to teach him Yiddish, and is again rebuked when he foolishly offers the boy non-kosher food. The rabbi, the teacher, is again put in the position of displaying his ignorance.

Driven by a sense of his own inadequacy as Jew and rabbi, Graetz, like one of the anxiety-ridden heroes of Philip Roth or Bernard Malamud, wanders the ghetto in search of the Jew within, thereby producing other ironies. Although he is engaged to a wealthy, dark-haired beauty from his own congregation, he falls in love with a blond *shikse*, a ghetto nurse who is not only the forbidden gentile but a socialist to boot. Ellen Stuart is accepted in the ghetto because she ministers to real needs; he, the Jew, is rejected as the slumming uptowner, a visitor from the enemy camp. To marry Ellen is to marry the Christian saint; to marry Ruth—which he does—is to fulfill his rabbinical, that is, his congregation's, expectations and, at the same time, solidify his own position in the Americanized German-Jewish community, a position he is no longer sure he wants. In this ironic reversal of the *shikse* theme, the prospect of intermarriage points away from, not toward, assimilation: the wealthy dark-haired Jewess, not the poor gentile socialist, is the way to American success.

Nyburg's rabbi-hero discovers what Abraham Cahan's entrepreneur-hero, David Levinsky, discovers—that assimilation has its psychic perils. To forge an American persona that denies the historical self is an act of betrayal, one that is accompanied by a sense of loss. To deny the parent is to deny that part of the self containing the parent.

While both *The Chosen People* and *The Rise of David Levinsky* take up this theme, Cahan's is a very different kind of narrative. The fable he employs is the up-from-the-ghetto tale found in Steiner, Brudno, and countless immigrant autobiographies: the fable of the movement out from the closed world of the *shtetl*, up from ghetto and sweatshop, and into the open, ambiguous world of the modern American city. It chronicles the hardships of the Old World childhood, the hope-laden voyage to America, the embittering experience of the New World ghetto, and, finally, the escape from poverty and the rise to American success. But Cahan tells it with relentless irony in the bittersweet voice of his unhappy millionaire. From his perspective at the top of the capitalist heap, Levinsky looks back over a life marked by an only-in-America metamorphosis that is nothing less than spectacular but that leaves him unsatisfied. His life has been a failure, he complains, because worldly triumph has not produced an end to the sorrows experienced in childhood. Success has in fact intensified them. Life in America has been an attempt to escape past deprivation. Wealth and position have isolated him from the objects of his desire—from love, companionship, and community. Hunger and loneliness, the legacies of his childhood, are the enduring conditions of his adulthood. Yearning has shaped him and he constantly returns to it. It becomes a reflexive, self-defining act, its own end. "The gloomiest past," he broods, "is dearer than the brightest present."[14] And yet he persists on a course that can only intensify his longings as it satisfies his ego.[15]

The first four sections of the novel—roughly one-sixth of it—chronicle Levinsky's childhood. What becomes apparent in these sections is that the division of his traditional (pious, familial) and modern (secular, acquisitive) self—the opposition that is formative to his lifelong dissatisfaction/yearning cycle—is rooted in his Russian past and not in American conditions. Each half of Levinsky's personality has been molded by two significant people in his childhood, one male, the other female. From his self-sacrificing mother and the otherworldly surrogate-father Reb Sender have come his veneration for family life, his piety, and his love for learning. This is one-half of the Russian legacy. The other consists of the influence of his friend Napthali, who introduced him to Russian literature and secular thought, and of the emancipated Jewish woman, Matilda, who provided his first sexual temptation and, appropriately, the ticket to America. Having drifted from the male influence of Sender to that of Napthali (sacred to secular learning) and from the female influence of his mother to that of Matilda (familial to sexual love), Levinsky was, in a real way, ready for America. Immigration did not engender the modernization of Levinsky, it nourished it.[16]

Desiring love and learning in America, Levinsky realizes neither. The dream of attending City College, New York's "secular temple," gives way to economic opportunity. The sweatshop labor that would have paid for his education goes instead into his capitalist venture. The acquisition of money, to the immigrant who set aside his reading of Charles Dickens and took up Herbert Spencer, becomes, in Levinsky's rationalization, a sign of his intellectual superiority— empirical evidence that he is one of the fittest.

The desire for love is similarly unfulfilled. He is attracted to women who remind him of the past, who will reconnect him with the world he has fled but still desires, women who combine the lost mother and the lost lover. Perpetuating the pattern of childhood deprivation, he fatally chases after women he cannot have, women, that is, who will not have him. One (Dora) is married; another (Matilda) is a socialist; and a third (Anna) is an idealist. The conditions of his life—and theirs—have made romance impossible. The women he can have, those, that is, who will have him, he rejects. A "believer in the cold, drab theory of the survival of the fittest," Levinsky nonetheless suscribes to the religion of family life. His fantasies turn on love objects that fuse the domestic, spiritual, and sexual. One takes the shape of a "table set for dinner. . . . Home and woman were one, a complex charm joining them into an inseparable force."[17]

In Cahan's earlier, shorter fiction as well, failures in love and sex are linked with the failure to fuse opposing traditional and modern selves. Jake Podkovnik, the clownish "allrightnik" of his first book, the novella *Yekl: A Tale of the New York Ghetto* (1896), divorces his orthodox Russian wife and marries the flashier Mamie Fein, puzzling at the end whether he has made the right decision. History tugs at Jake but never too hard. He see the past he has betrayed as "a charming tale, which he was neither willing to banish from his memory nor reconcile with the actualities of his American present."[18] In Cahan's fiction what has been betrayed can neither be forgotten nor retrieved. In his story "The Imported Bridegroom" (1898) the widowed Asriel Stroon, full of regret at having drifted from his faith, imports a talmudist from his native village to be husband to his daughter. Such a match will ensure him a place in heaven. The bridegroom-elect, however, makes other plans in America, and the old man is denied his bid to recoup his losses. In Cahan's many short stories of love and marriage in the ghetto, only one, "A Ghetto Wedding" (1898), offers the prospect of a permanent, fulfilling liaison.

In *The Rise of David Levinsky* characters from the Old World reappear in the New as they do in other immigrant novels. Here, though, they appear not to reveal how America has transformed them—from *shister* to mister or the reverse—but to show how America has transformed Levinsky. They function as mirrors throwing back disagreeable images. Contacts with the past are always causes for discomfort. Levinsky feels nostalgic when he meets a *landsman*, but his way of life makes impossible a rapprochement. Matilda, who kindled his sexual awakening in the village of Antomir, arrives in America as a socialist and is repelled by Levinsky as capitalist. Late in the novel he takes Gitelson, his "ship brother," to the Waldorf for lunch to mark the twenty-fifth anniversary of their arrival, his heart filled with sentiment. But Gitelson, a poor tailor, clumsy and ill at ease among the obsequious waiters and unable to read the menu, seems unreachable, even irrelevant in Levinsky's life. One of the operators in his plant, a man he knew as a boy in Russia, is an ardent union leader. Levinsky sentimentally retains him until the man's virulent, anti-capitalistic speeches force his hand and he fires him. A strike ensues and Levinsky becomes, to his workers, what Rabbi Graetz was to the ghetto Jews—a betrayer of his own people. Unable to reconcile the opposing mandates of the self—Jewish heart and American ego—he remains, despite his wealth, the unloved, hungry, lonely New World seeker.

IV

The 1920's produced other American-Jewish novels about the gaining of America and the loss of the integrated self. Samuel Ornitz's 1923 novel, *Haunch Paunch and Jowl*, invites comparison with Cahan's novel as a confessional account of the immigrant's rise from ghetto poverty, *Yidishkayt*, and rigid orthodoxy to wealth, power, and position in America. But while Cahan's novel turns on its narrator's unhappy discovery that the past cannot be bought off with money, that lunch at the Waldorf cannot satisfy hunger, Ornitz gives us a comic, urban picaro who scrambles his way to the top with a full belly and without a thought about the past. Levinsky is always looking back, measuring his gains against losses; Meyer Hirsch never looks back. Born literally between two worlds, on the boat to America, he steps out of the traditional world of his parents, the *cheder* and the *momme loschen*, and into the world of the street gang, the first rung on an American success ladder he mounts through careers in extortion and bribery, climbing to the top as judge of New York's Superior Criminal Court. If sex was the principal taboo of Levinsky's *shtetl* boyhood, it was among the most available and cheapest commodities to Hirsch's Ludlow Street gang, to whom the Jewish whores on Allen Street offered "cut rates." City College is not the "secular temple" it was to Levinsky, but the ticket from "wretches to riches." Gratification, not deprivation, marks Hirsch's rite of passage in the urban jungle.

Published as the "anonymous autobiography" of a New York politician, it is a relentlessly cynical book, and Ornitz's bitterness shows through every page of Hirsch's self-justifying account of his rise. Despite its comic adventures, it is a tough book, its toughness anticipating that of Michael Gold's 1930 memoir of a ghetto boyhood, *Jews Without Money*. Gold's book, however, points in an opposite direction on its final pages—toward its young hero's collectivist commitment. In doing so, it looks ahead to 1930's proletarian fiction, much of it the product of Jewish writers. Ornitz, whose later career as a screenwriter would end with his imprisonment as one of the "Hollywood Ten" following the House Un-American Activities Committee witch-hunt of the screen industry, offers no proletarian voice in this novel, but the whole work is an indictment of the power hunger of his protagonist and, more broadly, the capitalist system that offers grand rewards to the wily street fighter.[19]

Ornitz sets Hirsch off against three ancillary characters, each offering a gloss on his career. Throughout the book he yearns for the ghetto girl, Esther, a settlement worker who rejects him and marries a wealthy gentile social worker and philanthropist. Hirsch's metamorphosis, like Levinsky's, has alienated him from the love he seeks. He has chosen the wrong girl to fall in love with. A subplot concerning his uncle, Philip Gold, details a career that parallels Hirsch's. A sweatshop worker, victim of German-Jewish contractors, Gold turns first to socialism, but then, Levinsky-fashion, discovers he can beat the Germans at their own game by opening his own sweatshop and exploiting newly arrived immigrants. He rises from worker to owner and purchases his admission ticket to America by marrying the daughter of a rich German Jew, moving to Riverside Drive, joining the prestigious Fifth Avenue Temple, and becoming a force in Republican politics. A third character, Lionel Crane (born Lazarus Cohen), a member of Hirsch's boyhood gang, becomes a successful psychiatrist specializing in "race psychopathology." A product of the ghetto, he argues that the "Jewish question" will not be resolved until Jews learn to be invisible, to blend with the landscape, to free themselves of their neurotic insistence on their Jewishness. Cohen is the kind of Jew who will reappear later in the decade in Ludwig Lewisohn's fiction.

Before Lewisohn, though, comes Anzia Yezierska, the most significant Jewish writer of the twenties (Cahan wrote no more fiction after 1917). Between 1920 and 1932 Yezierska wrote six books about New York ghetto women trapped between Old World culture and New World urges. The recurring story she told was of the sensitive, intelligent woman, hungry for America, reaching out from the walls of the ghetto for love and a career, but finding that the American promise is bitter. Her heroines reject parents and tradition; they identify success with an American education, and, often enough, marriage with a wealthy Anglo-Saxon, a path that leads to more conflict. John Barnes, in *Hungry Hearts* (1920), and Henry Scott, in *All I Could Never Be* (1932), are Anglo-Saxon men of letters, American success models who represent to the immigrant heroines the ideal of what the New World can offer. But the relationships end in misunderstanding and confusion. In *All I Could Never Be*, for instance, the heroine is drawn to a sophisticated, urbane professor and tries to be like him, only to discover that what he is romantically drawn to is the Jewess as exotic, forbidden outsider. Her heroines find neither romantic love nor emotional satisfaction in America. They may realize, through a strong assertion of will, the dream of education and career, but they remain unfulfilled and hungry.

Yezierska first attracted attention with a long, two-part story, "The Fat of the Land," which the anthologist Edward O'Brien chose as the best story of 1919. The story attracted the attention of Samuel Goldwyn and landed Yezierska a Hollywood contract. Reprinted in her first collection, *Hungry Hearts*, it presents a ghetto mother, Hannah Breinah, who constantly complains of the hardness of her life. Life means hungry, dirty, squabbling children and unending work. A neighbor tells her that when the children are old enough to work, she "will have the fat of the land." The prophesy comes true. In the second part of the story the children are grown and successful, and she is ensconced in a plush Riverside Drive resident hotel, complete with maid and meal service. But in prosperity she is still miserable. The food "looks so fancy on the plate, but is nothing but straw in the mouth. I am starving, but I can't swallow their American eating."[20] And so she sneaks off to Delancey Street on the lower East Side to bargain for fish, smuggling the booty back to Riverside Drive. While the story has neither the aspiring America-hungry young heroine nor the romantic involvement with the American male, it establishes the tale Yezierska was to tell repeatedly: the escape from the ghetto and poverty that is no escape at all, the tale of hunger that knows no end.[21] At the same time, it foretells her own story, that of the "Sweatshop Cinderella," the woman transformed by success but unhappy and unfulfilled in her new life.

Her most autobiographical novel, *Bread Givers* (1925), follows these lines.

Like "The Fat of the Land," it is a two-part tale. In the first part Sara Smolinsky watches helplessly as her tyrannical, religious father self-righteously bargains off her three sisters to men they do not love, money-grubbers who will provide for him in his old age. The daughters are investments, commodities to be manipulated. The second part focuses on Sara's rebellion and return. Determined not to be another sacrifice, she leaves home, works to save money for an education and returns, college degree in hand. What she learns, though, is that the greater the distance she places between herself and her father, the more she is aware of the legacy: to deny the father is to deny the self:

How could I have hated him and tried to blot him out of my life? Can I hate my arm, my hand that is part of me? Can a tree hate the roots from which it sprang? Deeper than love, deeper than pity, is that oneness of the flesh that's in him and in me. Who gave me the fire, the passion to push myself up from the dirt? If I grow, if I rise, if I ever amount to something, is it not his spirit burning in me?[22]

Ludwig Lewisohn's *The Island Within* (1928) is another novel of Jewish return, tracing its author's own recoil from Americanization. Lewisohn, a German Jew, arrived in America at the age of seven, grew up in the South, and received an M.A. at Columbia University, but was one of those who found that Jews, particularly those with German surnames, were not welcome on English faculties. Discrimination and anti-Semitism convinced him that Jews could not be at home in America and pushed him toward Zionism. Arthur Levy, his psychiatrist-hero, is the American-born son of affluent, emancipated German Jews living on New York's upper West Side. The family's movement from traditional Judaism to secularism begins long before the generation of his parents. The first part of the novel summarizes four generations of family history in Europe by tracing the drift from orthodoxy in Lithuania to secularism, intermarriage, and commercial success in Germany, not without anti-Semitic encounters. Arthur Levy is similarly confronted by anti-Semitism. A sister is denied admission to a school because of Jewish quotas. An aristocratic gentile friend makes him aware that what America wants of Jews is not simply the abandonment of their history but the acknowledgment of a Christian history:

The Dawsons didn't only want the Levys to be loyal to their common present; the Dawsons wanted the Levys to give up imaginatively the Levy past and adopt the Dawson past. And the Levys did it; they did it. . . . Wouldn't they all hock their shirts for ancestors and cousins in Inverness? . . . You mustn't have any sentiment which wouldn't be yours if your people had in fact come from Inverness.[23]

As a novel about Jews living among, and competing with, Christians in the American city during what historian John Higham called "The Tribal Twenties," the decade of 100 percent Americanism and quota laws, it is a novel that inevitably has to be about both anti-Semitism and Jewish strategy for survival. "Protective mimicry," the adoption of "a technique of life that would insure gentile society'' is the strategy Levy is taught. When he complains to the family's sponsor in America about the treatment of Jews in mental institutions, he is admonished that Jews ought not to ''put themselves forward in any way that may be interpreted as a criticism of the existing order or its institutions.''[24]

Convinced that his own attachment to Judaism is only peripheral, he marries the agnostic daughter of a pastor; she turns out to be a sexually repressed, thoroughly neurotic woman. The *shikse*, in this 1920's version of the intermarriage story, is neither the emblem of Americanization nor the forbidden other, but now the Nordic iceberg, the emancipated but sexless new career woman for whom marriage is ''a pleasant companionship,'' not a ''deeper and more tragic union.'' Lewisohn is obviously playing one of the decade's favorite themes, the Freudian-inspired myth of the Puritan as repressed neurotic. The Jewish hero, portrayed as Freudian analyst, has won the *shikse*, but she comes portrayed as Freudian stereotype. Unable to display any passion, Elizabeth Knight is attracted to Levy because he has the sensuality she lacks. ''I love your Jewish darkness and ardor,'' she tells him. The irony is that she is attracted to his Jewishness only as long as he denies it. When he asserts it, she feels threatened. The marriage, based on the flimsy appeal of stereotype, collapses when the Jewish nature of Levy materializes. A distant cousin, a *Hasidic* Jew, shows up like an ancient messenger, and proceeds to tell Levy a thousand-year-old story of his people. Levy is aroused, but Elizabeth ''cringes at the symbol of something infinitely alien . . . of which her husband was a part.''[25] When she says, ''You didn't know you were going to resurrect the Jew in you,'' he responds: ''I didn't have to resurrect the Jew. I just put away the pretense . . . a stubborn, hard, protective core.''[26]

Lewisohn's fable of return closes the circle opened by Henry Harland forty-plus years earlier. For Harland, an Anglo-Saxon liberal posing as Jewish writer, the salvation of the Jew, and of America, lay in intermarriage, in the interbreeding of oldest and newest American stock. Amalgamation, not separatism nor cultural pluralism, would offer the best hope for a new, revitalized America. The Jew would enrich America if he could but free himself from the prison-house of ethnic identity. The exotic outsider would be the happy insider, Harland preached, and America would be the winner. Union with the American gentile is the destiny of the Jew, and his bizarre stories were meant as warnings of the peril of refusing that destiny. For Lewisohn, the Jew who took Harland at his word, who secured his Columbia degree in English letters only to find the gates of the academy shut, and whose first marriage was unhappily with a gentile woman, destiny lay in another direction. Lewisohn's America turned out not to be the crucible at all, as it was to earlier Jewish writers like Ezra Brudno, Elias Tobenkin, and Israel Zangwill.

But if Lewisohn's voice, along with those of Sidney Nyburg, Abraham Cahan, and Anzia Yezierska, effectively stilled the shriller, messianic assimilationist voices of pre-war immigrant writers, it was not the voice that would carry the decade of the thirties. With the crash, the Depression, and the mounting threat of European fascism, the American-Jewish writer of the thirties would have other priorities. The condition of the Jew in Christian America would continue to the present day to be the major theme of American-Jewish fiction, but for the writers of the thirties that concern would yield to, or merge with, a preoccupation with the very condition of America. Together with a host of socially dedicated poets, playwrights, painters, photographers, and critics, American-Jewish novelists would engage in the critical exploration of America itself that defined and shaped the intellectual commitment of the Depression decade. They became participants in that re-examination of all things American that gave the 1930's, that most self-conscious of native decades, its enduring legacy. Through narratives of ghetto childhoods like Michael Gold's *Jews Without Money* (1930) and Henry Roth's *Call It Sleep* (1934), or through proletarian novels of the awakening and conversion of the industrial worker, the American-Jewish writer of the thirties built on the foundation of the immigrant experience and established a modern Jewish literary and moral sensibility that would reach full maturity in the post–World War II "Breakthrough" of the Jewish writer as essential American. To return to Lawrence, "America has never been easy." The American-Jewish writer has not said it was.

NOTES

1. D. H. Lawrence, *Studies in Classic American Literature*, p. 5.

2. Abraham Cahan, *The Rise of David Levinsky*, p. 61.

3. Anzia Yezierska, *Children of Loneliness: Stories of Immigrant Life in America*, p. 38.

4. Samuel Ornitz, *Haunch Paunch and Jowl*, p. 3.

5. Leslie Fiedler, "Genesis: The American-Jewish Novel through the Twenties," p. 21.

6. See Philip Gleason, "The Melting Pot: Symbol of Fusion or Confusion?" pp. 20–46. Gleason demonstrates that the term was used euphemistically in these years to denote almost any view toward assimilation favored by those using it. Theoretically, it should be noted, assimilation can be divided into two broad types, melting-pot fusion and Anglo-conformity, but in common use the distinction blurs; melting pot has been used for both types.

7. See Randolph Bourne, "Trans-National America," pp. 86–97; and Horace Kallen, "Democracy versus the Melting Pot," pp. 190–194, 217–220. Kallen's position was restated in *Culture and Democracy in the United States*.

8. Fiedler, p. 28.

9. Frederick Cople Jaher, "The Quest for the Ultimate Shiksa," pp. 518–542. When I am not directly quoting Jaher, I have retained the more familiar English spelling "*shikse*."

10. Sidney Luska [Henry Harland], *As It Was Written, A Jewish Musician's Story*, pp. 105–106. For other enthusiastic assertions of what Jews can contribute to American life, see Hutchins Hapgood, *The Spirit of the Ghetto: Studies of the Jewish Quarter in New York*, and his brother Norman Hapgood's "The Jews and American Democracy," p. 201.

11. Israel Zangwill, *The Melting-Pot*, p. 199.

12. Edward Steiner, *The Mediator*, p. 249.

13. Sidney Nyburg, *The Chosen People*, p. 76.

14. Abraham Cahan, *Levinsky*, p. 526.

15. For an interesting account of the conflict between the overt and covert content of Levinsky's "autobiography," see Sanford Marovitz, "The Secular Trinity of a Lonely Millionaire: Language, Sex, and Power in *The Rise of David Levinsky*," pp. 20–35.

16. See David Singer, "David Levinsky's Fall: A Note on the Liebman Thesis," pp. 696–706. Singer applies to Cahan's novel Liebman's thesis that emigrating Eastern-European Jews were not in the main orthodox; he demonstrates that the breakdown of Levinsky's orthodoxy and piety occurred before the voyage and was not a product of it.

17. Cahan, *Levinsky*, pp. 376–377.

18. Abraham Cahan, *Yekl, a Tale of the New York Ghetto*, p. 54.

19. On Ornitz's career see Gabriel Miller, "Samuel Ornitz: A Hollywood Pastoral," pp. 81–85.

20. Anzia Yezierska, "The Fat of the Land," in *Hungry Hearts*, p. 218.

21. See Ellen Golub, "Eat Your Heart Out: The Fiction of Anzia Yezierska," pp. 51–61, on the use of hunger and food as metaphors for desire thwarted—for the "libidinal" language of desire.

22. Anzia Yezierska, *Bread Givers*, p. 286.

23. Ludwig Lewisohn, *The Island Within*, p. 167.

24. Ibid., pp. 192–193.

25. Ibid., p. 314.

26. Ibid., p. 346.

BIBLIOGRAPHY

Bourne, Randolph. "Trans-National America." *Atlantic Monthly*. 118. (July, 1916), pp. 86–97.

Cahan, Abraham. *The Rise of David Levinsky*. New York: Harper and Brothers, 1917.

———. *Yekl, a Tale of the New York Ghetto*. New York: Appleton, 1896.

Fiedler, Leslie. "Genesis: The American-Jewish Novel through the Twenties." *Midstream*. 4. (Summer, 1958), pp. 21–33.

Gleason, Philip. "The Melting Pot: Symbol of Fusion or Confusion?" *American Quarterly*. 16. (Spring, 1964), pp. 20–46.

Golub, Ellen. "Eat Your Heart Out: The Fiction of Anzia Yezierska." *Studies in American Jewish Literature*, ed. Daniel Walden. 3. (1983), pp. 51–61.

Hapgood, Hutchins. *The Spirit of the Ghetto: Studies of the Jewish Quarter in New York*. New York: Funk and Wagnalls, 1902.

Hapgood, Norman. "The Jews and American Democracy." *The Menorah Journal*. 2. (October 1916), pp. 201–205.

Jaher, Frederick Cople. "The Quest for the Ultimate Shiksa." *American Quarterly*. 35. (Winter, 1983), pp. 518–542.

Kallen, Horace. *Culture and Democracy in the United States*. New York: Boni and Liveright, 1924.

———. "Democracy versus the Melting Pot." *Nation*. 100. (February 18, 1915 and February 25, 1915), pp. 190–194, 217–220.

Lawrence, D. H. *Studies in Classic American Literature*. New York: T. Seltzer, 1923; rpt. New York: Viking Press, 1966.

Lewisohn, Ludwig. *The Island Within*. New York: Harper and Brothers, 1928.

Luska, Sidney [Henry Harland]. *As It Was Written, A Jewish Musician's Story*. New York: Cassell, 1885.

Marovitz, Sanford. "The Secular Trinity of a Lonely Millionaire: Language, Sex, and Power in *The Rise of David Levinsky*." *Studies in American Jewish Literature*, ed. Daniel Walden. 2. (1982), pp. 20–35.

Miller, Gabriel. "Samuel Ornitz: A Hollywood Pastoral." *Studies in American Jewish Literature*, ed. Daniel Walden. 2 (1982), pp. 81–85.

Nyburg, Sidney. *The Chosen People*. New York: Lippincott, 1917.

[Ornitz, Samuel]. *Haunch Paunch and Jowl*. New York: Boni and Liveright, 1923; rpt. New York: Pocket Books, 1968.

Singer, David. "David Levinsky's Fall: A Note on the Liebman Thesis." *American Quarterly*. 19. (Winter, 1967), pp. 696–706.

Steiner, Edward. *The Mediator*. New York: Fleming H. Revell, 1907.

Yezierska, Anzia. *Bread Givers*. Garden City, N.Y.: Doubleday, Page and Co., 1925; rpt. New York: Persea Books, 1975.

————. *Children of Loneliness: Stories of Immigrant Life in America*. New York: Funk and Wagnalls, 1923.

Zangwill, Israel. *The Melting-Pot*. New York: Macmillan, 1908.

FOR FURTHER READING

Primary

Bernstein, Herman. *In the Gates of Israel: Stories of the Jews*. New York: Taylor, 1902.

Cahan, Abraham. *The Imported Bridegroom and Other Stories of the New York Ghetto*. Boston: Houghton Mifflin, 1898.

Glass, Montague. *Potash and Perlmutter*. Philadelphia: Henry Altemus, 1910.

Lessing, Bruno [Block, Rudolph]. *Children of Men*. New York: McClure, Phillips, 1903.

Oppenheim, James. *Dr. Rast*. New York: Sturgis and Walton, 1909.

Secondary

Chametzky, Jules. *From the Ghetto: The Fiction of Abraham Cahan*. Amherst: University of Massachusetts Press, 1977.

————. "Main Currents in American Jewish Literature from the 1880s to the 1950s." *Ethnic Groups*. 4. (1984), pp. 85–101.

Engle, David. "The 'Discrepancies' of the Modern: Towards a Revaluation of Abraham Cahan's *The Rise of David Levinsky*." *Studies in American Jewish Literature*. 2. (1982), pp. 36–60.

Fine, David. "Attitudes toward Acculturation in the English Fiction of the Jewish Immigrant." *American Jewish Historical Quarterly*. 63. (September, 1973), pp. 45–56.

————. *The City, the Immigrant, and American Fiction, 1880–1920*. Metuchen, New Jersey: Scarecrow Press, 1977.

Girgus, Sam. *The New Covenant*. Chapel Hill: University of North Carolina Press, 1984.

Halper, Albert. "Notes on Jewish American Fiction." *The Menorah Journal*. 20. (Spring, 1932), pp. 61–69.

Harap, Lewis. *The Image of the Jew in American Literature*. Philadelphia: Jewish Publication Society, 1974.

Higham, John. "Introduction" to *The Rise of David Levinsky*. New York: Harper Torchbook Edition, 1960, pp. v–xii.

Howe, Irving. *World of Our Fathers*. New York: Harcourt Brace Jovanovich, 1976.

Kamel, Rose. "Anzia Yezierska, Get Out of Your Own Way: Selfhood and Otherness in the Autobiographical Fiction of Anzia Yezierska." *Studies in American Jewish Literature*. 3. (1983), pp. 40–50.

Kirk, Rudolph and Clara Kirk. "Abraham Cahan and William Dean Howells: The Story of a Friendship." *American Jewish Historical Quarterly*. 52. (September 1962), pp. 25–57.

Kress, Susan. "Women and Marriage in Abraham Cahan's Fiction." *Studies in American Jewish Literature*. 3. (1983), pp. 26–39.

Liptzin, Solomon. *The Jew in American Literature*. New York: Bloch, 1966.

Marovitz, Sanford. "The Lonely New Americans of Abraham Cahan." *American Quarterly*. 20. (1968), pp. 196–210.

Marovitz, Sanford and Lewis Fried. "Abraham Cahan: An Annotated Bibliography." *American Literary Realism, 1870–1910*. 3. (1970), pp. 197–243.

Rischin, Moses. *The Promised City*. Cambridge: Harvard University Press, 1962.

Rosenfeld, Isaac. "America, Land of the Sad Millionaire." *Commentary*. 14. (August, 1952), pp. 131–135.

Sanders, Ronald. *The Downtown Jews: Portraits of an Immigrant Generation*. New York: Harper and Row, 1969.

Schoen, Carol. *Anzia Yezierska*. Boston: Twayne Press, 1982.

————. "Anzia Yezierska: New Light on the Sweatshop Cinderella." *MELUS*. 7. (1980), pp. 3–11.

Sherman, Bernard. *The Invention of the Jew: Jewish-American Education Novels, 1916–1964*. New York: Thomas Yoseloff, 1969.

Syrkin, Marie. "Jewish Awareness in American Literature." *The American Jew: A Reappraisal*, ed. Oscar Janowsky. Philadelphia: Jewish Publication Society, 1964, pp. 211–234.

2

American-Jewish Fiction, 1930–1945

Lewis Fried

I

American-Jewish writers who came of age during the 1930's were often drawn to movements that claimed to interpret their history and experience. They lived in perilous times that called for explanations if not for certainty. The momentous redefinitions of national purpose caused, in part, by the collapse of progressive idealism after World War I, the Great Depression, the emergence of a vigorous socialist politics and the rise of European Nazism were disintegrative and interpretive crises for the American-Jewish community as well. Marxism, Zionism, liberalism, and a heterodox theology were seen as pathways to modernity. They could reorient and renew what many thinkers felt was an archaic Jewish life so that it would have a significant role to play in the American present. No less important, the American inclination to conceive of the future as open and the past as "a bucket of ashes" encouraged a number of American-Jewish writers to see their diaspora heritage as simply irrelevant to their circumstances. Assimilation was a welcome fact of their American existence.

This generation shared not a crisis of faith but crises about what they could know with certainty and act upon. The writers of this period came to no agreement about a common Jewish future, or for that matter no consensus about the value of the past, though they did agree generally upon one version of it, the story of the European emigration: flight from persecution, arrival in New York, a life of struggle, and a spiritually impoverishing success.

In other words, they were not a *Kreise* but they had common and commonizing experiences. In the main, they were urban, and accepted the opportunities of the city as the backdrop of their fiction. Having lived in a city of and in transition and being children of upheaval, they took change—conceptual and physical— as part of the substance of American life. They believed they had a stake in the making of a public culture and some version of the American future.

As they matured, they would be of the immigrant, Jewish past of their parents, but not in it. They might remember some Yiddish, or Hebrew, but they would devour Emerson and Thoreau to learn about a culture of man, or find that their mentors in writing were Turgenev and Tolstoy. Yiddish and Hebrew literatures were not taken as nourishing traditions.

The Depression swept them into hard times. As *writers* or aspirants, they found that the growing American left, especially the Communist party, was eager to encourage them. For one, the party seemed to have answers to the American crisis; its reading of European and American politics seemed to be convincing. The theses of Marxism—as the party saw them—could give writers a sureness of vision and judgment. The party's various claims about art and artists indicated the revolutionary significance of writing and its place in a new society. For another, left-wing periodicals usually fostered untried writers (the masthead of *The Anvil* proclaimed, "We prefer crude vigor to polished banality"; the *New Masses* published an immense amount of promising, and sometimes robustly awkward, writing). The John Reed Clubs helped would-be authors learn their craft as well as digest the guidelines of the party. Finally, the intellectual ferment of the left was compelling and familiar; it was part of immigrant Jewish life.

I want to sketch these major denominators with an eye toward their presence in the literature of this period.

Theology

This generation grew up with an insurrectionary theology—continuing the nineteenth-century struggles by Reform and nascent Conservative branches of American Jewry—that contested the prescriptive Judaism of Eastern-European immigrants. This group was the first significant generation of Jewish writers in America born to this portentous revolution. During these authors' lifetimes, the individual ceased to find Judaism at the core of his existence and came to expect that a theology would revolve around the self and its needs. A scientific biblical exegesis, based on modern philology, anthropology, and sociology, discerned underneath a mass of tradition an enduring yet modern Jewish spirit—so one argument goes. Reconstruction was not hypothetical in concept or in consequence. It affected, in a short time, the commitments of a generation to what it saw as a people and acted upon as individuals.

Writers of this group inherited, by the mid-thirties, a Judaism discontinuous with that of the past. The tenets of orthodoxy that regulated a substantial portion of European-Jewish deportment—that Judaism was a covenanted theological culture regulated by the system of *Halakhah* (law)—had no center of authority and judgment in America. American congregationalist influence, the spirit of American autonomy, and the disagreements of Jews themselves militated against this opportunity. Few individuals were able to speak compellingly enough about the significance of faith and ritual to a new secular generation. If there was a common faith that seemed to speak to the temper of progressive America, it was faith in man's ability to extend control over nature and society.

In America, redefinition of belief—in fact, of the scope and form of Jewish life—was an urgent project throughout this generation's life. A convenient landmark is Kaufmann Kohler's creed for Reform Judaism, *Jewish Theology Systematically and Historically Considered* (1918), in which he argued that "the Jewish religion has never been static, fixed for all time by an ecclesiastical authority but . . . is the result of a dynamic process of growth."[1] Kohler sought to distinguish the animating and irreducible theses of Judaism from their historically conventional form. His appeal to contemporary scientific methodologies—social and natural—was aimed at an audience comfortable with the thought that Judaism had no commanding principle inaccessible to reason.

By the time these writers were adults, efforts to define a contemporary American Judaism were commonplace: often found, for instance, in *The Menorah Journal* but reaching an apogee with Mordecai Kaplan's naturalistic *Judaism as a Civilization* (1934). Here, Judaism is examined in positivistic fashion emphasizing the historical, social function of its parts and their interrelationship. God is presented as a chronologically variable social idea that could best be replaced by the concept of a cooperative, filiating drive of nature. Jewish life is studied as a civilization, theology being but one part of it; God, as a struggling, ordering force of nature vaguely definable by physical law.

The line of inquiry from Kohler to Kaplan was consistent in consequence: orthodoxy had conceptually arrested an evolving Jewish existence. Orthodoxy had ignored the nature of Judaism's historically creative adjustments to circumstance. Finally, a religion that was dogmatic and formally archaic had nothing to say to a modern public. The implications were emphatic: Judaism had to be demystified and made to answer the questions of social and natural science.

Such radical American theological ventures redefined Jewish belief by stressing the autonomy of reason. Theological explication could—and did—pass into the hands of laymen essentially untrained in rabbinics: a not unprovocative effort ranging from Ludwig Lewisohn (who enticingly called his anthology of Jewish meditations *Rebirth: A Book of Modern Jewish Thought*, 1935) to Waldo Frank (whose interpretation of the Jewish heritage is entitled *The Jew in Our Day*, 1944). Therefore, it is not surprising to see that this generation's idea of "Jewishness"—in the largest sense of the term—promoted a self-given character, one predicated on the individual's need to translate the "truths" of Judaism into culture, to make Jewish theology serve personal, civic, and political causes and often to affiliate with Judaism only if it could be pressed into a necessary service.

It is worthwhile looking at the reflections upon the uses of Judaism toward the end of the Second World War when writers had more privilege than ever to argue for a return to orthodoxy and tradition. In February of 1944, the *Contemporary Jewish Record* presented the faith of these children of immigrants. Calling them "writers of Jewish descent," and arguing that they "are spectators no longer but full participants in the cultural life of this country," the editors of the journal asked them to discuss the influence of their heritage upon their work.[2] Interestingly, a number of writers contended that the legacy of Judaism was its passion for justice and ethic of universalism. Albert Halper observed that his Jewishness made him aware of the assaults on human decency: "Being a Jew has helped me to see the terrifying deadliness of the whole business."[3] Howard Fast claimed that part of a Jew's heritage is to "know intimately all the forces of hate and persecution."[4] Muriel Rukeyser spoke of Judaism as a "guarantee" against fascism as well as against "many kinds of temptation to close the spirit."[5]

In an explanation which saw the Jew and his predicament as constituting the human condition of the time, Delmore Schwartz wrote that the "fact of being a Jew became available to me as a central symbol of alienation, bias . . . and other characteristics which are the peculiar marks of modern life . . . the essential ones."[6]

Isaac Rosenfeld observed how the Jew's estrangement from society suggested a way to recover the totality of human relations. As he put it:

But alienation from society, like the paradox of the outsider, may function as a condition of entrance into society. Surely it is not a condition for the Jew's re-entrance into the world that has rejected him. But persecution may lead him, as it has in the past, to a further effort to envisage the good society.[7]

Elsewhere, Waldo Frank contended that the characteristic Jewish urge for justice is restated for modernity by Spinoza and Marx. Frank writes that "Marx is the man who most surely projected the prophetic aspiration of social justice into a cogent modern program . . . ." Spinoza's achievement was the "purifying of the knowledge of God into the God of inwardness, of substance and of action."[8] This Judeo-Marxist naturalism guaranteed the relevance of Jewish theology for any age by deriving social justice from the order of nature and culture.

After the war, in his own observation about a modern Judaism, Paul Goodman argued that the "disease of all real community in America is the most important cause of the specifically Jewish community illness."[9] His contentions—that Creation "justifies itself"; that "God is not a body"; that the "Messiah will come"; and that "all the rest is dubious and unessential" expressed his own idea of necessary Jewish theology. The unique and anticipatory dimension of experience prepares us for whatever may happen; the possibilities of human nature point to a richer engagement with the environment. As a result, the facts of self and world constitute an agenda for the essential Jewish community. For Goodman, sanctification becomes full engagement.

The only major authors of this period who allied their writing to somewhat conventional avowals of Jewish tradition (but not theology) were Ludwig Lewisohn and Meyer Levin. Lewisohn identified the Jewish self as a *Yidishe neshome*, a Jewish soul, but one in exile in the contemporary world. The non-Jewish environment contaminates this soul, making it forget its essential unity with a destiny and a Covenant. However, the land of Palestine can redeem the people of Israel both through a politics founded upon the justice of the prophets and upon uniquely Jewish social arrangements.[10]

His work, often an auto-da-fé, excoriates modern secularism and moral relativism. Lewisohn became a writer of boundary situations, speaking of the power of tradition and ritual to demarcate the integrity of Jewish existence from doubt and ambiguity. In 1925, in *Israel*, he contended that the Jewish people are one in fact—having their own literature, fable, and history. Nonetheless, a singular cosmopolitan history is part of their residence in exile: parochiality is inimical to the Jewish people. Being a Jew is an embodiment of this situation: living in every country but maintaining national characteristics without might; a renunciation of power and state militarism that indicates a unique and prophetic people. This ethic of quietism is practical; it works because this singular community has survived. (Lewisohn calls this Jews "being themselves.")

By the end of the decade, in a collection of essays entitled *The Answer* (1939), Lewisohn assessed the plight of world Jewry by examining the commitments Jews needed to make to each other and to a secularizing, pluralistic America. Acculturation jeopardized the relationship of the singular (Jewishness) to the universal (humanity). However, American democracy rooted in Jewish text and experience fosters on the part of Jewish citizens a loyalty to the Jewish people as well as the American nation. The particular and the universal preserve each other.

His novels, invariably didactic, dramatize these theses. *Stephen Escott* (1930) portrays the use characters make of their backgrounds to subsist ethically within America. Here, Jewishness is an antidote to the toxin of modernity. Jewish life is now a practice of ritual and compassion. *The Last Days of Shylock* (1931), an inelegant rambling book, depicts a Shylock who discovers that the strength of the Jewish tradition is peace, a Jewish peoplehood, and resignation to God's will. In *This People* (1933), a collection of short stories at times unfortunately given to Lewisohn's pronouncements about modern women, characters resolve their moral problems by acting upon the knowledge that they are members of the people of Israel: Israel as a transcendent culture and faith, but nonetheless a practical community in American life. In *Trumpet of Jubilee* (1937), an apocalyptic work, Lewisohn insists that human action must be subordinated to the law of God which makes for cooperation and peace without force. In *Breathe Upon These* (1944), Lewisohn's argument for a theology of activism, the Dorfsohns, German-Jewish refugees in America, represent the Jew who now sees the law of God within human struggle. Dr. Dorfsohn is an expert in optics and will work to develop bombsights. He urges his gentile hosts, the arid, shallow Burnetts, that man must struggle within and for the world. "If we will His victory," Dorfsohn states, "He will give it to us."

For Levin, who determined to be a novelist capturing the significant contemporary event, the richness of Jewish folk life and the promises of America brought him to the realization that he was "bicultural," that his nature was not so much divided as it was enhanced. His early works veer among then fashionable American subjects such as the city and the proletariat (*Reporter*, 1929; *The New Bridge*, 1933), his attraction to Zionist aspirations (*Yehuda*, 1931), and to the renewal of Jewish life in *Hasidic* parable (*The Golden Mountain*, 1932). These became projects to work through, not in, until he was able to accept the clash of his faith with his nationality or, more tellingly, to reconcile what he believed with what he did. *The Old Bunch* (1937) and *Citizens* (1940) resolve the issue of biculturalism: Levin traces the varieties of Jewish experience through his protagonists' consciousness of what America is.

His works, like Lewisohn's, transform messianic hopes into nationalist affirmations; the Jewish people must deliver themselves from a hateful world. They constitute the Messiah. Given their destiny and past, they are a people apart. While Levin termed himself godless, he wrote of the need to "confirm our belief in Torah" and spoke of the "mystic strain" that bound the people of Israel together. Community, he argued, while not shot through with divinity, was realizable as the social compact, a talmudic idea.[11]

Urbanization

For the most part, these writers took urban life and its numerous opposing values as normal in an era when the countryside still exerted a strong literary and cultural pull on the American imagination. They believed in the power of the city, by virtue of its democratic and democratizing institutions, to make life better, cooperative and shared. The conflict between neighborhood mores and the universalizing promises of city life was reconciled; they usually saw their Jewish past encouraging a progressive politics and culture. As a result, the city bound them to itself; it became the environment they knew—an immense physical and symbolic landscape that wed its heritage to their lives.

Growing up in the city was an education in passages, in journeying from a usually Jewish neighborhood (or state of affairs) to the urban public. When characters returned to their old neighborhoods years later, their moral commitments and allegiances to *Yidishkayt* were judged. Such writing, in the main, dealt with the significance of this odyssey, for it measured the uses of the past and the ability to use a common, public rhetoric. The question these works often asked is if an integrated self, one in touch with its Jewish heritage, had vanished in the vastness of American ambitions. The poignancy of recollection in Albert Halper's *On the Shore* (1934); the use of distance as a moral geography in Budd Schulberg's *What Makes Sammy Run?* (1941); and the attention to the dehumanizing landscape of opportunity in Jerome Weidman's *I Can Get It For You Wholesale* (1937) are examples of the strategic urban journey.

It is a commonplace by now to speak of the city as having a theological context, of its realizing a faith by letting its ethic be enacted. Given the intellectually dazzling and competing resources of the city, the *shul*, the *cheder*— even the congregationalized versions of *kehillah* (community)—were simply parts of the metropolis, more a mediation of the American scene than institutions apart. Whereas European-Jewish fiction depicted the indwelling nature of the sacred in the *shul*, for American-Jewish writing this house of worship was simply a house divested of its extraordinary character and seen as exposed to, if not captured by, American and secularizing interests. In Aben Kandel's caustic *Rabbi Burns* (1931), the temple is, literally, a Hollywood sham. In Edward Dahlberg's *Those Who Perish* (1934), the important Jewish institution is "Community House," which is the arena for political and sexual affairs.

The Depression

Like the early American passage through the Alleghenies, or the journey westward, or the making of cities, the Depression was shared and transforming. It wed ethnic groups and national regions to a common present. For the American-Jewish writer who wanted to realistically portray the environment he knew, the Depression gave him access to *the* American moment; it took him out of a literary province. His sensibilities, usually nurtured in hardship, could easily grasp the bewilderment and despair of other Americans, and they could all too easily understand the writer's portrayal of hard times. The story of the European-Jewish escape to America—a tale which by the end of the twenties had hardened into an almost mandatory litany—could be de-emphasized or abandoned. It was a theme, but no longer *the* theme of Jewish self-reflection. Catastrophe was now the avenue to a majoritarian literature. Devastation and upheaval were the themes of life for most people.

The American-Jewish writer now talked convincingly of the national scene—of people out of work, of poverty, of strikes—but Jewishness often became a literary incidental or a secular, communitarian idea. As such, it was an opportunity for the writer to situate a problem in a context he intimately knew: a realistic portrayal, for example, of family life in an urban American ghetto but an episode often devoid of a relationship to Jewishness qua Judaism. Instead, an exploitive capitalism that deprived the proletariat of its rights, that made law express the interests of the ruling class, and that disguised imperialism as patriotism became a subject that had found its moment. Witness, for example, Nelson Algren's *Somebody in Boots* (1935); Albert Halper's *The Foundry* (1934), *The Chute* (1937), and *Sons of the Fathers* (1940); and Isidor Schneider's *From the Kingdom of Necessity* (1935). Not surprisingly, the writer often gravitated to the left. It seemed to be sure in its reading of national and international politics. In its fight against fascism it was committed.

Strikingly, few if any American-Jewish novelists saw Zionism with its practical socialism as an answer for the Depression. Perhaps the only American-Jewish novelist of the period who presented in fiction the nature of the intentional, visionary Jewish community, the *kibbutz*, as an experiment withstanding the contradictions of capitalism was Meyer Levin. Briefly in *The Old Bunch*, but at length in *Yehuda*, Levin wrote of the *kibbutz's* democratic, socialist nature and its promise of a regulated, equitable life.

Prospects

American-Jewish writers of an earlier generation had written of the perils of de-Judaicization. Identifying the hardships of immigrants with what has been portrayed as *the* Jewish experience, they spoke of the pathos of their protagonists' lives in a secularizing, materialistic city. America had swallowed them, made them lose everything that defined them as Jews: study, faith, community, and often family. If they were a "peculiar" people, a chosen people, America had breached their identity.

For example, Abraham Cahan's eponymous protagonist of *The Rise of David Levinsky* (1917) laments that he is closer to his boyhood when he studied Talmud than to his present self, the lonely millionaire garment manufacturer. Bewildered by the opportunities of America surrounding her religious, almost feudal home, Anzia Yezierska's Sara Smolinsky, the narrator of *Bread Givers* (1925), wants to affirm her modern American identity and yet still be sympathetic toward her past. Imploring her aged father to live with her and her husband, she is callously rejected for not being Jewish enough. She reflects at the end of the novel: "But I felt the shadow still there, over me. It wasn't just my father, but the generations who made my father whose weight was still upon me."[12]

Whereas popular writers of the next generation would almost mechanically adopt this theme, more engaging novelists struggled with the significance of having a singular history in America. Without an allegiance to purposeful community, the idea of "chosenness" was devalued. Chosen—but by whom, and for what? How would this generation see the uses of the Covenant's promises within this present? After all, America had its own fable of destiny among nations.[13]

How would these writers find a usable tradition for their own lives—something that could enrich their sense of self and their writing? Without a continuous bringing of the Jewish past into the American present, the American-Jewish writer would be deprived of his historical community of judgment and voices. Without acceding to the immediacy of American life, though, could one address the contemporary audience? On the other hand, Yiddish writers who were at least linguistically bound together had no future. Their work could not reach a growing public; in time, their work would not be read at all.

American-Jewish writers responded to these questions by "categorizing" their Jewish past. They made Judaism a defined, marked area within their experience. Limiting its influence and scope, they enlarged their own autonomy. They or their protagonists would attempt to increase their freedom by opposing the institutions and myths of their environment, to break the hegemony of the past by making life more open to self-willed destiny, and less subject to the weight of tradition.

II

Four works taking up the subject of the past's interpretation and the need for a discontinuous future appeared in 1930: Michael Gold's *Jews Without Money*, Hyman and Lester Cohen's *Aaron Traum*, Charles Reznikoff's *By the Waters of Manhattan*, and Edward Dahlberg's American edition of *Bottom Dogs*. The protagonists of these novels break the expectations that their traditions and urban ghetto (in this case, the lower East Side, or as in Dahlberg's case the Jewish Orphan Asylum of Cleveland) offer them. Individuals of one exile or another—from place or from history—they demand a future free of tradition. As a result, author and character indicate that the meaning of the Jewish past is in process and redefined by American opportunities. *Bottom Dogs* goes beyond this by rejecting the authenticity of history. Freedom, autonomy, and will are not specious concepts, but they are uninventive and limited actualities. The range of human behavior is small enough so that action quickly becomes permutation and repetition. This present is a tedious variant of the past.

Jews Without Money by Michael Gold (Irwin Granich) is perhaps the best-known proletarian novel portraying Jewish life in New York's lower East Side. It is a memoir of a boy's growing consciousness and conscience. It is also a study in the impotency of Jewish life to maintain its humanizing ethic: the boy witnesses the death of his friends and sister; he is a silent partner in the suffering of his parents; he is tormented by the wish for deliverance. The anguish he bears for himself and those around him will have no end. Yet he is miraculously rescued from a life without hope; he hears a nameless man preaching that "a world movement had been born to abolish poverty."

For all its proletarian fervor, *Jews Without Money* is tacitly based on the Jewish tradition of exile and on the memory of the Covenant's promise of a sanctified life. The book is torn by the notion of a just habitation and the reality of the city-as-tribulation. The novel opens with—and is—an act of recollection that sustains the narrator's compassion. "I can never forget the East Side street where I lived as a boy," Gold's narrator begins, remembering a Jewish community without ethical restraints: parasitism and exploitation destroy Jewish fellowship and benevolence.

Amnesia is a new bondage. Gold's characters often forget what it is to be humane. Charity and compassion are weak insurrections within, but hardly against, the system of capitalism. Nonetheless, these small, personal revolts dramatize the last thing this sprawling population can cling to: a presentiment of the end of a Jewish way of being in America, a knowledge of the ease of sins against man.

A lamentation is the appropriate literary form for Gold's subject; it is a rhetorical strategy that can symbolically and imagistically draw upon the traditions of exile from place and separation of self from empowerment. In *Jews Without Money*, the lamentation portrays the estrangement, brought about by capitalism, of man from his nature and the alienation of the Jew from an ethical peoplehood and land. The lower East Side is now part of a city devastated by God's promised absence. The neighborhood is a wasteland reeking with garbage and excrement. Nature, the narrator remembers, mocks recollections of fecundity—a park outside the area, a few blades of grass growing in manure, a goat eating newspaper, and a horse dying on a street. If God exists, He cannot justify the punishment of His people with this creation, a New York that "is mythical, a city buried by a volcano. No grass is found in this petrified city, no big living trees, no flowers, no bird but the drab little lecherous sparrow, no soil, loam, earth. . . . "[14]

This fabled America is the promised land, yet these scenes of urban waste portray the Jewish community in decline and dispersion. The loss of rain, the degradation of nature, the scattering of the Jews—what could end this diaspora? Paradoxically, *Galut* is now an illegitimate historical concept. Exile and redemption, the sacred and the profane, are no longer categories of experience. They are terms that have no meaning other than literary.

Redemption is an individual choice, a human project that is man fabricating the conditions of his life. In other words, it is a conversion. The tarrying of the Messiah turns man into a passive historical creature. Marxism, on the contrary, delivers history to a people: free will and knowledge act upon nature. The workers' revolution can make the world rational—answerable to the demands of reason. Consequently, hope and deliverance will not be attributes of the religious future but the realities of secular experience. Marxism makes practical and complete a covenant of man for man. (To gauge the spirit of this claim in literature, it is well worth looking at Isidor Schneider's *From the Kingdom of Necessity*, a text that sees Marxism as the inevitable answer to a moribund Judaism. Schneider prefaced the work with Engels's line "It is the ascent of man from the kingdom of necessity to the kingdom of freedom.") Gold makes his point better. His characters are often good-hearted but feckless. They dream of a humane life but they can't bring it about. At the end of the book, Gold declaims:

> O workers' Revolution, you brought hope to me, a lonely suicidal boy. You are the true Messiah. You will destroy the East Side when you come, and build there a garden for the human spirit.
> O Revolution, that forced me to think, to struggle and to live.
> O great Beginning![15]

Gold's reworking of the first line of Genesis deliberately breaks its presentation of a transcendent Creator limiting creation. Instead, Gold celebrates the human appropriation of the world, one that man can make answer his wishes. His invocation to a "garden for the human spirit" and his proclamation that the Revolution taught him to "think, to struggle and to live" usurp Genesis's fable of Adam in Eden: it is now a usable past for the left. "Garden," "live," and "Beginning" constitute the Marxist prologue to an authentic human history.

The title of Reznikoff's *By the Waters of Manhattan* makes a claim to being a diaspora psalm for a new exile—America. The book traces the declining fortunes of the Volsky family in Russia. Sara Yetta, the daughter of Ezekiel and Hannah Volsky, is consumed by intellectual ambitions, but she is told that her obligations are otherwise: marriage and children. America is her escape. She emigrates, marries Saul Rubinow, works hard, and gets nowhere.

Their son, Ezekiel, something of a dreamer, opens a bookstore in the basement of a building—an ironic commentary upon the vastness of his mother's dreams and the reality of his intellectual life in America. He falls in love with Jane, a woman of Jewish-gentile ancestry. Despite his misgivings about his passion and commitment, he remains drawn to her, and the book closes with him on his way to see her.

This is no simple story. The book deals with the role of memory, its interpretive and binding powers, in America. And by interpretive, I mean Jewish communal sensibilities—a feeling for one's place and historical continuity in alien places and unique times—that make for creative adjustments on the part of Jews so that they can maintain rather than abandon their Jewish identity. Throughout the book, Sarah and Saul talk about the need to educate their children as Jews. They are dutiful to the values of their past, especially the concerns of Fivel, Ezekiel's great-grandfather: "I was to provide you with learning and to teach you to be upright."[16] In America, however, almost every inspiring motive in Sarah's life is suffocated. Remembering her own defeated hopes for an education, she argues, "We are a lost generation. . . . It is for our children to do what they can."[17]

Ezekiel belongs to this new exile, one that has not created its sustaining memory and autonomy. His generation knows Jewish life as struggle, but not as the realization of the sacred. He has no examples of an authentically Jewish way of being. For Ezekiel, it is not *Yidishkayt* but Western culture that is appropriated. His wisdom is democratic and literary—brought to any text. He is captured by books whose status changes from pedagogy to commodity. He is "liberated" in a way that his ancestors were not. His grandfather was a talmudic sage. Ezekiel owns a bookstore.

For Ezekiel, independence means a life apart from his daily existence. Ezekiel calls freedom "*his* [my italics] other life [that] would be like the ocean, without a master—except, perhaps, the moon."[18] His creation is this doubleness: he is an American character subsisting within competing presents and pasts. He does not find that his life is divided; he chooses a life that is so. He is partly Jewish but certainly American; intellectual but commercial; erotic but chaste; inclined towards the abstract but emphatically specific. The book ends with Ezekiel looking at his face: it is not ordinary, he realizes, but that of a swindler.

The book is written in what might be called a diction of exile in which imagery and tropes of *pasts* exist within the present. The work draws upon various literary traditions and sacred and secular histories such as an American diction, the cadences of the King James Bible, images of the contemporary commercial city, and events from the Bible. For example, Ezekiel thinks that he "would divide his life. So God divided the world into earth and sky. . . . The shop was land; on this he could build walls and houses, plant vineyards and fig trees. . . . ''[19]

Of Ezekiel's first day at the store, Reznikoff writes, ''It was morning and it was evening, the first day,'' and describes Ezekiel's walk to work: he ''went to the store . . . as calmly as a distant ancestor might have led his sheep to search for pasture. He did not know that there would be pasture, but he had found pasture before—'hitherto hath the Lord helped us'—and he looked about securely.''[20]

This strategy dramatizes the vastness of the American-Jewish historical present and its multiple, competing values. Composed of times and places, of modern and ancient tongues, of different ways of being, this rhetoric forces irony and detachment rather than literal commitment to the ruling dogmas of a time and place. That Ezekiel can choose and enact his version of autonomy, a juggling of incommensurate values, indicates the situation of the swindler who mediates several worlds yet is unable to discern his place in any of them.

Aaron Traum (the title alone is a presentiment of Aaron's speaking the prophecy of another, and by doing so realizing a dream) affirms America's promises. In this case, the dream literally is to embody the past. Aaron becomes a carver, a maker of personal idols, and thereby continues the struggle for self-expression his father, grandfather, and great-grandfather had undertaken. Ironically, his completion of these thwarted acts marks the sufficiency of a new Jewish life in America. Here, Aaron can keep the past only by inventing his own present. Paradoxically, his needs suspend the prohibition against making graven images; carving keeps his Jewish background from being forgotten in the maelstrom of America.

The book begins with an exodus: the flight across Russia into Germany, steerage passage to America, and resettlement in the lower East Side. ''It is only another step in the Eternal Exile,'' his grandmother tells him before they leave Russia. In the New World, he believes American fables of success. This land is where the cunning of diaspora leads. His sorrows connect him to other diasporas, but his future will redeem them. For example, having been fired from a job, Aaron ''found himself at the Catherine Street ferry. And like his forebears in Babylon, he sat down by the waters and wept.''[21]

He wants to be a ''real American workman,'' and shouts ''Take me, America!'' He longs to read (and finally does) Thoreau, Franklin, and Paine—the representatives of the radical and practical American imagination. Early in the book, his freedom becomes an American venture: he decides to rely upon himself.

By the time he is a young man, he has renounced a belief in God (his father, Saul, throws him out of the house), fought for a union, helped the socialist cause, passed a Regents examination with distinction, and worked in a lumber camp. Walking through a wood, he comes across a Jewish home, marries the girl he meets there, goes to medical school, and decides to leave it because of his urge to carve. The separation of hope from existence characterizing diaspora life is closed by American fulfillment. Aaron not only dreams, he dreams the right dreams. He gets what he wishes for.

Aaron's individuality connects him with the European-Jewish life of his family. After Saul dies, Aaron comes across a notebook of inventions and sketches in which his father had written, "Grandfather Eleazer sought the secret meaning of words. My father, David, was a whittler in wood, a maker of beautiful things. And I . . . ?"[22] Aaron wants to "piece together the alphabet of existence." His work heightens this feeling in others, for "there men came to seek him out— some to buy, some to share, some to dream again."[23]

The fable of American self-appointing opportunity that the Cohens developed must have certainly seemed like a fairy tale to the mass of immigrant Jews working in sweatshops but wishing (and laboring) for a better life. The triumphs of their collective struggles for a decent life were less celebratory than Aaron's. He nurtures self-reliance, intuition, and an education of the senses. He is, finally, American: anti-communitarian and self-informing.

Edward Dahlberg's *Bottom Dogs* despairingly searches for a myth that can redeem a helpless existence so that human will and choice may shape life. Proletarian writers of the thirties and forties relied upon several fables of liberation (the exodus from Egypt; the coming of the Messiah; the story of the grail) that revealed the significance of their characters' history. For Dahlberg's protagonist, Lorry Lewis—no foundling but a child sent by his Kansas City mother to the Jewish Orphan Asylum of Cleveland—there are no such fables. His orphanhood begins his estrangement from natural ties, community, and history.

The first paragraph of *Bottom Dogs* announces the characteristic existence of Lorry and Lizzie Lewis. They erupt from the text: without a past or controlling memory they are estranged from human fellowship. Indifferent to where they are, and to the idea of place itself, Lorry and his mother Lizzie are, literally, wandering Jews in the immensity of America.

Lizzie's work is the service of others: a situation that Dahlberg exploits to define her dehumanization of others. She is a lady barber, hair-switch seller, osteopathic healer, and later a masseuse, but her real talent is conniving. For Lizzie, people are reduced to objects or traits, such as sentimentality or generosity.

Lorry endures a childhood that emphasizes the opposition and incomprehensibility of community and solidarity: abandonment by his father, ascribed orphanhood, rejection, unemployment, and self-disgust. As a result, Lorry and Lizzie are less characters than *human* transactions with society. Mother and son barter their wishes and passions only to get a life of minimal psychological pleasure: bargains, they think, but only in the end do they realize that their haggling is to their detriment. Always on the lookout for a deal, they get fleeced and end by distrusting affection. Invariably studying words or phrases, they come to see speech and writing as negotiations of power and shrewdness; as artifacts that protect the self. Pathetically, they no longer understand the responses of others. The irony of the secularization of Jewish tradition is inescapable. The learning they cultivate ends without a glimpse of people and human fulfillment.

Sent to an orphanage by Lizzie, Lorry helplessly realizes his life is profoundly divorced from those around him. Language, ranging from the orphans' slang, to Herman Mush Tate's senseless rolling oratory of common words and Old Testament phrases, to Doc's appeals to New Testament hagiography and Old Testament figures, constitutes Lorry's experience of the world.

Bottom Dogs' collage of slang, common speech, and high diction lets Lorry (and Dahlberg) create a language that is talismanic and vital, transfiguring the barrenness of Lorry's life. Language becomes history: a symbolizing and humanizing medium that Lorry invokes to ward off the demons of his life. He lives within language and carries it beyond the moment. It is finally the tradition of his self; it confers his meaning and will on all things.

His resolve to learn Mush Tate's harangue is his subversive act: a descent into the drivel of humankind. Mush's "sure-fire" words collapse experience by making it, finally, nothing more than syllables. In high school, Lorry practices his lesson, so that words re-presenting the hopelessness and disorder he knows become cries for a deliverance from his life. Ironically, he nearly wins a literary club debate "from a girl who was intendin' to be a lawyer. Everybody said he sure dished out a mean vocab, that would have put a tear in Mush Tate's eye, in the debate: Resolved that the pen is mightier than the sword."[24]

Graduated from school, he wanders across America; nothing awaits him. The country he sees is at an end of days. History, he believes, is expurgation; its metaphor is vomit. Signs of yet another historical cycle nearing an end are the exile of chosen peoples. "His trip to the state bureau didn't come off so well; Salt Lake was dead, the man behind the desk informed him . . . but Lorry knew better; it was the Mormons dying out; history was vomiting all over itself again; look what happened to Spain when the Israelites were kicked out."[25]

Living in Los Angeles, he yearns to believe in something, to find some meaning for what is around him. Time replaces history; boredom, expectation. "Something had to happen; and he knew nothing would. . . ."[26]

III

The critical spirit of Jewish life in America, those elements of religious belief and historical memory that made for distancing from the American scene, helped make American-Jewish literature of this period a critique of a too-literal worldliness. On the one hand, the theological divisions of experience into the sacred and the profane and of history into exile and redemption made an account of existence without a holy dimension a disturbing one—too secular, too modern. On the other hand, the laboring day and the tenement provided lessons in commonsense empiricism for most Jewish immigrants. The world could easily be explained in materialistic terms. How could a novelist, without diminishing the interpretive claims of either system, reconcile the two as foundations for American-Jewish life? How could, in other terms, a writer draw upon the traditions of realism—literary and naturalistic—and at the same time capture empathetically the Hebraic world-view? Were these categories necessary for the contemporary American-Jewish writer or could a literature that was Jewish and American begin with other terms?

One answer was found in the nature of ordinary American-Jewish life. The commanding theology of Europe was replaced by the American cultivation of moral sentiments, of good character. The clash between the values of a progressive secularization and *Halakhah* became translated into the struggles for decency, not piety. Decency was the sign of the good man.

The willingness to grapple with American life on the basis of moral inclinations and recollections of tradition floods the American-Jewish novel with pathos. Characters are rarely sure of what they ought to do. Life in America was still too raw, too free of tradition, and too perplexing to confront without a stabilizing heritage and system of values. As a result, judgment is hard won, and often sensed as provisional. Daniel Fuchs's Williamsburg trilogy (*Summer in Williamsburg*, 1934; *Homage to Blenholt*, 1936; *Low Company*, 1937) portrays this situation as a loss of *Yidishkayt's* authority. His characters are forced to define the adequacy of moral responses outside the body of Jewish tradition, for what they remember is folklore and not text; they cultivate decorum. What binds the trilogy together is less the sense of place than an ethical sensibility withstanding the conventions of place. The protagonists find it either too difficult or inhumane to pass judgment on those who represent what life has forced upon them.

The decent man is at the heart of the trilogy. In *Summer in Williamsburg*, it is Mr. Hayman, who insists upon the need for integrity in the face of poverty. In *Homage to Blenholt*, it is Mr. Balkan, Max's father, whose absurd presence rebukes the vulgarity of an American capitalism that has victimized his son. In *Low Company*, it is Herbert Lurie, who recognizes that he cannot dismiss the small, grasping characters of Neptune Beach with an opportunistic morality. "It was not enough to call them low and pass on," he thinks.

For all of these figures the ethical imperative is to insist that we can sense, without the need for abstractions, what indecency and dehumanization are while preserving our obligation to act compassionately. Decency and the action it demands are possible in the worst of American situations. For these books, the worst of American situations is the undoing of empathy by dreams of wealth and success: in other words, self-undoing. Characters who succumb fall outside a now attenuated Jewish tradition and into a rapacious American existence.

The Williamsburg protagonists question their lot but are denied the practical means to change what is around them. Crucially, Fuchs's trilogy deals with the isolated, unhappy individual formally cut off from success. Philip Hayman and his father, Herbert Lurie, Max Balkan and his father remain "decent" because they gaze upon the American Dream as strangers. Fuchs does not confer triumphs upon them.

In *Summer in Williamsburg*, Philip Hayman, a boy of twenty attending City

College, finds his allegiances torn by friends and family—the mentors of his imagination. Williamsburg is a *Narrenschiff*. Philip is part of a circle of philosophes. Miller, a graveyard worker, advocates a naturalism that replaces reason with brute cause. Cohen, a lonely, suicidal individual, flits from political movement to aesthetic group—each promising happiness which he believes is sex. Mr. Hayman struggles against a coarsening America by trying to raise his children "with a Hebraic sense of propriety."

Yet Philip is also caught up in the gang wars—fought by rival bus lines—of Williamsburg. Papravel, Philip's uncle, happily pillages a rival company; Philip's brother, Harry, is a thug in Papravel's gang. Philip is the object of his uncle's opportunistic advice and his father's helpless concern.

In the course of the summer, Philip comes to understand that what he gazes upon can also transfigure him. He is bewildered by the sight of passions he has never known before. Whether there will be peace for those who live quietly and harmlessly is a daily question. Miller dies. Mr. Mahler is burned to death; Cohen perishes in the same fire. Meyer Sussman, a butcher, commits suicide. A nameless man hangs himself. Papravel's gang kills a policeman.

Mr. Hayman's propriety, it is understood, will keep him poor yet nourish his sagacity. Papravel's indecency will increase his wealth as well as his penchant for moralizing. Philip realizes that a rational piety, a reverence for the known order of things, is not the way out of Williamsburg. However, in a neighborhood resonating to the notes of individualism and exploitation, remaining aloof *is* moral action; it is a refusal to accede to the instincts of a lesser, profaning self. A cultivated indifference to the mundane is really a yearning for the sacred. Describing men studying the Talmud, Fuchs writes of the preservation of the human spirit amidst filth, of the learning that is meant to preserve Creation:

In our time we must admire and respect this fervor, this tradition. They are true heroes in a world of puppets and therefore we do not understand them. These old men who find synagogues in a tenement basement store with the terrible toilets facing the back yards. These old men . . . arguing in a straight line of tradition that extends over the world in width, in depth to the earliest times, in length to God himself [*sic*].[27]

Papravel's rugged individualism has the last word. Hiding from the police, he is taken for a man of manners by his landlady. When she reminds him that he won't be saved unless he is baptized, he retorts, "Just you leave this to me." But his reply has an earlier check. Philip's lament, "And what is to become of me?" is answered by his mother in a stereotypical fashion, but not without its insight: "Eat . . . Eat with bread. Don't touch only the fancy stuff." The decent, too, have an obligation to survive, and they must be prepared to live with the agony of a Williamsburg.

The ethical quietism of Philip and his father contrasts with the comic ambitions of Max Balkan, *schlimazel* and *luftmensch* in *Homage to Blenholt*. He also wills to break out of the trap he's in. Max, who claims to be an inventor, or a discoverer (only to find out his innovations have been long on the market), is broken by his desire to do something, to be someone. Admiring Blenholt, Commissioner of Sewers, a party hack and grafter, Max attends his funeral. For Max, Blenholt was a figure of grandeur and power. At the funeral, he gets caught in a fight and stepped on. Afterwards, he learns that his latest suggestion (onion juice) is already marketed and receives a complimentary bag of onions. Humiliation resigns him to a life without vaunting dreams. He decides to get married and hold a steady job.

The novel's resolution is failure of comic nerve on Fuchs's part: Max's test of spirit ends without any uncommon recognition, on his part, of what has essentially happened to him. He thinks his life will now be a series of compromises and surrenders; that his tragedy is abandoning his dreams of power, turning his back, Fuchs writes, upon "Xerxes, Darius, Caesar . . . [and] Blenholt who, as Max himself had meant to, had risen from nothing to majesty in America."[28]

For Max, the fall is a personal one; everyday life, as he sees it, reveals no majesty. Yet his decline's essential vulgarity is not that it dehumanizes him but that it lets him belittle others through his concessions. His failure, as always, is that of personality: he will now be serious, a "grown man," he thinks.

It is given to Mr. Balkan (who has had his brush with grandeur but only as an actor portraying characters his son dreams about—a Yiddish "King Lear, Macbeth and Tamburlaine") to see Max's loss as an insufficiency of self. The world is too large, too completed for Max's plans; he will have to work instead of dream. Max "would grow old and ageing, die, but actually Max was dead already for now he would live for bread alone."[29] Fuchs closes the novel with Mr. Balkan's inappropriate meditation, given Max's vacuity, that "this death of youth was among the greatest tragedies in experience and that all the tears in America were not enough to bewail it."[30]

A protagonist's inability to mature ethically within the nature of events in *Homage to Blenholt* is transformed in *Low Company*. Characters are defined by their willingness to understand the experience of others and to forgo judgment. *Low Company* begins with the prayer said on the Day of Atonement. "We have trespassed" is balanced by "O, Lord our God, forgive us for the sin we have committed in hardening of the heart."

Set in Ann's, a soda parlor in Neptune Beach, *Low Company* deals with the crises of its workers and customers: Herbert Lurie, involved with Dorothy, the cashier; Spitzbergen, the owner; Shorty, the cook; Karty, an inveterate gambler; and Shubunka, a brothel owner. These people are driven by obsessions and sentiments expressing the social drama of capitalism. Money is never far from their hearts, and their days are spent figuring out how to beat horses, or to avoid payoffs, or to make profits. Their affairs with others are determined by their financial success. Their virtues exist as exchange values. For example, Shubunka's generosity and punctiliousness are supported by his brothels; Shorty's putative savoir faire, by his cash; Lurie's morality, by his position.

Strangely enough, of all the characters in this book it is Shubunka who is most alert to the moral nature of situations. A target in a gang takeover of Neptune Beach's prostitution, he is, at first, genuinely bewildered by what is happening to him as if he is too small and ordinary a figure to be noticed. Yet this war makes Shubunka aware of how his daily life is parasitic on a brutal past, and how his moral appeal to it has been his excuse for pimping.

Wondering how much longer he can elude his would-be killers, he recites his sins from the liturgy of forgiveness. He concludes that "Evil was rewarded by evil and his punishment would be just."[31] Consoled by the thought that Jewish tradition ascribes an order to events, he thinks of his end as a seal upon his willed limitations; he could have chosen otherwise. He is a sign to Lurie that he, too, has hardened his heart to those around him. He could become like Shubunka, an individual who forgets the moral uses of his own suffering:

Lurie knew now that it had been insensible and inhuman for him, too, simply to hate Neptune and seek escape from it. This also was hard and ignorant, lacking human compassion. He had known the people at Ann's in their lowness and had been repelled by them, but now it seemed to him that he understood how their evil appeared in their impoverished dingy lives and, further, how miserable their own evil rendered them.[32]

IV

American life made accessible for the Jew the resources of a national culture, if not fully the opportunities for a public life. The culture of Christianity naturally suffused the writing of this generation, producing a symbology alien to the Eastern-European Jewish imagination. The writer's deployment of Jewish and Christian symbols argued for the universality of the *situation* of faith. It also emphasized the limitations of a specific Jewish representation of experience. Was this symptomatic of a distinct, emerging American-Jewish theology, one in which Judaism and Christianity would speak to the condition of faith rather than to the specifics of belief? Whether in the epigram from Corinthians opening Rosenfeld's *Passage from Home* (1946), or in Dahlberg's experiments with a literary polytheism in *From Flushing to Calvary* (1932), or in the interior drama of revolutionary Christianity in Joseph Freeman's *Never Call Retreat* (1943), or in Henry Roth's fusing of the Jewish and Christian traditions in *Call It Sleep* (1934), the American-Jewish literary imagination began to depict its characters in and not necessarily apart from a Christian world-view.

The work of the period that expresses these problems strikingly is *Call It Sleep*. The book commingles a third-person narrative voice with that of a young boy flooded by the energies, urban and hylic, of America. Moreover, the book's language is an attempt to render the characters' Yiddish *as if* it were English. As a result, the narrative is ironic and intrusive, suggesting the division between the privatizing Jewish community and its public life in the American-Christian environment. Not surprisingly, identity is protean and tested often through the conflict of languages and neighborhoods.

The book opens in May of 1907 when Genya Schearl and her two-year-old son, David, are reunited with Albert, husband and father, who has come to meet them on their arrival from Europe. The prologue describing this meeting introduces the themes of the book: deception (Albert had told Genya to deceive officials in Europe by claiming that David was only seventeen months old in order to save half the fare); identity (Albert is piqued that Genya did not recognize him at first); and, finally, a summation of the varieties of salvation that America makes possible (an icon of this new natural and social order ingathers light and darkness, liberty and subjection, the cross and the horizon). Roth (close to Kafka's lead in *Amerika*) describes the Statue of Liberty. ''Against the luminous sky the rays of her halo were spikes of darkness roweling the air; shadow flattened the torch she bore to a black cross against flawless light—the blackened hilt of a broken sword. Liberty. The child and his mother stared again at the massive figure in wonder.''[33]

As David grows, his need for order and the urgency to *know* this order are imperative. His everyday experience is too broken and incomplete to make any sense. A traumatic sexual initiation, a family life that is violent and suspicious, and a poverty that thins life to its edges fail to make David wiser or harder than his years. He seems unable to learn anything by experience; only an illumination can make a whole out of what surrounds him.

He turns his ignorance to his purpose; he believes that there must be a redemptive order surrounding him, awaiting him. He craves any indication of this, ''some sign, some seal that would forever relieve him of watchfulness and forever insure his well-being.''[34] Chancing upon whispered talk by his mother about her affair in a village with a gentile, David believes he is a bastard, part of an incomprehensible world. He is intrigued by Leo, an older, Catholic boy whose rosary suggests a transcendent existence. Reading Isaiah in *cheder*, and being struck by the prophet's purification with a coal, David's awe of the darkness of the tenement coal cellar and the sparks of trolley tracks is heightened. He feels that his existence is profane; he can be chosen. His sanctification is bound up with the riddle of his family, the Christian claim of both absorbing yet completing Jewish belief, and Isaiah's dramatic account of the divine fire encrusted by coal. Illumination, purgation, and redemption are refracted through images such as light, coal, and the crucifix. Bargaining for Leo's crucifix, David takes Leo to his aunt Bertha's house where Leo tries to seduce her step-daughter. David flees to his parents' apartment where his crazed father, fighting with Bertha and her husband, and piqued by Reb Pankower, insists that David is half-gentile. Running away, David throws a copper ladle onto the third rail of a trolley track and is burned.

In a grandiloquent passage describing David's visionary sleep, the fragments of his experience become fused. The images that he tried to make sense of are now revealed as parts of a whole. By thinking them, he affirms his life within their presence; by doing so, David masters them. Hebraic and Christological symbols of the holy become one. David, a castaway now from ordinary experience, dreams the sacred.

Nonetheless, Roth refuses to let *this* version of experience become *the* version. It is Reb Pankower who insists that the sacred must be divided from the profane: God's light is not to be found in trolley rails.

V

Before America's entrance into the Second World War, Nazism provoked no grand work by an American-Jewish novelist about the plight of European Jews or an American fascist temper. Edward Dahlberg's *Those Who Perish* (1934) and his eloquent address ("Fascism and Writers") to the first American Writers' Congress (1935), Lewisohn's *Trumpet of Jubilee* (1937), and Levin's *Citizens* (1940) are perhaps the most recognizable efforts to deal with these problems. Even given the pieces condemning Nazism and a domestic fascism in the left-wing press, American-Jewish writers had failed to relentlessly assess, publicize, and try to change the situation of world Jewry. In this, they were no more prescient, in the mid- and late thirties, than American Jewry as a whole or other American writers.

As long as a continuous Jewish presence in the world was assumed by American-Jewish writers, it could be ideologically depicted or captured in aesthetic experimentation, or even trivialized or ignored. The diverse, rich nature of world Jewry acted as a guarantee—within America—that a Jew's freely chosen identity and commitments did not imperil the body of Israel.

By the end of the war, American-Jewish writers *had* to reinvent the very concept of the totality of Israel. On the one hand, there could be no more Jewish learning from Europe; on the other, there would be no more European community that could transmit the Jewish past. In *The Menorah Journal* of 1945, Mark Wischnitzer pointed out that until the mid–1930's, America had not been deeply nourished by diaspora intelligentsia. Now, America would have to become a center for the preservation and transmission of the Jewish past and its culture—spiritual and material. America would succeed "Babylon, Spain, Poland and Russia."[35] No less important, it must create the Jewish future. But in America, despite the presence of seminaries and the survivors' confrontations with God's role in history, Jewish life became increasingly well known through (and as) organizations concerned with community and national problems rather than with keeping alive traditions of serious Jewish study and practice as part of everyday life.

Not only the past but the ability to understand its life was gone. Isaac Rosenfeld's commentary on Sholom Aleichem (Shalom Rabinowitz) is worth remembering for its poignant assessment of loss:

He [Sholom Aleichem] defined a peculiar intellectual and spiritual province of the Jews, revealing the hidden vitality of their religion and the historical viability of their culture.

It is a province which is lost to the majority of us today, who know nothing of such blessings, even as that which was once our world, with Kasrilevke its Jerusalem, was lost to the world that engulfed and destroyed it.[36]

American-Jewish writers would wait for some time to speak of the Holocaust and, more specifically, of themselves as a community of writers who were fundamentally dependent now upon a murdered people and a permanently incomplete future. An enduring community, some kind of enriching Jewish life with others, became a crucial subject bequeathed to another generation. The most inventive writer addressing the problem of community during this interim period was Paul Goodman. Commenting in 1947 on Goodman's place in American letters, Irving Howe called him a "Jewish intellectual alienated to the point of complete reduction."[37] Bisexual, Jewish, anarchist, and regionalist, Goodman seemed to be everywhere but fit in nowhere. Yet his estrangement from American society allowed him to have a good deal to say about alienation in general, and Jewish communities in specific. (Delmore Schwartz's caustic portrayal of Goodman's own youthful community and social ideas can be found in his "The World Is A Wedding," in the collection of stories of the same name, 1948.)

Goodman's community fiction is just that—writings about the need for a renewed fellowship, Jewish and universal. In this case, the fully Jewish is the fully human. His characters see redemption as an overcoming of the social and psychological obstacles that prevent them from realizing their nature. The title novella of *The Break-Up of Our Camp and Other Stories*, written between 1935 and 1947 but published in 1949, examines the fragility of an intentional, makeshift Jewish community that speaks to the incompleteness of modern communities. In this camp buried in the woods, legends and rites have to be invented to explain to the campers who they are; honor and fraternity can only be created on the basis of the group itself. Toward the story's end, ten counsellors recognize that each is the tenth man for the *minyan*. The intuition of impending disaster, conveyed through leitmotifs of loss and grief, makes the community an imperative: human nature as a whole is maintained by each person acting for everyone.

The Grand Piano (1942), the first book of *The Empire City* (1959), deals with the education of a contemporary American protagonist—an American hero named Horatio Alger, no less. Goodman audaciously makes this Jewish street kid incarnate the destiny of the nation. Goodman's Horatio wants to be a citizen— the rationally patriotic act of the age. He will become a member of the community of "Our Friends." Urbane, cynical, and yet idealistic, Horatio's and "Our Friends' " doings (lively, if not hopeful demonstrations of anarchism and gestalt therapy) are judged by commentary about the completion of idols drawn from Maimonides's *Mishneh Torah*. "Our Friends' " task in this book, and in the other Empire City novels, is to justify their creations.

In Isaac Rosenfeld's *Passage from Home* (1946), the clash between the family (the community in small) and a young boy makes possible his knowledge of himself and others. Fourteen-year-old Bernard, a Chicago boy, is in love with his aunt Minna for her spirited life which he believes makes her distant from his family, especially his father. Bernard's father, who is reluctant to even talk about Minna, embodies the continuity of Jewish existence for the boy, but more important, the continuity of human life in which fathers wish to have their destiny completed by their sons.

Leaving his father and step-mother's house, Bernard lives with Minna and discovers that her life is unconstrained. She has a husband—a well-kept secret; a lover—Cousin Willy, a Southern gentile; and an undying malice—years ago, she argues, Bernard's father assaulted her.

Returning home, and asked by his father why he left, he has no answer but senses that his father is afraid to ask about Minna's personal life. Bernard's reflection is his passage of understanding from a sense of his own emotional inadequacy to the difficulty of self-honesty: "My only hope had been to confess that I did not love him, to admit I had never known what love was or what it meant to love, and by that admission to create it. Now it was too late. Now there would only be life as it came and the excuses one made to himself for accepting it."[38]

The Passover theme, the freedom from bondage and the acceptance of the Covenant that limits the self, is the framework of the book. At the *seder*, Bernard gets drunk and thinks he is a sensualist. The sparkling lights of decanters remind him of "the original Egypt, colored and revived, the parting of the waters, the Red Sea agape, the journey through the desert."[39] His passage from home is his exodus, culminating in a recognition of the covenant the self makes with itself and with others.

In a celebrated passage, Bernard and his grandfather visit Reb Feldman and listen to him exhort his followers. The grandfather is "transformed into a new person" and the boy "shared the experience of that ecstacy."[40] Here, tradition is alive; embodying the boundaries of the law, it paradoxically helps the individual transcend a limiting secular existence. In contrast, Bernard's four weeks at Minna's, replete with Willy's tirades and the plodding counsel of Minna's husband, show how trying it is to live without human regard, to live only for one's passions.

At Minna's, he receives a package of clothes which also contains his father's *tefillin*. His father had never prayed in them, and in fact prayed only on the holidays. Bernard thinks that "this was the inheritance I had received from him. It was vacant of God, but it had the element, as of religious transmission, whereby we were united in feeling."[41] The "as of" is emphatic, and so is "united in feeling": an argument for a community more inclined to the Gospels than *Halakhah*. Bernard's realization takes us back to the book's epigram from Corinthians 1:13 ("When I was a child, I spake as a child . . . ") and to the Jewish and Christian traditions' fascination with language as creation which yet creates; with a truth that insists upon yet other truths. Bernard reflects, "Our lives contain a secret, hidden from us. It is no more than the recognition of our failing; but to find it is all of courage, and to speak of it, the whole of truth."[42]

As a graduate student, Rosenfeld had turned from his concerns with contemporary philosophy to a conviction, judging from his writings, that experience was not a matter of the consistency of logical propositions; that it resisted categorization and was, often, opaque. Writing could do some justice to its ambiguity. Not surprisingly, his own reviews mention the necessity of confronting the anxieties of our times that seem to be without a rational coherency and of defining the moral possibilities within undefined situations. I think this becomes one of the legacies that modern American-Jewish writers inherited. They, too, would turn away from a view that denied the complexity of the individual and experience. Ideologies for this new generation would have little appeal since they had morally failed to deal with the horror of the past. Their mechanical, reductionistic character held few hopes for the good community and a decent life.

Unlike the authors of the previous generation, contemporary writers now had a chance to move beyond the specifics of realism; witnessing a world destroyed, they had the opportunity to see how the plight of the modern Jew continued or spurned the ambitions of Western culture that spoke of fraternity, justice, and liberty. They were privileged to examine the Jew's response to a world in which human capabilities could no longer be judged by the values of classical philosophy and literature. They could contribute to a new Jewish culture that would invent again a version of its past.

VI

After 1945, that Jewish writers could subsist outside the traditions of their people was a point hardly raised. To paraphrase Gershom Scholem, would not all Jewish writers come to be regarded, and often self-regarded, finally, as Jewish? And would critics not talk freely and openly of a Jewish canon that was a literature apart from others? And would not the creation of this literature speak of the recovery of a humane life *in* the world and *for* it?

NOTES

1. Kaufmann Kohler, *Jewish Theology*, p. viii.
2. "Under Forty," *Contemporary Jewish Record*, pp. 3–36.
3. Albert Halper, "Under Forty," p. 24.
4. Howard Fast, "Under Forty," pp. 25–26.
5. Muriel Rukeyser, "Under Forty," p. 9.
6. Delmore Schwartz, "Under Forty," p. 14.
7. Isaac Rosenfeld, "Under Forty," p. 36.
8. Waldo Frank, *The Jew in Our Day*, p. 73.
9. Paul Goodman, "The Judaism of a Man of Letters," p. 241.
10. See Ludwig Lewisohn's *Israel* (1925) and *The Answer* (1939).
11. Meyer Levin, *In Search*, pp. 516–519.
12. Anzia Yezierska, *Bread Givers*, p. 297.

13. See Arnold Eisen's *The Chosen People in America* for a discussion of these questions.

14. Michael Gold, *Jews Without Money*, p. 25.

15. Ibid., p. 224.

16. Charles Reznikoff, *By the Waters of Manhattan*, p. 20.

17. Ibid., p. 146.

18. Ibid., p. 251.

19. Ibid., pp. 251–252.

20. Ibid., pp. 193–194.

21. Hyman and Lester Cohen, *Aaron Traum*, p. 46.

22. Ibid., p. 292.

23. Ibid., pp. 412–413.

24. Edward Dahlberg, *Bottom Dogs*, p. 115.

25. Ibid., p. 199.

26. Ibid., p. 269.

27. Daniel Fuchs, *Summer in Williamsburg*, p. 51.

28. Daniel Fuchs, *Homage to Blenholt*, p. 301.

29. Ibid., p. 302.

30. Ibid., p. 301.

31. Daniel Fuchs, *Low Company*, p. 254.

32. Ibid., p. 311.

33. Henry Roth, *Call It Sleep*, p. 14. The reader is also referred to Gordon Poole's "David in America: *dalla etnicita ebraica all'americanismo cristiano*," which has influenced my own reading of the text.

34. Roth, op. cit., p. 221.

35. Mark Wischnitzer, "The Road Ahead," p. 143.

36. Isaac Rosenfeld, "Sholom Aleichem II: The Blessings of Poverty," in *An Age of Enormity*, p. 80.

37. Irving Howe, "The Discovery of Sex," p. 196.

38. Isaac Rosenfeld, *Passage from Home*, p. 280.

39. Ibid., p. 14.

40. Ibid., p. 94.

41. Ibid., p. 201.

42. Ibid., pp. 279–280.

BIBLIOGRAPHY

Cohen, Hyman and Lester Cohen. *Aaron Traum*. New York: Charles Boni, 1930.

Dahlberg, Edward. *Bottom Dogs*. Private edition, London: 1929. 1930; rpt. San Francisco: City Lights Press, 1961.

Eisen, Arnold. *The Chosen People in America: American Jews and Their Lives Today*. Bloomington: Indiana University Press, 1966.

Fast, Howard, Albert Halper, Isaac Rosenfeld, Muriel Rukeyser, Delmore Schwartz, et al. "Under Forty." *Contemporary Jewish Record*. 7. (February, 1944), pp. 3–36.

Frank, Waldo. *The Jew in Our Day*. New York: Duell, Sloan and Pearce, 1944.

Fuchs, Daniel. *3 Novels by Daniel Fuchs*. New York: Basic Books, 1961.

Gold, Michael. *Jews Without Money*. 1930; rpt. New York: Avon, 1965. Corr. subsequent editions, 1968.

Goodman, Paul. "The Judaism of a Man of Letters." *Commentary*. 6. (September, 1948), pp. 241–243.

Howe, Irving. "The Discovery of Sex." *Commentary*. 3. (February, 1946), pp. 195–196.

Kohler, Kaufmann. *Jewish Theology Systematically and Historically Considered*. 1918; rpt. New York: Macmillan, 1923.

Levin, Meyer. *In Search*. Paris: Author's Press, 1950.

Lewisohn, Ludwig. *The Answer*. New York: Liveright, 1939.

———. *Israel*. New York: Albert and Charles Boni, 1925.

Poole, Gordon. "David in America: *dalla etnicita ebraica all'americanismo cristiano*." *Rothiana: Henry Roth nella critica italiana*. Firenze, Italy: Giunta, 1985, pp. 119–142.

Reznikoff, Charles. *By the Waters of Manhattan*. New York: Charles Boni, 1930.

Rosenfeld, Isaac. "Sholom Aleichem II: The Blessings of Poverty." Originally published in the *New Republic* of July 22, 1944; reprinted in *An Age of Enormity*. Cleveland: World Publishing, 1962, pp. 75–80.

———. *Passage from Home*. New York: Dial Press, 1946.

Roth, Henry. *Call It Sleep*. 1934; rpt. New York: Avon, 1962.

Wischnitzer, Mark. "The Road Ahead." *The Menorah Journal*. 33. (October-December, 1945), pp. 133–152.

Yezierska, Anzia. *Bread Givers*. 1925; rpt. New York: George Braziller, 1975.

FOR FURTHER READING

Primary

Bercovici, Konrad. *Main Entrance*. New York: Covici-Friede, 1932.

Bisno, Beatrice. *Tomorrow's Bread*. Philadelphia: Jewish Publication Society, 1938.

Brinig, Myron. *This Man Is My Brother*. New York: Farrar & Rinehart, 1932.

Ferber, Nat. *One Happy Jew*. New York: Farrar & Rinehart, 1934.

Fineman, Irving. *Hear, Ye Sons*. New York: Longmans, Green, 1933.

Gold, Michael. *Mike Gold: A Literary Anthology*, ed. Michael Folsom. New York: International Publishers, 1972.

Goodman, Paul. *The Facts of Life, Stories 1940–1949*, ed. Taylor Stoehr. Vol. III. Santa Barbara: Black Sparrow Press, 1979.

Hecht, Ben. *A Jew in Love*. New York: Covici-Friede, 1931.

West, Nathanael. *Miss Lonelyhearts*. New York: Liveright, 1933.

Zara, Louis, *Blessed Is the Man*. Indianapolis and New York: Bobbs-Merrill, 1935.

Secondary

Aaron, Daniel. *Writers on the Left*. New York: Harcourt, Brace & World, 1961.

Barrett, William. *The Truants: Adventures Among the Intellectuals*. Garden City, New York: Anchor Press/Doubleday, 1982.

Fiedler, Leslie. "The Two Memories: Reflections on Writers and Writing in the Thirties."

Proletarian Writers of the Thirties, ed. David Madden. Carbondale, Ill.: Southern
    Illinois University Press, 1968, pp. 3–25.
Halper, Albert. "Notes on Jewish-American Fiction." *The Menorah Journal*. 17. (April-
    June, 1932), pp. 61–69.
Nadel, Ira. *Jewish Writers of North America*. Detroit: Gale Research, 1981.
Rideout, Walter. "O Workers' Revolution . . . The True Messiah." *American Jewish
    Archives*. 11. (October, 1959), pp. 157–175.
Rosenberg, Harold. *Discovering the Present: Three Decades in Art, Culture, & Politics*.
    Chicago:University of Chicago Press, 1973.
Yedwab, Stanley. "The Jew as Portrayed in American Jewish Novels of the 1930's."
    American Jewish Archives. 11. (October, 1959), pp. 148–154.

3

American-Jewish Fiction
Since 1945

Bonnie K. Lyons

Saul Bellow, Bernard Malamud, Philip Roth, Tillie Olsen, Grace Paley, Cynthia Ozick, Herbert Gold, Joseph Heller, E. L. Doctorow, Stanley Elkin, Hugh Nissenson: the list of important American-Jewish fiction writers (of which this mini-list names only the most obvious) is staggering in both its variety and excellence. Indisputably, the emergence of American-Jewish fiction writers since World War II is, as Mark Shechner calls it, "a social movement that has had enormous literary consequence."[1] But is it more than a sociological fact? And does it make sense to talk about American-Jewish fiction rather than analyze the work of each writer separately?

Almost twenty years ago, Philip Rahv observed that "the American-Jewish writers do not in the least make up a literary faction or school" and warned:

the homogenization resulting from speaking of them as if they comprised some kind of literary faction or school is bad critical practice in that it is based on simplistic assumptions concerning the literary process as a whole as well as the nature of American Jewry, which, all appearances to the contrary, is very far from constituting a unitary group in its cultural manifestation.[2]

And recently Frederick R. Karl insisted: "[American-Jewish writers] are American writers, not Jewish writers, not members of a Jewish club, affiliated to each other not as Jews but as Americans. The distinctions among them are far greater than the similarities, and to speak of them as 'Jewish American' is to homogenize what should be particularized."[3] Karl's reduction of Jewishness to members of a Jewish club seems strikingly inappropriate, and ironically, while he rejects "Jewish writers" as a meaningful category, his entire book is based on the premise that the category "American writers" is viable, even though he himself repeatedly points out the back-and-forth influences and cross-pollination of European writers. Other critics, like Richard J. Fein, have suggested that Jewishness is so strong a unifying commonality that Jewish writers are "curiously trans-national," and, in a sense, "the works of Babel, Kafka, Singer and Malamud form one literature."[4] And Irving Malin has claimed that American-Jewish lit-erature is "the only movement in twentieth-century American literature as im-portant as the 'Southern Renaissance.' "[5]

Even writers who consider the category of Jewish writer valid have vastly differing conceptions of what makes a writer or work Jewish. Richard Fein has suggested that what links Jewish writers is not the common historical or religious background but the "internalizing of a people's insecurity"; that is, in Jewish literature, the "insecurity of a people has been personalized, converted to a nervous psychological energy."[6] Malin, on the other hand, has declared that "only when a Jewish (by birth) writer moved by religious tensions shows 'ul-timate concern' in creating a new structure of belief, can he be said to create 'Jewish' literature."[7] By traditional Jewish law Tillie Olsen is not a Jew since her mother was not Jewish, but who would want to remove her masterpiece "Tell Me a Riddle" (1961) from the canon of American-Jewish fiction?

My premise is that however thorny the questions about who is a Jew, what makes Jewish literature, and which writers are to be included, classifying lit-erature as American-Jewish literature, or looking at certain writers and works as American-Jewish, is a useful approach. All generalizations and categories are somewhat artificial, and indeed what is most valuable about each literary work is its unique qualities. But if these two qualifications are firmly held in mind, it is valid and instructive to trace common patterns and to look for unifying similarities.

Every writer writes out of a culture. That culture may be a battleground of conflicting visions and values, and the writer may either embrace or attack his cultural heritage. But a writer's work is necessarily a product of and response to a culture. In *Number Our Days* (1978), the acclaimed study of a community center of aged Eastern-European Jews living in Venice, California, Barbara Meyerhoff provides a useful tool for approaching American-Jewish culture and literature by applying Robert Redfield's distinction between Great Traditions and Little Traditions. The Great Tradition is the culture's formal laws and structures; for Jews, the Great Tradition is the formal Jewish law, study, and shared history that make Jews one people, *klal Yisrael*. The Little Tradition, on the other hand, is a local folk expression of a group's belief, unsystematized, not elaborately idealized, an oral tradition practiced constantly and often unconsciously by or-dinary people without external enforcement or interference. For Eastern-Euro-pean Jews and their descendants, which includes most American-Jewish writers, this folk culture or domestic religion is *Yidishkayt*. According to Meyerhoff, *Yidishkayt* is a matter of everyday life and mundane concerns but is "no less authentically Jewish because more homely than the Great Tradition of Hebrew and formal religion."[8]

What is central to the issue of the Jewishness of American-Jewish literature is the inheritance of *Yidishkayt*, a particular way of experiencing and reflecting the world. For brevity, I will simply summarize key aspects of *Yidishkayt* here.[9] What is central is the sense of a people, a cohesive group bound together by ties of memory and history, by outer limits and hostility and inner meaning and mutuality. Being a Jew means being part of a chosen people with a distinct sense of uniqueness, purpose, and calling. Because the Covenant is between God and a people, because Jewish immortality is traditionally seen in terms of survival of the group rather than the individual, because in historical fact the continuation of the Jews has been a *real* question, the world-view is deeply and pervasively social rather than individual, oriented toward the group rather than any one person. If the heart of the Protestant experience is the individual soul in relation to God and the heart of Catholicism is the church, then the heart of Judaism is the family—the biological family and the wider family of the Jewish people.

Jewish tradition and Jewish history, especially centuries of dispersion, exile, precariousness, homelessness, and powerlessness, gave rise to a distinct historical attitude toward humanity and heroes. Pervading Yiddish culture and literature is a questioning, in fact an underplaying, of conventional heroism, even a distinctly anti-heroic bias, no doubt in part based on clear perception of the self-destruction resulting from usually vain gestures—and a powerless victim's sense of how what passes for the heroic can be egotistical, narcissistic, and brutal. Simply surviving decently and living to tell the tale are often sufficiently problematic. And if heroes are absent or found wanting, the ordinary man is elevated, or at least evoked with love. *Dos kleine menshele*, the little man, with all his imperfections and foibles, is accepted and embraced. Likewise a wide range of human emotions, including ordinary, non-admirable feelings, is explored. The ordinary man struggling with his everyday problems is the core of Yiddish literature; the heroic individual and sharply climactic plot are conspicuously absent.

What is glorified in Yiddish life and literature is intellectual pursuit, not for its own sake but, ideally, as a route to God, a means of understanding. If the cultural ideal is a group of men deeply engaged in pursuing the precise nuance of a particular talmudic passage, engaged in a spirit of love of Torah, then what is relatively devalued is the world of nature, manual labor, indeed all solitary or physical pursuits.

This brief sketch can only suggest the heritage of *Yidishkayt*. To this, American-Jewish literature adds certain "modern" and "American" elements. Major themes of American-Jewish literature are the uneasy coming together of the American and the Jewish, the enormous problems of acculturation and assimilation, and the radical questioning of the traditions and values of both cultures. Economic and social change, the rapid, disorienting move from ghetto or *shtetl* to city to suburb, from street peddler and garment worker to doctor and professor—this is the external or social level of American-Jewish literature. The psychological or spiritual side of these narratives portrays a search for meaning or authority, an attempt to fill the void that accompanied rapid change, the loss of traditional values and meaning. Whatever deprivations and parochialism *shtetl* life in Europe entailed, it was at least a world of values, order, and meaning. The breakup of that world gave rise to doubt, anxiety, questioning, and guilt— emotions and themes which dominate American-Jewish literature and give rise to a tone of complexity, complaint, skepticism, and irony.

No single essay can do justice to the work of all the post-World War II American-Jewish fiction writers. Even a discussion of the careers of some of the prominent would be necessarily sketchy. More important, such an approach would do little to suggest the commonalities. Instead, I have selected a dozen themes that pervade contemporary American-Jewish fiction and shown how each is developed in one work or body of work. I have chosen examples from the work of Saul Bellow, Bernard Malamud, Philip Roth, Tillie Olsen, Cynthia Ozick, Grace Paley, and Edward Lewis Wallant. In this way, the reader is introduced to the dominating assumptions and themes, some of the major writers of the movement, and some of the central texts.

I begin by developing four pervasive attitudes concerning the specific moral nature of man: the affirmation of the common man, the moral code embodied in *menshlichkayt* as opposed to "manliness," the belief in man's mixed moral nature, and the idea of spiritual or moral turning, *t'shuva*. I then discuss eight related social and philosophical themes and assumptions concerning life and art: the use of specifically Jewish sources; cosmopolitanism and a universalist bent; the rejection of the extremes of romanticism and nihilism; a continuing preoccupation with time, history, and memory; belief in the centrality of the family; emphasis on intellect and spirit; celebration of talk for its own sake; and finally the underlying assumption that art is a humanistic enterprise.

1. *"DOS KLEINE MENSHELE"*: THE COMMON MAN

Dos kleine menshele, the little man or common man so fundamental to Yiddish literature, is also at the heart of contemporary American-Jewish literature. So central is the little man to this vision of the world that it is the focus of what are arguably the best play and novel by post-war American-Jewish writers— *Death of a Salesman* (1949) and *Seize the Day* (1956). Because Bellow's use of the theme can best be illuminated by comparison to Arthur Miller's play, I will discuss the novel in connection with the play. Unlike *Seize the Day*, nothing in the text of *Death of a Salesman* is about Jews. Indeed some critics, like Leslie Fiedler, have complained that in *Death of a Salesman* Miller created "crypto-Jewish" characters, that is, "characters who are in habit, speech, and condition of life typically Jewish-American, but who are presented as something else— general Americans."[10] I would suggest that what seems so Jewish is not the habits and speech of the characters but rather the vision of the world that the play embodies, especially its defense of the ordinary man. Both the novel and the play focus on a flawed and unsuccessful little man, and both works insist "attention must be paid." Both ask the reader to sympathize with the imperfect, weak man struggling to survive in a feelingless, competitive world beyond his capacity. Neither Tommy Wilhelm of the novel nor Willy Loman of the play is of the play is extraordinary or even particularly admirable. Both are in large part responsible for their miserable conditions. Willy's adultery was a betrayal of his long-suffering wife, and the revelation of his marital infidelity scarred his son Biff for years. Biff's insistence that the Loman family lived on lies and that Willy had the wrong dreams is affirmed by the play's overall structure. That is precisely the point: Miller asks the reader to love Willy despite his flaws and sins and to mourn for him despite all his weaknesses. The competitive business world is attacked precisely because it establishes a world of only two categories, winners and losers, and thus condemns little men like Willy to self-disgust and self-hatred. Willy's pitiful belief that he is worth more dead than alive is the reductio ad absurdum of the entire system. Similarly, Bellow insists that the reader identify with the overweight, pill-popping, weak, sentimental, confused Tommy Wilhelm and not his dapper, successful father.

The endings of the novel and play underscore the affirmation of the common man. At the end of the play, Willy is mourned not by the crowds he had hoped for, but by those who genuinely loved him. And Biff's epiphany of self-recognition balances Willy's suicide. By discovering and accepting himself for who he is, a "buck an hour" worker whose real satisfactions are nature and outdoor work, Biff embodies not only the essential worth of the common man but also the common man's ability to break through to the truth—and personal happiness. Thus Miller's play balances Willy's despairing suicide and Biff's psychological breakthrough; Bellow's novel ends with a concrete dramatization of Tommy's collapse and resurgence. Earlier in the novel, Tommy remembers a sudden, unsought feeling of general love that helped him to accept himself and to feel at one with humanity: "He was imperfect and disfigured himself, but what difference did that make if he was united with them by this blaze of love?"[11] While that was a fleeting, later minimalized memory, at the end of the novel, when Tommy weeps uncontrollably at the funeral of a stranger, his breakthrough is more profound and lasting. The very fact that it is slowly dramatized suggests its significance. It is important that this event occurs in a Jewish funeral chapel, because throughout the novel Tommy feels unfulfilled religious longing, discontent with his almost totally secularized life. The self-division signified by his many names—Tommy Wilhelm, Tommy Adler, Wilky, Velvel—is transcended by his grieving for the dead man in the funeral chapel. Identifying with the unknown, ordinary man, Tommy first thinks "a man—another human creature," then fully feels the weight of all his own woes and problems and soon "the source of all tears" springs open within him. At last hearing "the heavy sea-like music," he sinks "deeper than sorrow, through torn sobs and cries toward the consummation of his heart's ultimate need."[12] Thus the common man grieves for the common man and finds the common human comfort.

2. "MENSHLICHKAYT" VS. MANLINESS

One of American-Jewish writers' chief inheritances from *Yidishkayt* is the rich complicated ethic embodied in the code of *menshlichkayt*, which Irving Howe has defined as: "a readiness to live for ideals beyond the clamor of self, a sense of plebeian fraternity, an ability to forge a community of moral order even while remaining subject to a society of social disorder, and a persuasion that human existence is a deeply serious matter for which all of us are finally accountable."[13] This generally androgynous ideal is fitting for both men and women, although modified and expressed somewhat differently in each. It is in direct opposition to traditional American ideals of manliness. In particular, the aspects of American masculinity having to do with the body are conspicuously absent. There is no code of physical competence, no survival techniques, no outdoor skills, and no sexual virility. Likewise there is no toughness, no self-sufficiency, no longing for, let alone fulfillment of, freedom and solitude.

However bumbling, hapless, and self-defeating, all the protagonists in contemporary American-Jewish literature struggle with or toward this ideal of *menshlichkayt*. Often the tension between the two ideals of *menshlichkayt* and manliness provides the essence of the character's internal struggle. Indeed in much of Philip Roth's work this conflict is a central theme; often the hero feels torn between his unquiet conscience that demands *menshlichkayt* and his intuitive sense that the demands of responsibility, moderation, and moral maturity of *menshlichkayt* are depriving him of his spontaneity and sexuality.

Roth's early story "Defender of the Faith" (1959) depicts Nathan Marx's struggles with just these issues. The story opens "in May 1945 only a few weeks after the fighting had ended in Europe."[14] The last two years in Europe have anesthetized Marx, transformed him, so that now he has "an infantryman's heart" and can witness the "trembling of the old people, the crying of the very young, the uncertainty and fear in the eyes of the once arrogant" all "without feeling a thing."[15] Returned to the United States as a training instructor, Marx is almost immediately confronted by Sheldon Grossbart, one of his Jewish trainees who shrewdly manipulates Marx in order to wheedle favors. From the beginning Marx suspects Grossbart of deception; on the other hand, Grossbart reawakens his sense of his own past, his memories of family, New York streets, and synagogue. Grossbart's endearment, *leben*, to a fellow Jewish trainee evokes Marx's exclamation, "My grandmother's word for me!"[16] Marx, like Grossbart and his two Jewish friends, feels alien in this rural Missouri army camp where a *shul* is called "the Jewish Mass" and only guts count. After begrudgingly permitting Grossbart special privileges and half-heartedly defending him before the army officers, Marx comes to see that Grossbart's pleas for permission to attend Friday services instead of cleaning the barracks, to eat kosher food, and to celebrate a Passover *seder* have much less to do with religious fervor than simple self-interest. Furious when he discovers that Grossbart has persuaded another Jewish officer to have him sent to New Jersey instead of going to the Pacific front with the rest of his unit, Marx has this order countermanded. Using a Grossbart-type strategy, Marx calls a friend in Classification and Assignment and explains his motivation as a Jewish officer trying to do a favor for one of his Jewish privates who lost a brother in Europe and thus would "feel like a coward if he wound up Stateside."[17] In their last confrontation, when Grossbart furiously accuses Marx of anti-Semitism, Marx defends himself saying he did it "for all of us," resists an "impulse to turn and seek pardon" for his vindictiveness and accepts his position as a "defender of the faith." That is, having already proven himself a "man" in Europe through his physical courage and uncomplaining suffering, Marx, in the fictional present, struggles successfully to become a *mensh*.

3. MAN'S MIXED MORAL NATURE

Although every good person should strive to become a *mensh*, man's nature is ineluctably mixed, according to American-Jewish fiction. That is, man is seen as neither depraved nor noble, neither hopelessly fallen nor all good. Bellow has been the most overt about this essential mixed nature and at various times has defined man as "an animal of genius" and a "visionary animal." One of the dominant themes in his fiction and in American-Jewish fiction in general is an attempt to explore and define man, to ascertain what human potential is and how it is to be developed. A central statement of this theme occurs in *The Victim* (1947), where the old Yiddish journalist Schlossberg tells his fellow cafeteria sitters, "It's bad to be less than human and it's bad to be more than human!"[18] He explains that the motive behind trying to be more than human is the illegitimate attempt to escape death: "We only know what it is to die because some people die and, if we make ourselves different from them, maybe we don't have to?" Thus to try to be more than human is to express contempt for life: "More than human, can you have any use for life?" Schlossberg defines less than human as lacking in emotional response, inhuman absence of reaction.

In a typically Bellovian strategy the philosopher's dignity is undercut in several ways. The humble setting in a raucous cafeteria undermines the dignity of his speech. And even before he speaks, the reader is told that Schlossberg still supports a thirty-five-year-old son who "hasn't made up his mind about a vocation" and daughters who are "worse yet."[19] Moreover, his listeners tease him about making such a long speech and promise to fix him up with a theatrical agent. Nevertheless, Schlossberg's wisdom is central to *The Victim*, in which the central plot involves Asa Leventhal's growing sense of what it means to be human, his attempt to be neither superhuman nor subhuman, and in particular his developing awareness of problems of responsibility and guilt. Isolated, alienated, defensive, a product of an unhappy, impoverished immigrant family, Leventhal undergoes a dual moral and psychological journey. When he is alone in a palpably steamy New York one summer, his closed life is invaded by his sister-in-law Elena, who desperately seeks advice about medical care for her mysteriously stricken son, and by the down-and-out Kirby Allbee, a former acquaintance who accuses Leventhal of deliberately causing him to be fired from his job years ago following one of Allbee's anti-Semitic remarks. The two emotional invasions parallel the dual epigraphs. One from Thomas De Quincey's *The Pains of Opium* describes the "human face": the sea "appeared paved with innumerable faces upturned to the heavens; faces, imploring, wrathful, despairing; faces that surged upward by thousands, by myriads, by generations." The other, from *Thousand and One Nights*, is about a merchant who eats dates and throws away the stones only to be accused by an Ifrit of killing his son: "When thou atest dates and threwest away the stones they struck my son full in the breast as he was walking by, so that he died forthwith." The De Quincey epigraph underscores the question of human suffering embodied in Elena's woes; the one from *Thousand and One Nights* points to the problems of guilt and responsibility suggested by Allbee's accusations.

From his involvement with Elena and her family, Leventhal little by little grows to see the disproportion of some of his judgments (he considers her natural parental grief, madness), his own bigotry and stereotyping, and his own previous feelings of superiority to and alienation from his brother. The development and meaning of his relationship with Allbee is much more involved and enigmatic. Although Leventhal initially dismisses Allbee's charge that Leventhal ruined him as revenge for an anti-Semitic remark, he later accepts an indirect and incidental role in Allbee's decline. As Allbee increasingly takes over Leventhal's life, occupying his mind and his apartment, who is victim and who is victimizer becomes impossible to say. Only when Allbee tries to gas both of them, in what Leventhal calls "a kind of suicide pact without getting my permission first," does Leventhal finally break free.[20] In the epilogue which occurs years later, both men have grown. More prosperous, less recalcitrant, and less fearful, Leventhal has come to grips with the accidental and haphazard in life and accepts that even though people do not get their just rewards economically, maybe there is something beyond: "Possibly there was a promise, since so many felt it. He himself was almost ready to affirm that there was."[21] His wife's pregnancy symbolizes his more hopeful state. No longer a destitute drunk, Allbee too has made a better life for himself and grown more accepting of his own and the world's limitations.

Still neither can resist subtly insulting the other in the old ways. Allbee makes a mildly anti-Semitic remark ("I see you're following orders. 'Increase and multiply.' "),[22] and Leventhal counters by noting that Allbee is still drinking. When Allbee concludes that he is the type "that comes to terms with whoever runs things," Leventhal's last words in the novel are "Wait a minute, what's your idea of who runs things?"[23] Earlier Allbee's insinuation would have been that Jews have unfairly displaced Anglo-Saxons like himself. Now the question is left open, allowing a religious interpretation. While hardly an extraordinary man, not even "exactly affable," Leventhal has relinquished both his less than human feelinglessness and his more than human pretensions to become the perfectly guiltless victim. That is, in *The Victim*, Leventhal grows into his humanity, a mixed condition.

4. *"T'SHUVA"*: TURNING

T'shuva, turning, is central to the Jewish conception of human life and to contemporary American-Jewish fiction. The idea of turning to God or to the right path is connected with the Jewish conception of human redemption and underlies both the intrinsic hopefulness about humankind and the longing for messianic salvation which universal *t'shuva* will help bring about. Of course, in some ways *t'shuva* in fiction parallels the modern conception of epiphany in a character, but where epiphany is more a matter of consciousness, of recognition, *t'shuva* is both more spiritual and moral. And the result of the turn is either suggested or embodied in the fiction. Many of Bellow's novels hinge on a religious turning. For example, Herzog's letter to God ends his frenetic activity and compulsive letter writing, and Tommy Wilhelm breaks through past sorrow while mourning in a Jewish funeral chapel. Likewise, Philip Roth's *Goodbye, Columbus* (1959) ends with Neil Klugman's recognition of Brenda Patamkin's and, worse, his own shallowness and emotional dishonesty. Fittingly he looks at his own reflection in the window of Harvard's Lamont Library and penetrates his own facade. That he boards the next train south to return to work on the first day of the Jewish New Year underscores the fact that this is a moment of turning, an end and a beginning.

Almost all of Malamud's great stories and novels are about *t'shuva*, the turn, or, less frequently, a crucial failure to turn. In many the turn is double: one character's spiritual and moral movement brings about another's. In this way his stories suggest that human beings aid each other's growth. For example, in "The Mourners" (collected in *The Magic Barrel*, 1958), the old former candler, Kessler, who abandoned his wife and children thirty years previously, wakes up to the unfeeling monstrousness of his act when he is evicted by his landlord Gruber. The sudden memory "smote him to the heart and he recalled the past without end and moaned and tore at his flesh with his fingernails."[24] Seeing Kessler mourn, Gruber regrets his own harshness and decides that Kessler is mourning for him: "it was *he* who was dead." And as Gruber joins Kessler in mourning for their emotional deadness, their stony hearts, the smelly, filthy room becomes "drenched in daylight and fragrance."

But perhaps the best example of a Malamud *t'shuva* is the classic story, "The Magic Barrel" (1958). The opening words, "Not long ago," with the echo of "once upon a time," establish the partly fantastic atmosphere. Leo Finkle, a rabbinical student at Yeshivah University, having been advised that a wife would enhance his chances of finding a congregation, calls in a marriage broker, Pinye Salzman. Like the story itself, Salzman seems both absolutely realistic and concrete and partly fantastic, magical, allegorical. The pictures of the prospective brides that the matchmaker offers the rabbinical student disappoint him, but he finally agrees to meet Lily H., a "fine girl that she speaks four languages and has personally in the bank ten thousand dollars."[25] The meeting is critical in

Leo's development, for while he doesn't learn much about Lily, he discovers something about himself. Lily expects the rabbinical student to have felt a "sudden passionate inspiration" and to be "enamored of God."[26] Suddenly he confesses to her and to himself that he came to God "not because I loved Him but because I did not."[27] After the meeting Leo realizes that he has called in the marriage broker because he is incapable of finding a bride himself and not because this is the traditional Jewish marriage arrangement. Worse, he recognizes that except for his parents, he has never loved anyone. And in that deeply Malamudian formulation, "perhaps it went the other way, that he did not love God so well as he might, because he had not loved man."[28]

After a week of terrible suffering, which parallels the traditional week of Jewish mourning, the marriage broker reappears and leaves more pictures. Among them Leo finds a snapshot of a woman's face that speaks to him; her eyes suggest that she "had *lived* . . . had somehow deeply suffered."[29] Now the pursued becomes the pursuer; Leo goes in search of Salzman. Salzman claims the snapshot was a mistake, that the girl "is a wild one—wild, without shame," and that "This is my baby, my Stella, she should burn in hell."[30] Although initially terrified of her possible evil, Leo finally decides "to convert her to goodness, himself to God"[31] and insists on meeting Stella. When he humbly says perhaps he can be of some service, Salzman consents to arrange the meeting. Stella comes dressed in a white dress and red shoes, suggesting the dominance of innocence in her nature, and her eyes "clearly her father's—were filled with a desperate innocence."[32] As in a Chagall painting, "violins and lit candles revolved in the sky. Leo ran forward with flowers outthrust." As the story opens in winter and concludes in spring, these words suggest the turning, the awakening of the emotionally withdrawn, spiritually dead young man.

The last words of the story, "Around the corner Salzman, leaning against a wall, chanted prayers for the dead," complicate what would otherwise be an ecstatic conclusion. Whether Salzman believes both Stella and Leo are doomed or whether he mourns for their previously dead selves is unclear. Since Stella represents life in the story, it is possible that the two final tableaux represent the two sides of the life process—life and death. In any case, the story depicts a critical turning, one man's *t'shuva*. Leo does more than recognize his emotional and spiritual deadness; he changes himself and his life.

5. JEWISH SOURCES

Much American-Jewish literature is about the sociological and psychological dimensions of Jewish life, about being Jewish in America, and focuses on the Jew as Everyman—an ethnic one, but an Everyman. But some of the writing has been more particular, more specifically Jewish, and has emphasized the Jewish quality by relying on Jewish roots or sources. Some of Malamud's stories use biblical stories as a thematic focus; for example, "The First Seven Years" plays off Jacob and Rachel's marriage, and "Angel Levine" turns upon the biblical story of Job's suffering and test by God. Cynthia Ozick's self-definition as a Jewish writer (a more pronounced and conscious identification than has been made by any other major American-Jewish writer) is reflected in her brilliant use of specifically Jewish sources. In fact, in much of her best fiction Jewish sources are the fictional core. "Puttermesser and Xanthippe" (1982) is built around a striking piece of Jewish folklore, the golem, an artificially created human being endowed with life by supernatural means.[33] Not only is the novella *about* a golem, but its structure recapitulates the construction and destruction of a golem, the same reversal of procedures. The novel is symmetrically arranged in twelve numbered sections: the first six describe the positive creative movement, the making of the golem, Puttermesser's reign as mayor; the second six describe the unmaking of New York, Puttermesser, and the golem.

Another important Ozick story, "The Pagan Rabbi" (1971), is an extended meditation on its epigraph from *The Ethics of the Fathers*: "Rabbi Jacob said, 'He who is walking along and studying, but then breaks off to remark, "How lovely is that tree!" or "How beautiful is that fallow field!"—Scripture regards such a one as having hurt his own being.' "[34] Told in the first person by an unnamed narrator, the story is about a pious, brilliant rabbi, Isaac Kornfeld, who hanged himself; the story focuses on the causes, meaning, and effect of the suicide. Much of the story consists of the reading of Kornfeld's last letter, which is a tour de force, showing Ozick's remarkable ability to breathe life into the fantastic and to provide a convincing voice for ideas which are anathemas to her own. In his letter, Kornfeld describes his gradual conversion to pagan animism, his growing recognition that despite what Judaism taught, everything in life is holy, "Hence in God's fecundating Creation there is no possibility of idolatry."[35] In his letter, Kornfeld reports that in order to escape the human bondage of his soul/body prison, he decided to try to couple with some inhuman being so that the strength of the connection would wrest his soul to its freedom. This inhuman creature, the dryad Iripomonoeia, is a stroke of genius. She is a true flower child with skin as perfect as an eggplant's, leaf-life hands and feet, and the totally visible sexual parts of a flower. Stupendously lovely and joyous, she distinguishes only beauty or ugliness and playfully throws and catches Kornfeld's words like balls. The image of the beautiful child flower or flower child is more than delightful; through Iripomonoeia, Ozick underscores the connection between pagan aestheticism and contemporary literary experimentation, which like the dryad simply plays with language.

By coupling with the dryad Kornfeld succeeded in separating himself from his soul. But while he expected his soul to be delighted, he found it was an ugly, old man trudging along, as in the epigraph, reading as he walked, oblivious of the world of nature. Furious, Kornfeld grabbed his soul's *talis*, wound it around his neck and the tree, and died calling hopelessly for the dryad.

Linguistically, the story focuses on the word *fence* and its opposing connotations: negative, "to exclude or imprison," and positive, "to enclose, to protect." We learn that Kornfeld's wife Sheindel was born in a concentration camp and that when the Nazi guards were about to throw her against the electrified fence, an army mobbed the gate. At her orthodox wedding when the men and women danced separately, the women made a fence and the ecstatic Sheindel "fell against the long laughing row."[36] Most central is the idea of Jewish law as a fence, a fence which Kornfeld scaled in his pagan heresy. Thus when imposed from without, the fence is negative and terrible; when self-chosen, a source of protection and safety.

The story is balanced and subtle in its characterization. Although Sheindel's unforgiving pitilessness seems inhuman as compared with the narrator's understanding sympathy, the narrator's last act is to throw his house plants down the toilet. While Kornfeld comes to seem immoral or crazed despite his brilliance and religious passion, the representatives of the strict religious code are deeply unattractive. The narrator's and Kornfeld's fathers, both rabbis, were jealous and envious men who vied with each other "in demonstration of charitableness, in the captious glitter of their scholia, in the number of their adherents."[37] Both used their religion and their sons as extensions of their own egos. Most important of all, when one returns to the epigraph it seems entirely mild and sane. It says that one should not break off study to admire nature, not that one must never admire nature, that those who *do* incorrectly interrupt their study are to be regarded as having hurt their own beings, rather than as having committed a crime against others or against God.

6. COSMOPOLITANISM AND UNIVERSALISM

Like many good jokes, the old joke that cosmopolitanism is Jewish parochialism hits a nerve. Despite traditional Jewish particularism, one significant aspect of Jewish thought, especially in this century, has been an emphasis on the similarity of all human beings in their essential humanity and a commitment to one world brotherhood that transcends all distinctions and unites all human beings as human beings. Early in the century both in Eastern Europe and in this country, a considerable portion of the Jewish community considered itself socialist, and these Jewish socialists, whom Irving Howe celebrates in *World of Our Fathers* (1976), were dedicated to building a new society, a world-wide international community in which all human beings "would live without want in freedom and fulfillment."[38] The important point is that theirs was a socialism that was more than political and economic; it was founded on a profound idealism, an idea of human liberation and secular utopia. Opposed to traditional Judaism, socialist Jews transferred messianism, one of the traditional elements of Jewish experience, to secular dreams.

While deeply grounded in Jewish life and feeling, much contemporary American-Jewish fiction links its particular Jewishness to a quest for the universal; that is, it affirms things Jewish but as one—albeit one *special*—thread in the human fabric. Even Malamud, who in some ways is the most Jewish of writers, often uses his characters' Jewishness more as a metaphor than as a fact, and his definition of the good Jew and the good man often seem indistinguishable. Likewise, although Grace Paley's most frequent character, Faith, is recognizably Jewish, Paley carefully peoples her fictional New York with Puerto Ricans, blacks, and Chinese, and her pervasive political and social message is universalist. In Tillie Olsen's work this theme is quite dominant, and the most stirring example of a story that is both deeply Jewish and yet very explicitly committed to a universalist vision is her great "Tell Me a Riddle" (in the collection of the same name, 1961).

Olsen herself suggests this doubleness. She considers herself an atheist and proudly describes her father as "incorruptibly atheist to the last day of his life"; on the other hand, she says, "I still remain with the kind of *Yidishkayt* I grew up with."[39] What she means by her *Yidishkayt* is the Jewish socialist background which fostered two essential insights: first, "knowledge and experience of injustice, of discrimination, of oppression, of genocide and the need to act against them forever and whenever they appear," and second, an "absolute belief in the potentialities of human beings."[40]

Olsen's vision of the world parallels that of her character, Eva, in "Tell Me a Riddle." Eva is, on the one hand, a spiritual portrait of the artist as an old woman and, on the other, a wonderfully moving evocation of a segment of the Jewish community. That is, even Eva's insistence, "Race, human; religion, none," is a recognizably Jewish response.[41] Although "Tell Me a Riddle" attacks traditional Judaism and praises universalism, the story is a deeply Jewish story. Olsen has said that she began the story in order to celebrate a generation of revolutionaries, and her portrait of Eva and David is indeed a celebration of fervent Jewish revolutionaries during the early years of the century and of a time of boundless hopes and richly humanist fervor. The Yiddish-inflected speech and "old country curses" are obviously of Jewish origin. David's ideal, to retire in dignity and community to his workers' haven, evokes memories of Jewish Workmen's Circles. Even the bait with which David unsuccessfully tempts Eva to the home is particularly Jewish; he tells her there is a reading circle which studies Chekhov and Peretz, a Russian and Jewish author united by their understanding and love of the ordinary person, of basic, unimproved humanity.

Nonetheless, through Eva, Olsen repudiates traditional Judaism. When one of her children tells Eva that the hospital puts patients on lists so that "men of God may visit those of their religion" and that she is on the Jewish list, Eva responds: "Not for rabbis."[42] It is not that Eva denies being Jewish but that she refuses the religious views and consolation of the rabbis.

When asked by her daughter Hannah to light the Sabbath candles, Eva refuses and accuses Hannah of doing it for ignoble reasons: "Not for pleasure she does it. For emptiness. Because his [her husband's] family does. Because all around her do."[43] She calls Hannah's heritage and tradition "Superstition! From the savages, afraid of the dark, of themselves: mumbo words and magic lights to scare away ghosts." Eva's dismissive attitude toward ritual parallels that of her "real life" contemporaries: in the early years of the century young Jewish radicals held costume balls on Yom Kippur to flaunt their separation from a "benighted" past. What infuriates Eva most is Hannah's nostalgia for the past. For the forward-looking Eva the past means "dark centuries" when religion stifled women and encouraged the poor to buy candles instead of bread. It was when the poor chosen Jew was "ground under, despised, trembling in cellars" and later a Holocaust victim—"And cremated."[44] When her husband David asks whether the terrible victimization of the Jews is the fault of religion, Eva does not answer. But clearly she sees Judaism as a backward religion and has no faith in a God who permits his chosen people to suffer so excruciatingly. Instead of traditional religion she believes Hannah should teach universal humanism: "to smash all ghettos that divide us—not to go back, not to go back."[45]

Eva's undying faith in their youthful messianic hopes, "their holiest dreams," is the story's vision of a secular utopia. Both the vision and the faith in human possibility mirror Jewish socialism of the early years of the century and Olsen's own abiding *Yidishkayt*, "*that joyous certainty, that sense of mattering, of moving and being moved, of being one and indivisible with the great of the past, with all that freed, ennobled man.*"[46] Although Eva's sacred text is not the Bible but the *Book of Martyrs*, and Socrates, not Moses, is her hero, her vision embodies both the messianic hope and universalist world-view of a particular kind of secular Jew. This vision is one of the deepest tributaries in the stream of American-Jewish fiction.

7. THE MIDDLE ROAD: ANTI-ROMANTICISM/ANTI-NIHILISM

As American-Jewish fiction insists on man's mixed nature, so it walks the middle line between optimism and pessimism, complete hopeful affirmation and despair. Centuries of persecution preclude easy optimism, while hope and faith, whether in God or in a progressive future, have kept Jews from despair. Not only is this vision balanced and moderate in its estimation of man and the future, but it is deeply suspicious of the extremes. Both nihilism and romanticism are seen as wrongheaded and dangerous. As the American-Jewish novelist most interested in ideas and cultural questions, Bellow frequently takes the temperature of the culture and prescribes medication to eliminate fever or chill. Various novels attack one or the other negative extreme. In *Herzog* (1964) the problem is the chill of nihilism, and the novel repudiates both the intellectual nihilists, who flirt cheaply with fashionable wasteland despair, and the "practical" nihilists, ordinary people who chronically discount the possibility of values or meaning in the world. In *Mr. Sammler's Planet* (1970) the focus is on the feverish romantic excesses of the American sixties.

"Shortly after dawn, or what would have been dawn in a normal sky, Mr. Artur Sammler with his bushy eye took in the books and papers of his West Side bedroom and suspected strongly that they were the wrong books, the wrong papers."[47] This, the opening sentence of *Mr. Sammler's Planet*, establishes the tone and focus of the entire novel. The abnormal sky and the wrong books and papers suggest the negative terrain of the fictional present, the dangerously romantic sixties, and Sammler's singular bushy eye, both his disfigurement and his vision. As the title of the book suggests, *Mr. Sammler's Planet* is about one man's vision of the world, a blind world in which he, the one-eyed seer, is king of perception.

Sammler is the moral voice of the novel. Nearly as old as the century, Sammler, by virtue of his age, his diverse historical experience, his education and Holocaust survivor status, is a father figure and teacher to almost all the characters in the novel, most of whom tell him their secrets and hold him in a kind of awe. Even Sammler is aware that a certain wizardry is ascribed to him. Throughout the novel Sammler looks at almost all the other characters (many of whom are sixties types) from a superior position and finds them wanting in various ways.

Published in 1970, *Mr. Sammler's Planet* is clearly the product of an angry response to the sixties. It is full of the particulars of time and place and evokes exact physical scenes and the reigning cultural events of the decade. Through Sammler's reactions to the highly unsympathetic, even caricatured characters, especially Elya's aging children of the decade, Angela and Wallace, the novel strongly criticizes the romanticism of the time.

Its youth are seen as self-indulgent, brainless, spoiled, dirty, and anti-intellectual. When he lectures at Columbia, students revile Sammler for being an "effete old shit," saying "his balls are dry. He's dead. He can't come."[48] Sammler wants to escape "all this confused sex-excrement-militancy, explosiveness, abusiveness, tooth-showing, Barbary ape howling" into the "spiritual, Platonic Augustinian thirteenth century."[49] The two young men emblematic of the decade are both unappealing. Feffer is a charming, fast-talking self-promoter whose schemes finally seem thoroughly dangerous. Wallace, the young man in search of his identity who tries every profession in turn, is summed up as a "high IQ moron." The most violent attack is on Angela, who represents the sexually liberated woman: "In Angela you confronted sensual womanhood without remission."[50]

One of the major themes of *Mr. Sammler's Planet* is the attack on the decade's theory of "limitless demand—insatiability, refusal of the doomed creature (death being sure and final) to go away from this earth unsatisfied."[51] And the major form of crazed insatiability in the decade was sexual; according to Sammler, a sexual madness was overwhelming the Western world. The post-sexual hero denounces sexual excess in general, although he is much harsher on Angela, who represents uncontrolled female sexuality, than he is on the black pickpocket, who represents uncontrolled male sexuality.

Although all the excessive romantic types are repudiated, Sammler's (and through him the novel's) judgment of Elya is basically positive. In spite of Elya's faults (including performing illegal abortions for Mafia connections), he is presented as a good father, good man, and good Jew, interested in the Jewish past in Europe and the Jewish future in Israel. Suburbia and money have not spoiled

Elya. In fact, in Bellow's novel the usual hero's qualities are divided between Sammler and Elya: Sammler embodies what man should know; Elya, how man should act. Sammler is the spiritual and intellectual patriarch; Elya, the practical.

Despite Sammler's denunciation of the terrible "dark romanticism" of the sixties and his vision of New York as Sodom, a city of barbarity, crime, filth, and immorality, the novel ends with cautious affirmation. Sammler's last words are a prayer for his dead nephew Elya. The ending affirms a continuing faith in some basic truths about God and man. Sammler praises Elya for his eagerness "to do what was required of him," for his kindness, for having recognized and met the "terms of his contract." The last lines emphasize God's existence and man's duty: "the terms which . . . each man knows. . . . For that is the truth of it—that we know . . . we know."[52]

Overtly repudiating romanticism, the novel, through the example of Sammler, also rejects nihilism. Despite all he has experienced and seen—burial in a mass grave, digging himself out from the corpses including his wife's, hiding in a mausoleum in a Polish cemetery, barely existing like a half-starved animal in a forest, killing a German soldier who begged for his life—Sammler is not a nihilist. He affirms the old truths; even the Holocaust has not broken the terms of the contract between God and man. *Mr. Sammler's Planet* is then a novel of historical and intellectual judgment in which the errors of the past and present are revealed and the extremes of both romanticism and nihilism are denied.

8. TIME, HISTORY, AND MEMORY

In American-Jewish fiction, time, history, and memory define human life, make us human. This time-drenched universe is virtually opposite the mainstream of American literature and culture. While most American literature posits the United States as a new beginning, an Eden in which every man and every woman can see themselves as Adam and Eve, Jewish memory is long and profound. For the Jewish imagination Thoreau's ecstatic perpetual dawn is a terrifying amnesia, and the linked themes of time, history, and memory pervade American-Jewish fiction. For example, E. L. Doctorow's *The Book of Daniel* (1971) is about the growing historical sense and recovery of memory of the protagonist, Daniel Isaacson; and Jerome Weidman's story, "My Father Sits in the Dark" (1934), is about an immigrant Jew's enveloping memories of his old country childhood and his native American son's incomprehension.

It is not surprising that the themes of history, memory, and time are frequently focused on the most traumatic, devastating historical experience in modern Jewish history, the Holocaust. American-Jewish writers have tended to avoid evoking the Holocaust directly and to repudiate the nihilism that it implicitly suggests. Contemporary American-Jewish fiction writers who have written about the Holocaust include Bellow in *Mr. Sammler's Planet*, Malamud directly in many stories and indirectly in *The Fixer* (1966), Philip Roth in *The Ghost Writer* (1979) and "Eli, the Fanatic" (1959), and Susan Fromberg Schaeffer in *Anya*

(1974). In general, American-Jewish fiction writers have written about the Holocaust by focusing on a survivor who has come to this country. In this way they have struggled to bring together the American reality and European event, the unprecedented post-war material ease and relative psychological well-being on the one hand, and the most unfathomable monstrous event in Jewish history on the other.

One of the outstanding Holocaust novels, Edward Lewis Wallant's *The Pawnbroker* (1961) focuses its exploration of time, memory, and history on Sol Nazerman, a Holocaust victim living in New York. Employing the metaphor of seeing as a central organizing principle, it is about what Nazerman has seen in Europe and refuses to see in Harlem, his searing vision of the Holocaust and his current self-imposed blindness, his unwillingness to see. In the fictional present Nazerman's strange glasses and deformed body are signs of how the Holocaust has maimed him, physical signs of his psychological wounds.

Sol's response to his experience has been to try to blot it out of his consciousness, not to feel or remember. That attempted amnesia and armor of feelinglessness enable him to function minimally by day. But at night, especially when the anniversary of his family's destruction arrives, he is plagued by terrible dream memories of his wife's forced sexual abasement, and his daughter's and son's inhuman deaths.

Wallant's depiction of the other Holocaust survivors in the novel is basically negative. Sol's friend Tessie is slovenly and self-pitying; her aged father whining and querulous; the guilt-ridden survivor Goberman is pitiful, yet repulsive. These other survivors are decidedly unenlightened by their tragic experience; through their depiction *The Pawnbroker* clearly suggests that mere survival is not enough for wisdom or virtue.

Wallant's depiction of the members of Sol's suburban American-Jewish family is caustic, even occasionally stereotypical and unbalanced, because of their deadness to the past, their lack of memory, their ahistoricity. They refuse to see and feel what the Holocaust was; for them American life should be endlessly cheerful, and Europe a place for fancy cultural trips. Morton, the suffering would-be artist, is presented with sympathy, and the new relationship with Sol at the end of the novel suggests their hopeful future. But Sol's niece is a stereotypical bubble-headed Jewish American Princess; his brother-in-law is weak, dependent, smug, and full of liberal platitudes; and Sol's sister is a monster of vulgarity, willed superficiality, and cruelty, who rules her husband, uses her brother, and loathes her alienated son.

The major development of the novel is Sol's awakening, caused by the self-sacrificial death of his assistant Jesus Ortiz. There are clear indications that this awakening will enable him to function as an emotionally responsive human being; his going to mourn her father's death with Tessie is one sign. And the awakening that affects the present and future rests on a change in his attitudes toward the past, an accommodation of all the tragic suffering, an acceptance of past events. Sol's last words, ''rest in peace,'' are addressed to his dead loved ones. The religious mourning that ends the novel is then the deepest response to the Holocaust. Moreover, Nazerman's new father-son, teacher-pupil relationship with Morton suggests that Morton will lose his ahistoricity and will come to understand Sol's and the Jewish people's past, and this understanding will humanize and instruct him. Overall, *The Pawnbroker* demonstrates that history is the biography of the human race, and that while memory can be searing, coming to understand and accept the past is the only premise for a truly human future.

9. THE CENTRALITY OF FAMILY

In post-World War II American-Jewish fiction, family is the crucial bond that links—or chains—people together. In this fiction the family is the locus of narrative and the agent of meaning. From the earliest American-Jewish literature until the most recent, the family is the heart of human life. In the earliest important American-Jewish novel, Abraham Cahan's *The Rise of David Levinsky* (1917), the protagonist's emotional drama is one of orphanhood. Likewise, in Henry Roth's *Call It Sleep* (1934), the child's emotional life is a seesaw between his warm, protective mother and his tyrannical, paranoid father. Intense family feeling is a major theme in Bellow's work, and Philip Roth has evoked with complexity and depth both the tenderness, especially between father and son, and the suffocation, rage and guilt, of family life. Certainly family life is not always depicted positively in contemporary American-Jewish fiction, but it is always central.

One of the most affecting portrayals of family life and feeling is Malamud's "Idiots First" (1961), which depicts the last evening of a father, Mendel, and son, Isaac. The opening pages set the tone, as images of darkness and cold abound; Mendel's very clothing is "cold embittered."[53] When he winds his old watch, the sight of it nauseates him, because his idiot son's mind is like a stopped watch and because his last hours are ticking away. Mendel knows he is dying and resists, not because he loves life, but because he has one last mission to accomplish: he must put Isaac safely on the train to his uncle in California. That is, Mendel's last duty is toward his son, and who will accept this thirty-nine-year-old man-boy but his eighty-one-year-old great-uncle—a family problem, a family solution. Pursued relentlessly by Ginzburg, the Yiddish-accented angel of death, Mendel tries desperately to raise the last $35 for Isaac's ticket. Throughout their last hours, father and son are mutually solicitous: Isaac urges his father to sleep; Mendel helps Isaac put on his coat. Despite all Mendel's worries and anxiety, he can still share Isaac's simple delights, like the sight of the three gold balls of the pawnshop. And Mendel tries to keep Isaac's humanity alive by pointing out what is beautiful—the large moon and many stars.

The story depicts Mendel's last hours in a series of encounters, as he makes desperate efforts to raise the necessary money. When Mendel finally buys Isaac's ticket, the uniformed ticket collector, Ginzburg, says it is already past twelve and refuses to let them past the gate even though the train is still in the station.

What ensues is one of Malamud's great dialogues, a furious argument between a despairing, insistent father and the angel of death. Arguing that what happens to Isaac is not his problem, Ginzburg claims his responsibility is only "to create conditions. To make happen what happens."[54] Asked where his pity is, Ginzburg replies, "This ain't my commodity. The law is the law." At that, Mendel rises to his full stature and tells him about all his suffering, especially the pain "in a father's heart" waiting hopelessly for Isaac to grow up. Mendel's final cry is "You bastard, don't you understand what it means human?"[55] As they struggle together, Mendel sees the depth of his own terror mirrored in Ginzburg's eyes, while Ginzburg sees mirrored in Mendel's eyes "his own awful wrath." Then one of Malamud's miracles occurs: Mendel sees "a shimmering, starry, blinding light that produced darkness"—Ginzburg relents. Isaac helps his father up and together they totter toward the train. Their parting scene is almost unbearably tender. Hastily embracing his son, Mendel tells him " 'Help Uncle Leo, Issakil. Also remember your father and mother.' " Forced to entrust Isaac to the world, Mendel tells the conductor simply, "Be nice to him" and ascends the stairs "to see what had become of Ginzburg"; he is now ready to die.[56]

Ginzburg, the vividly humanized angel of death is an example of what Robert Alter has called "the habitual domestication of myth" in Jewish literature. That is, according to Alter, the last scene between Ginzburg and Mendel "could serve as an emblem of how this whole mode of imagination works, wresting a kind of concession from the ultimate powers by the very act of humanizing them, conceiving them in such a way that they will understand what it means to be human."[57]

Surely the story also domesticates the traditional Abraham and Isaac myth. In the biblical story, Abraham deeply loves his son, but accepting the mystery of God's commandment, faithfully consents to sacrifice his beloved son to God. His self-overcoming faith is the mark of his goodness. In Malamud's story Mendel is also sorely tried by God—with his poverty, ill health, the early death of his wife, and his idiot son. He has no fear of death and might in fact welcome it as a release. But he is faithful to his mission of finding a secure, loving place for Isaac, sending him safely to family. Surely it is this deep sense of family love and responsibility that moves Ginzburg, that humanizes the law, that brings forth the "shimmering starry, blinding light."

10. INTELLECT AND SPIRIT

Alfred Kazin has remarked on "the age-old Jewish belief that the only possible salvation lies in thinking well, which is thinking one's way to the root of all creation, thinking one's way to the ultimate reason of things."[58] The emphasis on intellect and reason pervades traditional Judaism, where knowledge of sacred texts and intellectual ability to analyze and discuss them are marks of highest distinction. But in traditional Judaism the intellect is not a totally separate sphere; it is a partner of the spirit, a means to a spiritual ideal. The extraordinarily high rate of literacy and experience with its sophisticated traditions (albeit about texts and questions the modern world rejects) made Jewish immigrants to this country a distinct group. This is reflected in the earliest American-Jewish fiction: David Levinsky aspired first to rabbinical study and later to secular intellectual achievement and, looking back, believes that the path from the *yeshiva* to City College was the correct one. Contemporary American-Jewish fiction is full of (mostly wrongheaded) intellectuals. Wallant's pawnbroker is a former philosophy instructor; many of Philip Roth's protagonists are professors or writers; and Ozick features intellectuals in almost all of her novels and stories.

Bellow's *Mr. Sammler's Planet, Humboldt's Gift* (1975), and *The Dean's December* (1982) are all dominated by intellectuals, but no book or character reveals Bellow's views of the relation between intellect and spirit more clearly than *Herzog* (1964). The novel focuses on the attempts of "that suffering joker," Moses Elkanah Herzog, to bring order to the chaos of his life and thoughts. In the complex three-part chronology (the fictional present at Herzog's Berkshire house; the recent past during which he compulsively raced between New York, Chicago, and Martha's Vineyard; and the distant past, including deeply felt childhood memories), the emphasis is on man thinking. Herzog thinks about his own follies, especially in relation to women, as well as about larger historical questions, and the two are intertwined; attempts to understand his own life necessarily involve Herzog in an investigation of the conditions of modern man. His frantic letter-writing to the great and the unknown, to the living and the dead, is both a symptom of his instability and a serious attempt to discover or invent significant order. While Herzog quips that *"What this country needs is a good five-cent synthesis,"* his struggle is to find a non-reductive intellectual position true to the complexity of reality he perceives.[59] A childhood friend's *"merely aesthetic critique of modern history! After the wars and mass killings,"* depresses and infuriates him.[60]

Herzog's commitment to reason and intellect is underscored by his contrasting reaction to women and sexuality. While much of the novel focuses on Herzog's attempt to come to terms with his unfinished emotional business with Madeline, his ex-wife, sexual relations are finally not seen as central or sufficient, let alone a source of wisdom. Remembering an early affair with an Oriental woman, Sono, he thinks, "*...I lacked the strength of character to bear such joy.*" Significantly, Herzog rejected this "life-giving pleasure" in the name of his Jewishness: "have all the traditions, passions, renunciation, virtues, gems, and masterpieces of Hebrew discipline and all the rest of it—rhetoric, a lot of it, but containing true facts—brought me to these untidy green sheets and this rippled mattress?"[61] And in the fictional present, Ramona, the high priestess of sex, is seen as alluring but not serious; early in the novel he writes her a mental letter suggesting, *"You think that sexual pleasure is all this spirit wants."*[62]

Neither sensual fulfillment (Sono) nor sexual drama (Ramona) is more than comfort or passing interest to Herzog, and ideas about the absolute value of profound sexual experience are totally alien. His sexual life is pale and superficial in comparison with his childhood life on Napoleon Street, which "offered him a wider range of human feelings than he had ever again been able to find."[63] In part this is the traditional value judgment of mind over body, but it also illuminates his position about the public versus the private life. Love is seen as "a female pursuit," while "the occupation of a man is in duty, in use, in civility, in politics in the Aristotelian sense."[64]

By the end of the novel, Herzog has not abandoned his intellectual efforts, but he has a more direct sense of the realm of the spirit. He still holds that "*the dream of man's heart*" is that "*life may complete itself in significant pattern*," but he has given up his endless intellectual analysis.[65] He no longer thinks that "explanation is a necessity of survival."[66] Having come to grips with his failed marriages, past mistakes, and fear of death, and accepting himself with all his strengths and flaws, he moves past the realm of reason to something like spiritual intuition: " *'Thou movest me. That leaves no choice.'* Something produces intensity, a holy feeling."[67] And with this final acceptance, of both the value and the limits of the intellect, "he had no messages for anyone. Nothing. Not a single word."[68]

11. THE CELEBRATION OF TALK

Bellow's first novel, *Dangling Man* (1944), established one of the major themes of post-war American-Jewish fiction when the protagonist Joseph announced his opposition to the current fashion of being tight-lipped and hard-boiled: "If you have difficulties grapple with them silently, goes one of their commandments. To hell with that! I intend to talk about mine, and if I had as many mouths as Siva has arms and kept them going all the time, I still could not do myself justice."[69]

This pronouncement clearly rejects the Hemingway ethic that praises action and is suspicious of words. Overall, American-Jewish fiction has repudiated Hemingway and his characters' notion that talking about your troubles is bad form and talking about your joys is diluting them. In fact, Lillian Hellman's acceptance of this closed-mouth code is one of the clearest indications of how "un-Jewish" her work is.

The necessity and value of talk for both self-expression and communication are frequently celebrated in American-Jewish fiction. A particularly vivid example is Grace Paley's short fiction. "Conversation," the jacket painting by Milton Avery which adorns Paley's recent collection, *Later the Same Day* (1985), makes explicit what has been implicit in her three short-story collections: the celebration of language in general and conversation in particular. Many of the titles of the stories point to this theme which pervades and unites the recent collection; two have the word language in their titles, others are entitled "A Man Told Me the Story of His Life," "The Story Hearer," "Zagrowsky Tells," and "Listening."

"Ruthy and Edie" is about old friends exploring and explaining their lives in rich conversation, and at the same time it is about a child coming to language. As the women talk, they recall childhood friendships and betrayals, share family news, mull over politics. Their ability to express themselves and share their feelings and thoughts through language is a delight and comfort to them, and the hours are not long enough for all they have to say. Just as the women's lives are expressed and enriched by conversation, Ruthy's granddaughter is just discovering these same potentialities. Her newest sentence, " 'Remember dat?' " is a milestone for memory, consciousness, and conversation: "Because for such a long time there had been only the present full of milk and looking. Then one day trying to dream into an afternoon nap, she sat up and said, Gramma, I boke your cup. Remember dat? In this simple way the lifelong past is invented, which as we know thickens the present and gives all kinds of advice to the future."[70]

Relishing her granddaughter's development, Ruthy sees words as the comfort and bulwark against time's ravages. She dreads Letty's "falling out of her brand-new hammock of world-inventing words onto the hard floor of man-made time."[71]

In "Zagrowsky Tells," the neighborhood druggist unpacks his heart by relating his tale of half-conscious bigotry and family woe. Izzie Zagrowsky says, "For a fact I didn't want her [Faith] to leave because since I already began to tell, I have to tell the whole story. I'm not a person who keeps things in. Tell!"[72]

Rather than "talking the whole thing away" as Hemingway characters fear, conversation in Paley's lovely formulation "thickens" experience. When Ruthy and Faith talk about Faith's love affair, they wryly extol the continuing, deepening power of conversation of women friends as opposed to the short life of sexual pleasure. When Ruthy asks why Faith describes her former lover at such length when the affair is over, Faith replies, " 'But the fun of talking, Ruthy. What about that? It's as good as fucking lots of times. Isn't it?' "[73] The two women praise a man for being " 'a true gossip like us.' " And when Ruth asks Faith about how she feels about the breakup of her affair, Faith says, "I couldn't talk to you about it, so it never got thick enough. I mean woofed and warped."[74]

Again and again, the stories assert the power of words to remember, rehash, discover, invent, express, share, attack, and defend. As one character says, "a few hot human truthful words are powerful enough . . . to steam all God's chemical mistakes and society's slimy lies out."[75] Because of the potency of language, misuse of words is extremely dangerous. In "The Story Hearer," Treadwell Thomas regrets having worked for the language division of the Defense Department, which he says "was organized to discontinue the English language as a useful way to communicate true facts."[76] Interviewing Thomas, another character asks, "Could you give us at least one expression you invented to stultify or mitigate?" At the words "stultify" and "mitigate," the narrator Faith screams, "You caught the disease."[77] She later asks the reader, "Don't you wish you could rise powerfully above your time and name? I'm sure we all try, but here we are, . . . speaking their narrow language."[78]

Words and conversation are finally central to naming both the world and the self. When a friend's daughter Abby dies, Faith insists on referring to her by name not as "the kid": "I wanted to say 'Abby' the way I've said 'Selena'— so those names can take thickness and strength and fall back into the world with their own weight."[79] And in the last story of the collection, "Listening," one of Faith's lesbian friends criticizes Faith for not naming her, for not "talking" about her in her fiction: "Listen, Faith, why don't you tell my story? . . . Where is Cassie? Where is *my* life?"[80] Thus two women talking about the power of language close the collection mid-conversation.

12. ART AS A HUMANISTIC ENTERPRISE

Contemporary American-Jewish fiction is based on some traditional beliefs about the nature of the world, human beings, and art. It assumes that however difficult to assess, the world and human life have meaning, that human beings can, to a degree, know the world, and that people must live with moral choice and responsibility. American-Jewish fiction does not necessarily mirror the world realistically; indeed fantasy is a major resource of Bellow, Malamud, Roth, and Ozick. But it is written on the premise that art communicates something about the nature of human beings and the world and that its spiritual, moral, and aesthetic qualities are an essential humanizing force.

All of these assumptions run counter to the reigning highbrow ideas about fiction, that is, to post-modernism. Although post-modernist fiction is not the most popular fiction of our time, its practitioners and defenders consider it the only intellectually defensible art and often attack writing outside its confines as middlebrow, repetitive, insufficiently new, or "critically naive." As opposed to American-Jewish fiction, post-modernist experimental fiction rejects the idea of meaning in both life and art; life and art are separate, equally meaningless realms. A distinct category, art provides neither a lamp nor a mirror for reality. To read literature is to enter a realm of words which may be elegantly or intricately arranged, but this arrangement bears no special relationship to the readers' lives, and readers are not to try to look through the words to a nameless vision informing them. Since history is seen as a unintelligible flux of phenomena, the efforts of the shaping or ordering imagination to discover or impose meaning are at best ridiculous or fraudulent. Donald Barthelme's post-modernist parody of Henry James in *Snow White* wittily suggests this overthrow of the older assumptions and stances:

Try to be a man about whom nothing is known, our father said, when we were young. Our father said several other interesting things, but we have forgotten what they were. . . . Our father was a man about whom nothing is known. Nothing is known about him still. He gave us the recipes. He was not very interesting. A tree is more interesting. A suitcase is more interesting. A canned good is more interesting.[81]

Parodying James's famous advice, "Try to be one of the people on whom nothing is lost," Barthelme then inverts all of James's ideas about psychology, character, and artistic authority. Character lacks plausible motive or discernible depth. Language is denied its traditional signifying power. James's idea of the importance of selection and arrangement to make material interesting is subverted: a canned good has equal status with human moral choice as valuable subject matter. While critics are divided about the value of post-modernist texts, many would agree with Frederick R. Karl, who recently praised John Hawkes, William Gaddis, John Barth, Thomas Pynchon, and Donald Barthelme for their daring newness and disparaged Bellow, Malamud, and Roth (along with Joyce Carol Oates, Ralph Ellison, and Walker Percy) as providing merely "literary events."[82]

Implicitly, all American-Jewish fiction depends on humanistic assumptions which contradict those of post-modernism. Indeed one of the principal values of American-Jewish fiction as a body of work is as a counterexample that questions or repudiates most experimental writing since World War II. The humanistic assumptions are explicit in Cynthia Ozick's essays in *Art & Ardor* (1983); they are some of the principal themes in Malamud's *The Assistant* (1957).

Frank Alpine's love affair and moral transformation in *The Assistant* are "told" through his relationship to literature. The stories a priest told him about St. Francis during his lonely, deprived childhood are the bedrock of his subsequent growth. Throughout the novel Helen's idea of herself is related to books and their humanistic value. Her New York University courses were "mostly lit courses" and her dream of finishing college and working as a social worker or teacher embodies a spiritual, not merely financial, aim. For her, education is not a means of getting on, and literature is connected with her belief that "Life *has* to have some meaning."[83] When their relationship is beginning, Frank is reading *The Life of Napoleon*; the choice reveals his desire for greatness which at that time is unconnected with values. As Helen tells him, others were great "in better ways." When Frank tells her he prefers to read the truth rather than fiction, she insists "It is the truth."[84] She urges Frank to read *Madame Bovary*, *Anna Karenina*, and *Crime and Punishment* as if "you could read in them everything you couldn't afford not to know—the Truth about Life."[85] At first Frank finds Raskolnikov distasteful with all his miseries and is surprised to find Raskolnikov is not a Jew. Later he has "this crazy sensation that he was reading about himself."[86] The initial revulsion and subsequent identification adumbrate the movement of the entire novel. Frank's first courtship gifts are a scarf and a copy of Shakespeare; deciding she can only accept one gift, Helen chooses the Shakespeare. After his many struggles in the novel, Frank's change and hopeful state at the end are both connected with books. When Helen refuses to see how much he has changed, how he has reshaped himself from a drifting, self-hating wastrel into a man of stern conscience, his remark to her is piercingly accurate: "Those books you once gave me to read . . . did you understand them yourself?"[87] His dream at the end is to help fulfill Helen's dream of finishing college. Later she signifies her recognition of his change and the possibility of their future together by saying, "I wanted you to know I'm still using your Shakespeare."[88]

And at the very end, Frank is in the grocery reading the Bible, thinking "there were parts of it he could have written himself."[89] Frank's growing recognition of the humanizing power of art is both a cause and effect of his radical internal development. From his initial rejection of fiction as untrue and thus without value, he comes to understand literature and its essential truth about himself and the human condition.

Contemporary American-Jewish fiction is then a coherent body of work; that is, there is something gained by grouping the individual writers and works in this way. Certain attitudes about what it means to be human and about the aims and possibilities of human life prevail in American-Jewish fiction. There are shared ideas about both life and art. Some of these ideas run counter to those of most American fiction; in particular, the American-Jewish vision of the individual as embedded in history and the family directly opposes the typical American conception of the American Adam, the solitary individual beginning a new day. And the underlying humanistic assumptions about the nature and value of art directly counter those of the current mode of experimental, postmodernist fiction.

Not every American-Jewish fiction embodies all of these themes and assumptions, and some of these themes are also found outside American-Jewish fiction. These ideas are, however, constitutive of American-Jewish fiction and are sufficiently widespread to make this category a useful one, especially given the abundance of examples. Discussion of American-Jewish fiction in these terms will, I believe, "thicken" the reader's response to the individual stories and novels and open the door onto some of the most intellectually, morally, and aesthetically satisfying fiction of our time.

NOTES

1. Mark Shechner, "Jewish Writers," p. 192.

2. Philip Rahv, Introduction to *A Malamud Reader*, p. vii.

3. Frederick R. Karl, *American Fictions 1940/1980: A Comprehensive History and Critical Evaluation*, p. 7.

4. Richard J. Fein, "Jewish Fiction in America," p. 407.

5. Irving Malin, ed., *Contemporary American-Jewish Literature: Critical Essays*, p. 3.

6. Fein, p. 415.

7. Malin, p. 7.

8. Barbara Meyerhoff, *Number Our Days*, p. 257.

9. For a fuller description of *Yidishkayt*, see the introduction to Irving Howe and Eliezer Greenberg, eds., *A Treasury of Yiddish Stories*, pp. 1–71.

10. Leslie A. Fiedler, *Waiting for the End*, p. 91.

11. Saul Bellow, *Seize the Day*, p. 92. This and all further quotations are from the Avon edition.

12. Ibid., pp. 127–128.

13. Irving Howe, *World of Our Fathers*, p. 645.

14. Philip Roth, "Defender of the Faith" in *Goodbye, Columbus and Five Short Stories*, p. 161. This and all further quotations are from the Modern Library edition.

15. Ibid.

16. Ibid., p. 174.

17. Ibid., p. 198.

18. Saul Bellow, *The Victim*, p. 121. This and all further quotations are from the Avon edition.

19. Ibid., p. 113.

20. Ibid., p. 249.

21. Ibid.

22. Ibid., p. 254.

23. Ibid., p. 256.

24. Bernard Malamud, "The Mourners" in *The Magic Barrel*, rpt. in *A Malamud Reader*, p. 402.

25. Bernard Malamud, "The Magic Barrel" in *The Magic Barrel*, rpt. in *A Malamud Reader*, pp. 477–478. This and all further quotations are from *A Malamud Reader*.

26. Ibid., p. 479.

27. Ibid., p. 480.

28. Ibid.

29. Ibid., p. 484.

30. Ibid., p. 487.

31. Ibid.

32. Ibid., p. 488.

33. Cynthia Ozick, "Puttermesser and Xanthippe" in *Levitation: Five Fictions*.

34. Cynthia Ozick, "The Pagan Rabbi" in *The Pagan Rabbi and Other Stories*.

35. Ibid., p. 21.

36. Ibid., p. 7.

37. Ibid., p. 3.

38. Howe, p. 323.

39. Unpublished Olsen interview with Naomi Rubin conducted in May, 1983.

40. Ibid.

41. Tillie Olsen, "Tell Me a Riddle" in *Tell Me a Riddle*, p. 80. This and all further quotations are from the Dell edition.

42. Ibid.

43. Ibid., p. 81.

44. Ibid.

45. Ibid.

46. Ibid., p. 113.

47. Saul Bellow, *Mr. Sammler's Planet*, p. 7. This and all subsequent quotations are from the Penguin edition.

48. Ibid., p. 42.

49. Ibid., p. 43.

50. Ibid., p. 31.

51. Ibid., p. 34.

52. Ibid., pp. 285–286.

53. Bernard Malamud, "Idiots First," in *Idiots First*, p. 403. This and all further quotations are from *A Malamud Reader*.

54. Ibid., p. 411.
55. Ibid., p. 412.
56. Ibid., p. 413.
57. Robert Alter, "Jewish Humor and the Domestication of Myth," *Defenses of the Imagination: Jewish Writers and Modern Historical Crisis*, p. 162.
58. Alfred Kazin, "Though He Slay Me," p. 3.
59. Saul Bellow, *Herzog*, p. 255. This and all further quotations are from the Fawcett edition.
60. Ibid., p. 96.
61. Ibid., p. 211.
62. Ibid., p. 26.
63. Ibid., p. 174.
64. Ibid., p. 119.
65. Ibid., p. 370.
66. Ibid., p. 392.
67. Ibid., p. 414.
68. Ibid., p. 416.
69. Saul Bellow, *Dangling Man*, p. 9. This quotation is from the World edition.
70. Grace Paley, "Ruthy and Edie" in *Later the Same Day*, p. 121. All further references to Paley's stories are from this book.
71. Ibid., p. 126.
72. Grace Paley, "Zagrowsky Tells," p. 161.
73. Grace Paley, "The Expensive Moment," p. 180.
74. Ibid., p. 190.
75. Grace Paley, "Friends," p. 73.
76. Grace Paley, "The Story Hearer," p. 138.
77. Ibid., p. 139.
78. Ibid., p. 140.
79. Paley, "Friends," p. 79.
80. Grace Paley, "Listening," p. 210.
81. Donald Barthelme, *Snow White*, pp. 18–19.
82. Karl, *American Fictions 1940/1980*, p. xxii.
83. Bernard Malamud, *The Assistant*, p. 43.
84. Ibid., p. 97.
85. Ibid., p. 106.
86. Ibid., p. 108.
87. Ibid., p. 234.
88. Ibid., p. 244.
89. Ibid., p. 245.

BIBLIOGRAPHY

Alter, Robert. *Defenses of the Imagination: Jewish Writers and Modern Historical Crisis*. Philadelphia: Jewish Publication Society, 1977.
Barthelme, Donald. *Snow White*. New York: Bantam, 1968.
Bellow, Saul. *Dangling Man*. New York: Vanguard, 1944; rpt. New York: Avon, 1975.
———. *Herzog*. New York: Viking, 1964; rpt. New York: Fawcett, 1977.
———. *Mr. Sammler's Planet*. New York: Viking, 1970; rpt. New York: Penguin, 1977.

————. *Seize the Day*. New York: Viking, 1956; rpt. New York: Avon, 1977.

————. *The Victim*. New York: Vanguard, 1947; rpt. New York: Avon, 1975.

Fein, Richard J. "Jewish Fiction in America." *Judaism*. 24. (Fall 1975), pp. 406–415.

Fiedler, Leslie A. *Waiting for the End*. New York: Dell, 1975.

Howe, Irving. *World of Our Fathers*. New York: Harcourt Brace Jovanovich, 1976.

Karl, Frederick R. *American Fictions 1940/1980; A Comprehensive History and Critical Evaluation*. New York: Harper & Row, 1983.

Kazin, Alfred. "Though He Slay Me." *New York Review of Books*. 15. (December 3, 1970), pp. 3–4.

Malamud, Bernard. *The Assistant*. New York: Farrar, Straus & Cudahy, 1957.

————. *Idiots First*. New York: Farrar, Straus, 1963.

————. *The Magic Barrel*. New York: Farrar, Straus & Cudahy, 1958.

————. *A Malamud Reader*, ed. Philip Rahv. New York: Farrar, Straus & Giroux, 1967.

Malin, Irving, ed. *Contemporary American-Jewish Literature: Critical Essays*. Bloomington: Indiana University Press, 1974.

Meyerhoff, Barbara. *Number Our Days*. New York: Simon & Schuster, 1978.

Miller, Arthur. *Death of a Salesman*. New York: Reynal and Hitchcock, 1947.

Olsen, Tillie. *Tell Me a Riddle*. Philadelphia: Lippincott, 1961; rpt. New York: Dell, 1971.

Ozick, Cynthia. *Levitation: Five Fictions*. New York: Knopf, 1982.

————. *The Pagan Rabbi and Other Stories*. New York: Knopf, 1971.

Paley, Grace. *Later the Same Day*. New York: Farrar, Straus & Giroux, 1985.

Roth, Philip. *Goodbye, Columbus and Five Short Stories*. Boston: Houghton Mifflin, 1959; rpt. New York: Modern Library, 1966.

Shechner, Mark. "Jewish Writers." *Harvard Guide to Contemporary American Writing*, ed. Daniel Hoffman. Cambridge: Harvard University Press, 1979.

Wallant, Edward Lewis. *The Pawnbroker*. New York: Harcourt, Brace & World, 1960.

FOR FURTHER READING:

Primary

Doctorow, E. L. *The Book of Daniel*. New York: Random House, 1971.

Elkin, Stanley. *A Bad Man*. New York: Random House, 1967.

————. *Criers and Kibitzers, Kibitzers and Criers*. New York: Random House, 1966.

————. *The Franchiser*. New York: Farrar, Straus & Giroux, 1976.

————. *Searches and Seizures*. New York: Random House, 1973.

Friedman, Bruce Jay. *Black Angels*. New York: Simon & Schuster, 1966.

————. *The Dick*. New York: Knopf, 1970.

————. *A Mother's Kisses* . New York: Simon & Schuster, 1964.

————. *Stern*. New York: Simon & Schuster, 1962.

Heller, Joseph. *God Knows*. New York: Knopf, 1984.

————. *Good as Gold*. New York: Simon & Schuster, 1979.

Kaplan, Johanna. *O My America!* New York: Harper & Row, 1980.

————. *Other People's Lives*. New York: Knopf, 1975.

Markfield, Wallace. *Teitlebaum's Window*. New York: Knopf, 1970.

————. *To an Early Grave*. New York: Simon & Schuster, 1964.

————. *You Could Live If They Let You*. New York: Knopf, 1974.

Neugeboren, Jay. *An Orphan's Tale*. New York: Holt, Rinehart & Winston, 1976.

————. *Sam's Legacy*. New York: Holt, Rinehart & Winston, 1974.

————. *The Stolen Jew*. New York: Holt, Rinehart & Winston, 1981.

Nissenson, Hugh. *In the Reign of Peace*. New York: Farrar, Straus & Giroux, 1972.

————. *My Own Ground*. New York: Farrar, Straus & Giroux, 1976.

————. *A Pile of Stones: Short Stories*. New York: Scribner's, 1965.

Potok, Chaim. *The Book of Lights*. New York: Knopf, 1981.

————. *The Chosen*. New York: Simon & Schuster, 1967.

————. *In the Beginning*. New York: Knopf, 1975.

————. *My Name is Asher Lev*. New York: Knopf, 1972.

————. *The Promise*. New York: Knopf, 1969.

Rosen, Norma. *At the Center*. Boston: Houghton Mifflin, 1982.

————. *Green: A Novella and Eight Short Stories*. New York: Harcourt, Brace & World, 1967.

————. *Joy to Levine!* New York: Knopf, 1962.

————. *Touching Evil*. New York: Harcourt, Brace & World, 1969.

Schaeffer, Susan Fromberg. *Anya*. New York: Macmillan, 1974.

————. *Falling*. New York: Macmillan, 1973.

————. *Love*. New York: Dutton, 1980.

Weidman, Jerome. *My Father Sits in the Dark and Other Selected Stories*. New York: Random House, 1961.

Secondary

Alter, Robert. *After the Tradition: Essays on Modern Jewish Writing*. New York: Dutton, 1969.

Greenspan, Ezra. *The Schlemiel Comes to America*. Metuchen, New Jersey: Scarecrow Press, 1983.

Guttmann, Allen. *The Jewish Writer in America: Assimilation and the Crisis of Identity*. New York: Oxford University Press, 1971.

Knopp, Josephine Zadorsky. *The Trial of Judaism in Contemporary Jewish Writing*. Urbana: University of Illinois Press, 1976.

Malin, Irving. *Jews and Americans*. Carbondale: Southern Illinois University Press, 1965.

Nadel, Ira Bruce. *Jewish Writers of North America: A Guide to Information Sources*. Detroit: Gale, 1981.

Pinsker, Sanford. *The Schlemiel as Metaphor: Studies in the Yiddish and American Jewish Novel*. Carbondale: Southern Illinois University Press, 1971.

Schulz, Max. *Radical Sophistication: Studies in Contemporary Jewish-American Novelists*. Athens: Ohio University Press, 1969.

Walden, Daniel, ed. *Twentieth-Century American-Jewish Fiction Writers, Vol. 28 of Dictionary of Literary Biography*. Detroit: Gale, 1984.

Wisse, Ruth. *The Schlemiel as Modern Hero*. Chicago: University of Chicago Press, 1971.

4

The Greening of American-Jewish Drama

Ellen Schiff

I

Jews have a long history of participation in American theatre. Almost from the start of what we today call the entertainment industry, Jews have played significant roles both behind the scenes and behind the footlights. In the years between the two World Wars, Jewish playwrights began to enjoy conspicuous success. However, in the fast-moving decades following the Second World War, American-Jewish drama has come of age. The repertory has matured and flourished as increasing numbers of talented writers have filled the stage with all manner of representations of American-Jewish life.

This vigorous growth results from a number of factors. Among them figures the increasing sophistication of Americans brought about by the war and its consequences. Certainly the Holocaust and Israeli statehood altered the notion of Jews in the popular mind, no longer so apt to conceive them as stereotyped comic or menacing figures. The same two paramount events prompted Jews to revise the way they perceived themselves. A sturdier self-image, combined with the post-war stability of American Jewry, enhanced the confidence and frequency with which Jewish artists began to speak out as Jews. That assurance was bolstered by the explosion of ethnic consciousness and ethnic pride during the sixties when many groups found their voices and raised them in self-celebration.

To the social and political influences that have fostered American-Jewish drama must be added shifting currents within the theatre itself. Ethnic appreciation has not confined itself to playwrights; it has proven a force at the box office too (witness, for example, the spectacular triumph of *Fiddler on the Roof*, 1965). That audiences were willing to buy tickets for plays on Jewish subjects led to the happiest of results: the establishment, beginning in the seventies, of Jewish producing companies and playwriting support groups which have since become a national phenomenon.

A final stimulus was provided by the dominant moods and subjects of post-war drama. On the one hand, there was the prevalence of alienation, neuroses, and hungering for bygone traditions, themes to which the Jewish psyche and creative imagination are especially hospitable. At the same time, the well-established popularity of biting humor and self-deprecation that typify so much Jewish entertainment continued undiminished, assuring the reception of satirical comedy.

While the achievement of the post-war decades provides the focus of this essay, it seems most useful to regard the current era of accomplishment in the context—if not as the result—of what we should consider the tradition of American-Jewish playwriting. That such an institution exists is not exactly a given. For example, the dramatists whom I queried in writing this study were far from unanimous about a definable tradition that reached into their work in any important way. Whereas one wrote me, "I feel strongly a part of the American-Jewish tradition in theatre," another stated that "the whole thing is too new and too young for a tradition to emerge," while a third was "never aware of a tradition." Having stepped back for a wider perspective and having seen and read scores of plays, I am persuaded that a tradition does indeed exist. Therefore, this essay seeks out continuity and connections between post–1945 American-Jewish drama and that of the decades which preceded it.

II

The American stage, from its beginnings largely derivative of the European *théâtre de boulevard*, did not become an innovative native institution until roughly the First World War. Louis Harap astutely observes that Jewish authors came to the stage in inverse ratio to mainstream American authors, who mastered fiction and poetry before they wrote important plays.[1]

In 1929, Elmer Rice became the first of a now impressive list of Jews to win the Pulitzer Prize for drama. In Rice's laureate play, *Street Scene*, a Jewish family figures among others in a multi-ethnic neighborhood made wretched and tense by the Great Depression. In *Counsellor-at-Law* (1931), Rice depicts the dilemma of a Jewish attorney caught between the Old World morality of his background and the prejudicial values of his powerful upper-class Yankee rival. Rice's preoccupation with the threat of fascism manifests itself in his impassioned *Judgment Day* (1934), based on the Reichstag Fire Trials, and again in *American Landscape* (1938), where a Bund group tries to buy land for a Nazi training camp in Connecticut. Finally, in the anti-Nazi *Flight to the West* (1941), Rice brings together characters who represent the gamut of political attitudes prevalent in the years just prior to America's entry into the war.

In many ways, Elmer Rice set the mood and the tone for subsequent American-Jewish playwriting. His mode is social realism. His subjects reflect the major concerns of immigrant and first-generation Jews: the pressure to "make it" in a materialistic America, a victory for which one often had to sacrifice dignity;

the susceptibility of the weak and poor to exploitation and degradation; and anxiety about the rise of belligerent nationalism in the countries whose harassment Jews in America had escaped. In treating these subjects, Rice was joined by a contemporary whose reputation surpassed his—Clifford Odets.

Much of Odets's pre-eminence is attributable to the accuracy with which he depicted onstage two additional matters of prime and enduring significance for Jews. The first is the tension generated by family life—particularly when under one roof live those who are psychologically still in the Old World, those whom the challenges of life in America render aggressive and insensitive, and those for whom the principal adversary is not Depression America but the Jewish family itself. The latter personae often embody Odets's second special interest, the struggle of the idealistic, creative soul for expression in a philistine society where "life is printed on dollar bills."

Odets treats virtually all these concerns in *Awake and Sing!* (1935), *Paradise Lost* (1936), and *Rocket to the Moon* (1938). The first of these is widely regarded as the earliest quintessentially American-Jewish play. Margaret Brenman-Gibson observes that with it, Odets moved "the drab lives of ordinary Jewish-Americans onto the stage so that they occupied it [as Alfred Kazin remarked after opening night] 'with as much right as Lear.' "[2]

One of the surest proofs of the significance of *Awake and Sing!* is the durability of its cast of characters, all of whom have become fixtures in American drama. Heading the list is Bessie Berger, prototypical *Yiddishe momma*, the indefatigable dispenser of hard-headed and hard-hearted decisions. Bessie's patience is tested by her idealistic Old World father and her ineffectual husband who never stops believing that the Messiah will come in the form of a hair restorative or a winning sweepstakes ticket. Manipulated by her mother into marriage with a gentle greenhorn, daughter Hennie—the archetype of yet another stage convention—ultimately abandons husband and child, having succumbed to the blandishments of a smooth talker. At the play's center stands the malcontent Ralph, a painfully young twenty-two-year-old, fervently determined to "take the world in two hands and polish off the dust."

Odets's concern with family infighting and the struggle of the dreamer for self-actualization recurs in plays without Jewish characters, e.g., *The Big Knife* (1949) and *The Country Girl* (1951). It crops up in his last published play, *The Flowering Peach* (1954), a reworking of the Noah story (made into a Danny Kaye musical, *Two by Two*, 1970). *The Flowering Peach* is a less successful vehicle for the delineation of the dreamer at odds with his family, partly because the play presents the Noah clan falsely not only as Jews, but as slick permutations of the fresh characters Odets had launched twenty years earlier.

One cannot discuss the career of Clifford Odets, or of many other pioneers of the indigenous American stage, without mentioning the influential role played by the Theatre Guild, especially in the twenties, and the Group Theatre in the thirties. Both of these producing companies dedicated themselves to cultivating native American talent as well as to artistic goals frequently inspired by the

European iconoclastic playwrights and vanguard theatres. In 1931, Harold Clurman, Lee Strasberg, and Cheryl Crawford broke away from the Guild to establish the Group. Its membership became a roster of Jewish luminaries: Morris Carnovsky, Stella and Luther Adler, Elia Kazan, Lee J. Cobb, Jules (John) Garfield among the headliners. The history of the organization has been recorded by Clurman in *The Fervent Years* (1945).

Among the playwrights whose work the Group Theatre produced, John Howard Lawson is not the best known. Yet Clurman once considered Lawson "the hope of our theatre."[3] Thoroughly political in his approach to art, Lawson had written for the Guild Theatre in 1925 an experimental work entitled *Processional*. He intended to put onstage something as distinctively American as jazz and to record "the color and movement of the American processional as it moves by us." However unique the work, it is populated by stereotypes, among them a ridiculous Jewish merchant and his alluring but disloyal daughter. The former is frankly characterized by Lawson as "the vaudeville type of Jewish figure." His Sadie is a joyfully unregenerate trollop: "I ain't a good little girl, I won't be," she explains, unnecessarily.

The play on which Clurman pinned the Group's hopes was *Success Story* (1932), the only one of Lawson's plays with significant Jewish content. The work focuses on the fanatic careerism of Sol Ginsberg, an early example of the Jew obsessed with "making it big." Lacking the gift for office politics and all patience with ethics, Ginsberg forges his way to power and wealth by will and blackmail.

"Making it" in America provided a theme for Ben Hecht in *The Front Page* (1928), which he wrote with Charles MacArthur. The work treats with dispassion the turmoil that failed to stir that era's inured policemen and cynical news reporters. In a much later work, *Winkelberg* (1959), Hecht tells the sad tale of an alienated and widely rejected poet. Winkelberg may well represent the Jewish "beats," just as Schwartz of *The Front Page* was doubtless modeled on Jewish newspapermen.

The social consciousness that has characterized American-Jewish drama from its beginning is effectively displayed in Irwin Shaw's *The Gentle People* (1939). This Brooklyn fairy tale plays out a hard-to-despise fantasy in which "justice triumphs and the meek prove victorious over violent men." Here two old immigrants, a Jew and a Greek, insist that their coming to America must be made to count in terms of personal freedom. Perhaps the most Jewish aspect of *The Gentle People* resides in its ironic demonstration of how good life can be and how awful it actually is.

Commitment to the rectification of injustices and the amelioration of misery is reflected in the works of many left-wing authors of whom Michael Gold (Irwin Granich) is typical. In *Money* (1929), Gold depicts both the fear of powerlessness that leads a poor man to steal from his *landsman* and the despair of his victim. The point of this extraordinary one-act play is the power of money to pervert human nature and to rive as well as to seal human bonds.

A very different order of expression of Jewish sensitivity to adversity comes from S. N. Behrman, many of whose politically oriented plays were presented by the Theatre Guild. One of these, *Rain from Heaven* (1934), looks at first like one of those English drawing-room comedies which bring together in the home of a beautiful, well-connected, and naughty lady a group of important people, all of whom, improbably, know one another. Not far beneath the surface, however, is evidence of the anti-Semitism rife among the power hungry who regard Jews as an economic threat and hence as personal menaces. Behrman's concern with the fate of Jews in Nazi Europe is again manifest in his collaboration with Franz Werfel in the delightful *Jacobowsky and the Colonel* (1944), in which a rabidly anti-Semitic Polish officer and a hapless but clever Jew become traveling companions in Pétain's France.

Behrman's plays, together with Rice's *Flight to the West* (1941) and Odets's *Till the Day I Die* (1935), number among the handful of works by Jews that dared to bring to the American stage the plight of European Jewry. (Lillian Hellman's two plays about the dangers of fascism, *Watch on the Rhine* [1941] and *The Searching Wind* [1944], for instance, are silent on the subject.) The most dramatic statement was made by Ben Hecht in the extravaganza *We Will Never Die*, first produced in Madison Square Garden on March 9, 1943.[4] This was an emotional celebration of Judaism and Jewish achievement throughout history. The necessity for a Jewish homeland was a dominant theme. The evening climaxed with the vow that the executioners of millions of Jews would be brought to judgment. At its conclusion, the Garden echoed with the *kaddish* recited by participants and spectators.

As this brief overview demonstrates, the first major American-Jewish plays were concerned with family life, upward mobility, and social and political observations. I do not mean to suggest that plays were written on no other themes, or that these were the only American Jews writing for the stage between the World Wars, or, least of all, that there was unanimity on any of these subjects. Dissent has always been a Jewish word.

Let one exception serve as representative. Jewish family life was not always portrayed by the pioneer Jewish dramatists as improverished, strife-ridden, and based in New York City. In his autobiographical *The Cold Wind and the Warm* (1958), S. N. Behrman dramatizes mostly the fun, the warmth, and the community of growing up in Worcester, Massachusetts, in the first decades of the twentieth century.

One of the characters in *The Cold Wind and the Warm* merits a few words of comment. She is the spirited and desirable young sensualist whom I find it appropriate to call the *belle Juive*.[5] Tracing her ancestry to spunky biblical foremothers (Esther, Jael, Judith), the *belle Juive* has over the centuries become a fixture in literature. She turns up early in American drama where she appears regularly as a self-indulgent voluptuary. In Behrman's play she is Leah, a passionate, independent woman who proudly refuses to marry her baby's father, or anybody else. We have already heard from Lawson's Sadie (*Processional*), surely a sister to Odets's Hennie Berger (*Awake and Sing!*) and Pearl Gordon (*Paradise Lost*). Their spokesperson might well be Stella in Shaw's *The Gentle People*, who declares, ''I don't want to give a damn about anything. I want to ride in open cars and drink champagne. . . . I don't want to spend all day cooking and playing bridge and changing diapers.''

We will want to keep an eye on the image of the *belle Juive*, as well as the other personae launched by the early Jewish dramatists, in subsequent American-Jewish drama.

III

Expanded images of Jews constitute only one of the contributions to American-Jewish drama made by the disparate writers brought together in this section. For one reason or another—usually because their work transcends the subgenre—none of them is best known as an American-Jewish dramatist. More immediately evident than their involvement with the Jewish stage is their renown in American literary life. Their number includes two Nobel Prize winners, this country's greatest living playwright, its most prolific dramatist, and three celebrated writers whose fame rests only partly on their work for the legitimate stage.

The Nobel laureates are Saul Bellow and Isaac Bashevis Singer. Readers of Bellow's novels will readily recognize the humor and pain in his five plays.[6] Equally familiar are the protagonists, typically engrossed in trying to get in touch with themselves. For instance, in *The Wrecker* (1956), Albert refuses a $1,000 bonus to vacate his condemned building because *he* wants to tear down the walls which have witnessed the major disappointments of his life. Albert is recognizably the less imaginative cousin of Bummidge, the anti-hero of Bellow's full-length *The Last Analysis* (1965), who attacks not plaster walls but the psychological barriers between himself and a crazy world he has allowed to pen him in.

Isaac Bashevis Singer has taken to adapting his fiction to the stage, beginning with *The Mirror* (1973), a play about a demonic seducer and the deserted wife he lures into temptation. A variation on that subject provides the plot of *Tiebele and Her Demon* (1978), which Singer wrote with Eve Friedman. With Leah Napolin, Singer dramatized *Yentl* (1977), the tale of a brilliant young woman who attains fulfillment as a Jew, but heartbreak as a human being, in her disguise as a *yeshivah* boy. The zaniness of the ''wise'' men of Chelm comes to the stage in *Shlemiel the First* (1984), edited for the stage by Sarah Blacher Cohen. The famous short story ''Gimpel the Fool'' has lent itself to dramatic treatment both as play (1963, adapted by David Schechter), and opera (1985, Singer's libretto translated by David Schiff). Not the least merit of all of these works is their preserving in theatrical dimension the destroyed *shtetlach* and their way of life, of which Singer is one of the last authoritative poets.

Arthur Miller inaugurated his distinguished career with a thoroughly Jewish play, and well into his career as America's premier dramatist, he returned to his heritage. As an undergraduate at the University of Michigan, Miller wrote the award-winning *No Villain* (1936).[7] The play concerns the refusal of a Jewish manufacturer to join his association's initiative in breaking a shipping clerks' strike. The strong-arm tactics of big steel companies are, for him, not "the way for Jewish men to act."

Enough has already been made of the putatively latent Jewish elements in *Death of a Salesman* (1949), which the present writer finds an unrewarding way to approach Miller's Pulitzer Prize–winning play.[8] *The Creation of the World and Other Business* (1972) and *The American Clock* (1980) make only superficial use of Jewish references. However, in *The Price* (1968), Miller shows that he knows how and when to create a superb Jewish persona, while both *Incident at Vichy* (1964) and *Playing for Time* (1980) testify to his interest in recording Holocaust history in dramatic form.

The characterization of eighty-nine-year-old Gregory Solomon is arguably the strongest formal element in *The Price*. He is an appealing composite of the Wandering Jew and Benya Krik, the Till Eulenspiegel of Yiddish folklore. In his latest role as a used furniture dealer, the aptly named Solomon is called in to give a price on the family furniture of two feuding brothers. He ends up giving them an authoritative estimate of the value of human relationships and of life itself.

Incident at Vichy accomplishes two very different goals. First, it effectively depicts the tensions and terror of a Nazi-ordered roundup of Jews for deportation. At the same time, the play demonstrates that as a result of Nazism, the word "Jew" has acquired a critical metaphorical meaning. As Miller's Jewish psychiatrist tells the Austrian prince who has mistakenly been arrested with him: "Part of knowing who we are is knowing we are not someone else. And Jew is only the name we give to that stranger, that agony we cannot feel, that death we look at like a cold abstraction. Each man has his Jew; it is the other."[9] Miller's redefinition of "Jew" is basic to the definitive expulsion from Eden which he writes about in *After the Fall* (1964). After Auschwitz, innocence is impossible.

Finally, *Playing for Time*, written for film and television, merits a few words. Here Miller translates into a script the memoirs of Fania Fénélon, a French nightclub entertainer who kept herself alive at Auschwitz as a member of the women's orchestra.

An entirely dissimilar note is sounded again and again by Neil Simon. As he has served up one comedy after another with a facility and an unerring aim at audience tastes that even his detractors have to acknowledge, Simon has hardly made a secret of his Jewishness. Nor has he—until very lately—made dramatic fodder of it either. In his most recent works, however, Neil Simon writes forthrightly as an American Jew.

Brighton Beach Memoirs (1984) depicts Simon's adolescence in that section of Brooklyn in the thirties. The dramatist puts himself onstage in the persona of Eugene Jerome, itchily pubescent, fixated on baseball and on recording in his diary every unvarnished detail of life in the Jerome household. This is a family we have met on the American stage before. At its center is a father whose first entrance is an ironic quotation from *Death of a Salesman*. Jack Jerome lumbers tiredly onstage, a heavy bag in each hand. But Jerome differs from Willy Loman in two important ways: he proclaims himself Jewish, and he is emphatically undefeated. He is not, however, entitled to any measure of insouciance. On the contrary, the Jeromes' situation is strongly reminiscent of the Bergers' in *Awake and Sing!*

Like Odets's play, *Brighton Beach Memoirs* takes place in a multi-ethnic New York neighborhood. These are Depression years; poverty plays a vital role in both works. At both addresses, too many disparate individuals are living on top of one another to permit much privacy or domestic tranquillity. Three generations share the Bergers' apartment, while the Jeromes have divided up their house to accommodate Eugene's widowed aunt and her daughters. Doubtless the most significant parallel is that each dramatist is not only writing out of his own life, but putting himself onstage.

The results could scarcely be more dissimilar. Odets's play lays bare the frustrations, resentments, and hostilities engendered by family life. "Bessie Berger," Odets states at the outset, "is not only the mother in this house, but also the father," and the efficacy with which she plays her thankless role leaves no room for her gentle husband to be anything but a dreamer and a *nebbish*. Each character is engrossed in a private preoccupation. Grandpa Jacob champions a radicalism he does not really understand as the solution to inequities he is imperfectly aware of. Bessie is absorbed with maintaining solvency and her own standards of respectability—as much a matter of pulling down the shades as of marrying off her pregnant daughter. It is no surprise that that young woman, Hennie, runs off without a word to her foreign-born husband, who is lost in his own quest for heart and hearth. These people are painfully unwilling or unable to talk to one another. Their hearts are full or breaking, yet they seldom say what is really on their minds. In the infrequent instances when they do, nobody listens. Tensions build and go undiscussed, as in the masterful haircutting scene (II, 1). Open communication is a rarity in the Berger home, and the alienation that these people suffer is largely of their own making. There is a bitter aptness to sentiment Jacob attributes to Marx: "Abolish such families."

That, essentially, is what Neil Simon does in *Brighton Beach Memoirs*. The externals may resemble Longwood Avenue in the Bronx, but despite the hardships, family life here is warm and caring. A big difference is made by the paterfamilias. The Old World–style fathers in *Awake and Sing!* are defeated by life in America. By contrast, Simon's Jack Jerome takes pride in working two jobs to support seven people. Although he drives himself to a heart attack, he derives genuine satisfaction in providing all he can. "If you're Jewish," he says at one point, "you've got a cousin suffering somewhere in the world." Indeed, the play ends with the family's resolve to take in some relatives who have just escaped from Poland. Jerome is responsible on another level as well. He is the family Solomon, a good listener and a fair arbiter.

Beneath Eugene's levity (and a residue of Neil Simon's characteristic slickness), the problems here are genuine and good solutions are not readily, if ever, forthcoming. Like the Bergers, the Jeromes live too close for comfort. Indeed, virtually every relationship in the play leads to a quarrel. But when the fray is over, the relatives are closer still. These are sensitive extroverts who care very deeply for one another, two crucial differences between the Jeromes and the Bergers. That Odets's medium is serious drama and Simon's comedy, which by definition constructs order out of chaos, does not make *Brighton Beach Memoirs* any less incisive a theatrical depiction of American-Jewish family life than *Awake and Sing!*

Brighton Beach Memoirs has a sequel in *Biloxi Blues* (1985), which follows Eugene Jerome into the Army in the forties. Simon mines the rigors and absurdities of basic training for their considerable comic potential. Where in *Brighton Beach Memoirs* Eugene Jerome as spokesman is also the center of interest, in *Biloxi Blues*, the inveterate diarist most often focuses attention on Arnold Epstein, whom he introduces as "the worst soldier in the U.S. Army—and that includes deserters."

Epstein is a bad soldier because, as he puts it, he's an intelligent human being who will not "capitulate to this lunacy." The "lunacy" is the countless inscrutable regulations of GI life, ardently enforced by a sadistic sergeant who makes no secret of his disdain for Jews. Where Private Jerome tries to keep a low profile and often waffles when he is challenged as a Jew, Epstein is almost foolhardy in protesting his principles and his identity. Time and time again, Eugene ducks the opportunity to stand up for his friend, only to rebuke himself later for his cowardice.

Eugene regards Arnold with the same respectful admiration he feels for his principled, self-assured brother Stanley in *Brighton Beach Memoirs*. Like Stanley, Arnold takes an interest in Eugene's education. When the fledgling writer's diary is discovered by his outraged barracks mates, Arnold chastises Eugene for his glibness as well as his fence-sitting. You have to take sides to make a contribution, Arnold cautions; you can't remain a witness. "Once you start compromising your principles, you're on your way to mediocrity," Arnold warns Eugene, reminding him that a writer's integrity is consequential because "people believe what they read." It is tempting to see these instances where Simon judges his own persona as an avowal that he has not publicly espoused what he believes; that, for example, in the interest of acceptance he has universalized where he might have Judaized his voice.

Whatever esteem for Jewish sensibility and ethics Simon expresses through *Biloxi Blues*'s Epstein is displaced by other concerns in his next autobiographical play. *Broadway Bound* (1986) dramatizes the struggles of Eugene Jerome and his brother Stanley to break into show business as comedy sketch writers. Casting about for material, the brothers find the stuff of comedy at their own Brighton Beach address. This time, though, it is not a wise-cracking teenager recording his family foibles in his notebooks or a budding author whom even basic training cannot distract from his diary. Here, would-be professionals wrest jokes for public consumption out of private matters such as what their father takes to be his involvement in the extra-marital affair that is tearing his marriage apart.

Broadway Bound is concerned with the pain Eugene and Stanley unwittingly cause their parents and with their realization that, however unwished the results, it is not completely accidental that they have been inspired by the distress of their parents' strained relationship. The testy, defensive Jack Jerome in this play bears little resemblance to the exemplary head of household of *Brighton Beach Memoirs*. *Broadway Bound*'s sympathies lie with Kate Jerome, no longer the wry, suspicious nag of the earlier play, but sorrowful, bitter—and tough. Neither the memories of a long-ago dance with George Raft—a dance she relives with Eugene in the play's most poignant moment—nor the expressed love of her antic sons get anywhere near her anguish at being betrayed. Except for a stereotypic grandfather who spouts left-wing clichés, a pale imitation of Jacob in *Awake and Sing!*, the family in *Broadway Bound* is one rarely seen on the American-Jewish stage and unprecedented in the work of Neil Simon.

That this play is the least comic of the trilogy and, indeed, of any that Simon has written is predictable. For the first time, he concentrates almost entirely on situations that defy the resolutions appropriate to comedy. While Simon has, at least for the moment, abandoned the inquiry begun in *Biloxi Blues* into the vitality and function of specifically Jewish values, he has continued to reflect on hard questions about the writer's integrity raised in that play. *Broadway Bound* considers the unavoidable compromise of principles faced by the artist in choosing between responsibilities to his art and to those he loves.

At least three prominent American-Jewish writers have earned acclaim in several genres. The late Paddy Chayefsky's fame as a television dramatist (e.g., *Marty*, *The Catered Affair*) should not eclipse his contribution to the legitimate theatre. His stage plays reflect a wide range of Jewish experience. For example, in *Gideon* (1961), he reworks the story of the hero of Judges to represent modern man's preference of earthly achievement to heavenly glory. *The Tenth Man* (1959) was inspired by one of the masterworks of the Yiddish theatre, S. Anski's (S. Z. Rapaport) *The Dybbuk* (1914). Chayefsky moves the story out of the mystical atmosphere of Anski's Eastern-European community to a synagogue struggling for existence in Mineola, Long Island. Concerned, like the original, with the working out of responsibility and guilt, the newer play lacks the dignity and frisson of the Anski work. However, *The Tenth Man* portrays effectively a corner of life in a pluralistic American-Jewish congregation where Judaism is for most people—here including the rabbi—no longer a way of life. In *Middle of the Night* (1965), Chayefsky treats intermarriage, an intensifying issue in American-Jewish life by mid-century. The lovers constitute a June-and-January couple, a device which permits the dramatist to depict several kinds of conflict provoked by the decision of a middle-aged widower (a role written for Edward G. Robinson) to gamble on unorthodox happiness.

Two of America's wittiest men divide their talents between the stage and other arts. One is the creator of the metaphysical cartoon, Jules Feiffer; the other, the ingenious author, actor, and filmmaker, Woody Allen. Feiffer and Allen share what is generally called a Jewish sense of humor—acerbic, carping, interrogative, self-conscious, black around the edges, and wickedly funny.

Feiffer ably endows characters and situations with the requisite dimensions for theatrical life in scripts that retain the series-of-frames effect of his pictorial satire. *Feiffer's People* (1969) and *Hold Me* (1977) are programs of sketches whose effectiveness depends on appropriate pacing, lighting, and the detached delivery of nameless personae. A conspicuous exception is the recurring figure of Bernard Mergendeiler, paradigm of anxiety. *Little Murders* (1967) makes its point about American life by having the banal episodes of a situation comedy cut short by incidents representing everyday American violence.

Feiffer's *Knock Knock* (1976) and *Grown Ups* (1982) have more unified plots. The former concerns the bucolic existence of two retired Jewish bachelors interrupted by such unexpected visitors as a vaudevillian genie and Joan of Arc. In form and content, *Grown Ups* is Feiffer's most conventional play. Its subject is a Jewish family whose members are especially adept at hurting one another. The most accomplished is Helen, a Jewish mother who, Feiffer says in his character notes, derives not from the stereotypic but "from another, less familiar tradition," a distinction he does not entirely observe. This thoroughly unpleasant individual criticizes everyone except her daughter, from whom she nonetheless withholds the respect she accords her son, the *New York Times* journalist. Like the stock Jewish mother, she pressures her children to measure up to her standards, chiefly through the application of guilt. Feiffer's play shows that the only way Helen's adult children can assert that they *are* grown-ups is to reserve the right to mess up their lives, to defy their Jewish parents by discomfiting them.

Woody Allen's plays are often more implicitly than overtly Jewish. This is not at all the same thing as, say, Neil Simon's endowing some of his characters with Jewish names but no real Jewish substance. An excellent example is *Death* (1975). Its protagonist, Kleinman, is wakened in the middle of the night and pressured into the search for a maniacal killer. Despite his wisecracks, Kleinman is frightened. He does not pretend to understand his place in this "plan," which seems to him as formless and menacing as the dark street where he is abandoned. Threatened by the police to supply information he does not have, Kleinman's consternation flares into terror when *he* is improbably identified as the killer. He is released, only to be immediately confronted by the real killer, a psychopath who resembles him. Like Bérenger in Ionesco's *The Killer*, trapped in a comparable situation, Kleinman tries unsuccessfully to reason Death out of murdering him.

Billed by Allen as a "comedy in one act," *Death*'s laughable moments and bitingly clever lines do not detract from the play as allegory. Allen writes here as a post-Holocaust Jew, haunted by the nocturnal summons which forced people out of their homes and into roles in a plan they did not understand—an innocence that failed to protect them from having to pay with their lives for being "wrong."

One of Allen's best plays, later a celebrated film, is *Play It Again Sam* (1968). There is another kind of Jewish subtext: if the protagonist's name and description were not evidence enough of him as Allen's alter ego, the writer himself played the role in the 1969 Broadway production. Allan Felix is anything but happy. Rather, he is nervous, shy, and insecure—this after years of therapy. He compensates for his disappointments and ineptitude by living much of his life in the movies. Logically, he is a film reviewer. At the center of his fantasy life stands that WASPish, macho embodiment of everything Allen is not, Humphrey Bogart. His dreams come true when his idol steps out of a TV film to act as his mentor. Unlike many Woody Allen scripts, this one ends on an upbeat when the modest hero is seen as outrageously fascinating by a lovely young Ph.D. in cinema as he himself finds Bogey.

No such happy resolution of dreams lies in store for the characters of *The Floating Light Bulb* (1981), the first play in which Allen offers a sustained depiction of Jewish family life. The central character is a shy adolescent named Paul Pollack who compensates for his bleak, quarrelsome family life and his loneliness by immersing himself in magic tricks. He is happiest when he is practicing his "act" alone in his room. Although his mother, Enid, understands his need to live in a world of Chinese boxes, she is too much the Jewish mother to leave well enough alone. Besides, she needs to offset her own dissatisfactions. She is married to an unfaithful, gambling husband and has learned to rely on the solace of alcohol. Enid tries to make what she decides is Paul's dream come true by arranging for a second-rate theatrical agent to see her son's tricks. But the young magician is too frightened to perform for the manager. Enid's frustrations mount until she turns her husband out, but not before that beset individual exhorts his son to "throw the first punch" as he claims he had done in the Navy to show harassers that "this is one Jew who's not afraid." But there *are* frightened Jews in *The Floating Light Bulb*, and nobody gets in the first or any other punch in a work full of pain and unfulfillable aspirations.

The works discussed in this section make a contribution to American-Jewish playwriting that goes far beyond the cachet lent to the subgenre by eminent writers. Their real importance lies in what their authors add from their own Jewish lives to the stock that enriches this drama. There is a widened scope and the flavor of more varied settings; for example, Singer's East European *shtetlach*, Bellow's Chicago, and the assorted New York scenes of Simon, Feiffer, and Chayefsky. There are expanded images of the Jew. While portraying Jewish dignity and self-respect, these writers are not afraid to depict as well the Jew as extraordinary exotic (Miller's octagenarian in *The Price*), cowardly (Private Jerome in *Biloxi Blues*), silly (all the men in *Shlemiel the First*), and ignoble (Chayefsky's Gideon, Feiffer's Jewish mother). Like Jules Feiffer, Woody Allen designs accomplished neurotics; in *The Floating Light Bulb*, he comes up with two characters rarely seen on the stage: the philandering, irresponsible pater-familias and—an even more radical portrait—the Jewish mother as alcoholic. Like the works of earlier dramatists, these plays demonstrate that Jewish problems are frequently universal problems: poverty, family dissensions, and guilt. Two contemporary issues are especially conspicuous: defining conflicting responsi-bilities and establishing personal morality and values in a world increasingly devoid of both. Finally, these works show that Jewish writers who have "made it" in America are sensitive to Jewish life and care enough about it to bring their observations to the stage. That same perceptivity and concern are impres-sively manifest in the art of the large group of up-and-coming dramatists currently expanding the repertory and enhancing the quality of American-Jewish theatre.

IV

In June 1980, the newly founded Jewish Theatre Association sponsored a conference and festival devoted to the theme "Exploring the Dimensions of Jewish Theatre." The magnitude and sophistication of this event took even its planners by surprise. Theatre artists came from all over the United States, and from Canada and Israel as well. There were performances, for example, by the Barking Rooster Theatre of Vermont, the New Artef Theatre of California, and the Jewish Heritage Theatre of Kansas. Four full days of panel discussions, workshops, play readings, and solo and group performances proclaimed the exuberant health of Jewish theatre as it entered the eighties.

The purview of this essay permits only passing mention of related subsequent developments, like the initiative to found a National Yiddish Theatre in New York, and the Conference on Jewish Playwriting in Pittsburgh in 1983. Nor is the activity confined to this country. The First International Conference and Festival of Jewish Theatre took place in Tel Aviv in 1982. A theatre section was included for the first time in the Ninth World Congress of Jewish Studies in Jerusalem in 1985. An international theatre conference sponsored by Hebrew University in Jerusalem was held in 1986.

While the contemporary vitality of American-Jewish theatre is correctly viewed as a major constituent of an international phenomenon, it is not difficult to identify the forces which nurture it on these shores. One center of activity is the National Foundation for Jewish Culture (NFJC), founded in 1960. The NFJC implements a gamut of scholarly and cultural projects. Among them is the Jewish Theatre Association (JTA). One of the JTA's most ambitious undertakings is a publication of inestimable value to anyone interested in American-Jewish theatre, and one to which the present study is enormously indebted. Edited by Edward M. Cohen, *Plays of Jewish Interest* (1982) is an annotated, cross-indexed listing of more than six hundred published and unpublished titles, including the finalists in the NFJC's playwriting competitions and information about Hebrew and Yiddish plays in translation.[10]

Two other organizations responsible for so much of the activity in American-Jewish theatre are, like the NFJC, based in New York: the Jewish Repertory Theatre and the American Jewish Theatre. The Jewish Repertory Theatre (JRT) housed in the 14th Street Emanu-El Midtown Y, has as its artistic director Ran Avni, one of the co-founders of the institution in 1972. Its associate director is Edward M. Cohen, director of the JRT's Writers' Lab and its Playwrights-in-Residence program, coordinator of the NFJC's annual playwriting contest, and editor of the above-mentioned *Plays of Jewish Interest*.[11] The American Jewish Theatre (AJT), which started out on Henry Street in 1974, now operates at the 92nd Street Y. Its artistic director is Stanley Brechner and its literary manager, Susan Nanus. To augment its New Play Program, the AJT created in 1984 a group for Jewish women playwrights, the Deborah Project. Nanus, its coordinator, identifies in the AJT's Fall 1984 newsletter the project's primary aim as the development and production of "new plays about the Jewish experience as seen through the eyes of the Jewish woman."

Together these associations play a role comparable to the European free theatres which contributed so importantly to the revolution of the dramatic arts at the end of the nineteenth century. Like Antoine's *Théâtre libre* in Paris and Grein's Free Theatre in London—as well as their American heirs, the Theatre Guild and the Group Theatre—the two Manhattan organizations nurture fresh talent in playwriting and production, while presenting works from the classic repertory of plays of Jewish interest.[12]

Because it has become almost impossible to pick up any major metropolitan daily paper without finding evidence of Jewish theatrical activity, writing about recent American-Jewish theatre is more akin to reporting the news than recording theatrical history. Lacking the necessary distance from so many careers in the making, the writer has no way of telling which plays will have staying power; which playwrights, the impact of Rice, Odets, and Miller.

Far more readily established is the wide spectrum of topics inspiring new plays. To provide a sampling of the variety and richness, and to demonstrate the enormous talent of contemporary American-Jewish dramatists, I have selected three especially popular topics. These plays about Judaism, the family, and assimilation represent a vast repertory. They also help to illustrate the growth of a sturdy tradition.

Judaism

Despite the widespread assimilation of American Jews in a secular society, Jewish dramatists go right on deriving nourishment from their roots. The Scriptures and rituals, traditions and legends of Judaism inspire plays so imaginative, one recalls with wonder the religion's fundamental antagonism to theatre. Two delightful examples are Norman Lessing's *36* and Shimon Wincelberg's *The Travels of Benjamin IV* . . . .

In *36* (1980), three irresistible New York *Hasidim* are directed by a Voice to locate the last of the 36 Righteous Ones. They find their man, an ostensibly gentile electrician named Joe Walski, working in a Reform synagogue in Cincinnati. Investigation into Walski's European childhood verifies his unsuspected special status. Joe and his pregnant Catholic wife Mary need a lot less convincing than the temple's spiritual leader. The rabbi's duties have shaken his faith: he describes himself as the MC of a social club. Establishing Joe's true identity not only restores the last *Lamedvovnik* to the world, it renews the rabbi's belief in God and the wonders of Judaism.

Shimon Wincelberg gives the astonishing title *The Travels of Benjamin IV to the Land Where Seldom Is Heard a Discouraging Word* ("a very nice and thrilling play with violence and music," [1969]) to a clever amalgam of nineteenth-century Americana and elements of Judaica. The songs are Western ballads transposed to a minor key and standards from the Yiddish theatre and the liturgy. The inspired hybrid characters include Nathan Shotness, mayor of Dodge City, ideally trained for the ruthless life of the Wild West by his earlier experiences with Cossacks in the Ukraine.

Benjamin IV is a sweet fifteen-year-old Philadelphian who consents to undertake a dangerous mission. He will carry a *Sefer Torah* donated by Sir Moses Montefiore (Sheriff of the City of London) to San Francisco. While the first three Benjamins of tradition were looking for some lost treasure, this one is searching for his father, lured to California by the gold rush. After adventures with America's premier stereotypes (Ozark mountain men, cowboys, Indians, and outlaws—anti-Semites to a man), the youngster is reunited with his father in San Francisco just in time for *Yom Kippur*. The end of the play is not a spoof; rather it asserts the enduring healing capacity of *Kol Nidre* and the tradition of reconciliation it preserves.

The New Year is joined by Passover in serving as the matrix of several plays. Ernest A. Joselovitz's *Triptych* (1977) depicts the reunion for a *seder* of three sisters who have not been together in the family home for fifteen years. As they set out the ritual foods and symbols, they vent their long-simmering resentments of one another and their uncaring parents. Once the stormy argument has cleared the air, the celebration of the familiar Passover service helps all three to realize that they have crossed a desert and can rely on one another for the love and support they need.

The *seder* in *Triptych* takes place in Los Angeles; the one in Lloyd Gold's *Passover* (1984), in north Georgia. The site is important because there is still little drama about Jewish life in the American South, and because Gold creates a Jewish mother who strikingly resembles Tennessee Williams's Amanda Wingfield. *Passover*'s Lucy Ashkenazy sounds like Amanda, for example, telling her eighteen-year-old daughter "the world is a toy for a pretty girl." Like Amanda, Lucy clings desperately to the happy past; in her case, before the premature death of her husband when she and the children were taken care of.

Lucy is a more stereotypical Jewish mother in the extravagant demands she makes on her children and herself. She lamely declines to invite her gentleman caller for the *seder* because "it's family time." The Ashkenazy family's fortunes take a dramatic turn for the better when the door opened for Elijah admits instead a repentant enemy who has been hounding them. Lucy realizes she must allow her children to live their own lives. She also resolves to rebuild her life as well and takes the first step by inviting her admirer in for matzoh ball soup.

The observance of *Shabbat* plays a small but significant role in Shirley Lauro's *The Contest*, which won first prize in the 1980 NFJC playwriting competition. The central dilemma is created by Lily Green. Like Gold's Lucy Ashkenazy, Lily lives in fantasies, often of the past. Her proudest achievement then was defying her father by graduating first in her class from a secretarial college which he had forbidden her to attend. But when Lily finds herself a needy widow, she lacks the self-confidence to go out and get a job. Over the years, Lily has become an inveterate entrant in commercial contests. She is also a perennial loser. Now, with her husband dead and the bills mounting, Lily makes a final attempt to strike it rich in a Wheaties contest with a fanaticism that costs her her sanity.

Like Blanche Dubois, another Tennessee Williams character, Lily depends upon the kindness of strangers, except that the strangers are her own family. This unhappy woman denigrates the people she needs, like her brother-in-law who takes genuine pleasure in contributing to the support of Lily and her musically talented daughter.

The Contest is a play about a family fragmented by the fanciful ambitions of a neurotic woman. The single experience of family togetherness comes in a Sabbath celebration. As the candles are lighted, the relatives "feel suddenly very close." They even break out the Mogen David wine reserved for Passover to toast life and Lily's latest "winning" jingle. *The Contest* demonstrates in its lovely Sabbath scene the bonds of a Jewish family which refuses to give up on one of its own, even one who fails to recognize the real prizes so close to her.

Despite its somber title, Stanley Taikeff's *Shivah* (1984) angers and shocks. The anger is provoked by a cast of remarkably loathsome individuals. Sonia Rosenstein must be the most odious Jewish mother on the American stage. Along with all the unpleasant stock traits, she is intolerant and malicious. There is poetic justice in her sitting on the couch instead of a mourner's wooden box because her *tuchis* hurts.

The rest of the family is no less self-indulgent and self-centered. Brought together reluctantly by the funeral of Sonia's brother Jake's wife, they lose little time in attacking one another. Jake's children refuse to sit *shivah* with their father because they have long avoided him. They recall quarrels between their parents that sometimes brought police to the house. Adulthood and professional success have not conferred any moral responsibility or mature esteem for their background, least of all for their Jewishness, which Jake's son, Irwin, pompously denounces as incompatible with the modern world.

The hypocrisy of these characters is apparent as they go through the motions of observing the prescribed rituals of mourning while mocking family respect and human decency. Sonia salves a vestigial conscience by paying a black nurse, who is caring for Jake's neighbor, to look in on her brother. Then she follows the others who have already gone back to their own lives, relieved to be done with Jake and his *shivah*.

Only then does it become apparent what has been so preoccupying the "bereaved" husband that he has remained mute throughout, seated on his wooden box, staring down between his legs. When the nurse comes into his empty apartment, he "talks" at last. He snaps a $50 bill at her, the signal for an established ritual. As she unzips Jake's pants, he literally comes alive as his *yarmulke* falls to the floor.

The personae and situations in *Shivah* lack the depth and balance one looks to find in art, if not in life. Nevertheless, the play shows how safe (and passionate) an American-Jewish dramatist feels in making observations about Jews who have buried both tradition and the moral principles on which it is based.

A strikingly original application of the Bible to contemporary American-Jewish life is made by Norma Rosen in her first play. The eponymous heroine of *The Miracle of Dora Wakin's Art* (1985) has counterparts throughout today's society: women who combine the demands of work they love with the traditional and ever-fulfilling female roles. Indeed, Dora Wakin has achieved renown as an "artist of wholeness" by expressing in her work love of family as well as love of her medium.

In maturity, Wakin's evolving sense of self leads her to her religious tradition. She enthusiastically describes her latest ceramics as depicting "some of the women of the Bible [who] just stepped out, joined hands and began to dance together." Clearly, Dora has danced with Miriam and Esther and Deborah who, as she puts it, "teach me who I am. When I free them into forms, I free myself too."

Rosen's play demonstrates the ways Wakin's husband, mother, and daughter react to the various stages of her career. Although her husband disapproves of her religious work, seeing it as a digression from the "serious" art world, these are devoted people who genuinely want to support Dora and often do. But they never understand that the true miracle of her art is that she has marshaled the inspiration, time, and energy to bring it into existence. Hence the central persona is bifurcated into roles for two actresses. Dora 1 is confined to bed with nervous exhaustion; she interacts with the family members whose concern comes close to strangling her. Dora 2 keeps her distance in her own space; she is the single-minded artist who drives on indefatigably.

The Miracle of Dora Wakin's Art is noteworthy for two reasons. It reflects onstage a concern to which society is finally paying merited attention: the dilemma of the artist who is also a family woman. Rosen's play also argues for creative devotion, however problematic, to the traditions which define and enrich Jewish life.

Family Life

The traditional centrality of family life in Judaism has quite naturally provided a major theme for the American-Jewish stage. As we have seen, some of the first great Jewish plays, beginning with *Awake and Sing!*, are candid views of average households. As the plays of Bellow, Feiffer, and Simon illustrate, the post–1945 theatre continues to find family life an intriguing subject which it treats in essentially two ways. Some plays look back on the domestic scene as it was in the first decades after the mass migration, but represent that sphere of activity in a present-day idiom. Another group of plays brings to the stage emphatically untraditional family situations reflecting post-war modifications in family life.

A prize-winning example of the retrospective scene viewed through a contemporary optic is Leah K. Friedman's *The Rachel Plays*. This pair of one-acts, which premiered at the American Jewish Theatre in 1985, is a series of episodes taking place in and around a New York tenement in 1939. The events are unified only as perceptions of the nine-year-old eponym. The incidents ring true: a lonely child so delighted to bring home a new friend, she forgets to step on the newspapers on the freshly washed kitchen floor; her entreaties for attention from a gruff father who has to be coaxed into tenderness; a mother perpetually trying to make do with too little of everything; and the alluring threat of an opportunistic insurance man who molests the child.

Such scenes from the thirties, for all that they are familiar and authentic, are reported through the point of view of a much later era. It takes the confidence of a woman playwright in the eighties to look so unblinkingly at the struggling immigrant father who demands the deference due a lord from a household he is barely able to support. The same feminine assurance is required to depict the confusion of the young wife who has not yet come to terms with her own sexuality before she has to begin dealing with her daughter's. The disjuncture between the attitudes within *The Rachel Plays* and those implicit in the dramatization is subtle and effective, and certainly the work's most original achievement.

The Rachel Plays won for Leah K. Friedman the NFJC's Playwriting Award for 1983. The following year, the award went to another retrospective of family life in the Bronx of the thirties, Arthur Sainer's *Sunday Childhood Journeys to Nobody at Home*. The work presents a series of episodes in which the family moves together in one way or another. There are the trips referred to in the title, outings which often end without a visit because nobody had a phone during the Depression, and chances were good that the intended hosts were themselves out visiting. There were wild rides with Uncle Willy, a maniacal driver. These excursions represent escape from the demands of the sweatshop and the terrors of the streets. Yet coming home—even on Sunday—is set forth as the greatest pleasure of all, largely due to a mother who protects the blue box from phony collectors and heals psychic and physical woes with chicken soup.

Pain and ugliness in this life are no less harsh for being left undeveloped: a second wife who, scorned by her husband's family, finally extracts revenge by kicking him out in his old age; a woman too moral to accept financial help from a now prosperous old beau looking to redeem an old wrong; a child who realizes too late that he did not say good-bye to his grandfather, whom he saw for the last time waiting for a cab to the hospital.

Like *The Rachel Plays*, Sainer's retrospective is seen from a contemporary point of view. The title suggests a journey to a home that now exists only in whatever Jewish souls it continues to nourish. Loving homage is paid, but not sentimentally. Rather, the use of Brechtian and Ghelderodian theatrical techniques—puppets, projections, legends, songs—deliberately encourages distance, and with it, a rational appreciation of the trip to the past.

Allan Knee's *Second Avenue Rag* (1980) draws on the incongruities between classic elements of immigrant life and the way these legends "play" today. The title applies equally well to the scraps of life the work stitches together, the syncopated rhythm of the action, and the treatment frequently meted out to the protagonist. This spirited comedy traces the lower East Side adventures of its Candide-like central figure in 1908.

Shlomo is a lovable *schlemiel*, predictably victimized. His chief tormentor is his father, given to taking in moribund boarders to share Shlomo's bed so that the poor fellow often wakes up next to a corpse. While awaiting advice from the editor of the *"Bintel Brief,"* to whom he regularly addresses himself, Shlomo has to get by on his charm and good nature. These are sufficient to stand him in good stead in sweatshop imbroglios and even in a brief, incredible involvement with his idol, Yiddish theatre star Bertha Kalish. In the end, Shlomo finds a woman he can love and take care of (she is pregnant by another man) and, at last, an answer from the *Forward*. *Second Avenue Rag* deliberately exploits every cliché in the repertory, and in doing so, shows that most of them still work.

A cluster of more current clichés—someone has dubbed them "the gripes of Roth"—provides the material for James Lapine's *Table Settings* (1979), a deft and funny exposé of the post-nuclear family. Because the characters are representative types, they are designated by role rather than name. "No one understands me" is a running motif and eating is a central issue. Many of the most painful scenes occur around the dinner table where Older Son and his wife and their two children talk, but not to each other. In another recurring scene, some member of the family (usually a male) seeks privacy under the table. The stereotypical Jewish urge to feed (the Mother opens the play by proclaiming, "Food is my passion! Food is my expression!") has been perverted. Even the Wife ("the ultimate *shiksa*"), the second best adjusted person in the family, handcuffs the Grandson to the table until he eats his seven lima beans. And in a bittersweet finale, the Younger Son, who has gotten out from under the family enough to get a job as a waiter, exacts fitting revenge on his family as they dine in his restaurant.

The problem is that the need to consume has gotten all out of proportion and hence, out of synch with the need to nourish others. Frustrated by the crazy, amoral world outside, bereft of sustaining values at home, these people take refuge in drugs, martinis, and loveless sex. Lapine's satire spares nothing. The most hopeful observation one can make is that this play about "the unshockable age . . . [where] everybody's done everything" still has the power to shock.

A different key characterizes Ernest A. Joselovitz's *Jesse's Land* (1980). The play is set in 1941 in the Connecticut River valley. Here Jesse Kletchik immigrated from Poland thirty-five years earlier. He has labored hard for his big house and considerable acreage. Problems arise when Jesse's son Sammi brings home Willa Newald, who has worked *her* way out of the New York slums.

Willa and Sammi would like nothing better than to start their life together in the rolling hills of the dairy farmland. However, the couple's dealings with Jesse deadlock whenever they raise the question of a place of their own. Jesse welcomes them under his roof. He will rent them a place, but he simply cannot give them land and the young couple cannot afford to buy any. As the gentle Sammi accurately puts it, "He sees that land like it's his own body."

Willa can respect Jesse's position because she too has fought for everything she has. Indeed, it is her tenacity and shrewdness, so like Jesse's own, that open him up to emotions he has never before admitted. In a moving final scene, Jesse, as humble as he can be, tries to persuade the young couple not to return to New York with their new son. Sammi and Willa know they have made the right decision when Jesse grandly presents what he considers a major concession, the deed to a rocky, waterless parcel he does not need. Like O'Neill's Ephraim Cabot, Joselovitz's Jesse Kletchik is left with the New England land he toiled so hard for and esteems even above human relations.

Jesse and Willa are fresh Jewish characters on the American stage. Jesse has never shed the identity he brought to this country thirty-five years before. Because he continues to think of himself as a vulnerable "Jew Polack," he cannot let down his guard, even to a loving family. For her part, Willa is as resolute and tough as *belles Juives* like Hennie Berger (*Awake and Sing!*) and Leah (*The Cold Wind and the Warm*). However, her self-discipline and decency, especially in arguments with her difficult father-in-law, contrast with their libertine self-centeredness. It is a tribute to the playwright's art that we can see Jesse as Willa does and so appreciate how much he needs his megalomania.

An even more unconventional woman is the heroine of Sybil Rosen's *Brink of Devotion* (1985). She is Sass Kaplan, an unmarried, forty-year-old entomologist, eight months pregnant by artificial insemination. She lives alone in "the tall pine forest in North Georgia, twenty miles out of Atlanta." A Ph.D., Sass is very much attuned to the wonders of life, eager to experience as many of them as she can, and more than slightly disillusioned with men.

Her solitary existence is punctuated when she offers to help Jodi, a teenager, and Lucky Starr, a gospel singer, who are running away together but have an accident near her house. Sass takes them in, then offers to keep them awhile if Starr will finish off the room Sass is building for her baby. As they negotiate terms, it becomes evident that Jodi is unusually bright and ambitious. Also, she is pregnant and miserable about it. Sass quickly becomes the mentor Jodi craves. It is a role the older woman is loath to undertake, but too considerate to refuse, especially when she sees that Starr is as unable to support a child as he is determined that Jodi will bear the baby. There is a striking statement about courage and responsibility here. Sass, who has confessed her fears about being a single mother and who wishes aloud that any man wanted her child as much as Starr wants Jodi's, will carry to term. By contrast, Jodi, who has the love of a man, however immature, recognizes that she can exercise her options. She asks Sass to take her to the Atlanta Women's Clinic the next day.

It is not just a new slant on American-Jewish life and one of the most unconventional mothers in all American-Jewish drama that Rosen gives us here. *Brink of Devotion*, like *Jesse's Land* and *Sunday Childhood Journeys to Nobody at Home*, gives motherhood a good name. In the former two, moreover, the more typical "woman of virtue" emerges as a gutsy fighter for well-defined principles that would doubtless bring a deep blush to the cheeks of her prototypes.

Up-to-date life-styles and contemporary versions of several established Jewish characters also form important components of Wendy Wasserstein's *Isn't It Romantic* (1983). The bittersweet comedy concerns two Manhattanites, girl-friends since childhood, just back in New York after Harvard to embark on their careers. Each has the potential for being a stock type: Janie Blumberg as a latter-day *belle Juive*, Harriet Cornwall as the cultivated WASP; in Wasserstein's talented hands, the characterizations are instead original and convincing. We get to know them through their parallel but hardly interchangeable experiences. For instance, each looks to her family for guidance, and especially to her mother for a role model, only to be disappointed for very different reasons.

Among the strongest features of the play is its incisive portrayal of modern Jewish parents who subscribe to one set of values while standing for a life-style based on an antithetical set. The Blumbergs are loving and genuine in encouraging Janie to forge her own career. Simultaneously and unwittingly, they send out undermining signals. They would love Janie to come into her father's business. More demoralizing, they make it clear that they want to see her married and settled down, by which they mean being taken care of by a husband.

Slim in her tie-dyed leotards, carrying a bag of raw green beans for energy between the dance classes she teaches, fond of proclaiming immodestly, "I am!" Tasha Blumberg represents a new breed of Jewish mothers. (Clearly only one decade separates her from the more *outré* Sass Kaplan of *Brink of Devotion*.) Tasha probably does not understand how fortunate she is: she became a liberated woman *after* she had the traditional security and fulfillments of husband, home, and family. The play does not fault Tasha; it simply makes the point that as a role model, this "mod" mother fails to understand the message she sends to her daughter.

In a scene that needed to be written for the stage, Janie tries to explain that the lesson of her mother's life is not what Tasha thinks it is, that she has indeed taught her *not* to be satisfied with the well-worn paths. ''Mother, think about it. Did you teach me to marry a nice Jewish doctor and make chicken for him; you order up breakfast from a Greek coffee shop every morning.'' Tasha starts to justify herself. Then her self-possession takes over. ''I'm a modern woman too, you know. I have my dancing, I have your father, and my beautiful grand-child and Ben [Janie's brother]. I don't need you to fill up my life.'' (Citations are from the unpublished ms.)

Tasha's icy blast sweeps fresh air across the American-Jewish stage. What Jewish mother has ever voiced such sentiments in the theatre? Compare Tasha's proud self-salute with the righteous self-pity of Bessie Berger: ''My whole life I wanted to go away too, but with children a woman stays home. A fire burned in *my* heart too, but now it's too late.''

As essential as Tasha's affirmation is, it reduces Janie to tears. Between this mother and daughter there stretches perhaps the widest generation gap in Amer-ican-Jewish life. Now Janie summons the courage to assert herself. In assuring her parents that she is not her mother's daughter for nothing, that she can take care of herself, Janie begins to convince herself as well.

Isn't It Romantic breaks new ground in yet another important way. It puts onstage the nice young Harvard-educated Jewish doctor—intent on reversing assimilation. Marty Sterling changes his name back to Murray Schlimovitz. He has decided to open his medical practice not on Park Avenue, but in Brooklyn. Like Janie, with whom he falls in love, Marty wants the things his parents have achieved. For him, that means not only a home and a family, but a wife who is not so engrossed in her own work she will not always put him first. This is not the bill Janie wants to fill.

The incompatibility of these two represents the difficult search by today's highly sophisticated young American Jews for ways to incorporate old values into new lives. With the characterizations of Tasha, Janie, and Marty and its treatment of issues basic to contemporary family life, *Isn't It Romantic* makes a major contribution to American-Jewish drama.

Assimilation

A whole chapter of the establishment of Jews in the United States is reflected in the distance between Murray Schisgal's greenhorns in *The Pushcart Peddlers* (1979), who shed their names as they come down the gangplank, and a character like Wendy Wasserstein's Murray Schlimovitz, who rejects his father's neu-tralized name for the Old World original.

The effects of the American melting pot (or pressure cooker) on the way Jews perceive themselves and are perceived by others as members of a pluralistic society are treated in a number of plays. School and military situations lend themselves particularly well to this consideration since both institutional settings homogenize individuals and thus put image and self-image squarely on the line.

Several dramatists, writing out of their own experiences, have depicted the encounters of Jews with America's most WASPish schools. In the one-act *Life Under Water* (1984), Richard Greenberg brings together Jews and preppies for a summer in the Hamptons. A more extended exploration of the subject occurs in Wendy Wasserstein's full-length *Uncommon Women and Others* (1977). The play portrays the overweight, curly-haired Holly Kaplan among her svelte blonde friends at Mt. Holyoke College, and then six years after graduation.

The issue is not discrimination. Feminism is a much more important question here than Judaism, yet the influence of the latter is unmistakable. While all these young women are bewildered by the disparities between their tradition-bound education and the opportunities newly opened to them, Holly finds even less direction after graduation than her classmates. Six years later, though the others may still be looking forward to becoming "pretty amazing" when they are in their forties, they have already made commitments to careers or relationships. By contrast, Holly, nagged by her parents to become—or to marry—a root-canal man, has not yet made any choices.

As we have seen, Wasserstein's subsequent play, *Isn't It Romantic*, explores the question of the support available to well-educated young people looking to find their place in late twentieth-century America. In both plays, Jewishness seems to be the source of debilitating sensitivity, contradictory family expectations—and a great, if self-deprecating, sense of humor.

Judaism provides a sturdier matrix in David S. Lifson and Martin Kalmanoff's comedy with music, *The Flatbush Football Golem* (1979), where the setting is the very antithesis of Mt. Holyoke College: Flatbush and its *yeshivah* (in this play, a Jewish college). The secular American life which insinuates itself into this thoroughly orthodox milieu is precisely what creates the plot complications.

The problem begins when Joshua Stein, a high school football standout, turns down scholarships from "almost all the Big Ten" because he is more dedicated to Torah than touchdowns. His decision to attend the *yeshivah* provokes the disappointment of his liberated, pre-med girlfriend and his sports fan father, Jacob. Because Joshua remains adamant, Jacob endows the *yeshivah* with a million-dollar football program. Thereupon ensues a comic scene in which the Flatbush team, in *tsitsith* and fur-lined helmets and spurred on by their coach's admonition that "5,000 years of history are looking down on you," loses, 45–0.

For once, tradition offers a ready-made solution. Joshua has a friend, Boruch, fortunately the descendant of Rabbi Loew of Prague, the most celebrated creator of a golem. On the sands of a Brooklyn beach, the two friends sculpt a six-and-a-half-foot golem, who strides forth to lead the *yeshivah* team to triumphs, and Joshua and Boruch into troubles with their love lives.

As it unfolds its fanciful tale, *The Flatbush Football Golem* makes room for a more realistic consideration: the unwillingness of modern young women from orthodox backgrounds to abandon their own goals for the traditional place in the shadow of dominant men. Joshua and Boruch's girlfriends make it clear that they have no intention of becoming their husbands' "golems." While the play does not work out the consequences of their resolution, it is apparent that the way women like these go about realizing themselves will shape Jewish lives far more significantly than the advent of a golem.

Drama about American Jews serving in the armed forces often shows the dynamics of establishing ethnic identity. In Arthur Laurents's *Home of the Brave* (1945), Private Peter Coen is traumatized when his best buddy, whose philo-Semitism he had never doubted, utters a racial slur just before he is shot. The script demonstrates that the malice of a frightened soldier who imprecates a comrade under fire, like the guilty relief of the survivor that another than he was killed, are perfectly normal reactions. However, Coen needs extensive psychotherapy to cope with what he interprets as betrayal and to see his own guilt as human rather than uniquely Jewish. By contrast, as we have seen in Neil Simon's *Biloxi Blues*, the Army has the stuff it takes to make not only men, but Jews.

Another perspective of the Jew in the service is explored in *Defender of the Faith* (1972), one of the three Philip Roth stories adapted for the stage by Larry Arrick. Here Sergeant Nathan Marx, just back from the European front, faces a new challenge in a training camp. He has to cope with the machinations of a Jewish rookie bent on manipulating Marx into granting special favors to three co-religionists. The appeals of the nineteen-year-old trainees open war-hardened Marx up to memories of Jewish home and family he is ready to recall. However, he is too good a soldier to be moved by sentiment and partiality. He defends his faith in America and the role of its soldiers of every religion by insisting that Private Grossbart and his two buddies share the fate of the rest of the company.

Because of his firsthand knowledge of wartime Europe, Sergeant Marx might even feel that American Jews in the military during the Second World War owe their country a little more than other citizens. That is emphatically the persuasion of Lieutenant Barney Greenwald, the Navy lawyer who successfully defends the man who has seized control of a mine sweeper in *The Caine Mutiny Court-Martial* (1954) by Herman Wouk. Instead of exulting over his victory, however, Greenwald feels sullied by having won his case at the expense of the reputation of the *Caine*'s Commander Queeg. Irrespective of his recent disturbed behavior, which had earned him the epithet Old Yellowstain, Queeg as a professional commands particular respect from Greenwald as a Jew. In the lawyer's eyes, America's career officers deserve full credit for saving her Jews from Hitler. As he explains to his shipmates:

See, the Germans aren't kidding about the Jews. They're cooking us down to soap over there. . . . So, when all hell broke loose and the Germans started running out of soap and figured, well, time to come over and melt down old Mrs. Greenwald, who's gonna stop 'em? Not her boy Barney. Can't stop a Nazi with a lawbook. . . . Old Yellowstain, maybe? Why yes, even poor sad Queeg. And most of them not sad at all, fellows, a lot of them sharper boys than any of us, don't kid yourself, you can't be good in the Army or Navy unless you're goddam good.[13]

In David Mamet's short work *Goldberg Street* (1985), an unnamed protagonist tells his daughter about visiting the site of his war service on the fortieth anniversary of the end of World War II. His being sent to France was the consequence of an anti-Semitic joke. Lost on maneuvers in Arkansas, he alone had figured out how to read a compass, a skill based less on having the requisite intelligence than on his certainty that nobody would come to find him. The scorn he earned for demonstrating an adroitness others envied resulted in his being "volunteered" for overseas duty.

But illustrating prejudice in the military is hardly the point of *Goldberg Street*. In a powerful curtain speech, Mamet's protagonist admits to complicity with the choice of post, and, even more painful, to still feeling closer to his own anti-Semitic society than to Zion. "They sent me for a joke," he remembers: "Because I read the compass. I was glad to go. I knew they thought me ludicrous. Our shame is that we feel they're right. (Pause) I . . . have no desire to go to Israel. (Pause) But I went to France."[14]

Mamet examines the price the assimilated Jew pays for absorbing the prejudices of American society in *The Disappearance of the Jews* (1982). The play depicts the disenchantment with their lives of two boyhood friends, now in their thirties. Their regrets fix on how detached they are from their Jewish roots. Bobby is sorry he married a non-Jew, especially because that means his blond son is not Jewish. Joey has given the matter more imaginative thought. He longs to live in a society whose best minds are devoted to Talmud so they can be appealed to for Truth when it is required. Rather than working in a restaurant, he feels he should be using his strength farming, out in the cold. Joey's fantasies about "the life we were supposed to live" make him wish for the joy and rituals of life in the *shtetl*, even for experiencing the Holocaust. Bobby will not let his friend trivialize the fate of European Jewry by romanticizing it, but he, in turn, would not have minded being part of the Jewish movie empire in the great years of Hollywood.

Like most of us, these old friends are not very objective about themselves. Joey, for example, who has grandly declared that Jews have inflamed anti-Semites through the centuries by being too high-minded to be violent, admits dreaming that he has shot his family to live freely as a contemplative in the Canadian woods. They are lucid enough to know that their vagaries are unrealizable. Bobby and Joey are coming to grips with just how far their mediocre lives have strayed not only from the inspiration of Judaism, but from what they had always imagined they would make of themselves. Laments Joey: "I'm going to die like this. A schmuck. I know that there's power in me. But it's not coming out. It's never coming out. The only bar between me and what I would like to do is doing it. I'll never do it, though."[15]

The Disappearance of the Jews refers to more than the unsubstantial ties between assimilated Americans like these and Judaism. Mamet's title also comments ironically on the lack of stimulus or opportunity for Jews in an indifferent, if not always tolerant, America, to be as visible as they have under less favorable circumstances.

V

The abundance and variety of plays represented here demonstrate how American-Jewish drama has come of age in the years following the Second World War. Given the extensive body of works that already exists and the impressive number of playwrights confidently expanding it, it is time to look back over the last six decades to identify those unifying values, shared attitudes, and common ideas which can be seen as constituting a tradition.

The first element of the tradition is immediately evident: American Jews are involved in an enduring love affair with the theatre. The focus in this essay on plays and playwrights could easily be broadened to include the Jewish performers, directors, producers, impresarios, dramaturges, angels, and, of course, audiences who have played such a significant role in the growth and shaping of American theatre. The phenomenon is all the more remarkable for the fact that Jewish involvement in theatre runs counter to rabbinical strictures and traditional cultural practices.

The single theatrical activity admitted by orthodox Judaism was the *Purim* play. Originally based on Bible stories, the plays, as they evolved through the centuries, began to incorporate secular materials and refer specifically to the lives of the Jews they entertained. A direct line runs from the familiar world represented by this folk theatre through the Yiddish stage and into American-Jewish drama. It is particularly apparent in the style that has dominated the American-Jewish stage from its beginning, social realism. The art of the Jewish dramatist writing in English has characteristically been devoted to visual as well as psychological versimilitude. Indeed, realism stands as the second element of the tradition of American-Jewish drama.

However, in representing Jewish life onstage, dramatists have sometimes adopted what one of the Deborah Project members terms "the realistic style, but not the realistic form." She was talking about "breaking time and space," as, for example, Leah K. Friedman does in *The Rachel Plays*. There are other such disjunctions with literalism: Arthur Sainer's integration of puppets with people in *Sunday Childhood Journeys to Nobody at Home*, or Norma Rosen's divided protagonist in *The Miracle of Dora Wakin's Art*, for instance. Some of the most conventionally realistic plays incorporate symbolic, even expressionistic, devices.

A third characteristic of American-Jewish drama is its preoccupation with family life. As the preceding pages have demonstrated, playwrights find many other aspects of American-Jewish life stageworthy, but often incorporate family situations even when they are not the focal point of the play.

There is a crucial distinction to be made here. The family is hardly a subject peculiar to the American-Jewish stage. Drama from *Oedipus Rex* to *Mourning Becomes Electra* exploits the rich potential of family life. However, in American-Jewish drama, the family is something more than an appropriate context in which a group of disparate individuals is brought together. It is an institution which prescribes conventions for interaction and engenders certain expectations—both within the play and from audiences—as to how characters should behave. A good deal of dramatic power resides in disappointing those expectations, as plays like *Shivah*, *Table Settings*, and *Grown Ups* illustrate. Prevalent in the work of the early dramatists, family life goes right on inspiring plays, doubtless because of its continued importance in American-Jewish life.

There have been important modifications over the years. The most apparent are in the structure of the family itself. Contemporary households built by a single parent (Sybil Rosen's *Brink of Devotion*) or by homosexuals (Harvey Fierstein's admirable *Torch Song Trilogy*, 1981), join the more traditional family units portrayed on the stage. It does not seem excessive to observe that family life in secular America functions as the last stronghold of peoplehood. It is also in the depictions of family life that the moral underpinnings of American-Jewish drama are the most evident.

Drama about family life has followed American Jews out of New York's lower East Side to the suburbs and across the country. The fanning out of Jewish life across the American continent parallels the original immigration to these shores in that it creates some of the same kinds of problems. Just as the first generations of Jews in America had to salvage what they could from a way of life to which they could not return, so subsequent Jews have had to cope with vast changes in American society and in their own lives which make the certitudes of an immigrant society—however chafing or resented—unavailable or unworkable. The resulting quest for values is a dominant theme in American-Jewish drama and constitutes a fourth element of the tradition.

The breakdown of established value systems and the search for new ones are announced in *Awake and Sing!* The play's central figure, Ralph, repudiates both the opportunism and the futile idealism he sees around him and vows "to get more from life." The subsequent fifty years of American-Jewish drama have shown Jews "getting more from life" in ways that have frequently alienated them from their ethnic roots. (There is a nice prefiguration in Moe and Hennie's vow to send Easter eggs back to Bessie Berger.) Sometimes this is a matter of intermarriage and assimilation, as in David Mamet's *The Disappearance of the Jews*. Other times it is the pursuit of success in business; witness the evolution of Brooklyn's Schlimovitz Kosher Dairy Restaurants into the nationwide Sterling Tavernes in Wendy Wasserstein's *Isn't It Romantic*. Most often it is simply the changes wrought by time which make a traditional life impractical.

Yet in a number of plays we have seen characters rediscover their Judaism and with it a surer identity as well as the missing sense of belonging. Principles and practices of Jewish life—as often a cultural as a religious concept—are shown coming to the support of characters in Joselovitz's *Triptych*, Rosen's *The Miracle of Dora Wakin's Art*, and, ironically, the rabbis in Chayefsky's *The Tenth Man* and Lessing's *36*. Other plays celebrate, even as they criticize, bygone days when the old values were operative, e.g., Knee's *Second Avenue Rag* and Friedman's *The Rachel Plays*.

The business of squaring changing life-styles and redefined gender roles with Judaism is conveyed onstage largely through characters. The personae who populate American-Jewish drama are for the most part modeled on Jews in society. Such accuracy in drawing character deserves to be cited as a fifth element of the tradition. That may appear a modest accomplishment until one considers the handful of formulaic, one-dimensional stage Jews that dominate Western drama from the middle ages until the present century. Jewish playwrights (not just in this country) have been instrumental in reversing or inverting the stereotypes. Certainly they have brought to the scene warm, attractive individuals we recognize from life, from Behrman's big-hearted Aunt Ida (*The Cold Wind and the Warm*) to Wouk's high-principled lawyer (*The Caine Mutiny Court-Martial*). At the same time, Jews have not shrunk from making unflattering portrayals, from Odets's insensitive Sam Katz (*Paradise Lost*) to the despicable family in Taikeff's *Shivah*.

But drama does not thrive on ordinary folks, and the crowd of new-style Jews who fill American-Jewish drama also contains a number of fabulous standouts (e.g., the obdurate father in *Jesse's Land*; the glib diarist in *Biloxi Blues*) and new stock types, e.g., the Jew as neurotic, as thwarted artist, as libidinous adventurer.

A pair of clichés that has been enthusiastically adopted by Jewish and gentile playwrights alike is the Jewish mother and the *belle Juive*. These characters figure in the plays of Odets, Behrman, Lawson, and Shaw, as in American entertainment generally. Although subsequent playwrights have hardly banished them from the stage, they have often transformed them into more fully dimensional characters. Among others, Lauro, Allen, and Norma Rosen present mothers who have little in common with the *Yiddishe momma*; while Lifson, Wasserstein, and Joselovitz show us young Jewesses who are emphatically not *belles Juives*.

On balance, the wide variety of Jews in contemporary plays are recognizably the descendants of the more authentic characters of pioneer works. They are less a response to the old question, "Is it good for the Jews?" than to "Is it true of them?" One of the significant achievements of American drama is ridding the stage of many of the foolish and malign ethnic stereotypes too long cherished by it; to this achievement Jewish playwrights have made an important contribution.

Such a breakthrough could not have been made everywhere in the world. A final element of the tradition of American-Jewish drama is its active appreciation of its milieu. Since John Howard Lawson's *Processional*, which sought in 1925 to celebrate the range of peoples that make up American society, American-Jewish playwrights have made it apparent that they know where they are and what that means. From the start, Jews have represented themselves as a self-respecting, integral part of American society. Whether they insist on their rights, like the old men in Shaw's *The Gentle People*, or serve in the armed forces gratefully, like Wouk's Barney Greenwald or reluctantly, like Simon's Arnold Epstein, characters created by Jewish authors bespeak their awareness of the freedoms and opportunities enjoyed by this country's Jews.

Those advantages, coupled with the Jewish tendency to messianism in social crusading, led American-Jewish dramatists to establish themselves early on as spokespersons for the oppressed and exploited. The practice has never flagged. It is especially apparent in large groups of plays there is not enough room in this essay to discuss. For example, the anti-Semitism condemned on stage by Rice, Behrman, and Hecht expands in plays about the Holocaust, as well as those about bias that persists in our country. Jewish solidarity with all who are persecuted and harassed, stated originally by Lawson, Odets, and Gold, finds latter-day expression in works about labor problems and those about blacks and Jews. Rice's and Odets's plays about Depression America where families are dumped into the street have been followed by drama about inner-city decay and violence. Shaw's and Gold's voices championing the poor and defenseless echo in plays about the vulnerability of the old to society's indifference and the viciousness of urban life. While no one could deny that American-Jewish drama sometimes contributes to the solipsism so fashionable in recent theatre, it has at the same time kept alive the tradition of American Jews speaking out in the name of justice and equality. In this propensity, as in its enduring concern with the integrity of the family, American-Jewish drama manifests what I have earlier called its moral underpinnings.

The greening of American-Jewish drama in the post–Second World War years is intimately allied with the growth of American-Jewish theatre, that is, the network of professional, community, and university theatres and producing groups all over the United States. While I have tried to impart a sense of this development in Part IV, readers are urged to consult Edward M. Cohen's introduction to *New Jewish Voices* for a full and uniquely informed overview of Jewish theatre today.

Nourished by its roots in the *shtetl* and Second Avenue, cultivated by six decades of dedicated artists, American-Jewish drama has grown vigorous and multiform. The confidence, versatility, and sophistication of the institution belie its youth. Nor is the greening of Jewish drama in the United States an isolated phenomenon. All over the post–1945 world, from Canada to Israel, writers are creating significant work for the stage out of their Jewish lives. Indeed, that the enormous accomplishment of Jews in the theatre—as in all the secular arts—comes only in the sixth millennium of Jewish history may be its most dramatic achievement of all.

NOTES

1. See Louis Harap's *Dramatic Encounters: The Jewish Presence in Twentieth-Century Drama, Humor, Poetry and the Black-Jewish Literary Relationship*, p. 79.

2. Margaret Brenman-Gibson, *Clifford Odets: American Playwright*, p. 651.

3. Harold Clurman, *The Fervent Years*, p. 87.

4. Ms. in Katherine Cornell Room, Performing Arts Section, Lincoln Center, New York Public Library. See Robert Skloot, "*We Will Never Die*: The Success and Failure of a Holocaust Pageant," pp. 167–180.

5. See Ellen Schiff, "What Kind of Way Is That for Nice Jewish Girls to Act? Images of Jewish Women in Modern American Drama," pp. 106–118.

6. In addition to the works mentioned here, there are three one-act comedies: *A Wen, Orange Soufflé*, and *Out From Under*. See Keith Opdahl, "The 'Mental Comedies' of Saul Bellow," in *From Hester Street to Hollywood*, pp. 183–196.

7. Miller's preoccupation with this play is apparent in his revising and retitling it: *They Too Arise* (1936), *The Grass Still Grows* (1939). Ms. of *They Too Arise* in Performing Arts Section, Lincoln Center, New York Public Library.

8. For example, Mary McCarthy faults Miller for insufficiently particularizing Willy and Linda Loman, giving them Jewish speech cadences but not corroborating their ethnicity in any other way. See Mary McCarthy's *Theatre Chronicles, 1927–1962*, pp. xix, xxi. Also, Henry Popkin cites with approbation George Ross's " 'Death of a Salesman' in the Original," (*Commentary*, 11. [February, 1951] pp. 184–186), which argues convincingly the Jewish elements in *Death of a Salesman*; see Popkin, "Arthur Miller: The Strange Encounter," in *American Drama and Its Critics*, ed. Alan S. Downer, p. 221. See also Enoch Brater, "Ethics and Ethnicity in the Plays of Arthur Miller," in *From Hester Street to Hollywood*, pp. 123–136, and Ruby Cohn, "The Articulate Victims of Arthur Miller," in her *Dialogue in American Drama*, pp. 68–96.

9. Arthur Miller, *Incident at Vichy*, p. 105.

10. Available from the National Foundation for Jewish Culture, 122 East 42nd Street, Suite 1512, New York, NY 10168. Inquire for current price.

11. In addition to *Plays of Jewish Interest*, Cohen has edited a collection of plays produced by the JRT with an introductory essay about Jewish theatre in America and his insider's view of what is happening on the modern Jewish scene, *New Jewish Voices*.

12. For further information on these two professional Jewish theatres as well as the activities of Jewish community theatres across the United States, see Hannah Grad Goodman's lively series in *Hadassah Magazine*: "Just Off Broadway" (November 1984), pp. 58–60; "Jewish Fringe Theater" (December, 1984), pp. 55–57; and "A Dramatic Flowering" (March, 1985), pp. 50–53. The series begins with an overview of an older and still vital scene, "Yiddish Theater: The Show Goes On" (October, 1984), pp. 48–50.

13. Herman Wouk, *The Caine Mutiny Court-Martial*, pp. 93–94.

14. David Mamet, *Goldberg Street*, p. 6.

15. Reprinted from the unpublished ms. by permission of the author, copyright 1982 by David Mamet.

BIBLIOGRAPHY

Bellow, Saul. *The Last Analysis*. New York: Viking, 1965.
———. "Orange Soufflé." *Esquire*. 64. (October, 1965), pp. 30–31, 134, 136.

————. "Out from Under." Unpublished.

————. "A Wen." *Esquire.* 63 (January, 1965), pp. 72–74.

————. "The Wrecker." In *Seize the Day.* New York: Viking, 1956.

Brenman-Gibson, Margaret. *Clifford Odets: American Playwright.* New York: Atheneum, 1981.

Clurman, Harold. *The Fervent Years.* 1945; rpt. New York: Hill and Wang Dramabook, 1957.

Cohen, Edward M., ed. *New Jewish Voices.* Albany: State University of New York Press, 1985.

————. *Plays of Jewish Interest.* New York: Jewish Theatre Association, 1982.

Cohen, Sarah Blacher, ed. *From Hester Street to Hollywood.* Bloomington: University of Indiana Press, 1983.

Cohn, Ruby. *Dialogue in American Drama.* Bloomington: University of Indiana Press, 1971.

Downer, Alan, ed. *American Drama and Its Critics.* Toronto: University of Toronto Press, 1965.

Goodman, Hannah Grad. "A Dramatic Flowering." *Hadassah Magazine.* 66. (March, 1985), pp. 50–53.

————. "Jewish Fringe Theater." *Hadassah Magazine.* 66. (December, 1984), pp. 55–57.

————. "Just Off Broadway." *Hadassah Magazine.* 66. (November, 1984), pp. 58–60.

————. "Yiddish Theater: The Show Goes On." *Hadassah Magazine.* 66. (October, 1984), pp. 48–50.

Harap, Louis. *Dramatic Encounters: The Jewish Presence in Twentieth-Century American Drama, Poetry, and Humor and the Black-Jewish Literary Relationship.* Westport, Connecticut: Greenwood Press, 1987.

Hecht, Ben. *We Will Never Die.* Ms. in Performing Arts Section, New York Public Library.

McCarthy, Mary. *Mary McCarthy's Theatre Chronicles, 1927–1962.* New York: Farrar, Straus, 1963.

Mamet, David. *Goldberg Street: A Collection of Short Plays and Monologues.* New York: Grove Press, 1985.

Miller, Arthur. *Incident at Vichy.* New York: Viking, 1965.

————. *They Too Arise* (unpublished revision of *No Villain*). Performing Arts Section, New York Public Library.

Opdahl, Keith. "The 'Mental Comedies' of Saul Bellow." In *From Hester Street to Hollywood,* ed. Sarah Blacher Cohen. Bloomington: University of Indiana Press, 1983.

Popkin, Henry. "Arthur Miller: The Strange Encounter." In *American Drama and Its Critics,* ed. Alan S. Downer. Toronto: University of Toronto Press, 1965.

Ross, George. " 'Death of a Salesman' in the Original." *Commentary.* 11. (February, 1951), pp. 184–186.

Schiff, Ellen. "What Kind of Way Is That for Nice Jewish Girls to Act? Images of Women in Modern American Drama." *American Jewish History.* 70. (September, 1980) pp. 106–118.

Skloot, Robert. "We Will Never Die: The Success and Failure of a Holocaust Pageant." *Theatre Journal.* 37. (May, 1985), pp. 167–180.

Wouk, Herman. *The Caine Mutiny Court-Martial.* New York: Samuel French, 1954.

FOR FURTHER READING

Cohn, Ruby. *American Dramatists, 1960–1980*. New York: Grove, 1982.

Coleman, Edward D. "Jewish Prototypes in American and English *Romans* and *Drames à Clef.*" *Publications of the American Jewish Historical Society*. 35. (1939), pp. 227–280.

———. "Plays of Jewish Interest on the American Stage, 1752–1821." *Publications of the American Jewish Historical Society*. 33. (1934), pp. 171–198.

The Drama Review. Jewish Theatre Issue (T87). 24. (September, 1980).

Fisch, Harold. *The Dual Image: The Figure of the Jew in English and American Literature*. New York: KTAV, 1971.

Goldstein, Malcolm. *The Political Stage: American Drama and Theater of the Great Depression*. New York: Oxford University Press, 1975.

Harap, Louis. *The Image of the Jew in American Literature: from Early Republic to Mass Immigration*. Philadelphia: Jewish Publication Society, 1974.

Sandrow, Nahma. *Vagabond Stars: A World History of Yiddish Theater*. New York: Harper and Row, 1977.

Schiff, Ellen. *From Stereotype to Metaphor: The Jew in Contemporary Drama*. Albany: State University of New York Press, 1982.

———. "Shylock's *Mishpocheh*: Anti-Semitism on the American Stage." In *Anti-Semitism and American History*, ed. David A. Gerber. Urbana: University of Illinois Press, 1986.

Weales, Gerald. *Clifford Odets: Playwright*. New York: Bobbs-Merrill, Pegasus, 1971.

5

American-Jewish Poetry:
An Overview

R. Barbara Gitenstein

If a student conducted an overview of the criticism of American-Jewish literature, he would discover that almost all the commentary is about fiction. In fact, almost all the criticism is about fiction written by males who were born in urban areas, usually urban areas of the Northeast. This hypothetical student might come to the conclusion from such an overview that there are no American-Jewish writers who are women, no writers who have lived in towns smaller than Chicago— and surely no writers who are poets.

Recently, it has been gratifying to notice that critics have come to see that all these other American-Jewish creators do exist—have been writing since about the same time as the New York City male fiction writers. Indeed, these other American-Jewish writers are more apt to lead the reader to recognize the ambivalence inherent in the dual identity of any American Jew. In other words, these overlooked writers are the ones most likely to reveal the psychological strains of the hyphenated status of the ethnic American. It is remarkable that the absence of these categories (women, rural or suburban writers, and poets) went almost unnoted for all these decades. Particularly surprising is the lack of notice of the poets.

Jewish culture is as patriarchal and anti-feminist as any other Western culture. Thus, its oversight of women writers is quite in keeping with the rest of Western culture. Jewish intellectual culture in America is just as prejudiced against rural values as the rest of America. Since the nineteenth century, only the South of America has valued rural qualities. The emphasis on urban, Northeastern writers, therefore, is simply another manifestation of the defeat of Jeffersonian values. But the oversight of poetry is really quite peculiar. Poetry has been a significant feature of every type of Jewish literary experience in and out of exile. What could be so devastatingly prosaic about the American culture that it would by definition destroy the more than four-thousand-year-old poetic inspiration? As Saul Bellow has said, America is overburdened by facts, by material existence, and simpler minds than Bellow's make this material obsession, our lowest common denominator, the determinant of our aesthetics.[1] But Saul Bellow would not argue that this realistic and utilitarian spirit destroys poetic inspiration, merely that it makes poetry difficult to write.

The tradition of Jewish poetry reaches back to biblical times. No reader of *Tanakh* can be unaware of the poetry of the *Psalms*, the prophetic books, or the Song of Songs. The post-biblical poetry of the canonical Book of Daniel and Ecclesiastes continued the tradition; and throughout the Middle Ages, the period of European expansion, the *Haskalah* (Enlightenment), and the modern age, religious and secular poetry continued to appear in Hebrew in almost every country in which Jews settled. The great Sephardic poets of the medieval period, such as Solomon ibn Gabirol and Judah Halevi, are merely examples of that long and respected tradition of Jewish poetic inspiration in an exilic setting. Even in languages other than Hebrew, Jews wrote poetry worthy of study and memory. This includes poets of other especially Jewish languages, such as those who wrote in Yiddish. The Yiddish literary tradition began at least as early as the fourteenth-century epic poems and biblical translations. During the nineteenth century there were some Yiddish poets of note, but for the most part nineteenth-century Yiddish literature is prose narrative.

However, after World War I some of the most exciting new Yiddish writers (whether they were living in America or in Europe) were poets. Many of these early twentieth-century poets were experimenting with Modernism, Imagism, and Expressionism in much the same way as the English-language poets of the day. Furthermore, during the nineteenth and early twentieth centuries, Jews who were assimilated enough into non-Jewish cultures so that they could write in languages such as German, Russian, and French began gaining reputations in literary traditions that were not particularly Jewish. Thus, the nineteenth-century Western literary heritage is marked by such Jewish poets as the Russians Boris Pasternak and Osip Emilyevich Mandelshtam; the Germans Heinrich Heine and Hugo von Hofmannsthal; and the Frenchmen Edmond Fleg, Tristan Tzara, and Isidore Isou. In other words, the tradition of poetry by Jews in Jewish languages and in non-Jewish languages is long and reputable; and if we accept as a premise that poetry is one of the forms of man's highest inspiration, were it not present in America, its absence would be a grave condemnation of American culture. But we need not feel so chastened. The poets have been here all along; however, the critics have taken an extra century to acknowledge their existence.

The presence of Yiddish-language poetry in America is a fascinating commentary on the acculturation of the Jews in modern Western society in general and in America in particular. This special tradition includes many poetic types: experimental poetry, typical of the early twentieth century (found in the *In zikh* group, the Introspectivists, like Jacob Glatstein [Yankev Glatshteyn] and A. Glanz-Leyeles [Glanz; Glantz]), socially responsible poetry (such as the sweatshop poems of Abraham Reisen [Reyzin]), mystical poetry (such as the work of Aaron Zeitlen), and narrative poems (such as those by Chaim Grade).

Yiddish poets in America responded to the events of the twentieth century in an especially visceral and poignant fashion. Many of these writers were continually confronting the issues of assimilation and anti-Semitism in their lives and families. Simultaneously, they were devouring the Western literary heritage (i.e., that tradition that is not only Eurocentric but Christian, and male, and narrow, that all of us learned in our high school and college literature classes as THE literature of our culture) with a freshness and exuberance that has rarely been matched in other groups. They took these paradigms from the master culture and re-formed them into a Jewish poetry in the most imaginative, though innocent, fashion possible.

But most interesting to our study here is the presence and vitality of American-Jewish poetry in English. This tradition began in the mid-nineteenth century with the conventional hymns and sonnets of the Sephardic poets, Penina Moise and Emma Lazarus. The tradition continued into the early twentieth century when the dialogue between Modernism and the Jews first began, a dialogue that is still apparent in such poets as Hyam Plutzik and John Hollander. Further, it shows itself in the impulse to redeem ancient Jewish sources in modern America, in works by such poets as Jerome Rothenberg and David Meltzer.

Penina Moise (1797–1880), a daughter of Southern Jewry, wrote nineteenth-century hymns that were greatly admired by her contemporaries. Their presence in Reform hymnals of today indicates her continued popularity. These hymns follow the usual form and thematic patterns of typical American hymns of her day. Her works sound as if they might have been heard in churches throughout the South and the North. They are usually iambic tetrameter quatrains with an a a b b rhyme scheme. The language is high poetic diction; the tone is respectful in the Christian sense of that word (no Jewish familiarity with *Yahweh* in her poetry). The messages are those of acceptance of God's will and mysterious ways—even when those ways mean poverty, blindness, and spinsterhood.

A much better known and more accomplished poet of this time was Emma Lazarus (1849–1887). Her first poetry was published in 1866 and met with the praise of no less a literary light than Ralph Waldo Emerson. These poems and the poetry and prose that she published in the 1870's were conventional and she seemed disinterested in any subjects that could be deemed particularly Jewish. But after reading George Eliot's *Daniel Deronda*, Lazarus turned her attentions almost exclusively to Jewish subjects and poets. Her English translations of such greats as Heinrich Heine, Judah Halevi, and Solomon Gabirol reveal a serious dedication to her newfound Jewish identity. Her 1882 collection, *Songs of a Semite*, includes some passionate poems about the Jewish experience of survival, poems such as the long verse narrative "The Dance to Death," about the massacres of Jews in Europe during the years of the Black Death. Her 1887 collection of prose poems, "By the Waters of Babylon," her periodical essays, and the 1882–1883 tract, *An Epistle to the Hebrews*, illustrate her feelings of brotherhood with Jews of different cultures (such as the new American immigrants from Eastern Europe) and her propethic plans for the rebirth of a vital Jewish culture in America and Palestine. But it is for her penning of that moving Italian sonnet "The New Colossus" that she will be best remembered. This 1883 sonnet, which stands engraved at the base of the Statue of Liberty, greets American immigrants as they enter a new land of golden opportunity, a land that sees the refuse of Europe as the promise of America. Her optimism and patriotism are as much features of nineteenth-century American expansionism and cult of progress as of her sense of Jewish peoplehood, but Lazarus's concern for the new Jews of America was the concern of a Jew for another Jew.

In terms of audience and tone, the true twentieth-century successors to Emma Lazarus are not poets but the novelists of the 1960's and 1970's, Saul Bellow and Bernard Malamud. These novelists, even in their clearly Jewish subject matter, are writing with the Christian audience in mind. Surely they expect Jews to read their works as well, but they are quite conscious of the Christian public, and they are anxious to receive praise from the Christian centers of culture. Lazarus, even as she wrote of anti-Semitism and the brotherhood of Jews, reveled in the compliments of Emerson, Longfellow, and Whittier—not in the readership of any Jews. And one cannot avoid noting that her muse for Jewishness was the novel by a nineteenth-century Victorian.

In the twentieth century, the American-Jewish poets also had to confront gentile culture. And they confronted that culture not as Jewish apologists but as acculturated defenders of Jewishness. The foundational question for these poets derives from their dialogue with Modernism about its relationship to their personal inspiration and intellectual credentials. Even in contemporary times, when we are seeing a greater distance from the Modernism of Eliot and Pound, American-Jewish poets still seem haunted by their tie to this seminal twentieth-century movement. When this dialogue is about form, the answers can be found in the formalistic poetry of Irving Feldman, John Hollander, and Anthony Hecht as well as in experiments with form which deconstruct our formal expectations such as Objectivist poetry (George Oppen, Carl Rakosi, Louis Zukofsky, and Charles Reznikoff), monologues (Delmore Schwartz), and oral-based poetry (Jerome Rothenberg and David Meltzer).

When this dialogue with Modernism is more personal, the poets concern themselves with the politics and humanity of the great Modernists and the consequence of their essential anti-Semitism on the modern American mind, the literary canon, and its paradigms. Further incursions of the general *Weltanschauung* of twentieth-century America upon American-Jewish poetry included the impact of the women's movement on the growing presence and awareness of women poets, the influence of contemporary theories of ethnic celebration and identity by all American minorities, the impulse to expand the canon of American and Western literatures to include subterranean cultures not valued by previous canon makers (such as those found in folk art, in women's work, in minority existence, and in secret, usually mystical, societies), and the influence of the historical reality and philosophical and ethical consequences of the Holocaust. In fact, then, these writers are interacting and responding to the features of the twentieth century in America, features that we would have to note as influential on the art and consciousness of any American writer of the day.

It is inaccurate, therefore, to call American-Jewish poets a school, for they do not agree upon a credo, nor do they share a complex of ideas or attitudes. Their ideas of form and subject matter are almost as various as the span of traditions in American letters. But what these poets do share are an awareness and an interest in being Jewish and in things Jewish. These might not be an awareness and an interest that permeate every poem by any of these authors, and the awareness and interest might not be positive or complimentary. But there is a significant proportion of the work by American poets of Jewish descent that can and should be identified as American-Jewish poetry. By identifying some shared geographical features of the poetry as a whole and pointing out certain landmarks of publication, I wish to describe the landscape of this poetry.

The first identifiable group of American-Jewish poets in the twentieth century is the Objectivist Group. Though nothing in their published credos argues their Jewishness, overlooking the Jewish descent of every major proponent of the movement would be wearing blinders. For the Objectivists (George Oppen, Carl Rakosi, Louis Zukofsky, Charles Reznikoff, and tangentially William Carlos Williams), the poem was an artifact important in and only in itself. Reality could be created only by words, and created particularly well by words in poetic form. Imagism's elevation of the power of the image and the vitality of free verse were the structural features of Objectivism. These theorists argued in the true spirit of Modernism that form and meaning were inextricably entwined and that the form offered coherence in the contemporary world.

For our purposes, the most important of these poets is Charles Reznikoff (1894–1976). He was surely one of the more prolific of the Objectivists and probably the most easily comprehended. Further, excepting Williams (who was an Objectivist for only part of his career), Reznikoff was the most influential of the group. Finally, of the Objectivists, only Reznikoff publicly identified himself as an American, urban, Jewish poet. His Jewish sense of identity is central to the inspiration and subject choice of his poetry. We can see this Jewish influence on his prose writings as well: three novels, *By the Waters of Manhattan* (1930), *The Lionhearted* (1944), and *The Manner "Music"* (1977); a collection of prose pieces, *By the Waters of Manhattan: An Annual* (1929); three historical pieces, *Testimony* (1934), *Early History of a Sewing Machine Operator* (1936), and *Family Chronicle* (1963); and several translations and editions. However, his sense of himself as a Jew, an exile Jew—exiled from Israel, from his Jewish past, and from Russia—permeates his poetry. Reznikoff published more than nineteen individual volumes and collections of poetry, beginning in 1918 and spanning the next approximately sixty years.

In 1976–1977, Black Sparrow Press published a two-volume collection of Reznikoff's poetic canon. Now the student of American-Jewish literature has in convenient form selections from more than twelve of Reznikoff's previous publications. These volumes include poetry from his earliest collection (*Rhythms*, 1918) and from his last, unpublished collection. The second volume contains the best poetry, such poems as "A Short History of Israel," "From the Apocalyptic Ezra," "Lesson in Homer," and "Autobiography: New York." A simple observation of these titles suggests the breadth of influence on Reznikoff. References to masters of British literature (for instance, Keats), to Icelandic saga, and to episodes of American history appear in his work alongside references to his favorite Jewish literature—the Talmud and the Torah. He also knew about more esoteric texts, as evidenced by his translation of the apocalyptic Ezra cited above. Reznikoff wrote about Jewish survival and exilic existence; he set his poems in biblical Israel, nineteenth-century Russia, and twentieth-century America. In other words, in his poetry we see details from his autobiography as well as from his readings.

The poetics of his art, even the latest of his poetry, agrees with his early espousal of Objectivism. In fact, we can see in his last published collection, *Holocaust*, not included in the two-volume Black Sparrow edition, how successful his mature vision of Objectivism could be. Published in 1977, this epic is based on the documents of the Nuremberg trials and Eichmann's trial in Jerusalem. The twelve-part poem echoes epic structure (epics are usually twelve or twenty-four chapters). In addition, the scope of the setting is broad, as broad as Hitler's ambition; the action is heroic in the dignity of those who resist and those who survive; the supernatural is present in the form of the Nazi killing machine; the style is as elevated and the tone as objective as any epic in the literary tradition; and the hero is the Saving Remnant, the small portion of Jews that God has promised His People will survive every new pogrom and every new Haman. In fact, the poem ends with those representative Jews escaping from Denmark to Sweden. Perhaps the peculiar distance of Objectivism makes this Reznikoff poem the most successful extended American comment on the Holocaust. Only by a pretense of distance can the American poet respond to the Holocaust's horror.

Throughout the century other American-Jewish poets responded to Modernism, its concerns with form and alienation. In the earlier group, that is those poets who are associated with the period of the Second World War and the early fifties, Delmore Schwartz (1913–1966) and Karl Shapiro (1913–   ) are the most memorable. Schwartz has recently reappeared on center stage of the American literary consciousness in the person of Bellow's portrait of Von Humboldt Fleisher (*Humboldt's Gift*, 1975). This loving, humorous, but painful portrait of a friend's disintegration into alcoholism and psychosis and the almost concurrent publication of James Atlas's biography of Delmore Schwartz (*Delmore Schwartz*, 1977) have done a great deal to open the door to the mystery of Schwartz, who was a great inspiration to the poets and novelists of the fifties and sixties. Schwartz's psychological exposure and guilt-ridden reminiscences influenced Saul Bellow and John Berryman among others of his contemporaries. He is best remembered for his often dreamlike short fiction that chronicles his own insecurities in a typical New York Jewish household during the Depression (see especially "In Dreams Begin Responsibilities").

In his collection of poetry, *Summer Knowledge: New and Selected Poems, 1938–1958* (1959), however, there are some impressive examples of his poetry. The monologue "Jacob" is an interesting case in point. Jacob muses on the status of being born second, but being born with a gift. His gift was intelligence and its primacy, which brought with it guilt. Joseph re-enacts his father's suffering as the preferred son. In both histories, Jacob learns the injustice of love and the lovelessness of justice.

Karl Shapiro, born the same year as Schwartz, is a writer of many parts. He is a poet, a critic, an editor, and a teacher. In fact, wearing multiple hats is not unusual for the poets who follow him (such as Hollander, Plutzik, Feldman, and Hecht). Indeed, many poets from the fifties to the present have assumed the role of academic poet and thereby gained acclaim from the bastion of gentile culture, the Academy. Despite this position, these poets often assume the role of Jewish spokesman.

Shapiro's earlier poetry is more traditional in form, more Jewish in content, and in fact more successful than his later poetry. The collection for which he is most likely to be remembered is his *Poems of a Jew* (1958), in which is collected "Alphabet." Here he delineates the contrasting modes of existence—gentile and Jewish. The Jewish mode is a strict one, a fiery one, but unlike the gentile Celts and Romans, the Jews still survive as a culture and a nation, despite a two-thousand-year exile. His early Jewish subject poems, such as "Alphabet," "Synagogue," "A Travelogue for Exiles," and "The Jew," follow traditional metrical forms. Later, Shapiro turned to open-ended verse, admitting the influence of such Americans as Walt Whitman and William Carlos Williams. The attraction to free verse and iconoclastic formal experiments suggests a parallel with Reznikoff. However, Shapiro's poetry of this later period is not great poetry. His literary criticism of this period is. He has written thought-provoking and intelligent responses to both the Modernist poetics of Pound and Eliot and the form consciousness of the New Critics of the 1950s.

In Shapiro's criticism of Modernism (see for instance, *Essay on Rime*, 1945, and *Beyond Criticism*, 1953), he comments about the impact of the anti-Semitic beliefs of Pound and Eliot on their poetics. He, like so many other twentieth-century American-Jewish poets, is unable to divorce himself from these great lights of the modern age. On the other hand, he, like so many other twentieth-century American-Jewish poets, is unable to forgive these poets for their anti-Semitism.

The most delightful expression of this conflict is that found in Hyam Plutzik's "For T. S. E. Only," in his 1959 collection *Apples from Shinar*. In this personal dialogue with the spirit of Eliot, Plutzik reminds Eliot that he engaged in name-calling when he stooped to the anti-Semitic slur against Bleistein. Plutzik invites Eliot to see his prejudice and to join with all Jews in weeping over their exilic existence in the twentieth century. The poem is full of allusions to Eliot's masterpieces, to "The Love Song of J. Alfred Prufrock," *The Wasteland*, and *The Four Quartets*. Clearly, it is the poem of an Eliot aficionado and clearly his feelings are hurt. In the end, Eliot is characterized as a prideful eagle, and Plutzik calls him what Eliot called someone else, somewhere else: "You, hypocrite lecteur! mon semblable! mon frère!" Such ambivalence can be seen in many of the poets of Jewish descent who have gained some acclaim during the last twenty-five years, poets like Irving Feldman, Anthony Hecht, and John Hollander.

The most recent generation of American-Jewish poets has undoubtedly produced the richest and most diverse literature. Continuing into the present, poetry by the academic, professorial, usually formalistic artist flourishes in the careers of Hecht, Feldman, and Hollander. But the tradition of poetry that depends on the highly personal and open-ended free verse of Walt Whitman, communicated through the Objectivist glass, also appears in the poetry of Jack Hirschman, Jerome Rothenberg, and David Meltzer. Furthermore, in perhaps the last ten years or so, a group of American-Jewish women poets has come to their art with allegiances fruitfully divided by a consciousness of their double minority status. These poets include Chana Bloch, Rose Drachler, Susan Mernit, and Marcia Falk.

Anthony Hecht (1923–   ) experiments with many traditional forms and reveals in this formal experimentation as well as in the subject matter of his literature his erudition. Like Karl Shapiro, Hecht was early influenced by Wallace Stevens and W. H. Auden. During the year 1947–1948, Hecht came under the influnce of New Criticism in the person of John Crowe Ransom. Unlike Shapiro, however, Hecht has continued to display his interest and expertise in formal experimentation. The variety of his four collections includes parodies of Western masterpieces (such as "The Dover Bitch"), translations (of Joseph Brodsky), poems of urban New York ("Apprehensions"), and poems of Jewish diaspora existence. This last category is the most fruitful for our discussion.

A characteristic poem of this group, "Exile" (1968), draws parallels among three Josephs—the Joseph of *Genesis*, sent into exile by his jealous brothers, where his inspired dream reading not only saved his life but also afforded him luxuries he did not expect; the Joseph of the Christian Testament, baffled by his situation, lost to himself, and finally to the Jewish people; and the contemporary Joseph Brodsky, sent into exile by his communist brothers, where his poetry saved him and gained him acclaim, a Joseph baffled by his exile and his strained relationship to Jewish peoplehood and communism.

Hecht's most extensive treatment of Jewish exilic life is the long poem "Rites and Ceremonies" (1968). This four-part poem relates several seminal episodes of government-sanctioned anti-Semitism and ends with a prayer for forgiveness. Section 1, "The Room," begins with a modern version of the *"Amidah"* prayer, celebrating the power of God: requesting His healing of the sick, His granting of wisdom, His destruction of slanderers, His re-establishment of Israel and of peace. Hecht's version also alludes to Job and his suffering. The room of the title and therefore the place in which this "*Amidah*" is prayed is the room in which the Jews were gassed in the Nazi death camps. The prayer section ends with a vision of the cross on the belt-buckle of the SS. The second half of section 1 describes the clawing of the people as they perished and the indifference of the world outside, a world in which the Catholic Church "deplored" the death machine. At the point of death, the Psalmist's call to God is remembered, "And He has heard me out His holy hill."

"The Fire Sermon," section 2, alludes to the Western literary heritage, to such canonical poets as Eliot (note the title), and Coleridge (references to "The Rime of the Ancient Mariner"), and to the historical episode of 1349 in Strasbourg when 2,000 Jews were burned as scapegoats for the Black Death. The last six stanzas of this section allude to the sixteenth-century *kabbalistic* metaphor of Isaac Luria, in which the sparks of creation and existence must be returned to the original, pure stasis. If these sparks are returned, the Messianic Age, the Ingathering of Exiles, and the end of Jewish pain will be accomplished. The image of the sparks that flew up from the bonfires in which Jews were martyred in Strasbourg thereby becomes for Hecht the possible sparks that can effect restitution of perfection.

Section 3, "The Dream," is a formal exercise in iambic pentameter in which the majority of stanzas are five-line stanzas, with a rhyme pattern a b b a b or a b a a b. This form and the subject of the poem, exile in Rome, suggest the sixteenth-century French poet Du Bellay, exiled to Rome, who wrote verse of much the same form and tone about his experience and his desire to return to Anjou, his homeland. "The Dream" notes the similarity of exilic feelings of displacement and disjointedness.

The final section, "Words for the Day of Atonement," turns from all other historical experience and describes the American-Jewish circumstance, a circumstance best identified as "a wilderness of comfort," a place where we can assume a false position of pride in our purity. Hecht's conclusion contains many references to the services of *Yom Kippur*, particularly to the *Ne'lah* service, in which the penitents request forgiveness for their sins. Hecht prays for the continuance of the Saving Remnant—not only those who survived the Holocaust, but those who will survive the next anti-Semitic attack. These Jews shall pray to God in the new death camps and they shall be saved as before, but the Jews of today and of America must repent for their own sins. They cannot assume the pure and martyred status of either the Saving Remnant or the victims of the Nazi Holocaust. The power of this poem as an expression of contemporary Jewish ethical sensibility is illustrated by the inclusion of this last section of "Rites and Ceremonies" in the most recent Reform prayer book for the High Holidays.

Another prolific academic writer of contemporary poetry is Irving Feldman (1928–   ). Currently a professor at SUNY-Buffalo, Feldman has published at least four major collections of poetry. His Jewish subject poems range from poetry about the history of Jewish literature ("The Apocalypse Is a School for

Prophets," 1972) to autobiographical meditations on American-Jewish existence ("Works and Days," 1961, and "Wandering Jew," 1961) to imaginative rumi-nations on the Holocaust ("The Pripet Marshes," 1965, and "To the Six Mil-lion," 1965). For example, "The Apocalypse Is a School for Prophets" inverts the unusual wisdom of the Biblical scholars that prophecy preceded the apocalyp-tic, that the apocalyptic represented a degradation of the prophetic spirit.[2] In fact, Feldman argues, in order for there to be a prophetic temper, there has to be the apocalyptic destruction. Instead of the prophets as seers and spokesmen of the people, for Feldman they are "misanthropic" and celebrators of a "zombi-verse." His discomfort with prophecy stems from its denial of human physicality.

"Works and Days" is an autobiographical account in three sections. The first, "The Ark," describes Feldman's move out of his home (a home where the Depression and depression reign) to the large, gentile, and friendless city. He has left the sadness of his schooling in pogrom and anti-Semitism only to discover loneliness in the city. The ark of this short introductory section is the ark on which he, like Noah, travels; it is also the ark of the Covenant, which he has rejected, the ark in which the Torah is protected. The section ends with his flight away from the ark of Noah, perched on Ararat, while he, in the form of the crow that never returned, flies into the open world—the world of pain.

Section 2, "Wrack," is divided into seven shorter lyrics. The first lyric, like section 1, is in iambic tetrameter quatrains, rhyming a b a b. At first, the world of wrack seems survivable. Filled with excess sensuality, this world does not seem particularly painful. In "Crow," however, Feldman's minority existence, his Jewishness in the midst of gentileness, expressed in unevenly metered, rhymed couplets, is not a comfortable existence. The rest of section 2 returns to iambic tetrameter. The tone of the section grows in threat and destructive suggestiveness. For instance, the very last lyric is entitled "Apocalypse" and describes the landscape of New York City as the landscape of the final destruction of the world, complete with blasts of doom and the red of a final sunset. In this conclusive lyric, Feldman refers to himself again as the "prodigal crow," a miserly and miserable bird of pain. The section ends with the vision of the ark, a memory that allows Feldman to speculate on return and hope.

The third section, "Return" is divided into three promising lyrics: "Lullaby," an appropriate allusion to the diaper image of the ark's sail that ended section 2; "Arabian Night," a reference to magic as an attractive but empty source of hope; and "Crystal," which explicates Feldman's circumspect return to tradition. This final lyric uses natural images to describe a crystalline source for meaning. Feldman equates the crystal of prophetic answers with the humanly produced crystal of the salt in tears. However, Feldman compares the poet's return to that of Tiresias, a prophet, a seer—but a blind one. Feldman ends expressing a desire to build and return, but recognizing that he will be doing so in ignorance and blindness, for "who will teach me to build?"

Feldman's Holocaust poems are powerful, distinctively American meditations on the meaning of the Holocaust. In fact, Sidra DeKoven Ezrahi calls "The

Pripet Marshes'' the most successful use of the American existential reality of our relationship to the European Holocaust.[3] In ''The Pripet Marshes,'' Feldman speculates in free verse, in almost Whitmanesque lines, about the possibility of his American-Jewish family's involvement in the Holocaust. He transports his people from the Brooklyn where they really lived to the place of their ancestors in the Ukraine. What if they had been in the Pripet Marshes instead of on the streets of New York City? They would have looked different; they would have spoken differently. He imagines these real friends and family members in an imaginary *shtetl* moments before the storm troopers invaded the community in order to gather up the Jews and send them to Auschwitz. But here his imagination stuns him—they would die. Feldman snatches these imaginary transports from the Ukraine. When the motorcycles of the Nazis speed through his imagined town, the Germans find no one. However, every Jew in the twentieth century, including Irving Feldman, knows that this is all imagination. In fact, every single one of the counterparts to his Jewish family was gathered up, was transferred not to some Platonic safe home but to Auschwitz, where most of them were murdered or died.

Another contemporary American-Jewish poet who has gained a deserved reputation for writing formal poetry is current Yale professor John Hollander (1929–   ). Until recently, Hollander was not associated with Jewish subject poetry. A close review of his over sixteen volumes of poetry indicates that this lack of association makes good sense, because most of his poetry that would be identified as Jewish appears in his later writing. Hollander is one of the most respected contemporary American poets, not just for his Jewish poetry, but for his entire canon. He, for instance, was one of the few contemporary poets included in the 1982 Frank N. Magill *Critical Survey of Poetry*. He has illustrated his expertise as a critic and versifier in critical analyses of Milton as well as in masterful exercises of verse form, even texts of forms like his 1982 *Rhyme's Reason*.

In his 1978 collection, *Spectral Emanations*, Hollander published some poetry that reveals his imaginative control of formal verse as well as of Jewish subjects. ''The Loss of Smyrna'' assumes the point of view of the seventeenth-century pseudo-messiah, Shabbatai Zevi. Hollander sets the poem on the boat as Zevi returns to his home, Smyrna, after having been exiled by his own community for his outrageous behavior in the study house. He returns in hope of solace and comfort, but finds that his return is a disappointment. Shabbatai Zevi realizes that total freedom, the consequence of his version of the transformation of Judaism, is not true freedom; it is license. In the final vision Hollander echoes the apocalyptic cry in its most despairing form. He writes of a seventeenth-century confidence man, but from his references to contemporary circumstances (e.g., Biloxi, Mississippi, and Radcliffe graduates), his comments seem directed toward our search for freedom which, for Hollander, is nothing more than anarchy.

Perhaps the most sophisticated and complex contemporary use of Jewish sources in American poetry is ''Spectral Emanations,'' Hollander's seven-section explication of reality, based on the sixteenth-century *kabbalah* of Isaac Luria. The poem begins with an extract and a commentary identifying Hollander's hyphenated identity—the extract is from the late romance of Nathaniel Hawthorne, *The Marble Faun*, referring to the decorations of the Temple in Jerusalem. Hollander's inspiration for the poem is Jewish, but it is a Jewish inspiration filtered through the eyes and experiences of an American: an American writes of a Jewish artist in Europe, Hawthorne writes of Miriam in the nineteenth-century romance. The ambiguous relationship of this Jew of fiction to John Hollander in the halls of academe is rich in implications for the poem. Hollander provides an allegory, a parable (the terms of Miriam's understanding of the symbols of the ancient Temple), concerning the ontology and epistemology that constitute reality. The seven colors (which offer titles for the seven sections) that make up white light symbolize the aspects of reality: red, orange, yellow, green, blue, indigo, and violet. Each section contains first a poetic portion of seventy-two lines, followed by a prose commentary on the meaning of the color as a symbol for an aspect of reality.

In a "Prologue," Hollander leads the narrator through seven chambers, but never allows him into the final sanctuary. The poem begins with the red vision of war. The specifics of this section are those of the 1973 *Yom Kippur* War, but the red of life, death, and dirt is the real substance of "Red." "Orange" describes the material and sensual portion of reality; "Yellow" is the fading of such physicality, a spiritual and artistic rendition of existence; "Green" is simple and fertile nature, the most comfortable aspect of reality; "Blue" dwells on the color of the sky, as the dome that spreads over our daily existence; "Indigo" describes the different faces of goddesses, the different judgments of female power; "Violet" tells of endings, nights, fires, and ultimate things.

Each of these sections offers varieties of stanzaic, metrical, and rhythmic versions of the required seventy-two lines. The prose commentaries following the sections are quite various: some are narrative, some are meditative, some are speculative and critical. Thus in the form as well as in the substance of this exquisite poem Hollander delineates the varieties of existence and interpretations of existence that make up a true and complete reality.

Unlike the new formalists who strain under the traditional strictures of form, the new avant-garde is not so closely tied to academic settings. Three of the most distinctive voices of the group are the California-based poets who are associated with the Tree Book enterprise: Jack Hirschman, David Meltzer, and Jerome Rothenberg. These three are not members of a single school. Some rather obvious differences should be noted before a discussion of individual examples of these poets begins. Hirschman's most powerful poetry centers on the contemporary political flaws of American society, particularly his 1960's poems about the Vietnam War and the assassination of Jack Kennedy. The other two poets are not especially political, except in their identification with minority groups and with the oppressed. They reject the given wisdom of the mainstream, the Western heritage, and in that sense, surely Rothenberg and Meltzer are political.

Nonetheless, they rarely comment on specific political events. The events that do appear in their poetry are central to some ethnic consciousness, to some comment on social identity, but not to political action. The guru of the group, Rothenberg, describes his theory of "Ethnopoetics" as a poetics that depends on the paradigms and ideals of subterranean and rejected cultures, an oral-based poetry. Ethnopoetics provides the theoretical context in which we can read all of this poetry. Meltzer, married to neither political causes nor theoretical contexts, is the freest spirit of the group and in many ways the most inspired.

Jack Hirschman (1933–   ), dedicated to unconventional style and to criticism of American society, is quite knowledgeable of the Western tradition which he so often criticizes; he has a Ph.D. from the English literature program of Indiana University. A translator particularly well known for his translations of Jewish sources, Hirschman creatively rewrites these texts so that they become his poems. Such translations indicate his knowledge of Jewish sources and Jewish languages, as well as his poetic ability. These translations have appeared in Rothenberg's creative anthology *A Big Jewish Book* (1978) and a number of Tree publications, such as the collection of the thirteenth-century mystic Abraham Abulafia. Of the twelve collections and monographs by Hirschman, the one that contains the largest number and the best examples of his original poetry based on Jewish subjects and texts is *Black Alephs: Poems 1960–1968* (1969). Here are poems that allude to Abulafia, Isaac Luria, the *Zohar*, the Talmud, and *kabbalistic* numerological devices.

One of the most effective poems in this collection is "Ascent." Using the mystical methods of number and letter manipulation to derive ontological truths, Hirschman manipulates the English transliterations of the Hebrew letters *samek*, *feh*, and *resh*, and relates these sounds to sounds and words in other languages. Thus, beginning with *sapheir* in Hebrew, a rabbi derives the word for numbers, then to the Greek *sphairai*, meaning "spheres," to *siphoor*, meaning "permitted to narrate to it," to *sephirah*, meaning a limit or end, to the town Sephar, to the words *sepher* of the early mystical text, *Sepher yetzirah*, and ending with the English word *sapphire*. In other words, through this mystical mode of explanation Hirschman moves from the intellectual foundation of human communication in mathematics or language (Hebrew numbers are indicated by Hebrew letters) to the dome of heaven; from Hebrew, through Greek, to English; from the classical ages to contemporary times.

David Meltzer (1937–   ) is author of more than thirteen collections of poems and translations of Jewish esoteric texts as well as at least nine prose collections, and the editor of one of the most imaginative small presses of today. His poetry formally owes much to Whitman: that is, its open-ended form and free verse rely on the prophetic position of the poet. In both his shorter poem "Abulafia" (1969) and his longer meditation "Tohu" (1973), Meltzer writes about his personal inspiration, as well as the generic question of poetic inspiration. In the shorter reference to Abulafia, the American poet recognizes his identity with the medieval *kabbalist* who thought of himself as a messianic aspirant. For both Abulafia and Meltzer, the sound of words and the manipulation of the language form the poetics of a mystical art. In "Tohu," Meltzer begins with a reference to the *Zohar* passage that describes a place that has no form or color, the place of inspiration, where he stands and tries to sing with angels. However, interrupted by the material realities of contemporary America, he loses his inspiration and now only reminisces about inspiration. He sings as Whitman did in "Out of the Cradle Endlessly Rocking" of a recollection of a transmuting event: the conversation with angels who tell him of apocalyptic texts and truths.

Jerome Rothenberg (1931–   ), author of more than twenty-five collections of poetry and translations, is the most important theorist of the avant-garde writers of Jewish-American poetry. Early on he defined the term "deep image," a term associated with American poets as diverse as Diane Wakoski, Robert Bly, Louis Simpson, and James Wright. This counterpoetics shares a great deal with the early movements of Imagism and Objectivism; the deep image is an image that permeates the form and content of a poem to explain its power. More recently, Rothenberg has coined the term "Ethnopoetics," and then proceeded to create poetry to illustrate this elevation of oral, ancient, pagan traditions. In this spirit Rothenberg has produced several collections of ethnic or national poetic and sacred texts from cultures not represented well in the mainstream European cultural tradition. Thus, he has edited *Shaking the Pumpkin* (1971) and *A Big Jewish Book*, both imaginative and creative collections, commentaries on Native-American and Jewish cultural heritages. Rothenberg's poetry and editing reveal his eclectic and counterpoetic concerns, but his interest in Jewish sources is particularly apparent in the poetry. Though we could discover Jewish influences on Rothenberg's canon from the beginning, his most sophisticated and effective poetry of a Jewish concern can be found in two later collections, *Poland/1931* (1974) and *Vienna Blood* (1980).

The largely autobiographical *Poland/1931* contains seven subsections of poems concerned with Rothenberg's personal, cultural, and family heritage. Of Polish-Jewish descent, the poet writes of his ancestral homeland and of other Polish-American Jews. The two most engaging sections, both originally published as monographs, "Galician Nights; or A Novel in Progress" and "Esther K. Comes to America," center on the character Esther K. She is a Polish-born Jew who becomes a modern-day soothsayer and spiritual advisor on the lower East Side of New York City. She becomes transformed into the *Shekinah*, the female principle of God, a role she plays opposite another immigrant Jew, the failed messianic aspirant, Leo Levy. Her cosmic significance is reinforced by the inclusion in "Esther K. Comes to America" of Rothenberg's translation of a Lurianic hymn to *Shekinah*. In this hymn the female principle of God is identified with Bride Sabbath. United, these female divinities are celebrated as sources of inspiration—spiritual and artistic—in fact as salvational powers. They are associated with joy and productivity. The *Shekinah* is God's highest crown, His holiest Holy, and on Sabbath her powers are awesome. On the day of rest, the *Shekinah* holds the promise of all the universe in her hands, for instead of the

Messiah waiting in chains (as legend holds he should until his appearance at the Messianic Advent), on Sabbath through the powers and mercies of the *Shekinah*, only hostile powers, demons, "sleep in chains."

The complex and eclectic three-section poem "Abulafia's Circles" included in the 1980 *Vienna Blood* is one of the most imaginative contemporary American renditions of Jewish sources. This poem is a meditation on Jewish messianism. Beginning with one of the most bizarre, yet spiritualized, versions of Messiah in Jewish history, the poem emphasizes the *kabbalah* and life of Abraham Abulafia. The poet notes the thirteenth-century mystic as a master of linguistic manipulation, an activity of which the later messianic candidates and Jerome Rothenberg (as well as his literary followers) are so fond. For the medieval Jew, the Hebrew language and its letters explained the mystery of the universe. In other words, a Hebrew letter in both its phonetic and mathematical significance was a principle of existence. To understand the Hebrew language was to understand cosmology and ontology. Thus, Abulafian *kabbalah* prescribed a pattern of meditation on certain letters of the alphabet (those that made up what was called the seventy-two-letter name of God) in order for one to attain the special knowledge of the mystic.

Rothenberg begins his poem citing that philosophical and mystical principle as it was found in Abulafia, but also recognizing its various mutations in contemporary Western experience. He sees it in the art of Hannah Weiner, in the lives of Mafia thugs, the actions of a Chaplin character, in the rejection of Hitler's murderings, and in the sexually charged relationships of men and women. The second section, "The Secret Dream of Jacob Frank," ostensibly relates the life of a successor Messiah of the eighteenth century. The passionate sexuality and strange habits of this historical messianic movement are described and are paralleled with other messianic impulses. Frankist attraction to the Catholic worship of Mary is aligned with Frank's questionable relationship with his daughter, whom he called his *Shekinah*. The final section, "The Holy Words of Tristan Tzara," turns from leaders often discussed in the religious or spiritual realm to a leader and revolutionary of the artistic world. Rothenberg sees the iconoclastic nature of Dada and its leader as messianic and transformative in the very same fashion as Abulafia's *kabbalah* and life. In fact, Dada's attitude toward language and letter significance is not very far from the mystical interpretation of language and letter significance in Abulafian *kabbalah*. Finally, "Abulafia's Circles" becomes a treatise on poetic inspiration and an argument in favor of the poet's prophetic powers, powers that Rothenberg argues he himself wishes to assume. The poem ends with the narrator of the poem seeing someone, the poet, the new leader of the new poetics, leaping into the saddle of a horse and rushing after Tzara who really is Frank who really is Abulafia who really is the Messiah.

The presence of American-Jewish women poets as such is not a new phenomenon. The two nineteenth-century poets discussed at the beginning of this essay were women. Further, all contemporary women poets do not share the same attitudes toward feminism or women's literature. In other words, I am not so convinced that discussing women poets separately does them full justice. But I do so because recently their numbers have grown to be so remarkable and their production is so impressive. There are, for instance, several women who have been most often associated with fiction who should be cited here—writers such as Erica Jong, Cynthia Ozick, and Susan Fromberg Schaeffer. All three of these writers have written some noteworthy poetry. Indeed, in the case of Jong, her poetry outstrips her fiction in almost every way. This is not true of Ozick and Schaeffer, both of whom seem serious-minded in both fiction and poetry. Schaeffer is equally adept at both genres. Ozick excels in fiction and knows that, so she has written very little poetry.

Other writers who are known as poets can be represented by four examples: Rose Drachler (1911–1982), Linda Pastan (1932–), Marcia Falk (1946–), and Susan Mernit (1950–). Drachler wrote formal verse that derived its inspiration from her sense of herself as a Jew and as a woman. For her, the Jewish religion was a human and spiritual celebration of life. In ironic fashion, Drachler sees the Jewish divinity as the sensual God and the Greek divinity as an all-too-human and insensitive male chauvinist ("Athens and Jerusalem," 1977). "The Choice" (1977) recognizes the beautiful ambivalence of the status of the Chosen People.

Linda Pastan has to date published four separate volumes of poetry. These are quiet and melancholy meditations on the difficult existence of a contemporary American-Jewish woman. She articulates her acceptance of her job as mother and wife along with an almost irresistible desire to escape ("Knots," 1975). Poems on the Jewish calendar and liturgy reveal their peculiar hyphenated appearance in America ("Passover" and "Yom Kippur," 1971).

Falk and Mernit represent even more complex reactions of women to the Jewish tradition. Marcia Falk is an accomplished poet and translator. Her rendition of the Song of Songs (1977) reveals the erudition of the Hebrew scholar as well as the spirit of a poet. By re-establishing in English the clear Hebraic indications of the sexuality of the multiple speakers in Song of Songs, Falk returns to the dialogue much of its sexual and religious power. Therefore, her recent project, *A Book of Blessings* (1988), an attempt to remove sexist language from the prayers without damaging their spirit, should be met by scholar, rabbi, and Jew with gratitude and admiration. And were the traditional community of Jews not so defensive and so overwhelmingly represented by those who mistakenly see rabbinic male tradition as the only norms for Judaism, this gratitude and admiration would be forthcoming. But when Falk published her first rendition, the "Kiddush," in *Moment* (March 1985), the vituperative response found in the letters in the subsequent months of that magazine would disabuse any idealist of such a positive response being made public. The positive letters were censored either by being drastically excerpted or by being overlooked altogether. The significance of this event is in its revelation about the Jewish community's discomfort with the feminist movement. The American-Jewish woman feels her divided loyalties most painfully—she is an American, she is a Jew, she is a woman—each aspect of herself pulling in another direction. The American-Jewish woman is the Jew of the American-Jewish community.

Susan Mernit represents an interesting exception in American-Jewish women's poetry. Though these poets might allude to *kabbalah*, most do not write of the experience from the inside out. They do not write as true initiates. In *Angelic Alphabet* (1975), Mernit does just that. She explicates (in a fashion similar to that found in Hollander's "Spectral Emanations," though not with his formalistic concerns) a complex understanding of reality. She divides her poem into twelve sections, nine of which are named for the Lurianic faces of God in creation. After a full description of both the hidden and the revealed presences of God in creation, Mernit ends with three commentary sections on the methods, the uses, of this *kabbalah*. She sees the meaning of all things in a cosmic unifying principle that fertilizes and empowers our existence.

In an essay such as this, I wanted to take notice of the following things: the variety of the poetry, the value of individual poets and poems, the theories that underlie the major groupings of the poets, and the rationale for the oversight of this most fertile and exciting collection of American-Jewish writers. If there is one quality shared by these poets, ranging from the mid-nineteenth century to the late 1980's, from the poetics of formalism to the counterpoetics of oral poetry, from the political to the personal, from the Modernists to the anti-Modernists, it is the confrontation with their hybrid existence. How to be a Jew and an American (sometimes there is the additional question: how to be a woman)? Surely these very same concerns have interested the fiction writer, but not with the same intensity. Some of this intensity is the simple consequence of the genre: poetry is condensed, intense expression. Thus, by definition these creative artists can express that painful and fertile pull, that "sweet hell," in Whitman's terms, the source for inspiration in all of American-Jewish art.

NOTES

1. Saul Bellow, "Facts That Put Fancy to Flight," *Opinions and Perspectives from the New York Times Book Review*, p. 235.

2. I use the term "apocalyptic" as a noun to denote the literary genre; it is the term in common use by biblical scholars. The apocalypse is the event.

3. Sidra DeKoven Ezrahi, *By Words Alone*, pp. 210–213.

BIBLIOGRAPHY

Bellow, Saul. "Facts That Put Fancy to Flight." *Opinions and Perspectives from the New York Times Book Review*, ed. Francis Brown. Boston: Houghton Mifflin, 1964.

Ezrahi, Sidra DeKoven. *By Words Alone: The Holocaust in Literature*. Chicago: University of Chicago Press, 1980.

FOR FURTHER READING

Selections by Individual Poets

Bloch, Chana. *The Secrets of the Tribe*. New York: Sheep Meadow Press, 1981.

Drachler, Rose. *The Collected Poems*. New York: Assembling Press, 1983.

Falk, Marcia, trans. *The Song of Songs: Love Poems from the Bible*. New York: Harcourt Brace Jovanovich, 1977.

———. *This Year in Jerusalem*. Brockport, New York: State Street Press, 1986.

Feldman, Irving. *Lost Originals*. Chicago: Holt, Rinehart and Winston, 1972.

———. *Magic Papers; and Other Poems*. New York: Harper and Row, 1970.

———. *The Pripet Marshes and Other Poems*. New York: Viking, 1965.

———. *Works and Days and Other Poems*. Boston: Atlantic Monthly Press Little, Brown, 1961.

Hecht, Anthony. *Hard Hours*. New York: Atheneum Press, 1967.

———. *Millions of Strange Shadows*. New York: Atheneum Press, 1977.

Hirschman, Jack. *Black Alephs: Poems 1960–1968*. London: Trigram Press, 1969.

Hollander, John. *Spectral Emanations: New and Selected Poems*. New York: Atheneum Press, 1978.

Lazarus, Emma. *Songs of a Semite*. New York: Office of *The American Hebrew*, 1882.

Meltzer, David. *Tens: Selected Poems, 1961–1971*. New York: McGraw-Hill, 1973.

———, ed. *The Path of the Names: Writings by Abraham ben Samuel Abulafia*. London: Trigram, Tree, 1976.

Mernit, Susan. *Angelic Alphabet*. Berkeley: Tree, 1975.

Pastan, Linda. *A Perfect Circle of Sun*. Chicago: Swallow Press, 1971.

Plutzik, Hyam. *Apples from Shinar*. Middletown, Connecticut: Wesleyan University Press, 1959.

Reznikoff, Charles. *The Complete Poems*. 2 vols. Santa Barbara: Black Sparrow Press, 1976.

———. *Holocaust*. Santa Barbara: Black Sparrow Press, 1975.

Rothenberg, Jerome. *Poland/1931*. Santa Barbara, California: Unicorn Press, 1970.

———. *Vienna Blood and Other Poems*. New York: New Directions, 1980.

Schwartz, Delmore. *Summer Knowledge: New and Selected Poems, 1938–1958*. New York: New Directions, 1959.

Schwartz, Howard. *Gathering the Sparks: Poems 1965–1979*. St. Louis: Singing Wind Press, 1979.

Schaeffer, Susan Fromberg. *The Bible of the Beasts of the Little Field*. New York: E. P. Dutton, 1980.

Shapiro, Harvey. *Battle Report: Selected Poems*. Middletown, Connecticut: Wesleyan University Press, 1966.

Shapiro, Karl. *Poems of a Jew*. New York: Random House, 1958.

Collections

Chapman, Abraham, ed. *Jewish-American Literature*. New York: New American Library, 1974.

Malin, Irving and Irwin Stark, eds. *Breakthrough: A Treasury of Contemporary Jewish-American Literature*. Philadelphia: Jewish Publication Society, 1963.

Rothenberg, Jerome, with Harris Lenowitz and Charles Doria, eds. *A Big Jewish Book: Poems & Other Visions of the Jews from Tribal Times to Present*. Garden City, New York: Anchor Press, Doubleday, 1978.

Schwartz, Howard and Anthony Rudolf, eds. *Voices Within the Ark: The Modern Jewish Poets*. Yonkers, New York: Pushcart Press, 1980.

6

Yiddish Dreams in America

Joseph C. Landis

Collective dreams, unlike private ones, are a public affair and simpler to explore since their content tends to be more overt than latent. The wishes they reflect seem more obvious to the eye. It is not difficult to observe, however, that when wishes are held with such tenacity as to border on illusion, the corrections administered by reality are often bitter. Such certainly was the case with the European dream of America, which was from the outset imbued with illusion. Columbus's confusion of desire with reality became a pattern for many who followed him in thinking about America. But it took four centuries for that contrast between expectation and event to find its marvelously ironic embodiment in the Yiddish-speaking immigrant's wry exclamation, *"Kolombuses medine!"* (Columbus's country), a phrase that embraces simultaneously a whole range of feelings between admiration and despair. During the years that intervened between Columbus and the Jewish rediscovery of his *medine*, there were, of course, other visions of America and its people.[1] The New World had, on the one hand, been regarded as a wilderness where brutish savages roamed a Hobbesian wild— or at best, a land where pathetic creatures dwelt, untouched by the benefits of civilization or Christianity or both. At the other end of the spectrum was the romantic view of the "noble savage" (a phrase John Dryden originally intended for the primitive Europeans), or, in William Wordsworth's formulation, "that pure archetype of human greatness." Needless to say, the awareness of America invaded the consciousness of the Yiddish world too late for it to enter into that classic-romantic dispute. Before the nineteenth century, there was hardly a Jew in Eastern Europe who knew "that there was any such place as America."[2] By the time America became known to Eastern-European Jews through Khaykel Hurvits's immensely popular Yiddish adaptation (Berditchev, 1817) of J. H. Campe's *Die Entdeckung von Amerika* (The Discovery of America), the New World had outgrown earlier fictions and been clothed in newer visions. It had become the land of personal liberty and limitless freedom of opportunity. In the dreams of the oppressed of Europe, in the very folklore of Europe, it had become the golden land; to Eastern-European Jews, too, America had become *di goldene medine*: in Isaac Meyer Dick's (1814–1893) phrase, "a Utopia or better still a land of fable."[3]

Yiddish dreams of the new utopia grew in Eastern Europe in proportion as waking life became a nightmare. The political dislocations following the three partitions of Poland in the 1790's; the succeeding social and personal penalties imposed on Russian Jews as the Czarist empire attempted to consolidate itself into a modern state; the economic consequences of Russia's emergence from a quasi-feudal economy—all acted like the movement of great geologic plates on the Eastern-European Jewish world: *shtetl* walls began to crumble and its inhabitants sought escape. By a happy coincidence, there was *di goldene medine* (golden land).

Sholom Aleichem (Shalom Rabinowitz, 1859–1916), with his genius for sensing and expressing what lay nearest the heart of the ordinary Jew, gave simple expression to this Jewish dream in 1892 in one of his few poems, "*Shlof, mayn kind*" (Sleep, My Child), which was soon set to music and quickly became so popular that it was mistakenly included as a folk song in the first major collection of Yiddish folk songs, which appeared in 1901.[4]

> Sleep, my child, my consolation,
> Sleep and hushabye
>
> In America, your father
> Oh, my dearest son,
> You are still a little boy
> Sleep and hushabye
>
> America is, for everyone,
> A land of luck, they say,
> And for Jews—a Paradise,
> Something beyond price.
>
> There they eat, as daily fare,
> Khale, oh my son.
> There I'll cook you chicken soup,
> Sleep and hushabye.

At last we meet the American dream we all know, the Jewish version of the official myth of America, available to one and all, a land of *chaleh* and chicken soup even on weekdays, a paradise for Jews, and entirely free of cost except fare. Well, not entirely free. A bill would be sent later.

The story of the flight to the *goldene medine* is by this time, over a century after its beginning, a familiar one. The first large wave of immigration began, following the oppressive anti-Jewish laws of May 1881 and, as would be expected, included mainly those who had nothing to lose—the poorest, the un-skilled, the minimally educated—as well as those who had everything to lose—the young revolutionaries and idealists who had thrown themselves into Russian libertarian movements and were either wanted or about to be wanted by the Czarist police.

The first wave of immigrants that arrived in the New World met the full fury of American industrialization and its bitter extremes. It was the age of the robber barons, and of what Lincoln Steffens called the shame of the cities, the age of the rich and the age of exploitation of the poor. In response to these shocks, a Yiddish literature arose in the New World whose spokesmen were immigrant young men who shared the lives and sufferings of their fellow newcomers to a land with few Jews like themselves, where illusions were traded for bitter realities.

The roots of the new literature, despite its immigrant origin, were to a re-markable degree American. The sources, the character, often the very voice of the Eastern-European Yiddish literature, on the other hand, had been and con-tinued to be derived from the parables, tales, and traditions of the Bible, the Talmud and commentaries, from the parables of *Hasidic tsadikim* (righteous men), most notably Reb Nachman of Bratslav and the *Baal Shem Tov* (Master of the Good Name, founder of *Hasidism*, 1700–1760) himself, from the unbroken flow of a religious tradition absorbed from infancy in home and *kheyder* (religious school), a flood from the past which even the powerful impact of *Haskalah* (Enlightenment) writers and intellectuals on modern Yiddish literature could not diminish. It is symbolic that Mendele Mokher Sforim (Sholem Yankev Abra-movitch, 1835–1917), dubbed the "grandfather" of Yiddish literature by the great Yiddish writer Sholom Aleichem, should have spent nearly forty years of his life as director of a *Talmud Torah* in Odessa. Modern Yiddish literature, "officially" born in 1864 with the serial publication of Mendele's *Dos kleyne mentshele* (The Common Man), arose in the context of this millennial tradition, which had produced a stable way of life, one that provided a refuge and a solace, bounded from year's end to year's end, from birth to death by prescribed patterns of behavior and obligation, of joy and sorrow.[5]

Modern Yiddish literature was initially almost wholly a small-town literature. It grew out of the *shtetl*, and its major subject was the *shtetl*. It admired the *shtetl*; it satirized the *shtetl*; and it revolted against the *shtetl*, as it sought the broader horizons of the modern world. Fathered by the *Haskalah* that had spread eastward from central Europe, proclaiming the separation of faith and culture, the Eastern-European Jewish Enlightenment sought the total uplifting and mod-ernization of Jewish life, economic, social, political, cultural.

By contrast, the roots, the circumstances, and the shapers of the Yiddish literature that arose in America about a score of years after the "birth" in Eastern Europe were wildly different. The immigrants of the eighties and nineties were mainly not intellectuals speaking to or revolting from the *shtetl* world. They were, by and large, not steeped in traditional learning, and, having emigrated, in great proportion, as youngsters in their teens, they had not sunk tap roots into the archetypal way of life. Their American milieu was not a *shtetl* but the metropolis. They were oppressed, not by the intellectual stultification of quasi-medieval small-town life, but by the economic exploitation of a modern, burgeoning free-enterprise industrial, urban world. They were neither petty traders nor *shtetl* craftsmen; they were largely factory workers, proletarians.

It was in this urban setting, whose horizon was bounded by tenements, that Yiddish literature in America arose. Morris Winchevsky (Vinchevski [1856–1932]), sometimes called the "grandfather" of Yiddish literature in America, Joseph Bovshover (1873–1915), David Edelstadt (Edelshtadt [1866–1892]), Morris Rosenfeld (1862–1923), and dozens of less talented poets, mostly shop workers themselves, created a working-class literature that voiced the pathos and the indignation of their fellow "slaves of the machine."[6]

Many of these proletarian writers had little contact with the substantial Yiddish literature that was developing in Russia, especially during the eighties and nineties. While the young writers in Russia were paying homage to Grandfather Mendele Mokher Sforim, and appearing in the periodicals published by Sholom Aleichem, Y. L. Peretz (1852–1915), and others, and gravitating to Warsaw to consult with Peretz, who had increasingly become the ideological center of the new renaissance in Yiddish, Joseph Bovshover in America was writing poetry under the influence of Shelley, Emerson, Whitman, and Markham, about whom he also wrote essays. And Morris Winchevsky, who had sojourned in London before coming to New York, brought with him his admiration for Thomas Hood and William Morris. As Leon Kobrin (1872–1946), himself a contemporary writer noted: "Our Yiddish-American literature has its own history. It is not a continuation of the older Yiddish literature in Russia. (In fact, we who created American Yiddish literature had no knowledge at all of Yiddish literature in Russia at that time.)"[7]

Out of the American asphalt rose the cries of the poets. Filling their imagery with the clichés of radical verse in English, Winchevsky, Bovshover, and Edelstadt, revolutionary in their outlook, summoned the masses to arise, to revolt, to raise the red flag of freedom, to throw off their chains, to usher in the new dawn.

A prophet of revolution, Bovshover proclaimed that he would come

> like fiery lava,
> like a storm from the north,
>
> because freedom cannot forever be fettered by chains.[8]

In another personification, he thundered that he would loom like a lighthouse "till his sleeping brothers rise."[9]

And Edelstadt rallied the masses:

"Awake!"
How long will you suffer as slaves? How long will you toil to enrich those
who rob you of bread? How long will you bear the yoke of oppression?
Let the bells of freedom ring out and summon the oppressed to struggle.
And all will bloom
And love and feel
In that free and golden May.
Brothers, enough
Before tyrants to kneel,
Swear that you must be free![10]

If the poetry of these two decades was public, declamatory, hortatory—sometimes bombastic and sentimental—it was so because the poets were mainly
workers whose private woes coincided with the suffering of the multitudes and
whose poetry was the public voice rather than the private lyric. So overwhelming
was the initial shock that private feelings were molten into those of the mass,
and the qualities of the response were derived from its very immediacy. The
prose writers, many of them self-educated, produced fiction that was crude and
primitive, but popular. Their work was direct and immediate, as hortatory as a
demonstration placard. Like their audience, many of the writers were ordinary
workers, uneducated even in Jewish matters. When they strove for elegance,
they turned, not in the manner of their European confreres to Bible and Talmud
for references, metaphors, and telling phrases, but to Germanized forms which
have come to be known as "*daychmerish.*" But for the most part their writing
was simple and direct, their construction unsophisticated, their themes obvious,
and their strength in the realistic depiction of the everyday world and in their
romantic exhortations to change it.

More shocking, however, than the economic exploitation and the physical
degradation was the even greater affront to the self, the sense of dehumanization
that assaulted the immigrant in every aspect of his being. He was no stranger
to poverty and suffering; he was familiar with all degrees of hostility to Jews;
but he was thoroughly unprepared for a total indifference to his very humanity.
That spiritual assault struck at his sense of personal worth and dignity; it thrust
upon him values that made a mockery of those in which he had been reared,
and it created a generation chasm between "greenhorn" parents and native
children. Fresh from a *shtetl* culture that was stable, integral, supportive, whole,
and committed to mutual responsibility, the immigrant found himself plunged
into an urban, highly mobile, competitive, indifferent, fragmented world in which
he was merely an easily dispensable hand.

He had come here with unspoken suppositions of astonishing credulity. Implicit in the *shtetl* dream of the *goldene medine* that the immigrant brought with
him was the assumption, unformulated, unverbalized, yet very real, nonetheless,
that American freedom would somehow be joined to a Jewish community life;
that he would be coming to a world which, however different, would still be
familiarly Jewish. The assumption, though incredibly naive, was just as incre-

dibly real. The discovery that it was an illusion produced a shock of maximum intensity. Even when conditions improved as the decades rolled along, new waves of immigrants, fresh from the Jewish world of Eastern Europe, still felt the same affront inflicted by the indignities of a world whose life-style and values were so hostile to the world they had left. If the red banners and exhortations to revolt appear less frequently in the literature of the new century, the anger at Columbus's *medine* continues, nevertheless, in middle-brow as well as in popular culture, in such widely repeated lyrics as Shloyme Shmulevitch's (1868–1943) outraged "Ellis Island" which denounced that brutal tyrant of rejection, the "Isle of Tears,"[11] and Yankev Leyzerovitch's (1893–1967) lacrimonious "*Dem pedlers brivele*" (The Pedlar's Letter, an example of a whole epistolary genre that arose)[12] and his sardonic "*Di grine kuzine*" (The Green Cousin, perhaps the most famous of Yiddish popular songs) with its bitter last line, "The hell with Columbus's country."[13]

Alongside the revolutionary and denunciatory currents, but reflecting the same reality, flowed a third stream—longing for home. Mikhl Kaplan's (1882–1944) monologue "*Tsurik aheym*" (Going Home), in which Moyshe Yosel explains his decision to return to his native Vlednik, is a highly popular example of the type. As though picking up the green cousin's outcry, Moyshe Yosel erupts:

> May he burn in hell, that Columbus!
> It's a land for a fiend to find!
> A hell, on my word of honor,
> A flaming, blazing fire!

> I'm going home to Vlednik.
> I'll saunter into the square
> Earn a couple of pennies
> and not have to work hard at all.

> And live in contentment and honor
> And be respected by folks.[13]

Ah, Vlednik—where, as Robert Burns had put it in his day, "a man's a man for a' that"!

If the Yiddish dream of the *goldene medine* was in so many ways similar to the dreams of other immigrant groups, it was, however, in essential ways utterly unique. One aspect of this difference is apparent in the decision to return "home"—which, incidentally, many an immigrant acted upon and many more cherished to their dying days. For an Italian or a German or a Russian to return home was to return to his own land and his own people and to a friendly world no matter how hard the conditions there. The Jewish immigrant, however, had left a country that was not his own, surrounded by a sea of dangerously hostile people not his own, and subject to squires and governments not his own. That he even entertained the thought of returning is an index of the intensity of the spiritual affront he endured.

Alongside the realistic fiction and didactic poetry, an entertainment literature, much of it imitative of popular literature in English, began to appear, at first hawked in the streets in penny installments, then as a regular newspaper feature. Wildly escapist, it was, in Jacob Gordin's phrase, "a Noah's Ark of nonsense and junk."[14] The list which Alexander Harkavy compiled of sixty-five Yiddish novels published in America before 1898, included such titles as *Indian Prince*, *California Gold Miners*, *Heroes of the Night*, *The Black Hand*, *Between Love and Millions*, *A Daughter's Revenge*, *White Slavery*, along with translations of Jules Verne.[15] If the penny dreadfuls represent an escape from a difficult reality, they also suggest a measure of acceptance, of coming to terms with a new life and finding a place in it. And they also indicate that, however hard life was, the immigrant's economic level was higher than it had been "at home": here he was able to buy the installments as they appeared. And if such purveyors of these dime novels as Getsel Zelikowitch (1863–1926), Moyshe Seifert (1859–1922), David Moyshe Hermalin (1865–1921), and Johann Paley (1871–1907)—the most widely read—sinned against literature, they also served it well, for they prepared an audience for works of quality.[16] Once he became aware that the American reality was substantially different from the Yiddish dream of the *goldene medine*, the immigrant "greenie" Jew, now a little "*oysgegrint*" (ungreened), began to restructure and adapt some of that reality to his dream and his dream to the reality.

Unique among immigrants in his situation, the immigrant Jew was also unique—indeed, therefore unique—in his response to it, he began to shape a Jewish environment. Amazingly, within a mere decade—by the 1890's—the contours of an American-Jewish world began to emerge. The dream of the *goldene medine*, a shattered illusion to the newcomer, began to acquire a large measure of reality as his condition improved. As the century drew to a close and the immigrants found a place for themselves in the new land, Jewish life began to acquire stability and to re-create a surrogate *shtetl* world in the Jewish enclaves of the great cities. The immigrant who arrived at the turn of the century came to a Jewish world which had already developed a substantial measure of stability, a structure of institutions, a sense of community life, with its *landsmanshaftn*, its press, its theatre, its literature—in short, a culture and a linguistic base. As early as 1890, an editorial in the *Yidisher Herold* had proudly proclaimed: "Here in America, especially in New York, we now have the era of Yiddish."[17] To the immigrant fresh from the tyranny of Russia, New York seemed to be a city in which the thread of the Jewish past was not broken. The new arrival witnessed a vibrant Jewish way of life.

By the turn of the century many of the sweatshop poets of the eighties and nineties, those socially committed spokesmen for the people, had either ceased writing poetry or had died. Even Morris Rosenfeld had already done his best work and seemed to be trying to recapture his earlier passion.

With the new century, other voices—Yehoash (Solomon Bloomgarden [1872–1924]), A. Liessen (Liesin [1872–1938], born Valt), Avrom Reisen (Reyzin [1876–1953])—were beginning to be heard, and Jacob Gordin (1853–1909), having single-handedly created what was widely heralded as the golden age of a Yiddish theatre in America (which was only a scant two decades old), now reigned as the acknowledged reformer of the Yiddish stage. Indeed, the stage had become normalized. Pop-art "*shund*" (vulgar) for the groundlings shared the stage with serious drama.

When a new wave of Jewish immigrants began to inundate the American shore after the shattering Kishinev pogrom in 1903 and the failure of the Russian Duma in 1905, a busy, thriving *Jewish* world was already in existence on the old East Side of New York. The new wave of immigrants was also different in kind. It began to bring scores, hundreds, thousands of young men and women, products of a developing modern secular Yiddish culture in Eastern Europe, who were familiar with the substantial Yiddish literature that had developed there during the quarter-century that had elapsed since the first wave crashed onto the American shore and who had heard a different drummer—Yitskhok Leybush Peretz, the "father" of modern Yiddish literature. Many dreamed of careers as Yiddish writers. Some had even been to Tsegliana #1 in Warsaw, where Peretz (later dubbed somewhat grandiloquently the Prince of the Ghetto, by Maurice Samuel) lived and presided over a literary Yiddish salon on Saturday afternoons and where that doyen of modern Yiddish literature had read their work and encouraged them. Avrom Reisen recalled the exaltation of a literary afternoon at Peretz's:

> When days are gray, my mind returns
> To Peretz-house, to hours I loved,
> When young folks used to gather there,
> Their people's finest flower.
>
> The door bell rang, the guests arrived,
> And soon they sang their joyous songs,
> Like Hassidim at their Rebbe's house,
> "Beloved Rebbe, live and teach us."
>
> There it was—a new "Hassidish,"
> Wordly free and worldly Yiddish.[18]

(*Hassidish* was the title of one of Peretz's best-known collections of stories, depicting *Hasidic* life and morality.)

The new mood of the time was reflected in a *new* dream of the *goldene medine*. I. J. Schwartz (1885–1971), who in later years tried to shape some of that American-Jewish experience into a Yiddish verse epic called *Kentucky*,[19] recalled those ecstatic times half a century after the fact in a conversation with fellow poet and critic Abraham Tabachnik (1901–1970):

I came to America in 1906. It was the time of the great mass immigration. There was an endless stream of young people, among them scores of talented people. . . . We came here during a time of great hopes. Do you recall that time at the beginning of the century? *I have several times tried to depict that great, grandiose time, when an entire people moved to a new land, a new environment, under a free sky. . . . We were dazzled, we were winged* [italics mine].[20]

Not since Wordsworth remembered his youth in revolutionary France has a time been recalled with such exhilaration.

In this new and contoured world of the early twentieth century, there arose a clamor of new voices, a group of young writers who expressed the fresh mood of the American Jewish community. The spirit of the new century was heard in the literary revolt of the *Yunge*, the varied band of young rebels who had little in common except their rebellion against the public and social poetry and fiction of the nineteenth century. Prominent among them were Mani Leyb (Leib [1883–1953], born Brahinsky), Zishe Landau (1889–1937), Reuben Eisland (Ayzland [1884–1955]), Halper Leivick (Leyvik [1888–1962]), Joseph Opatoshu (1886–1954), David Ignatoff (1885–1954), and Berl Lapin (1889–1952). Though these young men brought with them, as some of their predecessors had done, the influence of European literature, and though, unlike their predecessors, they were well-read in Yiddish literature and schooled in Jewish learning, it was soon America that spoke through them in rich and supple Yiddish, which they liberated from "*daychmerisms.*" Beyond any doubt, for them America was home; none dreamed of returning to Europe. They had brushed the Eastern-European dust from themselves forever and looked—or wished to look—with unqualified love upon their new home.

Perhaps the most outspoken and extreme of these rebels was Zishe Landau, an arch-individualist who dismissed the nineteenth-century American Yiddish poets as a mere literary branch of the labor movement and who asserted the primary responsibility of the poet to express himself, rejecting the notion that the poet had any responsibility to be a spokesman for the mass. Is it only the times that are heard in Landau's declaration of individuality? Or are there not echoes of Emerson and Whitman and the great American dream of the unfettered self, of Emerson's dismissal of the "foolish hobgoblin of little minds," in Landau's remark to a contemporary critic who chided him for his inconsistency and self-contradiction: "I am aware of the contradictions. Who cares about your logic? Contradiction is the logic of my soul, my need, my custom. . . . We who have any kind of individuality, we, the brave lads and bold adventurers, we assert our right to step on every logic and culture, and we treat all standpoints, ideas, opinions, and convictions—foreign or native—like children's toys."[21]

If Landau's language was extreme, his spirit was, nevertheless, shared by his fellow rebels. Their revolt was not merely the product of a generation gap, a repudiation of predecessors by young Turks; nor was it merely a literary revolt, for theirs was a movement without any real manifesto. The revolt of the *Yunge*, in contrast to the revolution sought by their proletarian predecessors, was essentially an affirmation of America, of a new life, a new home, a new freedom, a determination to be American.[22] Years later, Melech Epstein (1889–1979), journalist, biographer, labor activist, recalled it all much more simply: "To me as to an overwhelming majority of my fellow Jews, America was home."[23]

It is hardly surprising that these young people, having forever given up any hopes for Jewish life in Russia, should come to the new world dazzled by the American dream of the sweet land of liberty and opportunity. What is breathtaking is the new *Yiddish* dream they brought with them, the dream of creating in America a literature in Yiddish—even more—of living in a culturally creative Jewish community whose literature would be Yiddish! They were not thinking of a halfway house on the road to assimilation, nor were they expecting to be a cultural colony of the old country, nourished by its spiritual exports. They were thinking of an American segment of a unique world people, united by a Yiddish language and by a cultural tradition, a culture and a language that would be joined in a great interchange of Yiddish culture and creativity. This dream was in essence Peretz's view of the direction Jewish life should take in the modern secular world. It was the view that won a major victory at the historic language conference which took place in Czernowitz, Rumania, in 1908. In reality that conference, despite its lively debates, achieved nothing beyond a statement, but that statement was enough to fire imaginations for nearly half a century.

The dispute between Yiddish and Hebrew that occupied so much time at the conference and that rocked Jewish life on the threshold of the twentieth century was in one way or another a continuation of a nearly two-hundred-year-old quarrel between adherents of the two languages. That historic and in many ways destructive conflict was, however, not merely a linguistic quarrel; it was one of the battlefields of two contending views of the nature of Jewish identity, of Jewish continuity. It was at Czernowitz that a small assemblage of mainly young people of magnificent *khutzpa*, representing only themselves, leaving no organization to realize their adopted resolutions, decided that Yiddish was eminently deserving of being recognized and proclaimed as *a*—not *the*, as some participants had urged—language of the Jewish people. This proclamation by a group of young intellectuals, who were resolved formally to elevate Yiddish from *jhargonhood* to the status of a language, thereafter became a rallying cry of Yiddish culturists and an expression of their spirit.

If 1897 was a watershed year in modern Jewish history, because it witnessed the founding of two polar organizations—the Jewish socialist Bund in Poland and the Zionist Congress in Basle, Switzerland—whose conflicting ideologies dominated Jewish intellectual life over the four ensuing decades, 1908 is, in a subtler sense, also a year to remember for the two polarized forces that came to expression. It was not only the year of the Czernowitz conference; it was also the year when Israel Zangwill's play, *The Melting-Pot*, opened to very few cheers except those of President Theodore Roosevelt. But presidential approval gave a name to a concept of American unity. The process, the desideratum of our national life, enshrined on our very coinage, *e pluribus unum*, now had a popular designation for its cultural counterpart. We were reminded: America was not only the sweet land of liberty; it was also the land where our fathers died—even if they had to do so retroactively.

In the very teeth of this America, the young men and women of the second great wave of Jewish immigration proclaimed their Peretz-inspired dream of creating a modern Yiddish literature, a modern Yiddish culture. Literary and cultural critics and historians in English and in Yiddish record the path and quality of Yiddish literature and culture in America as though the entire enterprise were sane. With our matter-of-fact acceptance of its existence, we fail to perceive its madness, marvelous though that madness is. We never ask the question that should have been obvious—why did they persist in writing in Yiddish rather than in English as other immigrant groups soon did? We accept without the slightest expression of surprise the fact that thousands upon thousands of young intellectuals came to this country to live in a world where they chose to remain foreign: to read a foreign press, to teach in foreign schools, to create a foreign literature, and, above all, to commit their lives to the perpetuation here of this foreign culture, without the slightest suspicion that a dream of cultural autonomy born in the multi-national states of the two great European empires might not thrive in a new WASP-spawned world committed to a single nationality within the borders of the state. Of all the Yiddish dreams, this may well have been the noblest, the grandest, and surely the maddest.

The *Yunge*, like the overwhelming majority of those who were a part of the great Yiddish modernist movement, were hardly aware of the magnitude—or magnificent folly—of their enterprise. Of course it was possible in America! Even a half century later, Joseph Opatoshu, himself one of that varied crowd of young writers, in trying to explain the appearance of Young America, still regarded it as a purely literary revolt, a rejection of tradition that found a later parallel in American literature. "The answer was of course that these youthful writers considered this revolt the only way to liberate Yiddish literature from traditional sentimentality."[24] It still did not occur to him to wonder aloud about the very viability of the Peretz dream and of a Yiddish literature in America! He still saw only the literary revolt, American Yiddish writers—the *Yunge* and the later *Inzikhistn* (Introspectivists) alike—"united in their protest against the mediocrity and irresponsibility existing among their fellow Jews."[25] A decade after Opatoshu's appraisal, Abraham Tabachnik observed: "The *Yunge* were not so much exponents of a new ideology as of a new psychology. Something took place in Jewish life at that time, something matured socially and culturally, which made the rise of poets like the *Yunge* inevitable. They felt differently, saw differently, heard differently."[26] Surely, underlying what they felt and saw and heard was the unuttered, unformulated—because so obvious to them— conviction that in the freedom of America the Peretz notion of Yiddish cultural autonomy was beyond question: the modern era in Jewish peoplehood was here.

In spirit, they were not foreigners. They were natives, and they asserted their kinship. To H. Royzenblatt (1878–1956) in "Amerike," America was "our soil," where the spirit of "Jefferson, Lincoln, John Brown and Paine had wandered." Whitman and Poe and Emerson had written "On our land and under our sky."

> And you and I? Children of another world—
> On the stretches of this lovely land
> We built our new abode
> We wandered long and came here late, so late,
> But—free and broad the shore still stretches,
> And tomorrow, tomorrow new cities will be built.
> Translucent skies will hang forever over us
> And endless, endless is the line of crystal days.[27]

The same spirit of love, of rejoicing in a land where the Yiddish dream is possible, is to be found in Aaron Glantz-Leyeles's (Glantz; Glanz [1889–1966]) paean "To Thee, America": "I love the dream of the truth that's called America."

> I'm one with the audacious sky-line of Manhattan,
> The mighty rivers, canyons, prairies, woods primordial,
> I'm one with the roaming autos that seem the earth to flatten,
> I'm one with all the things that ring and bravely call: America!
>
> I hail the youthful fervor, the breath of dauntless spaces,
> The free and hopeful voices, dialects and speeches manifold,
> The blend harmonious of peoples, tribes and races—
> From sunny south to northern snows, what strength
>   what pride, behold—America![28]

The eyes of the new generation of dreamers and writers looked beyond the ghettos of the great cities to the broad horizons of the new land. David Ignatoff began to write fiction about the West. So did Isaac Raboy (1882–1944): " . . . who is not the *galut* Jew of the great cities. In him runs the blood of the old-time healthy Jews who lived close to nature . . . who perceived that there is too much of the gray and the workaday in the life of the great cities and went off to the open freedom of broad fields to sing of the beauty of the prairies."[29]

A thrill of exhilaration and pride ran through a group of them as they settled into what was then a new section of New York in the process of being built up:

. . . the most beautiful section of the Bronx—the achievement of energetic and enterprising Jews. In this neighborhood, while it was still quite rural, young Jewish writers conceived their songs, their stories, their novels. And if they felt gratified to cleave to the soil, with its flowers and living creatures, they were even more pleased to associate with the dynamic men who were building homes, streets, cities. This joy in nature and this dynamism enlivened their writings.[30]

How little the Old World understood of these new developments, of the new home in the New World, can be seen from the tone of the greeting sent by Mendele Mokher Sforim to the New York *Yidishes Tageblat* for its March 20, 1910, anniversary issue. It reads in part:

How are you Sisters, how are you Brothers, in the new land whither you have wandered far from home? As a leaf is in autumn, in the storm, in the cold, so have you been cast away far from your old home, having left there forever all that is so dear to your hearts. . . . Woe unto the fallen leaf that is driven and buffeted by the wind. . . .
Yes, my Dear Ones, you have been storm-tossed and I have remained here. But what sort of remaining has this been? . . . Broken-hearted, I have yearned, and I have worried endlessly about my poor forsaken sisters and brothers. . . .

The first generation of American Yiddish writers had been untouched by the influence of Mendele in Odessa or of Sholom Aleichem in Kiev or of Peretz in Warsaw, which were becoming major centers of literary activity. The second generation refused to follow their patterns. "There is a rhythm in the United States that is alien to Europe,"[31] remarked Opatoshu, and American Yiddish writers were responding to that rhythm in their poetry, in their experimentation, in their new forms and their new subject matter. Whitman's catalogues are puny in comparison to the geographical atlas of America that could be compiled from the works of American Yiddish writers. They turned to America with love and with hope; and they created verse and prose as patriotic as any that has ever been written in this country. The Peretz dream was real.

Meanwhile, literary revolt followed upon literary revolt. The concentration on self of the *Yunge* was, a decade or so later, denounced by the expressionist *Inzikhistn*. Urban and intellectual, they emphasized the importance of ideas and rejected the concentration on self and mood. And they proclaimed their derivation from the American Imagists. But for all their literary declarations, "The fathers of the Inzikhistn—Leyeles, Glatstein, Minkoff—would have felt just as much at home among the members of Young America (i.e., the *Yunge*), and vice versa."[32] They shared a common dream of a culturally creative Yiddish world on American soil, a dream that seemed no dream at all. And for two decades and more, much more, it glowed and summoned almost without rebuke from reality.

In the years after World War I, however, doubts began to surface. A large uneasiness about the prospects for Yiddish and Yiddish culture, about the continuation of the Yiddish renaissance in America, began to darken the mood of Yiddish culturists here. If the first two decades of the century seemed to thrill with the spirit of optimism, the twenties began to give freer expression to underlying, persistent doubts.[33] As the twenties drew to a close, Shmuel Niger (Shmuel Charney, Samuel Niger [1883–1955]), addressing a group of student

activists, was urging that their "work among students is the crown and justification of our cultural activity in this country. Your duty is the hardest and the
finest activity of all duties; your duty is to build a bridge to the future, and I
hope that you will be brave, believing, and energetic builders."[34] Other writers
and critics addressing the same group reiterated the hope that its members would
be able to attract the estranged young Jewish men and women back to Yiddish
and Yiddish culture.[35] But in all their words of encouragement there is heard
more anxiety than hope.

If the broad river of American Yiddish literature during the first three decades—
indeed, during the first three quarters—of the twentieth century reflects the
naturalization of Jewish life in America, it also reveals an ambivalence towards
the American home, sharp doubts about the prospects for the dream of a Yiddish
cultural world. The affirmation of America, the sense of belonging here runs
deep and strong after the *Yunge* asserted themselves. The American landscape
is painted with love and wonder. The great cities, the overpowering natural
wonders, the exhilarating sense of freedom strike sparks in the Yiddish imagination. But along with the acceptance there is a sense of disquiet, of not being
wholly at ease in Zion, a disaffection that goes beyond that alienation which is
indigenous to literary creativity. It goes beyond the protests against the oppression
of blacks; beyond the outcries on behalf of Sacco and Vanzetti; beyond the
proletarian sympathies in such plays as Leivick's *Shmates* (Rags), *Shop*, or *Keytn*
(Chains); beyond the sharp criticism of American values in Lamed Shapiro's
(1878–1948) short stories and the gentle satire in Ossip Dymov's (1878–1959)
Bronx Express. It is evident in these works, as it is also evident in the deep
concern about intermarriage and assimilation in such novels as David Pinski's
(1872–1959) *Arnold Levenberg* and *The Generations of Noah Edon* and in Sholem Asch's *East River*. This sense of uneasiness in popular culture re-creates
the old East Side as a *shtetl* surrogate and finds expression in theatre songs such
as one Ludwig Satz made popular, singing "Oh, my! Life is sweet / I'm back
again on Attorney Street," as though it were a reprise of "I'm going home to
Vlednik."

There is palpably a heightened awareness of the price America continually
demanded: surrender of ethnic and moral identity—the bill tendered by the land
of the free for the freedom it allows. The sanguine expectation of the development
of a Jewish folk life in America, of the growth of a Jewish cultural world here
did not long survive the act of immigration. Worries grew increasingly grave
about the fate of Jews as a cultural entity, about the sense of Jewish commitment—an uneasiness about Jewish destiny that is the underlying concern of the
overwhelming majority of Yiddish writers and that constitutes the mainstream
of Yiddish writing This is the broad river upon which literary manifestos and
revolts are but paper boats; and it is this concern that finds repeated and troubled
expression. It is central to the historical novels of Joseph Opatoshu and to the
triple-decker novels of I. J. Singer (1893–1944) and Sholem Asch (1880–1957).
Unlike their nineteenth-century European counterparts, these novelists do not

hold up for critical examination the way we live now nor do they strive to depict a Jewish society. They are troubled by such questions as how did Jews get here and what lies in store; they are concerned with movement, not stability; history, not social mobility. Once the timeless traditional world of the *shtetl* is shattered, time and place, modernity and geography are thrust upon the Jewish experience and the Jewish consciousness. And from American soil, past and present began to look different; the future—disturbing.

And therefore the note of *shtetl*-longing first struck earlier in the century is heard again with renewed strength, and during the 1920's a rose-colored haze again begins to envelop the *shtetl* world that was left behind. Its traditions, its holiday warmth, its people (recalled as moral and pious despite their poverty), its wholeness, its meaningful existence—all these contrast with the well-known ills of an urban, indifferent, competitive, alienating world. It is this American platform that provides Peretz Hirschbein (1880–1948) with the perspective for his idyllic portraits of Jewish farmers in *Green Fields* (1916) and accounts for the very great popularity of the play; in this perspective is seen the Old World in so much of the poetry of Joseph Rolnik (1879–1955), Reuben Eisland, and Mani Leib, of the later fiction of Israel Metzker (1901–1984), and of untold volumes of memoirs. It is this perspective that is evident in scores of popular musicals that played in the Yiddish theatres along New York's Second Avenue, the Yiddish Broadway. *"Mayn shtetele belz"* became the most popular of the *shtetl* songs of nostalgia; it was, however, only one of dozens that were sung about the long-lost hometowns and peaceful fields and mighty woods of Rumania, Galicia, Poland, or Russia. But the longing for an integral Jewish world, whether Vlednik or Belz, was unsubdued in belles lettres as well as in popular literature, a longing that was, in its own terms, an expression of the growing fear of the failure of the Peretz dream, the great dream of a flourishing Yiddish cultural community.

Those on the political left who shared the Peretz dream and looked for Yiddish redemption as part of a proletarian restructuring of the world perhaps remained sanguine longer than most and blamed the middle-class orientation and the acceptance of bourgeois values by Yiddish writers for the limitations of Yiddish literature and culture. In 1945, Yitskhok Alkhonen Rontch (Rontsh [1899–1985]), a left-of-center literary critic, surveying the development of the Yiddish novel in America, commented that the great Yiddish novel of the American Jewish experience had not yet been written. His remarks grew out of a time when critics still awaited "the great American novel" and out of a conviction then current in Rontch's circles that great American Yiddish fiction should grow out of those democratic traditions and common-man sympathies that Granville Hicks had earlier traced in the American novel (*The Great Tradition*, 1935). With keen disappointment Rontch observed that "The Yiddish novel in America has yet to be born."[36] The Yiddish novel of American Jewish life had up to that time depicted the negligible number of Jews who had made it and had ignored the huge majority who were workers. The cause of this neglect he ascribed largely to Abraham Cahan (1860–1951), whose *The Rise of David Levinsky* (1917), despite its rich portraits of ordinary Jews, concentrates on Levinsky the capitalist. This "Ab. Cahanism" Rontch found embodied in the novels of Sholem Asch (*Chaim Lederer's Return*, 1927), David Pinski (*Arnold Levenberg*, 1928; *The Generations of Noah Edon*, 1931),as well as in those of a number of lesser lights whose heroes were all successful entrepreneurs. The heroes of the younger novelists, he noted with puzzlement, are all defeated. They are always running away. They return to Jewish nationalism and tradition. And the novelists themselves are pessimists.

It did not then strike Rontch that perhaps *Levinsky is* the great American Yiddish novel, despite the irony of its having been written by a Yiddish writer in English; that perhaps the failure of a success whose price is loss of cultural identity *is* the essential theme of the American-Jewish experience; that perhaps the failure of spirit and the surrender of values are parallel expressions of the failure of the great Yiddish dream of a thriving world of Yiddish culture; and that perhaps this realization underlies the pessimism he deplored among the younger novelists.

If a romantic faith in the viability of the Yiddish dream in America with or without social revolution remained an occasional mood or a current of varying strength, the rising tide of Nazism during the thirties and the later revelations about the Holocaust gave a powerful impetus to the current of pessimism. The anxieties of the twenties were succeeded by the shattering impact of the Hitler decade. If Rontch in 1945 was still looking for a renewed flowering of the great Yiddish dream, Yankev Glatshteyn (Jacob Glatstein [1896–1971]) along with most of his literary colleagues was pouring his wrath and contempt upon the false promises of the West that had fostered a dazzling dream of modern culture, which he and his comrades had lovingly adopted and shaped to their own needs and that was now betraying that dream with a horror whose dimensions were more terrible than anyone yet suspected. As early as 1938 he had hurled back into the teeth of the world its phony modernity, its blithely hawked illusion of civilization and culture. "Good night, wide world," he crooned, as though opening a lullaby, and then thundered, "Big, stinking world," as he proclaimed his repudiation of the unclean culture of the West and his return to the dusty humanity of the traditional Jewish world.[37]

And when the full panorama of hell was at last revealed, the very security of the American refuge became a source of unendurable guilt and anguished impotence. If, along with H. Leivick, they could lament, *"Ikh bin in treblinka nit geven"* (I was not in Treblinka), American Yiddish writers could nonetheless never escape it. The horror of those years brought to bitter fulfillment the powers of Leivick, Glatshteyn, and others who in their youth had been proud rebels and dreamers; and it also ended the blind love affair with America and American optimism.

Since the Holocaust, America has appeared far less frequently as either subject or hope in American Yiddish writing. The predominant subject is the destroyed world of the *shtetl*, that Jewish world which had given birth to those giddying hopes of a greater Yiddish world. Since the Holocaust, the great Yiddish dream, the Peretz dream, has been much subdued. Post–World War II poetry and prose are more concerned with the recent past than with the present. Fiction is more likely to deal with the Old World than with the New. The destruction of that world created a mood of mourning and farewell, the desire to erect a monument to its memory.

This elegiac literature mourns not only the annihilation of the old home; it mourns even more the waning of the great Yiddish dream and the enormousness of that blow. It is especially strong in poetry, whether in such works as Glatshteyn's *Shtralndike yidn* (Radiant Jews) or, more recently, in Eliezer Greenberg's (1896–1977) *Gedenkshaft* (Memorabilia), in which he recalls with astonishment and pain: "How great were the riches we once possessed / How great were the riches we have lost!" and reminds us of Avrom Reisen's lines: "There was so little then— / Why is there so much left?"

This elegiac note is struck again and again, whether in the verse of Chaim Grade (1910–1982) or Meyer Shticker (1905–1983) or of a dozen other poets of stature.

During the sweatshop years, writing about the *shtetl* was a longing for a still living world. During the teens, twenties, and after, the longing became a nostalgia which no one seriously considered bringing to fulfillment. After Auschwitz, nothing remained but to elegize a world whose loss forever altered the course of Jewish history and Yiddish culture and to recall a vanished Motherland (in more ways than one), a lost Atlantis which, with all its flaws and failings, was an admirable world whose traditions endowed life with human decency and dignity and warmth. This mood is detectable not only in Yiddish writing, though it is strongest there. Its echoes are detectable in the American-Jewish community at large and occasionally in American-Jewish fiction in English. That world is still continually evoked by Isaac Bashevis Singer (1904–   ), who is caught in a web of ambivalence, caught between his longing for the lost God-fearing world and its God whom he could not love yet could not reject, and his modernity as a Yiddish writer who could not wholly share the secular Peretz dream of a modern Yiddish culture and yet could not wholly reject it for that longed for pious world, which had no place for Yiddish writers.

The achievement of Yiddish literature in America has been towering, especially in poetry and fiction, and its dreams have shared the glories of Quixote. While dreaming its Jewish version of the American dream of freedom, it has been inescapably American. Every Yiddish writer who came here absorbed something of the spirit of America and underwent the experience of America: the hope of America, the pain of America, and ultimately, the ambivalence of America.

Eras rarely end abruptly. They blend into new eras and fructify them. While the era of the Eastern-European-born Yiddish writer is drawing to a close, a new involvement with Yiddish is evident in the American-Jewish community and among Jewish students on the American campus.

Among Yiddish writers themselves the moods range from I. B. Singer's oft-asserted optimism to deepest, bitter pessimism. The center holds in shades of gray. In "With You," A. Luria turns his back on Royzenblatt's delight with "our land," and as though in counterpoint to Mendele's pitying letter of 1910, addresses his fellow poets, living and dead:

> All of us,
> Those
> Whom time
> Banished here to an alien shore,
> To an alien table,
> To an alien door—
> To you my greeting,
> To you my tear.
> We are one,
> Of the same clay,
> Flesh of flesh and bone of bone.
>
> Like you I bear
> The alien taint:
> An alien sky weighs on my head,
> An alien tree rocks me to sleep.
> An alien star, through the wind,
> Into my window blinks blind.
>
> And one-alone, I am sustained—
> We're equal partners in our pain. . . . [38]

On the other hand, Kadye Molodowsky (1894–1975) refuses to yield though disaster impends:

> Perhaps I am my generation's last.
> That's no concern of mine.
> I do not prepare the seeds of time.
> My day, my only day was given me on loan.
> When it will be recalled cannot be known.
>
> Light your light and be its keeper.
>
> And if your light is burning, you must bear.
> The fire's brightness and the fire's wounds.
>
> And it may be there is no final generation.
> It's no concern of yours.
> Light your light and be its keeper. [39]

And again:

> And what will be—
> If the flyers return
> And say that no sky exists?
> Then where should I look,
> If not higher, above?
>
> How shall I stand the grayness of rain?
> The dusts of stoney streets?
> Where will I find a haven from wrongs?
> And who will help me to write these songs?
> If nothing at all is up there?
>
> But I won't believe what the flyers say,
> I won't believe what they say . . .
>
> For I have seen an angel,
> Not once, but many a time.
> And he has rescued me
> From threatening woes.
>
> And I won't trust the flyers,
> I won't trust them.
>
> And what will be
> If the flyers return
> And deny that there is a heaven?
> The home of God's righteous?
> And how will I manage
> To cross paper bridges
> If not with God's righteous?
>
> But I will not heed the flyers,
> I will not heed them.
>
> For I have seen God's righteous,
> Not once but many a time.
>
> So I won't even look at the flyers,
> Neither notice nor look at the flyers,
> Only those can reach up to heaven
> Who weave the heavenly blue,
> And have climbed up miracles like steps
> And know eternity's ways.[40]

In a similar vein of stoic acceptance is Eliezer Greenberg's

"In Days of Deepest Grief"

In days of deepest hopelessness and grief
When no darkness could be darker,
Suddenly a voice from deep within begins to sing aloud
With mercy most consoling, in purest grace and light.

The voice begins caressing me and scolding, angry, sharp
What did you think it meant to be a poet
Among a folk oppressed?
Picking words of honey, dipped in foaming wine,
Amid melodious voices and the twanging of a harp?

That's not what fate decreed.
The fate of song is fate of folk.
God let you be a poet, writing Yiddish verses.
What reason then for wonder or for curses?
Your poem must be faithful to that need
And share the fate of language and of folk.[41]

In the same spirit, Moyshe Shifris, grim but doggedly persistent, speaks for all the Yiddish writers who are determined still to beat their luminous wings—even in the void, hopefully not in vain—as he defends the contemporary Yiddish writer's last redoubt, his indifference to destiny and thereby his triumph over it:

... And even if
The last Yiddish reader
Should disappear
And no one ever ask
For a Yiddish book—
I will not cease
My Yiddish song to sing.[42]

NOTES

1. This chapter is not intended as a survey of Yiddish literature in America. It is an account of the fate of some Yiddish hopes—economic and cultural—as reflected in American Yiddish literature. Unless otherwise indicated, all translations are by the author. Biographical dates are given if information is available.

2. Shmuel Niger, "America in the Works of Isaac Meyer Dick," p. 63.

3. Ibid., p. 64.

4. See Shoel Ginzburg and Perets Marek, *Yidishe folkslider in rusland*, Petersburg, 1901.

5. See *Kol ha' mevaser* (Voice of the Messenger). 2. No 45 (November 12, 1864); No. 6 (February 4, 1865).

6. See M. Bassin's collection *Yidishe poezie oyf amerikaner motivn* and the much larger anthology *Amerike in yidishn vort* by Nachman Mayzel (Meisel).

7. Leon Kobrin, *Fun daychmerish tzu yiddish in amerike*, p. 28. In English, see *Yiddish*. 2. (Winter-Spring 1976), p. 47.

8. J. Bovshover, *Gazamlte shriftn* (New York: Hebrew Publishing Company, 1923), p. 34.

9. Ibid., p. 104.

10. Translated by the author from David Edelstadt; can also be found in *Songs of the American Jewish Experience*, compiled and arranged by Neil Levin, p. 95.

11. Ibid., pp. 58–59.

12. Ibid., pp. 80–81, 92–93. Leyzerovitch's pen name was Yankele Brisker.

13. Mikhl Kaplan, *Geto klangen*, p. 19.

14. Elias Schulman, *Geshikhte fun der yiddisher literatur in amerike, 1870–1900*, p. 89. Schulman's book is a guide to the literature of this period, as is N. B. Minkoff's *Pionern fun der yidisher poezye in amerike* (New York, 1956).

15. Ibid., pp. 89–90.

16. Ibid., pp. 62–90.

17. Shlomo Noble, "The Image of the American Jew in Hebrew and Yiddish Literature in America, 1870–1900," p. 96. See also Hutchins Hapgood, *The Spirit of the Ghetto*, rev. ed. (New York: Funk and Wagnalls, 1909).

18. *"Varshe."* For full text and English rendering, see the *Forward*. (July 11, 1986), p. 19.

19. For a translation by Gertrude Dubrovsky of chapter 1 of *Kentucky*, see *Yiddish*. 2. (Winter, Spring 1976), pp. 93–107, and for an interview with Schwartz regarding the translation, see Gertrude Dubrovsky, "Between a Yiddish Poet and His Translator," Ibid., p. 67–92.

20. I. J. Schwartz, "About Myself and My Generation" (an interview with A. Tabachnik, in Yiddish), p. 35.

21. Noyekh Shteynberg, *Yung amerike*, pp. 44–45.

22. See especially Joseph Opatoshu, himself one of the young rebels, relating the revolt of the *Yunge* to a parallel development in American literature in "Fifty Years of Yiddish Literature in the United States," pp. 72–73.

23. Melech Epstein, "Pages from My Stormy Life—an Auto-biographical Sketch," *American Jewish Archives*, p. 137.

24. Opatoshu, op. cit., p. 78.

25. Ibid., p. 79.

26. Abraham Tabachnik, *Dikhter un dikhtung*, p. 162.

27. Mayzel, op. cit., p. 236.

28. In a musical setting by Lazar Weiner, "To thee, America" became "a Cantata for Solo, Mixed Chorus and Piano (or orchestra)." The English version is by Glantz-Leyeles himself.

29. Shteynberg, op. cit., p. 83.

30. Opatoshu, op. cit., p. 79.

31. Ibid., p. 80.

32. Ibid., p. 79; See also Jacob Glatstein, "Thinking Back," pp. 33–36.

33. Shmuel Niger, one of the most prolific and generally regarded as the greatest of Yiddish literary critics, dealt with this problem in a number of his essays.

34. Elias Schulman, *"A kultur tkufe"* (A Cultural Period), p. 102.

35. Ibid.

36. I. A. Rontch, *Amerike in der yidisher literatur*, p. 7.

37. For a full translation by Etta Blum, see her *Jacob Glatstein: Poems* (Tel Aviv: I. L. Peretz Publishing House, 1970), pp. 39–40.
38. A. Luria, *"Mit aykh"* (With You), *Yidishe kultur*, pp. 44–45.
39. Kadye Molodowsky, *"Tsind on dayn likht"* (Light Your Light), *Likht fun dornboym* (Light of the Burning Bush), pp. 143–144.
40. "Un vos vet zayn" (And What If), ibid., pp. 97–98.
41. Eliezer Greenberg, *"In teg fun tifn tsar"* (In Days of Deepest Grief), p. 64.
42. Moyshe Shifris, *"Un ven afile"* (And even if), p. 8.

BIBLIOGRAPHY

Bassin, M. *Yidishe poezie oyf amerikaner motivn* (Yiddish Poetry on American Themes). New York: Alveltlekher yidisher kultu kongress, 1953.

Blum, Etta. *Jacob Glatstein: Poems*. Tel Aviv: I. L. Peretz Publishing House, 1970.

Bovshover, J. *Gazamlte schriftn* (Collected Writings). New York: Hebrew Publishing Company, 1923.

Dubrovsky, Gertrude. "Between a Yiddish Poet and His Translator." *Yiddish*. 2. (Winter, Spring 1976), pp. 67–92.

———, trans. *Kentucky*, Chapter I. *Yiddish*. 2. (Winter, Spring 1976), pp. 93–107.

Epstein, Melech. "Pages from My Stormy Life—an Auto-biographical Sketch." *American Jewish Archives*. 14. (November 1962), p. 137.

Ginzburg, Shoel, and Perets Marek. *Yidishe folkslider in rusland* (Yiddish Folk-Songs in Russia). Petersburg: n.p., 1901.

Glantz-Leyeles, Aaron. *To Thee, America*. New York: Transcontinental Music Corporation, 1942.

Glatstein, Jacob. "Thinking Back." *Yiddish*. 3. (Spring, 1978), pp. 33–36.

Greenberg, Eliezer. *"In teg fun tifn tsar."* *Gedenkshaft*. New York: Lavdi, 1974, p. 64. ("In Days of Deepest Grief," *Memorabilia*).

Hapgood, Hutchins. *The Spirit of the Ghetto*, rev. ed. New York: Funk and Wagnalls, 1909.

Kaplan, Mikhl. *"Tsurik aheym."* *Geto klangen* (Ghetto Sounds). New York: Internatsionale bibliotek farlag, n.d., p. 19.

Kobrin, Leon. *Fun daychmerish tsu yidish in amerike* (From Daytshmerish to Yiddish in America). New York: Leah Kissman Literary Foundation of the YKUF, 1944, and in English, *Yiddish*. 2. (Winter, Spring 1976), p. 47.

Levin, Neil. *Songs of the American Jewish Experience*. Chicago: Board of Jewish Education of Metropolitan Chicago, 1976.

Luria, A. *"Mit Aykh."* *Yidishe kultur* (Yiddish Culture). 44. (October, 1982), pp. 44–45.

Mayzel, Nachman. *Amerike in yidishn vort* (America in Yiddish Literature). New York: Yidisher kultur farband, 1955.

Mendele, Mokher Sforim. *"Dos kleyne mentshele."* *Kol ha' mevaser* ("The Common Man," *Voice of the Messenger*). 2. No. 45 (November 12, 1864); 3. No. 6 (February 4, 1865).

Molodowsky, Kadye. "Tsind on dayn likht." *Likht fun dornboym* (Light from the Burning Bush). Buenos Aires: Farlag Kiyom, 1965, pp. 143–144.

———. *"Un vos vet zayn."* *Likht fun dornboym*. Buenos Aires: Farlag Kiyom, 1965, pp. 97–98.

Niger, Shmuel. "America in the works of Isaac Meyer Dick." *YIVO Annual of Jewish Social Science*. Vol. 9. New York: YIVO, 1954, pp. 63–71.

Noble, Shlomo. "The Image of the American Jew in Hebrew and Yiddish Literature in America, 1870–1900." *YIVO Annual of Jewish Social Science*. Vol. 9. New York: YIVO, 1954, pp. 83–108.

Opatoshu, Joseph. "Fifty Years of Yiddish Literature in the United States." *YIVO Annual of Jewish Social Science*. Vol. 9. New York: YIVO, 1954, pp. 72–73.

Reisen, Avrom. "Varshe." *Forward*. (July 11, 1986), p. 19.

Rontch, Yitskhok Alkhonon. *Amerike in der yidisher literatur*. New York: Y. A. Rontch Book Committee, 1945.

Schulman, Elias. *Geshikhte fun der yidisher literatur in amerike, 1870–1900* (History of Yiddish Literature in America, 1870–1900). New York: I. Biderman, 1943.

Schwartz, I. J. "About Myself and My Generation" (an interview with Abraham Tabachnik, in Yiddish). *Di zukunft* (The Future). 69. (January 1964), p. 35.

Shifris, Moyshe. "*Un ven afile.*" *Yo, yidish* (Yes, Yiddish). New York: YKUF, 1975.

Shteynberg, Noyekh. *Yung amerike* (Young America). New York: Farlag lebn, 1917.

Tabachnik, Abraham. *Dikhter un dikhtung* (Poet and Poetry). New York: Committee of Friends, 1965.

7

American Yiddish Literary Criticism

Hannah Berliner Fischthal

The earliest Yiddish writers in America (dating from about 1880) were more than writers—they were people with a mission. In the newspapers for which they wrote, on their lecture tours, in the sweatshops and on the streets of the lower East Side of New York, they felt it their duty, their obligation, to educate and to enlighten the Yiddish-speaking public. Literature would help bring freedom and a better world. Life would copy art. In its sense of responsibility to its readers and in its desire to continue the great tradition of learning brought over from Europe, American Yiddish literary criticism has become a very unique criticism indeed.

Yet in spite of the fact that the Jewish people have always prided themselves on being the people of the book, true literary criticism was not born easily. The writers were immigrants, strangers in their new country, an ocean away from loved ones and "home." The adjustments they had to make were countless. There were economic problems, religious problems, social problems. Apart from the fact that the earliest Yiddish writers were forced by necessity to work long and miserable hours in the sweatshop, there were also literary problems that had to be hurdled. The Yiddish language itself had to be cleaned up, stylized, freed of German words and unbecoming syntax. The Czernowitz Conference in which Yiddish was declared as a national language of the Jewish people did not take place until 1908. And few immigrants knew of Mendele Mocher Sforim (Sholem Yankev Abramovitch), Sholom Aleichem (Shalom Rabinowitz), or I. L. Peretz writing on the other side of the sea. Fiction, poetry, drama, and criticism had to be developed, almost anew, on native grounds.

Once started, Yiddish literature flourished and quickly matured. Poetry especially developed with lightning speed in America. For quite a while, however, literary criticism lagged far behind. This was true even in Europe. "When Yiddish fiction had already such giants as Mendele Mocher Sforim, I. L. Peretz, and Sholom Aleichem, and had a whole generation or even generations of writers who enriched Yiddish literature with weighty, important, wide encompassing works, we in the critical field of Yiddish had no separate, important works and no noteworthy or distinguished critical writers."[1]

America, by the 1880's, had a similar problem: renowned poets (Morris Winchevsky [Vinchevski], Morris Rosenfeld, David Edelshtadt [Edelstadt]), but no literary critics. From time to time a writer would publish a book review or an essay about literature; journalists wrote about everything else, so they wrote about literature, too. But these articles tended to be didactic, and scarcely touched the literature itself.

Both the literature and the articles of the day were utilitarian. All writing was meant to help in the fight for socialism. Critics examined a literary work for its ideas. "A literary creation was declared important only when it had a socialistic idea," records Elias Schulman.[2] Every writer had to serve the working class. Whether a poem, story, or essay—all genres had the task of helping to eliminate capitalism and build in its place a new society. For the critics, only realism was acceptable. Almost at one with its audience, Yiddish literature portrayed the hardships of the immigrants' lives. It also had the higher goal of speaking out for a better life.

A few examples will suffice to emphasize the didactic nature of this literary criticism. L. Budyanov, writing for *Di naye tsayt* (The New Time) in 1898, asserted that not only must a poet create a realistic portrait of the real world, he must also portray "the social building which he helps to construct."[3] Abraham Cahan wrote on a myriad of subjects in a popular, simple style specifically for the benefit of his readers. In his *"Kritishe shtudyen fun zhargonishe maysterverk"* (Criticial Studies of Yiddish Masterpieces) printed in the *Tsukunft* (Future) in 1896, Cahan states that Sholom Aleichem would have been more artistic and more worthwhile had he written with a socialistic motif.[4] Sweatshop Poet David Edelshtadt, in an essay entitled *"Zhargonishe dikhter"* (Yiddish Poets), states that good critics "teach the public to judge correctly on how much this or that poet understands the spirit of his times and on how correctly human nature, beauty and humanism, warmth and freedom, love and hate . . . are mirrored in the writers' works."[5]

Although Edelshtadt and others wrote with some sensitivity about literature, the idea of actually examining a work on its own terms had not yet penetrated the Yiddish literary world in America.

JOEL ENTIN

Joel Entin (1874 or 1875–1959) was a remarkable transition figure in the history of Yiddish literary criticism. He arrived in America in 1891 and began to publish literary criticism, theater criticism, and other articles five years later. At a time when Yiddish literature in America was rallying the people for socialism, nationalism, anarchism, or Zionism, Entin instead began to use a formalistic-aesthetic approach to literature and drama. He was the only Yiddish-

American critic of his day who had studied literature formally; at Columbia he had taken courses in philosophy, literary aesthetics, comparative literature, psychology, and anthropology. Entin was privileged to be acquainted with movements in world literature that were unknown to his contemporaries. Critical of the official Yiddish poetry of his time, he preceded by twelve years the derisions of Zishe Landau when he censured "the nationalist and socialist movements which had their own rhyme departments."[6]

Indeed, the *Yunge* (Young Ones: members of the Yiddish-American literary movement whose main purpose was to free Yiddish literature from didacticism and propaganda) were undoubtedly influenced by Entin. As early as July, 1910, in *Literatur*, the anthology he helped to edit, Entin wrote an interesting piece about symbolism in world literature. He discussed the character, philosophy, background, and aspirations of symbolism. This essay accomplished a great deal for Yiddish literature in America; it surely influenced the *Yunge*.

Entin also did much to encourage romantic sensibilities in Yiddish literature, another concept the *Yunge* later developed. In 1909 he published "A *yidisher romantism*" (Jewish Romanticism) in *Troymen un virklekhkayt* (Dreams and Reality). Yiddish writers, at this point, were still committed to realism. (Looking back, we may find most of this material sentimental or melodramatic or both, but anything dealing with the troubled life of the worker was considered realistic at the time.) Instead of the "cold and dry" poetry of his day, Entin wanted to see beauty and feeling in literature. A person's soul, for instance, "should immerse itself in the mystical shine of the world past and future."[7] He saw a basis for romanticism in the Jewish religion, in Jewish history, and in Jewish folklore, for which he had great respect. Entin envisioned marvelous possibilities for Yiddish literature, would it deliberately allow romanticism to permeate it.

Like other Yiddish writers, Joel Entin did not write from a secluded ivory tower. From 1905 to 1915 he wrote for the *Varhayt* (Truth), a daily that appealed to a great number of the more educated Yiddish readers and boasted of such contributors as Chaim Zhitlovsky, Nachman Syrkin, Dov Ber Borukhov, and Sholom Aleichem. Entin co-edited the second volume of *Yugnd* (Youth, 1908), an early anthology composed by the *Yunge*. In addition, he co-edited the *Yidisher kemfer* (Jewish Fighter), the weekly organ of the Labor Zionists, from 1916 to 1920. Although he did not declaim his political viewpoints, he was driven to spread knowledge to his people, and to refine their tastes. He helped prepare the way for the *Yunge*; and when others called them decadent and worse, Entin remained their staunch defender and supporter.

B. RIVKIN

The most original, unorthodox, and controversial theories in the whole of Yiddish literary criticism were crafted by B. Rivkin (born Baruch Abraham Weinryb, 1883–1945). Rivkin didn't analyze a text; he sought a more grandiose project. Rivkin expected Yiddish literature not only to fulfill a purpose for the

Jewish people, it had to fulfill "great purpose." In other words, Yiddish literature was expected to transform itself into the religion of the Jewish people, the territory of the Jewish people, the means of continuity for the Jewish people. These themes, though often undeveloped, were repeated throughout his works.

Rivkin's best-known work is *Grunt-tendentsn fun der yidisher literatur in amerike* (Basic Tendencies of Yiddish Literature in America, 1948). This is a philosophic, abstract tome which cannot be lightly digested. Not having their own territory, Jews unwittingly created a would-be, quasi-territory, a literary territory, says Rivkin. This territory has its own traits, which become transformed into laws. The Jewish people have a special talent for such transformations. They can take the psychological powers they've inherited and collected over the generations and transfer them to literature. Religious belief can also be converted into art. Yiddish literature is then to serve the people as a substitute religion; it must "extend the Jewish sky over their [Jewish] heads; without this cover over their heads they are not yet even Jews, only raw meat, which America's stomach must first cook and digest."[8]

Rivkin's writings have been both praised and criticized. YIVO (*Yidisher Visnshaftlekher Institut*; Yiddish Scientific Institute known as YIVO Institute for Jewish Research) never awarded any recognition to him because of his undocumented theories, his abstractions, and his mystical beliefs in bringing the Messiah. Other literati, however, rallied to Rivkin's side. A. Mukdoyni, for example, remarks that Rivkin "doesn't have the cold and dead objectivity of a vivisectionist."[9] I. E. Rontsh (Rontch) states that Rivkin "was too creative" to be subservient to dates, numbers, facts.[10]

Grunt-tendentsn was part of the Federal Writers' Project of *Zamlbikher* (Collected Books). Most Yiddishists at the time agreed that Rivkin did breathe new life into Yiddish criticism. He certainly valued the Yiddish word and saw more purpose to it than any one could have thought possible in those days. Rivkin was not happy with the state of Yiddish criticism as it was. It took "too modest a role," he complained: "Yiddish criticism is specially called on to be not only a co-creator, but also the spiritual leader of [Yiddish] literature, the organizer of its consciousness, its idea-feeder. . . ."[11]

Although original, there are problems with Rivkin's work which cannot be overlooked. Itche Goldberg takes strong exception to Rivkin's thesis on early Yiddish-American literature, namely, that it was born with fundamental flaws, "without Yiddish air in which to breathe, and without soil—without roots in the Jewish disposition."[12] Abraham Tabachnik asks if literature "has no other functions in a modern, blackened, and complicated society other than serving as 'substitute religion'?" Tabachnik prefers Rivkin's treatments of individual authors to his general opinions on the traits of Yiddish literature. His essay on Libin, says Tabachnik, "is a pearl of criticism." [13] Ever-sensible Samuel Niger remarks that Rivkin's ambition for Yiddish criticism is a "little too big and too hot."[14] He also notes Rivkin's lack of any clear definitions of his eloquent theories. And Jacob Glatstein (Yankev Glatshteyn), who appreciates Rivkin's "orchestral style for his thoughts," speaks disparagingly of Rivkin's belief that literature can bring the Messiah.[15]

Yet what devotion this penniless scholar brought to the literature he loved! He wanted to redeem the Jewish people through Yiddish literature. He spent all his creative years on this, his holy mission.

SAMUEL NIGER

Samuel Niger (Shmuel Niger, born Shmuel Charney, 1883–1955) was the first Yiddish critic to really read literature for itself, not for how much or how little it reflected certain ideas. During his thirty-five years in America, Niger turned out articles and essays about Yiddish books and writers, most of them for *Der tog* (The Day). He defined a critic simply as "a reader who becomes a writer."[16] To be a good reader one has to be an active reader, a creative reader. The task of the critic is to make the reader interested in the literary work being discussed, not necessarily to make him agree with the critic. "His function," states Niger, "is not to teach us *what* to read, but *how* to read."[17]

Niger writes at length on the purpose of criticism. In *Kritik un kritiker* (Criticism and Critics), which came out in 1959, he has a chapter entitled "Criticism— Its Main Value, Its Goals, Its Means, Its Problems." To evaluate criticism, one must ask if the critic has shone light on the work, if it is now easier to enter the writer's world. "Did the critic, in other words, make the reader's innermost contacts with the writer's creativity richer and cleaner, fuller . . . ?"[18]

He deplores the so-called criticism that simply searches for errors. "The readers that enjoy looking for mistakes don't enjoy reading. They are bad readers, and thus they're also bad critics." True criticism isn't just negative. Nor is it only praiseful. "It is creative and it teaches readers to be creative, too."[19]

"Artistic criticism," to use Niger's terminology, is all-encompassing, like art. He feels that purely aesthetic or formalist criticism is just as one-sided as idea or content (social, ethical, etc.) criticism. The synthesis is the criticism to which the artistic critic strives. In other words, Niger employs many methodologies in his criticism. What is important is the impression a work leaves upon him. "I am a person who has an impression of a book, of a writer, and I bring out my impression," he states.[20] Niger's style is logical, responsible, conservative. The methods he employs vary with each work. In an essay on Bal-Makhshoves (1873–1924), the so-called "Father of Yiddish Criticism," Niger writes:

The *ideal* of artistic criticism is not aesthetic, not ethical, not philosophical and not any kind of specialized and artistically isolating criticism, but such that should give us the individual picture and the characteristic synthesis that the critic has gotten from the work as a whole, in the unity of its various elements.[21]

N. B. Minkoff, in *Zeks yidishe kritiker* (Six Yiddish Critics, 1954), points out that when Niger writes of Lamed Shapiro, his style becomes nervous, staccato-like. When he writes of Hirsch David Nomberg, his style is slower, the sentences longer. When he writes of Sholem Asch, he becomes a bit sentimental; and when he writes of Isaac Leib Peretz, his style, like Peretz's, is impressionistic-laconic. Often, Niger reflects the style of the author of whom he writes.

If Niger's critical theories weren't brilliant enough to emblazon world literature, they most certainly did shine a steady light on Yiddish literature and literary criticism. "In the wine-garden of our Yiddish literature," writes Hyman B. Bass, "he was a faithful gardener who watched and planted and guarded over even the hardest, in the bitterest years. . . . "[22]

Now and then Niger was criticized for not appreciating the symbolism and expressionism that broke into the stream of Yiddish literature. To the best of his abilities, however, he did try to understand the avant-garde, and he did praise Jacob Glatstein and the literary criticism of N. B. Minkoff. He sincerely wanted to appreciate everything that was genuine and creative.

Jacob Glatstein had vilified Niger in the twenties. He later repented, however, of his youthful, fiery attacks. In 1955 he admitted to Tabachnik:

Sh. Niger wrote negatively about my Chinese poems in my latest book. I have nothing against Niger. He is one of the most honest of critics. I fought him some twenty-five or thirty years ago, but we corresponded extensively after that and we are the best of friends. His opinions are entirely honest. He admitted in a letter to me that he finds it difficult to judge modern poetry. When a critic says that he cannot respond favorably to modern poetry, that it's not for him, I don't think that such a man, at his age, should be required to get used to a diet that he finds difficult to digest.[23]

In *Dertseyler un romanistn* (Storytellers and Novelists, 1946), Niger has authoritative essays on earlier Yiddish writers in America. In *H. Leivick* (*H. Leyvik*) (1951) there are thirteen essays on the great poet, including such topics as "From Individual to Social and National Lyric," "Synthesis of Personal and Social Motifs," "From Unrest to Calm, From Struggle to Happiness," "Back to Lyrical Romanticism," and "Reality and Death, Dream and Reawakening."

Yidishe shrayber fun tsvantsikstn yorhundert (Yiddish Writers of the Twentieth Century, 1972), is an important two-volume collection of essays written by Niger over the years 1920–1955. Volume 1 discusses Bialik, Yehoash, Frug, Pinski, Einhorn, Leivick, Opatoshu, Halpern, Mani Leib (Leyb, born Brahinsky), Rolnick, Liessin (Liesin, born Valt), Segal, Roizenblatt, Ravitch, and Zeitlin. Volume 2 contains essays on Glatstein, Manger, Sutskever, Grade, Schwartz, Auerbach, Boraisho, Kulbak, Molodowsky, Steinberg, Korn, Zychlinsky, Raboy, I. J. Singer, I. Bashevis Singer, Metzker, Spiegel, Erik, and Weinreich.

Niger also published the very successful studies of *Sholem Asch* (1960), *I. L. Peretz* (1952), and *Mendele Mocher Sforim* (1936). For thirty-five years he contributed weekly critical articles to the Sunday edition of *Der tog*. In addition, he co-edited the literary monthly *Tsukunft* from 1941 to 1947, thus helping to maintain the journal's high quality and influence. Niger fulfilled many other public functions for the Yiddish world. He was a pillar of YIVO, and he was active in CYCO (the Central Yiddish Culture Organization). In 1948 he helped found the Congress for Jewish Culture. He also undertook to co-edit the encyclopedic *Leksikon far der nayer yidisher literatur* (Handbook of the New Yiddish Literature); he died, however, when the first volume was in press.

Like those American Yiddish writers before him, Niger knew criticism is not an individual function but a social duty. He was "an enlightener, an educator of the people, a pedagogue of great social responsibility."[24]

BENJAMIN JACOB BIALOSTOTZKY

B. J. Bialostotzky (1892–1962), Yiddish poet, folklorist, and critic, emigrated from Lithuania to Pittsburgh in 1911, where he worked in a clothing sweatshop until 1915. In 1916 he moved to New York, where he taught in Yiddish schools, co-edited *Der yidisher kemfer*, the daily *Di tsayt* (The Time), and *Di kinder velt* (The Children's World). He also wrote poetry and articles about poetry and poets for *Shriftn* (Writings), *Tsukunft*, and *Der veker* (The Alarm Clock). In 1922, for example, he published *"Motivn fun arbet un kamf in der yidisher poezye"* (Motifs of Work and Struggle in Yiddish Poetry) in the socialist *Veker*. In that same year he began writing for the *Forverts* (*Forward*).

In 1932 his *Lider un eseyen* (Poems and Essays) appeared. The second volume of this collection contains Bialostotzky's discussions of poetry that set him apart, for example, from Niger. In "The Relation of Word to Word," Bialostotzky explains that he has "tried to ascertain the sense and the contents of rhyme. Also its origins. Immersing myself in this matter, I have seen three definite rhyme-groupings of words according to content, meaning, and image.... "[25] Topics included in this chapter are "Study-Essay about Rhyme in Language and Poem," "Word and Picture," "How Old Is the Rhyme?" "The Contents of the Rhyme," "The Three Rhyme Groups," "About Rhymes Between Words That Stem from Hebrew with Other Yiddish Words," and "A Few Words about the Developments of Yiddish Rhyme in General."

Bialostotzky takes poetry very seriously. He understands the technical problems involved in creating verse better than any Yiddish critic before him. Like Niger, Bialostotzky is a good reader, a creative reader, a reader who looks at the work itself. In that same second volume of *Lider un eseyen*, Bialostotzky includes an amusing fable entitled "Seven Critics." Here he wittily portrays seven different kinds of critics, each of whom tries to fit a certain writer into his own made-up categories; all fail to see the actual writer who literally escapes them. The moral of the story is quite clear: a critic should not approach a literary work with preconceived notions. Each work must be examined on its own grounds.

A wider known volume of literary criticism by Bialostotzky, *Kholem in vor* (Dream in Reality), was published in 1956. Most of the essays in this interesting, perceptive, and well-written work deal with Yiddish poetry, "the joy and the comfort of my life!"[26] The essays are thematically bound. "The figure of the poor man in Yiddish poetry," containing twenty-two essays, is

a cross-section of Yiddish poetry from the days of Winchevsky-Rosenfeld-Edelshtadt-Frug until today. Bridging this with the figure of the poor man, in all of his transformations, through the miraculous shrine of Yiddish poetry, I have meanwhile taken a glance in the separate rooms and chambers—directions, poetic groups—of this shrine.[27]

Bialostotzky sees a continuity in Yiddish poetry, an ongoing process of "modernism" which started with the first socialist poets. These Sweatshop Poets broke with the earlier *Haskalah* (Enlightenment) poetry of Israel Aksenfeld and Eliakum Zunser, and thus were modernists. The *Yunge* between 1910 and 1915 turned away from the ghettoish East Side life, turned away from the socialistic motif and also from the talmudic legends of Yehoash and the Rabbi Akiva poems of Liessen. They were modernists, too. "Modernism is not a term affixed to any one epoch, to any one time," Bialostotzky states.[28]

Bialostotzky was a staunch nationalist, as both his poetry and essays demonstrate. Like the other Yiddish critics, he wished to strengthen both Yiddish literature and the intellectual level of Yiddish readers. He accomplished both.

NOCHUM BORUCH MINKOFF

N. B. Minkoff (1893–1958), was a poet-critic who regarded literary criticism as a scientific discipline. He attempted objective evaluations and classifications of writers and works. Together with Jacob Glatstein and A. Glanz (-Leyeles; Glantz), Minkoff revolutionized Yiddish literature by issuing the first manifesto of the *Inzikh* (Introspectivist) movement. This alone would have made him a most important figure in the world of Yiddish letters; his literary criticism, too, however, adds great merit to this noteworthy Yiddish intellectual.

His published volumes of criticism include *Yidishe klasiker poetn* (Yiddish Classical Poets, 1939); *Zeks yidishe kritiker* (Six Yiddish Critics, 1954); *Literarishe vegn* (Literary Ways, 1955); and the three-volume *Pyonern fun der yidisher poezye in amerike* (Pioneers of Yiddish Poetry in America, 1956).

Zeks yidishe kritiker contains informative, well-written essays on critics Alexander Tsederboym, Joseph Judah Lerner, Joshua Chana Ravnitzky, Joel Entin, Bal-Makhshoves, and Samuel Niger, the classical Yiddish critic. Hyman Bass calls the volume "an example of serious, responsible, and creative critical work."[29]

Pyonern fun der yidisher poezye in amerike is a sympathetic, well-researched and documented scholarly study of twenty-two of the Sweatshop Poets in America. Minkoff thematically arranges the early poems into five basic motifs: (1) poems of need and empathy; that is, the need of the oppressed and exploited, and empathy for them; (2) poems of battle for socialism; (3) satires; these include the poems unmasking the three enemies of man—capitalism, the state, and the

powers that help them; (4) social lyrics, such as Bovshover's "*Mayn frayndin*"
(My Friend), which is symbolic and sorrowful; (5) poems of high romanticism
mixed with socialism, poems of sacrificial symbolism. Minkoff's thesis that he
is dealing with what he terms the "socialist era in the Yiddish literature of
America" is entirely sound.[30]

Minkoff was thoroughly devoted to the service of Yiddish literature. Shlomo
Bickel even bemoans the fact that Minkoff's erudition falls upon "a people
without a Yiddish university," that Minkoff wrote for imaginary students and
imaginary Yiddish professors.[31] Minkoff, however, continued to serve *Yidishkayt*, as did Bickel for that matter, all his life.

SHLOMO BICKEL

Shlomo Bickel (1896–1969) was an eminent essayist, memoirist, novelist,
and literary critic. In *Shrayber fun mayn dor* (Writers of My Generation, pub.
1958–1970), a monumental three-volume work dealing with the writers of his
time, Bickel discusses his two main literary themes. His main concern is that
of the individual versus society: on the one hand, "the idea of free thought, and
on the other hand, immersion in the burden of good deeds toward society, which
leads to feeling secure in the warm nest of *my* people and *my* country."[32] His
other main theme deals with the separation between the Jewish corner and the
wide world: "I have in the course of the decades of years of my conscious life
always felt soulful spaciousness in the Jewish niche and claustrophobic in the
wide world. . . . I never had the desire to jump the fence into the wide world."[33]

Of course, Bickel is not naive about the possibly false security of the Yiddish
nook.

Certainly I, like every one of us, am not blind to the tragic plight of our Jewish niche
on the waves of so much evil and also on the waves of so much freedom. We here in
the great freedom of America feel how our Yiddish creative area becomes tinier, and we
see the red shine of an epoch that sets in the great ocean of our thousand-year-old history.[34]

Bickel's work is often pessimistic. His criticism developed after the Holocaust,
after every Jew's expectations and hopes had been brutally shattered. "There
are peoples without literature. Our Yiddish literature is the exceptional publication of a literature without a people," he laments.[35] Whereas Yiddish writers
at the turn of the century could and did proclaim that great revolutions would
shake the social order and emancipate everyone, writers in the mid-century could
only grieve and mourn. In fact, Bickel has no regard for those whom he calls
the "almost-poets of the pioneer generation," and he adds that perhaps N. B.
Minkoff, in his remarkable history of the pioneer poetry in America, ought not
to have wasted his talents on the early Sweatshop Poets. "From a literary-
historical point of view it would not be a sin to forget them, and it might even
be a bit of a good deed to not remember them," he sardonically remarks.[36]

Like Bialostotzky, Bickel is more analytical than Niger. Like Niger, however, he does not approve of the formalism which separates the work from the writer. Instead, Bickel is more intimate, a critic who loves to tie his analyses to memories of encounters and experiences.

Bickel's world-view was necessarily shattered by the horrors of this century, yet his love, devotion, and service to Yiddish and *Yidishkayt* never wavered. "Certainly our unrest is large," he writes. "But can this very unrest decrease our desire for creativity, decrease our faith in the eternal value of our Yiddish world?"[37]

JACOB GLATSTEIN

Like N. B. Minkoff, Jacob Glatstein (1896–1971) was a poet, a founder of the *Inzikh* (Introspectivist) literary movement, and a critic. There the analogy ends, however, for Glatstein soared above Minkoff in poetry; in fact, Glatstein is probably the greatest Yiddish poet of all time. His literary criticism is not as well-documented and scholarly as Minkoff's, yet it, like his poetry, is brilliant, creative, and lively. Great literary personalities such as Samuel Niger, Sh. D. Singer, Shlomo Bickel, Eliezer Greenberg, and Hyman Bass concur on Glatstein's almost magical use of language. Niger, for example, admits being won over by Glatstein's originality. He says that Glatstein is not as patient a reader as a critic ought to be, but he's more playful and sharp-witted than critics generally are: "His thoughts are incendiary, not quietly glowing. His speech is a zigzag of lightning. His most expressive tool is the incisive remark. . . . I always read him with profound eagerness."[38]

It is interesting to note that Glatstein, in his youth, had insulted Niger mercilessly. In *"An Ode tsu der kritik"* (An Ode to Criticism), for example, which first appeared in *In zikh* (1928), Glatstein brashly rants against "unartistic, tasteless Sh. Niger." He calls him a critic "who babbles . . . helpless, colorless, and gaseous words. . . . "[39] Later on, however, as Glatstein and Yiddish literature matured and moved beyond the fervor of *Inzikhism*, he was able to regret, privately and publicly, his early attacks on Niger and a number of writers of the establishment toward whom he had been disrespectful. Glatstein's dissidence had been part of the literary revolution he had helped to bring forth. In an early, brilliant piece of criticism, *"A shnel-loyf iber der yidisher poezye"* (A Quick Tour of Yiddish Poetry, 1920), for example, Glatstein harshly attacks Mani Leib and Zishe Landau, leading poets of the *Yunge* school, for being overrefined, for being too involved in the poetry and not concerned at all with content. Rationality, decorum, the fixed forms of poetry, and tradition—these were challenged by Glatstein in the 1920's. Glatstein and the other *In zikh* poets modernized Yiddish literature by making way for introspection, for urbanity, for free verse and new rhythms.

In later years, when Glatstein came to formulate his own theories of criticism, a primary stipulation was that a critic ought not to be abrasive. His essay *"Kritik far a novine*" (Criticism for a Change, 1963) is very specific about this. Indeed, he grew to be just such a critic—one who did not condemn a writer but rather tried to appreciate whatever positive talents there were. And in a later essay on Niger in *In tokh genumen* (Sum and Substance, 1947), Glatstein even adds that "criticism—Niger probably found out long ago—is a thankless task."

There are six excellent volumes of essays by Glatstein. (Sometimes they are listed under the name of Gladstone.) *In tokh genumen* is the title of three of the volumes, published in 1947, 1956, and 1960. *Mit mayne fartog-bikher* (With My Daybreak Books, 1963), *Oyf greyte temes* (Upon Ready Themes, 1967), and *Prost un poshet* (Plain and Simple, 1978) are the other three volumes.

OTHER YIDDISH CRITICS

There are a number of other critics who deserve mention. Alexander Mukdoyni (b. Alexander Kappel, 1877–1958), was primarily a theatre critic for *Der morgn zhurnal* (The Morning Journal) but he also published occcasional articles on literature. Relying on intuition rather than logical analysis, Mukdoyni's critiques deal directly with the very essence of a work. His fiery language could be as hurtful as it could be laudatory.

Kalman Marmor (1879–1956) was a literary historian and critic of early American Yiddish literature. Marmor wrote for over thirty Yiddish and Hebrew journals, and edited or co-edited fifteen Yiddish journals and newspapers. He fought for the recognition of proletarian literature and demonstrated countless times how the early Sweatshop Poets provided the fundamental bases for later Yiddish literature in America. He also showed the intrinsic value of labor poetry itself. *Der onheyb fun der yidisher literatur in amerike* (The Birth of Yiddish Literature in America, 1944), *Dovid Edelshtadt* (1950), *Yoysef Bovshover* (1952), and *Mayn lebns-geshikhte* (My Life History, 1959) are representative of his published works.

Abraham Coralnick (1883–1937), who began writing for *Der tog* in 1915, and then became its co-editor in 1920, wrote essays on a multitude of subjects, including literature.

Nachman Meisel (Mayzel [1887–1966]) was a prolific writer who composed more than forty books and hundreds of major articles. He was also editor of *Yidishe kultur* from 1939 to 1964. Meisel's published volumes include *Doyres un tekufes in der yidisher literatur* (Generations and Ages in Yiddish Literature, 1942), *Forgeyer un mit-tsaytler* (Forerunners and Contemporaries, 1946), and *Tsurikblikn un perspektivn* (Looking Back and Perspectives, 1962).

Eliezer Greenberg (1896–1977), well-known to the English reader as the Yiddish half of the successful (Irving) Howe and Greenberg team, was a poet and critic. He wrote sensitive studies of H. Leivick *Tsentrale motivn in H. Leyvik's shafn;* (Central Motifs in H. Leivick's Works, 1961) and Jacob Glatstein, *Glatstein's freyd fun yidishn vort* (Glatstein's Joy of the Yiddish Word, 1964), among others. His *Moyshe Leib Halpern in ram fun zayn dor* (Halpern in the Frame of His Generation, 1942), is an excellent study of the poet.

Also a poet and a literary critic in the strict sense of the term, one who devoted his critical career to an intense study of the poetry written by the *Yunge*, was Abraham Tabachnik (1901–1970). His *Dikhter un dikhtung* (Poets and Poetry, 1949) is the definitive study of the period. Tabachnik demonstrated a deep understanding of contemporary American literary criticism. A major study needs to be made of this critic.

Irving Greenberg (Ber Grin in Yiddish) is another poet-critic concerned with the continuity of Yiddish literature. His published critical volumes are *Fun dor tsu dor: literarishe eseyen* (From Generation to Generation: Literary Essays, 1971) and *Yidishe shrayber in amerike* (Yiddish Writers in America, 1963).

Hyman Bass published an important volume of thirty-eight critical and pedagogical essays, *Shrayber un verk* (Writers and Works, 1971). Bass discusses works of Niger, Edelshtadt, Bovshover, A. Reisin (Reyzin), S. Leivick, Glanz, Opatoshu, Mani Leib, Leyzer Wolf, Chaim Grade, Glatstein, Minkoff, Bickel, and others. A main thesis of his writing is that modern Yiddish literature is a link in the chain of Jewish writing stemming back to the Old Testament.

Indispensable in the field of early American Yiddish literature is Elias Schulman's scholarly *Geshikhte fun der yidisher literatur in amerike, 1870–1900* (History of Yiddish Literature in America, 1943). Schulman (1907–1986) was awarded the coveted Itsik Manger Prize for 1986. He had founded and edited, together with Eliezer Greenberg, *Getseln* (Tents), a periodical of poetry and criticism. His *Portretn un etyudn* (Portraits and Studies, 1979) contains articles on Glanz, Niger, Coralnick, Aaron Zeitlin, I. J. Schwartz, Alexander Harkavy as an editor, Sholom Aleichem's debut in America, the beginning of Yiddish literature in America, the main currents in Yiddish literature in America in the twentieth century, I. B. Singer, and two articles on Chaim Grade, among others. Schulman had also published *Avrom Reisin vi a redaktor* (Reisin as an Editor), and most recently for *Bay zikh* (By Oneself), *Der oyfkum un antviklung fun di yunge* (The Rise and Development of the *Yunge*) in installments which began in 1983 and are still continuing at the date of this writing. Schulman was additionally a co-editor of the *Lexikon fun der nayer yidisher literatur* (Handbook of the New Yiddish Literature), to which he had contributed some seventy-five biographies. He had been a weekly contributor to the *Forverts* from 1971 until his death.

The stress on the continuity of Yiddish literature is the main and repeated focus of Itche Goldberg's *Eseyen* (Essays, 1981). Goldberg, who won the Itsik Manger Prize for literary criticism in 1985, is the present editor of the fine literary and cultural monthly *Yidishe kultur* (Yiddish Culture). *Eseyen* contains studies of, for example, Nachman Meisel, Kalman Marmor, Zisha Weinper, Irving Greenberg (Ber Grin), Chaver Paver, I. B. Singer, I. L. Peretz, and Itsik Manger. The essays on Peretz and Manger are especially fine. There are also excellent comprehensive essays such as ''The National Face of the First Worker-Poets in

America'' and "On the Threshold of the Second Century: 100 Years of Yiddish Literature and Press in the U.S.A." Goldberg's own prose is poetic. He writes, for example, that Ber Grin "plays with adjectives the way a child plays with a pouch of beads."[40] Goldberg has edited or co-edited dozens of textbooks and anthologies; he has written poetry, operettas, and short stories. He additionally edited, introduced, and wrote twenty-six biographical chapters for *Undzer dramaturgye* (Our Drama, 1961), a large anthology of plays including works by such Americans as Jacob Gordin, Peretz Hirschbein, David Pinski, Sholem Asch, Moshe Nadir, H. Leivick, and Philip Bimko. In all his endeavors, Goldberg demonstrates his great devotion to and concern for Yiddish literature.

Much criticism of Yiddish literature in America today is done in English. It is not in the scope of this article to discuss the studies that have been made of Yiddish poetry and prose in languages other than Yiddish. But there is one inescapable fact that must be mentioned— the English writer, no matter how knowledgeable he may be, is a step removed from the literature. Yiddish critics, no matter what their political or religious viewpoints, are all involved in the literature they discuss in a way that no outsider can duplicate. The Yiddishists write out of their deep convictions of the importance of their subject, out of the necessity of preserving and loving and passing on the literature so central and dear to their lives, so crucial to the golden chain of continuity. They are impassioned writers, writers with a mission.

GUIDE TO BIBLIOGRAPHY OF AMERICAN YIDDISH LITERARY CRITICISM

This bibliography is a basic outline of American Yiddish criticism. I have tried to include works generally considered the most important and representative and those most readily available. A mere listing of all the Yiddish critical articles published in this country would be a project requiring years of research, and it would most certainly fill up scores of volumes. The thousands upon thousands of articles "are scattered over the seven seas," as it is said in Yiddish, for many are located in scores of newspapers, little magazines, journals, and books which are not easily found. Also included in this bibliography are some American Yiddish works about critics and criticism.

For authors' names I have used the spellings provided by the Library of Congress. In some instances the Yiddish name differs from the English. For example, the poet known as Leyeles in Yiddish is referred to as Glanz in English. Irving Howe resolves this conflict by employing the name "Glanz-Leyeles." For bibliographical purposes, however, I find the Library of Congress designation to be more expedient. Note, however, that I have listed—where called for— critics Samuel Charney and B. Weinryb under their more prominent pseudonyms; Shmuel (Sh.) Niger and B. Rivkin. For titles, I have complied with the system of transliteration provided by YIVO, the Yiddish Scientific Institute. In trans-

literation of Yiddish, it is standard practice to capitalize only the initial letter of
the first word. I have translated or annotated entries wherever necessary.

For convenience, this bibliography is subdivided into the following categories:
(1) Newspapers and Magazines, (2) Criticism of Literary Movements, (3) Criticism of Specific Writers, (4) Criticism in General, (5) Collections of Various
Kinds of Critical Articles, including Encyclopedias, (6) Bibliographies, and (7)
Selected Sources in English.

Newspapers and Magazines

Yiddish newspapers and magazines are the primary sources for Yiddish literary
criticism. The main papers to be consulted are the *Yidishes tageblat* (Daily News),
Morgn zhurnal (Morning Journal), *Varhayt* (Truth), *Arbayter tsaytung* (Workers'
Newspaper), *Yidishe folk-tsaytung* (Jewish People's Newspaper), *Emes* (Truth),
Di fraye arbeyter shtime (Free Worker's Voice), *Ovnt blat* (Evening Page), *Tog*
(Day), *Frayhayt* (Freedom), and *Forverts* (Jewish Daily Forward).

There are hundreds of other American Yiddish publications. Some of the more
valuable ones are *Yidisher kemfer* (Jewish Fighter), *Naye lebn* (New Life), *Naye
land* (New Country), *Literarishe velt* (Literary World), and *Feder* (Pen). *Literatur, Shriftn* (Writings), *Inzl* (Island), *In zikh* (Introspection), and *Getseltn*
(Tents) are excellent literary magazines. Current magazines of note are *Tsukunft*
(Future), *Afn shvel* (On the Threshold), *Yidishe kultur*, and *YIVO bleter* (YIVO
Pages).

Important sources in English are YIVO papers, the *American Jewish Yearbook*,
and the journal *Yiddish*.

Criticism of Literary Movements

The best works of criticism on literary movements include Nochum Boruch
Minkoff's *Pyonern fun yidisher poezye in amerike: dos sotsyale lid* (Pioneers of
Yiddish Poetry in America: The Social Poem), a sympathetic study of the Sweatshop Poets; and Abraham Tabachnik's *Dikhter un dikhtung* (Poets and Poetry),
an excellent study of the *Yunge*.

Among the sources in this category, listed alphabetically by author, are the
following:

Bader, Gershom. *"Inzikhistisher amoratsizm."* *Yidishes tageblat* (March 29, 1920), p. 4.
    [Introspectivist Ignorance]
Birnboym, Y. *"Der zhurnal 'In zikh'."* *Pinkis far der forshung fun der yidisher literatur*,
    vol. 2. Ed. Hyman Bass. New York: Congress for Jewish Culture, 1972. pp. 28–
    49.
[The Journal *In zikh*]
Eisland (Ayzland), Reuben. *"Ikh ze far zikh a bild fun draysik yor tsurik."* *Der tog*
    (November 7, 1944), p. 7.
    [I See Before Me a Picture of Thirty Years Ago; by a leading member of the *Yunge*]

Entin, Joel. *Di zayl in fun der nayer yidisher literatur*. New York: Jewish National
Workers' Union, 1919.
[The Pillars of the New Yiddish Literature; on romanticism]
———. *"Tsvishn mizrakh un mayrev."* *Literatur* (July, 1910), pp. 10–15.
[Between East and West; on symbolism]
———. *"A yidisher romantism."* *Troymen un virklekhkayt*, ed. Y. Adler and Y. Slonism.
New York: A. Karlin, 1909.
[A Jewish Romanticism]
Glanz, Aaron. *Labirint*. New York: M. N. Meisel, 1918.
[Labyrinth; includes tenets of Introspectivism]
Goldberg, Itche. *"Dos natsyonale ponim fun di ershte arbeter-poetn in amerike"* (1976).
Eseyen. New York: Yidisher kultur farband, 1981, pp. 163–188.
[The National Face of the First Worker-Poets in America; on Sweatshop Poets]
Minkoff, Nochum Boruch. *Pyonern fun yidisher poezye in amerike: dos sotsyale lid*. 3
vols. New York: Grenich, 1956.
[Pioneers of Yiddish Poetry in America: The Social Poem; on Sweatshop Poets]
Niger, Samuel (Sh.). *"A naye rikhtung in der yidisher poezye."* *Der tog un di varhayt*
(March 14, 1920), p. 9.
[A New Direction in Yiddish Poetry; on Introspectivism]
———. *"Teorye un praktik."* *Der tog un di varhayt* (March 28, 1920), p. 9.
[Theory and Practice; on Introspective Poetry]
———. *"Vegn der 'inzikh' teorye."* *Der tog un di varhayt* (March 21, 1920), p. 9.
[About the "Introspective" Theory]
Rontch, Isaac Elchanan. *Di pyonern fun yidishn arbeter lid in amerike (Morris Winch-
evsky, Morris Rosenfeld, David Edelshtadt, Yosef Bovshover)*. New York: Bronx
Yiddish Mitlshul, 1950.
[Pioneers of the Yiddish Workers' Poem in America]
Schulman, Elias. *"Der oyfkum un antviklung fun di 'yunge',"* installments in *Bay zikh*
(Tel Aviv), vols. 22, 23–24, 25, 26, 27, 28–   (June, 1983–   ), various pp.
[The Rise and Development of the *Yunge*]
Tabachnik, Abraham. *Dikhter un dikhtung*. New York: David Ignatoff Literature Fund,
1949.
[Poets and Poetry]

Criticism of Specific Writers

Eliezer Greenberg's *Moyshe Leib Halpern in ram fun zayn dor* (Halpern within
the Frame of His Generation) is a wonderful study of the poet. Excellent essays
on early American Yiddish writers can be found in Shmuel Niger, *Dertseyler
un romanistn* (Storytellers and Novelists). Representative critical studies of specific writers include the following:

Bass, Hyman B. *"Dr. Shloyme Bickel—der kritiker un memuarist (1896–1969)."* *Shrayber un verk: literatur-kritishe un pedagogishe eseyen*. Tel Aviv: Hamenora, 1971,
pp. 463–475.
[Bickel—Critic and Memoirist]

————. "*N. B. Minkoff: der dikhter un kritiker* (1893–1958)." *Shrayber un verk: literatur-kritishe un pedagogishe eseyen*. Tel Aviv: Hamenora, 1971, pp. 456–62.
[Minkoff: Poet and Critic]

————. "*Shmuel Niger un Bal-makhshoves*." *Shrayber un verk: Literatur-kritishe un pedagogishe eseyen*. Tel Aviv: Hamenora, 1971, pp. 41–67.

Bialostotzky, Benjamin Jacob. *Moris Rozenfeld, 1862–1923*, illus. Aba Lilien. New York: Kinder-ring of Ed. Dept. of Workmen's Circle, 1941.

————. *Y. L. Perets tsum finf un tsvantsikstn yortsayt*. New York: Central Yiddish Culture Organization, 1940.
[Twenty-fifth Commemorative Year: Y. L. Peretz]

Bickel, Shlomo. "*B. Rivkin, shrayber mit emune in yidishn vort: a rede gehaltn baym oyfdekn di matseyve* (June 30, 1946)." *B. Rivkin: lebn un shafn*, comp. Mina Rivkin. Chicago: L. M. Shteyn, 1953, pp. 185–188.
[Rivkin, Writer with Faith in the Yiddish Word]

————. "Dr. A. Mukdoyni" (1956). *Shrayber fun mayn dor*. New York: Matones, 1958, pp. 215–221.

————. "I. Bashevis." *Shrayber fun mayn dor*. New York: Matones, 1958, pp. 358–366.
[I. B. Singer]

————. "*Mayne iker ideyen*" (1956). *Shrayber fun mayn dor*. New York: Matones, 1958, pp. 11–15.
[Bickel's Main Ideas]

————. "N. B. Minkoff." *Shrayber fun mayn dor*. New York: Matones, 1958, pp. 222–231.

————. "Sh. Niger." *Shrayber fun mayn dor*. New York: Matones, 1958, pp. 239–256.

————. "Sholem Asch's *stil*" (1945). *Shrayber fun mayn dor*. New York: Matones, 1958, pp. 377–382.
[Asch's style]

————. *Shrayber fun mayn dor*. 3 vols. New York: Matones, 1958; Tel Aviv: Hamenora, 1965, 1970.
[Writers of My Generation]

————. "Yankev Glatstein: *di proze*" (1956). *Shrayber fun mayn dor*. New York: Matones, 1958, pp. 115–121.
[Glatstein: Prose]

————. "Yankev Glatstein: *gezamlte lider*" (1957). *Shrayber fun mayn dor*. New York: Matones, 1958, pp. 108–115.
[Glatstein: Collected Poems]

Bickel, Shlomo and L. Lehrer, eds. *Shmuel Niger bukh*. New York: YIVO, 1958.
[Includes bibliography]

Boraisho, Menachem. "Sholem Asch: *der kuntsler un der preydiker*." *Der tog* (December 19, 1948), p. 6.
[Asch: The Artist and the Preacher]

Entin, Joel. *Di zayln fun der nayer yidisher literatur*. New York: National Workers Union, 1919.
[The Pillars of New Yiddish Literature]

————. *Itskhok Leybush Perets: der shenster templ-zayl fun der nayer idisher literatur*. New York: Yiddish National Workers Union, 1952.

[Peretz: The Finest Pillar in the Temple of New Yiddish Literature]
Faynberg, Leon. *Yidish*. New York: Saulzon Publishers, 1950.
[Poems about important Yiddish poets]
Glatstein, Jacob. "B. Rivkin." *B. Rivkin: Lebn un shafn*, comp. Mina Rivkin. Chicago:
    L. M. Shteyn, 1953, pp. 63–70.
[Reprinted from *Yidisher kemfer* (June 22, 1945), p. 8.]
———. *"Dr. Mukdoyni's kritik"* (1942). *Prost un poshet*. New York: Fanny Gladstone,
    1978, p. 316.
[Mukdoyni's Criticism]
———. "Fame of Bashevis Singer." *Congress Bi-weekly* 32 (December 27, 1965),
    pp. 17–19.
———. *"Moses*: Sholem Asch's Poorest Book." *Jewish Frontier* 18 (November, 1951),
    pp. 21–23.
———. "Sh. D. Zinger." *Prost un poshet*. New York: Fanny Gladstone, 1978, pp. 350–
    355.
———. *"Sholem Asch un zayne kristlekhe bikher."* *Prost un poshet*. New York: Fanny
    Gladstone, 1978, pp. 145–157.
[Asch and His Christological Books]
Goldberg, Itche. *"Ber Grin der kritiker"* (1971). *Eseyen*. New York: Yidisher kultur
    farband, 1981, pp. 292–298.
[Irving Greenberg the Critic]
———. *"Kalman Marmor"* (1957). *Eseyen*. New York: Yidisher kultur farband, 1981,
    pp. 151–160.
———. *"Nachman Meisel der kritiker"* (1968). *Eseyen*. New York: Yidisher kultur
    farband, 1981, pp. 123–133.
[Meisel the Critic]
Greenberg, Eliezer. "The Central Role of Jacob Glatstein in Modern Yiddish Literature."
    Trans. Elliot Palevsky. *Yiddish*. 1. (Summer, 1973), pp. 54–62.
———. *Moyshe Leib Halpern in ram fun zayn dor*. New York: M. L. Halpern &
    Workmen's Circle Branch 450, 1942.
[Halpern within the Frame of His Generation]
———. *Tsentrale motivn in H. Leyvik's shafn*. New York: Central Yiddish Culture
    Organization, 1961.
[Central Motifs in Leivick's Works]
———. *Yankev Glatstein's "Freyd fun yidishn vort."* New York: Central Yiddish Culture
    Organization, 1964.
[Glatstein's *Joy of the Yiddish Word*]
Greenberg, Irving. *"Yidishe shrayber in amerike*. New York: Yidisher kultur farband,
    1963.
[Yiddish Writers in America]
Kahn, Mikhal. *"Yoysef Bovshover: zayn lebn un zayn shafn."* *Gezamlte shriftn: poezye
    un proze*, by Yoysef Bovshover. New York: Fraye arbayter shtime, 1911, pp. iii–
    xxviii.
[Bovshover: His Life and Works]
Katz, Moshe. "Dovid Edelshtadt." *Dovid Edelshtadt: Shriftn*. London: Arbayter fraynd,
    1909; New York: Fraye arbayter shtime, 1925, pp. iii–xxv.
Lieberman, Chaim. *Sholem Asch un kristentum: an entfer oyf zayne misyonerishe shriftn*.
    New York: Om, 1950.

[Asch and Christianity: An Answer to His Missionary Writings; a vicious attack on
    the writer]
Marmor, Kalman. *Dovid Edelshtadt*. New York: Cooperative People's Publishers, 1942.
————. *Dovid Edelshtadt*. New York: Yidisher kultur farband, 1950.
————. *Mayn lebns geshikhte*. New York: Yidisher kultur farband, 1959.
    [My Life History]
————. *Yoysef Bovshover*. New York: Kalman Marmor jubiley komitet, 1952.
Meisel, Nachman. "*Amerike in di verk fun Sholem Asch*." *Yidisher kultur farband
    almanakh*. New York: Yidisher kultur farband, 1961.
    [America in the Works of Sholem Asch]
————. "*B. Rivkin—der kritiker, der entuziast*." *B. Rivkin: Lebn un shafn*, comp. Mina
    Rivkin. Chicago: L. M. Shteyn, 1953, pp. 223–238.
[Rivkin—the Critic, the Enthusiast]
————. *Tsum hundertstn geboyrntog fun Moris Rozenfeld: zamlung*. New York: Yidisher
    kultur farband, 1962.
[On the 100th Birthday of Morris Rosenfeld]
Minkoff, Nochum Boruch. *Avram Reyzn: der dikhter fun lid*. New York: Badn, 1936.
    [A. Reisin: Poet of the Song]
————. "David Pinski." *Di goldene kayt*. 12. (1952), pp. 21–35.
————. *Nochum Boruch Minkoff (1893–1958)*. New York: N. B. Minkoff bukh komitet,
    1959.
————. "Sh. Niger." *Zeks yidishe kritiker*. Buenos Aires: Yidbukh, 1954, pp. 293–
    344.
————. "Yoyl Entin." *Zeks yidishe kritiker*. Buenos Aires: Yidbukh, 1954, pp. 171–
    223.
————. *Zeks yidishe kritiker*. Buenos Aires: Yidbukh, 1954.
[Six Yiddish Critics]
[Rivkin—Temperamental Literary Critic]
Mukdoyni, Alexander. "*A bukh vegn Sholem Asch*." *Der morgn-zhurnal*. (February 4,
    1951), p. 10.
————. "*B. Rivkin's verk*." *B. Rivkin: Lebn un shafn*. Comp. Mina Rivkin. Chicago:
    L. M. Shteyn, 1953, pp. 169–176.
[Rivkin's Works: rpt. from *Der Morgn-zhurnal* (December 23, 1951), p. 9]
————."*B. Rivkin—der temperamentfuler literatur-kritiker*." *B. Rivkin: lebn un shafn*,
    comp. Mina Rivkin. Chicago: L. M. Shteyn, 1953, pp. 160–162.
[A Book about Sholem Asch; on Lieberman's *Sholem Asch un kristentum*]
Niger, Sh. (Samuel) "*Amerike in dertseylungen fun A. M. Dik* (1814–1893)." *YIVO
    bleter*. 38. (1954), pp. 106–116.
    [America in the Stories of I. M.Dik]
————. *Dertseyler un romanistn*. New York: Central Yiddish Culture Organization,
    1946.
[Storytellers and Novelists]
————. "*Dikhter un kritiker*." *Geklibene shriftn*, vol. 2. New York: Jewish Culture,
    1928.
[Poets and Critics]
————. *H. Leyvik, 1888–1948*. Toronto: Gershon Pomerantz, 1951.
————. "Kritik—'literatur-farvaltung.'" *B. Rivkin: lebn un shafn*, comp. Mina Rivkin.
    Chicago: L. M. Shteyn, 1953, pp. 145–151.

[On Rivkin; rpt. from *Der tog* (August 14, 1949), p. 6]

―――. *Kritik un kritiker*. Buenos Aires: Congress for Jewish Culture, 1959.

[Criticism and Critics]

―――. *"Meshiyakhistishe kritik." B.Rivkin: lebn un shafn*, comp. Mina Rivkin. Chicago: L. M. Shteyn, 1953, pp. 152–159.

[On Rivkin's Messianic Criticism; rpt. from *Der tog* (August 28, 1949), p. 5]

―――. *Sholem Ash: zayn lebn,-zayne verk: byografye, opshatsungen, polemik, brif*, comp. Melekh Ravitch. New York: Sh. Niger Book Committee, Congress for Jewish Culture, 1960.

[Asch: His Life, Works, Biography, Evaluations, Polemics, Letters]

―――. *"Der sotn"* (1936). *Yidishe shrayber fun tsvantsikstn yorhundert*, vol. 2. New York: Congress for Jewish Culture, 1973, pp. 299–303.

[Satan; on I. B. Singer's *Satan in Goray*]

―――. *"Der sotn hot dos vort"* (1943). *Yidishe shrayber fun tsvantsikstn yorhundert*, vol. 2. New York: Congress for Jewish Culture, 1973, pp. 303–309.

[Satan Has the Floor; on I. B. Singer's *Satan in Goray*]

―――. *Yidishe shrayber fun tsvantsikstn yorhundert*. 2 vols. New York: Congress for Jewish Culture, 1972.

[Yiddish Writers of the Twentieth Century]

―――. *"Y. Opatoshu's 'Mi un furem'"* (1936). *Yidishe shrayber fun tsvantsikstn yorhundert*, vol. 1. New York: Congress for Jewish Culture, 1972, pp. 226–231.

[Opatoshu's "Efforts and Form"]

Olgin, Moissaye Joseph. *Yitskhok Leybush Perets*. New York: Yidisher kultur farband, 1955.

[on Peretz]

Pat, Jacob. *Shmuesn mit yidishe shrayber*. New York: Marstin Press, 1954.

[Conversations with Yiddish Writers]

Ravitch, Melech. "I. J. Singer." *Jewish Book Annual*. 26. (1968), pp. 121–124.

Reisin, Abraham. *"B. Rivkin's nayer gang in publitsistik un kritik"* (1946). *B.Rivkin: lebn un shafn*, comp. Mina Rivkin. Chicago: L. M. Shteyn, 1953, pp. 44–52.

[Rivkin's New Steps in Journalism and Criticism]

Rivkin, B. *H. Leyvik, zayne lider un dramatishe verk*. Buenos Aires: Yidbukh, 1955.

[Leivick, His Poems and Dramatic Works]

――― *"Opatoshu's hoypt-oyftu." Undzere prozayiker*. New York: Yidisher kultur farband, 1951, pp. 243–254.

[Opatoshu's Main Accomplishment]

―――. *Undzere prozayiker*. New York: Yidisher kultur farband, 1951.

[Our Prose Writers; includes discussions of Leon Kobrin, David Pinski, Abraham Reisin, Jonah Rosenfeld, Peretz Hirshbein, David Ignatoff, Joseph Opatoshu, Mendele, Peretz, I. J. Singer, Boruch Glassman, B. Epelboym, and P. Bimko]

―――. *Yidishe dikhter in amerike*. 2 vols. New York: Central Yiddish Culture Organization, 1947; Buenos Aires: Yidbukh 1959.

[Yiddish Poets in America]

―――. *Yoysef Opatoshus gang*. Toronto: Gershon Pomerantz Essay Library, 1948.

[Opatoshu's Way]

Rivkin, Mina Bordo, comp. *B. Rivkin: lebn un shafn*. Chicago: L. M. Shteyn, 1953.

[Rivkin: Life and Works]

Rontsh, Isaac Elchanan. "*B. Rivkin—der ontsinder fun yidishn vort.*" *B. Rivkin: lebn un shafn*, comp. Mina Rivkin. Chicago: L. M. Shteyn, 1953, pp. 96–100.
[Rivkin—Kindler of the Yiddish Word]
Schulman, Elias. "*Avrom Reyzn vi a redaktor.*" Installments in *Bay zikh* (Tel Aviv). 9–19. (1977–December 1981), various pages.
[Reisin as an Editor]
———. *Portretn un etyudn.* New York: Central Yiddish Culture Organization, 1979.
[Portraits and Studies]
Shtern, Sholem. "*Talantful un farshidnartik is geven der dikhter un eseyist B. J. Bialostotzky.*" *Yidishe kultur.* (August-September, 1985), pp. 28–31.
[Talented and Diversified Was the Poet and Essayist Bialostotzky]
Singer, Sh. D. *Dikhter un prozayiker: eseyen vegn shrayber un bikher.* New York: Ed. Dept. of Workmen's Circle, 1959.
[Poets and Prose Writers; essays about writers and books]
———. "*Yankev Glatshteyn.*" *Pinkis far der forshung fun der yidisher literatur*, vol. 2. Ed. Hyman Bass. New York: Congress for Jewish Culture, 1972, pp. 11–27.
[Jacob Glatstein]
Spivak, Charles David. "*Erinerungen fun Cahan's grine tsaytn.*" *Yubileum shrift tsu Ab. Cahan's 50th geburtstog, Dec. 11, 1910.* New York: Jubilee Committee, 1910.
[Reminiscences of Cahan's Early Years]
Starkman, Moshe, ed. *Shlomo Bikl yoyvl-bukh.* New York: Matones, 1967.
[Bickel's Anniversary Book]
Tabachnik, Abraham. "*B. Rivkin.*" *B. Rivkin: lebn un shafn*, comp. Mina Rivkin. Chicago: L. M. Shteyn, 1953, pp. 239–261.
———. "*A Conversation with Jacob Glatstein.*" Trans. Joseph C. Landis. *Yiddish.* 1. (Summer, 1973), pp. 40–53.
[Taped 1955]
———. *Der man fun lid.* New York: M. Shkyarski, 1941.
[Man of the Poem; Zishe Landau]
———. *Der mentsh in khulem: di dikhtung fun Meyer Shtiker.* New York: Marstin Press, 1962.
[The Man in a Dream: The Poetry of Meyer Shticker]
Tenenboym, Sh. "*Avrom Reyzn der poet: likoved zayn 70-yoriker geburtstog yubiley.*" *Shnit fun mayn feld: eseyen, dertseylungen, miniaturn.* New York: Sh. Tenenboym, 1949, pp. 255–260.
[Reisin the Poet: In Honor of His 70th Birthday]
———. "*B. A. Weinrib—B. Rivkin—Mark Taleron: Necrologye.*" *Shnit fun mayn feld: eseyen, dertseylungen, miniaturn.* New York: Sh. Tenenboym, 1949, pp. 154–156.
———. "*Verter vegn Sholem Ashn.*" *Shnit fun mayn feld: eseyen, dertseylungen, miniaturn.* New York: Sh. Tenenboym, 1949, pp. 154–156.
[Words about Sholem Asch]
———. "*Yoysef Opatoshu's kurtse dertseylungen.*" *Shnit fun mayn feld.* New York: Sh. Tenenboym, 1949, pp. 353–368.
[Opatoshu's Short Stories; negative remarks]

Criticism in General

Indispensable general critical studies of American Yiddish literature include B. Rivkin's *Grunt-tendentsn fun der yidisher literatur in amerike* (Basic Tendencies of Yiddish Literature in America) and Elias Schulman's *Geshikhte fun der yidisher literatur in amerike: 1870–1900* (History of Yiddish Literature in America). Also see:

Baranov, M. *"Fun vanen hobn zikh genumen poetn?* (*nokh Herbert Spencer*)." *Arbayter tsaytung*. (March 20, 1896), p. 4, and (March 27, 1896), p. 6.
[From Where Do Poets Come? (After Herbert Spencer)]
——. *"Vos iz poezye?" Arbayter tsaytung*. (March 13, 1896), p. 7.
[What Is Poetry?]
Bialostotzky, Benjamin Jacob. *"Motivn fun arbet un kamf in der yidisher poezye." Der veker*. (June 10, 1922), pp. 17–20.
[Themes of Work and Struggle in Yiddish Poetry]
Bickel, Shlomo. *Detaln un sakh-haklen: kritishe un polemishe bamerkungen*. New York: Matones, 1943.
[Details and Summaries: Critical and Polemical Remarks]
Bovshover, Joseph. "Vegn poezye." *Gezamlte shriftn: poezye un proze*. New York: Fraye arbayter shtime, 1911, pp. 281–309.
[About Poetry]
Edelshtadt, David. "Printsipenlozikayt fun der zhargonishe literatur in amerike." *Dovid Edelshtadt: shriftn*. London: Arbayter fraynd,1909; New York: Fraye arbayter shtime, 1925, pp. 381–385.
[Lack of Principles of Yiddish Literature in America]
——. *"Zhargonishe dikhter." Dovid Edelshtadt: Shriftn*. London: Arbayter freynd, 1909; New York: Fraye arbayter shtime, 1925, pp. 386–391.
[Yiddish Poets]
Entin, Joel. *Vos iz literatur?* New York: Yidish-natsyonaler arbeter farband, 1919.
[What Is Literature?]
Glanz, Aaron. *Velt un vort: literarishe un andere eseyen*. New York: Central Yiddish Culture Organization, 1958.
[World and Word: Literary and Other Essays]
Glatstein, Jacob. *"Kritik far a novine." Prost un poshet*. New York: Fanny Gladstone, 1978, pp. 34–37.
[Criticism for a Change; rpt. from *Yidisher kemfer*. (August 16, 1963), pp. 9–10].
——. *"An ode tsu der kritik." Prost un poshet*. New York: Fanny Gladstone, 1978, pp. 108–110.
[An Ode to Criticism]
——. "Of Yiddish and Yiddish Poetry" (Interview). *Keeping Posted*. 17. (December, 1971), pp. 8ff.
——. "Short View of Yiddish Poetry" (1920). Trans. Joseph C. Landis. *Yiddish*. 1. (Summer, 1973), pp. 30–39.
——. "Thinking Back." Trans. Henry Goodman. *Yiddish*. 3. (Spring, 1978), pp. 33–36.

Goldberg, Itche. *"Oyf der shvel fun tsveytn yorhundert* (100 *yor yidishe literatur un prese in di fareynikte shtatn)"* (1970). *Eseyen.* New York: Yidisher kultur farband, 1981, pp. 189–206.
[On the Threshold of the Second Century (100 Years of Yiddish Literature and Press in the U.S.A.)]

———. *"Dos drite oyr fun der yidisher literatur."* *Yidishe kultur.* (June-July, 1985), pp. 18–21.
[The Third Ear of Yiddish Literature]

Goodman, Saul Lederman. *Traditsye un banayung: eseyen 1944–1966.* New York: Matones, 1967.
[Tradition and Renewal]

Ignatoff, David. *Opgerisene bleter: eseyen.* Buenos Aires: Yidbukh, 1957.
[Torn-off Pages]

Marmor, Kalman. *Der onheyb fun der yidisher literatur in amerike (1870–1890).* New York: Yidisher kultur farband, 1944.
[Birth of Yiddish Literature in America]

Meisel, Nachman. *Doyres un tekufes in der yidisher literatur: bletlekh tsu der geshikhte un tsu der kharakteristik fun der yidisher literatur.* New York: Yidisher kultur farband, 1942.
[Generations and Ages in Yiddish Literature: Pages on the History and Characteristics of Yiddish Literature]

———. *Forgeyer un mit-tsaytler.* New York: Yidisher kultur farband, 1946.
[Forerunners and Contemporaries]

———. *Tsurikblikn un perspektivn.* Tel Aviv: Y. L. Peretz, 1962.
[Looking Back and Perspectives]

Minkoff, Nochum Boruch. *Literarishe vegn.* Mexico: Culture Commission, Yiddish Central Committee, 1955.
[Literary Ways; essays]

Niger, Sh. *Bleter geshikhte fun der yidisher literatur,* comp. H. Leivick. New York: Sh. Niger bukh komitet of Congress for Jewish Culture, 1959.
[Pages of History of Yiddish Literature]

———. *Fun mayn togbukh,* intro. Hyman Bass. New York: Congress for Jewish Culture, 1973.
[Diary and Literary Notes]

———. *Kritik un kritiker.* Buenos Aires: Congress for Jewish Culture, 1959.
[Criticism and Critics]

———. *Leyzer, dikhter, kritiker.* New York: Yidisher kultur farband, 1928.
[Readers, Poets, Critics]

———. *Shmuesn vegn bikher.* New York: Farlag Yiddish, 1922.
[Discussions about Books]

———. *Di tsveyshprakhikayt fun undzer literatur.* Michigan: Louis La Med Foundation for the Advancement of Hebrew and Yiddish Literature, 1941.
[The Dual Languages, Hebrew and Yiddish, of Our Literature]

———. *"Vegn dem onheyb fun der nayer yidisher literatur."* *Tsukunft.* (June, July, August, September, 1944), various pages.
[About the Birth of Our New Yiddish Literature]

Olgin, Moissaye Joseph. *In der velt fun gezangen; a bukh vegn poezye un poetn.* New York: Forverts, 1919.

[In the World of Song; A Book about Poetry and Poets]

Opatoshu, Joseph. "*50 yor yidishe literatur in di fareynikte shtatn.*" YIVO bleter. 38. (1954), pp. 39–50.

[50 Years of Yiddish Literature in the U.S.A.]

———. "Yiddish Literature in the United States" (1949). Trans. Shlomo Noble. *Voices from the Yiddish*, ed. Irving Howe and Eliezer Greenberg. Ann Arbor: University of Michigan Press, 1972, pp. 306–315.

Rivkin, B. *A gloybn far umgloybike*, comp. Mina Rivkin, ed. Aba Gordin. New York: David Ignatoff Literature Fund, 1947.

[A Belief for Non-Believers]

———. *Grunt-tendentsn fun der yidisher literatur in amerike*, comp. Mina Rivkin. New York: Yidisher kultur farband, 1948.

[Basic Tendencies of Yiddish Literature in America]

Rontch, Isaac Elchanan. *Amerike in der yidisher literatur*. New York: I. A. Rontch Book Committee, 1945.

[America in Yiddish Literature]

Rozshanski, Samuel. *Yidishe literatur—yidish lebn*. Argentina, IWO, 1973.

[Yiddish Literature—Yiddish Life]

Schulman,Elias. *Geshikhte fun der yidisher literatur in amerike: 1870–1900*. New York: I. W. Biderman, 1943.

[History of Yiddish Literature in America: 1870–1900]

———. "*Veltlekhe motivn in der alter yidisher literatur.*" *Bay zikh*. 21. (December, 1982), pp. 78–93.

[Worldly Motifs in Old Yiddish Literature]

Tabachnik, Abraham. "Tradition and Revolt in Yiddish Poetry." Trans. Cynthia Ozick. *Voices from the Yiddish*, ed. Irving Howe and Eliezer Greenberg. Ann Arbor: University of Michigan Press, 1972, pp. 289–299.

Collections of Various Kinds of Critical Articles Including Encyclopedias

Most indispensable is the *Lexikon fun der nayer yidisher literatur*, 7 vols. (New York: Congress for Jewish Culture, 1968). Other collections include the following:

Bass, Hyman B., 147 ed. *Pinkis far der forshung fun der yidisher literatur un prese*, vol. 2. New York: Congress for Jewish Culture, 1972.

[Yiddish Literature and the Yiddish Press]

———. *Shrayber un verk: literarishe-kritishe un pedagogishe eseyen*. Tel Aviv: Hamenora, 1971.

[Writers and Works: Literary-Critical and Pedagogical Essays]

Bialostotzky, Benjamin Jacob. *Fun di shtamen*. New York: Education Committee of Workmen's Circle, 1939.

[From the Stems]

———. *Kholem in vor: eseyen*. New York: Committee (n.p.), 1956.

[Dream in Reality: Essays]

———. *Lider un eseyen*. 2 vols. New York: Tsvaygn, 1932.

[Vol. 2: Essays]

Bickel, Shlomo. *Der yidisher esey: a zamlung*. New York: Matones, 1946.
   [The Yiddish Essay: A Collection]
———. ed. *Pinkis far der forshung fun der yidisher literatur un prese*, vol. 1. New
   York: Congress for Jewish Culture, 1965.
   [Yiddish Literature and the Yiddish Press]
Coralnik, Abraham. *Shriftn*. 3 vols. New York: Coralnik farlag komitet, 1938–1940.
   [Writings: Vol. 1: Characters and Thoughts; Vol. 2: Ideas and Jews; Vol. 3: Moods
   and Pictures]
Entin, Joel. *Gezamlte shriftn*, ed. S. Shapiro. New York: Pinkhis Gingold Publishers of
   the National Committee of Yiddish Elementary Schools, 1960.
   [Collected Writings]
———. intro. and ed. *Idishe poetn; hantbukh fun idisher dikhtung*. New York: Folkshul
   organizatsye fun idish natsyonaln arbeter farband un poali zion, 1927.
   [Yiddish Poets; Handbook of Yiddish Poetry]
Glatstein, Jacob. *In der velt mit yidish: eseyen*. New York: Congress for Jewish Culture,
   1972.
   [In the World with Yiddish: Essays]
———. *In tokh genumen: eseyen (1945–1947)*. New York: Matones, 1947.
   [Sum and Substance]
———. *In tokh genumen: eseyen (1948–1956)*. New York: Yidish-natsyonaln arbeter
   farband, 1956.
———. *In tokh genumen: eseyen (1949–1959)*. Buenos Aires: Yidbukh, 1960.
———. *Mit mayne fartogbikher*. Tel Aviv: Y. L. Peretz, 1963.
   [With my Daybreak Books; *In tokh genumen 1958–1962*]
———. *Oyf greyte temes*. Tel Aviv: Y. L. Peretz, 1967.
   [Upon Ready Themes]
———. *Prost un poshet: literarishe eseyen*, comp. Berl Kahn. New York: Fanny Glad-
   stone, 1978.
   [Plain and Simple]
Goldberg, Itche. *Eseyen*. New York: Yidisher kultur farband, 1981.
   [Essays]
Greenberg, Irving. *Fun dor tsu dor: literarishe eseyen*. New York: Yidisher kultur farband
   and Ber Grin bukh komitet. 1971.
   [From Generation to Generation: Literary Essays]
Leivick, H. *Eseyen un redes*. New York: Congress for Jewish Culture, 1963.
   [Essays and Speeches]
Niger, Sh. *Geklibene shriftn*. 3 vols. New York: Jewish Culture, 1928.
   [Selected Writings; vols. 1–2: Readers, Poets, Critics; Vol. 3: Sholem Aleichem]
Ravitch, Melekh, Yankev Pat, and Zanvil Dyamant, eds. *Almanakh "Yidish"*. New
   York: Congress for Jewish Culture, 1961.
Reisin, Zalman. *Lexikon fun der yidisher literatur, prese un filologye*. 4 vols. 3d ed.
   Vilna: B. Kleckin, 1927–1929.
   [Handbook of New Yiddish Literature, Press and Philology]

Bibliographies

E. H. Jeshurin undertook the important task of compiling Yiddish bibliographies. Among these are the following:

Jeshurin, E. H. *"B. Rivkin biblyografye."* *B. Rivkin: lebn un shafn*, comp. Mina Rivkin.
    Chicago: L. M. Shteyn, 1953, pp. 306–336.
    [Lists hundreds of articles by Rivkin]
————. *"B. J. Bialostotzky biblyografye."* B. J. Bialostotzky. *Lid tsu lid*. New York:
    n.p., 1958, pp. i–xxv.
————.·*"Nokhum Borukh Minkoff bibliografye."* *Nokhum Borukh Minkoff (1893–1958)*.
    New York: N. B. Minkoff Book Committee, 1959, pp. 314–348.
————. *"Shmuel Niger bibliografye."* *Kultur un dertsiyung*. 26. (February, 1956),
    pp. 36–39.

Selected Sources in English

A few sources in English are quite helpful. Among these are the following:

Encyclopaedia Judaica. 16 Vols. Jerusalem: Keter; New York: Macmillan, 1971.
Howe, Irving. "The Culture of Yiddish." *World of Our Fathers*. New York: Harcourt
    Brace Jovanovich, 1976, pp. 417–551.
Howe, Irving, and Eliezer Greenberg, eds. *Voices from the Yiddish*. Ann Arbor: University
    of Michigan Press, 1972.
Liptzin, Sol. "The Rise of Literary Criticism." *The Maturing of Yiddish Literature*. New
    York: Jonathan David, 1970.
Madison, Charles. *Yiddish Literature: Its Scope and Major Writers*. New York: Schocken,
    1971.

NOTES

1. Nachman Meisel, *"B. Rivkin—der kritiker, der entuziast,"* in B. Rivkin, pp. 223–
224. This quotation and all future quotations are my own translation, unless otherwise
noted in the bibliography.
2. Elias Schulman, *Geshikhte fun der yidisher literatur in amerike*, p. 73.
3. Ibid., p. 78.
4. Ibid., p. 75.
5. In *Dovid Edelshtadt*, p. 386.
6. *"Literarishe iberzikht,"* *Di yugnd*. 2. (1907). Landau expressed this sentiment in
the Introduction to the anthology *In zikh* (1919), when he made his famous witty remark
that Sweatshop Poetry had been "the rhyme department of the Jewish Labor Movement."
7. N. B. Minkoff, *"Yoyl Entin."* *Zeks yidishe kritiker*, p. 199.
8. B. Rivkin, *Grunt-tendentsn*, p. 295.
9. Alexander Mukdoyni, *"B. Rivkin—der temperamentfuler literatur-kritiker,"* in *B.
Rivkin*, p. 161.
10. I. E. Rontch, *"Der ontsinder fun yidishn vort,"* in *B. Rivkin*. p. 97.
11. Rivkin, *Grunt-tendentsn*, p. 276.
12. Ibid., p. 61.
13. Abraham Tabachnik, "B. Rivkin," in *B. Rivkin*, pp. 245, 251.
14. Shmuel Niger, *Kritik un kritiker*, p. 148.
15. Jacob Glatstein, "B. Rivkin," in *B. Rivkin*, p. 65.
16. Shmuel Niger, *Kritik un kritiker*, p. 125.

17. Ibid., p. 127.

18. Ibid., p. 119.

19. Ibid., p. 132.

20. [Jacob] Yankev Pat, *Shmuesn mit yidishe shrayber*, p. 223.

21. N. B. Minkoff, *Zeks yidishe kritiker*, p. 304.

22. Hyman B. Bass, "*Shmuel Niger un Bal-makhshoves*," *Shrayber un verk*, p. 43.

23. Abraham Tabachnik, "A Conversation with Jacob Glatstein," p. 52.

24. Bass, "Niger un Bal-makhshoves," p. 65.

25. Benjamin Jacob Bialostotzky, *Lider un eseyen*, vol. 2, p. 5.

26. Benjamin Jacob Bialostotzky, *Kholem in vor*, p. 9.

27. Ibid.

28. Benjamin Jacob Bialostotzky, "In the Beginning Days," *Kholem in vor*, p. 435.

29. Hyman B. Bass, "*N. B. Minkoff: der dikhter un kritiker*," *Shrayber un verk*, p. 457.

30. N. B. Minkoff, *Pyonern*, p. 14.

31. Shlomo Bickel, "N. B. Minkoff," p. 222.

32. Shlomo Bickel, "*Mayne iker ideyen*," p. 11.

33. Ibid., p. 13.

34. Ibid., p. 14.

35. Bickel, "N. B. Minkoff," p. 222.

36. Ibid., pp. 224, 225.

37. Bickel, "*Mayne iker ideyen*," p. 14.

38. Niger, *Kritik un kritiker*, p. 141.

39. Jacob Glatstein, *Prost un poshet*, pp. 109, 110.

40. Itche Goldberg, "*Ber Grin*," *Eseyen*, p. 297.

BIBLIOGRAPHY

Bass, Hyman B. *Shrayber un verk*. Tel Aviv: Hamenora, 1971.

Bialostotzky, Benjamin Jacob. *Kholem in vor: eseyen*. New York: Committee (n.p.), 1956.

———. *Lider un eseyen*, vol. 2, New York: Tsvaygn, 1932.

Bickel, Shlomo. *Shrayber fun mayn dor*. vol. 1. New York: Matones, 1958.

Edelshtadt, David. *Dovid Edelshtadt: shriftn*. New York: Fraye arbayter shtime, 1925.

Glatstein, Jacob. "B. Rivkin." *B. Rivkin: lebn un shafn*, comp. Mina Bordo Rivkin. Chicago: L. M. Shteyn, 1953, pp. 63–70.

———. *Prost un poshet*. New York: Fanny Gladstone, 1978.

Goldberg, Itche. *Eseyen*. New York: Yidisher kultur farband, 1981.

Meisel, Nachman. "*B. Rivkin—der kritiker, der entuziast*." *B. Rivkin: lebn un shafn*, comp. Mina Bordo Rivkin. Chicago: L. M. Shteyn, 1953, pp. 223–238.

Minkoff, Nochum Boruch. *Pyonern fun yidisher poezye in amerike: dos sotsyale lid*. 3 vols. New York: Grenich, 1956.

———. *Zeks yidishe kritiker*. Buenos Aires: Yidbukh, 1954.

Mukdoyni, Alexander. "*B. Rivkin—der temperamentfuler literatur-kritiker*." *B. Rivkin: lebn un shafn*, comp. Mina Bordo Rivkin. Chicago: L. M. Shteyn, 1953, pp. 160–162.

Niger, Samuel. *Kritik un kritiker*. Buenos Aires: Congress for Jewish Culture, 1959.

Pat, Jacob. *Shmuesn mit yidishe shrayber*. New York: Marstin Press, 1954.

Rivkin, B. *Grunt-tendentsn fun der yidisher literatur in amerike*, 1936; rev., comp. Mina
    Bordo Rivkin. New York: Yidisher kultur farband, 1948.
Rontch, Isaac Elchanan. *"Der ontsinder fun yidishn vort." B. Rivkin: lebn un shafn*,
    comp. Mina Bordo Rivkin. Chicago: L. M. Shteyn, 1953, pp. 96–100.
Schulman, Elias. *Geshikhte fun der yidisher literatur in amerike: 1870–1900*. New York:
    I. M. Biderman, 1943.
Tabachnik, Abraham. "B. Rivkin." *B. Rivkin: lebn un shafn*, comp. Mina Bordo Rivkin.
    Chicago: L. M. Shteyn, 1953, pp. 239–261.
———. "A Conversation with Jacob Glatstein," trans. Joseph C. Landis. *Yiddish*. 1.
    (Summer, 1973), pp. 40–53.

8

A Question of Tradition: Women Poets in Yiddish

Kathryn Hellerstein

I

In 1928, Ezra Korman, a teacher and literary critic living in Detroit, Michigan, published a volume of Yiddish poems by women, entitled *Yidishe dikhterins: antologye* (Yiddish Women Poets: Anthology). Clothbound, lavishly illustrated, replete with introductions, notes, and bibliographies, this book collected poems by seventy women who published between 1586 and 1927. The earliest figures represented in Korman's anthology wrote popular devotional poetry in Krakow and Prague. The poets after the *Haskalah* (Jewish Enlightenment) in the late nineteenth century wrote on national and social themes, using metaphorically the images and conventions of devotional literature. The more recent poets composed lyrics in America and in the Soviet Union, under the influence of socialism and cosmopolitan modernism. From the evidence of Korman's collection, a reader would assume that in 1928 women poets were a significant presence in Yiddish literature.

In fact, Korman's volume was the first of its sort to be published, and since then, there has not been another like it in Yiddish.[1] Women poets have been sporadically included in anthologies of Yiddish poetry and of English translations from Yiddish.[2] A few articles have appeared over the decades discussing women poets in Yiddish. What has accumulated is an as yet uncatalogued, but fairly extensive, literature of critical essays, memoirs, and reviews in Yiddish on some of the individual women poets. However, there has been until recently almost no treatment of women poets in Yiddish which picks up where Korman left off. Since the controversial dispute on the subject in the 1910's and 1920's, from which Korman's anthology emerged, the topic has remained virtually unexplored. The questions to be asked of this literature now, in light of the new methods and perspectives of feminist literary criticism of the 1970's and 1980's, are quite different from the questions asked of it in the earlier period. The subject needs a fresh start. Within its limited confines, the following essay cannot adequately cover all the issues or the writers. Yet it will attempt to sketch out some of the terms and questions that such a new work might undertake.

I will begin by surveying the secondary literature in English. From the perspective of the social historian, there is a good introductory essay by Norma Fain Pratt, covering the careers of fifty Yiddish women writers.[3] Recent histories of Yiddish literature and culture, such as the classics, *World of Our Fathers* (1976) by Irving Howe, and *Against the Apocalypse* (1984) by David G. Roskies, make a few passing references to one or two women writers.[4] Most feminist studies of Jewish women focus on historical, psychological, sociological, religious, or philosophical questions.[5] Even works devoted specifically to Jewish women and literature omit Yiddish poetry; they most often concentrate on the depiction of women characters in biblical, rabbinic, and Israeli prose, writtten in Hebrew, or American-Jewish fiction, written in English.[6]

From the literary perspective, there has not been a systematic or comprehensive consideration of the poetry itself. It is hard, then, to begin with authentic generalizations about poetry by women or the place of this work in the tradition of Yiddish literature. Instead, I choose to touch on specifics. This essay, part of a larger work in progress, will shed some light on Yiddish poetry by women, by considering Korman's anthology as an artifact of a women's poetic tradition in Yiddish.

II

To determine whether in fact there is a tradition of women's poetry in Yiddish, we must consider generally how the idea of a literary tradition developed in modern Yiddish poetry. We necessarily begin with a discussion of tradition and the modern. In his introduction to the 1984 Hebrew University edition of the biblical poems of Itzik Manger, Chone Shmeruk notes that "T. S. Eliot's essay of 1919, 'Tradition and the Individual Talent,' is the classic point of departure for any discussion of the problem of literary traditions in modern literature."[7]

Eliot argues that tradition and poetry are mutually dependent: poetry invents the tradition in which it stands, for the dead inform the living, while the living reform the dead.[8] Accordingly, the traditional writer transcends time by means of a historical sense, while the value of the individual talent is attributed to its context: " . . . [the poet] is not likely to know what is to be done unless he lives in what is not merely the present, but the present moment of the past, unless he is conscious not of what is dead, but of what is already living."[9] Eliot dismisses an idea of time and tradition as an irreversible, linear movement from past to present, from old to new. Rather, he articulates a simultaneity of the dead and the living in a metaphor that makes literary works themselves alive and part of the organism of tradition. In contrast to Eliot's integration of past and present stands a contradicting contemporary "notion of [modern art as] radical performance" which becomes "in some modern aesthetics a theory of anti-art, an act of negation denying the formal significance of perpetuated, monumentalized expression.''[10]

The Yiddish modernist movements incorporated this violent break with the past and the poet's attempt to redefine the present in radically different terms. At the same time, these movements embodied Eliot's idea of a living tradition as the seeking of connection, if not with the immediate literary past, then with strains of Yiddish literature remote from the self-conscious act of writing poetry in the American city. These strains include genres such as folk songs, ballads, and popular devotional literature for women that the poets had known directly in their former lives in the *shtetlekh*, or that they came to know indirectly through "a new scholarship" of Old Yiddish literature.[11] The poet's urges to destroy and to invent a literary past are both means to justify the artistic act of writing poetry in Yiddish at that present moment. Because of the contradictions inherent in the peculiar ideological, historical, and cultural situations of the Yiddish writers, often in modern Yiddish poems of the early twentieth century, these paradoxical tendencies co-exist.[12]

The tendency to revise the literary past can be seen clearly in the two modernist Yiddish movements in America, first the *Yunge* in the 1910's and later the Introspectivists in the 1920's. Each of these groups set out to establish new criteria for a consciously modern Yiddish poetry to override the unselfconscious thematic, formal, and didactic conventions of national and social poetry of the late nineteenth century. Each group set forth its ideas about poetry implicitly and explicitly in anthologies. The *Yunge* composed manifestos which set up an ideology of poetry that stood against ideology and emphasized the individualism of poetic voice and experience. Ironically, this emphasis on the individual was made with self-sacrificing zeal to adhere to the ideals of individuality and in the rhetoric of the very political ideologies the poets eschewed.

Initially, in the early nineteen-teens, the *Yunge* published their avant-garde poetry in *zamlbikher*, or miscellanies, such as *Shriftn* (Writings, 1911, 1914, etc.); *Di naye heym* (The New Home, 1914); *East Broadway* (1916). In contrast, in the late teens, as the members of the young avant-garde of Yiddish poetry matured and published their own books of poems, *antologyes*, or anthologies, began to appear in Yiddish. These anthologies differ from the *zamlbikher* in that they suggest a need to define a historical literary tradition into which the current poets can fit themselves, rather than presenting the current literature being written. The historical anthology of Yiddish poetry stands as a statement of literary purpose. It embodies T. S. Eliot's idea of tradition and the individual talent. But the idea of where the individual talent fits into the tradition, and how that individual in the present can alter the past, varies from anthology to anthology. Each anthology implies its own ideology of Yiddish poetry.

The rebellious early moderns, known as the *Yunge*, rejected the idea that the poet must serve the Yiddish language and the Jewish people's political and national causes, as preached and practiced in the 1890's and 1900's by such labor poets as David Edelstadt (Edelshtadt) and Morris Rosenfeld. Ruth Wisse formulates their situation in terms of "the paradox that shaped [the] art" of these self-defined literary orphans, who were "rootless, without tradition."[14] The works of Moyshe-Leyb Halpern, Mani Leyb (Leib, born Brahinsky), and Halper Leyvik (Leivick) reflect both ironically and respectfully the merging of a re-created folk voice in Yiddish poetry with the effects of the poets' recent exposure to European and American poetry.

The resulting aesthetic and ideological tensions are evident in the anthologies of poetry in the early part of this century, which evince the way Yiddish literature was inventing its own history. One anthology, assembled and introduced by Zishe Landau, represented Yiddish poetry in America until the year 1919. Landau's *Antologye* is representative of the conflict the *Yunge* perceived between the individual poetic voice and experience, and the powerful pull of and need for a collective context for that voice.[15] This conflict between the individual and the collective endeavor is found in the earlier *zamlbukh*, *East Broadway* compiled by M. L. Halpern and Menachem in one of its two centerpiece sequences of poems, Halpern's "*A nakht*" (A Night) and H. Leyvik's "*In shney*" (In Snow), the former of which presents a narrator whose "I" is simultaneously and paradoxically that of the isolated psyche and of the historically collective Jewish people.[16] Halpern's poem presents the disintegrating logic of historical continuity and of ideology, including socialism and Jewish nationalism, and questions the place of the individual within them.

In light of this work, Landau's anthology is revealing. Arranged alphabetically, poets are assigned in groups of two and three each to a letter of the Yiddish alphabet. Yet the anthology claims to represent Yiddish poetry in America until the year 1919. The contrast between the arrangement and the purpose embodies the tension between the aesthetic and the didactic demands upon Yiddish poetry. The historical, representative aims suggest that the anthology seeks to present a canon of poets and poems. In contrast, the alphabetical, rather than the chronological, arrangement of the poems emphasizes the ordering powers of language itself by means of its most elementary components. This emphasis on language is strengthened by the illustrations of Z. Movd, in which each letter of the alphabet is centered and decorated by the names of the poet or poets who begin with it. The convenience of alphabetical order becomes a symbolic badge: the tyranny of history is superseded by the ordering powers of language.

Landau's selection of poets includes the older generation, such as the socialist poets Morris Rosenfeld and A. Liesin (Liessen, born Valt), born in 1862 and 1870, respectively, and the already classical voice of Yehoash (Sh. Bloomgarden) born in 1872. The poets of the *Yunge* (born between 1879 and 1889) are presented in a modest selection of poems by Moyshe-Leyb Halpern, more generous representations of Mani Leyb and Halper Leyvik, and extensive selections of poems by Reuven Ayzland (Eisland), Zishe Landau, and Joseph Rolnik. Two very young poets are presented, Reuven Ludvig (born 1895) and A. Nisenson (born 1897), and two poets whose work had recently first appeared in 1917, Celia Dropkin ["*Mayn vayse shney printsesin*" (My White Snow Princess) and

"Kh'hob zikh gezen in kholem" (I Saw Myself in a Dream)] and M. Afranel. Fradl Shtok, the only other woman poet, is represented by one sonnet, the last poem in the collection.

Landau's introductory remarks make clear his priorities in presenting Yiddish poetry in this anthology. Poetry should not be the "shrieking epithets, impossible exaggerations . . . [which] characterize" bad, political poetry in Yiddish.[17] In Landau's words, the political obligations of socialism and nationalism in "the childhood of the Jewish settlement in America" limited the Yiddish poetry of the late nineteenth century. At first, in the 1880's, the Yiddish audience tolerated only the themes of social hope and suffering, and by the turn of the century, Jewish "national tones" were also allowed. This subject matter, while it reflected the difficult lives of the Yiddish-speaking population, tyrannized Yiddish poetry: "Until the beginning of our century," Landau writes, "it was shameful to write poems other than social. . . . "

Landau characterizes Yiddish poets of the late nineteenth century as "the rhyming departments" of the socialist and nationalist movements. However, with the poetry of Yehoash, which paid attention to language and literary sensibility, Yiddish poetry made advances which allowed for the development of the *Yunge*, the poets who, grouped around the *zamlbikher*, practiced "poetry for its own sake." Landau emphasizes the individuality of these poets, who, in a concert of varied voices, advanced the efforts and broadened the scope of Yiddish poetry.[18] His intention in the anthology is to present the varied image of Yiddish poetry in America, "an image of what a ragged fragment of the Jewish people created during its first forty years in its new home."[19]

Landau's metaphor for the development of Yiddish poetry is that of the coming-of-age of a young man. He describes the labor poet David Edelstadt, in terms of having taken the "baby steps," as Yiddish poetry learned how to walk. He later describes the advances of the subsequent generation, the *Yunge*, in terms of the adolescent and assimilationist act of learning how to shave one's beard. In this impressionistic "biography" of Yiddish poetry, Landau deliberately shies away from making a monolithic historical proclamation of the collective aims and achievements of Yiddish poetry. Rather, he presents his anthology as a selection of quality, representing the thirty best poets who literally had come of age in America. Landau's account, by personifying the development of the poetry, embodies the modernist valuation of the individual sensibility.

Yiddish poetry moves further from the collective obligation with the *Inzikhistn* (Introspectivists). Building on, while turning against, the defining terms of the *Yunge*, the modernist *In zikh* anthology, manifesto, and later journal declared a program for the writing of poetry in the present and future. Unlike the *Yunge*, these writers did not simply react against social and cultural demands on poetry by limiting poetry to its own aesthetic circumference. Rather, the Introspectivists dug deep into the very words they wrote to confront in their fundamental state the roots of the Yiddish language, and through those roots, the culture itself.

The original Introspectivist manifesto, which appeared as the introduction to the anthology, *Introspektive lider* (Introspective Poems, 1920), set forth an aesthetic theory of poetry which is, in essence, ahistorical.[20] Valuing the continuities and eternal truths embedded in poetic form, this manifesto argued that all good poetry of all periods and kinds is "Introspectivist," which means, "looking inward INTO THE SELF. And through that looking within one's own spirit, the world is reflected in the poet's soul, sung and versified."[21] The new movement intended consciously to develop this quality. Some fifty-eight years after the manifesto appeared, Yankev Glatshteyn (Jacob Glatstein) recalled the Introspectivists' dual tendencies toward and away from literary tradition, in contrast to the outright "revolution" of the *Yunge*: "Although the Yunge were the true revolutionaries, the Introspectionists [sic] were rebels in the tradition of Yiddish culture and continuity. . . . This is how I see the difference between the two fruitful revolutions in Yiddish poetry. We were traditionalists in all our achievements and innovations."[22] By allying themselves with what they perceived as a universal aspect of good poetry, the authors of this manifesto placed themselves as timely advocates within a timeless tradition of poetry.

The methods of Introspectivist poetry emphasize the individuality of expression in each poem. This individuality is differentiated from that of the *Yunge* in that the Introspectivists embedded that uniqueness of vision not in the personality of the poet, but in the form and rhythms, the nuances and connotations of the language the poet calls forth: "In truth, form and content are one and the same. . . . One is not divided from the other. . . . Each poem is in reality a singular experience, a uniqueness. Because of this, two poems cannot actually have the same rhythm. This, according to our conception of poetry, is impossible."[23] Taking a stand against conventional ideas of the form of poetry, and reflecting an awareness of vers libre, which was very much in the literary air of the times, the Introspectivists dismissed rhyme, as well: "The melodiousness of a poem needs also to be a purely individual one, and it can be achieved without rhymes, which must necessarily lead to a certain stereotypicality—rhymes are, when all is said and done, limited in quantity and quality."[24] Yet there is an ideological impact in these formal concerns, for in the uniqueness of a poem's suggestiveness hovers "a little remnant of [the poet's] past incarnation, or of his hereditary 'I'—these are all the paths and the labyrinths of his soul, he must set foot on them, because they are HE, and only through the own, inner, true, introspective 'I' lies the path that leads to creation and to redemption."[25]

"Introspection" is the means for the poet to descend deeper into the self through particularly poetic aspects of the Yiddish language—its sounds—in order to find within the self, through this familiar medium, the exotic and the extraordinary territories upon which poetry borders. The manifesto emphasizes the poem as poem, the integrity of the artifact, rather than of the poet and his/her ideas, experiences, or ideologies. This manifesto does not attempt to restrict or direct the content appropriate to poetry, as did the statements of the *Yunge*. Rather, it redefines the poem as a self-contained entity in formal terms. There is not a conflict between the aesthetic and the political here—both of which are ideologies—but rather an acknowledgment of the linguistic medium from which the poem is made.

In the same issue of *In zikh*, Yankev Glatshteyn has an essay, "*A shnel-loyf iber der yidisher poezye*" (A Run-through of Yiddish Poetry), in which he delineates the folk origins of the Yiddish poem and its problematic development in the hands of the dispersers of the *Haskalah*.[26] He traces the development of Yiddish poetry across the literature of the medieval troubadors, wedding jesters, and theatre songsters, through what he considers the primitive efforts at the individual poetic voice, by Abraham Goldfaden, who "tried to sing about himself," and Avram Reyzen (Reisin), to a dismissal of the *Yunge*.[27] Glatshteyn holds that although "the first five or six of the Yunge" were a liberating force for Yiddish poetry, most of their poems were of "pure moods" and lacked content.[28] Through a metaphor of music-making, he attacks the *Yunge* for their ultimately empty musicality: "When those who had instructed themselves in the smoothness and sonorousness of making a poem joined the orchestra, and joyously signed their names to contentlessness, and began to rhyme moodily, the orchestra began to screech with emptiness and nothingness. It became . . . a chaos."[29]

Glatshteyn's article then surveys the history of Yiddish poetry from the folk poem to the *Yunge*, emphasizing the development of the individual voice and point of view in the poem. Loping through literary history, he makes the case for the necessity and timely contribution of the Introspectivists, who take Yiddish poetry a step further. Whereas the excerpted Introspectivist manifesto provides a theory of aesthetics and poetics for the journal, Glatshteyn's article provides a historical account of the Yiddish poetic tradition into which the Introspectivist poets, who adhere to the tenets of formalism and musicality, the linguistic and experiential particularity of the poem, fit in a culminating, climactic way. The Introspectivists proclaim formalist values, but fit themselves into a progressive, linear idea of historical tradition.

The tension between the individual poet and the collective, the aesthetic and the didactic, in Yiddish poetry swings back toward the collective obligation of the poet in M. Bassin's monumental historical anthology of 1917, the deluxe *Antologye: finf hundert yor yidishe poezye* (Anthology: Five Hundred Years of Yiddish Poetry), representing poets in Yiddish from 1410 through 1916.[30]

The first volume encompasses Yiddish poetry from 1410 through 1885, from the first poem, "*Shabes-lid*" (Sabbath song), by Reb Zelmelin, who died around 1456, through the folk-like poems of A. M. Sharkanski, who immigrated to America in 1887. The second of the three parts of the volume contains folk poetry which, Bassin explains in his introduction, usually is considered to be "the oldest form, the root of poetry," but which in Yiddish is not. Along with the folk songs which are sources for modern Yiddish poetry, the first volume has other scholarly apparatus—a glossary of archaic Yiddish words found in the poems and bibliographic and linguistic notes on the poetry. The second volume presents the modern period. It begins in the 1890's with Morris Rosenfeld and ends with M. Bassin himself, emphasizing the individuality of the poets with biographical notes and portraits.

Bassin's introductory remarks indicate that, in contrast to the exclusive selectivity of the Landau and the *In zikh* anthologies, his edition intends to be as inclusive and representative of all the kinds of Yiddish poetry as possible. In a second introduction to the work, the scholar B. Borokhov states his hope that Bassin's anthology will begin to fill the lack of a classical tradition in Yiddish poetry, ensuring that the "Yiddish muse" is not left orphaned and vulnerable to dilettantes. Borokhov's remarks emphasize how the individual poets fit into the overall development of the collective tradition. In this idea, he contradicts the *Yunge* ideal of individualism in the poetic voice. Ironically, in Borokhov's view, the individual is subsumed by the overall good. Inadvertently, Borokhov reverses the idea of the development of a Yiddish poetic tradition from the discriminating, modernist practice and theories of the *Yunge* and the Introspectivists to the values of the collective. This emphasis on the cultural collective implicitly corresponds to the ideologies of socialism and Jewish nationalism, which the modernist poets were decrying. The idea of literary tradition that Borokhov states and that Bassin's anthology embodies is a political and nationalistic statement about the ends of Yiddish poetry. In this scheme, poetry serves the greater ends of peoplehood and national culture. This emphasis stands in opposition to the ideas of poetry that motivated the major poets of that time.

In these three anthologies, there are so few women poets represented that it appears that they had a negligible role in the various notions of tradition. Bassin sees fit to include eight women poets in 500 years of the literature: Geleh, Yehudit, Roza Y., Zelda Knizshnik, Anna Rapport, Paula R., Sore Reyzen, and Fradl Shtok. Landau includes two, Fradl Shtok and Celia Dropkin, whom he presents meagerly. The first issue of the *In zikh* journal, quoted above, begins with two poems by Celia Dropkin.[31] In this context, we see that Korman's anthology of women poets in Yiddish, while it emulates Bassin's, answers the earlier volume's major omission.[32]

The scarcity of women poets in these earlier collections may not appear to be significant until we consider that Korman was able to collect the works of seventy women poets over roughly the same five centuries covered in Bassin's work. Once we know that there were many women writing poetry in Yiddish at the time these anthologies appeared, we begin to formulate questions: *within this culture, which traditionally places the collective peoplehood before the individual in literary expression, how does the modernist role of the poet as maker of linguistically and experientially unique poems differ for men and for women? Does the modernist idea of the poet generally distinguish between the public and the private voice? Is the "public" private voice of the poet considered the domain of men rather than women?*

III

Inventing a literary tradition in Yiddish, the poets and anthologizers of poetry cast a retrospective eye across the preceding decades to compose the history necessary to validate their work. What Bassin's heavy march and Glatshteyn's quick race through the centuries neglected to account for, though, was the devotional literature for women that had been published in Yiddish since the sixteenth century and which was the bread and butter of literate experience for most Jewish women. The neglect of these materials also implies the neglect by these tradition-makers of the role of women as readers and writers in the Yiddish language.

However, this absence was not universal in the nineteen-teens and twenties. At that time, an unbalanced, twofold discussion arose, exploring in fits and starts the role of women in Yiddish literature. On the one hand, this interest fell within the general effort among Yiddishists, linguists, folklorists and ethnographers in Russia and Poland to preserve the folk and oral manifestations of Yiddish culture and literature.[33] For instance, Sh. Niger (Shmuel Charney, Samuel Niger) published a scholarly monograph on Yiddish literature and the female reader in 1913, "*Di yidishe literatur un di lezerin.*"[34] On the other hand, there was a popular, contemporary concern with the burgeoning number of women poets and writers who were submitting work for publication and the questioning of the role of women in the general creativity of Yiddish literature.[35] This popular interest culminated in Ezra Korman's *Yidishe dikhterins: antologye*, in 1928.[36] Yet the condescending critical response to this anthology in the most prestigious literary paper, *Literarishe bleter*, published in Warsaw and Vilna, reveals the inability of the evolving self-defined literary tradition of Yiddish poetry to accept the work of women: the inventors of this tradition repelled literary work by women because, as their prose implies, Yiddish was viewed negatively by a culture that valued Hebrew as the sacred language, available almost exclusively to men. The Yiddish language was perceived as the medium for a literature written only for women and uneducated men.[37]

Sh. Niger's monograph on Yiddish literature and the female reader opens by challenging this prejudice, by asking that if "literature in Yiddish was in the beginning a literature only for women and ignorant men," then were women and ignorant men the only sources for the Yiddish maxims and witticisms, often so sharply profound?[38] Despite the disparagement implied here, Niger presents a descriptive history of the impact and significance of the fact that the majority of readers for which early Yiddish books were published were women. Although women by necessity mastered the skills necessary to earn a living for their families, while their husbands studied Torah, they had a peculiar kind of economic power, because it was infused with economic exploitation and a religio-cultural double standard, whereby an *eyshes khayl*, the conventional epitome of a valorous, clever, and active woman, could at most hope to be her husband's "*fusbenkele in gan eyden*" (footstool in the world to come).[39] Moreover, in synagogue, women were kept in a "spiritual ghetto," because they knew no Hebrew, the holy tongue, in which prayer took place. According to Niger, early Yiddish literature developed out of necessity, to serve as an intermediary between the women and the holy words of prayer and the Law.[40]

Niger examines the literature of the sixteenth through the nineteenth centuries:

the supplicatory prayers for women, the *tkhines*, translations of Hebrew prayers into Yiddish, and translations of the *Khumash* (Torah), *Tanakh* (Torah, Prophets, Writings), commentary, and interpretive materials. In this analysis, Niger contrasts the Hebrew texts for men with the Yiddish texts for women, discovering that the female readership influenced the content and form of the latter. The texts in Yiddish for women deal with "womanly matter"; are less concerned with analysis, law, and interpretation than they are with stories, legends, and morals; and take on a style and conventions that are particularly geared toward the female readership.[41] It is curious that stories are considered "womanly" by Niger, given the value attributed to narrative in the rabbinic tradition of *Midrash*. Perhaps Niger considers stories "feminine" because they convey principles implicitly by evoking emotion and depicting action without logical argument or explanation. These "feminine" features of content and form penetrate into the worldly, non-Jewish "belletristic" literature that appears in Yiddish in the sixteenth century and onward, as well.[42]

Niger's concern with the way the female readership shaped Yiddish literature has several implications for his contemporary literary audience. One of these implications has to do with the way women are perceived as the audience and subject for Yiddish poetry; another has to do with how women are received as poets. A. Glanz (-Leyeles; Glantz)—who was to become, with Glatshteyn and Minkoff, one of the leading Introspectivist poets and theorists—wrote an article for the New York newspaper *Di fraye arbeter shtime* (The Free Worker's Voice) on October 30, 1915, called "*Kultur un di froy*" (Culture and Woman).[43] In it, Glanz complains that the latest collections of poetry and philosophical writings offer nothing new, that they simply repeat themselves, "page after page."[44] He blames this cultural lag on the absence of "Woman" from the creative scene.

Transferring the terms of Marxist analysis from class to sex, Glanz blames an over-emphasis of the individual in modernism for the inability of male artists to be original: "The male sex, the principal producer and principal beneficiary of culture, perhaps has already become obsolete, perhaps already has given everything that he alone in independence could give, as expression of his separate individualism. Man wants to say the new word, but he cannot. He doesn't have it."[45] In answer to the impotence and infertility of the male artist alone, Glanz holds forth the creative woman, whose female "I" he finds to be tragically absent from contemporary literature. The problem, as Glanz sees it, is that the one-sidedness of male art leaves male artists without a context. The advent of women poets will, he predicts, give male poets a context and a counterpart to respond to. According to Glanz, the presence of women poets will help Man "find his real place, find himself." As T. S. Eliot states the poet's need to define himself in relation to "what is already living from the past," so Glanz reorients that task in sexual terms. Both these poet-critics suggest that great poetry emerges not from the renegade, isolated individual, but from the one who is conscious of the larger cultural tradition into which the individual's work fits and which it changes with its presence.

To describe how poetry works best in context, Glanz relies on a sexual metaphor. This metaphor of male sexual impotence and infertility extends the metaphor Landau employed to describe the development of Yiddish poetry as the growth of a boy, from his first baby steps to the rite of passage into modern manhood, marked by the boy's shaving his beard. In Glanz's metaphor of sexual potency, Yiddish poetry is reaching for a further maturity. No longer a bachelor, the literature figuratively will marry and reproduce. In this hoped-for marriage, although man and woman are equals, they are by no means identical: "They are entirely different versions of the same species." Glanz urges that women writers empower the literature with the qualities peculiar to their sex: " . . . And if Woman is meant to play a significant role in the culture . . . she must find herSELF."[46]

In Glanz's dichotomy, men rule the domain of logic and reason, while women possess intuition, the faculty that Glanz believes is necessary for artistic creation. Reversing the derogatory formula Niger invoked, that Old Yiddish literature was written only for women or men who are like women in their ignorance, Glanz implies that the true artist is necessarily a woman or like a woman. In his words, the woman artist alone has the ability to make Yiddish culture great: "Thus, as we see, the female soul is not inferior to but different from the male soul. If [Woman] wants to make the culture great, she must comprehend and begin to create in her own sphere; she must stop imitating Man."[47]

Yet in this call to power, Glanz has set forth a paradox: on the one hand, he calls for women to find their own, original voices in poetry, and on the other hand, he requests this originality and independence for the sake of men: "Women's poetry will create a new world and become a blessing for men."

The trouble with Glanz's theory of women's creativity is that it is based only on what he considers inherent sexual attributes—the concreteness of motherhood as a model for intuition and the generosity of creation. Glanz's initial metaphor of poetic creativity as sexual reproduction, then, limits the possibilities for women's creativity. His model provides only the culture of sexuality, not any sort of temporal, literate culture, as a context for the potential poetry by women. The men poets, he intimates, have come to a standstill, to their impotency, over a period of time. To their history, men need to add the component of a new sexual context. But for the women, Glanz provides no history, no past. Without a conscious past, an awareness of tradition, according to T. S. Eliot, the individual talent will not write good poetry.

Glanz holds, then, that what Yiddish culture lacks in 1915 is the felt presence of cultural creativity by women. He sees Yiddish poetry at a standstill, made stagnant by the dominant voices of men who depend on the faculties of logic and lack the special gift of intuition on which true poetry depends, and which only women inherently, naturally possess. His complaint, though, that the women poets have not yet found their own artistic identities and modes, proved hypocritical. For, as Norma Fain Pratt points out, Glanz actively discouraged the original contributions of women when he confronted them: he wrote, for example, a harsh review of Fradl Shtok's short stories when they first appeared in 1919, thereby fostering, it seems, her subsequent silence and mental breakdown.[48]

The idea that women had something special to contribute to Yiddish culture was acknowledged in a saccharine and idealizing way in Nahum Sokolov's *Yidishe froy* (Jewish Woman), published in New York in 1918.[49] Unlike Glanz's idealization of the special artistic potentialities of women in Yiddish, Sokolov's treatise celebrates the biblical matriarchs as models for the merely "ordinary" creativity of homemaking and mothering. Determining that the hearth is the domain of women, Sokolov actually venerates the lack of public cultural expression for any especially female creativity.

In contrast to Glanz's prediction of women's promising creative role in Jewish cultural life and Sokolov's glorification of the lack of such a communal female presence, Ezra Korman asserted and assessed the actual contribution of women poets in Yiddish.[50] The anthology *Yidishe dikhterins* is his case.[51] Korman was a teacher.[52] He was a literary critic.[53] He was a poet.[54] He was the editior of two collections, *In fayerdikn doyer—zamlung fun revolutsionerer lyrik in der nayer yidisher dikhtung* (In Fiery Duration—Collection of Revolutionary Lyrics in New Yiddish Poetry, Kiev, 1921), and *Brenendike brikn—antologye fun revolutsionerer lyrik in der nayer yidisher dikhtung fun ukraine* (Burning Bridges—Anthology of Revolutionary Lyrics in the New Yiddish Poetry of the Ukraine, Berlin, 1923).[55]

Korman as an anthologizer fit into the contemporary efforts to define a tradition for Yiddish poetry. In his lengthy, scholarly introduction, Korman indicated his intention to canonize the women Yiddish poets, whom he had culled from current papers and journals and from earlier ambitious efforts to canonize Yiddish literature, including the first literary encyclopedia of Yiddish literature, Zalman Reyzen's (Reisin) *Leksikon fun der yidisher literatur un prese* (Lexicon of Yiddish Literature and Press), edited by Sh. Niger, and published in Warsaw in 1914; M. Bassin's historical *Antologye: finf hundert yor yidishe poezye* (1917); Max Erik's 1926 study of *"Brantshpigl—di entsiklopedye fun der yidisher froy in 17tn yorhundert"* (Brantshpigl—The Encyclopedia of the Jewish Woman in the 17th Century); and Sh. Niger's article on *"Yidishe literatur un di lezerin"* (first published in 1913), two of which I have discussed earlier here.[56] He cites these works in footnotes to the introduction, and discusses at some length the textual and bibliographic variants of the early poems that his anthology shares with Bassin's.[57]

Korman's anthology resembles the Bassin anthology in its massiveness, its chronological span, its format, and its apparatus. Whereas the Bassin volumes featured sketched portraits of each poet, Korman tipped in photographs of each modern poet and facsimile reproductions of the significant pages from some original books of poems, such as the first and last pages of Toybe Pan's seventeenth-century poem (a prayer for God's mercy in time of plague), a variant version of that poem, and a photo-montage of the title pages of modern collections of poems.[58] In the apparatus at the end of the volume is a section on "Biographies and Bibliography,'' including a biographical sketch of each poet and a 232-title bibliography.

This bibliography deserves mention. Divided into two main sections, "Sources" and "Literature," it lists books of poems by individual authors, anthologies, handbooks, collections and periodical publications, studies and literary histories, articles and reviews, a bibliography of Old Yiddish literature, and translations of Yiddish poems by women into Hebrew, English, and Polish. With this bibliography, Korman accomplishes several tasks. First, by documenting the sources for all the authors he has included in his anthology, Korman establishes his own credentials and the validity of his research. Second, he shows how widely published, how present in their contemporary world, these poets were. Third, he establishes the range of audience these women poets had, for they appeared in anthologies, the specialized collections of literary movements, political and literary journals, daily newspapers, and even in a short-lived weekly journal for women, *Froyen zshurnal-vokhnblat* (Women's Journal-Weekly).[59] These were published in the centers of Yiddish culture, such as New York, Montreal, Warsaw, Vilna, Moscow, Kiev, Lodz, and in less obvious places, such as Los Angeles, Chicago, and Cape Town, South Africa. Fourth, he provided an invaluable tool for future readers of Yiddish literature in an era long after most of the ephemeral publications, the newspapers and journals, had been discarded, along with many of the Yiddish books themselves.

We can read the bibliography for a portrait of the moment, as well. For instance, Korman lists only thirteen books poems by individual authors: Miriam Ulinover, *Der bobes oytser* (My Grandmother's Treasure; Warsaw, 1922); Anna Blokh, *Poezye fun a litvishe(r) meydel in afrike* (Poetry by a Lithuanian Girl in Africa; South Africa, 1921); Roza Gutman, *Far gor dem noen(t)stn. lider* (Especially for the Closest; Berlin, 1925); Ida Glazer-Andrus, *In halb-shotn* (In Half-Shadow; New York, 1922); Leah K. Hofman, *In kinderland* (In Childland; New York, 1921, 2d ed.); Pesi Hershfeld, *Kareln* (Carols; Chicago, 1926); Khana Vurtsel, *Hundert lider* (A Hundred Poems; New York, 1927); Rashel Veprinski, *Ruf fun fligl* (Call of Wings; New York, 1926); Khana-Layeh Khaveydanski, *Gedikhte un aforizmen* (Poetry and Aphorisms; Ponevezsh, 1922); Roza Yakubovitsh, *Mayne gezangen* (My Songs; Warsaw, 1924); Yudika, *Naye yugent* (New Youth; Kovne, 1923); Kadya Molodowsky, *Kheshvandike nekht. lider* (Nights of Heshvan. Poems; Vilna-Warsaw, 1927); Sore Reyzen, *Lider* (Poems; Vilna, 1924). In contrast, Korman lists 126 entries under "Collections and Periodical Publications." What we see from this is that in the 1920's there was a small flurry of books published by women poets. This bibliography, though, is not complete, for among the biographies, Korman mentions at least one book, Paula R.'s *Der malakh un der sotn: poeme* (The Angel and the Devil: Poems; Warsaw, 1908), which does not appear in the bibliography.[60]

In contrast, a comparatively large number of books of poems had been published by men by 1928, implying a Yiddish canon.[61] Of the women poets that Korman includes, at least two of the most talented, Celia Dropkin and Anna

Margolin (Rosa Lebensboym), each was to publish a single volume within the next ten years. The second books of Miriam Ulinover and Roza Yakubovitsh are described in Korman's notes as finished but as of 1928 not yet published. I have not been able to determine whether these second books ever appeared.[62]

The Introduction sets forth Korman's ideological position. By presenting, together with modern Yiddish poetry by women, or "the modern women-poetry" (der moderner froyen-dikhtung), examples of the works of women writers (froyen-farfasterins) who wrote in Old Yiddish (yidish-taytsh), Korman hopes to show the connection between the beginnings of a new Jewish literature in the sixteenth century, which marked the beginning of a new epoch of Jewish life, and the current period, in which the buds of that early period had blossomed. He emphasizes the creativity of women, old and new. Although Korman explicitly denies a continuous poetic tradition between the women poets of the early and later periods, he implies a line of influence. Old Yiddish poetry for and presumably by women, in Korman's words, "is immeasurably huge and incomparable," while modern poetry by women is merely a "thin thread" continuing that heritage which still affects the modern women poets. The Old Yiddish literature has an abiding influence over the moderns, because, Korman argues, there has been no single great modern voice to override it, restructuring the relationship of the new to the old. Significantly, although Korman states that the old literature of women in Yiddish outweighs the new, his selections in the anthology reverse this judgment, for the anthology emphasizes in numbers the proliferation of the modern and presents only four examples of the old literature.

As if in answer to Glanz's call of 1915, Korman considers the new women's literature as a positive development for the growth of Yiddish literature and culture in general: "Un ver kon nevuies zogn vos unzer tsukinftike froyen-shafung trogt mit zikh un far der literatur?" (Who can prophesy what our future female creativity bears within itself and for the literature?)[63]

Curiously, like Glanz, Korman attributes the unique creativity of women to the processes of biological productivity. These processes are implied in the phrasing of the preceding quotation, which suggests a connection between poetry and pregnancy. In the verb trogn mit, "to carry, to bear" in a general sense and specifically in relation to childbearing, Korman draws an analogy between the making of poems and the making of babies, both of which are froyen-shafung, "women's creation." This analogy at once attempts to characterize women's poetry as having a special nature to distinguish it from poetry written by men, and to stereotype it or limit it. Feminist literary theorists of the later part of the twentieth century have dealt with this analogy, but in 1928, when Korman's volume represented the first compilation of Yiddish poetry by women as an entity unto itself, this analogy served as point of departure for a critic to classify poetry by women in either elevated or in deflated terms.[64]

The nexus of the creative power of women as writers and as progenitors within the context of Jewish life and language provides a focus for a rich controversy among the critics and within the works of the poets themselves. The vicious, witty exchange of barbs printed during the summer and fall of 1927 in *Literarishe bleter* between poet-critic Melekh Ravitsh and two young women poets who had not yet published their first books, Kadya Molodowsky and Malka Heifetz Tussman, on the subject of *"Meydlekh, froyen, vayber—yidishe dikhterins"* (Girls, Women, Wives—Yiddish Poetesses), balances metaphors of gentile romantic chivalry with Jewish chaste virtue (*tsnies*); flirtation with seduction; and pregnancy with infertility and miscarriage.[65]

Both Molodowsky and Tussman castigate Ravitsh for trivializing the efforts of women poets in Yiddish. It seems no accident that these two women developed into two of the most prolific and original of the Yiddish poets, each of whose works contend directly with the conflicting forces of Judaism, modern secularism, and sexuality.[66] In the ironic play on her own position as a woman poet, flirting in her figurative petticoat with the hypocritically "chivalrous" Ravitsh, Tussman asserts that indeed, the more of a woman one is, the more a poet. According to Tussman, the fires of creation in the woman poet are only smoldering, waiting to be awakened. She depicts the woman poet as having two heritages, female and male, the modesty of the virtuous grandmother and the fire of the pious grandfather. Juxtaposing these sources of strength and inspiration, which connote the order and values of the old religious life, with the sexual powers of a modern American woman, Tussman taps into the essential terms of tradition in Yiddish poetry.

There was no escaping the connection between writer and sexual being when discussing poetry by women. A year later, Melekh Ravitsh's outrageous review of Korman's anthology begins, "My dear, patient, infatuated, polygamist, Ezra Korman!"[67] Discrediting Korman as an editor by attributing to him personal, sexual motives in his literary judgment and choices, Ravitsh also discredits the poets themselves. Perhaps his viciousness is due to professional envy of Korman, which he disguises as a critical attack. Kadya Molodowsky, in her response to Ravitsh's 1927 anonymous group review of works by individual women poets, mentioned that Ravitsh had stated in print his intention to publish an anthology of Yiddish women poets, "and with pictures!"[68]

According to Ravitsh's review, an editor's ideal "principle is not to want to be original, but obviously to include a poet's best-known poem, as long as it is also simultaneously *his* best" [emphasis mine]. Ravitsh reveals here his sense of the conservative role of an anthology. It should represent and perpetuate a canon, an idea of tradition established by popularity and fame. In Ravitsh's prose, the poet worth anthologizing is designated by the masculine pronoun, *zayn* (his). "His" poems should already have achieved some fame, for they are "well-known poems." It seems that an unknown poet, who may well be a woman poet, has no place in an anthology, and, conversely, that there is no justification for an anthology of unknown poets.

Ravitsh's idea of an anthology is predicated, then, on the idea of a canon of communally agreed-upon "classic" texts. For Ravitsh, an anthology is the stronghold of conventional tradition, and tradition in Yiddish literature is itself a static, given body of works. Ravitsh's idea of the anthology as conservator of a tradition stands in contrast to the revisionary program of the *Yunge* and the Introspectivists, represented earlier here by Landau's introduction to the *Antologye* of 1919 and the introduction to *In zikh* of 1921. Yet Ravitsh's vaguely modern, destructive idea of a canon also stands in contrast to the 1917 anthology of Bassin and Borokhov, which attempted to establish a five-hundred-year-long canon including obscure works. Mostly what Ravitsh objects to, though, is the idea of a women's tradition within Yiddish poetry that brings the devotional literature dangerously close to the secular, politically correct Yiddish poetry that Ravitsh himself writes.

A month later, in November, 1928, Sh. Niger published a more responsible review of Korman's anthology in the *"Bikher velt"* column of *Literarishe bleter*, which he called *"Froyen-lyrik"* (Women-Lyric).[69] This review differs fundamentally from Ravitsh's in that Niger states that there is a tradition of "women's poetry [which] now occupies an acknowledged place in Yiddish poetry." Yet, although Niger affirms the anthology and the women poets by arguing for a women's tradition, he cannot resist the urge to belittle *froyen-shafung*, the creativity of women, commenting that the forty-odd women in Korman's anthology who began to publish poetry after the First World War "might have been able to do more useful things."[70]

Like Glanz, in his article of 1915 on women and culture, Niger attributes to the female writer a sensibility that differs from that of the male writer. The new "women's poetry" is "still too young to be able to boast of great and ripe talents." Nonetheless, Niger acknowledges the "gifted Yiddish women poets, [whose] chief virtue is that they are WOMEN in their poetry." He argues that the woman poet can contribute a necessary femininity, a softness and gentleness to counteract the harshness of the war years.

This specialized feminization of poetry has a limited value, for the poems connote a collective voice. Like critics among the *Yunge* and the Introspectivists, Niger attributes the advanced development of literary style to the degree to which the individual voice can elevate itself above the collective. This "women's poetry" lacks the "artistic universalism, in which we sense more the personality of the poet than the collective to which he belongs." Yet Niger differs from all the critics we have considered, for in this review he acknowledges that Jewish women comprise as valid a collective voice in Yiddish poetry as the working class or the Jewish nation. Since "women's poetry" has not yet achieved "artistic universalism," Niger argues, "its importance, therefore, lies in the fact that this poetry conveys a sense of the feminine disposition." Niger characterizes the "feminine disposition" in this "group poetry, a type of folklore of the female sex," as "sincere and straightforward." Its chief virtue is that it preserves "that element of feeling, that intimate tone" which "have become such a rarity in male verses since the war." Like A. Glanz thirteen years earlier, Niger depicts women poets as the providers of what contemporary men poets no longer had. Yet while Niger praises the women for preserving in lyric poems feelings and sensitivity missing from the deadly cerebral post-war Yiddish poetry, simultaneously he finds limitations in that lyricism attributable to the female sex. Equating the "eternally womanly " with the "eternally lyrical," Niger places the woman poet in a double bind.[71] Her poetry is by its nature, by the natural functions of women, circumscribed. Like Ravitsh, Niger reviewed the anthology only through generalizations about the poets as women.

The individual poets in the anthology that Korman draws attention to in his introduction differ from those Niger brings forth in his review. Unlike Niger, Korman emphasizes the typical, in his intent to establish the lineage and development of poetry by women.

In the first part of his introduction, Korman discusses the literature *af yidish-taytsh* (in Judeo-German), dating from *Sefer mides* (Morality Book, published in 1542) and the *Mayse bukh* (Book of Tales, first published in Basel, 1602), through the eighteenth century. Korman cites the translations and compendiums that enabled women to study and pray, such as the *Taytsh khumesh* (the translation of the Pentateuch into Yiddish; Prague, 1608); the *Tsenerene* (Yiddish translation and elaboration on the Pentateuch; first known edition, Basel, 1622); and the *tkhines* (the supplicatory prayers in Yiddish, some of which were composed by women for the significant moments in the lives of women—for blessing *Shabbes* candles, for childbirth, for recitation at the *mikve* and at the graves of family members—from the sixteenth century onward).[72] He deals, as well, with other works created by Jewish women themselves, such as *musar-sforim* (morality books), composed and translated by women, *tfiles* and *droshes* (prayers and sermons), which, like some of the *tkhines*, were composed in rhymed verse, and even lyrics and poems, "which the pens of women possessed."[73] He discusses the four poets of the *yidish-taytsh* period, Royzl Fishls, Toybe Pan, Geleh, and Khana Ka"ts (Kohen-Tsadik), by providing bibliographic detail, explicating the devotional nature of the poems and emphasizing that the publication of works in Yiddish by women poets during the sixteenth and seventeenth centuries allowed Jewish women to recognize their creative possibilities.[74]

Korman follows the conventional reading that modern Yiddish literature developed with the Enlightenment in the second half of the nineteenth century, but argues that the *Haskalah* "hardly affected the life of the Jewish woman, who remained a mute witness; therefore, the Haskalah brought with it only half of a liberation."[75] Korman attributes the emergence of a new, lively literature by women to the consequences of secularism in the 1890's—political engagement and the development of the Yiddish theatre in Poland and Russia where women took to the stage. Initially, he states, Yiddish culture absorbed the voices of the modern, "*nayveltike*" (new-wordly) women along with the traditional in Yiddish. Soon, though, the modern voices dominated the traditional, causing both cultural pain and joy, as the public of Yiddish-speaking women cast off the old pieties of the *tkhines*: "Thanks to the girls, women, and mothers who were actresses and political activists, the matriarchs dimmed and slipped into the shadows, leaving the modern Jewish woman with sighs, tears, and a new kind of pleasure that had been up to this time as foreign to her as the foreignness of idolatry.''[76]

Korman's anthology, then, embraces an idea of simultaneous movement toward and away from women's tradition. On the one hand, the entire body of modern poetry by women exists only because the familiar biblical matriarchs of the *tkhines* and *tsenerene* withdrew into the shadows, as actresses and activists took the spotlight and introduced Jewish women to the foreign pleasures of secular ''idolatry.'' On the other hand, the very ability of these new women to find their voices and even to conceive of writing in Yiddish depended upon this devotional literature for women. The dependence of the new, the secular, the revolutionary poets on the religious literature against which they actively define themselves is a paradox which extends throughout Korman's historical introduction and within the language and structure of many Yiddish poems by women. This paradox is another example of the way modern Yiddish literature reappropriates the past, at once subverting it and reclaiming it. David G.Roskies has pointed this out in reference to Jewish literature responding to catastrophe.[77]

Korman argues for the progress of Yiddish women's poetry from 1899 to 1927 by placing individual women poets in the context of their contemporaries. Roza Goldshteyn, whose first poem appeared in *Yudishn folks-blatt* in 1888, is discussed in terms of her contemporaries, the labor poets, David Edelstadt, Morris Vinchevski (Winchevsky) Sh. Frug, and Morris Rosenfeld, to emphasize how her work was typical of the times, in its nationalist and socialist themes: ''The disappointing belief in the earlier gods and the turn of the intellectuals to the Folk after the bankruptcy of assimilationist ideology, these are the themes and motifs of Yiddish poetry of this period.''[78]

Unlike the cyclical relationship of present and past in Glatshteyn's idea of tradition, Korman's sense of the history of Yiddish literature is linear and ''progressive.'' Therefore, Korman's emphasis condescends in the comparison of Yiddish poetry in 1888 and the ''improvements'' evident in 1927. For example, he characterizes Frug as ''a cantor without a cantor's desk,'' akin to the sentimental poet of the Russian people, Nadson, and likens to Frug's works Roza Goldshteyn's, which treat the Jewish people sentimentally. In one of Goldshteyn's poems, ''*Di yidishe muze*'' (The Yiddish Muse), the muse is depicted as the embodiment of the wandering Jewish people who provides the sorrow of the diaspora to the poet as inspiration.[79]

The margin of ''improvement'' that Korman acknowledges lies in the change in Yiddish poetry from the collective first person to ''the personal '*ikh*' '' (I) of the poet. Anna Rapport's poems, written and published in America from 1893 onward, reflect the conflict between the two possibilities of emigration for the Jewish poet—either to the ''Golden Land'' of America or the ''Promised Land'' of *Eretz Yisroel*. Korman calls her ''the modern Deborah, celebrating America in song,'' and praises her poems for evoking the collective experience of immigrants with the immediacy of a personal ''I.''

Korman connects modern Yiddish poetry with modern Hebrew poetry. Both the pseudonymous Paula R. (1906) and Yehudit (1907) wrote after the failure of the 1905 revolution in Russia and the second wave of pogroms. Their verse, like that of Goldshteyn and another poet, Zelde Knizshnik, was characterized by "ideal language and colors" which expressed individual moods and feelings in terms of the collective. Yehudit writes "not about herself, but in the language of the majority," and her poems show the influence of Bialik's Hebrew poem of the pogroms, "City of Slaughter." Despite this "language of the majority," Yehudit's poems reveal a greater sense of self than do those of her predecessors. Her works herald a new age of deepened individualism, like those of Yehoash, Liesin, and Reyzen, whose poems develop "individual lyricism and intellectual singularity beyond the tears of Morris Rosenfeld." He quotes these lines from her poetry, which praise the new and argue for discarding the old:

> Enough! Don't write old-fashioned poems,—
> They are not yours . . .
> They've had their day! . . . They can't revive.
> Your poem now rings false.[80]

Korman argues that the individual voice in modern poetry has a complicated relationship to the folk tradition. A woman poet whose poetry alludes to or imitates conventions and tones of folk poetry, he suggests, seeks to hide her individuality behind the *tsnies* ("modesty" or "virtue") of Jewish peoplehood. As an example, Korman offers mixed praise to the aforementioned Paula R. for the new tone she introduces to Yiddish poetry through the folk motif: "In the disguise and modesty of folk-language, one can afford to speak to the world about one's own feelings and experiences and, with that popular virtue, cover oneself as if with a veil."[81]

Although Korman depicts this modesty as a weakness in the poems of Paula R., this weakness promises strength, for he asserts, the good poet will learn to use the folk medium effectively. For Korman, then, the individual voice of the modern woman poet is necessarily connected to the collective voice of the Jewish people. The best poetry keeps these two forces in balance.

Korman praises Roza Yakubovitsh, who began writing in Poland in 1910, for her simultaneous respect for the "patriarchal" knowledge of Jewish suffering in the diaspora and for the revitalizing lessons of personal rebellion.[82] He mentions Sore Reyzen, Yakubovitsh's contemporary, whose later lyric poems show signs of possessing "the personal I." Yet Korman's sense of the modern, which he values most, comes clear when he discusses "the personal 'I'," unveiled in an original way in the poetry of Fradl Shtok. Shtok was a poet from Galicia, who began writing in America with a sense of high culture in her literary form and content. According to popular belief, Shtok introduced the sonnet and the sonnet cycle into Yiddish poetry.[83] Her diction and quality of imagination were innovative. The *Yunge*'s concept of "*reyner dikhtung*" (pure poetry) as written by Mani Leyb, and to a lesser degree by Moyshe-Leyb Halpern and H. Leyvik,

influenced the poetry of Fradl Shtok. Korman praises her poem *"Baym yam"*
(By the Sea) for its "individual poetic vision" and the "personal 'I'." Korman
characterizes Shtok's sonnet sequence as daring in its eroticism and bitterness.
Here is an example:

> My friend, my terrible friend, how you are evil,
> And proudly chaste as any saintly John
> Who made the nights of the king's daughter sleepless.
> And as she hated him, I hate you now.
>
> Your face is not as pale and cool as ivory,
> Your hair does not curl, writhing like young snakes,
> Your youth's heart is not as pure as any other's—
> So why am I engulfed by buring hate?
>
> I hate you. I reiterate it now:
> And as I dance the sinful dance once more,
> I gesture at the bidding of the devil.
>
> And for my dance he'll show his gratitude
> With pay well worthy of a sinful heart:
> He'll give me what I crave—your lilac tongue.[84]

Although Korman mentions that Shtok also published a novel and short stories,
he avoids discussing her sudden silence and subsequent breakdown which, as
Norma Fain Pratt has explained, was in part a response to the devastating reviews
her short fiction received in the Yiddish press, most notably from A. Glanz in
Der tog, in 1919 and 1920.[85]

In contrast to his views of the passive folk voice of Paula R., Roza Yakubovitsh's "gentle rebellion," and Fradl Shtok's modern sensibility and "personal
'I,' " Korman holds up the poems of Miriam Ulinover as having nearly achieved
the ideal balance between the traditional folk and the modern personal voices in
poetry.[86] Praising this European poet for her innovative poetic style and substance, he presents "her poems, written in a folklike, romantic tone, and wrapped
in a thin veil of naive folk mysticism," as "approaching the classic." These
poems, from *Der bobes oytser*, are "a monument to the Jewish woman of the
past . . . making luminous the customs and obsolete ways of Jewish life of more
than one hundred years ago."[87]

Korman emphasizes the cultural distance the poet and critic have traveled
from the traditional Jewish ways of life. Only from his safely modern perspective
as critic can Korman praise Ulinover's poems, based on the tales, maxims, and
utterances of her *"elter bobe fun iber hundert yor,"* her more than hundred-
year-old great-grandmother, who is "the poetic inspiration [for the] first self-
possessed woman poet in the new Yiddish literature."[88] Yet, despite his tone
of seeking protection in the modern and his implied faith in the progress of

progress—that whatever poetry is more recent is better than that which came earlier—Korman presents here a point central to the question of how women's poetry fits into the idea of tradition in Yiddish poetry. By attributing Ulinover's achievement as the first "self-possessed" woman poet in modern Yiddish to the "poetic inspiration" of the great-grandmother, Korman acknowledges that the "muse" of Yiddish poetry is situated as much in the oral traditions of women's lives and their lived customs as in the modern world where individualistic notions of love and beauty vie with socialist-nationalist ideologies. This sense of a religio-cultural tradition lived by women in Yiddish is what distinguishes Korman's sense of good modern poetry in the light of tradition. Differing from this are revisionist ideas of poetic tradition expressed aesthetically by Landau for the *Yunge*, formalistically by Glatshteyn for the Introspectivists, and historically by Bassin and Borokhov.

Like Korman, Sh. Niger valued the strong poetic voice able to maintain a balance between the opposing forces pulling at the modern Yiddish poet: the folk and the modern, the religious and the secular, the collective and the individual. In his 1928 review of women's poetry in *Literarishe bleter*, discussed earlier, Niger examines the work of two poets from Korman's anthology who had recently published books, Rashel Veprinsky's *Ruf fun fligl* (Call of Wings; New York, 1926), and Kadya Molodowsky's *Kheshvandike nekht* (Nights of Heshvan; Vilna, 1927).[89] In this review, he holds up Veprinsky as an example of the eternally feminine lyricist. To Niger, she is representative of "women's poetry," for her lines are characterized not by "the force and sap of deep roots," "the fullness of fruit," but rather by "the charm of blossoming, the pale promise of unripeness":

> Truth is in naked fall,
> In your fingers, like naked branches,
> In the uncovered fields,
> In the full fruits that keep still.
>
> The splendor of plants does not stir me,
> Like the young girlish blossoms;
> Truth is in naked fall
> And the fruit is sweet, not the petals.

And:

> Your tired head droops on my neck,
> Like an unconscious rose,
> I don't feel its weight,
> I feel only the breath
> That rolls from your mouth,
> The white, soft rose petals
> That spill apart
> Over my dress.

And:

> I see . . .
> The fringes hang unevenly
> At the edge of the cloth
> And dangle uselessly . . .
> Chopped, yellowish piano keys,
> Pale fingertips, little ears—
> Little lips half-stretch—
> Stretch uselessly . . .
> And so the poem begins
> With me.

Niger characterizes these lines, which he quotes without identifying the particular poems, as "accidental" in their "clear and expressive moods." However, what he considers "not accidental" are "the vague, nostalgic, delicately astonished lines, which could have been written by the collective hand of lyrically inclined Woman, and not necessarily by [Veprinsky's] own, individual hand."[90]

In contrast, Niger treats Molodowsky as "individual, rich, and diverse," containing and yet transcending the "old love and nostalgia motif " of the generalized woman poet. In her poems, "*Froyen-lider*" (Songs of Women) and "*Alte vayber*" (Old Wives), "eternal motherhood speaks" alongside "our old mamas," who recite *tkhines*. Niger characterizes Molodowsky's contribution in terms of collective Jewish and collective female traditions. Molodowsky's speaker fights the force of her familial matriarchs, the generations of mothers, who seek to shape her life in the present day. When she summons forth the matriarchs of the Bible, Sarah, Rebecca, Rachel, and Leah, through the filter of the *tkhines*, Molodowsky turns askew the comfort each of the Mothers offers to the streetwalkers, the poor brides, the barren women, and the unmarried. The poem forces to its surface the conflict between the traditional comfort and the timeless yet peculiarly modern sorrows of the woman writing poetry in a world beyond the boundary of that tradition:

> For poor brides who were servant girls,
> Mother Sarah draws forth from dim barrels
> And pitchers sparkling wine.
> Mother Sarah carries with both hands
> A full pitcher to whom it is decreed,
> And Mother Sarah's tears fall
> Into a small goblet for whom it is decreed.
>
> For high-born brides now poor,
> Who blush to bring patched wash
> Before their mothers-in-law,
> Mother Rebecca leads camels
> Laden with white linen.

For those . . .
Whose hands are thin from yearning
For a soft small body
And for the rocking of a cradle,
Mother Rachel brings healing leaves.

For those who cry at night in lonely beds,
And have no one to share their sorrow,
Who talk to themselves with parched lips,
To them, Mother Leah comes quietly,
Her eyes covered with her pale hands.[91]

Molodowsky creates a dialectical relationship between the force of the religious traditions and the forces of nature, working on and within the Jewish woman who has stepped into the modern, secular world:

Nights when I'm awake
And one by one my days stand before me,
My mother's life comes to me.
And her emaciated hands
Wrapped in virtuous nightgown sleeves
Are like a God's fearful script on white parchment,
And the words of Hammappil,
The prayer for falling asleep, grow angry
Like fiery coals quenched by her quiet plea,
And they shrivel her mouth like a withered plum.
And her tears come drop by drop like a meager drizzle.
And now that I am a woman,
And wear brown silk décolleté
With my head bare.
And my own life's misfortune has hunted me down,
And like a crow falling upon a chick,
My room is lit up all night,
And I throw my hands to my head
And my lips recite a quiet, simple
Plea to God.
And tears come drop by drop like a meager drizzle.[92]

In "*Opgeshite bleter*" (Fallen Leaves), Molodowsky places a strict limit on the power of longing.[93] Through the initial image of an old *siddur* (prayerbook) for women, the poem separates the traditional Jewish past from the speaker's present state of disbelief. At the end, a metaphor of a page torn loose tentatively binds together the past and the present. Niger describes Molodowsky's gift for such binding in the following passage:

Kadya Molodowsky has brought into Yiddish poetry THE JEWISH WOMAN with her old Jewish/Yiddish traditions. Like Miriam Ulinover, she spins further (and more forcefully) the thread of the ancient Yiddish woman-lyric, the lyric of *taytsh-khumash* and *tsenerene*. In a poem—a letter—she says:

> I stretch both arms, like reins
> And pull the wagon.
> In harness together with me
> Thirty-odd children from lowly streets.
> We cry often,
> We laugh often,
> We heave heavily the dear old alphabet
> In stylish and tedious classes.

. . . She has the beauty and grace of truth. But she is so deeply rooted in the soil of the generations that her personal truth grows together with the truth of the environment. Her most intimate experiences braid themselves in with Jewish ways of life. . . . [94]

Yet Niger's praise for Molodowsky's ability to assert for her individuality through tradition implies the double bind in which the woman writer has been placed:

Kadya Molodowsky identifies explicitly with Jewish nationalism, but that does not impede her. —To the contrary, it helps her to express her feelings and thoughts, which have a universal value. She is deeply feminine both in her motifs and in her —not fixed—rhythm, but there is here something generally human in her poetry, and she is already worthy of a place in the Yiddish lyric, not only in the lyric of the Yiddish woman. [95]

Niger is condescending about poetry written by women. His assessment of Molodowsky's gifts suggests that she is "feminine" in her rhythms and motifs, yet that she also conveys something "generally human" and universal. Despite the "femininity" expressed in the form and content of the poetry, Niger implies, Molodowsky's poems rise to a general standard of excellence. Yet the last sentence denotes that there are two standards by which to measure excellence: that of the Yiddish lyric and the less significant standard of the woman's lyric in Yiddish.

The double standard is carried further in Niger's conclusion, in which he examines Molodowsky's tropes:

In her epithets and similes two characteristic traits draw themselves to one's attention. On the one hand, she calls forth traditionally Jewish ideas ("Nights like this are all *yortsayt* [death anniversary] nights." "Villas—*agunes* [abandoned wives]." And so forth.); on the other hand, she likes comparisons which have to do with nonhuman creatures. (Worries approach like "tired horses with heavy heads . . . " "When his little hands are cuddled to her breasts like small chicks." "Like bees stinging around my heart . . . " "Like drowsy rabbits around my bed," "And drop like butterflies to the dress," and so forth.) She is woven into the historical tradition and united with nature—she drinks from two deep springs. She is a WOMAN POET, not only a woman's woman poet. [*Zi iz a DIKHTERIN, nisht nor a froyen-dikhterin.*][96]

According to Niger, these two "springs" of culture and nature paradoxically both give the woman poet her strength and limit her in her endeavors. In fact, the "weakness and unripeness" in Veprinksy's poems quoted earlier from Niger seem to lie in the predominance of conventionalized figures of nature: the autumnal tree, the drooping rose. Although Veprinsky does use the conventional figures in an original way, they are not integrated with figures of Jewish culture, while in Molodowsky's poems, the unexpected analogies of nature and culture work together. What Niger values in Molodowsky's work is her joining of these two realms in her poems.

I find it striking that both culture and nature are the terms that the Yiddish critics use to define women poets. While nature governs their creativity as sexual procreators, culture controls and measures that biological creativity in terms of restraint. In traditional Jewish culture, this restraint takes the form of virtuous modesty (*tsnies*), obedient fecundity, and the laws and rituals of marital purity (*niddah*). Niger, like other critics, chooses only this terminology of nature and culture to describe and evaluate the poems written by women. Poems by women, then, tend to be read primarily in reference to the writer's sex, whether regarded as a strength or a weakness. As of 1928, Yiddish did not possess a critical vocabulary for reading poems by women as poems.

Niger makes the distinction in his last sentence between *dikhterin* and *froyen-dikhterin*—a woman poet who is a poet, and a woman poet who is a poet for and like other women poets. Although praising her, Niger cannot avoid the slur implicit in his categorization of Molodowsky as a woman poet. He cannot call her a *dikhter*, because the gender-inflected language would make that noun incorrect. He wants to de-emphasize Molodowsky's femaleness in what he senses as its derogatory influence on her poetry, while maintaining the necessary acknowledgment of how her womanhood informs her poetry in a positive way. In other words, Niger sees the fact that Molodowsky writes as a woman who is a poet as both an attribute and a detriment. Because he inherits the double standard of his culture, he infuses his literary criteria with contradictory forces which at once value and devalue a specific women's poetic tradition within the recently defined general tradition of Yiddish poetry.

IV

This cultural double vision raises the question of whether, in fact, "women's poetry" stands outside the general Yiddish tradition. Is that "general tradition" of "artistic universalism" synonymous with a "men's tradition of poetry?" In other words, can only the exceptional woman poet transcend the "women's tradition" and enter the general (i.e., men's) tradition of Yiddish poetry? Why do the critics not define the general tradition by choosing among all Yiddish poets, good and less good, female and male? Where do mediocre men poets fit in? Finally, if "woman's poetry" is an entity unto itself in Yiddish, what are its characteristics? Is Niger's "womanly lyricism" the limit?

Responses to these questions lie in the poetry itself, read on its own terms. Two poems, by Anna Margolin and Malka Heifetz Tussman, provide rich material. Anna Margolin's *Lider* (Poems; New York, 1929) allusively seeks to establish traditions for Yiddish poetry outside Judaism. Poems such as "*Ikh bin amol geven a yingling*" (I Was Once a Boy) and "*Fargesene geter*" (Forgotten Gods) are couched in images from Greek and Roman culture.But because the Yiddish language is rooted in Judaism, the poems reflexively return to that which they try to escape.[97] In another poem, "*Yorn*" (Years), women are a metaphor for the passing years:[98]

> Like women, much loved yet never sated,
> Who walk through life with laughter and with anger
> In their eyes of fire and agate—
> So are the years.

> And they were also like actors
> Who mouth Hamlet half-heartedly for the market,
> Like noblemen in a proud country
> Who seize rebellion by the nape.

> And see, how demure they are now, my God,
> And mute as a crushed clavier.
> They grasp at just anybody's impulse and mockery as at love
> And seek you, not believing in you.[99]

Through nouns imported into Yiddish from English and Spanish, *aktyorn* (actors) and *gransinyorn* (noblemen), Margolin depicts the passing of *yorn* (years) by calling forth the traditions of Western Europe, in which Shakespeare and nobility figure allusively. In the first two stanzas, the years are personified as having been like sensual, insatiable women; like high-class actors playing Hamlet halfheartedly in inappropriately low places; like noblemen who easily quell rebellion by force. This string of similes escalates the degree of power possessed by the passing of years, from the private realm of love to the public demonstrations of drama and politics, from the female to the male.

In the last stanza, the poem addresses the present moment. Now, the poet tells us, the years are silenced and broken. This final personification of the years returns to the desperation of the women of the first stanza. The unsated desire of the much-loved women implicitly results in the muteness of a broken instrument. This muteness leads the women to misapprehend experience, misreading mockery for love, and cynically to seek a God whom the poet addresses yet in whom they (and implicitly she) do not believe.

Through the feminizing figure, "*Yorn*" plays out an ambivalent version of tradition. The passing years themselves accumulate in human memory, and through that accumulation, become tradition. Although the poem lists metaphors for that tradition, which include the power of Western art and society made evident in words and acts of men, in the end it returns to the privateness of inarticulate desire and shattered faith, to silenced women. The figure of years as broken, sensual women undermines the cumulative force of the tradition of Shakespeare and Cervantes in which this Yiddish poem seeks to stand. It is no accident that the poem ends on the question of belief in God, for the poem is written in a Yiddish voice, which is a voice of Judaism in the uncertainity of modern history. That doubting, Yiddish voicing of Judaism is, by nature, undeniably and implicitly female.

Margolin's speakers embody a conflict between Jewish and classical non-Jewish traditions and a merging of female and male identities. These contradictory forces join the cultural dilemma of the modern Yiddish poet with the sexual dilemma of the woman poet. Such a rich connecting results in a tension that differs starkly from the diverse efforts of Yakubovitsh, Ulinover, and Molodowsky. Their poems attempt to reconcile the question of tradition by integrating the old texts of devotion, specifically of women's devotion which is bound up in the conventions of women's biological creativity, with the poetry that emerges from the expressly modern life of a Jewish woman.

Contradictory as these trends are, they imply that communal culture is necessary to poetry. This sense of poetry's cultural context contrasts to the universalism of sexual isolation that emerges from the erotic, private poems by both Fradl Shtok and Celia Dropkin (*In heysn vint* [In Hot Wind; New York, 1935, 1959]). Whereas Margolin's poems set gentile and pagan cultures against Judaism, and Molodowsky's poems try to reconcile the old Jewish life with the new, these erotic poems set women apart from men. This sexual separation pares away the anxiety about tradition by isolating love in a sensory rather than a temporal framework. The speaker's ambivalent desire for the Other is the source of creativity in all these poems, whether the Other is defined as exotic, obsolete, or male.

This pursuit of the Other culminates in the extreme communion of creativity depicted in the poems of Malka Heifetz Tussman, where the poet's power of creation is seen as the chaotic underside of God's creation. We see this in *"Midbar vint"* (Desert Wind), where the speaker finds half-terrifying and half-alluring the dazzling, barren, feminized chaos of *toye-voye*, the state of the earth in *Genesis* 1:2, before God separated light from darkness and imposed order, and in *"Duner mayn bruder"* (Thunder My Brother), where the forceful disorder of nature is kin to the forbidden otherness of the poet's work:

Thunder my brother
My powerful brother,
Stones rolling on stones—your voice.
Like a forest, forceful, your voice.

What pleasure you take in making mountains rattle,
How happy you feel
When you bewilder creeping creatures in the valley.

Once
Long ago
The storm—my father—
Rode on a dark cloud,
And stared at the other side of the Order-of-the-Universe,
Across to the chaos.
I, too,
Have a voice—
A voice of fearsome roaring
In the grip of my muteness.

And there are commandments
Forbidding me:
"Thou shalt not,
Thou shalt not"
O thunder,
My wild unbridled brother.[100]

The poet, in assessing her lineage, sees through to the other side of God's order. Yet she voices that vision in conflict with herself. Like the thunder's, the poet's voice is "of fearsome roaring / In the grip of my muteness." These poems set up a tension between the force of God and a contrary creative force in nature, kindred to the poet. Setting the poet's work in opposition to God, these poems try to understand the work of God in the chaotic terms of human creation. When the poet prays, it is to a deity that emerging from within Jewish tradition has been created in the image of the poet.[101]

These trends in which sexuality is linked to creativity and creativity to devotion suggest one of the major concerns of Yiddish poetry in the modern era—to legitimate the individual voice defining itself in tension against and within the forceful currents of tradition.

V

Korman's anthology is significant because it attempts to separate and canonize Yiddish poetry by women at a time when many women were publishing poetry in journals, but few had yet published books.[102] The anthology gave a stability and coherence to this body of works. Its chronological scope suggests a twofold message: that individual women poets are a significant presence in Yiddish literature and that there is a separate tradition of women's poetry within the larger tradition of Yiddish literature.

This anthology is a kind of prism for us to hold up to the light of Yiddish;

through its refraction, we can see the distinct colors of the individual poets and the way they fit together in the spectrum. The anthology implies that in 1928, Yiddish poetry in general was thriving; and that within that general thriving, women held their own place. In fact, that suggestion is misleading, as a look at other anthologies of the time and at the critical response to this anthology reveals. The Korman anthology gathers a diversity of poems by women that defy simple categorization, although there are repeated themes and conventions. These poems reflect the limitations and the variety of Yiddish poems in general, especially the modernist shift from collective, political poetry to aesthetic, individualist poetry in the nineteen-teens and twenties. The poetry of this and the subsequent decades embodies the tension between the communal and the individual responsibilities of the Yiddish poet. While peculiar to Yiddish poetry in particular and Jewish poetry in general, these tensions are also characteristic of modern European and American poetry. In this sense, the poems by women in Korman's anthology reflect the development of modernism in twentieth-century poetry. However, the women poets work out these tensions in ways that seem to emerge from the particular experiences of being female and Jewish within the Yiddish language.

Korman's anthology demonstrated that women had published Yiddish poems since 1586. Many of the responses to this fact, when the anthology appeared, denied the value of this literature and dismissed the tradition of women's poetry. Yet this dismissal, though unfortunately effective, was weak: for the exact nature of this tradition was not fully perceived or understood by Korman's contemporaries. Half a century later, the real work commences, as we begin to read and re-evaluate the lives and works of the women poets in terms of the general field of Yiddish poetry. However the tradition set forth in Korman's anthology may be apprehended across the decades and in translation, the fact is that Yiddish poetry by women documents a realm of Jewish experience that otherwise would remain unknown.

NOTES

[All translations in this essay are mine unless otherwise noted.]

1. The only other work that in any way resembles Korman's anthology is Shmuel Rozshanski, ed., *Di froy in der yidisher poezye: 315 Lider fun 136 Poetn; fragmentn fun forsharbetn tsu der kharakteristik un zikhroynes* (Woman in Yiddish Poetry: 315 Poems from 136 Poets; Fragments by the Deceased toward the Characterization and Memories). However, this anthology, which covers only the modern period, is arranged thematically and impressionistically. It includes as many poems *about* women as it does poems *by* women.

2. Selected Yiddish anthologies: M. Bassin, ed., *Amerikaner yidishe poezye: antologye* (American Yiddish Poetry: Anthology), pp. 253–266. M. Bassin, ed., *Antologye: finf hundert yor yidishe poezye* (Anthology: Five Hundred Years of Yiddish Poetry), vol. 1, p. 79; vol. 2, pp. 49–50, 121, 125, 134, 203, 299–303. Nachman Mayzel, ed., *Amerike in yidishn vort* (America in the Yiddish Word), pp. 147, 158, 287, 421, 465, 501, 611,

647, 652, 660, 751, 753, 776, 800, 857, 863, 869. Zishe Landau, ed., *Antologye: di yidishe dikhtung in amerike biz yor 1919* (Anthology: Yiddish Poetry in America until 1919), pp. 51–52; 172. Anna Margolin, ed., *Dos yidishe lid in amerike, 1923: antologye* (The Yiddish Poem in America, 1923), p. 5. Mattes Deutch, Ben Sholem, Shloime Schwartz, eds., *Antologye: mitvest-mayrev, 1932–1933* (Anthology: Midwest-West, 1932–1933), pp. 44–45; 95–102; 103–104; 105–110; 156–158. Selected Yiddish miscellanies (*zamlbikher*): Moyshe-Leyb Halpern and Menachem, eds., *East Broadway*. Ben Sholem et al., eds., *Yung chicago: a zamlung, 1922.* (Young Chicago: A Collection). William Abrams and Kalman Marmor, eds., *Revolutsionerer deklamator* (Revolutionary Declaimer). Dovid Ignatov, ed., *Shriftn: a zamlbukh* (Writings: A Collection), 1914, no. 3. Joseph Opatoshu, ed., *Di naye heym: ershtes zamlbukh* (The New Home: First Collection). Abraham Rintsler, ed., *Yung-Yisroel: zamlung* (Young Israel).

Selected English anthologies: Joseph Leftwich, ed., *The Golden Peacock: An Anthology of Yiddish Poetry*, "Women Poets," pp. 737–780; Howard Schwartz and Anthony Rudolf, eds., *Voices Within the Ark: The Modern Jewish Poets*, p. 244, 248, 252, 254, 279, 301, 312, 317, 334, 335, 360, 366, 374; Irving Howe and Eliezer Greenberg, eds., *A Treasury of Yiddish Poetry*, pp. 60–162, 168, 230–231, 236–238, 284–289, 297–298, 302–306; Melanie Kaye/Kantrowitz and Irena Klepfisz, eds., *The Tribe of Dina: A Jewish Women's Anthology*; and Benjamin and Barbara Harshav, eds., *American Yiddish Poetry*, pp. 592–627.

3. Norma Fain Pratt, "Culture and Radical Politics: Yiddish Women Writers, 1890–1940," pp. 68–90.

4. Irving Howe and Kenneth Libo, *World of Our Fathers: The Journey of the East European Jews to America and the Life They Found and Made*, pp. 453, 454, 634. David G. Roskies, *Against the Apocalypse: Responses to Catastrophe in Modern Jewish Culture*. A. A. Roback, *The Story of Yiddish Literature*, pp. 293, 294, 295. Sol Liptzin, *The Maturing of Yiddish Literature*, pp. 40, 101, 180–186, 191. Charles Madison, *Yiddish Literature: Its Scope and Major Writers*, pp. 319ff., 200. Yitzhak Kahn, *Portraits of Yiddish Writers*, trans. Joseph Leftwich, pp. 159–173, 175–186.

5. Charlotte Baum, Paula Hyman, Sonya Michel, *The Jewish Woman in America*. Lucy Dawidowicz, "On Being a Woman in Shul," pp. 46–57. Elizabeth Ewen, *Immigrant Women in the Land of Dollars: Life and Culture on the Lower East Side, 1890–1925*. Blu Greenberg, *On Women and Judaism: A View from Tradition*. Susannah Heschel, ed. and intro., *On Being a Jewish Feminist: A Reader*, Introduction, pp. xiii–xxxvi. Cynthia Ozick, "Notes toward Finding the Right Question," pp. 120–151. Liz Koltun, ed., *The Jewish Woman: An Anthology*. *Response*, vol. 18. Kathy Peiss, *Cheap Amusements: Working Women and Leisure in Turn-of-the-Century New York*.

6. See Elizabeth Koltun, ed., *The Jewish Woman: New Perspectives*, pp. 217–282; Arthur Green, "Bride, Spouse, Daughter: Images of the Feminine in Classical Jewish Sources," pp. 248–260; and Claire R. Satlof, "History, Fiction, and the Tradition: Creating a Jewish Feminist Poetic," pp. 186–206. There is some treatment of early Yiddish letters, diaries, and devotional literature written for women; see Sondra Henry and Emily Taitz, *Written Out of History: Our Jewish Foremothers*, pp. 152–173, 184–196.

7. Chone Shmeruk, "*Medresh itsik* and the Problem of Its Literary Traditions," pp. v–xxix.

8. Twenty years later, in 1939, Cleanth Brooks restated this idea in reference to the poets of the American South: "Indeed, every past is dead which is unconnected with

the present—the past of the literary vacuum. Conversely, a present which is nothing but the immediate present of sensation—the present unrelated to history—is not even the present. It is apt to be merely a collection of sensations, or at best, unrelated images. The problem presented by an attempt to hold on to a tradition is, thus, ultimately a problem of sincerity or integrity. . . . '' Cleanth Brooks, ''The Modern Poet and the Tradition,'' in *Modern Poetry and the Tradition*, pp. 75–76.

In 1960, J. V. Cunningham, in contrast with Eliot, argues that tradition produces literary forms:

A tradition is the body of texts and interpretations current among a group of writers at a given time and place. . . . the principles that determine the realization of what [the poet] regards as a particular literary form—the appropriate subject, devices, and structure—are principles located in that tradition. It follows from this that a literary form is not simply an external principle of classification of literary works, . . . nor is it an Idea. It is rather a principle operative in the production of works. It is a scheme of experience recognized in the tradition and derived from prior works and from the descriptions of those works extant in the tradition. It is, moreover, a scheme that directs the discovery of material and detail and that orders the disposition of the whole.

Tradition and Poetic Structure, pp. 62–63.

9. T. S. Eliot. ''Tradition and the Individual Talent,'' pp. 38–39, 44.

10. Malcolm Bradbury and James McFarlane, ''Movements, Magazines and Manifestos: The Succession from Naturalism,'' p. 193.

11. Chone Shmeruk, quoting Aharon Zeitlin in ''Introduction,'' *Medresh itsik*, p. ix, note 12.

12. See Kathryn Hellerstein, ''Moyshe-Leyb Halpern's Subversive Ballads,'' *Prooftexts* (Fall, 1987).

13 . Halpern's first book is *In New York* (1919). Leyvik published three early collections of poems: *Hintern shlos* (1918); *Lider* (1919); *In keynemn land* (1916–1921; 1923). Mani Leyb published three volumes in 1918: *Balade*, *Lider*, and *Yidishe un slavishe motivn*.

14. Ruth Wisse, ''*Di Yunge* and the Problem of Jewish Aestheticism,'' pp. 269–270.

15. Zishe Landau, *Antologye: di yidishe dikhtung in amerike biz yor 1919*.

16. For a discussion of Moyshe-Leyb Halpern's ''*A nakht*'' as the simultaneous embodiment of the modern individual and the historical collective voice, see my doctoral dissertation, ''Moyshe-Leyb Halpern's *In nyu york*: A Modern Yiddish Verse Narrative,'' pp. 671–689.

17. Zishe Landau, *Antologye*, p. i.

18. Ibid., p. vi.

19. Ibid., p. vii.

20. ''*Introspektivizm*,'' pp. 1–10.

21. Ibid., pp. 1–2.

22. Jacob Glatstein, ''Thinking Back,'' trans. Henny Goodman, pp. 33–36.

23. ''*Introspektivizm*,'' p. 6.

24. Ibid., pp. 9–10. Note in the same issue, N. Minkov, ''*In zikh*,'' pp. 10–15.

25. ''*Introspketivizm*,'' p. 10.

26. Yankev Glatshteyn, ''*A shnel-loyf iber der yidisher poezye*'' (A Run-through of Yiddish Poetry), pp. 19–28.

27. Ibid., p. 22.

28. Ibid., p. 28.

29. Ibid.

30. M. Bassin, ed., *Antologye: finf hundert yor yidishe poezye*, 2 vols.

31. Celia Dropkin, *"Du erniderigst mikh haynt"* (Today You Humble Me) and *"Mayne hent"* (My Hands), p. 11. Dropkin published poems in Yiddish journals besides *In zikh*, such as *Di naye velt, Poezye*. Her manuscripts and correspondence are housed in the Genazim Biobibliographic Institute, Tel Aviv, and in the Melekh Ravitsh Archives, Jewish National and University Library, Jerusalem. Her books are *In heysn vint: lider* (In a Hot Wind: Poems, 1935) and the expanded, posthumous edition, *In heysn vint: Poems, Stories, and Pictures* (1959).

32. A question which seems central to the issue of where and how women poets fit into the self-defining traditions of Yiddish poetry in the early twentieth century is this: how does the public and the private voice differ for men and women poets, especially in the context of Yiddish, where the precedent for the communal obligations of the poet is so powerful? It seems that the efforts of Landau and Ayzland to write a program for individualism, which the Introspectivists follow up on in formalist terms in their insistence on the linguistic and aesthetic uniqueness of each poem, work against what a feminist critic, Jeanne Kammer, calls, in her essay "The Art of Silence and the Forms of Women's Poetry," "the cultural hierarchy of vocal strength: the male voice carries more 'universal' authority than the female" (p. 159). Kammer explains this cultural hierarchy thus: "For the woman poet, perhaps, the model is oracle, not bard; the activity seeing, not singing" (p. 164).

33. For a dramatic account and interpretation of the efforts of S. Anski (Shloyme-Zanvl Rapaport) to collect folk literature and folk art before and during the First World War, see David G. Roskies, *Against the Apocalypse: Responses to Catastrophe in Modern Jewish Culture*, pp. 133–162.

34. Sh. Niger, *"Di yidishe literatur un di lezerin,"* pp. 35–107. See also Solomon B. Freehof, "Devotional Literature in the Vernacular," pp. 1–43; Israel Zinberg, "Popular Literature; *Tze'enah U-re'enah"* and "Historical and Travel Literature; Memoirs and *Tehinnot*," pp. 119–139, 241–259.

35. For a recent survey of fifty women Yiddish poets from a cultural-historical perspective, see Pratt, pp. 68–90.

36. Ezra Korman, ed. and intro., *Yidishe dikhterins: antologye*.

37. Chava Weissler translates this conventional Yiddish and Hebrew phrase, which often appeared at the beginning of religious Yiddish books from the seventeenth century on, in a richly allusive way: " . . . women and 'men who are like women in not having much knowledge.' " Chava Weissler, "Issues in the Study of Women's Religion: The Case of Ashkenazik Jewish Women," p. 7, quoted by permission of the author.

38. Sh. Niger, *"Di yidishe literatur un di lezerin,"* p. 37.

39. Ibid., pp. 49; 51–52.

40. Ibid., pp. 52–53.

41. Ibid., pp. 55–68.

42. Ibid., pp.69–73.

43. A. Glanz, *"Kultur un di froy,"* pp. 4–5. Brought to my attention by Pratt, p. 77, note 18.

44. A. Glanz, *"Kultur un di froy,"* p. 4.

45. Ibid.

46. Ibid.

47. Ibid. The copy of the article I read at YIVO was torn, and the word "different" was illegible. From the context, I read the fragment, "AN- . . . ERS", as *andersh* (other, alternate, different).

48. Pratt, p. 79.

49. Nahum Sokolov, *Yidishe froy*, pp.1–22.

50. *dikhterins*. I have been deliberately inconsistent in translating this word. Niger uses it in the context of the Yiddish word for poets in general, which is conventionally the masculine form of the noun, *dikhter*. In his review he uses the feminine noun with a tone of matter-of-fact respect. Ravitsh, in contrast, in both his reviews, gives the word a mocking tone by repeating it insistently and lewdly. I have translated *dikhterin* "poetess" in the Ravitsh reviews, because I think that the archaism best conveys his attitudes and intentions in using it. But I hesitate to use "poetess" in Niger's review, or in the letters of Molodowsky and Tussman, because they intend neither mockery nor archaic condescension and *politesse*.

51. Ezra Korman, ed., *Yidishe dikhterins: antologye*, pp. vii–xii, xxvii–lxv, 5–335.

52. According to Malka Heifetz Tussman, Berkeley, California, telephone interview, December 1985.

53. Korman's reviews are "*Vegn miriam ulinovers 'Der bobes oytser'* " and "*Vegn glazer-andrus 'In halb shotn,' celia dropkins un rashel veprinskis lider.*" Cited in Korman, *Yidishe dikhterins: antologye*, p. 373, no. 215.

54. Korman's original poetry appeared as *Shkye: lider* (Sunset: Poems). Poems also appeared in Mattes Deutch, ed., *Antologye: mitvest-mayrev*, pp. 152–155, 197. The biography on p. 197 states that Korman, born in 1888 in Kiev, began to write in 1910 for Sh. Godelik's *Almanakh*. He wrote journalism for various European and American newspapers, and published poems in the journals *Milgroym* (Pomegranate), *Kultur* (Culture), and *Yidish* (Yiddish). He also compiled bibliographies of Sh. Niger and A. Tseytlin for Zalman Reyzen's *Antologye*.

55. Ezra Korman, ed., *In fayerdikn doyer—zamlung fun revolutsionerer lyrik in der nayer yidisher dikhtung* (1921), and ed. and intro., *Brenendike brikn—antologye fun revolutsionerer lyrik in der nayer yidisher dikhtung fun ukraine* (1923, second edition of *In fayerdikn doyer*). Cited in Ezra Korman, "*Kvaln un literatur*" (Sources and Literature), *Yidishe dikhterins: antologye*, p. 360, nos. 16, 17.

56. Max Erik, "*Brantshpigl—di entsiklopedye fun der yidisher froy in 17th yorhundert*" and "*Bleter tsu der geshikhte fun der elterer yidisher literatur un kultur*" (Pages toward the History of Old Yiddish Literature and Culture). Cited in Ezra Korman, *Yidishe dikhterins: antologye*, p. xxx, note 3.

57. Korman, *Yidishe dikhterins: antologye*, pp. xxvii; xxxi–xxxii; xxxiii–xxxv.

58. Ibid., pp. lxvii–lxxxiii; 357.

59. *Froyen zshurnal-vokhenblat* (New York, 1922). Cited in Korman, *Yidishe dikhterins: antologye*, p. 364, no. 73.

60. Korman, *Yidishe dikhterins: antologye*, p. 350.

61. Among the earlier generation of labor poets, editions of the collected works of Morris Rosenfeld and David Edelstat had appeared in 1908 and 1909, signaling a self-conscious making of a canon. Of the *Yunge*, Moyshe Leyb Halpern had published his two collections of poems; Mani Leyb at least twelve books of poems, children's poems, and other writings; Reuven Ayzland had published one volume of poems and several of translations; Zishe Landau had published a play, the anthology of 1919, and translations.

Of the Introspectivists, Yankev Glatshteyn had published three books; A.Glanz-Leyeles had published at least six volumes, including poems, plays, and scholarship.

62. See Dov Sadan, "Guardian of the Treasure: On Miriam Ulinover" [Hebrew], pp. 1–8. Includes a bibliography of nine articles in Yiddish on Ulinover: Mirl Ardberg-Shatan, "Miriam ulinover" (1956); Yehemial Briks, "*Miriam ulinover*" (1953) and "*Literatn in ghetto*" (Men of Letters in the Ghetto, 1963); Yitskhok Goldkorn, "*Miriam ulinover*" (1959); Yitskhok Zilberberg, "*Fartretn fun interesante froyen*" (Encounters with Interesting Women, 1955); Sh. D. Zinger, "*Miriam ulinover, tsu ir zekstn yortsayt*" (For the Sixth Anniversary of Her Death, 1950) and "*Vegn shrayber un bikher*" (About Writers and Books, 1959); Rikuda Potash, "*Der goyrl fun tsvey lider*" (The Fate of Two Poems); Khaim Leyb Fuks, "*Lodz shel maalah*" (1972); Leo Finkelshteyn, "*Di eyshes khayl in poyln*" (The Woman of Valor in Poland, 1947) and *Megillat poyln* (The Scroll of Poland, 1947).

63. Korman, *Yidishe dikhterins: antologye*, p. xxix.

64. See Susan Stanford Friedman, "Creativity in the Childbirth Metaphor: Gender Difference in Literary Discourse." Also see Estella Lauter, *Women as Mythmakers: Poetry and Visual Art by Twentieth Century Women*, pp. 13–17, 131–223. See also Julia Kristeva, "Semiotics of Biblical Abomination," pp. 90–112. Kristeva discusses the prohibitions for the menses and childbirth in terms of keeping "a being who speaks to his God separate from the fecund mother . . . that phantasmic power of the mother, that archaic Mother Goddess" (p. 100). This separation of the art of language through prayer from the creativity of the female body contradicts the childbirth metaphor of the Yiddish critics.

65. Melekh Ravitsh, "*Meydlekh, froyen, vayber—yidishe dikhterins*," pp. 395–396. All the materials cited from *Literarishe bleter* and other Yiddish journals and newspapers were found at YIVO Institute for Jewish Research. I thank the librarians for their assistance and generous cooperation. Kadya Molodowsky, "*Meydlekh, froyen, vayber, un . . . ne-vue*" (Girls, Women, Wives, and . . . Prophecy), p. 416. Malka Heifetz Tussman, "*An entfer melekh ravitshn af 'Meydlekh, froyen, vayber—yidishe dikhterins.*' " *Literarishe bleter*, May 27, 1927 (An Answer to Melekh Ravitsh concerning 'Girls, Women, Wives— Yiddish Poetesses' in *Literary Leaves*), manuscript of letter that appeared in *Literarishe bleter* August, 1927, pp. 1–3 (unnumbered). Manuscript in the Melekh Ravitsh Archives at the Jewish National and University Library, Hebrew University, Jerusalem. Quoted by permission of Malka Heifetz Tussman.

66. Malka Heifetz Tussman's seven books of poetry are the following: *Lider* (Poems, 1949); *Mild mayn vild* (Mild My Wild, 1958); *Shotns fun gedenken* (Shadows of Remembering, 1965); *Bleter faln nit: lider* (Leaves Do Not Fall, 1972); *Unter dayn tseykhn* (Under Your Sign, 1974); *Haynt iz eybik* (Today Is Forever, 1977); *Un ikh shmeykhl: lider un proze* (And I Smile: Poems and Prose, manuscript, 1986). She has also written essays, children's poetry (*Shabbes-oyps*, n.d.), and translated poetry into Yiddish. Tussman was awarded the prestigious Israeli Itsik Manger Prize for her poetry in 1981. Her poems and prose have appeared in *Di goldene keyt* (Tel Aviv, 1948–1985), *Tsukunft* (New York), *Literarishe bleter* (Warsaw), *Antologye* (Chicago, 1933), *Amerike in yidishn vort* (New York, n.d.). "Triolets" first published in *Studio*. 4, no. 2. (October-December, 1934), Farlag Aleyn, New York, pp. 207–208. Letters and manuscripts in Melekh Ravitsh Archives at Jewish National and University Library (Jerusalem), Genazim Biobiblio-graphic Institute (Tel Aviv), YIVO Institute for Jewish Research (New York), and in the author's possession.

Kadya Molodowsky's works include: *A shtub mit zibn fentster* (A House with Seven

Windows, stories, 1957); *Af di vegn fun tsion* (On the Roads from Zion, essays, 1957); *Ale fentster tsu der zun: shpil in elef bilder* (All Windows to the Sun: Play in Eleven Images, 1938); *Baym toyer, roman* (By the Gate, novel, 1967); *Der melekh dovid aleyn iz geblibn* (Only King David Remains, poems, 1946); *Dzshike gas: lider* (Dzshike Street, poems, 1933, 1936); *Freydke: lider* (Freydke, poems, 1935, 1936); *Fun lublin biz nyu york: togbukh fun rivke zilberg* (From Lublin to New York: Diary of Rivke Zilberg, 1942); *In land fun mayn gebeyn: lider* (In the Land of My Bones, poems, 1937); *Kheshvandike nekht: lider* (Nights of Heshvan, poems, 1927); ed., *Lider fun khurbn: antologye* (Poems of Destruction, anthology, 1962); *Likht fun dornboym: lider un poeme* (Light from the Thornbush, poems, 1965); *Malokhim kumen keyn yerushalayim: lider* (Angels Come to Jerusalem, poems, 1952); *Martsepanes: mayselekh un lider far kinder* (Marzipans: Tales and Poems for Children, 1970); *Mayselekh* (Tales, 1930–1935); *Nokhn got fun midbar: drame* (After the God of the Desert, drama, 1949); *Pithu et hasha'ar: shirei yeladim* (Open the Gate: Poems for Children, Hebrew translations, 1979); *Yidishe kinder: mayselekh* (Jewish Children: Tales, 1945).

Molodowsky was awarded the Itsik Manger Prize for her poetry in 1965. In addition to her prize-winning poetry and writings for children, her novels, plays, and collections of essays, she founded and edited the journal *Sviva* (Environment, New York, 1955–1974). Individual poems by Molodowsky appeared in *Yidishe dikhterins: antologye*, *Literarishe bleter* (Warsaw), *Aygns* (Kiev, 1921), *Tsukunft* (New York), *Signal* (Moscow, 1930's), *Fraye arbeter shtime* (New York). Manuscripts and correspondence in YIVO Institute (New York), Jewish National and University Library (Jerusalem), Genazim Biobibliographic Institute (Tel Aviv), and private collections.

67. Melekh Ravitsh, *"'Den mir hobn zunshtn keyn andri (mekhaye) in der velt':* *E. Korman—Yidishe Dikhterins: Antologye"* (Then We Have Hardly Any Other Pleasure in the World: E. Korman—Yiddish Women Poets: Anthology), pp. 830–831.

68. Kadya Molodowsky, *"Meydlekh, froyen, vayber un . . . nevue,"* p. 416.

69. Sh. Niger, *"Froyen-lyrik,"* pp. 909–910.

70. Ibid., p. 909.

71. The concept of the double bind of the woman poet was first articulated by Suzanne Juhasz, *Naked and Fiery Forms: Modern American Poetry by Women, A New Tradition*, pp. 1–6. For analyses of poets' solutions to the double bind, see Alicia Ostriker, "The Thieves of Language: Women Poets and Revisionist Mythmaking," pp. 68–90; Wendy Martin, "Anne Bradstreet's Poetry: A Study of Subversive Piety," pp. 19–31; Jeanne Kammer, "The Art of Silence and the Forms of Women's Poetry," pp. 153–164; and Estella Lauter, *Women as Mythmakers: Poetry and Visual Art by 20th Century Women*, pp. 1–20.

72. See Chava Weissler, "The Traditional Piety of Ashkenazic Women." Also, Israel Zinberg, "Historical and Travel Literature; Memoirs and Tehinnot," and "Popular Literature; *Tze'ena U're'enah,*" pp.119–139; 229–259. Also, Solomon B. Freehof, *Devotional Literature in the Vernacular*.

73. Korman, *Yidishe dikhterins: antologye*, p. xxx.

74. Ibid., pp. lxiv–lxv.

75. Ibid., p. xlvii.

76. Ibid., pp. xlviii–xlix.

77. See David G. Roskies, *Against the Apocalypse: Jewish Cultural Responses to Catastrophe*, pp. 17, 77–108, 225–257, 283, 289.

78. Korman, *Yidishe dikhterins: antologye*, p. L.

79. Ibid., p. li.

80. Ibid., pp. liv–lvi.

81. Ibid., p. lvi.

82. Roza Yakubovitsh, *Mayne gezangen* (My Songs, Warsaw, 1924). *Lider tsu got* (Poems to God, not published, as of 1928).

83. Conversation with Malka Heifetz Tussman in Berkeley, California, September, 1978. Fradl Shtok published her sonnets in groups, for example, the eight sonnets in the anthology, *Di naye heym* (New York, 1914). However, Abraham Tabatchnik argues that this is a popular misconception that originated with Bassin's *Antologye: finf hundert yor yidishe poezye*; rather, Morris Vinchevski was the true innovator, writing sonnets between 1892 and 1908. Abraham Tabatchnik, *"Fradl shtok un der sonet"* (Fradl Shtok and the Sonnet), pp. 505–508.

84. Fradl Shtok, "Sonnet," in Ezra Korman, *Yidishe dikhterins: antologye*, p. 98.

85. Pratt, pp. 78–79.

86. See also Ezra Korman, *"Vegn miriam ulinover's 'Der bobes oytser,' "* cited in Korman, *Yidishe dikhterins: antologye*, p. 373, no. 215.

87. Korman, *Yidishe dikhterins: antologye*, pp. lxiii-lxiv.

88. Ibid., p. lxiv.

89. Sh. Niger, *"Froyen lyrik,"* pp.909–910.

90. Ibid.

91. Kadya Molodowsky, *"Froyen-lider,"* VI, in *Kheshvandike nekht: lider*, pp. 16–17. Also in Korman, *Yidishe dikhterins: antologye*, pp. 192–193. This translation first appeared in *Grove*. (Spring, 1982), pp. 36–37.

92. Kadya Molodowsky, *Kheshvandike nekht*, p. 19. In Korman, *Yidishe dikhterins: antologye*, pp. 194–195. This translation first appeared in *Imagine*. 1. (Summer, 1984), pp. 74–75.

93. Kadya Molodowsky, *"Opgeshite bleter,"* *Kheshvandike nekht*, p. 21. In Korman, *Yidishe dikhterins: antologye*, pp. 195–196.

94. Sh. Niger, *"Froyen lyrik,"* pp. 909–910.

95. Ibid.

96. Ibid.

97. I am indebted to David Stern, who commented that the classical influence in the Yiddish poems of Margolin bears a resemblance to the classicism of the Hebrew poet Saul Tchernikhovsky (1875–1943). See T. Carmi, ed. and trans., *The Penguin Book of Hebrew Verse*, pp. 133–134, 516–521.

98. The opening of *"Yorn"* is reminiscent of Ralph Waldo Emerson's sonnet "Days," except that Emerson fills time with promise as the figurative procession of women, while Margolin's figure of the woman-like years connotes disillusionment.

99. Anna Margolin, *"Yorn,"* in Korman, *Yidishe dikhterins: antologye*, p. 217. There is another translation of this poem by Ruth Whitman, in Howard Schwartz and Anthony Rudolf, eds., *Voices Within the Ark: The Modern Jewish Poets*, p. 313. "Yorn" also appears in *Tikkun*. 2. (Nov.–Dec. 1987), p. 30.

100. Malka Heifetz Tussman, *"Duner mayn bruder,"* *Bleter faln nit*, p. 34. Kathryn Hellerstein, trans., "Thunder My Brother," in Benjamin and Barbara Harshav, *American Yiddish Poetry*.

101. Malka Heifetz Tussman, *"Midbar vint,"* *Unter dayn tseykhn*, pp. 41–42. Kathryn Hellerstein, trans., "Desert Wind," in Benjamin and Barbara Harshav, *American Yiddish Poetry*. Malka Heifetz Tussman, *"In onheyb,"* (In the beginning) *Haynt iz eybik*, p. 57.

102. The collections at YIVO Institute for Jewish Research in New York City and the National Yiddish Book Center in Amherst, Massachusetts, yield evidence that far more volumes of Yiddish poetry by women have been published since the 1950's than in the preceding decades. A full-scale study of this body of literature has yet to be done.

BIBLIOGRAPHY

Time for the research and writing of this essay was made available through the support of the National Endowment for the Humanities Travel to Collections Grant (June–July, 1985), the National Endowment for the Humanities Fellowship for College Teachers (Spring, 1986), the Lipman Foundation Travel Grant (August, 1985), and the Wellesley College Faculty Research Fund (Summer, 1985). I would like to acknowledge the invaluable help I received from the librarians at the YIVO Institute for Jewish Research in New York, Dina Abramovitsh and Jack Weinstein; the Hebrew University and Jewish National Library Manuscripts Division, in Jerusalem; and the Genazim Biobibliographic Institute, in Tel Aviv.

Abrams, William and Kalman Marmor, eds. *Revolutsionerer deklamator*. New York: International Workers Order, 1933.

Ardberg-Shatan, Mirl. "Miriam ulinover." *Montrealer heftn* (Montreal Notebooks). 2 (July, 1956).

Bassin, M., ed. *Amerikaner yidishe poezye; antologye*. New York: Committee, 1940.

———. *Antologye: finf hundert yor yidishe poezye*. 2 vols. New York: Dos bukh, 1917. Foreword and Old Yiddish glossary, B. Borokhov. Portraits, S. Zagat. Illustrations, Y. Likhtenshteyn and Z. Movd.

Baum, Charlotte, Paula Hyman, and Sonya Michel. *The Jewish Woman in America*. New York: New American Library, 1976.

Bradbury, Malcolm and James McFarlane. "Movements, Magazines and Manifestos: The Succession from Naturalism." In *Modernism: 1890–1930*, ed. Malcolm Bradbury and James McFarlane. Sussex, England: Harvester Press (Penguin), 1978.

Briks, Yehemiel. "*Literatn in Ghetto*." *Unzer veg* (Our Way) (June–July, 1963).

———. "Miriam Ulinover." *Keneder odler* (Canadian Eagle). (March 2, 1953).

Brooks, Cleanth. *Modern Poetry and the Tradition*. Chapel Hill: University of North Carolina Press, 1979.

Carmi, T., ed., and trans. *The Penguin Book of Hebrew Verse*. New York: Penguin, 1981.

Cunningham, J. V. *Tradition and Poetic Structure*. Denver: Alan Swallow, 1960.

Dawidowicz, Lucy. "On Being a Woman in Shul." In *The Jewish Presence: Essays on Identity and History*. New York: Harcourt Brace Jovanovich, 1978, pp. 46–57.

Deutch, Mattes, Ben Sholem, and Shloyme Schwartz, eds. *Antologye: mitvest-mayrev, 1932–1933*. Chicago: Farlag tseshinski, 1933.

Dropkin, Celia. "*Du erniderigst mikh haynt*" and "*Mayne hent*." *In zikh*. 1. (January, 1920), p. 11.

———. *In heysn vint, lider*. New York: Published by the author, 1935.

———. *In heysn vint, Poems, Stories, and Pictures*. New York: The Author's Children, 1959.

———. Manuscripts and correspondence in Genazim Biobibliographic Institute, Tel Aviv, and in Melekh Ravitsh Archives, Jewish National and University Library,

Jerusalem. Poems in *Yidishe dikhterins: antologye*, ed. Ezra Korman (Chicago, 1928). Poems in Yiddish Journals: *Di naye velt*, *Poezye*, *In zikh*.

Eliot, T. S. "Tradition and the Individual Talent." In *Selected Essays of T. S. Eliot*, ed. and intro. Frank Kermode. New York: Harcourt Brace Jovanovich; Farrar, Straus and Giroux, 1975.

Erik, Max. "*Bleter tsu der geshikhte fun der elterer yidisher literatur un kultur.*" Cited in *Yidishe dikhterins*, ed. Korman.

———. "*Brantshpigl—di entsiklopedye fun der yidisher froy in 17tn yorhundert.*" *Tsaytshrift* (Periodical), Book I, Minsk, 1926.

Ewen, Elizabeth. *Immigrant Women in the Land of Dollars: Life and Culture on the Lower East Side, 1890–1925*. New York: Monthly Review Press, 1985.

Finkelshteyn, Leo. "*Di eyshes khayl in poylin.*" *Tsukunft* (Future). (November, 1947). Cf. Sadan, Dov entry.

———. *Megillat poyln*. New York, 1947. Cf. Sadan, Dov entry.

Freehof, Solomon B. "Devotional Literature in the Vernacular." *Central Conference of American Rabbis*, 1923. Reprinted from *Yearbook*, vol. 33, pp. 1–43.

Friedman, Susan Stanford. "Creativity in the Childbirth Metaphor: Gender Difference in Literary Discourse." Paper presented in Session 202, "The Body-Soul Bond in Poetry by Contemporary American Women," Modern Language Association Convention, Chicago, December 28, 1985. *Feminist Studies*. 13. (Spring, 1987), pp. 49–82.

Froyen zshurnal-vokhnblat. New York, 1922.

Fuks, Khaim Leyb. "*Lodz shel maalah.*" *Ayen bemafatkha Hashamot*. (1972). Cf. Sadan, Dov entry.

Glanz, A. "*Kultur un di froy.*" *Di fraye arbeter shtime*. (October 30, 1915), pp. 4–5.

Glatstein, Jacob (Yankev Glatshteyn). "Thinking Back." Trans. Henny Goodman. *Yiddish*. 3. (Spring, 1978), pp. 33–36.

Glatshtyen, Yankev. "*A shnel-loyf iber der yidisher poezye.*" *In zikh: monatlikher zshurnal far introspektiver literatur*. 1. (January, 1920), pp. 19–28.

Goldkorn, Yitskhok. "*Miriam ulinover.*" *Vidershtand*. (January, 1959). Cf. Sadan, Dov entry.

Green, Arthur. "Bride, Spouse, Daughter: Images of the Feminine in Classical Jewish Sources." In *On Being a Jewish Feminist: A Reader*, ed. Susannah Heschel. New York: Schocken, 1983, pp. 248–260.

Greenberg, Blu. *On Women and Judaism: A View from Tradition*. Philadelphia: Jewish Publication Society, 1981.

Halpern, Moyshe-Leyb. *In nyu york*. New York: Farlag Vinkl, 1919.

Halpern, Moyshe-Leyb and Menachem, eds. *East Broadway*. New York: Literarisher Farlag, 1916.

Harshav, Benjamin and Barbara, eds. *American Yiddish Poetry: A Bilingual Anthology*. Los Angeles: University of California Press, 1986.

Hellerstein, Kathryn. *Moyshe-Leyb Halpern's "In New York": A Modern Yiddish Verse Narrative*. Ph.D. diss., Stanford University, 1981. University Microfilm, Ann Arbor, Michigan. Chapter 5, pp. 671–689.

———. "Moyshe-Leyb Halpern's Subversive Ballads." *Prooftexts*. (Fall, 1987).

———, trans. "Songs of Women VI." Kadya Molodowsky. *Grove*. 6. (Spring, 1982), pp. 36–37.

————, trans. "Songs of Women VIII." Kadya Molodowsky. *Imagine*. 1. (Summer, 1984), pp. 74–75.

Henry, Sondra and Emily Taitz. *Written Out of History: Our Jewish Foremothers*. 2d ed. Fresh Meadows, New York: Biblio Press, 1984.

Heschel, Susannah, ed. and intro. *On Being a Jewish Feminist: A Reader*. New York: Schocken, 1983.

Howe, Irving and Eliezer Greenberg, eds. *A Treasury of Yiddish Poetry*. New York: Holt, Rinehart and Winston, 1969.

Howe, Irving and Kenneth Libo. *World of Our Fathers: The Journey of the East European Jews to America and the Life They Found and Made*. New York: Harcourt Brace Jovanovich, 1976.

Harshav, Benjamin and Barbara Harshav. *American Yiddish Poetry*. Los Angeles: University of California Press, 1986.

Ignatov, Dovid, ed. *Shriftn: drites zamlbukh*. New York: Farlag Amerike, 1914.

"Introspektivizm" (selected from the foreword to the *zamlbukh introspektive lider*. New York: Farlag M. N. Mayzel, 1920). *In zikh: monatlikher zshurnal far introspektiver literatur*. 1. (January, 1920), pp. 1–10.

Juhasz, Suzanne. *Naked and Fiery Forms: Modern American Poetry by Women, A New Tradition*. New York: Harper and Row, 1976.

Kahn, Yitzhak. *Portraits of Yiddish Writers*, trans. Joseph Leftwich. New York: Vantage Press, 1979.

Kammer, Jeanne. "The Art of Silence and the Forms of Women's Poetry." In *Shakespeare's Sisters: Feminist Essays on Women Poets*, ed. Sandra M. Gilbert and Susan Gubar. Bloomington: Indiana University Press, 1979, pp. 153–164.

Kaye/Kantrowitz, Melanie and Irena Klepfisz, eds. *The Tribe of Dina: A Jewish Women's Anthology*. Montpelier, Vermont: Sinister Wisdom Books, 1985.

Koltun, Elizabeth, ed. *The Jewish Woman: New Perspectives*. New York: Schocken, 1976.

Koltun, Liz, ed. *The Jewish Woman: An Anthology*. *Response*. 18. (Summer, 1973).

Korman, Ezra. *Shkye: lider*. Chicago: L. M. Stein, 1932.

————. *"Vegn glazer-andrus 'In halb shotn,' celia dropkins un rashel veprinskis lider."* *Bikher velt*. 6. (Warsaw, 1922).

————. *"Vegn miriam ulinovers 'Der bobes oytser.' "* *Bikher velt*. 1. (Warsaw, 1922).

————, ed. and intro. *Brenendike brikn—antologye fun revolutsionerer lyrik in der nayer yidisher dikhtung fun ukraine*. Berlin: Yidisher Literatur Farlag, 1923.

————, ed. *In fayerdikn doyer—zamlung fun revolutsionerer lyrik in der nayer yidisher dikhtung*. Kiev: Farlag Melukhe, Farlag Kultur-Lige, 1921.

————, ed. and intro. *Yidishe dikhterins: antologye*. Chicago: Farlag L. M. Stein, 1928.

Kristeva, Julia. "Semiotics of Biblical Abomination." In *Powers of Horror: An Essay on Abjection*, trans. Leon S. Roudiez. New York: Columbia University Press, 1982, pp. 90–112.

Landau, Zishe, ed. *Antologye: di yidishe dikhtung in amerike biz yor 1919*, illus. Z. Movd. New York: Farlag Yidish, 1919.

Lauter, Estella. *Women as Mythmakers: Poetry and Visual Art by 20th Century Women*. Bloomington: Indiana University Press, 1984.

Leftwich, Joseph, ed. *The Golden Peacock: An Anthology of Yiddish Poetry*. London: Robert Anscombe, 1939.

Leyvik, Halper. *Hintern shlos*. New York: Farlag Dr. K. Forenberg, 1918.

————. *In keynemn land: lider un poeme*. Warsaw: Farlag Kultur-Lige, 1923.

————. *Lider*. New York: Farlag Inzel, 1919.

Liptzin, Sol. *The Maturing of Yiddish Literature*. New York: Jonathan David, 1970, pp. 180–186.

Madison, Charles. *Yiddish Literature: Its Scope and Major Writers*. New York: Schocken, 1971.

Mani Leyb, *Balade*; *Lider*; and *Yidishe un slavishe motivn*. 3 vols. New York: Farlag Inzel, 1918.

Margolin, Anna, *Lider*. New York: Published by author, 1929.

————. Poems and articles in Yiddish weekly *Der tog* (New York). Manuscripts and correspondence in YIVO archives. Poems in Yiddish journals *Shriftn, Di naye heym, In zikh*.

————. ed. *Dos yidishe lid in amerike, 1923: antologye*. New York: Published by author, 1923.

Martin, Wendy. "Anne Bradstreet's Poetry: A Study of Subversive Piety." In *Shakespeare's Sisters: Feminist Essays on Women Poets*, ed. Sandra M.Gilbert and Susan Gubar. Bloomington: Indiana University Press, 1979, pp. 19–31.

Mayzel, Nachman, ed. *Amerike in yidishn vort*. New York Yidisher Kultur Farband, 1955.

Minkov, Nakum Borekh. "*In zikh*". In zikh: *monatlikher zshurnal far introspektiver literatur*. 1. (January, 1920), pp. 10–15.

Molodowsky, Kadya. *Af di vegn fun tsion*. New York: Pinchas Gingold Publishing Foundation of the National Committee of the Jewish Folk Schools, 1957.

————. *Ale fentster tsu der zun: shpil in elef bilder*. Warsaw, 1938.

————. *A shtub mit zibn fentster*. New York: Farlag Matones, 1957.

————. *Baym toyer, roman*. New York: Central Yiddish Culture Organization, 1967.

————. *Dzshike gas: lider*. Warsaw: Di "Literarishe bleter," 1933, 1936.

————. *Freydke: lider*. Warsaw: Di "Literarishe bleter," 1935, 1936.

————. *Fun lublin biz nyu york: togbukh fun rivke zilberg*. New York: Farlag Papirene Brik, 1942.

————. *In land fun mayn gebeyn: lider*. Chicago: Farlag L. M. Shteyn, 1937.

————. Individual poems in *Yidishe dikhterins: antologye* (op. cit.), *Literarishe bleter* (Warsaw), *Aygns* (Kiev, 1921), *Tsukunft* (New York), *Signal* (Moscow, 1930's), *Fraye arbeter shtime* (New York). Manuscripts and correspondence in YIVO Institute (New York), Jewish National and University Library (Jerusalem), Genazim Biobibliographic Institute (Tel Aviv), and private collections.

————. *Kheshvandike nekht: lider*. Vilna: B. Kletskin, 1927.

————. *Likht fun dornboym: lider un poeme*. Buenos Aires: Farlag Poaley Tsion Hitakhdut, 1965.

————. *Malokhim kumen keyn yerushalayim: lider*. New York, 1952.

————. *Martsepanes: mayselekh un lider far kinder*. New York: Bildungs-Komitet fun Arbeter-Ring and Farlag CYCO, 1970.

————. *Mayselekh*. Warsaw: Yidishe Shul Organizatsye fun Poyln, 1930–1935.

————. *Der melekh dovid aleyn iz geblibn*. New York: Farlag Papirene Brik, 1946.

————. "*Meydlekh, froyen, vayber, un . . . nevue*." *Literarishe bleter*. 4. (June 3, 1927), p. 416.

————. *Nokhn got fun midbar: drame*. New York: Farlag Papirene Brik, 1949.

————. *Pithu et hasha'ar: shirei yeladim*. Hebrew translations by Nathan Alterman,

Leah Goldberg, Penyah Bergshteyn, and Avraham Leyvinson. Israel: Hakibbutz Hameuchad, 1979.

———. *Yidishe kinder: mayselekh*. New York: Tsentral-Komitet fun di Yidishe Folks-Shuln in di Fareynikte Shtatn un Kanade, 1945.

———, ed. *Lider fun khurbn: antologye*. Tel Aviv: Farlag I. L. Peretz, 1962.

———, ed. *Sviva*. New York: 1955–1974.

Niger, Sh. "*Di yidishe literatur un di lezerin.*" *Der pinkes*. Vilna, 1913. Reissued, Vilna, 1919. In *Geklibene verk fun sh. niger, volume 2: bleter geshikhte fun der yidisher literatur*. New York: Sh. Niger Book Committee of the World-Wide Jewish Culture Congress, 1959, pp. 35–107.

———. "*Froyen lyrik.*" *Literarishe bleter*. 5.46. (November 16, 1928), pp. 909–910.

Opatoshu, Joseph, ed. *Di naye heym: ershtes zamlbukh*. New York: Literarisher Farlag, 1914.

Ostriker, Alicia. "The Thieves of Language: Women Poets and Revisionist Mythmaking." *Signs*. 8. (Autumn, 1982), pp. 68–90.

Ozick, Cynthia. "Notes toward Finding the Right Question." In *On Being a Jewish Feminist: A Reader*, ed. Susannah Heschel. New York: Schocken, 1983, pp. 120–151.

Peiss, Kathy. *Cheap Amusements: Working Women and Leisure in Turn-of-the-Century New York*. Philadelphia: Temple University Press, 1986.

Potash, Rikuda. "*Der goyrl fun tsvey lider fun miriam ulinover.*" Cf. Sadan, Dov entry. Publication information unavailable.

Pratt, Norma Fain. "Culture and Radical Politics: Yiddish Women Writers, 1890–1940." *American Jewish History*. 70. (September, 1980), pp. 68–90.

Ravitsh, Melekh. " '*Den mir hobn zunshtn keyn andri (mekhaye) in der velt*': E. Korman—'*Yidishe dikhterins: antologye*.' Farlag L. M. Shteyn. Chicago, 84 un 390 zaytn." *Literarishe bleter*. 5. (October 19, 1928), pp. 830–831.

———. "*Meydlekh, froyen, vayber—yidishe dikhterins,*" *Literarishe bleter*. 4. (May 27, 1927), pp. 395–396.

Rintsler, Abraham, ed. *Yung-yisroel: zamlung*. Haifa: Yung-Yisroel, 1957.

Roback, A. A. *The Story of Yiddish Literature*. New York: YIVO, 1940.

Roskies, David G. *Against the Apocalypse: Responses to Catastrophe in Modern Jewish Culture*. Cambridge: Harvard University Press, 1984.

Rozshanski, Shmuel, ed. *Di froy in der yidisher poezye: 315 lider fun 136 poetn; fragmentn fun forsharbetn tsu der kharakteristik un zikhroynes*. Buenos Aires: Literatur Gezelshaft baym YIVO in Argentine, 1966.

Sadan, Dov. "Guardian of the Treasure: On Miriam Ulinover" [Hebrew]. In *Der bobes oytser*, by Miriam Ulinover. Jerusalem: Mossad Harav Kook, 1975. Hebrew translations by Yehoshe Tan Pei, pp. 1–8. Bibliography.

Satlof, Claire R. "History, Fiction, and the Tradition: Creating a Jewish Feminist Poetic." In *On Being a Jewish Feminist: A Reader*, ed. Susannah Heschel. New York: Schocken, 1983, pp. 186–206.

Schwartz, Howard and Anthony Rudolf, eds. *Voices Within the Ark: The Modern Jewish Poets*. New York: Avon, 1980.

Shmeruk, Chone. "*Medresh itsik* and the Problem of Its Literary Traditions." In *Medresh itsik*, by Itsik Manger, ed. and intro. Ch. Shmeruk, intro. D. Sadan, glossary Ch. Turniansky, M. Wolf. 3d ed. Jerusalem: Hebrew University of Jerusalem, Yiddish Department, Magnes Press, 1984, pp. v–xxix.

Sholem, Ben, et al., eds. *Yung chicago: a zamlung, 1922*. Chicago: Farlag Yung Chicago, 1922.

Sokolov, Nakhum. *Yidishe froy*. New York: American Zionist Federation, 1918.

Tabatchnik, A. *"Fradl shtok un der sonet." Dikhter un dikhtung* (Poets and Poetry). New York: Published by author, 1965, pp. 505–508.

Tussman, Malka Heifetz. *"An entfer melekh ravitshn af 'Meydlekh, froyen, vayber— yidishe dikhterins.' Literarishe bleter, May 27, 1927."* Manuscript of letter, Melekh Ravitsh Archives at the Jewish National and University Library, Hebrew University, Jerusalem, July, 1927.

———. *"An entfer melekh ravitshn af 'Meydlekh, froyen, vayber— yidishe dikhterins,' Literarishe bleter, May 27, 1927." Literarishe bleter*, August, 1927, n.p. available.

———. *Bleter faln nit*. Tel Aviv: Farlag Yisroel Bukh, 1972.

———. *Haynt iz eybik: lider*. Tel Aviv: Farlag Yisroel Bukh, 1977.

———. *Lider*. Los Angeles: Malka Heifetz Tussman Bikh Komitet, 1949.

———. *Mild mayn vild: lider*. Los Angeles: The Author, 1958.

———. *"Shabes-oyps: kinder lider."* Unpublished book manuscript, courtesy of the author, n.d.

———. *Shotns fun gedenkn*. Tel Aviv: Farlag Hamenora, 1965.

———. *Unter dayn tseykhn: lider*. Tel Aviv: Yisroel Bukh, 1974.

———. *"Un ikh shmeykhl: lider un proze."* Unpublished book manuscript, courtesy of the author, 1986.

———. Poems and prose in *Di goldene keyt* (Tel Aviv, 1948–1985), *Tsukunft* (New York), *Literarishe bleter* (Warsaw), *Antologye* (Chicago, 1933), *Amerike in yidishn vort* (New York, n.d.). "Triolets" first published in *Studio*. 4, (October–December, 1934), Farlag Aleyn, New York, pp. 207–208. Letters and manuscripts in Melekh Ravitsh Archives at Jewish National and University Library (Jerusalem), Genazim Biobibliographic Institute (Tel Aviv), YIVO Institute for Jewish Research (New York), and in the author's possession.

Ulinover, Miriam. *Der bobes oytser*. Jerusalem: Mossad Harav Kook, 1975.

Weissler, Chava. "Issues in the Study of Women's Religion: The Case of Ashkenazic Jewish Women." Unpublished essay, copyright by the author, 1986.

———. "The Traditional Piety of Ashkenazic Women." In *A History of Jewish Spirituality*, ed. Arthur Green. Philadelphia: Crossroads, 1986.

Wisse, Ruth. *"Di Yunge* and the Problem of Jewish Aestheticism." *Jewish Social Studies*. 38. (Summer-Fall, 1976), pp. 269–270.

Zilberberg, Yitskhok. *"Fartretn fun interesante froyen"* (Encounters with Interesting Women). *Di prese* (The Press). (March 26, 1955).

Zinberg, Israel. "Popular Literature; *Tze'enah U-re'enah*" and "Historical and Travel Literature; Memoirs and *Tehinnot*." In *A History of Jewish Literature: Old Yiddish Literature from Its Origins to the Haskalah Period*, trans. and ed. Bernard Martin. Cincinnati: Hebrew Union College Press; New York: KTAV, 1975. Vol. 7, pp. 119–139; 241–259.

Zinger, Sh. D. *"Miriam ulinover, tsu ir zekstn yortsayt"* (For the Sixth Anniversary of Her Death). *Kultur un dertsiung* (Culture and Education). (December, 1950).

———. *"Vegn shrayber un bikher"* (About Writers and Books). *Unzer veg*. (April, 1959).

FOR FURTHER READING

Aschkenasy, Nehama. *Eve's Journey: Feminine Images in Hebraic Literary Tradition*. Philadelphia: University of Pennsylvania Press, 1986.

Bar-El, Judith. "The National Poet: The Emergence of a Concept in Hebrew Literary Criticism (1885–1905)." *Prooftexts*. 6. (September, 1986), pp. 205–220.

Brayer, Menachem M. *The Jewish Woman in Rabbinic Literature: A Psychological Perspective*. Hoboken, N.J.: KTAV, 1986.

Ecker, Gisela, ed. *Feminist Aesthetics*. Trans. Harriet Anderson. Boston: Beacon Press, 1986.

Homans, Margaret. *Bearing the Word: Language and Female Experience in Nineteenth-Century Women's Writing*. Chicago: University of Chicago Press, 1986.

Korn, Rachel. *Paper Roses*. Trans. Seymour Levitan. Toronto: Aya Press, 1985.

Mitchie, Helena. *The Flesh Made Word: Female Figures and Women's Bodies*. New York: Oxford University Press, 1987.

Ostriker, Alicia. "American Poetry, Now Shaped by Women." *New York Times Book Review*. March 9, 1986, pp. 1, 28, 30.

Ostriker, Alicia. "Writing like a Woman." *Poets on Poetry*. Ann Arbor: University of Michigan, 1983.

Ozick, Cynthia. "Toward a New Yiddish." In *Art and Ardor: Essays*. New York: E. P. Dutton, 1984, pp. 154–177.

Perloff, Marjorie. "Recharging the Canon: Some Reflections on Feminist Poetics and the Avant-Garde." *American Poetry Review*. 15. (July–August, 1986), pp. 12–20.

Robinson, Lillian S. "Treason Our Text: Feminist Challenges to the Literary Canon." *Tulsa Studies in Women's Literature*. 2. (Spring, 1983), pp. 83–98.

Tabatchnik, Avrom. "*Traditsye un revolt in der yisiher poezye*." *Dikhter un dikhtung*. New York: Published by author, 1965, pp. 402–413.

von Hallberg, Robert, ed. *Canons*. Chicago: University of Chicago Press, 1984.

9

Makers of a Modern American-Jewish Theology

Arnold Jacob Wolf

The life of the American-Jewish religious community at the end of the twentieth century is chaotic and poorly differentiated. For one, Reform Judaism, the oldest of the post-Emancipation doctrines, has broken with the system of traditional Jewish law. Some Reformers follow the classical line of their earliest predecessors while others are influenced by the existentialism of Martin Buber and/or Franz Rosenzweig. And these thinkers, in turn, owe much to the rationalism of Hermann Cohen, their mentor. For another, Conservative Judaism is torn between what Mordecai Kaplan called timid Reform and diffident neo-Orthodoxy. The issue of women in the rabbinate represents this split. Finally, Orthodoxy itself is divided among the neo-Orthodox followers of Samson Raphael Hirsch (the eminent nineteenth-century German rabbi), *Hasidim* of various sorts who have found an unexpected home in America, and miscellaneous groups of believers who tend to be increasingly isolationist and increasingly conservative. At present, Orthodoxy finds its best, most coherent, and most persuasive spokesman in America in the compelling Joseph B. Soloveitchik.

The thinkers who are described in this chapter are not Orthodox, but they share little else than being outside this category. Non-Reform is marked by individual statements, fascinating though hardly conclusive, by the writers I shall discuss.

It was Mordecai Kaplan who, early in our century, found all the old systems worn as well as dangerous and who relentlessly criticized their pretensions to finality. We must, because modern American-Jewish theology inevitably does, begin with him.

MORDECAI M. KAPLAN

The most important American-Jewish theologian is undoubtedly Mordecai Kaplan. By now, a few years after his death in 1983 and more than a hundred years after his birth in 1881, his ideas and the movement he created, Jewish Reconstructionism, are more alive and more influential than they have ever been. While critics have refuted his ideas again and again, there seems to be no doubt that his modernist version of Judaism is the de facto religion of a great many American Jews. His blend of Émile Durkheim, John Dewey, and a pastiche of Jewish tradition, as much as could be accepted by many a twentieth-century person, is attractive and inspiriting to them, even if it seems inconsistent and puerile to a few.

Kaplan's magnum opus, *Judaism as a Civilization* (1934), the work we shall be analyzing, is a seminal text, one that changed American-Jewish thinking permanently. Kaplan began with the notion that contemporary Judaism is, as much as it is anything else, a problem. It is not simply a religion or a tradition, which could be accepted or rejected by an American Jew. It has become deeply and painfully problematic. Judaism has become a burden. It seems, for good reason, to be an outworn faith. Since we no longer believe in a world-to-come, the central motivation for obeying traditional commandments, namely, to gain immortality, is lost and no possible alternative could supplant the long-lost expectation of the resurrection of the dead.

American Jews are at home in America. Democratic nationalism inevitably leads to assimilation. America is inevitably more important to Jews than is their Judaism. The claim of work and politics erodes religious practice and implies religious negligence. Empiricism, the true American philosophy, and scientism, the true American faith, refute traditional Jewish supernaturalism. They deny quite explicitly any possible idea of Jewish chosenness:

The modern man who is used to thinking in terms of humanity as a whole can no longer reconcile himself to the notion of any people, or body of believers, constituting a type of society which may be described as belonging to a supernatural order. This is essentially what the doctrine of "election" has hitherto implied. . . . But nowadays when only present achievement tends to satisfy the human spirit, the doctrine of Israel's election, in its traditional sense, cannot be expected to make the slightest difference in the behavior or outlook of the Jew. From an ethical standpoint, it is deemed inadvisable, to say the least, to keep alive ideas of race or national superiority, inasmuch as they are known to exercise a divisive influence, generating suspicion and hatred.[1]

Existing Jewish denominations have not solved the dilemmas of modernism, and they never will. What Kaplan calls "Reformism" is a mere colorless ethicism, a collection of platitudes that neither satisfy nor explain. Reform Judaism placed God above Torah and above the peoplehood of Israel, precisely at a time when God has become a problematic idea. Reformist ethics is mere bourgeois morality served up to middle-class, middle-brow, mediocre minds. Its notion of spiritual genius to explain what once was called revelation is self-serving and unprovable. Judaism in this version can no longer legislate nor explain nor comfort nor convoke. It is part of our problem, not of its solution.

Still, Kaplan concedes that Reform Judaism does have a conscious direction, which places it above its sisters. It is honestly post-medieval, no longer pretending to believe in Sinaitic revelation. It is self-critical and self-correcting. Its prayer book "unconsciously reflects the present apathy and skepticism toward prayer . . . [and is consciously] used as a mere introduction to the rabbi's discourse."[2] Reform ideology is an excellent "shock-absorber" to cushion the unprecedented buffeting of modern thought. It fails utterly, however, to deal with the problem of evil. This failure betrays a final lack of seriousness which dooms Reformist theology.

Kaplan's critique of Conservative Judaism is that, in essence, it does not exist. It is either the right wing of Reform or the left of neo-Orthodoxy. It is equivocal and vacillating, weak-kneed and unpersuasive. It makes a principle out of moderateness and plays on mere nostalgia instead of assisting creativity. It reduces revelation to conscience. It is either tepid Orthodoxy or tepid Reform.

For the neo-Orthodox (Kaplan cannot imagine an old-fashioned Orthodoxy that would survive in America, wrongly as it turns out), all the old myths are true. Human criteria are irrelevant to a revealed Torah, and the spirit of the age has no privilege against millennial Judaism. Still, the neo-Orthodox do temporize: they pretend that *galut*, exile, is a good thing. They abandon the need for creative legislation and attenuate traditional *halakhah* (legal process). They are, above all, intellectually dishonest, pretending to believe what their grandparents did, but themselves unconsciously modernizing and halfheartedly transforming what they accept only verbally but never in their hearts.

Kaplan's famous alternative proposal is that Judaism is an evolving, religious civilization. It is no mere religion, neither Orthodox nor Reform. It is not unchangeable. It is not theoretical, but the *lived experience* of the Jewish people; it is *all* that they think and do. No moment of our history is privileged; no text is, in principle, more sacred than any other. What we believe is epiphenomenal to who we are.

Kaplan begins his reconstruction of Jewish thinking, with a reformulated Zionism. The fact that Jewish national rebirth emerged not out of any of the religious movements but in profound opposition to them is itself a proof of their desuetude. Zionism is the only truly fertile idea in modern Jewish life. It points to the need for a Jewish religious expression that will be more honest and more radical than any that the century of Emancipation has produced. New thinking will include "*a history, literature, language, social organization, folk sanctions, standards of conduct, social and spiritual ideals, esthetic values, which in their totality form a civilization.*"[3]

Judaism is a way of life, not a complex, "an experience of infinite variety." Its center is in *Eretz Yisrael*; the land that will become the Jewish state. But even in the diaspora, we are a polity, "a state within a state." We constitute a separate American ethnic religion; we are hyphenated Americans. There will be no melting pot, but only a nation of nations. We Jews, surely, must live in two civilizations, and our need for American pluralism is crucially important to Americans other than ourselves.

Jewish history must be demythologized. The God of the Hebrew Bible was "paradoxical"; he was God of the whole world and yet "content to put up with one little rebellious people for his nation." He was too personal for us to accept any longer and too demanding for us blindly to obey. Rabbinic Judaism introduced notions of resurrection and other-worldliness after the traumatic defeat of the Jewish nation and the exile of the Jewish folk. It tried to rationalize, but succeeded only in constricting, a once full-blown Jewish civilization. Until modern times Jews were an abnormal people, suffering under religious tyranny both from without and from within. The great community shrank steadily to a pseudo-church, and our great ideals were systematically attenuated and became insignificant. The idea of the chosen people unsuccessfully covered over the fact of Jewish defeat and dissolution.

We are not chosen and our religion is not revealed. Our theology must be reinterpreted in the light of the best and latest modern thinking; that happened over and over again in our history. Discontinuity is the secret of Jewish survival, and reinterpretation was a characteristic of our ancestors as it must become of ourselves. They did not imitate, and imitating them as persons, we must not imitate their ideas: *"Reinterpretation of religious values is spiritual metabolism. It is a form of the law of growth which, by an uninterrupted transfer of life from the old to the new, renders vital change a very means to vital sameness and continuity."*[4]

God is not a superhuman Person. *"God is the life of the universe, immanent insofar as each part acts upon every other, and transcendent insofar as the whole acts upon each part."*[5] Each Jew must produce his or her own idea of God, faithful to one's own need for self-fulfillment as well as to "elements of the heritage." Religion must no longer preoccupy us, precisely so that spiritual regeneration becomes possible again. We are, after all, a folk religion, and our people must assemble and reform if we are to throw up new religious ideas that could claim our allegiance. We build upon "the accumulated momentum and emotional drive of man's previous efforts to attain greater spiritual power,"[6] but we ourselves must make our future faith. "Ethical and spiritual strivings" in our tradtion must be disengaged from "the mass of traditional lore and custom" by each of us alone and by all of us together.

God may once have seemed to be "the Creator of the universe. Now we must consider God the creative principle of the universe." Blind acceptance of traditional ideas must and will be replaced by *"a vital interest in the objects upon which those beliefs were centered. If, for the maintenance of interest in those objects it is necessary to abandon the traditional view concerning them, Jews should not hesitate to do so, and to replace those beliefs with whatever type of ideas is likely to sustain their interest."*[7] Concern is the modern substitute for commitment.

What once were *mitsvot*, commandments, are now to be seen as folkways. These must be invented, rediscovered, reworked, or otherwise reconstructed. Innovation of positive obligations, some but not all of them ethical in nature, will follow the successful aestheticization of older practices. A Hebrew renascence will give us new books and new opportunities. A Jewish homeland will send us new tasks and a bold new inspiration. Group discussions will replace sermons. Group ideals will destroy the patriarchal forms of old-fashioned Jewishness. We can create a new version of our history, free from supernaturalism: "a history every stage of which is understood in the light of all the preceding stages, a history in which as much importance is attached to the subtler forces of will and mind as to the more evident ones which operate in economic factors and political events."[8]

Kaplan's version of Judaism was to prove paradigmatic and controversial at the same time. Many Jews could no longer accept traditional Judaism, and his new theology kept them close to the Jewish community while they worked out their idiosyncratic, personal systems. Personal autonomy together with a love for tradition kept a generation or two loyal even if unbelieving. Reform and Conservative Judaism became de facto varieties of Reconstructionism. More recently, the Reconstructionist movement has created a rabbinical school and is a powerful claimant to status as an alternative American-Jewish system.

But critical analysis of Reconstructionism undermines its credibility. It is too naturalistic, too naive, and too "folksy" to convince post-modern Jews. If Judaism is whatever we want it to be, who, in the end, needs to be a Jew at all? If God is only our idea of God, He can hardly be considered divine. If we are not chosen, how can or why should we live beyond the Holocaust? If the state of Israel is far from perfect, or even perfectible, how can it be our unique model or our goal? If folkways attract, they still cannot really command, and in the late twentieth century, we feel a profound need for a direction that comes from beyond all our failed communities. Perhaps, in the end, the Torah *is* revealed morality and authorized obligation and, perhaps, God is far, far more than any of our ideas of Him. Still, it is Mordecai Kaplan who set the agenda for most of the rest of American-Jewish theology, even if his successors have cast doubt upon both his coherence and his credibility.

EMIL FACKENHEIM

The intellectual career of Emil Fackenheim falls into two distinct parts. The first—including the late forties, the fifties, and the beginning of the sixties—produced a series of elegant, somewhat technical, essays on Jewish philosophy which betrayed a finely honed discipline and a comprehensive grasp of the Frankfurt school of Jewish thinking, a school which included Martin Buber and Franz Rosenzweig among others.

The Frankfurt school both culminated and criticized a liberal Judaism in central Europe which had been growing powerfully for a hundred years. While never becoming itself a neo-Orthodoxy, it facilitated a clear rediscovery of classical texts and renewed old commitments. It preached a return to the sources of Judaism. It proclaimed the collapse of modern rationalism around the time of the First World War, and presaged a Jewish existentialism which holds that Jewish existence precedes any abstract ideas that the Jewish religion has ever held. Buber and Rosenzweig agreed with Kierkegaard that religious "immediacy after reflection" precludes both neutrality and certainty. They spoke for a leap of actionable faith, a risky attempt to become a Jewish person without prior reservation. They were deeply critical both of Christian claims to certainty and of mere philosophic criticism itself. In a sense, the younger Fackenheim (like many of the rest of us in American-Jewish theology) was neither more nor less than the successor of Buber and Rosenzweig, perhaps also their epigone.

Fackenheim proclaimed *Midrash* (Jewish interpretation of the Bible and, more broadly, all Jewish religious imagination) as the best source of our theological reconstruction, since Judaism has produced no direct parallel to the great Christian system builders. *Midrash* taught him the rejection of mysticism, skepticism, and all vaguely universalistic claims of earlier Jewish liberals. Story should replace system. As it was in the first century of our era a response to the catastrophe of the Roman destruction of Jerusalem, so in our time *Midrash* could be an adequate answer to the traumas and terrors of this century. The *midrashic* Hebrew expression *"c'v'yachol"* means not only "as it were," but also importantly asserts that nothing about God and His revelation is certain, but that, nevertheless, much is true.

Fackenheim faces, squarely and intelligently, the problem of autonomy which recurs again and again in modern Jewish thought. In "Quest for Past and Future," reproduced in his collection of the same name (1968), he tries to correlate a Kantian insistence that human beings must be free to make their own choices with the manifest obligation in Judaism to make our will bend to God's. He describes our obedience as a free response to God's presence which both entails responsibility and still ensures personal freedom. "We must choose between Judaism and the belief in autonomy" as an absolute.[9] But it is precisely the Torah and experience of God that liberate human capacity. God shares our human life-with-our-neighbors, neither dominating nor disappearing from our decision making. To believe is to be at once more bound and more emancipated than to doubt. God may be our Master, but He is also, pre-eminently, our true Liberator.

Nor need we surrender the traditional images of God found in *Midrash* and in Jewish philosophy. "God does not require demythologizing."[10] The old categories may be refurbished and reaffirmed. After all our modern reservations, God is still Judge, Redeemer, Father, and King. He remains omnipotent and independent, despite His condescending to us in full dialogic relationship. We meet Him in love and in fear, in freedom and in surrender, paradoxically but not irrationally. The most important truth that God means is: we are never radically alone.

Fackenheim admits paradox without reveling in it. He is not surprised that our categories do not fully and consistently explain divinity, nor that our scientific models exhaust revelation. Reason cannot refute faith but can only raise questions that are important to answer. Torah specifies. It offers not information but response to existential query. It is not just an expression of human feeling, but rather the deepest, if still inadequate, truth of which we are capable. The Torah must not be read literally, as if it were a menu or a formula, but profoundly, like a letter from a beloved friend or like a mysterious communication which is needful and which can be understood.

Modernist claims to progress and to the superseding of older religious ideas are merely a presumption which the facts do not support. If progress were indeed continuous and inevitable, then God would be powerless, *de trop*, and Judaism would be outmoded instead of exemplary. But the twentieth century unmasks such false theories of progress once and for all. The Messiah is not the automatic culmination of time and history. Rather, the idea of the messianic is a sign of our need for God's redemption. The failure of progressive ideas of revelation and human history is finally apparent, and we are left with "a return, in principle, to traditional supernaturalism."[11]

Mystery does not erode in our scientific era. Human pretensions are unmasked, undone by human sin. Finally, we are mysterious and tragic if not redeemed by God. True Jewish messianism is a blend of tragedy and faith, of accomplishing and waiting, of national survival and universal hope. Our age is a time between the ordinary and its ultimate apocalyptic transfiguration. The root experiences of the Jewish people were never more desperately needed to decode both our suffering and our yearning.

Perhaps the final possible *midrash* is the story of Auschwitz, a great turning point in Fackenheim's own thinking but also in the whole history of humankind. Fackenheim, a survivor of early concentration camps and in his own self-understanding essentially a survivor, came more and more to believe that the Nazi period was profoundly paradigmatic in every sense. In his books *God's Presence in History* (1970) and *The Jewish Return into History* (1978) he marked a new stage in his thinking about catastrophe. The demons of Auschwitz cannot be put to rest by human reason, which never really understands its scandal, nor by progressive philosophy which comprehends them as mere throwbacks, nor by a claim of Jewish genius which denies the uniquely terrible fate and signification of the Jews, seeing us as merely one gifted people among others.

Philosophic secularism "is breached because internalized absolutes either cannot single out or else cannot remain absolute." The Jewish secularist is brought short "by a Voice as truly other than man-made ideals—an imperative as truly given—as was the Voice of Sinai."

Jewish martyrdom signifies. It legitimates protest against a good God but refutes any atheism which knows no superhuman power at all. It speaks, as does the earlier *Midrash*, of a God in exile. It unites secular and believing Jews peacefully as Hitler himself earlier did by violently killing them all together. It entails profoundly; it commands the survival of the Jews, the newest and most encompassing command. In his most well-known idea that deserves to be quoted at length, Fackenheim claims:

Jews are forbidden to hand Hitler posthumous victories. They are commanded to survive as Jews, lest the Jewish people perish. They are commanded to remember the victims of

Auschwitz lest their memory perish. They are forbidden to despair of man and his world, and to escape into either cynicism or otherworldliness, lest they cooperate in delivering the world over to the forces of Auschwitz. Finally, they are forbidden to despair of the God of Israel, lest Judaism perish. A secularist Jew cannot make himself believe by a mere act of will, nor can he be commanded to do so. . . . And a religious Jew who has stayed with his God may be forced into new, possible revolutionary relationships with Him. One possibility, however, is wholly unthinkable. A Jew may not respond to Hitler's attempt to destroy Judaism by himself cooperating in its destruction. In ancient times, the unthinkable Jewish sin was idolatry. Today, it is to respond to Hitler by doing his work.[12]

The Holocaust is an agenda. It is the possibility of *"tikkun olam,"* the reparation of our world. From the *anus mundi*, the world's asshole, Auschwitz, emerges unexpectedly but unmistakably a new commandment: our first duty is to survive. Amid persisting trauma, terrifying mystery, we are led to *t'shuvah*, return, repentance, a more profound rootedness. The Nazi period was the true "heroic age of the Jews" in which we finally became, under duress, one people. Constantinian, triumphalist Christianity failed utterly while we Jews were united in a meta-Zionist identity. Of course, our own faith, too, was inadequate to make sense of the terror. Post-Holocaust thinking is still too unmoved and too separatistic. But we will never be what we were before Auschwitz, which was to be our death warrant, but instead began to signify our declaration of independence from the world.

Jewish experience must be remythologized. The Holocaust and the re-creation of the State of Israel are, literally, epoch-making events which imply the end of Jewish escapist universalism and the crisis of modern secular liberalism in the West. Israel, the concrete state of Israel, is the hope for our survival and of our self-understanding. Our primary identity is Jewish, now and forever. The United States and the West have proven unworthy of our trust or respect. We refuse to be oppressed or merely tolerated again. We are returning to history as active masters of our own destiny, for we are living in a historic time between Sinai and a messianic age which may both be trans-historic but are no longer decisive for us. It is not just the worst peoples who hate us but, especially, the best in our diaspora lands, including the Third World (radicals, socialists, true Christians). When we reproduce Jewish children, when we continue to study the Torah, when we simply support the United Jewish Appeal, we demonstrate more theological power than all their much vaunted idealism.

There, the enterprise of Jewish theology culminates, for Fackenheim, in Jewish politics. It embraces specific associational and specifically Zionist tasks. A Messiah who could have come to Auschwitz, but did not, leaves us desperately alone but also free to master our own destiny. In this latter phase of his thinking, Fackenheim is less concerned with God's power than with the need to survive His powerlessness. If Israel rebuilds, it can begin to make over the world. Our gospel is hope through power, the redemption of mankind beginning with our own self-emancipation. A Jew who deserts this enterprise is a traitor not only to his people but to mankind's deep need for Jewish survival. Again, Fackenheim should be quoted at length:

This is a *novum* in the human condition, without parallels inside Jewish history or outside it. . . . Only one thing is clear and devoid of all obscurity: one cannot authentically cope with one's Jewish identity crisis without facing the *novum* in all its starkness and uniqueness. It is said that this is the first time in Jewish history when a Jew can cease to be a Jew without having to become something else, and that therefore the present Jewish identity crisis can authentically be solved by the dissolution of Jewish identity. It is not obvious that the conclusion follows from the premise. A generation ago Franz Rosenzweig knew that he could not authentically become a Christian without first knowing the Judaism he was about to leave. He never left, and subsequently helped write a new page in Jewish history. No Jew today can authentically abandon his Jewish identity without first asking whether in so doing he helps close the book of a history that should be closed, or abandons those who write a new page that cries out to be written; whether he leaves the ranks of pointless past victims or joins the ranks of possible future murderers and bystanders; whether he serves the cause of God and man or betrays it.[13]

We may not be able to follow Fackenheim's long journey from post-liberal theology to sophisticated neo-chauvinism. He may, perhaps, have been undone and not, as he believes, enlightened by long reflection on the Holocaust. Our great commandment should, perhaps, not come from Adolph Hitler, after all. But any Jewish thinker who now wishes to be heard must deal with Fackenheim's proud *cri du coeur* and, to be sure, our best younger thinkers have done exactly that.

RICHARD L. RUBENSTEIN

"We live in a time of the death of God" wrote Richard Rubenstein, the most protean of American-Jewish thinkers in his important book *After Auschwitz* (1966). During the short-lived period of "death of God theology," Rubenstein served as the prime Jewish exemplar. But with a difference: not only was he careful to speak of a "time of the death of God" rather than in terms of God's actual demise, but he also spoke of that time tragically, with a profound sense of loss. For Rubenstein, the fall from immanence, the end of illusion and even, finally, of hope, is a cultural fact which should occasion no joy. When he quoted the radical crypto-*Hasidic* Zalman Schachter saying "if there is a God, He doesn't exist," Rubenstein claimed no humanistic triumphalism, no relieved sense of freedom from constraint.

The key to his idea of the death of God is a relentless reading-out of the Holocaust, one attempted by no Christian death-of-God theologian, at least before Rubenstein. In a meeting with Probst Grüber, an anti-Nazi church leader in Germany, who asserted that the destruction of the Jews was the will of God, Rubenstein was sharply confronted with the contradictions between a traditional view of God and His acts in human history against an honest description of the terrible events of the Nazi period. Something had to give. The old God was either a monster or an incompetent. After Auschwitz, Jews, at least, could never *simply* believe in Him again. And it would be better for us all if Christendom would surrender its biblical view of the Jewish people as a uniquely chosen folk:

As long as we continue to hold to the doctrine of the election of Israel, we will leave ourselves open to the theology expressed by Dean Grüber, that because the Jews are God's Chosen People, God wanted Hitler to punish them.

There is a way out, and Reconstructionism has pointed to it. Religious uniqueness does not necessarily place us at the center of the divine drama of perdition, redemption, and salvation for mankind. All we need for a sane religious life is to recognize that we are, when given normal opportunities, neither more nor less than any other men. . . .

We began with a question, whether the Christian Church's attitude involves it in a process which in times of stress incites to the murder of Jews. To this question we must now append a further question, whether the way Jews regard themselves religiously contributes to the terrible process. The tendency of the Church to regard Jews in magic and theological terms encourages the view that the vicissitudes of Jewish history are God's will. If we accept his theological premises, there is no way of avoiding Dean Grüber's conclusion that God sent Hitler. But how can we ask Christians to give up these premises if we continue to regard ourselves in this light? . . . There is, however, no doubt that the simple capacity of Jew and Christian to accept their own and each other's humanity lies at the core of any possibility of reconciliation between the two great faiths of the Western world.[14]

The Holocaust marks the end of liberal optimism as well as Orthodox messianism, both of which had tempted Rubenstein in his earlier career. As he describes his intellectual journey in an autobiographical fragment, *Power Struggle* (1974), he had been variously a Unitarian, a Reform Jewish rabbinical student, a Conservative rabbi, a disciple of the brilliant, ultra-Orthodox Rav Hutner, a disillusioned philosophical radical, and a neo-conservative in politics who steadily disengaged himself from the Jewish community. Since the publication of that revelatory, if also carefully self-disclosing, volume he has become professor of religious studies at Florida State University and a close personal associate of the Reverend Sun Myung Moon. None of these episodes was lightly experienced. None of them was merely for the sake of experience. Each of them resulted in publications of note (except the last), and a drastic revision of deeply felt positions of an earlier time. His liberal Judaism was partly a cultural, even social-climbing, move, but it taught him how to read the sources and led him to a more traditional period of confrontation with Judaism under Rabbi Abraham Heschel, Harry Wolfson of Harvard, and a small group of famous Orthodox rabbis and thinkers. But none of these could hold him for long.

Rubenstein moved inexorably toward a repudiation of all current and traditional Jewish options or alternatives. The Holocaust seemed finally to mean the breakdown of all earlier systems and every mediating interpretation. God, for him, is a "holy nothingness," an image he borrows from a Jewish mystical tradition with which he could hardly identify consistently. There are no transcendent standards, no resting places in the vicissitudes of history. "Nothingness is the Lord of creation." The Bible and rabbinic imagination are both metaphors for what we can no longer claim, and their repudiation is essential for our recovery. In the words of I. B. Singer, "death is the Messiah," and Richard Rubenstein is willing to go to the end in facing that awful truth.

Jewish ethics can no longer be followed complacently. The Jewish people must go from claiming chosenness to unconcealed naked self-interest. There is no God to protect or defend us; we must accept the revolutionary Zionist idea which teaches us to defend ourselves. "Never Again," the motto of the Jewish Defense League (and Meir Kahane's *Kach* party in Israel), means exactly what it says; Rubenstein agrees. The next time the world tries to destroy the Jews, the Jews should and will destroy the world. Once, long ago, Johanan ben Zakkai made a deal with the world-historical powers that we would renounce sovereignty if they would protect our lives and our right to our beliefs. They broke that agreement. Now we are morally free to do literally anything we must do to ensure our own survival. In a world of realpolitik, Jews must be the most realistic of all the nations. If we are not for ourselves, who will be for us? And, after the camps, we have no need to be for anyone but ourselves. The State of Israel is our only hope, and Jews must do whatever they can do to protect its self-interest and the lives of our brothers and sisters there. Any group that will not ally itself with our survival will no longer receive our support. Doubtful as it may seem to many of us, Rubenstein believes Jews can go it alone and may very well have to do just that.

Jewish religion becomes, for him, a religion without God. That does not mean a less religious but, in a strange way, even a more religious community. Because we can no longer believe in a Redeemer, we must fashion the rituals of our own redemption. Rubenstein is powerfully influenced by Freud, but turns him on his head. Just because religion is an illusion (not a *delusion*, of course), it is all the more important. Just because biblical faith is untenable, the pagan sources of Jewish peoplehood and religion are more available than ever and far more necessary. For example, the ceremony of *Bar Mitzvah*, which is both late and equivocal in Jewish tradition, takes on a strong new importance:

Bar Mitzvah is a *rite de passage*. It allows a young man to formalize his passage from childhood to adolescence and incipient manhood. It confirms him in his newly acquired masculine role. The disappearance of such a ritual would diminish the extent to which the community compels recognition of the new stage the young man has reached in the timetable of life. . . . There is renunciation of the infantile and acceptance of the reality of the passing of time in the ceremony. Bar Mitzvah reconciles the boy with his father through a reinforcement of identification. . . . Not only does the ceremony formalize the child's entry into manhood, it also is the occasion of the parents' entry into middle age. Parents are as much in need of a *rite de passage* as are children. . . . In short, Bar Mitzvah is a puberty rite.[15]

Rubenstein adds, "We err when we stress the distance we have traveled from the ways of primitive man."[16]

This is not the only possible example of a revival of religious practice without God. The dietary laws, prayers for the rebuilding of the Temple and its bloody cult become models for sublimation of an awful human desire to kill. The synagogue and the community will root us in our own bodies and in our own sexuality, he hopes. Traditional worship is an unconscious validation of our most needful fantasy, but not the I-Thou dialogue that Buber had—in vain—described. Jewish religion has no theological validity, but it has far more psychological power than Feuerbach or the Marxists could have dreamed. There is no God but we, Israel, are still "His" people.

If Rubenstein's avowed Jewish neo-paganism refutes the Jewish religion of most of his contemporaries, it is far more bitterly an attack on Christianity after its terrible failure in Nazi Europe. Christianity is, for him, the seedbed of Fascist anti-Semitism. It has nourished disasters of all kinds by its otherworldly inattention to human passions and to human needs. It has pretended to be a religion of saints but has left the world to the demons. Pagan realism would have been far more successful in "the age of triage," a time when Christians are still singing hymns while they rush headlong to the lifeboats.

Jewish paganism understands the sadness of sexuality, the brutality of humankind, the agony of living and dying alone. It is much stronger than the existentialism which preceded it and much more chastened than the German phenomenology which misunderstood it. It leads us to a love of our fate and a courageous willingness to live out a tragic existence. Jews, above all, have nothing to lose after six million of us were done to death. The old consolations are too dangerous for our new time. A much older pagan wisdom may help us to live through a nuclear threat. But death is irresistible and will conquer us all in the end.

EUGENE B. BOROWITZ

The most prolific of all contemporary Jewish theologians, Borowitz is the author of ten books and more than thirty articles, founding editor of *Sh'ma* magazine, professor at Hebrew Union College-Jewish Institute of Religion in New York and has taught at many universities, including Harvard and Princeton. A master of many disciplines, Jewish and humanistic, he is the true successor of Claude Montefiore, the great liberal British scholar. He is also the successor of Reform thinker Kaufmann Kohler as the semi-official theologian of American Reform Judaism. His expertise extends to ethical problems, especially those connected with sexuality, and to education, the field in which he first became eminent.

A kind of *summa* of Borowitz's thought is his recent book, *Liberal Judaism* (1984), which, like much of his work, is both accessible and exceedingly careful. Together with two recent essays on the "autonomous self," it represents the best statement of why he remains a liberal in spite of his criticism of older versions of Reform, why he insists on the right to choose at the same time that he has consistently led his colleagues into more and more obedient Jewish commitment.

God, for Borowitz, creates an agenda. God means learning, thinking, and doing. He is indispensable to true choice and even to true selfhood. A Jew must place no value ahead of Judaism by which the latter may be judged. A Jew is a solitary conscience who is also bound mysteriously to his/her people and committed to its survival above (almost) everything else. He is a Zionist, if that means not blindly following Israeli policy but bending every effort to strengthen and to ennoble Jewish existence in the "Land of Israel" and in the diaspora. The Jew believes Israel is a chosen people whose holiness is, however, not a fact but a duty. Each Jew now is post-modern, in the sense that his old mythologies of progress and universal goodwill are unmasked forever, but he must never fall into cynicism or despair.

Borowitz's liberal Judaism is resolutely personal, that is, resolutely autonomous. It embraces, with an enthusiasm that is hard to emulate, the values of a permanent pluralism. He believes in doing what one can and starting where one is. His humane realism is shocking in a theology as sophisticated as his, and there is no question that he speaks for multitudes when he says, for example:

"If you don't do it the Orthodox way you might just as well not do it at all," is the antithesis of liberalism. For us, creative adaption is the chief sign of Judaism's vitality. Rituals, appealing largely to the affective side of us, will necessarily be chosen, in part, as subjective judgment—and communities appear to have sensibilities as do individuals. Liberal Judaism will therefore always have a variety of practice among individuals, and some difficulty in reaching community agreement for joint observances. From the liberal perspective, such pluralism is not only healthy but desirable; from it, particularly from the creative energy it releases, arise the new forms which keep Judaism alive.

We need to keep this subjective factor in mind when we seek to determine what rituals we will practice. Some simply appeal to us and I believe we need have no more justification for them than that. A problem arises when we are put off by observations. Then we must inquire whether they do not "work" for us or whether something in us prevents our religious growth. . . . I counsel that, unless a rite seems inherently unacceptable, you try it long enough to feel comfortable with it. Only then can you make a fair decision whether it can "work" for you.

There are some Jewish rituals which, by their nature, I could not observe or recommend to others to follow.[17]

In our commitment to pluralism we are not free to shame our fellow-Jews who behave differently, nor to minimize their own quest for God and His Torah, even when ours seems much more responsible than theirs. We have no guru to lead us, as the Lubavitchers do, no code that will be binding in all circumstances as the *Shulhan Aruch* (Code of Jewish Law) is for many traditionalists, no authoritative group to make decisions for us. We stand within a community, deeply within it, irrevocably within it, but in the end we stand alone. There is no super-personal obligation, but there is duty:

Within each area of Jewish observance Reform Jews are called upon to confront the claims of Jewish tradition, however differently perceived, and to exercise their individual autonomy, choosing and creating on the basis of commitment and knowledge.

Your freedom to choose what you will do is the precious premise of your humanhood, and your modernity consists mainly in acknowledging and acting upon it. As moderns who are Jews, we are called upon to use our freedom in terms of the "claims of Jewish tradition" upon us, for we are part of our people's millennial relationship with God. I have begun each chapter of this book with a survey of our Jewish heritage in joyous fulfillment of this Reform Jewish obligation. Not everyone will read the Jewish tradition the same way and thus "hear" the same call being made to them. We are too individualistic for that and it is too complex for such uniformity. We should then approach it and decide out of the depth of "knowledge" which befits a significant decision. We should also do so in terms of our deepest "commitment," for, when we ask about religious duties, we are speaking of the service of God. Then whatever we choose from the past or create for the present should rest upon us with the full force of commandment. For only by being false to ourselves and what we believe will we be able to ignore or transgress it.[18]

Borowitz is not afraid to be specific even when he must express his conclusions with a continuing tentativeness. He deals with sex and war and money and drinking and psychotherapy and child-rearing, the many issues that trouble us all, and he attempts to bring Jewish wisdom to bear upon each of them. He is wise and moderate, perhaps moderate to a fault. Jewish ethics is neither permissive nor ascetic in his view. It is not a matter of feeling good, but of doing good—whatever we may feel. It is always a metaethics, a doing that is also a way of believing, one that requires faith as well as skillful discrimination. Jewish ethics is universal, in the sense that it applies to all people without prejudice, and it is particularistic in that it obligates Jews in uniquely demanding ways. It is creative, and must now look creatively at issues of women's liberation, the covenanted community, and the limits of Jewish self-protection. It requires an elite to lead and to demand. It is hopeful and messianic, but also chastened by our traditional sources and by our unsettling century. It is at the crossroads of personal choice and Jewish obedience to God.

In two essays, both published in 1984, "The Autonomous Self and the Commanding Community" and "The Autonomous Jewish Self," Borowitz tries to clarify his paradoxical view. He demolishes the idea of absolute individualism which he finds rooted in Rousseau and somewhat dangerous even in Kant. The Cartesian *cogito* and the Leibnizian monad are models for an individualism no Jew can affirm. With Kant we believe in a moral law, but for us the emphases are not only on our autonomous choice but on our rational commitment to a law which we did not create. We are not as confident in our reason as was Kant, and so we must find a direction in which our minds and choices may be transformed. Marx has convinced us that reason often rationalizes class privilege and personal whim, that man is truly a species-being and that society often knows better than the individual what the individual needs. The ethical nationalism of Ahad ha'Am (lit. "One of the People"; Asher Ginzberg, 1856–1927) points Borowitz toward Martin Buber's philosophy of dialogue. And Sartre's final venture into a kind of Jewishness points Borowitz toward an escape from the lost self of existentialism, reminiscent of the earlier spirit (if not the letter) of Hermann Cohen.

Buber teaches us that our self is always in relationship, that we exist, so to speak, in the space between our "selves" and the other. Engagement modifies individualism. Hence, no moral judgment is entirely private. We act always and only in partnership with others and with God. Our task is to transmute society (a collection of atomic individuals) into community (a commune of relational persons). The name of that experience is covenant, or, in specifying the particularly Jewish experience that began at Sinai, Covenant. It deals with the "it" in the spirit of the I-Thou. It materializes spirit and spiritualizes the world of things. It follows no abstract Law, but it is always lawful. It obeys no punitive Other, yet responds again and again to the personal call of Otherness. We are to hold ourselves ready for a revelation of God's Torah which can come anywhere and anytime, but only *we* can know what it signifies for us. Autonomy means autonomy beside God; it means autonomy within a community which we ourselves must build over and over again.

"The self gains its worth not from itself, but from its relationship with God," who obliterates our selfishness. We cannot bypass community nor eschew the modifying wisdom of family, group, people, world:

I believe that we modern Jews properly exercise our autonomy only when we do so in terms of our relationship with God as part of the people of Israel and as the latest expression of its long Covenant tradition. Two intensifications of our general human sociality arise from this situation. As in all religions, the most utterly fundamental human bond is at stake here, namely, that with God. Hence our religious communities and responsibilities should properly be invested with profound devotion and commitment. Moreover, because of the ethnic base of its Covenant, Judaism emphasizes the social means by which this relationship is lived.[19]

All of Borowitz's wisdom is spoken modestly and with almost too much care. He believes less than he thinks he should believe, but never in nothing. He teaches more than he is certain of, but he is virtually certain of something. His faith and his doubts are very modern. His sophisticated confrontation of both bespeaks a fine technical skill, even if, in the end, we cannot follow him into naked liberalism. It is almost as if we are personally unworthy of his confidence in us, and must structure our own Judaism more obsessionally in order to survive. Or, perhaps, it is Borowitz who is too trusting and even too typical to change.

The autonomous Jewish self of the essay of the same name (1984) is more than an ethical being. He/she must stand in relation to a millennial tradition.

Jews must live not only by the covenant but by their own, special Covenant. We cannot do so without the help of God, a God who both cares and judges, who knows and is infinitely involved. We are historically rooted, but we need not, indeed cannot, be Orthodox Jews. Orthodoxy seems, to Borowitz, to violate the will of God when it appears to discriminate against *mamzers* (children of forbidden unions) and abandoned wives. The Orthodox model, for Borowitz, is almost inevitably hard-line, which seems to him more authentic, but also more convenient for him to dismiss. He agrees with Buber, not Rosenzweig, in holding that no Jewish law can ever be imposed upon a Jewish self. Liberal *halakah* (law) must be richly personal, if also communally created on Jewish ground. Borowitz personally feels commanded not to perform intermarriage, but he will not condemn his colleagues who feel authorized to unite a Jew and non-Jew "by the laws of Moses and Israel."

Is there not here some hint of intellectual dishonesty? Are there no limits, not only to what we refuse, but also to what we refuse to justify? Is his autonomy, perhaps, too reckless, even after he modifies it by learning, commitment, and demanding personal self-discipline? Or are we who criticize mere hypocrites who claim to an obedience we are unable regularly to practice? I believe that Borowitz has failed to justify systematically the liberal version of Judaism, but for me, and for so many others, no better alternative is available. His failure is as close as we have come to making our own choices not only reasonable but defensible in God's great world which stretches infinitely beyond all our lives.

STEVEN S. SCHWARZSCHILD

Steven Schwarzschild has manifested both an astonishing virtuosity and a single-mindedness during thirty years of writing about Judaism and Jewish philosophy. His output is diverse, ranging from social issues like peace and capital punishment through foreign policy and Christian thought to esoteric studies of prayer and Messiah. His mentor has always been and still remains Hermann Cohen, the great German-Jewish thinker who died almost seventy years ago but whose ideas remain seminal not only for Schwarzschild but for the most important contemporary Jewish thinkers. Cohen's neo-Kantian, post-liberal Judaism has inspired Schwarzschild to feats of imagination hardly paralleled by any of his contemporaries. He has published no complete book, but his essays are very broadly conceived and his fecundity increases with each decade.

The basic outlook of Schwarzschild reflects an ethical monotheism carried to its conclusion, which drives to the very limits the basic principle of Judaism as he sees it. This means, among other claims, that everything is ultimately rational in Judaism—including, and perhaps most especially, its version of mysticism.[20] Judaism is an idea, one which can be appropriated by Jews who try to do so, and which has consequences that can be not only spelled out but lived out, too. Against all obscurantist readings of Judaism, Schwarzschild describes a clear, lucid, rather complicated, version of monotheistic rationalism, one with unmistakably concrete outcomes.

One of the latter is that everything in Judaism must be humane. Judaism gives no warrant to any sacred egoism, nor to any merely prudential self-protection. Judaism *is* concern for humanity, not theoretical and mealymouthed, but revolutionary and categorical. Whatever in Judaism does not accord with that concern for humanity is not authentic, and what does *is* authentic insofar as it accords with a strict ethical humanitarianism. But this ethical emphasis has surprisingly traditional implications—for instance, an emphasis on messianism, earlier in Schwarzschild's career even on the personal messiah, though more recently, a return to the belief in the final unification of humanity in a messianic age. Messiah means not so much Jewish survival and power as the linking of all God's children in one brotherhood, which signifies the final oneness of His name. All our labor before that time is for the sake of and in anticipation of a messianic love of the human species.

One implication of Schwarzschild's radical ethical stance is a re-emphasis of Jewish laws against usury, laws which both parallel and inspired Marxist socialism.[21] Judaism, for Schwarzschild, is the refusal to live off the surplus labor of the worker, adamant refusal to sweat the poor for the enrichment of the propertied. The biblical laws, expanded by the rabbis in theory even as they moderated them in practice, make it clear that the wealth of all the people is to be held in common and that egalitarianism is the will of God. Schwarzschild has consistently spoken for equality between the classes and races and, during his tenure as editor of *Judaism* (1960–1969), opened the pages of that distinguished journal to its most varied, radical, and gifted collaborators.

Ethical monotheism also implies a radical critique of Christian incarnationalism.[22] Nothing marks Jewish uniqueness more than its unwillingness to conceive of a God in human flesh or a world that is already redeemed. Judaism will not and cannot enshrine or worship a world that is, since it is always laboring for a world that is yet to be. Nature is not divine, and God is not human. Spinoza and Hegel, who carried Christian incarnationalism to its logical conclusion in a pantheistic quietism, are for Schwarzschild the great antagonists. They glorify the world that is, claiming for it an inevitability and a value that Judaism cannot admit, thus accepting the present as the real and the real as the ultimate.

For Schwarzschild, on the other hand, nature is only the arena for possible human achievement and solidarity. Jewish aesthetics always prefers the "unnatural," the potentially ethical, the possible and not the given, the task and not the setting.[23] Messiah is always coming and the ethical is an infinite obligation, an asymptote that, like God, moves away from us as we infinitely approach it. Faith is not a feeling but a task: "to perfect the world under the kingship of the Almighty," Whose power is the correlate of our own obligation. Christianity errs in emphasizing religion as salvific; Judaism is primarily the demand of a just God that we perform His commandments, all of which are basically ethical and all of which lead us beyond the world as it is to that humane kingdom that we must construct.

Another of Schwarzschild's targets is liberal humanism, which he considers complacent and acquiescent amid the travails of history. Not only is its optimism centered on man himself, a dubious hero, but it also reflects class bias, the allrightnik as philosopher. Rather, says Schwarzschild, the human self must be created, not merely discovered and celebrated.[24] It must be challenged to exist by profound claims that come from beyond humankind but can raise us up toward the infinite. Our task will not be clarified by ethical simplicities. The meaning of monotheism is far more profound and complex than any humanism imagines. Schwarzschild is deeply interested in traditional forms of Judaism, because in them he often sees a more instructive form of ethical theology, but he also traces the most orthodox back to his hero, Hermann Cohen, even when connections with Cohen seem most improbable at first glance.[25] Humanism fails as a goad to human self-transcendence. Nothing, in the end, is more radical than naked tradition, if understood properly and driven to its conclusion without fear or favor.

Schwarzschild also opposes all nationalism, especially Jewish nationalism. The Covenant between God and the Jewish people subverts any interpretation of our religion as a defense of ourselves, in the style of Fackenheim or Rubenstein. Power, in fact, erodes whatever makes Jewish loyalty worthwhile. It cannot be that we have survived the vicissitudes of four millennia simply to be another Bulgaria or Colombia, nurturing a little patriotism while ignoring the most influential and powerful ethical system that the world has ever known. The European-Jewish symbiosis was not, as some assert, an illusion; our religion and our people helped create the great civilizations of the West and inspired them with radical ideas of God and humanity. Of course, we were victims of the West's most atavistic reaction, but we are also the only hope that the world has for a future, especially in the atomic age. Pacifism, internationalism, and socialism are not for Schwarzschild mere abstractions; they are the flesh and blood of Jewish religiosity.[26]

Jewishness, including Jewish languages, Jewish aesthetic judgment, Jewish ways of teaching non-Jewish subjects—all of this is a way of mediating Judaism. To be Jewish is not so much to do something as to do everything in a certain way. The Yiddish language puts a premium on being a *mensch*, which signifies not a "macho" male, but a compassionate human being. Talmudic law universalizes most precepts for the sake of *shalom*, and that means not just getting along with non-Jews, but, more important, bringing wholeness and integrity to the world. God is known not as He is, but by what He does and for what He means us to do. Maimonides's negative theology is a way of saying that we cannot know what God means to Himself, but we can precisely know what He wants us to do, "to perfect the world under His kingship."

What have we obtained then as a result of our analysis of Maimonides' philosophical ethics that we are not likely to have been aware of before?

We can now be sure that, for reasons of religious/Jewish moral perfectionism and using an essentially Platonizing approach, Maimonides teaches an ethical Aristotelian moderateness only as an initial and lower stage of ethics. This is still an ethic derived from and thus bound to existing society. From this he goes on to a higher and ultimate stage of moral radicalism, which is determined by *imitatio Dei*. Here moral reason, not sociology, defines the good. The transition from the lower to the higher stage is in fact a cognitive achievement, that is, by coming "to know God" men come to act as God acts, or, to put it differently, philosophy reverses "the Fall of Adam" and messianically rehabilitates prelapsarian perfect man. This, then, is an eschatological, or regulative, ethical epistemology, which, as such, also extends the values of the full knowledge of "the good" to all men universally. If one were to try to bring all this into one short formula for the Maimonidean categorical imperative it might be this: learn to know (philosophical-rationally or religiously) how God acts so as to emulate him, and spread this knowledge to all men to the same end.[27]

It is impossible to summarize so manifold a philosophy as Schwarzschild's, which I believe is the most brilliant and fruitful of any that have grown on American soil, though, of course, nurtured by ancient Jewish and modern European roots. He is scholarly, sometimes pedantic, often too elaborate and self-conscious in his formulations. But there is a startling simplicity and conviction to all his central theses. He is a successor and epigone of Hermann Cohen, even of Maimonides. He closes an epoch in European-Jewish thinking which has had its last burst of glory on American soil.

NOTES

1. Mordecai M. Kaplan, *Judaism as a Civilization*, 1934 ed., p. 43.

2. Ibid., p. 112, quoting Rabbi S. S. Cohon.

3. Ibid., p. 178.

4. Ibid., pp. 381–382.

5. Ibid., p. 316.

6. Mordecai M. Kaplan, *Judaism as a Civilization*, 1957 enlarged ed., p. 386.

7. Ibid., 1934 ed., p. 410.

8. Ibid., 1934 ed., p. 485.

9. Emil Fackenheim, "The Dilemma of Liberal Judaism," in *Quest for Past and Future*, p. 139.

10. Emil Fackenheim, "A Jew Looks at Christianity and Secularist Liberalism," op. cit., p. 275.

11. Emil Fackenheim, "Judaism and the Idea of Progress," op. cit., p. 91.

12. Emil Fackenheim, *God's Presence in History*, p. 84.

13. Emil Fackenheim, *The Jewish Return into History*, pp. 229ff.

14. Richard L. Rubenstein, *After Auschwitz*, p. 58.

15. Ibid., p. 234.

16. Ibid.

17. Eugene B. Borowitz, *Liberal Judaism*, pp. 423–424.

18. Ibid., p. 331.

19. Eugene B. Borowitz, "The Autonomous Self and the Commanding Community," p. 52.

20. Steven S. Schwarzschild, "An Introduction to the Thought of R. Isaac Hutner," pp. 235–277.

21. Steven S. Schwarzschild, "Karl Marx's Jewish Theory of Usury," pp. 7–40.

22. Steven S. Schwarzschild, "The Lure of Immanence—The Crisis in Contemporary Religious Thought," pp. 70–99.

23. Steven S. Schwarzschild, "The Unnatural Jew," pp. 347–362.

24. Steven S. Schwarzschild, "The Tenability of Hermann Cohen's Construction of the Self," pp. 361–384.

25. Cf. "An Introduction to the Thought of R. Isaac Hutner," esp. pp. 251–256.

26. Cf. Schwarzschild's "The Question of Jewish Ethics Today," pp. 29–36 (Sh'ma. 7.127) and pp. 118–127 (Sh'ma. 7.134).

27. Steven S. Schwarzschild, "Moral Radicalism and 'Middlingness' in the Ethics of Maimonides," pp. 65–94.

BIBLIOGRAPHY

Borowitz, Eugene B. "The Autonomous Self and the Commanding Community." *Theological Studies*. 45. (1984), pp. 34–56.

———. *Liberal Judaism*. New York: Union of American Hebrew Congregations, 1984.

Fackenheim, Emil. *God's Presence in History*. New York: New York University Press, 1970.

———. *The Jewish Return into History*. New York: Schocken Books, 1978.

———. *Quest for Past and Future*. Bloomington: Indiana University Press, 1968.

Kaplan, Mordecai M. *Judaism as a Civilization*. New York: Macmillan, 1934.

———. *Judaism as a Civilization*. Enlarged ed. New York: Reconstructionist Press, 1957.

Rubenstein, Richard L. *After Auschwitz*. Indianapolis: Bobbs-Merrill, 1966.

Schwarzschild, Steven S. "An Introduction to the Thought of R. Isaac Hutner." *Modern Judaism*. 5. (1985), pp. 235–277.

———. "Karl Marx's Jewish Theory of Usury." *Gesher*. (1978), pp. 7–40.

———. "The Lure of Immanence—The Crisis in Contemporary Religious Thought." *Tradition*. 9.1–2. (Spring–Summer, 1967), pp. 70–99.

———. "Moral Radicalism and 'Middlingness' in the Ethics of Maimonides." *Studies in Medieval Culture*. 11. (1977), pp. 65–94.

———. "The Question of Jewish Ethics." *Sh'ma*. 7.127. (December 24, 1976), pp. 29–36, and 7.134. (May, 1977), pp. 118–127.

———. "The Tenability of Hermann Cohen's Construction of the Self." *Journal of the History of Philosophy*. 13. (July, 1975), pp. 361–384.

———. "The Unnatural Jew." *Environmental Ethics*. 6. (Winter, 1984), pp. 347–362.

FOR FURTHER READING

Berkovits, Eliezer. *Faith after the Holocaust*. New York: KTAV, 1973.

Borowitz, Eugene B. *Choices in Modern Jewish Thought*. New York: Behrman House, 1983.

————. *Choosing a Sex Ethic*. New York: Schocken, 1969.

————. *Contemporary Christologies: A Jewish Response*. New York: Paulist Press, 1980.

————. *The Mask Jews Wear*. New York: Simon and Schuster, 1973.

Cohen, Arthur. *Arguments and Doctrines*. New York: Harper & Row, 1970.

————. *The Natural and the Supernatural Jew*. New York: Behrman House, 1979.

Fackenheim, Emil. *Encounters Between Judaism and Modern Philosophy*. Philadelphia: Jewish Publication Society, 1973.

Frank, Waldo. *The Jew in Our Day*. New York: Duell, Sloan and Pearce, 1944.

Gordis, Robert. *Judaism for the Modern Age*. New York: Farrar, Straus and Cudahy, 1955.

Herberg, Will. *Judaism and Modern Man*. New York: Farrar, Straus and Young, 1951.

Heschel, Abraham Joshua. *God in Search of Man*. Philadelphia: Jewish Publication Society, 1956.

Kaplan, Mordecai M. *The Future of the American Jew*. New York: Macmillan, 1948.

————. *The Meaning of God in Modern Jewish Religion*. New York: Reconstructionist Press, 1937.

Lamm, Norman. *Faith and Doubt*. New York: KTAV, 1971.

Petuchowski, Jacob J. *Ever Since Sinai*. New York: Scribe Publications, 1961.

Rubenstein, Richard L. *Eros and Morality*. New York: McGraw-Hill, 1970.

————. *The Religious Imagination*. Indianapolis: Bobbs-Merrill, 1968.

Schwarzschild, Steven S. "J. P. Sartre as Jew." *Modern Judaism*. 3. (February, 1983), pp. 39–73.

Soloveitchik, Joseph B. *Halakhic Man*. Philadelphia: Jewish Publication Society, 1983.

————. "The Lonely Man of Faith." *Tradition*. 7. (Summer 1965), pp. 5–67.

Steinberg, Milton. *Anatomy of a Faith*, ed. Arthur Cohen. New York: Harcourt, Brace, 1960.

Wolf, Arnold J., ed. *Rediscovering Judaism*. Chicago: Quadrangle, 1965.

Wyschogrod, Michael. *The Body of Faith*. New York: Seabury, 1983.

10

Zionist Ideology in America

David Polish

In its earliest stages, American Zionism concentrated on justifying the burgeoning movement philosophically. The confrontation between Zionism and anti-Zionism evoked ideological conflict. As the crisis of Jewish existence intensified during the Nazi period and through World War II, the issue of Zionism shifted from ideology to pragmatics—how to save Jews through fulfilling the Zionist program.

After the Second World War, the diaspora, which had long been the seat of Zionist authority, began to yield to the newly created state. This generated a relatively new issue: the place of the diaspora and its relationship to the state.

Finally, varieties of Zionist belief and expectation—spiritual, social, political—have been constant subjects of discourse in Zionist thought. While the idiom of discourse has changed, the issues are at least as intensely debated as ever. These varieties of Zionist experience will inform this essay.

Both as an idea and as a movement, Zionism took root in the United States together with the first waves of Jewish immigration from Eastern Europe. Paradoxically, some of the most eloquent and profound spokesmen came from Western Europe and from within the capital of anti-Zionism—American Reform Judaism. Except for Richard Gottheil, these intellectual pioneers have been given scant attention in the most authoritative texts on American Zionism. Until recently their undeserved obscurity has helped perpetuate a distorted perception of Reform Judaism and, even more, a diminished version of American Zionist thought. Zionism has always concerned itself with two issues, the political condition of the Jewish people and its spiritual condition. Homelessness was the common cause of both the oppression and the ambiguous identity of many Jews. The early Zionist pioneers confronted both issues as inter-related.

EARLIEST ZIONIST IDEOLOGISTS

Caspar Levias (1860–1934)

Two of the foremost and earliest Zionist ideologists in American Jewry were a Reform scholar and a Reform rabbi, members of the Central Conference of American Rabbis which, at its inception (1889), was uncompromisingly anti-Zionist. One of them was Caspar Levias, a professor at the Hebrew Union College in Cincinnati. Subsequently dismissed from the Hebrew Union College for his "heretical" views, Levias was to write a definitive statement, his "The Justification of Zionism" (1899), which not only challenged Reform theology on the issue of Jewish nationhood but also drew a definitive outline for future Zionist ideology.

Professor Levias asserted that he was "not aware" of previous efforts to deal with the problem "from the point of view I have taken here." His contribution was unique in its appraisal of the mission theory of Reform Judaism. Instead of attacking it, as Zionists had before him, he appropriated it for his Zionist ideology. The mission theory (Judaism as a "light to the nations") had been propagated by Reform theologians as the chief philosophic justification for opposing Zionism. Zionism was a narrow particularism. Reform Judaism represented a humanity-embracing universalism. Both were incompatible. Zionism was concerned exclusively with a Jewish people (which according to Reform thinkers was non-existent), while universalism was concerned with the fate and destiny of all humanity. Zionism kept alive that brand of Jewish parochialism which is identified with a particular plot of ground and a particular set of ritualistic and ceremonial practices. Reform Judaism enshrined the prophets of Israel who called out their message of justice and righteousness to all people. It was therefore the mission of Reform Judaism to bring the prophetic message to non-Jews, particularly in the Western world.

Caspar Levias turned the mission theory on its head and demonstrated that it could be advanced most effectively through a Jewish people which enjoyed a national base from which to reach out to the world with its prophetic message. Levias did not depend on the usual argument that Jewish prophecy was deeply rooted in concern for the Jewish people and its land. He indicated that anti-Zionists could, with equal cogency, show how Jewish prophets denounced the Jewish people and predicted its destruction. Since these arguments militated against each other, he had recourse to four special positions. First, he argued, with irony, that the supporters of the mission theory prefer to apply it to non-Jews rather than to their fellow Jews. Thus the exclusionary practices of German and *Sephardi* (descendants of Spanish Jewry) Jews against one another as well as against Jews of other ethnic derivations seem to indicate that they preferred to have as few Jews around them as possible. He contended that it is the concern of Zionism to care for homeless Jews, but since a Jewish state would be able to accomodate only a comparatively small number, enough remain in the lands of diaspora to enable the continuation of the Jewish mission. Second, a Jewish state, however small, would not be unworthy of the Jewish people, as anti-Zionists argue. By enabling Jews to find refuge from their oppressors, even a small Jewish state would advance rather than hinder "the realization of a common humanity." Third, Levias presents the social philosophy of Aristotle, who conceives of man as a political and social creature. Individualism, on which anti-Zionists lay great stress, is an artificial conception, and cannot be realized except in an organized society. The logical derivative of this is a nationhood. Fourth, the de-nationalized ghetto Jew suffers from a spiritual trauma because he has become victim both of an oppressing and of an overpowering Christian milieu. The Jew has unmistakably great spiritual qualities but they are suppressed and distorted by an alien and hostile environment. They can flourish best in a uniquely Jewish environment, and this means Jewish nationalism. "If you deny this particular genius, then what becomes of your mission?" Levias asked.

Levias dismissed the optimistic anticipation of Reform Judaism that historical progress and expanding emancipation are inevitable: did anyone predict the anti-Semitism of the Dreyfus case or the anti-Jewish riots of Germany?

Levias countered anti-Zionists by demonstrating the irrelevance of their argument. Their long-range messianic aspirations in no way invalidated the need for immediate relief of Jewish oppression: Palestine offered peace; the Cossacks and Junkers, abuse.

Side by side with this political argument, Levias advanced a spiritual argument, which is the incompatibility of Judaism and Christianity as long as Judaism is embedded in a Christian environment.

Levias discredited the theory that the most effective solution to the Jewish question is assimilation. He began with the premise that anti-Zionists advance the cause of assimilation because it would create and nurture "a common humanity," which would be superior to ethnic and religious differentiations. His first argument against this is that assimilation will succeed in lowering rather than raising the spiritual content of the common denominator. Second, if nationalism were to disappear and a "higher" form of world government were to take its place, the result would only be a global nationalism more questionable than even local nationalisms. It would incorporate into itself all of the evil of former national states. Finally, cultural and ethical differentiations are preferable to a melting down of all cultures and ethical systems into a single conglomerate.

For Levias, the essence of universalism lies in each religious and cultural group being privileged to retain its own identity. For Jews to merge their identity with the rest of humanity, and thereby presumably advance the cause of universalism, is a contradiction in terms:

From the above it follows that a cosmopolitan religion is an impossibility, that the watchword "a common humanity," is but a meaningless jingle, and that the mission of Israel is to further the nationalization of all groups of humanity; of course, of their own first of all. If the Jews wanted to assimilate with the nations, a cosmopolitan religion being impossible, they could only do it by adopting Christianity in one form or another, something that no man, even the most visionary, can ever expect to happen. The hope of assimilation, therefore, turns out to be a sad delusion.

One of the speakers remarked that he cared only for Judaism, but not for the Jews. As I have shown above, religion is not transferable, and does not exist in the abstract. Religion is not a bundle of intellectual ideas, but a complex phenomenon of a given nation's soul-life, which must disappear with the disappearance of the people. Without Jews there can be no Judaism; as the ancient rabbis said: "Israel, the Torah, and God form one indivisible whole." Judaism could very well get along without theologians, but we could not have Judaism without Jews.[1]

Finally, Levias demonstrates the compatibility of universalism and national-ism, both for Jews and non-Jews. The prophets were intensely nationalistic and enthusiastically universalistic:

Universalistic religion, as can be seen, does not conflict with nationalism. If, now, we claim, and rightly so, that our religion is just as universalistic as the Christian is, then why should we fight shy of confessing that we are a nation. . . . why should Jews not be able to form a separate nation? . . . It is evident that the inference drawn from the premises posited by a universalistic religion, that we are not a nation, is just as rational as the inference from the same premises, that we must all have red hair.[2]

Levias subordinated the theory and theology to the more compelling realities of both Jewish necessity and thought. He suggested that Reform is predicated more upon a theoretical system than upon an authentic Jewish tradition: "Should my deductions, though, standing the test of scientific criticism, disagree with somebody's theology, I would repeat the fearless statement that Isaac M. Wise . . . made . . . namely, that somebody would have to revise this theology."[3]

Bernard Felsenthal (1822–1908)

Even though the earliest deliberations of the Central Conference of American Rabbis were heavily informed with anti-Zionist pronouncements, it has been generally overlooked that some of the most seminal Zionist thought was produced within the very same Central Conference. The far-reaching appeal of this thought, particularly that of Bernard Felsenthal, which influenced Richard Gottheil and Stephen S. Wise, suggests that the Reform movement from its very inception held the dual and paradoxical position of its official anti-Zionism, as well as a profoundly original pro-Zionist view. In view of this, a serious reconsideration of Reform history in relationship to Zionism is called for.

Even fair and objective Zionist thinkers tend to overlook this complex rela-tionship. Nevertheless, Mordecai Kaplan (1881–1983; founder of Reconstruc-tionism) gives inferential credit to this many-sided problem in his *Judaism as a Civilization* (1934), where he cites Felsenthal's observation that Judaism "is the sum total of all the manifestations of the distinctively Jewish national spirit."[4]

Much of Felsenthal's Zionism is political and reflects the tenor of Theodor Herzl's influence and the Zionist Congress in Basle in 1897 as well as subsequent Congresses in 1898 and 1899. In setting forth the objectives of Zionism, Felsenthal places rescue from persecution at the very top of the agenda: *"The aim and object of the Zionistic movement is, to create a legally secured home in Palestine for poor, persecuted Israelites who have no secure homes,*—to create a home where these poor can enjoy undisturbedly life, liberty and freedom of conscience, and where they can live a life worthy of human beings."[5]

Felsenthal's second and equally trenchant argument is directed against those who continue to refer to America as their Zion. This contention is not nearly so much a glorification of America (as well as an oversimplification of its presumably utopian character), but a cynical disregard of the vast majority of Jews living under oppression in Europe. For Felsenthal and his fellow Zionists, the essence of Zion is its capacity to gather in those who seek to flee from persecution. As long as America remained a sanctuary only for privileged Jews while others were victims of persecution, calling it Zion represented contemptuous exclusivism against the oppressed:

And please do not look down contemptuously from the heights of your better social and financial standing upon these Polaks and Russaks and Lithuaks. I have met great numbers of them who, despite their having been brought up in poverty and having experienced in their native country nothing but misery and tyranny and baiting and bitter hatred, have become as genuinely cultured as many of you are, and have as pure souls and as noble characters and as idealistic aspirations as you have. Some of these Polaks have indeed a perfect right, condescendingly to say to you: An American Jew, or a German Jew, if he behaves well, is just as good as a Polish Jew.[6]

Finally, Felsenthal resorts to the same arguments employed by Levias, who rejected the concept of inevitable historical progress. For many Reform leaders, the existence of Jewish persecution did not necessarily represent a refutation of their historical optimism. They dealt with this "blip" in their utopian vision by affirming its temporary and fleeting nature. His response is devastating and prophetic:

"There is no real persecution of the Jews anywhere, at least not a lasting one, not a deeprooted [sic] one. Tomorrow, or on the next day, the sun of justice will send its bright rays down upon the Russian and Roumanian Jews, too. Let the Russian and Roumanian Jews only have a little patience, let them have faith in Humanity. Don't despair, because for a short while the clouds hang low." And so forth. O, these phrases! O, these phrasemongers! The Jews have been patiently waiting and patiently hoping these many centuries—in vain! . . . "Have faith in Humanity! Wait till to-morrow!"—This tomorrow may be at a *very* distant day, it may occur after a thousand years or more; it may never come.[7]

Richard J. H. Gottheil (1862–1936)

From its very beginnings, the Zionist conception was beset by debate as to whether the movement should pursue a purely political course or whether it should be guided by the impulse to revive the spiritual qualities of Judaism and the Jewish people. Engaged in this issue was Richard Gottheil, professor of Semitic languages at Columbia University and former president of a federation of American Zionists which appeared before the outbreak of the First World War. He was a son of Rabbi Gustav Gottheil, the rabbi of the Reform Temple Emanuel in New York, and he became the intellectual as well as Zionist mentor of Rabbi Stephen S. Wise.

Gottheil sought to synthesize the political and spiritual aspects of Zionism and in fact argued that both are inherent in Zionist ideology. As Gottheil put it: " . . . the moment Herzl came into real contact with the Jewish people he issued the parole: 'Zionism means a return to Judaism prior to a return to a Jewish land,' even though he might not have understood the word Judaism in the same manner as Ahad ha'Am [lit. "One of the People"; Asher Ginzberg, 1856–1917, the Eastern-European formulator of this principle], or others."[8]

Gottheil recognized that the need for spiritual restoration was indigenous to Zionism. He understood the need for a diversified and pluralistic Jewish culture under Zionism and in a sense anticipated the later development of this concept:

Jewish life cannot be unilateral in its development. The Jews coming to Palestine will have passed through the sieve of various civilizations, will have acquired varied experiences, which have become a part of their being. Above all, the authentic voice of the Synagogue has spoken in various tones to its different members and in diverse notes. They will come with divergent views of life, which they cannot be asked to relinquish when living together.[9]

Nevertheless, having obtained the synthesis between the spiritual and the political, Gottheil stresses that the spiritual aspects of Zionism can be obtained only on the sound foundations of a political structure. Morality without a political society and prophecy without the strong directing hands of kingship are unrealized visions only.

The assumption that the diaspora will continue as a normative phenomenon in Jewish life was made by Gottheil thirty-six years before the creation of the State of Israel. As the process of loss of Jewish identity and the relationship among the various Jewries in the world intensified, he saw Israel as the unifying agent. A unified religion is no longer possible in the modern world and this must be replaced by a "physical center" that "will serve as a point toward which the thoughts, aspirations and longings of the Diaspora Jews will converge, and from which they will draw, each in his own measure, that sufficiency of moral and religious strength that will enable them to resist the encroachments of their surroundings."[10]

The central tenet of anti-Zionism was from the beginning the fear that Jews might be accused of maintaining not merely double loyalties but contradictory loyalties to Israel and to the lands of their citizenship. One response offered to this claim, coming primarily from Jews in lands of Western emancipation, is that all nationalities are ethnically pluralistic and that the modern world does not expect individuals and groups to abrogate their unique traditions and commitments. Gottheil expressed this for his time and ours when he wrote:

The state cannot demand that the individual shall relinquish his peculiarities, his traditions, his family relationship. Nor can it ask of any group to give up its historic associations, its connection with other groups of the same race or of the same religion living elsewhere. It can only demand that as citizens all elements shall put the needs of the state in which they live in the forefront of their thought and render to it and to the ideals for which it stands the best effort they are capable of.[11]

STRATEGIES

Prior to the Second World War, the centers of Zionist intellectual and political leadership outside of what was then Palestine were to be found in Eastern Europe and Great Britain. The story of the Balfour Declaration, culminating in its promulgation in 1917, is primarily the story of British Zionism, with significant but clearly secondary support from the United States. The latter was certainly a prelude and a foreshadowing of what was yet to come, but the dominant role of Zionist leadership was played out in Europe and the primary actors in that role were European Jews. With the outbreak of the Second World War, the latent intellectual and political powers of American Jewry began to coalesce into an unprecedented instrument, culminating in the Biltmore Platform of 1942 (calling for the creation of Israel), around which the organized strength of American Jewry was to be rallied, and the convening of the American Jewish Conference in 1943.

It should be clear that this mass effort which has never since been duplicated was in a large measure a response to the inability of American Jewry and the reluctance of the Allied Forces to act decisively in behalf of the victims of the *Shoah* (Holocaust). Not only the upheaval of the war but the unfolding of the horrifying destruction of European Jewry was the galvanizing force for the creation of a Jewish state. It emerged from the despair, the frustration, and the guilt over the failure to save the victims of the death camps. In the context of his Zionist leadership and activity, Rabbi Abba Hillel Silver (1893–1963) evokes this awareness. Speaking before the World Zionist Congress in Basle, Switzerland, on December 10, 1946, he said,

American Jewry also tried to assist in the rescue of European Jewry. . . . This called, of course, for governmental action. Unfortunately, in this regard they were far from successful. . . . The whole world, and not only America, remained blind to the ruin and outrage of our people. . . . I believe that much of the failure to achieve results, on the part of the American Jewish organizations which concerned themselves with this problem, was due to their lack of coordination, their working at cross purposes, their tardiness, and the political involvements of some of their leaders which kept them from exposing forcibly the do-nothing policy of the Government.

Realizing that it had been singled out by destiny for grave and unprecedented responsibilities . . . American Jewry resolved to organize itself on a representative national scale for effective action. . . . [This is the] story of the organization and convocation of the American Jewish Conference. . . . [12]

Since the creation of the State of Israel, American Zionist thought has been distinguished by its pragmatism. While pure ideology has manifested itself on occasion, it has not been American Zionism's most singular characteristic. Nevertheless, Zionist theoreticians and philosophers who address themselves to ideological issues on the American scene played an important role in preparing American Jewry for the activist phases of the Zionist movement. It goes without saying that historical events played a compelling role. The devastating consequences to Eastern-European Jewry of the First World War, the rise of Hitler, the *Shoah*, the events in Palestine prior to the creation of the State—all revolutionized Jewish life and history. But up until the creation of Israel, American Jewry had been wracked by conflict over Jewish nationalism. Anti-Zionists abounded within Reform and Orthodox Judaism and within secular, Yiddishist, and socialist circles. The debate was acute and did not come to an end until the State of Israel was born. It represented a struggle for the mind and soul of American Jewry, and ideology helped prepare the ground for historical events which were altogether non-partisan. Disaster alone could not have directed the energies of the Jewish people toward the creation of a state. Just as Theodor Herzl (1860–1904, the father of modern Zionism) converted the tragedy of Jewish life into a political instrument, so did the ideologists for Zion prepare American Jewry both for confrontation with its opponents and for impending catastrophe.

In addition, Zionist ideologists who developed their thought on American soil and often in the idiom of a native or naturalized American Jewry, helped create an ambiance for indigenous thought. There was an abundance of European-Zionist speculation which made its way through American-Jewish life, but for American Zionism to attain a maturity of its own, it required thinkers who either grew up in America or adopted America. This proved to be more than a cultural or a psychological advantage. With the onslaught of the *Shoah*, American Jewry overnight became the political and intellectual center of Zionism outside Palestine. The spiritual resources of the American-Jewish community, having been cultivated for almost half a century, became indispensable for the national struggle that was to be waged.

The objectives of American Zionism under Rabbi Abba Hillel Silver's leadership were large. Until compelled by the imminent prospects of the United Nations' decision (1947) to create both a Jewish and an Arab state, American Zionists together with Zionists throughout the world fought for the realization of Jewish statehood in the entire area of the "Land of Israel." Thus, Silver stated: "Zionism is not an immigration or a refugee movement, but a movement to establish the Jewish State for a Jewish nation in the land of Israel. The classic textbook of Zionism is not how to find a home for 100,000 Jewish refugees. The classic textbook of our movement is *The Jewish State*."[13]

Representing the World Zionist Movement, Silver appeared twice before the United Nations to defend the right of the Jewish people to statehood in the land of Israel. On April 28, 1947, he appeared before the General Assembly, and again on September 23, when he stated: "Twenty-five years ago a similar international organization recognized the historic claims of the Jewish people, sanctioned our program and set us firmly on the road of realization. We were not then regarded as intruders or invaders. . . . The statesmen of the world faced the tragic problem of Jewish national homelessness and they set about to solve it."[14]

Maurice Samuel (1895–1972, Yiddishist, Zionist author, and biographer of Chaim Weizmann), paid special tribute to American Jewry as a primary factor in the creation of Israel:

It goes without saying that there would have been no Israel, either, if Jewry had not been saved by America. The creation of an American Jewry of these dimensions was an absolute prerequisite to the creation of the Jewish State. Historically speaking, Israel is the child of America not less than of the Jewish people and England.

But the extent of America's help is not appreciated. We know of course that the mere existence of American Jewry encouraged England to initiate the plan of a Jewish homeland; we know that the continuous expressions of interest and benevolence which came from leading Americans had a deterrent effect on England when she wanted to retract; we remember also the role America played in precipitating the last stages; we also think of the funds contributed by American Jewry, and, latterly, of American grants-in-aid and credits. What we do not understand and appreciate is America's role *as the providential selective factor* in the creation of the Jewish State.[15]

SPIRITUAL COMPONENTS IN ZIONIST THOUGHT

Most histories of Zionism present it as an offspring of nineteenth-century nationalism. Little attention is given to the religious impulses of Judaism which yearned to restore the land of Israel. These were dismissed as aspirations alone, having the most tenuous relationship with the political eruptions accompanying Zionism, which in turn owed its dynamism to national strivings in Europe. Yet one must not overlook the fact not only that the national aspirations of the Jewish people were kept alive for centuries by their religion, but that these aspirations frequently broke out in pre-Zionist undertakings which were aborted. These nevertheless demonstrated the vitality of the national component in the Jewish religion and the spiritual-ethical factors in Zionism, factors which in the earlier period of American Zionism were regarded as indispensable. This was emphasized by Horace Kallen (1882–1974) in his *Zionism and World Politics* (1921).

For Kallen, Zionism represents a movement of enormous spiritual and moral force confronting Christianity and secular modernity. It is rooted deeply in the Jewish past and derives authentically from the Jewish Bible.

For Kallen, two biblical components are indigenous to modern Zionism: the ancient connection to the land and the prophetic passion for righteousness. Moreover, Jewish messianism, unlike Christian messianism, derives from and moves within history. Jewish messianism is committed to redemption within historical time:

Already in the beginnings of the Messianic legend there had been a potential differentiation between an earthly and a heavenly Messiah. The failure of the earthly Messiahship of the leader of the little sect that later developed into the Christian multitude led to the immediate compensation of the other-worldly ideal which is the Messiahship of the Christian; salvation from evil and happiness both became heavenly things: earth was regarded as a trial and a transition, to be abandoned and spurned. The Messiah was God and the Son of God, miserable on earth but omnipotent in the universe. This ideal denial of real failure the Jews had refused to accept. They fought and hoped on for twelve hundred years. And when, finally, misfortune and the contagion from their intellectual and emotional setting made other-worldliness a part of their outlook, it did not become the overruling part.[16]

Kallen's thesis is not abstract. He attempts to apply it to the realities of the Zionist enterprise, to its contemporary social and economic issues. Thus he states:

In the very nature of the case, the land and other natural resources and the public utilities of a Jewish Palestine must come under public control and be developed for public use. A new, large, and swift settlement of self-supporting Jews does not seem to be possible under any other conditions. That such a socialization would meet with resistance from the vested Jewish interests already established in Palestine is of course a foregone conclusion. But it is equally foregone that such resistance could be broken down either by force or persuasion.[17]

He extended these principles to include the entire political infrastructure.

In retrospect, Kallen's perceptions bear the mark of utopianism. In 1958, following a visit to Israel, his vision becomes somewhat dimmed but not obliterated as he writes:

The total impression I left Israel with, was of a somewhat strayed Utopian fellowship of believers, intrepid, embattled, and unyielding, working and fighting with every means within their reach, to transubstantiate the image of the things they hope for into the actualities they live with, to transvalue the faith which is the evidence of their things unseen into the visible events and tangible facts of everyday existence. Be the outcome of their struggle what it may, it presently discloses an ethos of valor and devotion which seems to me a moving testimony to what is most hopefully human in mankind's struggle for its own humanity.[18]

Maurice Samuel wrote in similar fashion, stressing the religious and biblical less than did Kallen, but the socialist more. He thereby placed the roots of Zionism in modernity rather than in antiquity:

The kibbutzim demanded an immediate total transformation in the lifeways of its members. It was assumed that as soon as a society was created free from the profit motif [sic], the psychological and moral effects would at once become operative. . . . The family may serve as an instance.

As Marxists the *Chalutzim* saw in the old family life many evils implanted in it by the capitalistic and pre-capitalistic history of man: the degradation and enslavement of the wife and mother; the tyranny of the father, himself a slave in the outer world when he was not a slave-driver; the egotistical separateness of this little primitive, biological unit in the larger social setting; the debasement of sexual ideals in the struggle for possession and prestige—and others. A socialist life meant the end of these evils. Family life—for that would still exist—would have new forms within which the old evils simply would not arise. . . .

And as with the family, so with the community of property, with equality of reward for labor, with the absence of the acquisitive impulses.[19]

(It must be noted that, having written this in 1953, Samuel was not able to observe some of the transformation of kibbutz life, both organizationally and to a lesser extent, ideologically.)

As president of the Zionist Organization of America and as a leader in the World Zionist Movement, both of which were clearly devoted to political objectives, Rabbi Solomon Goldman (1893–1953) laid particular stress on the cultural and spiritual aspects of Zionism. Implicit in all forms of Zionism is the need for statehood, without which the inner life of the Jewish people could not be developed, but Goldman went further and stressed that political statehood without spiritual regeneration would not represent a true fulfillment.

Our cities and our colonies, our villages and our farms, our gardens and our orchards stand on land we ourselves recreated. Nowhere in the world, at no time in history, has any people achieved such an amazing transformation of a land in so short a period of time. But even as we have revitalized the soil, we have revivified the language. We have made the language of liturgy, psaltery, and prophecy the language of bacteriology, relativity, micro-biology, the chemistry of complex molecules, non-Euclidian geometry and the Calculus of Variations.[20]

Even those who perceived Zionism in spiritual terms nevertheless accepted as axiomatic the need for a political structure in which the moral and spiritual powers of the Jewish people could be released. Among them was Hayim Greenberg (1889–1953), whose Zionism was contained in a profound philosophical and ethical system. Yet for him, as a socialist Zionist, spiritual values required statehood as a prerequisite. In 1943, as the conflict intensified between Zionists and anti-Zionists (those who rejected the concept of Jewish peoplehood and

Jewish statehood in absolute terms), he argued in his essay "Concerning Jewish Statehood": "But if statehood is such a nasty business that we Jews must wash our hands of it, why consider only our own purity? Why not undertake the task of ridding the entire world of states? . . . A people without a state is not above statehood but beneath it, and if statehood be despicable (as some of its manifestations certainly are), then statelessness is even worse."[21]

Hayim Greenberg's essay "The Meaning of Zionism" (1922), although written two years before his arrival in the United States, represents an essential component of his message to American Jewry in whose midst he lived for the remainder of his life. He sees Zionism as the product of a dual rebellion, first against the ghetto and second, against assimilation. For too long the Jewish ghetto had come to be regarded as "a peculiar Jewish 'oasis' in the 'wilderness' of the nations of the world."

As for assimilation, Judaism retained a spiritual strength which overcame in large measure assimilating trends.

The assimilationist idea was not realized. . . . Jewry had such deep organic roots that no assimilationist passion was capable of eating them away without leaving a trace. . . . The entire organism of the Jewish people had already been so imbued from time immemorial with national elements rooted in it and cherished for centuries, that no "operation," however bold and decisive, could free the people from these elements all at once.[22]

Nevertheless, assimilation made certain social contributions to the idea of Zionism that cannot be dismissed. Unlike the ghetto which effectively isolated the Jewish people from the outer world in a moral and cultural sense, assimilation compelled the Jewish people to confront the world and resolve the Jewish problem in the light of that reality. Encounter and confrontation forced the ghetto Jew into an inescapable relationship with reality:

The Ghetto was incapable of producing an effective Zionism; assimilationism produced it. . . . Assimilation annihilated that social and personal asceticism that the isolated and armored world of the Ghetto had clung to, and—what was even more important—it cut Jewry off from any road back into the world of the ascetic Ghetto. It gave form and expression to those demands that had been leading an underground life in the Ghetto; it increased the number of those demands and heightened their acuteness. . . . The new universally human requirements that assimilation nourished in Jewry later became . . . an organic part of its national requirements. . . . Jewry was compelled to seek paths for [its] satisfaction beyond the boundaries of the Ghetto—in the creation of its own territorial center, in *Zionism*.[23]

Like national movements everywhere, pre-Israel Zionist thought appears in retrospect to have romanticized the realities which were to ensue. Statehood gave Zionist ideology a more somber cast. That the Jewish state would not measure up to the utopian and messianic vision of Zionist prophets should have been predictable. That some thinkers were apprehensive about the future indicates that their glowing expectations were rooted in conscious and unconscious misgivings. Yet, as Greenberg strikingly pointed out, in a world where statehood is not an unmixed blessing, realism as well as sound moral judgment demand that the Jewish state should not be the only one to be dismantled or rendered indefensible. There can be no isolated utopias in a dangerous world.

Does this invalidate the prophetic hopes of earlier Zionist thinkers? This can best be answered by yet another question. Can the expectations of the biblical prophets of Israel for a world of peace and social righteousness be invalidated by the realities of a world in constant battle and embroiled in human repression? The expectations of the early founders of Israel, like those of the early founders of America, have proved to be elusive, but both states are the better because the expectations continue to animate the consciousness of the respective nation's people. The internal social and moral contradictions of Israel are far from resolved, but unless they are rejected by the people, the early visions of founders and thinkers abide as guides to the future.

An important clue is to be found in this observation. Unlike European-Zionist thought, which to a great extent drew on social and economic systems for its various rationales, such as Marxism in varying shadings, American-Zionist thought was not so doctrinaire. Its spokesmen appealed to biblical and prophetic tradition. They summoned Zionism to Jewish authenticity and Jewish spirituality, a message which may not have been as appealing to its time as it may be to the contemporary situation. While much of earlier Zionism took pride in its secularism, we may speculate that contemporary Zionism might rescue itself from disintegration by turning once again to the spiritual and ethical insights of the Jewish religious tradition. In Israel today, Jews who are not fettered to a politicized religious system but who at the same time are devoutly and traditionally religious, are struggling to apply the ethical and social principles of biblical and rabbinic Judaism to the issues of statehood (economics, international relations, property, labor, etc.) in a democratic, religiously pluralistic, and religiously uncoerced society. Thus, the religious component, understood in a voluntaristic and unrepressive content, could prove to be a transforming factor for Israel, for diaspora Jewry and for Zionist thought.

STATE AND DIASPORA

Until the Emancipation, when the Jews of Western Europe achieved civil equality, there was no distinction between the concept of exile and diaspora. All Jews considered themselves in *galut* (exile). The period of post-Emancipation American Jewry brought about a distinction between the two concepts. For the greater number of American Jews, America had obliterated the concept of exile in the United States where Jews enjoyed the greatest degree of political and economic freedom as well as civil rights in their history. Instead of exile, they accepted the principle of diaspora which indicated that they occupied lands outside of their traditional homeland, but chose to do so freely rather than being compelled by oppression and historical misfortune. Consequently, they felt comfortable in their adopted and native land, and at the same time felt obligated to come to the aid of fellow Jews who indeed lived in *galut* in lands of persecution. The diaspora became a place where Jews, including Zionists, felt that they were not only living in freedom but were able to develop a high degree of Jewish vitality. In *Judaism as a Civilization*, Mordecai Kaplan called this "living in two civilizations."

With the rise of the State of Israel, Israelis almost uniformly believed that American Jews were deceiving themselves for they did indeed live in *galut*. The 21st World Zionist Congress in July 1951 kindled a sharp debate over this issue. In Melvin Urofsky's words:

The Congress touched off the major Zionist ideological debate of the decade. The Israelis, almost without exception, insisted that Jews outside the state lived in *galut*, and the only remedy for that situation was massive *aliyah*. In 1957, at the special Jerusalem Ideological Conference, one Israeli after another rose to offer changes on this theme; Halper Leivick [Leyvik]: "A Jew who for one reason or another is not in Israel—the land from which his people was driven and to which it was bound to return—is in exile. Even America is, in my opinion, complete *Galut*." Yitzhak Tabenkin: "There is such a thing as *Galut*, and the Jews of America are also in one. . . . For this reason we say to the Jews: 'Leave the Diaspora and don't take generations to do it; do it within a period of one generation!' " Shmuel Yavnieli: "*Mene, mene, tekel upharsin!* This should be written on the walls of every Jewish home." Golda Meir: "We have nothing against Jews in the *Galut*. It is against *Galut* itself that we protest."

For most Jews in the United States, the debate over exile or dispersion had little personal impact, but in the context of relations between the new Jewish state and the American Jewish community, it held enormous significance. If American Jewish leaders accepted the Israeli viewpoint that all Jews living outside the Jewish state were in *galut*, then that automatically placed American Jewry in a permanently inferior and subsidiary role vis-á-vis Israel. If one denied *galut*, and insisted on the legitimacy of the Diaspora for Jewish life, then one could argue for a partnership between Israeli and Diaspora Jewries. Among articulate Jewish leaders in the United States, spokesmen represented all points of view.[24]

Before the creation of the State of Israel and particularly during the Second World War, the pre-eminent issue roiling in organized Jewish life was the need for a Jewish state. Although most American Jews supported the idea of Jewish statehood, an opposition (the American Council for Judaism), strong enough to gain the attention of the American government and the American public, strenuously fought the idea. With statehood achieved, the issue underwent overnight obsolescence, but it was replaced by another—the problem of the viability and the desirability of the diaspora.

This issue pre-dated the State of Israel: in fact, it was indigenous to Zionist thought. From at least the time of Theodor Herzl, there was a division between those like Herzl who believed that following the creation of statehood, the diaspora would wither away, and others like Jacob Klatzkin (1882–1948) who not only believed in historical determinism in this context but also advocated that the process be accelerated wherever possible. Another position, defended chiefly by Ahad ha'Am and his followers, advocated the principle that the Jewish state would serve as the chief source of spiritual and cultural nourishment for the diaspora for an indeterminate period of time.

Statehood transformed the issue from a philosphical to a practical one. Overwhelmingly, political and intellectual leaders in Israel advanced the position that life in diaspora was at best tenuous and that a necessary consequence of statehood required that lands of oppression should be divested of their Jews, that the diaspora of the West be reduced. While a difference of opinion persisted as to the longevity of that diaspora, it was generally agreed (at least at the beginning) that like all dispersions in Jewish history, its life expectancy would be limited. At the World Zionist Congress in 1978, a report from the American Commission on Zionist Ideology was presented to the Israeli counterpart of that Commission. Numerous meetings by representatives of both commissions had been held in an attempt to hammer out a position on the question of the diaspora. It was finally agreed that, without attempting to define the life expectancy of the diaspora, it should be the responsibility of world Zionism to encourage it to endure creatively for as long as possible. At the joint meeting preceding the presentation of the final document to the Plenary Session of the World Zionist Congress, a fierce debate ensued in which it was strongly suggested that under no circumstances must Zionism countenance even the possibility of the endurance of the diaspora. Nevertheless, the intent of the statement, attenuated as it became during the discussion, was adopted and presented to the Congress where it likewise was approved. This represented a significant departure from classical Zionist thought. However, in the official proceedings of the World Zionist Congress, this decision does not appear.

On the American scene, intellectual advocates of the tenability of the diaspora took their stand. Foremost among them was Mordecai Kaplan, architect of the concept of Judaism as a "religious civilization," and, significantly, propounder of the principle that in that civilization Israel occupies the central position. Nevertheless, Kaplan was a strong advocate of the need for maintaining a rich diaspora existence as a corollary (secondary to Israel, to be sure) to the Jewish state. Symbolic of his conviction was his decision after many years of residence in Israel, to come back to the United States so that he might be buried on American soil as a diaspora Jew. In his *Judaism as a Civilization*, he outlines the principle of the capacity of Jews outside the land of Israel to live simultaneously in two civilizations. He writes:

The Jew who is satisfied to live in two civilizations, in his own and in that of the country of his adoption, but wants the two civilizations to play an equal part in his life, would have to live in a country where Jews are granted minority rights. If he wants to live as a Jew only, and to be free of the need of reckoning with the civilization of any other people, he will have to go to Palestine. . . . In a country like America, Jewish life cannot possibly occupy in the consciousness and activities of the Jew a place co-ordinate with that of American life. The majority of Jews are prepared to retain their Jewish individuality provided they can do so without surrendering the primary place in their lives held by Americanism. This condition can be met. No civilization has a right to monopolize the life of its adherent when he cannot find self-fulfillment, or express himself completely, through it. These considerations confirm the possibility of Jewish survival outside Palestine.[25]

Twenty-five years later, Kaplan gave added urgency to his position, possibly due to the newer realities of statehood as well as the devastation of the *Shoah*, which apparently confirmed rather than weakened his concern for the survival of the diaspora. He cited an official warning by British Zionists at a convention following the establishment of the State of Israel that the "Jews of the *Golah*" and those of Israel would become divided; the State of Israel and the body of Jewry would be different entities.[26]

Kaplan argued for reconstituting the Jewish people as a world-wide entity, thereby redefining its historical status in relationship to the world. He made the radical proposal that the prayer "Gather us from the four corners of the earth and lead us proudly to our Land" should be set aside because "were Jews to take that tradition seriously, they would have to regard themselves as aliens in every country of the world outside Eretz Yisroel."[27] Kaplan vigorously rejected that branch of Zionism which advances the doctrine of "*shelilat ha-golah*" (negation of the diaspora). That doctrine is predicated on the warning that just as other diasporas were destroyed or undermined by anti-Semitism, the same is inevitably true of present-day diasporas.

For Kaplan, the State of Israel contributes not only to the ingathering of Jews but also to the sacred element which is inherent in the unity of the Jewish people everywhere. The return to Zion is the catalyst by which the return to the Jewish people and the restoration of a life of holiness to the people are made possible.

On the other hand, Maurice Samuel inveighed against an extreme form of Israeli rejection of the diaspora and charged Israel with attempting to deny the spiritual and cultural attainments of the diaspora. He urges that "American Jewry must counteract Israel Jewry's growing illusion that it can stand before the world as an immediate self-resurrection of the bi-millennial past."[28]

For Professor Salo Baron (b. 1895), author of the multi-volume *A Social and Religious History of the Jews*, diaspora is a normative phenomenon in Jewish history. He points out that during the time of the Second Jewish Commonwealth, two-thirds of the Jews in the world chose to live outside the territory of Israel. He also indicates that those Jews willingly and devotedly identified with their homeland, sending it their financial and spiritual support, and being content to relate to it in a secondary capacity. Also, Baron regards the diaspora as normative because he foresees it continuing for an indeterminate period of time.

For Baron, one of the most important justifications for Zionism, rather than the defense against anti-Semitism alone, is the need to prevent assimilation and preserve the unity of the Jewish people everywhere. Emancipation became a threat to Jewish unity and served as a means of fragmenting Jews throughout the world. On the one hand, it was the means for giving Jews opportunities and skills for creating nationhood anew, but on the other hand, it served as an instrument for undermining Jewish identity and unity.

Because of this, Baron stresses the need for world Jewry, and particularly American Jewry, to play the role of partners in Israel's national enterprise. While this in fact was not the role of ancient Jewry with which Baron draws certain analogies, the contemporary realities of Jewish life call for a closer collaboration between the diaspora and Israel. This collaboration must not only enable Israel to flourish, but must help create a global, spiritual, and cultural creativity which will inform and enrich diaspora Jewry:

I think it is one of the great tasks of the State of Israel, in partnership with the Diaspora, to find new ways in which Jews living in the countries of equality of rights, can at the same time be creative and fruitful as Jews. Since as a matter of historical necessity, it is impossible for Jews to vanish from the world, let us not make the mistake of thinking that ways will not be found. . . . let us continue building a great world culture which for all its historic antecedents is essentially new, the culture of an eternal people scattered throughout the world, which is at the same time a partner in the world's cultures and a partner—a real partner, not a mere helper—in the political, and even more the cultural and religious, achievements of that increasing part of Jewry which is concentrated in the State of Israel.[29]

Ludwig Lewisohn (1882–1955), who came to Judaism and Zionism comparatively late in life, also pressed the case for a special relationship between the diaspora and a Jewish state. Writing in *Israel* (1925), he urged the affirmation of the diaspora.

Palestine, it must never be forgotten, does not exist for itself alone. It exists for itself; it exists for the Jewish people everywhere in the world. By the time we have brought three millions of Jews to Palestine there will probably be almost as many left in the dispersion as there are today. The difficulties of intercommunication must be reduced to a minimum. The life that streams forth from Palestine must be, in the largest possible measure, a life immediately intelligible to great masses of the Jewry of the world. Intelligible or, at least, accessible.[30]

Lewisohn borders on the romantic and utopian—certainly from our present perspective. He dismisses the possibility that a Jewish state could become a mirror image of other states by referring to it as a "fancied difficulty." His defense of the principle that a Jewish state will differ from all other states is fairly representative of much of Zionist thought of his time:

The concept state has lost its rigidity. The Jewish people through its agency does in fact administer the government of the Jew in Palestine today in all matters that pertain to civilization. We colonize, educate, sanitate. We deal with all economic problems. We do not exercise the political functions of the state. . . . We are, in fact, building up an organization in Palestine which may be called a state or not, as one pleases, but which has nothing to do with force. Perhaps this sort of organization *is* the state of the future.[31]

Within a half century Lewisohn's utopianism was to be demolished. Among those who recognized the blessings of the American diaspora, but at the same time were apprehensive as to what the future might yield, was Abba Hillel Silver, certainly one of American Judaism's most devoted defenders. In 1942 he stated: " . . . our lives as American Jews have now fallen into the well-known pattern of Israel's millennial experience in Diaspora. . . . And American Jews also have come to share, however reluctantly, the common and inescapable destiny of their fellow Jews in the rest of the world."[32]

Almost euphoric about Israel, Horace Kallen nevertheless makes Israel more dependent on the diaspora than the reverse. While ascribing similar possibilities for survival and similar risks of extinction, unlike other observers, he finds Israel in greater need of sustenance through the diaspora:

Indeed, in the present crux of global affairs, the Jewish communities of the free world could live on without Israel, but Israel cannot live on without them. Its dependence on them is critical, while their commitment to it is the commitment of parents to children, which they can meet only as they are stong and wise and skilled enough to produce both what will sustain and enhance their own powers and bring those of Israel to the freedoms of self-help and self-support.[33]

While some may have seen elements of exile in even the most benign of diasporas, others differed. Rabbi Abba Hillel Silver, for example, argued that the question "Will Judaism survive the diaspora?" be answered with "Will democracy survive?"[34]

Yet in authentic Jewish thought, such a moderate term as diaspora did not exist. The exact word was *galut*, exile. *Galut* meant being an oppressed and humiliated stranger. The only way to overcome *galut* was to escape it. On a theological plane, *galut* meant a disabling defect in the moral world. The mystics from Isaac Luria (1534–1572) in Safed to Yehuda Loeb ben Bezalel (c. 1525–1609) in Prague believed that the expulsion of Israel from its land created a crippling imbalance in the cosmos, causing God's female consort (*Shekhinah*) to go into exile.

Thus national restoration had at stake the correction of the world (*tikkun olam*). This concept was secularized by Zionism which taught that there can be only one solution to the Jewish question, the liquidation of the diaspora. It was a spawning ground for anti-Semitism. Herzl stated the proposition ruthlessly. Jews must get out. Those who do will live. Those who stay behind will perish. With varying degrees of harshness, Zionism has stood for the end of *galut*, physically. There is also a spiritual side which in its own way contends that *galut* represents a moral flaw in the universe. Aaron David Gordon (1856–1922), the philosopher of Labor Zionism, taught that through redeeming himself by joining forces with nature, the Jewish laborer in *Eretz Yisroel* will realize his cosmic identity and contribute to the improvement of the world.

Nonetheless, history and the actuarial tables appear to be on the side of classical Zionism. Every diaspora community in our history has shriveled and disappeared. Zionism argues that Western Jewry, especially North American Jewry, is not immune. It will take a little longer, but it will happen. Intermarriage or anti-Semitism or both will do the job. This makes Jewish existence outside of Israel exile. By indulging in messianic fantasies, European Jewry sublimated its despair and repressed its resentment against its culturally and physically distorted condition. Out of this sense of resentment came various messianic movements, all failures, but nevertheless manifesting rebellious stirrings within ghetto Jewry "in proclaiming the principle of deliverance from the galut." These elements headed by their messianic leaders anticipated the consequences that were bound to be brought about by "the realization of Israel's dreams. . . . The outbursts of the messianic movements were the threatening harbingers of the further destruction of the Ghetto. With all its solidarity the ghetto was bound slowly to outlive itself and to collapse from its own internal decomposition."[35]

This sense of exile as an existential as well as physical reality was prevalent in Eastern Europe, but exile as a psychological and spiritual state of alienation in the midst of democratic, Western society, is rarely found in contemporary Zionist thought. Yet for a small minority of American Jews, the concept of *galut* has retained validity in a psychological sense. While it was acknowledged that American Jews enjoyed constitutionally guaranteed freedoms in a land where no tradition of officially sponsored anti-Semitism prevailed, the very existence of Jews outside the land of Israel presented them with spiritual and identity problems which could be defined only in terms of *galut*.

Ben Halpern (b. 1912), a foremost Zionist thinker, particularly in Labor Zionist circles, presents a significant metaphysical perception of exile. Paradoxically, he sees it as a negative constant in Jewish history, while at the same time recognizing that it adds significance to Jewish life outside of Israel. Central to the issues he raises is his "consciousness of Exile" (as a metahistorical concept) "and the essential element that gives meaning to Diaspora Jewish life."[36]

In spite of his continuing adherence to a secularism which is nevertheless informed with the religious influence of Mordecai Kaplan, Halpern insists on addressing "Exile [as] the idea that makes sense of Jewish history to this day, so that without a sense of Exile, Jewish experience loses its meaning."[37] The classical Reform denial of exile, thus offering Judaism's opportunity to bring a light to the nations, and the Orthodox view as a "cult . . . masking a weak surrender, " are both dismissed by Halpern. He presents the Zionist perception which neither denies nor submits to exile but totally rejects it. In place of these unworthy versions Zionism stresses "the motif of Redemption" within "the picture of contemporary Jewish history." Stripping away the ideological superstructure, Halpern's Zionism is that of Herzl and Klatzkin, who saw nothing valid in exile and defined Zionism as the eradication of exile. For Halpern, then, the centrality of exile in Jewish thought turns out ultimately to be nothing more than an anti-value, a black hole in the Jewish universe. By insisting that this be confronted rather than evaded or transmuted, Halpern makes a significant contribution to Jewish religious thought, but by attributing the meaning of "Jewish experience" to a malignant factor—*galut*—he deprives that existence of all intrinsic content.

In Judaism, while the centrifugal drive out of exile was a given and a constant, redemption meant far more than release from exile. It represented a comprehensive system of religious, ethical, political, and social elements which would be activated, within the context of the tradition of which early Zionists (to cite Halpern) were vaguely aware. While the objective condition of exile was unacceptable, many of its derivatives, especially the religious content, were rejected by secular Zionists. And this is one of the problematics of secular Zionism with which Halpern only obliquely comes to grips. He does establish an identity with cultural Zionism, which bears a striking resemblance to Kaplan's Judaism as a religious civilization, but he does not seize the implications of this factor and attempt to construct an alternative to a failed secularism. Instead, he continues to cling to salvation through community, as though community bereft of redeeming religious components is possible.

Halpern's essential thesis is embodied in the concept of *metahistorical* exile. This suggests a factor which does not submit to historical solution. It suggests that even national restoration for the entire Jewish people will not release it from the fullness of exile. This should have disturbing implications for a secular Zionist, an issue which Halpern confronts by defining it, but which he does not resolve. For a religious Zionist, exile means that even when political fulfillment has been achieved, it represents not redemption but only the doorway to it, not messianism but only the footsteps leading toward it. Exile in a religious context represents a cosmic imbalance to which the Jew is especially sensitive, an imbalance for which national restoration is a prerequisite but not a surrogate. Unlike physical exile (which continues to possess Jewish life, as in the Soviet Union), there exists inner exile which can enslave a people occupying its own territory and also living in unprecedented freedom in the American diaspora. The freedom of the latter is always contingent, and this endows all of diaspora with the intimations of exile.

Even more, the inner moral conflicts which agitate Jewish life everywhere, including Israel, prevent the lifting of the stigma of exile from a people whose sense of chosenness compels it to be acutely sensitive to the paradox of incompleteness, even in the midst of restoration. It should be added that restoration is not yet redemption.

Nevertheless, the fact remains that Halpern's perception presents an opportunity which many who have become thoroughly politicized have failed to grasp. Zionism may have arrived at an intellectual impasse because it has allowed itself, even its presumably religious wing, to cut itself off from the religious, not cultic (as Halpern correctly identifies it) enterprise. This enterprise is nothing less than the authentic Jewish fusion of nationhood and religion. The amputation of these inseparable components both by Zionism and Reform in the nineteenth century, and the imposition upon Zionism by Orthodoxy of a coercive, bureaucratic clericalism, distorted the Jewish vision of redemption. That distortion now requires corrective measures.

PROSPECTS

One approach to the dilemmas of diaspora and state, exile and ingathering, is to define new Israeli Jewry and Israel as components of an organic entity, the "Jewish People." All Jews committed to the "People's" survival are involved in Israel's destiny and should have a legitimate voice in helping shape it. Upon the creation of the state, the issue erupted concerning the relationship of American Zionism with the State of Israel. As long as it was still potential, the struggle for its realization commanded the collective powers of the Jewish community of Palestine and of diaspora Jewry, which was coming increasingly under the leadership of American Jewry. The American-Jewish community and the community of Palestine worked as one and as equal partners in behalf of their common objective. Power was evenly distributed. Once Israel came into being, it was generally assumed that with national sovereignty would come full determination by the newborn state of its affairs, and even its right to help shape—if not to determine—significant aspects of diaspora policy.

For those in America who played dominant roles in the creation of the State, it was not an easy matter now to defer to the primacy of Israel. For Israeli leaders, it was inconceivable that power and authority should be shared with others, however devoted, in the diaspora. Some American Zionists who claim a consultative role, however limited, in Israeli decision making, use the following argument: the existence of Israel or diaspora is imperilled by threats to the other. We present a double thesis. First, the diaspora and Israel are inherently part of one another; they are both subordinate parts of the greatest entity of all, *Am Yisroel* (the Jewish People). The State of Israel is central to Jewish life today not only because it makes Jewish survival possible in Israel, but because it has rescued the entire "Jewish People" everywhere and has helped give individual Jews everywhere reason to live. Israel as a place of refuge is a given, but not everyone understands that Israel does not and should not exist apart from the "Jewish People" of which it is a part but not an isolated entity. The State of Israel exists for the sake of the "Jewish People"; the "Jewish People" does not exist exclusively for the sake of Israel. The objective of Zionism should not be to empty the diaspora of as many Jews as possible and then let Israel go its own way, but to preserve the diaspora so that *Am Yisroel* might live. Jews are, in Herzl's words, a People, one People.

Second, it follows that Jews are unique within the world; they are a "People" that occupies both a state and a diaspora. Late in his life, Mordecai Kaplan proposed that the "Jewish People" through its leaders enter into a covenant declaring its status as a world-wide body, yet having a center in Israel, and certifying this fact in the United Nations. While Jews are unique in this respect, the trend in our world moves increasingly in this direction. Nations are establishing their own diasporas—world-wide bases where their industries, welfare agencies, political, and cultural personnel enter into different worlds and are at the same time bound to their native lands. As the globe continues to shrink, people will increasingly be citizens of their homelands and members of their own special voluntary diasporas.

It should follow that Jews, as members of a single people whose center is Israel, are entitled to a consultative relationship with Israel even as it has in fact exercised a consultative relationship with diaspora. The term is consultation, not policy-making, because it should be understood that each entity is ultimately responsible for its own decisions. Whether such a Jewry outside Israel can long endure globally is beyond speculation and fervent wishes.

If it can be convincingly demonstrated that the diaspora has no future, then Zionism has no future, and the priorities of the diaspora should be reordered. Jews should then devote themselves to transferring to Israel in planned fashion those of their resources that they can feasibly confer upon it. This they are not now prepared to do.

Diaspora (read American) Jewry faces the paradoxical condition of being devoted to Israel and at the same time insisting on its own survival. Such a paradox could not have been supported by classical, political Zionists. But some American Jews, if they are Zionists, are beset by concern that they live in *galut*. The non-Zionist entertains no such doubts. The Zionist is torn by the conflict between his conviction that the American experience is historically different, and his apprehensions, bolstered periodically by grim fact, that the unprecedented defenses against the *galut* may prove to be all too vulnerable.

The issue of *shelilat ha-golah* is not merely an academic exercise but a mischievous one. If spiritual Zionism did not reckon with the Holocaust, neither did classical political Zionism, which regarded the end of the diaspora with enthusiasm. But Israel, standing alone in this post-Holocaust age, would not be a liberated but an isolated state, reduced to what its adversaries, in their ultimate strategy, have long envisioned. Yet at the Zionist Congress in 1979, it was clear that a substantial number of Israelis argued for the *shelilat ha-golah* syndrome. It is therefore all the more significant that with surprisingly little debate, the Congress endorsed the position that diaspora life is a "reality" and that Zionism strengthens "Jewish life and self-realization." This marks a radical departure from previous Zionist thought. It puts an official quietus on *shelilat ha-golah*. It acknowledges that there is a strong diaspora and it recognizes that it has a right to exist. To reject viability is to prophesy and to hasten disintegration, which for Israel as well as American Jewry must be opposed as vigorously as possible.

There are derivatives of this position, more far-reaching than may be contemplated or presently conceded. One is that the *galut* plays a critical role in the survival of the "People" and the "State." Another is that the "People," not the "State," is the ultimate goal of statehood. The third derivative is that an alternative to mutual dependency as presently obtains, is authentic collaboration for as long as this can be sustained. This is far more demanding on the state than the terms suggests. It does not mean assistance alone, but assistance as the product of consultation.

This contention brings us to yet another argument: the diaspora should have a voice in Israel's internal affairs. This claim is refuted by Israelis on the grounds that Jews outside Israel lack the qualifications to have such a voice, that they may only give support and intercede on behalf of Israel. For example, there are indeed limited non-political areas, such as fiscal, economic, and educational matters where diaspora Jews do have the opportunity of consulting with Israelis. The reconstituted Jewish Agency is an example of common decision making in these areas. Moreover, Israel is a sovereign state and non-Israelis would be intruding in its internal political affairs and infringing on its sovereignty. Finally, Israel alone must assume the obligation and consequences for its decisions, just as Israel's people incur the physical jeopardy of their decisions.

Responses to such arguments are based largely on radical changes in the Jewish world and in world affairs in general. The contention concerning infringement on sovereignty does not adequately consider the unique condition of Israeli sovereignty which could become a paradigm in a changing world order. Sovereignty in principle and in reality no longer is, if it ever was, an absolute. National entities are increasingly involved in sharing their sovereignty, though not surrendering it, to be sure. Even though the sharing is conditional, its existence is in itself significant. The NATO relationship comes to mind.

Nevertheless, the diaspora-Israel relationship cannot by definition require equal sacrifice. This is presently true, yet not necessarily true for all time. There is no doubt that American Jewry has enjoyed a secure and privileged sanctuary since the founding of Israel, and in full awareness of this, has been reluctant to press its views on Israel. Yet it is becoming increasingly evident that Israel's struggle for security and the retention of its sovereignty will significantly affect the position and the condition of American Jewry. All of this emphasizes that Jews are a people linked not only by intangible spiritual and ancestral bonds, but in the twentieth century, Jews are linked by a global connection which gives their relationship to Israel a configuration never contemplated by classical Zionism.

The Jewish polity is a living, immutable demonstration that the State of Israel came into being through the efforts of both the Jewish settlers in the land and the "Jewish People." In large measure the state exists for the sake of the "People" as well as for its own sake. While there may not be another entity or relationship quite like that of "Jewish People-State of Israel," it is a reality and its validity should be recognized structurally as well as conceptually. Since this entire entity is engaged in a common struggle for survival, it would be an error to insist on total compartmentalization. I stress the word "total" because it must be recognized that there are areas where this principle cannot be applied—decisions of war, defense, and international relationships.

The proposal for a consultative relationship could be construed by some as an advocacy of dual loyalties. Aside from the fact that this charge already is advanced without benefit of consultative status, it should be met not by denial but by the observation that dual loyalties are not to be equated with conflicting loyalties. The growing complexity of global relationships could see increasing signs of more pluralistic relationships. While nationalism becomes more intense on one level, it becomes more interconnected, often in apparently paradoxical configurations, on another level.

It is not within the province of this chapter to outline the structure and methodology of the consultative process. It would, admittedly, be difficult, but within Jewish and Zionist history, this consideration should not in itself invalidate the attempt to outline such a process. What should be considered is that this proposal is being presented with growing conviction on the American scene and has adherents in Israel as well.

Most recently, Zionist ideology is being subordinated to diaspora demands for greater participation and consultation in Israeli affairs. The following principles underlie this assertiveness: distinctions between Zionism and non-Zionism are non-existent, therefore all Jews have legitimate claims to intimate involvement in Israel's affairs; diaspora Jews do not have to live in Israel in order to share with it a common destiny, therefore the viability of the diaspora is valid both for its own sake and for the sake of Israel. Thrown back on the defensive, Zionists are returning to an anti-diaspora (read anti-*galut*) polemic which intends to make a sharp distinction between Zionists and benefactors of Israel. The negation of the diaspora is again becoming pronounced. This could reduce the ranks of Zionists, but it could also help restore the distinctiveness of Zionist principles which have always represented a minority position.

Are the factors here presented sufficient to assure an identifiable Zionist presence on the Jewish scene, especially when even bodies such as the non-Zionist American Jewish Committee advocate the principle of consultation? There is no way of knowing. Perhaps, except for structure, Zionism, even in its renewal, is destined to be absorbed by a Jewish community, bent on appropriating the Zionist idea. In that case, there still remains the Zionist principle that *galut* is *galut*.

NOTES

1. Caspar Levias, "The Justification of Zionism," p. 186.

2. Ibid., p. 188.

3. Ibid., p. 191.

4. Mordecai Kaplan, *Judaism as a Civilization*, p. vii, citing Emma Felsenthal, *Teacher in Israel*, p. 212.

5. Bernard Felsenthal, "Some Remarks Concerning Zionism," p. 48.

6. Ibid., p. 49.
7. Ibid.
8. Richard Gottheil, *Zionism*, p. 193.
9. Ibid., pp. 194–195.
10. Ibid., p. 207.
11. Ibid., p. 212.
12. Abba Hillel Silver, *Vision and Victory*, pp. 108–109.
13. Ibid., p. 123.
14. Ibid., p. 149.
15. Maurice Samuel, *Level Sunlight*, pp. 246–247.
16. Horace Kallen, *Zionism and World Politics*, pp. 15–16.
17. Ibid., p. 316.
18. Horace Kallen, *Utopians at Bay*, p. 290.
19. Samuel, p. 86.
20. Solomon Goldman, *Undefeated*, p. 117.
21. Hayim Greenberg, "Concerning Jewish Statehood," *The Inner Eye*, vol. 1, pp. 170–171.
22. Hayim Greenberg, "The Meaning of Zionism," *The Inner Eye*, vol. 2, pp. 55–56.
23. Ibid., pp. 56–57.
24. Melvin Urofsky, *We Are One*, pp. 259–260.
25. Mordecai Kaplan, *Judaism as a Civilization*, p. 216.
26. Mordecai Kaplan, "The Next Step in Zionism," p. 31.
27. Ibid., p. 32.
28. Samuel, p. 266.
29. Salo Baron, "The Dialogue Between Israel and the Diaspora," pp. 243–244.
30. Ludwig Lewisohn, *Israel*, pp. 220–221.
31. Ibid., pp. 235–236.
32. Silver, p. 212.
33. Kallen, *Utopians at Bay*, pp. 288–289.
34. Silver, p. 229.
35. Hayim Greenberg, "The Meaning of Zionism," *The Inner Eye*, vol. 2, pp. 52–53.
36. Ben Halpern, *The American Jew*, p. 100.
37. Ibid., p. 101.

BIBLIOGRAPHY

Baron, Salo. "The Dialogue Between Israel and the Diaspora." Pt. 3. *Forum for the Problems of Zionism, World Jewry, and the State of Israel*. 4. (Spring, 1959), pp. 236–245.

Felsenthal, Bernard. "Some Remarks Concerning Zionism." *Hebrew Union College Journal*. 4. (1899), pp. 48–53.

Felsenthal, Emma. *Bernard Felsenthal: Teacher in Israel*. New York: Oxford University Press, 1924.

Goldman, Solomon. *Undefeated*. Washington, D.C.: Zionist Organization of America, 1940.

Gottheil, Richard. *Zionism*. Philadelphia: Jewish Publication Society, 1914.

Greenberg, Hayim. *The Inner Eye*. 2 vols. New York: Jewish Frontier Association, 1953–1964.

Halpern, Ben. *The American Jew*. New York: Schocken Books, 1983.

Kallen, Horace. *Frontiers of Hope*. New York: Arno Press, 1977.

———. *The Struggle for Jewish Unity*. New York: American Jewish Congress, 1933.

———. *Utopians at Bay*. New York: Theodor Herzl Foundation, 1958.

———. *Zionism and World Politics*. 1921; rpt. Westport, Connecticut: Greenwood Press, 1975.

Kaplan, Mordecai. *Judaism as a Civilization*. New York: Macmillan, 1934.

———. "The Next Step in Zionism." *Forum for the Problems of Zionism, World Jewry, and the State of Israel*. 4. (Spring, 1959), pp. 29–41.

Levias, Caspar. "The Justification of Zionism." *Central Conference of American Rabbis. Yearbook*. 9. (1899), pp. 179–191.

Lewisohn, Ludwig. *Israel*. New York: Boni & Liveright, 1925.

Samuel, Maurice. *Level Sunlight*. New York: Alfred A. Knopf, 1953.

Silver, Abba Hillel. *Vision and Victory*. New York: Zionist Organization of America, 1949.

Urofsky, Melvin. *We Are One*. Garden City, New York: Anchor, 1978.

FOR FURTHER READING

Hertzberg, Arthur, ed. *The Zionist Idea*. Philadelphia: Jewish Publication Society, 1959.

Laqueur, Walter. *A History of Zionism*. New York: Schocken, 1976.

Polish, David. *Israel—Nation and People*. New York: KTAV Publishing House, 1975.

———. *Renew Our Days*. Jerusalem: World Union for Progressive Judaism, 1976.

Sachar, Howard. *The Course of Modern Jewish History*. New York: Dell, 1977.

Urofsky, Melvin. *American Zionism from Herzl to the Holocaust*. New York: Doubleday, 1975.

11

American-Jewish Autobiography, 1912 to the Present

Steven J. Rubin

I

Autobiography is both an affirmation of personal identity and a record of social history. By its very nature, it is an assertion of the power of the individual; its purpose is to express subjective awareness. At the same time, autobiography is inescapably historical, reflecting the wider concerns of society and culture in general. It is this essential duality—the fact that autobiography exists as both history and literature—that has made it an especially rich mode of minority expression. As James Olney, in his essay "Autobiography and the Cultural Moment," points out,

... autobiography—the story of a distinctive culture written in individual characters and from within—offers a privileged access to an experience (the American experience, the black experience, the female experience, the African experience) that no other variety of writing can offer.[1]

Like other minority writers, many Jewish authors have turned to autobiography in an effort to understand and define the ethnic experience in America, as well as their own individual images as American Jews. In the case of the Jewish immigrant writers like Ludwig Lewisohn (1882–1955), Anzia Yezierska, (1885–1970), and Mary Antin (1881–1949), all of whom wrote autobiographies, the task was further complicated by the ambiguous relationship between past and present identities, between Old World customs and New World values. Autobiography, therefore, offered a means of defining an uncertain identity within a new and often alien culture. More important, it provided a vehicle for linking personal history with that of the group—with an entire social process. In re-creating the inherent truths of their lives, writers such as Antin and Yezierska re-created the collective truths of their people. "It is because I understand my history, in its larger outlines, to be typical of many," explained Mary Antin in the "Introduction" to her autobiography, *The Promised Land* (1912), "that I consider it worth recording. . . . Although I have written a personal memoir, I believe that its chief interest lies in the fact that it is illustrative of scores of unwritten lives."[2] In this sense, the immigrant author is typical of autobiographers in general who, according to William Howarth, wish "to carve public monuments out of their private lives."[3]

In the great majority of immigrant autobiographies, the theme of change—of transformation of self—clearly dominates. The author who wished—as did Mary Antin—to chronicle the specific aspects of this rebirth, found in autobiography the perfect form for the development of such themes as freedom, the re-creation of self, and the possibilities of man. The element of voyage, in fact, is a common aspect of autobiography, metaphorically suggesting the author's subjective movement toward self-discovery and rebirth. In the case of immigration, the process itself—the actual voyage from one country to another and the establishment of a new life in a strange land—is inherently existential and thus provided both the ideal metaphor and the perfect subject for autobiography. As Mary Antin states: "I was born, I have lived, and I have been made over. Is it not time to write my life's story?"[4] For Mary Antin, as for other immigrant authors, the autobiographical "act," as well as the example of immigration, serves as proof of selfhood; one reinforces and reflects the other.

Mary Antin's *The Promised Land* is the paradigmatic dramatization of the exodus of hundreds of thousands of Jews from Czarist Russia. It is ostensibly the optimistic story of those who arrived in America eager to shed their outdated customs and who willingly accepted the values and manners of the New World. It is generally considered to be the classic story of assimilation, of transformation, and of hope. It is, as one critic notes, similar to Benjamin Franklin's *Autobiography* in both tone and purpose: "Franklin's optimistic story of freedom and progress. . . . an immigrant's version of the same hopeful story."[5] Yet a close look at *The Promised Land* reveals both the author's regret over the loss of her past, as well as her hope for the future—an ambivalence that was to characterize American-Jewish literature for years to come.

Born into the vanished world of the European *shtetl*, Mary Antin begins the story of her life with an account of her early estrangement from her native Russia: "When I was a little girl, the world was divided into two parts; namely, Polotzk, the place where I lived, and a strange land called Russia."[6] She recounts that as a young girl she learned to accept "ill-usage from the Gentiles as one accepts the weather." "The world was made in a certain way," she reasons, "and I had to live in it." As the daughter in an orthodox family, she also comes to understand the inferior role assigned to the Jewish woman:

After a boy entered heder, he was the hero of the family. He was served before the other children at table, and nothing was too good for him. If the family were very poor, all the girls might go barefoot, but the heder boy must have shoes; he must have a plate of hot soup, though the others ate dry bread. . . . It was not much to be a girl, you see. Girls could not be scholars and rabbonim.[7]

Soon, however, Mary—inquisitive and rebellious by nature—begins to question "the medieval position of the women of Polotzk," as well as the laws of orthodox Judaism. She begins to doubt her father's strict observance of religious custom; she becomes increasingly dissatisfied with her teachers' explanations. Although Mary often disrupts the Rabbi's religious instruction with difficult questions ("Rebbe, when was the beginning? . . . Reb' Lebe, *who made God?*"), she receives only admonishment. One day she decides to challenge God's presence by openly disobeying the commandment against carrying objects on the Sabbath. Venturing out into the street with a handkerchief securely in her pocket, she awaits God's fury: "An age passed in blank expectancy. Nothing happened! Where was the wrath of God? *Where was* God?"[8] Clearly, "Mashke," as she was called, was already eager to leave her Old World beliefs behind.

The first half of *The Promised Land*—that part of the autobiography which takes place in Russia—is mostly dominated by images of darkness and confinement, of memories of epidemic cholera and long, cold winters. While she is a young girl in Russia, Mary's thoughts are dominated by fears of persecution, of kidnap, of imprisonment, and of the dreaded pogroms. Once it is learned, however, that Mary's father (who had earlier journeyed to America) has arranged for his family to follow: "A million suns shown out for every star. The winds rushed in from outer space, roaring in my ears, 'America! America!' "[9] As Mary leaves the Old World behind, her description of herself and her surroundings changes dramatically; now she is Icarus flying close to the sun: "I rushed impetuously out of the cage of my provincialism and looked eagerly about the brilliant universe. . . . I know I have come on a thousand feet, on wings, on winds, and American machines."[10]

Upon her arrival, the young "Mashke" becomes "Mary" and quickly divests herself of her European customs, her ghetto clothes, and her foreign accent. In every respect, America meets her high expectations: four years after her arrival, she is admitted to the Boston Latin School and is soon befriended by the daughters of the city's elite. Edward Everett Hale also becomes a friend, and she is given free access to his library. Eventually she attends Barnard College, has her poems published in American newspapers, and associates with statesmen and civic leaders. The book ends with an exclamation of exultation and optimism: "America is the youngest of the nations, and inherits all that went before in history. And I am the youngest of America's children, and into my hands is given all her priceless heritage, to the last white star espied through the telescope, to the last great thought of the philosopher. Mine is the whole majestic past, and mine is the shining future."[11]

The Promised Land, with its positive portrayal of American society and the process of assimilation, is seen by most critics as a naive and unrealistic portrayal of the difficulties of immigration and acculturation, the story of a woman who too eagerly surrendered her past, her culture, and her religion for the promise of America. To be sure, Antin's purpose in writing the story of her life is to dramatize the process of rebirth and by so doing demonstrate the superiority of her new self. From the opening pages, the author strives to let the reader know that she is not now what she once was. In the first half of the narrative, for example, Antin continually refers to her former self in the third person: "the little philosopher," "this pious child," "the pupil." The first-person autobiographical mode is thus altered to introduce the historical and to underscore the estrangement the present narrator now feels from her past persona. Yet one is left with the impression that Antin insists too much on the triumph of her transformation, for the descriptions of her life in Russia reveal an underlying and subtle mood of loss, regret, and nostalgia.

While past events are often recounted with irony and condescension (the Jews of Polotzk are described as "medieval" in their religious faith, hiding behind a wall of their own devotion), they are just as often remembered lovingly and lyrically. Antin recalls the past in order to relive it, to experience in adulthood "the flavors of past feasts." There is a sense of lost innocence and childhood joy, for example, in her descriptions of visits to her grandfather's house by the Dvina River: "On the hither bank of that stream, as you go from Polotzk, I should plant a flowering bush, a lilac or a rose, in memory of the life that bloomed in me one day that I was there."[12] And despite the gloom of the ghetto, Antin describes the "joy of sabbath" and the other Jewish holidays as a time of idyllic happiness:

The festivals were observed with all due pomp and circumstance in our house. Passover was beautiful with shining new things all through the house; *Purim* was gay with feasting and presents . . . ; *Succoth* was a poem lived in a green arbor; New Year thrilled our hearts with its symbols and promises. . . . The year, in our pious house, was an endless song in many cantos of joy, lamentation, aspiration, and rhapsody.[13]

Despite the narrator's later emphasis on the positive aspects of her "release" from the prison of her former self, the past is not seen as deficient—or at least not entirely so—but as an object of both love and scorn, of nostalgia as well as irony. This apparent duality would seem to contradict much of the book's overly optimistic conclusion and the author's insistence on her own present contentment. Yet these inconsistencies are explainable when *The Promised Land* is read not as doctrine but as self-interpretation, as a re-creation of lived experience, and as the equivalent of Mary Antin's own unresolved feelings about her new identity. In a general sense, it is also a replica of the entire process of immigration and acculturation, and, as such, voices themes similar to those expressed in American-Jewish fiction in general during the same period. Accordingly, the past is seen as intellectually and materially inferior—as a time of confinement and limitation—but also as a time of familial warmth, of meaningful ceremony, of childhood happiness, of love and of caring. Mary Antin did indeed rush to cast

off the trappings of her past life, but she also understood—perhaps intuitively—
that there was a price to pay.

While Mary Antin might have unconsciously and subtly voiced her objections
to life in the New World, others among the generation of immigrant writers
were more overt in their protests against assimilation. Finding themselves cut
off from their native roots and at the same time excluded from the mainstream
of American culture, many struggled to maintain their religious identity within
the chaos and confusion of the New World. Although some among the immigrant
generation, like Mary Antin, sought to shed the vestiges of their European past
as quickly as possible, others, feeling a deep sense of loss, embraced peoplehood
and their own Jewish heritage. Among those writers in the early part of the
century who chose to portray Judaism and Jewish life in a positive light and to
thus eschew the more secular aspects of American society was Ludwig Lewisohn,
a German-American Jew who, having first been converted to both the religion
and the culture of America, returned with a deep commitment to all things Jewish.

Up Stream (1922) is the first and the most self-revealing of Lewisohn's three
autobiographical works, and the one that most clearly traces his assimilation into
American life and his subsequent disillusion and return to his Jewish roots. The
title suggests the movement of salmon who, having matured, swim upstream—
against the current—to find their breeding ground.

Born in Berlin in 1882, Lewisohn recalls his early childhood in Europe with
nostalgia and love, much in the same way as Mary Antin recounted her past
life. Unlike Antin, however, Lewisohn was born into a cosmopolitan German
family who ''seemed to feel that they were German first and Jews afterwards.''
Although Lewisohn's grandfather was a rabbi, he was clean-shaven, dressed in
the latest fashions, and maintained ''a whimsical contempt for the ritual law.''
Lewisohn's fondest memories were of Christmas, not of the Jewish holidays
which, when observed at a relative's house, seemed to the young Lewisohn ''a
little weird and terrifying and alien.''

After a particularly damaging commercial failure, Lewisohn's father decided
to migrate with his family to America, eventually settling in Charleston, South
Carolina, in 1889. Here, in spite of their immigrant background, the Lewisohn's
managed to enter the mainstream of Southern Christian life. They preferred the
company of their more refined Christian neighbors to that of the less educated,
coarser Jewish immigrants. The young Lewisohn was soon enrolled in the local
Baptist Sunday school and often attended Catholic mass with a friend of the
family. '' . . . I accepted Jesus as my personal Savior,'' Lewisohn recalled, ''and
cultivated, with vivid faith, the habit of prayer in which I persisted for many
years.''[14] In religion, family, and education, Lewisohn followed all things American: ''It was clear then that, at the age of fifteen, I was an American, a Southerner
and a Christian.''[15]

Graduating with a M.A. in English literature from Charleston College, Lewisohn (with the aid of a scholarship from ''the gentleman of Queenshaven''—

Lewisohn's fictional name for Charleston), set off to earn a graduate degree from Columbia University in New York, and it was here that he discovered for the first time the reality of what it meant to be a Jew in America. Although he did better than most of his colleagues in graduate school, Lewisohn alone was refused a second-year fellowship. Nevertheless, he persevered on his own only to encounter another, more significant setback. As his studies reached their conclusion, no offers for teaching were forthcoming. One by one, his friends at Columbia were called in to the chairman's office to discuss teaching appointments and vacancies in departments across the country; he was not. Finally, out of desperation and frustration, Lewisohn sent a questioning letter to Professor Brewer (George Rice Carpenter), asking for an explanation. Carpenter replied that it was "sensible" for Lewisohn to examine his future plans, but that Carpenter could not encourage his young student, explaining "how terribly hard it is for a man of Jewish birth to get a good position." "While we shall be glad to do anything we can for you," he concluded. "I cannot help feeling that the chances are going to be greatly against you."[16]

The incident, which forms the climax of *Up Stream*, is for Lewisohn both traumatic and epiphanic, resulting in an understanding of his own identity as well as an immediate bond with other "outsiders" of his race: "I ate nothing till evening when I went into a bakery and, catching sight of myself in a mirror, noted with dull objectivity my dark hair, my melancholy eyes, my unmistakably Semitic nose. . . . An outcast. . . . And for the first time in my life my heart turned with grief and remorse to the thought of my brethren in exile all over the world. . . . "[17]

The second half of *Up Stream*, that which describes Lewisohn's return to Judaism, is somewhat anticlimactic. Political and social polemics are mixed with personal memoir, as Lewisohn describes his troubled years after his departure from Columbia: his work as a researcher for Doubleday, Page and Company (which he regarded as drudgery), his mostly unhappy marriage to Mary Arnold Child Crocker (an English-born, Christian, divorced woman, twenty years his senior), his early attempts at writing fiction, and the publication and commercial failure of his first serious novel, *The Broken Snare* (1908). "I was beaten, broken, breadless," Lewisohn recalled; "I was a scholar and forbidden to teach, an artist and forbidden to write. Liberty, opportunity. The words had nothing friendly to my ear."[18]

In 1910 Lewisohn finally received an instructorship in German (which he regarded as a backdoor entry into university teaching) at the University of Wisconsin. A year later he moved to Ohio State University as an assistant professor, again in German. *Up Stream* describes the author's six-year stay in Columbus, Ohio, in mostly acrimonious terms. Lewisohn attacks what he perceived to be the philistinism, materialism, and narrow-mindedness of the people of middle America. As a Germanist who had written a scholarly book in praise of modern German literature, Lewisohn was needlessly harassed by the local townspeople when World War I began. Disappointed by the university's failure to come to his defense, Lewisohn finally decided to leave Columbus in 1917.

The last chapters of *Up Stream* are devoted to Lewisohn's diatribes against the war itself and against the war spirit in America. There are also persistent attacks against what Lewisohn believed to be the extreme assimilationist tendency in American culture. Lewisohn argues instead for a culturally pluralistic society and for the preservation of a multi-ethnic culture:

The doctrine of assimilation, if driven home by public pressure and official mandate, will create a race of unconscious spiritual helots. . . . the lover of those values which alone make life endurable, must bid the German and the Jew, the Latin and the Slav preserve his cultural tradition and beware of the encroachments of Neo-Puritan barbarism—beware of becoming another dweller on an endless Main Street. . . . [19]

In spite of its occasional excesses, *Up Stream* is an authentic and moving document of self-discovery and self-definition. It is also one of the first literary works by an American Jew to refute the then widely held belief in the value of assimilation and acculturation—popularized in part by such works as Mary Antin's *The Promised Land* and Abraham Cahan's *The Rise of David Levinsky* (1917). As Seymour Lainoff states in his study of Lewisohn: "*Up Stream* reversed the trend expressed by Mary Antin, who, in her autobiography, *The Promised Land* (1912), advocated the complete assimilation of American Jews, and Lewisohn's book encouraged Anzia Yezierska and other Jewish writers to assert their own ethnic identity."[20]

Lewisohn wrote two other autobiographies, *Mid-Channel* (1929) and *Haven* (1940), both of lesser literary merit and interest than *Up Stream*. *Mid-Channel* covers the years 1924–1929 and attempts to further chronicle Lewisohn's return to his Jewish origins, but the how and why are never clearly demonstrated. Moreover, the book suffers from a general lack of focus, theme, and purpose— moving randomly as it does from Lewisohn's defense of his personal life, to attacks upon puritan Christian values, to an account of his trip to Palestine in 1925.

Haven was written jointly by Lewisohn and Edna Manley, his second wife, and covers a period of less than a year in their life together. Written in letter and diary form, with alternating sections by each, the work is mostly personal and of interest more to the Lewisohn scholar than to the general reader.

Nevertheless, the inferior quality of these two later works should not diminish the achievement of *Up Stream*, both in terms of its power and eloquence and in terms of its importance to the development of American-Jewish literature. Without the example of Lewisohn to show them the way, writers such as Yezierska, Henry Roth, Daniel Fuchs, and Meyer Levin might not have had the courage to pursue their own literary voyage of self-discovery as both Americans and Jews in "the promised land."

The career of Anzia Yezierska, as Irving Howe points out in *World of Our Fathers* (1976), represents in extreme the tragic dilemma of a generation of American-Jewish immigrants. Having rejected the Old World values of her parents (specifically those of her stern, orthodox father), Yezierska could find no suitable ones to replace them. Confronted on the one hand by her father's rigid devotion to religious law and by the materialistic opportunism of America on the other, she was forced, as Howe states, "to confront at their stiffest, the imperatives of both Jewish and American culture."[21] The former proved to be too restrictive, especially for a young, independent woman who wished to become a writer. The latter, she discovered, could provide no solid foundation for a meaningful life. Like others of her generation who sought self-expression in art, Yezierska spent much of her life alone, lost between two cultures. Perhaps more clearly than any other work by an American-Jewish immigrant, *Red Ribbon on a White Horse* (1950) dramatizes the acute psychological strain of Americanization—and the tragic sense of isolation and loss that were its by-products.

Published when Yezierska was close to seventy years old and mostly a forgotten writer, *Red Ribbon* is "fictionalized" autobiography. Although actual events are recounted in a first-person narrative, they are often manipulated to suit the author's purposes and the overall structure of the book. Similarly, real characters exist alongside occasional fictional ones. In short, Yezierska arranged and selected events in order to create a pattern that would reveal her own travail as well as the collective struggle of her generation.

The three sections of *Red Ribbon* dramatize respectively Yezierska's pursuit of literary fame, love, and sense of community. In each, she is eventually frustrated and defeated, partly through her own idealism and partly because of the insensitivity of those she encounters. Perpetually in the background of her struggle is the unforgiving figure of her devoutly religious father, who neither understood nor approved of her life as a writer: "Only in America could it happen—an ignorant thing like you—a writer! What do you know of life? Of history, philosophy? What do you know of the Bible, the foundation of all knowledge? . . . You're a *meshumeides*, an apostate, an enemy of your own people."[22].

In spite of her father's admonishments, Yezierska continued to write, first in her one-room, basement apartment on Hester Street ("the pushcart center of the East Side"), and then, as luck would have it, in Hollywood. Part 1 describes the events surrounding Samuel Goldwyn's offer of $10,000 for the movie rights to Yezierska's first collection of short stories, *Hungry Hearts* (1920), and a job as a Hollywood scriptwriter.

Penniless at the time (she had to pawn her dead mother's shawl for carfare and a telephone call to her agent), Yezierska is thrown overnight into the glamorous world of Hollywood. Impressed at first, she soon discovers opportunistic producers, callous editors, and jaded writers. Her eventual decision to leave is based partly on her disappointment, but more significant are the overwhelming guilt and remorse that she begins to experience at having abandoned her people and her ghetto past. Her dilemma is that of an entire generation. As a poor, Jewish immigrant, she had only one wish: to escape the poverty and ignorance of the lower East Side. Yet as an immigrant, she remains rooted in the Jewish community, and nowhere else in America was she able to find acceptance or a sense of belonging. Moreover, the immigrant world of Hester Street provided her with the background, language, and experience which animated her work. Cut off from that milieu, she was unable to write.

The brief second section of *Red Ribbon* describes Yezierska's life after Hollywood: her return to New York (although not to Hester Street), and the one brief, meaningful relationship in her life. As a young writer, Yezierska had become intimately involved with John Dewey, the philosopher and educator (fictionalized as John Morrow in *Red Ribbon*). Although the affair was short-lived and supposedly never consummated, Yezierska was deeply hurt and angered by his decision to sever their friendship. As her pursuit of success and literary fame proved a disappointment in part 1, so, too, her search for love ended in failure in part 2.

Two central events dominate part 3: the author's involvement in the Writer's Project of the Works Progress Administration (WPA) and her brief stay in a small New England village. Once again, the events recounted are true, although one of the main characters in Yezierska's account of the WPA is invented, and the actual order of the two is reversed to place greater emphasis on the latter— her stay in New England.

With the help of an $800 inheritance from an old friend, Yezierska, after years of struggling in anonymity and poverty, decides to settle in Arlington, Vermont (fictionalized in *Red Ribbon* as Fair Oaks, New Hampshire). Here in rural America she hopes to recapture the sense of community she had lost long ago. For a time she is encouraged by the hospitality of her new neighbors. '' . . . I could slough off my skin,'' she thinks, ''and with this new home begin a new life.''[23] Not unlike Lewisohn, however, she is alert to the reality of her identity as a Jew. And when she attends the local Thanksgiving Day pageant, she begins to understand that her efforts have been futile, that she will remain irrevocably alienated: ''an outsider wherever I went.''

The book concludes with the author on her way back once again to New York, secure at last that she can find meaning within herself and within her own Jewish traditions. On the train, she recalls the image of her father, his bitter tirades against her, and the gulf that separated them during his lifetime. Yet now, remembering his devotion to his God and to his ideals, she thinks of him with new understanding and sympathy: ''a man in love with God all the days of his life.'' Remembering one of his many angry outbursts, she recalls being struck, even in his (and her) fury, ''by the radiance that the evils of the world could not mar. I envied his inward peace as a homeless one envies the sight of home.''[24]

''In my end is my beginning,'' wrote T. S. Eliot in ''East Coker,'' and so it seems it was for Yezierska. Unable to establish her place in secular America, incapable of accepting the values of materialism, Yezierska turned at last to what she believed to be her true heritage—not necessarily as it had been practiced by her father—but one that would surely be closer to his world than to Hollywood's.

Yezierska's experiences all end in failure, and the book's last three paragraphs, those that delineate the author's transformation, seem forced and inauthentic, contradicting as they do both the tone and content of the entire work: "The power that makes grass grow, fruit ripen, and guides the bird in its flight is in us all. . . . Yesterday I was a bungler, an idiot, a blind destroyer of myself, reaching for I knew not what and only pushing it from me in my ignorance. Today the knowledge of a thousand failures cannot keep me from this light born of my darkness, here, now."[25]

Despite Yezierska's newfound optimism, *Red Ribbon* remains above all else a chronicle of failure, of the author's struggle and inability to integrate the particular aspects of her personality with those of the collective American psyche. In the end, Yezierska does seek a connection with the past, although the specifics of that connection are never fully defined. Moreover, the book's final chapter, with its emphasis on the memory of the author's deceased father, indicates, as Howe claims in *World of Our Fathers*, "a final reconciliation, of sorts." And there is surely significance in the fact that Yezierska chose an old Yiddish proverb, one that her father was fond of quoting, as the title of her work: "Poverty becomes a wise man like a red ribbon on a white horse."

II

As the process of Americanization progressed, the sons and daughters of immigrant Jews moved as rapidly as possible to shed the trappings of their greenhorn parents and to thus partake in the richness of American life. Along with new prosperity and acceptance came a decline in traditional religion, of community ties, and of family. Many moved without remorse toward a future that ignored their heritage; others felt a deep sense of loss for an irretrievable past.

The note of nostalgia and regret that was heard in autobiographies and novels of immigrant writers became a dominant chord in the many memoirs published by the children of Jewish immigrants. As Allen Guttmann observes: "Once the children and grandchildren of the immigrant generation had moved from the urban *shtetls* of Chicago and New York to America's wider world, they . . . were able to indulge themselves in moments of regret."[26] Of the dozens of personal memoirs written during this time, many were little more than nostalgic pictures of a particular time and place. A few, like Alfred Kazin's *A Walker in the City* (1951), were moving accounts of the ambiguities and difficulties of assimilation.

Born in the Brownsville section of Brooklyn in 1915, Kazin was one who "made it" in America. The son of an immigrant house painter, Kazin quickly succeeded in the wider intellectual world of Manhattan: first as a book reviewer and then as an editor of the *New Republic*; later as an author, critic, and teacher. *A Walker in the City* is the first of three autobiographical works that Kazin has written to date, and the one that most clearly evokes his early life in Brownsville and its relationship to his present self.

The book contains two conflicting themes, and the author establishes them both before the narrative begins. Kazin uses as his frontispiece Alfred Stieglitz's famous photograph of crowded immigrants on board ship, "The Steerage." Yet the epigraph of *A Walker in the City* is from Whitman's poem, "Crossing Brooklyn Ferry": "The glories strung like beads on my smallest sights and hearings— / on the walk in the street, and the passage over the river." Thus the reader is very early presented with the two aspects of Kazin's personal history and the two motifs he wishes to develop. On the one hand are his immigrant past and the richness of his Jewish culture, which he presents with lyrical affection. On the other is all that lies "beyond Brownsville," the history of America, the poetry of Whitman and Emily Dickinson, and the paintings of Thomas Eakins and Winslow Homer. The book is about the immigrants in Stieglitz's photograph, many of whom settled in Brownsville. But it is also about Kazin's own escape from his ghetto roots, and his great desire to enter Whitman's America: "the great world that was anything just out of Brownsville."

A Walker in the City is divided into four chapters, each signifying a particular landscape within Kazin's past and present Brownsville. The book's structure is not linear, but emerges Proustian-like, as Kazin links physical sensation with the emotional past: the sights, sounds, smells, and tastes of the present transport the author back into his past.

The first chapter, "From the Subway to the Synagogue," derives its title from the direction the present narrator takes as he returns to Brownsville, descends from the subway to the street, and strolls slowly toward his old synagogue. On the way, he pauses at each personal landmark: his old school, "I went sick with all my old fear of it"; Belmont Avenue, with its open street market; Pitkin Avenue, "Brownsville's show street"; and finally the old synagogue, "one of the oldest things in Brownsville and in the world." All that Kazin encounters and all that he remembers are rendered in specific, concrete terms. Again, like Proust's *Remembrance of Things Past*, sensations evoke memory, and what is remembered is recounted with great attention to detail, revealing, as Allen Guttmann notes, "an almost obsessive desire to see in the present a past that was."[27]

The second chapter, "The Kitchen," recalls Kazin's nuclear family, specifically his mother, a dressmaker, continually working at her sewing machine, "stitching" the family together: "All my memories of that kitchen are dominated by the nearness of my mother sitting all day long at her sewing machine, by the clacking sound of the treadle against the linoleum floor. . . . The kitchen was her life. Year by year, as I began to take in her fantastic capacity for labor and her anxious zeal, I realized it was ourselves she kept stitched together."[28]

Kazin evokes the memory of past intimacy to reinforce his present dislocation. Yet the solidarity of the immigrant family is only one aspect of the wider theme of peoplehood expressed throughout: "So it was: we had always to be together: believers and non-believers, we were a people; I was of that people. Unthinkable to go one's own way, to doubt or to escape the fact that I was a Jew. . . . The most terrible word was *aleyn*, alone.''[29]

The second half of *A Walker in the City*—chapter 3, "The Block Beyond," and chapter 4, "Summer: The Way to Highland Park''—concentrate on the other side of Kazin's dichotomy, the Whitmanesque America that lies "beyond Brownsville": "*Beyond* was anything old and American—the name *Fraunces Tavern* repeated to us on a school excursion; . . . the very streets, the deeper you got into Brooklyn, named after generals of the Revolutionary War—Putnam, Gates, Kosciusko, DeKalb, Lafayette, Pulaski.''[30]

"Beyond," too was the world of American art and literature: the poems of Whitman and Dickinson, the paintings of Thomas Eakins, Albert Pinkham Ryder, John Singer Sargent, John Sloan, and Winslow Homer. But even as Kazin declares his desire to embrace "my city, my country," the book's tension reasserts itself, for in the last pages Kazin expresses once again his dominant fears of permanent alienation, of existing always on the periphery of mainstream American culture: "I felt then that I stood outside all that, that I would be alien forever. . . . ''[31]

Despite his anxieties, Kazin, the adult, was to easily and quickly enter the world outside Brownsville. In 1942, nine years prior to the appearance of *A Walker in the City*, Kazin published the first of many critical and scholarly works, *On Native Grounds*, a highly praised study of American literature. That same year, at the age of twenty-seven, he became an editor of the *New Republic*. In addition to *A Walker in the City*, Kazin published two subsequent autobiographies: *Starting Out in the Thirties* (1965), loosely a sequel to his first work and covering the years 1934–1940, and *New York Jew* (1978), which continues his story from 1940 to 1978. Both are highly readable and lively accounts, not only of the details of Kazin's personal life, but those of his cultural and social milieu as well. As Kazin became more confident of his role as a critic and a scholar within the wider sphere of America, he worried less about the ambiguities of Jewish identity and less about the loss of his Brownsville heritage. For the last several decades, Kazin has indeed been one of the dominant figures in American literary life, one of the few "New York Intellectuals" (to use Irving Howe's term) to achieve fame outside that city.

For the first generation of Jewish writers to be born in this country, the American-Jewish experience was difficult to describe; the social, intellectual, political, and economic freedom that Jews had achieved by mid-century only served to complicate the story. For writers like Alfred Kazin, lost for a time between the old and the new, autobiography offered a means of re-creating the past, of telling how it was and why it was important. Others, like Meyer Levin (1905–1981)—the author of some fifteen novels—sought in autobiography a means of defining his ambiguous relationship to two cultures, a task with which he had struggled throughout his career. *The Old Bunch* (1937), Levin's best novel, portrayed the attempt of a group of Jewish characters to fight their way out of Chicago's West Side ghetto and into the mainstream of American society. *In Search*, published in 1950, is Levin's own dramatization of the conflicting interplay between secular Americanism and Jewish consciousness. Levin's "search" was therefore for a basis of understanding not only of his own identity, but on a larger scale, of how a Jew functions within a majority culture that is not historically his own.

The basic dichotomy of Levin's existence and the central issue of the book is stated early: "Was I an American, or a Jew?" Levin asks; "Could one be both?"[32] *In Search* is, as Levin asserts at the outset, "a book about being a Jew." It is a long work—over five hundred pages; the tone is mostly confessional, and the mood is one of self-examination. The events of the past, both political and personal, are recounted from the vantage point of the present and interpreted through Levin's acute sense of Jewishness. Levin is a novelist who has roots in America, in the Jewish traditions of the past, and in Israel. In almost every episode he attempts to assess each of these factors in order to develop some kind of personal equilibrium.

The book is divided into three parts, each representing one aspect of the synthesis of his personality: Europe, America, and Israel. The headings also reflect Levin's physical movement, his journey from Chicago to his roots in Eastern Europe, and then to Israel and an acceptance of a new, bicultural identity. Levin's odyssey back to Poland ("the source land of European Jewry") and then forward to a Zionistic future in Israel metaphorically suggests the author's subjective movement toward self-discovery. Levin's journey is circular in nature, leading him out of isolation and back into the community of man. He must return to Vilna, the place of his parents' birth, to understand his own identity as a Jew, before he can move toward the future and comprehend the full meaning of peoplehood and the land of Israel: "I had to . . . touch Poland before I was free. . . . Then my own journey would be rounded and complete."[33]

Part 1, "America: The Self-Accused," begins with Levin's early memories of life in Chicago where social tensions between hostile minorities brought him to a premature sense of alienation: "My dominant childhood memory is of fear and shame at being a Jew."[34] One learns of Levin's boyhood on the West Side of Chicago, his editorship of his high school newspaper, his literary group at the University of Chicago, and his first writing apprenticeship with the *Chicago Daily News* where he was able to rub elbows with some of Chicago's finest writers: Ben Hecht, Maxwell Bodenheim, and the young John Gunther. His early efforts at fiction are described: short stories published (almost ashamedly) in "Jewish" journals and his first "American" novels, *Reporter* (1929) and *Frankie and Johnny* (1930). Part 1 also tells of Levin's early association with Zionism, his first trip to Palestine, and his stay on a collective farm near Haifa, the experience of which formed the basis of his novel *Yehuda* (1931).

In addition to the recounting of personal experiences, *In Search* is a firsthand report of much of the literary and political history of three decades. Levin describes, for example, his short-lived experience with the Spanish Civil War, his growing apprehension over the threat of Fascism in Europe, and the events leading up to World War II. Part 1 concludes on the eve of the war, and Levin's premonition of the horror that was about to take place.

Part 2, "Europe: The Witnesses," is dominated by the story of the Holocaust and Levin's own discovery of the tragic fate of six million European Jews. Although the shortest of the three sections, it is in many ways the heart of the book. Levin's melancholy yet obsessive odyssey through Hitler's crematoria understandably became one of the most significant experiences in his life and helped solidify his commitment to the future of world Jewry. Yet Levin acknowledges the impossibility of expressing the ineffable emotional trauma of the survivors:

From the beginning I realized I would never be able to write the story of the Jews of Europe. This tragic epic cannot be written by a stranger to the experience, for the survivors have an augmented view which we cannot attain; they lived so long so close with death that on a moral plane they are like people who have acquired the hearing of a whole range of tones outside normal human hearing.[35]

Instead Levin gives a moving account of what he discovered as he traveled through the sites of Hitler's death camps and of his own strained emotions as he learned of the millions dead and the living dead who emerged. " . . . I am sick of telling their stories," Levin writes of the survivors, "for there is no issue from their dreary tales. . . . It isn't a fourth of the Bulgarian Jews and a fifth of the Polish Jews and a third of the French who survived; they all have death inside."[36] All this transcends memoir to become history that is at once personal and universal. Levin articulates his link, not only with the dead of Auschwitz and Dachau, but also with the whole of the Jewish past and its future.

In Part 3, "Israel: The Released," Levin specifies the implications of this connection with Jewish history and his relationship to the new nation of Israel. This last section recounts his filming of a documentary (*The Illegals*, 1948) about the Jewish underground to Palestine. The clandestine flight of the Jewish survivors and Levin's involvement with the *Bricha*, as it was called, is told in detail. We learn of the difficulties and dangers that were part of the exodus, the multitude of heroic and tragic episodes experienced by the voyagers, the seizure of the ship by the British while Levin covertly filmed the encounter, and the subterfuge by which the film was hidden from the British military. The style is objective and reportorial; but Levin's purpose is ultimately personal, as he describes his sense of responsibility to the European survivors and his urgent need to be part of the future of Israel.

The book closes with some philosophical reflections on the relationship between Israel and America, and with a call for mutual understanding and support between the world's two largest Jewish communities. Having his roots in both, Levin naturally wants to build a bridge between them. For his part, his "search" is concluded in Israel where his earlier doubts have been replaced by a renewed commitment to Judaism. The central dichotomy of his life—his Jewish and his American identity—is resolved through an ultimate acceptance of his "biculturalism": "I do not . . . feel that I am in an issueless dilemma as an American and as a Jew, and that I must renounce one culture or the other. . . . we know that there can be successful bicultural and multicultural personalities, and I do not see why the modern Jew shouldn't strive for such a realization, if it gives the best expression to all that is in him."[37] Furthermore, Levin concludes, Jewish civilization will continue to flourish because of a living Israel, a land which will stand as a metaphor for the survival of the Jewish people as well as for universal justice.

Despite Levin's optimistic conclusion, his need to somehow see a purpose to the chaotic events of the first half of the twentieth century seems forced and unrealistic. Israel did indeed arise out of the horror of the Holocaust, but Levin searches in vain for a cause and effect relationship. As with so many Jews who lived through the age of Hitler (and surely Levin's involvement was personal and traumatic), Levin had to live with the knowledge of enormous atrocities and somehow try to justify the ways of God to man. Explanations, however, are mostly impossible, and his seem at times contrived.

Moreover, Levin's claim to have resolved his particular identity problem and to have embraced the Jewish aspects of his personality does not negate the self-doubting tone of the rest of the book. Levin is troubled throughout by a feeling of guilt, of inferiority, and by his inability to "make it" in a gentile world. Levin's early "fear and shame at being a Jew" is hardly mitigated as an adult: "For all my labor in the last years to fit myself into the world pattern, I was still a little member of my clan, over-anxious, self-centered, insecure, the eternal bright and troublesome Jew."[38]

Nevertheless, the importance of *In Search*, like Lewisohn's *Up Stream*, lies not in its philosophical conclusions but in the author's ability to reveal both the nature and the significance of his particular journey toward self-discovery. Like all good autobiography, *In Search* maintains a balance between individual awareness and historical truth, between self and the world. Levin has told the story of what being a Jew means to him and why his connection to the Jewish past and future is important for him, and ultimately for us.

III

The critical and popular success of the American-Jewish writers of the 1950's and 1960's did much to affirm the presence of Jews in American literature. Moreover, the works of such talented authors as Bernard Malamud, Saul Bellow, and Philip Roth helped to establish our definition of American-Jewish fiction. But as Jews became more Americanized, their literature became more an expression of individual talent than of ethnicity. For the past several years, for example, Malamud, Bellow, and Roth have gone their separate literary ways, having little if anything to do with the old themes of marginality and identity. Their writing not only has been accepted by the majority culture but has become an important component of that culture. As the 1960's drew to a close, it was generally acknowledged that the so-called American-Jewish Renaissance was also nearing completion. As Leslie Fiedler observed as early as 1964:

... the moment of triumph for the Jewish writer in the United States has come just when his awareness of himself as a Jew is reaching a vanishing point, when the gesture of rejection seems his last possible connection with his historical past; and the popular acceptance of his alienation as a satisfactory symbol for the human condition threatens to turn it into an affectation, a fashionable cliché.[39]

Indeed, by the late 1960's, most American-Jewish writers were no longer concerned with the proverbial ethnic themes of alienation and acculturation. Interestingly, however, in the past decade several important American-Jewish authors have chosen to redefine and reaffirm their traditional connections to their Jewish heritage.

Just as several decades of successful American-Jewish novels legitimized that particular genre and allowed those who followed the freedom and security to pursue a more eclectic course, the same can be said of American-Jewish auto-biography. The recent generation of writers, no longer concerned with the anx-ieties of belonging or the ambiguities of assimilation, have moved further and further away from the themes and subjects that dominated what we have come to associate with minority literature. Whereas writers of the immigrant generation sought in autobiography a means of linking individual identity with that of the group, and while writers at mid-century used the autobiographical mode to recall what it was like to grow up in the Jewish ghettos of Brownsville and Chicago's West Side, those who have chosen to write autobiography in the last twenty years have had very different—and often divergent—priorities. Some works, like Leslie Fiedler's *Being Busted* (1969) and Norman Podhoretz's *Breaking Ranks* (1978), are politically motivated and need not be of great concern to us in this study. By contrast, Herbert Gold's *My Last Two Thousand Years* (1972) is a personal and imaginative work which returns to questions of Jewish identity— of what it means to be a Jew historically and in present-day America. Still others, such as Podhoretz's earlier *Making It* (1967), Kazin's *Starting Out in the Thirties* (1965) and *New York Jew* (1978), and Irving Howe's *A Margin of Hope* (1982), are chronicles of the literary and sociopolitical climate of their times, as well as personal histories.

Starting Out in the Thirties, Kazin's second autobiography, is a straightforward account of the author's early years of writing and editing, of "starting out" in the wider cultural world of Manhattan. The book's structure is linear and rela-tively simple. Each chapter represents one year and is entitled accordingly: "Part I, 1934," "Part II, 1935," and so forth through 1940 (with the exception of Part V, which covers two years, 1938–1939). The work concludes with a very short epilogue, dated 1945.

Unlike *A Walker in the City*, which is a highly subjective account of places and persons meaningful primarily to the author, *Starting Out* dramatizes events both personal and historical. Family characters again figure in the narrative. For example, the tragic ending of Kazin's unmarried cousin Sophie (abandoned by the one man that took an interest in her, she goes mad and spends the last twenty years of her life in an institution, unable to recognize anyone) forms the nucleus of "Part IV, 1937," and loosely functions as an objective correlative for other, less personal tragedies. Kazin's mother is present too, as are his new bride Natasha and a host of other friends and acquaintances. Yet personal events are juxtaposed throughout with those of literary or cultural import. *Starting Out* contains, for example, many portraits of the leading literary and intellectual figures of the thirties—including James T. Farrell, Mary McCarthy, Nathanael West, Malcolm Cowley, Mark Van Doren, Philip Rahv, Otis Ferguson, and John Chamberlain—and thus captures firsthand the cultural climate of the times. Kazin also writes convincingly of his passion for literature: his excitement, for instance, at the first appearance in America of such "committed" European political novels as Malraux's *Man's Fate* and Silone's *Fontamara*, both of which were published in this country in 1934.

Starting Out, therefore, is perhaps more rewarding as social and intellectual history than as a chronicle of an articulate and sensitive artist struggling with the ambiguities of his identity as a Jew and as an American. Interestingly, however, the central theme of isolation in *A Walker* has not been resolved and is again expressed in *Starting Out*. "Lonely you were born," Kazin laments at the outset of his second autobiography, "and lonely you would die—you were lonely as a Jew and lonely in a strange land."[40] And although there are few such personal confessions, as Kazin recounts his growing success and acceptance in the world "beyond," *Starting Out* concludes with a startling and forceful image of peoplehood and suffering that suddenly brings the reader full circle back to Brownsville, back to Stieglitz's immigrants. In the spring of 1945, Kazin sat in a London theatre, watching the newsreels of the liberated concentration camps. He recalls his reaction:

One day in the spring of 1945, when the war against Hitler was almost won, I sat in a newsreel theater in Piccadilly looking at the first films of newly liberated Belsen. On the screen, sticks in black-and-white prison garb leaned on a wire, staring dreamily at the camera; other sticks shuffled about, or sat vaguely on the ground, next to an enormous pile of bodies, piled up like cordwood, from which protruded legs, arms, heads. A few guards were collected sullenly in a corner, and for a moment a British Army bulldozer was shown digging an enormous hole in the ground. Then the sticks would come back on the screen, hanging on the wire, looking at us.

It was unbearable. People coughed in embarrassment, and in embarrassment many laughed.[41]

Kazin could not have ended his book on a more moving note, nor one that better clarifies for the reader why Kazin was moved to write a book such as *A*

Walker in the City in the first place, why it was necessary for him to recapture the past of his parents' generation—and to link his own history with the tragic history of the diaspora.

Kazin's third autobiography, *New York Jew* (1978), continues where *Starting Out* left off and recounts events up to 1978. Somewhat different in tone and style, *New York Jew* is nevertheless linked thematically with Kazin's two earlier works. Here, for instance, Kazin explains in full his choice of Stieglitz's photograph as frontispiece for *A Walker in the City*:

> I was another slave to Stieglitz's eye. I had become one from the moment I had seen his great photograph "The Steerage" and had imagined my mother as the woman who dominates the composition as she stands on the lower deck draped in an enormous towel, her back always to me. In some way Stieglitz's photographs of old New York possessed my soul, my unconscious past. His was the New York my mother and father had stumbled along as frightened young immigrants. My mother seemed to me frozen forever on that lower deck.[42]

New York Jew is primarily a portrait of the contemporary New York literary and cultural scene; but again and again Kazin moves back in time to explore earlier, more personal issues. Written thirty-three years after the incident that dramatically concluded *Starting Out in the Thirties*, *New York Jew* once more bears witness to Kazin's shock at having discovered the horror of Nazi extermination. For Kazin, the Holocaust would become "the nightmare that would bring everything else into question, that will haunt me to my last breath."[43] Yet Kazin, like Levin, is struck throughout by "the impossibility of finding words for Jewish martyrdom." "I felt," Kazin states at the conclusion of *New York Jew*, "the residual cruelty of the Holocaust. The Jews could not state their case without seeming to overstate it. The world was getting tired of our complaint."[44]

In 1970, Kazin was moved to visit Belsen on the twenty-fifth anniversary of its liberation, and from there, on to Israel "to sweeten the pill." But even here, Kazin worries about Jewish survival: "There is no ease in Zion. There is never any safe homecomings for Jews."[45] Once again, Kazin recalls the image of Stieglitz's Jews and of their—and of his parents'—"overpowering sense of effort, of strain, of will" to survive, be it here in the promised land or in the ghetto of Brownsville.

Although Kazin repeatedly returns to the themes implied in Stieglitz's photograph, *New York Jew* is above all else an intellectual memoir of the literary happenings during the period from 1942 to 1978. Covering as it does over a quarter of a century, *New York Jew*, compared to Kazin's two earlier autobiographical works, is overly long, discursive, and anecdotal without the benefit of a strong narrative line. But the sections dealing with issues of Jewish identity—specifically the Holocaust and Israel—are impassioned and eloquent. More significant, *New York Jew* again demonstrates Kazin's commitment to exploring those subjects and themes that are of particular concern to American Jews.

The autobiographic form, what Kazin called "personal history," allowed him to create "situation rather than plot" and thereby address issues that have been largely ignored by contemporary American-Jewish novelists.[46] Kazin's delineation of the Jewish aspects of his American personality is a significant aspect of his individual story, of his "personal history." Yet Kazin is not alone among American-Jewish autobiographers who have chosen to recount the events of their lives and their understanding of self and society in relation to intrinsically Jewish concerns.

Among the first generation of writers to be born in America, both Kazin and Meyer Levin rely heavily on the motif of return: Kazin to his version of the *shtetl* (Brownsville), and Levin to the birthplace of his parents in Poland and then to Israel. Herbert Gold's *My Last Two Thousand Years* (1972) is another personal account of Jewish return and renewal. Like Levin, Gold discovers at mid-life (he was born in 1924) that one cannot cut oneself off from the past without sacrificing the future. *My Last Two Thousand Years* is Gold's record of that discovery, of his retrieval of Jewish consciousness, of his giving birth, as he states, "to the Jewishness within myself."

Gold, the successful author of over a dozen works of fiction, begins his autobiography with a statement outlining his spiritual turning and return: "By a wide and narrow road I found my way back to an allegiance I didn't possess. Born a Jew in Lakewood, Ohio, I embraced the belief and accusation: America is enough."[47] Like Podhoretz, Gold had spent his life "making it," pursuing the rewards of success in America: "health, love, money, luck, and words." But unlike the self-promotional tone of Podhoretz's *Making It*, *My Last Two Thousand Years* is a painful, careful reassessment of the worth of that success. In reviewing his life, Gold takes stock not only of his assets but of the empty spaces as well: "In the community of girls and the commerce of culture, I forgot I was a writer, a Jew, a man. . . . Like the Hassidic folk singer, I was elsewhere than at home in the Diaspora."[48]

Gold begins to think through the details and circumstances of his life: graduate study, teaching positions, publication successes, two marriages and numerous affairs, travels throughout Europe and Israel. Yet without community or any recognizable purpose, Gold concludes that his past life has been one of disconnection and inauthenticity. "I was dying," Gold concludes, "I could tell by the smells around me."

But Gold is eventually able to emerge renewed from the disarray of his former existence. What saves Gold from total disaffection is the eventual knowledge that he is a Jew and as such shares a history both tragic and beautiful with others of his race: "I did not suddenly learn the faith of my fathers, but I learned the lesson of this faith. It wouldn't shut up my complaining, either, no more than it shut up the complaining of my fathers. But now I also had the reassurance of history which they had given me through their sons and daughters."[49]

Throughout his wanderings Gold encounters fellow Jews in strange places: an ancient tailor in Haiti; a Hungarian-Jewish refugee aboard a steamship to Jerusalem; old, forgotten Jews in Moscow; and young, optimistic *Sabras* in Israel. Despite the trauma of the past and the difficulties of the present, they all seem to share the same stoic, simple response to life and history as that expressed to Gold by an elderly Holocaust survivor in Paris: " 'I lived. I lived.' he said, still not believing it. 'I'm alive.' " In the lesson of Jewish survival, Gold finds hope and compassion: "I was moved by my kind."

Although Gold's basic autobiographical question—"What is a Jew, and why am I that thing?"—is not completely answered in *My Last Two Thousand Years*, the issues of Jewish history and continuity are brought into sharp focus. By the end of *My Last Two Thousand Years*, Gold in Jerusalem is uplifted by his newly discovered connection to Jewish history and to his Jewish faith which links him to past generations: "Being a Jew has come to seem like having a child: I have given birth to the Jewishness within myself. I did not choose it; it has been given me; but I share in the power and pain which it has offered. I am a part of history, not merely a kid on a street corner or a man making out okay. The suffering of others is mine, too."[50]

In *Fathers* (1967), an autobiographical novel, Gold raises the issue of Jewish identity and perhaps answers the question sufficiently in terms of those of the past generation. In *My Last Two Thousand Years* Gold again moves backwards into Jewish history, but only as a means of conveying his present self forward into the community of Jews and of man. Gold offers no definitive answers to the problems of identity. But as is also true for Levin and Kazin, Gold's understanding of himself as a Jew relies on the relationship between the Jewish past and the Jewish present. " . . . I'm not sure what my destiny as a Jew means," Gold concludes, "—or what the destiny of the Jews means—except that it is a unique fate, a peculiar devotion to world and spirit wrapped together. And that I have at last become what I was when my Old Country father and mother in Cleveland submitted to nature and conceived me."[51]

Norman Podhoretz's *Making It* (1967) is the story of its author's quest for, and attainment of, literary fame, success, and money. Podhoretz's up-from-the-ghetto story is one of self-congratulation rather than self-doubt and self-examination. It is also a lively account of contemporary intellectual and sociopolitical events.

There are several obvious comparisons between *Making It* and Kazin's autobiographies. Like *A Walker in the City*, *Making It* chronicles its author's passage from the Jewish section of Brooklyn to the more exclusive reaches of Manhattan. "One of the longest journeys in the world," Podhoretz states at the outset, "is the journey from Brooklyn to Manhattan. . . . " Like Kazin, Podhoretz sought to escape the narrow and limited world of the Jewish ghetto. And like Kazin and Gold, Podhoretz comes to understand that he cannot leave behind the remnants of a past that has become part of his present.

The book's central theme, however, is not identity. *Making It* is essentially a celebration of success in America, the proud boast of a brash young man who wishes to confess the "dirty little secret" of his ambition. Podhoretz wants to share with the world his discovery that "it is better to be a success than a failure. . . . it was better to be rich than to be poor. . . . it was better to be recognized than to be anonymous."[52]

Podhoretz's journey from Brooklyn (where he was born in 1930) to Manhattan took him first to Columbia University, where he was befriended by Lionel Trilling, and where—in his final year—he won a Kellert Fellowship and a Fulbright to continue his studies at Clare College, Cambridge. Upon his return to the States, at the age of twenty-three, Podhoretz became a monthly contributor to *Commentary*. After two years in the Army, he returned to the journal, eventually becoming associate editor and then in 1960—after much infighting and some political intrigue—editor before his thirtieth birthday. Throughout, Podhoretz's unrelentling pursuit of literary fame and distinction dominates his persona, as, for example, in this account of the importance attached to New York social invitations:

Parties were sometimes fun and sometimes not, but fun was beside the point: for me they always served as a barometer of the progress of my career. There were other landmarks besides my first party at Lillian Hellman's. There was my first weekend at Philip Rahv's house in the country; . . . there was my first invitation (at last!) to Hannah Arendt's annual New Year's Eve party; . . . there was my first small dinner party at Mary McCarthy's. . . . And for the sake of these things too, I drove myself to write.[53]

One can easily become offended (or bored) by Podhoretz's repetitive admission to obsessive career climbing. But the author is obviously enjoying his "confessions," and the reader tends to overlook the less substantive aspects of the narrative. More significantly, Podhoretz's climb to literary prominence and his easy adjustment to his success reveal an aspect of the Jewish intellectual personality previously unarticulated in American-Jewish autobiography. As Alvin Rosenfeld in "Inventing the Jew: Notes on Jewish Autobiography" has correctly noted, Podhoretz was one of the first of his generation (that is, American Jews to be born in this country) to understand that the Jewish intellectual can achieve secular success without losing his connections to his Jewish heritage and without agonizing over the inherent contradictions: " . . . with Podhoretz we begin to see an alternative to the Jew as *merely* secular intellectual and catch glimpses of something more, of options within the intellectual life that permit and encourage a return to Jewishness while fully maintaining a stake in the world."[54]

Whereas Kazin and Levin in the 1950's, for example, seemed to dwell on their sense of alienation and exclusion, Podhoretz in the mid-sixties moves easily between the old and the new. As a young man, Podhoretz attends both Columbia University and the Jewish Theological Seminary across the street. As an adult, he becomes the editor of *Commentary*, one of the nation's leading intellectual journals, which also happened to be published under the auspices of the American

Jewish Committee. And although Podhoretz believed *Commentary* needed to be "more general than Jewish in emphasis," he recalled that "it remained explicitly Jewish in part of its contents and identifiably Jewish in the intellectual style. . . . "[55]

By the 1980's, the notion of cultural pluralism had gained wide acceptance. But in the 1960's, Podhoretz was one of the first, as Rosenfeld states, to "show us the affinities, rather than the inevitable separations, between intellectual and Jew."[56] Nevertheless, in *Making It*, this synthesis is inferred more from Podhoretz's demeanor than from any statements he makes. In a 1985 article, however, Podhoretz clearly spelled out the circumstances of the new cultural pluralism he had felt two decades earlier:

No longer was complete assimilation the price of "making it" in America. On the contrary: continued attachment and loyalty to the ethnic culture came to be regarded as a positive value and a personal virtue. In this new climate, it became possible, even easy, to stake a claim in the larger American world and to participate fully in the common culture without cutting the lifeline to one's ancestral roots.[57]

A far cry, it would seem, from the experiences recounted by Ludwig Lewisohn and Anzia Yezierska.

The concept of cultural pluralism and of the "Jewishness" of the New York intellectual becomes a major theme in another recent autobiography, Irving Howe's *A Margin of Hope* (1982). Howe, the quintessential "New York intellectual," had previously set down his recollection of the New York literary and sociopolitical scene, first in his 1968 article for *Commentary*, "The New York Intellectuals, " and again in a section of *World of Our Fathers* (1976). In *A Margin of Hope* Howe delineates explicitly that which was left implicit by Podhoretz: the relationship between one's Jewish roots and the life of the modern intellectual.

A Margin of Hope is Howe's rumination over those forces—both historical and personal—that helped form him as a writer, a socialist, and a Jew. Howe's analysis of intellectual and political currents over five decades (specifically the growth and decline of socialism and radical politics in America) occupies the major portion of the book, but his thoughts about his identity as a Jew give *A Margin of Hope* its individuality and its pathos.

Born of impoverished immigrant parents in 1920 in the Bronx, Howe acknowledges his early ties to the past and to the language of his parents:

In the early thirties—by then I was entering my teens—the East Bronx was still a self-contained little world. . . . Yiddish was spoken everywhere. The English of the young, if unmarred by accent, had its own intonation, the stumbling melody of immigrant speech. A mile or two from my building—I did not know it then—there lived a cluster of Yiddish writers. . . . At the corner newsstands the Yiddish daily, the *Forward*, sold about as well as the *News* and the *Mirror*. . . . [58]

For Howe, the world of culture and ideas was a liberation from the ghetto, as well as "a high calling." Howe retells the now familiar story of a pilgrimage from the outer reaches of New York to the inner circles of Manhattan. His particular journey begins at City College ("where ideology grew wild") and an early involvement with radical politics. After graduation, he spent several months editing *Labor Action*, a four-page weekly socialist tabloid, until he was drafted into the Army and sent to serve out his term of duty in Alaska. Upon his release, Howe returned to New York and to writing for the "movement." Eventually, he placed an essay in *Commentary* on Isaac Rosenfeld's *Passage From Home*— and others followed. By the late 1940's Howe was writing for Dwight Macdonald's *Politics* and on occasion for *Partisan Review*, until he landed a steady job as a book reviewer for *Time*. In the meantime, he began his eclectic career as an author and a critic, publishing books on Sherwood Anderson on the one hand, and Walter Reuther and the United Auto Workers on the other. After Howe had spent several years at *Time*, there came an academic appointment at Brandeis, the editorship of *Dissent*, and many more books.

Throughout *A Margin of Hope*, Howe talks seriously about the issues of politics, literature, the history of ideas, and—in one central chapter—his Jewish identity. As a secular Jew, Howe questions his "authenticity." Early in his career, he gave little thought to the problem: "Some of us like, say, Rahv and me were a strange breed. We knew we were Jews. We had no choice but to remain Jews. . . . But we had no taste for and little interest in Judaism as religion."[59]

After the war, however, the reality of the Holocaust led "to timid reconsiderations of what it meant to be Jewish" and the acknowledgment that "the problems" of Jewish identity cut more deeply: "Our earlier failure to face them with sufficient candor had left us their victims, had made us 'inauthentic' Jews who gave the Jewish 'situation' neither serious thought nor unblocked emotion."[60]

Howe begins, therefore, to acknowledge his relationship to his past and to his religion, a process he labels his "reconquest" of Jewishness. He is quick to point out, however, that this "reconquest" is not merely the nostalgic turning of a middle-aged man back to his roots. It is rather an existential act, "an ordeal of the will," to use Howe's term, intended to bring the author closer to his own beliefs—no matter how unorthodox they may be—and to his past.

Howe's repossession of his Jewish consciousness manifests itself first by a devotion to the "lost cause" of Yiddish literature, "to preserve a Jewish culture derived from the Judaic past." In the early fifties Howe began to edit and translate Yiddish poetry and fiction with the poet Eliezer Greenberg. As a result, he discovered not only the beauty of Yiddish poetry but a direct connection with his own history: " . . . reading more deeply in the Yiddish poets helped me to feel at ease, if not with myself, then at least with my past. . . . Yiddish poetry . . . helped me strike a truce with, and then extend a hand to, the world of my father."[61]

Concomitant with this renewed interest in the past was Howe's increased empathy with the State of Israel, a bond that he did not feel at the time of its birth. Howe was not "one of those who danced in the streets when Ben Gurion made his famous pronouncement that the Jews, like other peoples, now had a state of their own."[62] But by 1967, Howe—almost ashamedly—admits his pride and "thrill" at Israel's victory.

Nevertheless, Howe's "reconquest" is both limited and, by his own admission, problematic: "How much easier my 'reconquest of Jewishness' would have been if God, with or without a clap of thunder, had appeared one day to tap me on the shoulder and declare me his own!"[63] What Howe has become, he finally concludes, is a "partial" Jew, true to himself, if to no organized group, "savoring the goodness of the thinning tradition of Yiddish" and acknowledging his place in the "net and memory of expectation" that has formed Jewish life and tradition throughout history.

In the end Howe offers no solutions to the "problems" of Jewish identity. Nor does he put forth any program for younger Jews: "they would have to improvise and scamper about, like others before them." "My own hope," Howe concludes, "was to achieve some equilibrium with that earlier self which had started with childhood Yiddish . . . and then turned away in adolescent shame."[64]

There is no ultimate "conquest" of the Jewish self in A Margin of Hope. But there is understanding that is, even within its limitations, both human and profound. As such, the book goes beyond the political or intellectual memoir to become true autobiography: an affirmation of identity, a testament to a life lived, and a full and honest explanation of how the author came to be the person he now is.

IV

"Autobiography," James Olney maintains, "renders in a peculiarly direct and faithful way the experience and the vision of a people. . . . "[65] Its study offers a revealing—albeit highly individualistic—portrait of the intellectual and emotional history of that people. In spite of the eclectic nature of each of the works examined in this study, all share certain concerns and preoccupations, perhaps best epitomized by Howe's ultimate insistence on a "repossession" of the Jewish aspects of his personality. He was not the first to do so, for a generation earlier, Ludwig Lewisohn and Anzia Yezierska also sought a reconciliation with their past religious and cultural traditions. Like Howe, Levin, Kazin, Gold, and to a lesser extent Podhoretz have demonstrated a particular interest in exploring Jewish identity in relation to their faith, to their collective history, and to recent world events. And although it is too early to determine how the next generation of Jewish writers will assess their own lives (should they choose to write autobiography), it is apparent that for the last twenty years, American-Jewish autobiographers have chosen, as Irving Howe has envisioned, "to extend a hand" to the world of their fathers.

NOTES

1. James Olney, "Autobiography and the Cultural Moment: A Thematic, Historical, and Bibliographical Introduction," p. 13.
2. Mary Antin, Introduction, *The Promised Land*, p. xiii.
3. William L. Howarth. "Some Principles of Autobiography," p. 92.
4. Antin, op. cit., p. xi.
5. James Craig Holte, "The Representative Voice: Autobiography and the Ethnic Experience," p. 33.
6. Antin, *The Promised Land*, p. 1.
7. Ibid., pp. 32–33.
8. Ibid., p. 125.
9. Ibid., p. 162.
10. Ibid., p. 181.
11. Ibid., p. 364.
12. Ibid., p. 86.
13. Ibid., p. 74.
14. Ludwig Lewisohn, *Up Stream: An American Chronicle*, pp. 50–51.
15. Ibid., p. 77.
16. Ibid., p. 122.
17. Ibid., pp. 122–123.
18. Ibid., p. 145.
19. Ibid., p. 240.
20. Seymour Lainoff, *Ludwig Lewisohn*, p. 121.
21. Irving Howe, *World of Our Fathers*, p. 270.
22. Anzia Yezierska, *Red Ribbon on a White Horse*, pp. 216–217.
23. Ibid., p. 203.
24. Ibid., p. 217.
25. Ibid., p. 220.
26. Allen Guttmann, *The Jewish Writer in America: Assimilation and the Crisis of Identity*, p. 88.
27. Ibid., p. 90.
28. Alfred Kazin, *A Walker in the City*, pp. 66–67.
29. Ibid., p. 60.
30. Ibid., p. 90.
31. Ibid., p. 172.
32. Meyer Levin, *In Search*, p. 69.
33. Ibid., p. 370.
34. Ibid., p. 5.
35. Ibid., p. 173.
36. Ibid., p. 175.
37. Ibid., p. 536.
38. Ibid., p. 171.
39. Leslie Fiedler, *Waiting for the End*, p. 66.
40. Alfred Kazin, *Starting Out in the Thirties*, p. 45.
41. Ibid., p. 166.
42. Alfred Kazin, *New York Jew*, p. 140.

43. Ibid., p. 39.
44. Ibid., p. 436.
45. Ibid., p. 424.
46. Alfred Kazin, "The Self as History: Reflections on Autobiography," p. 36.
47. Herbert Gold, *My Last Two Thousand Years*, p. 7.
48. Ibid., p. 195.
49. Ibid., p. 223.
50. Ibid., p. 245.
51. Ibid., p. 246.
52. Norman Podhoretz, *Making It*, p. xi.
53. Ibid., pp. 247–248.
54. Alvin Rosenfeld, "Inventing the Jew: Notes on Jewish Autobiography," p. 147.
55. Podhoretz, op. cit., p. 309.
56. Rosenfeld, op. cit., p. 147.
57. Norman Podhoretz, "English is the Escape Passage from Ethnic Ghetto," *Tampa Tribune* (October 13, 1985), p. 3-C.
58. Irving Howe, *A Margin of Hope: An Intellectual Autobiography*, p. 2.
59. Ibid., p. 252.
60. Ibid., p. 258.
61. Ibid., pp. 267, 269.
62. Ibid., p. 276.
63. Ibid., p. 277.
64. Ibid., p. 269.
65. Olney, "Autobiography and the Cultural Moment," p. 13.

BIBLIOGRAPHY

Antin, Mary. *The Promised Land*. Boston and New York: Houghton Mifflin, 1912.
Fiedler, Leslie. *Waiting for the End*. New York: Stein and Day, 1964.
Gold, Herbert. *My Last Two Thousand Years*. New York: Random House, 1972.
Guttmann, Allen. *The Jewish Writer in America: Assimilation and the Crisis of Identity*. New York: Oxford University Press, 1971.
Holte, James Craig. "The Representative Voice: Autobiography and the Ethnic Experience." *Journal of the Society for the Study of the Multi-Ethnic Literature of the United States* (MELUS). 9. (1982), pp. 24–46.
Howarth, William L. "Some Principles of Autobiography." *Autobiography: Essays Theoretical and Critical*, ed. James Olney. Princeton, New Jersey: Princeton University Press, 1980, pp. 84–114.
Howe, Irving. *A Margin of Hope: An Intellectual Autobiography*. New York: Harcourt Brace Jovanovich, 1982.
———. *World of Our Fathers*. New York: Harcourt Brace Jovanovich, 1976.
Kazin, Alfred. *New York Jew*. New York: Vintage Books, 1979.
———. "The Self as History: Reflections in Autobiography." *The American Autobiography: A Collection of Critical Essays*. ed. Albert E. Stone. Englewood Cliffs, New Jersey: Prentice-Hall, 1981, pp. 31–43.
———. *Starting Out in the Thirties*. Boston: Little, Brown, 1965.
———. *A Walker in the City*. New York: Harcourt, Brace, 1951.
Lainoff, Seymour. *Ludwig Lewisohn*. Boston: Twayne Publishers, 1982.

Levin, Meyer. *In Search.* 1950; rpt. New York: Pocket Books, 1973.

Lewisohn, Ludwig. *Up Stream: An American Chronicle.* New York: Boni and Liveright, 1922.

Olney, James. "Autobiography and the Cultural Moment: A Thematic, Historical, and Bibliographical Introduction." *Autobiography: Essays Theoretical and Critical,* ed. James Olney. Princeton, New Jersey: Princeton University Press, 1980, pp. 3–27.

Podhoretz, Norman. "English Is the Escape Passage from Ethnic Ghetto." *Tampa Tribune.* (October 13, 1985), p. 3-C (1985 News America Syndicate).

————. *Making It.* New York: Random House, 1967.

Rosenfeld, Alvin. "Inventing the Jew: Notes on Jewish Autobiography." *The American Autobiography: A Collection of Critical Essays,* ed. Albert E. Stone. Englewood Cliffs, New Jersey: Prentice-Hall, 1981, pp. 133–156.

Yezierska, Anzia, *Red Ribbon on a White Horse.* New York: Charles Scribner's Sons, 1950.

FOR FURTHER READING

Angoff, Charles. *When I Was a Boy in Boston.* New York: Beechhurst Press, 1947.

Bellow, Saul. *To Jerusalem and Back: A Personal Account.* New York: Viking Press, 1976.

Charyn, Jerome. *Metropolis.* New York: Putnam, 1986.

Chyet, Stanley F., ed. *Lives and Voices: A Collection of American Jewish Memoirs.* Philadelphia: Jewish Publication Society of America, 1972.

Cowan, Paul. *An Orphan in History: Retrieving a Jewish Legacy.* Garden City, New York: Doubleday, 1982.

Diamond, Sigmund. *In Quest: Journal of an Unquiet Pilgrimage.* New York: Columbia University Press, 1980.

Eisenberg, Azriel, ed. *The Golden Land: A Literary Portrait of American Jewry, 1654 to the Present.* New York and London: Thomas Yoseloff, 1964.

Fiedler, Leslie A. *Being Busted.* New York: Stein and Day, 1969.

Goldstein, Israel. *My World as a Jew: The Memoirs of Israel Goldstein.* New York: Herzl Press, 1984.

Hecht, Ben. *A Child of the Century.* New York: Simon and Schuster, 1954.

Jastrow, Marie. *Looking Back: The American Dream Through Immigrant Eyes.* New York: W. W. Norton, 1986.

Lisitzky, Ephraim E. *In the Grip of Cross-Currents,* trans. Moshe Kohn and Jacob Sloan. New York: Bloch, 1959.

Neugeboren, Jay. *Parentheses: An Autobiographical Journey.* New York: Dutton, 1970.

Podhoretz, Norman. *Breaking Ranks: A Political Memoir.* New York: Harper and Row, 1979.

Ribalow, Harold U., ed. *Autobiographies of American Jews.* Philadelphia: Jewish Publication Society of America, 1965.

Rosenberg, Bernard and Ernest Goldstein, eds. *Creators and Disturbers: Reminiscences by Jewish Intellectuals of New York.* New York: Columbia University Press, 1982.

Sanders, Ronald. *Reflections on a Teapot: The Personal History of a Time.* New York: Harper and Row, 1972.

Simon, Kate. *Bronx Primitive: Portraits in a Childhood.* New York: Viking Press, 1982.

————. *A Wider World: Portraits in an Adolescence.* New York: Harper and Row, 1986.

12

Images of America in American-Jewish Fiction

Sanford E. Marovitz

The images of America reflected and refracted through myriad writings of American-Jewish authors over approximately the past century are no less varied than the authors who created them. Any attempt to reduce these images to a single composite portrait of the country would lead either to so general or so confusing a vision as to be nearly meaningless, either an easy symbol for a multi-faceted ideal or a palimpsest with innumerable and often incompatible colors and forms.

But to deny the presence of a uniform national vision is not to deny the existence of certain themes and features common to the writings of many American-Jewish authors which deal directly or indirectly with a specifically American milieu. Among these, from the earliest enduring fiction published in the last decade of the nineteenth century to that of the present, the most important theme by far explores the question of *identity*. "Am I or do I want to be a secularized American, an assimilated Jew, or a Jewish alien on the margin of a secular national culture reflective of a chiefly Christian past?" The identity of a Jewish character is determinable not alone through self-knowledge but through his or her relation to *home,* that is, to the United States or any small part of it, whether adoptive or otherwise, whether the character is first-generation American or later. Thus it may be seen that the choices confronting American Jews seventy-five to a hundred years ago were considerably different from those faced by American Jews of the past quarter century, but the question of identity has not disappeared. The choices now are more subtle and often less consciously made, but they generate frustrating ambivalences and often constitute the central moral issues of contemporary American-Jewish fiction.

Three other themes in which a vision of America is prominent are corollary to that of identity. First is the *money* theme, which comprises both the need of money for subsistence in the proletarian fiction of Michael Gold, Tillie Olsen, and Anzia Yezierska as well as the drive for wealth and power in the writing of Abraham Cahan, Samuel Ornitz, and Budd Schulberg. Although they have not avoided the creation of distasteful and even repugnant Jewish characters, a forthrightness for which they have often drawn sharp criticism from embittered Jewish readers, the authors employing this theme include in their fiction no Shylocks, Fagins, or Svengalis, those gentile caricatures that have contributed markedly to the Jewish stereotype still evolving in the anti-Semitic imagination. The quest for wealth and power is rarely the dominant theme, and even when it is central, a psychological issue is usually embedded within it—as with Levinsky's irresolvable ambivalence in Cahan's *The Rise of David Levinsky* (1917) and Sammy Glick's insatiable compulsion for *more* in Schulberg's *What Makes Sammy Run?* (1941). Both Levinsky and Sammy have fled backgrounds in which their lives were largely governed by Hebrew traditions in narrowly Jewish communities where poverty was typically so severe that bare subsistence was often in question. Ironically, the warmth of faith through tradition and community in the European *shtetl* and urban American tenement was characteristically accompanied by the cold barrenness of poverty in the same environment, and these two extremes were not compatible in the minds and hearts of many immigrants. The tension between them provided a second corollary theme, the traditional role of the Jewish *community* under compelling new circumstances of displacement in America. This idea is especially pertinent in fiction that deals with the lives of immigrants from Eastern Europe around the turn of the last century, but it has reappeared in modified form among more recent writers as well, including Isaac Bashevis Singer, Cynthia Ozick, and Chaim Potok, among whom tradition and community are treated with great sympathy.

The third theme evolves from the turmoil generated by the conflict inherent in the quest itself. Unless a character can be comfortable in hypocrisy—no conscience, no turmoil—neither side of the warring psyche permanently gives way to the other. Under certain circumstances one set of values dominates, and under others the opposing set takes hold. The conflict may be depicted in terms of practical versus ideal, secular American versus Orthodox, innovative versus traditional, and so forth. Whatever the pairing, when the two sides are represented as extreme in the same mind and both are attempting over an extended period of time to prevail, the psyche itself ultimately succumbs, and a *mental breakdown* results. Such is the case, for example, with Saul Bellow's eponymous hero Herzog, Philip Roth's Portnoy and Kepesch in *Portnoy's Complaint* (1969) and *The Breast* (1972), and E. L. Doctorow's Susan and Daniel Isaacson in *The Book of Daniel* (1971). Also, variations on the theme of psychological breakdown and derangement appear in this fiction, for they are not always attributable primarily to a Jewish identity crisis, though a character's Judaism may be a factor, as with David Schearl's father in Henry Roth's *Call It Sleep* (1934) and Sol Nazerman in Edward Lewis Wallant's *The Pawnbroker* (1961). In another of Wallant's novels, however, *The Children at the Gate* (1964), and in Nathanael West's *The Day of the Locust* (1939), the characters who suffer the breakdowns are not Jewish at all. In most of these novels, America as setting plays a singularly violent role.

Finally, a regional theme that has been largely overlooked in American-Jewish fiction is *the West,* the huge expanse of America that lies roughly between the Mississippi and the Pacific. Because with few exceptions, Jewish authors in this country have lived and worked in the urban East, little attention has been given to an overview of their individual pictures of the West, and no comprehensive grasp of their American images can be attained without considering those. Because the identity theme and its corollaries also appear in this fiction with a different regional setting, they contribute significantly to a specifically western vision in American-Jewish fiction.

THE FIRST HALF CENTURY

Jewish fiction in America originated on the East Coast, most notably in New York at the end of the nineteenth century. By the time that mass Eastern-European immigration began about 1880, New York City already held a population of some eighty thousand Jews, but within the next thirty years nearly twenty times that number would enter the United States from Europe, and most of these, too, would settle in and around several nuclear tenement areas of New York. Among the first wave of Russian immigrants to arrive on this continent was a young Jewish socialist who had been educated in Vilna, the intellectual center of Lithuania, before he assumed a position as provincial leader. Finding himself under suspicion for his socialist activities, the twenty-two-year-old Abraham Cahan fled to America in 1882, the same year that Emma Lazarus published *Songs of a Semite,* the first book of Jewish poems written by an American Jew. Cahan was soon to become the most influential Yiddish editor and journalist in the nation, an advisor to immigrants on issues ranging from labor problems to domestic squabbles and personal hygiene, with much of his counsel appearing in the pages of the *Forward,* of which he was editor for nearly fifty years.

Cahan's first story in English, "A Providential Match," was read and praised by William Dean Howells following its initial publication in 1895 (it was also included three years later in Cahan's *The Imported Bridegroom and Other Stories of the New York Ghetto*). In this story, Rouvke Arbel immigrates to America, becomes a successful peddler after a few years in the Bowery, and changes his name to Robert Friedman, which he has printed on a business card. Quickly Americanized, he nevertheless suffers from a "stretching" heart, consequently hires a *shadchen* (marriage broker), and pays to have a bride brought to him from the Old World. When she arrives, however, she steps from the boat, her arm entwined with that of a Russian student, and the distraught bachelor is left with neither the girl nor the costs of bringing her over. He is back where he began but poorer. Such loneliness and longing characterize many of Cahan's figures. Occasionally, as in "A Ghetto Wedding" and "A Sweatshop Romance," two lonely hearts find each other, but often at least one of the principals is left in despair, as in "The Imported Bridegroom," "Circumstances," and "A Providential Match." On the one hand, America offers freedom to move in one's own direction, but on the other, it reduces or undermines the security that comes through a community tightly knit with the customs and rituals of one's faith.

The despondency is particularly striking in Cahan's two American novels. *Yekl: A Tale of the New York Ghetto* (1896) was praised by Howells when he read it in manuscript, but despite his recommendation, Cahan found it so difficult to publish in English that he resorted to bringing it out serially in Yiddish before it was finally accepted by an American publisher (D. Appleton). Though a sensitive young man when he first arrives in America, Yekl is anxious to slough off the green horns of an immigrant and become a Yankee as quickly as possible. First goes his Yiddish name in favor of Jake; then, after sending for his wife and child, he forsakes them in the New World, probably dooming himself to a bleak future with a new spouse he had met in a dance hall. He has been Americanized.

For an author immersed in worldly affairs, a man who was writing English fiction in his fourth language (after Yiddish, Russian, and German), *Yekl* is a good novel, even an extraordinary one, but it is short and relatively crude. In *The Rise of David Levinsky* (1917), the crudeness is nearly gone; indeed, *Levinsky* is certainly the first major American-Jewish novel and one of the most important ethnic novels published in this country. It is a long, encyclopedic work narrated by an egocentric millionaire with enough money to buy anything but love and peace of soul. Levinsky is in many ways a despicable character, a robber baron and adherent of Herbert Spencer's theory of Social Darwinism. Levinsky was a talmudic scholar before leaving his native Russia for America, but once he is situated in the United States, he rapidly embarks on a passage of commercial and social exploitation that nearly dehumanizes him. Through a combination of industry, knavery, shrewdness, risk, and luck, Levinsky transforms himself from a penniless immigrant into a plutocratic industrialist, and although his ethical standards are often far from admirable, fundamentally this rich, hypocritical, secularized Jew commands more than a little of the reader's sympathy and respect. Why? Not only has he succeeded amid fierce competitors whose commercial behavior and moral values are akin to his, but also the persistent ambivalence to which he is subject reflects that of many twentieth-century American readers, thus making him an easy character with whom to identify. They, too, suffer from a spiritual dislocation; having cut themselves away from the faith of their past, they have nevertheless found no binding or directional force that provides a truly gratifying and fulfilling emotional equivalent. A million dollars cannot sustain a hungry soul, Levinsky discovers, but Cahan does not condemn America for giving him the opportunity to learn it for himself.

Although Cahan was the most compelling American-Jewish fiction writer of his generation, others with varying degrees of talent were publishing novels and stories on Jewish themes early in the century. Some of the stories in Herman Bernstein's collection, *In the Gates of Israel* (1902), seem derivative of Cahan's tales but lack his power; in "A Ghetto Romance," for example, Shimshen has come from Russia to "the heart of the [New York] Ghetto," where he works sixteen-hour days heaving flour barrels. In America for three years, Shimshen is still but twenty-five; he is lonely and nostalgic. After learning that Esther, whom he loved when they were children, has also come to America, he is deeply stirred; his longing for her reawakens and merges with the recollection of "the very prayers he once loved and knew so well by heart." "He felt that something was stirring within his breast—rising, as it were, from a long-protracted sleep—and it seemed to him as though Sabbath candles illumined his soul, and something carried him onward, onward, until he suddenly found himself beside one of the neighboring synagogues."[1] The story, which turns more heavily upon coincidence than credibility will allow, is one of the many in Bernstein's collection that employs the "overriding theme" that Stanley F. Chyet has identified in early American-Jewish fiction; he calls it "the wrench of change"—emigration from a dying feudalistic, tradition-based, familiar, and generally rural European culture to a democratic, capitalistic, rapidly developing urban one.[2] As the fiction suggests, especially that which deals with the immigrants who had recently come from Eastern Europe, a severe sense of alienation affected even the most optimistic and adaptable new American Jews. They felt the effects of ties new and old, but from the old ones they had all but broken away, and the new were still so tenuous and superficial as to provide little moral or psychological stability.

Artistically more successful than Bernstein and contemporary with him were Elias Tobenkin, Sidney L. Nyburg, and James Oppenheim. Tobenkin's *Witte Arrives* (1916) relates the success through Americanization of an ambitious young Jewish immigrant who comes as a child to a small town in the Midwest from Russia, attends college, and from there goes to ever larger cities—"N____," Chicago, New York—to work for newspapers. Although he feels a tie to his Jewish past, after his wife dies he prepares to marry again but out of the faith, which clearly reveals the extent of his American assimilation. In *The Chosen People* (1917), published the same year as *Levinsky,* Sidney L. Nyburg, a native of Baltimore, explores several controversial issues of his day including Zionism, the relation of racial to religious Judaism, and the apparently unbridgeable chasm between the well-to-do Jewish socialites of German descent and the downtown Russian Jews. The central figure of this novel is a naive and idealistic young Reform rabbi who serves to a large extent as a community figurehead in the synagogue where he is employed; his nemesis is a secularized Jewish attorney, a skeptic, who professes that the only viable course for the Jewish people lies in Zionism. *The Chosen People* is a particularly noteworthy novel not only for its thematic complexity but also for its Baltimore setting; from it comes a rare glimpse of Jewish life outside the major northern cities early in the century.

Nevertheless, the conflicts are not unique to Baltimore or the South, for they deal with the same basic problems that the Jews face in New York and Chicago. The Yiddish-speaking Orthodox living in poverty on the East Side are employed by the culturally if not socially assimilated Reform Jews uptown, and both groups are ultimately subject to the dictates of Baltimore's wealthy gentiles. If the problems are similar, the pace of life is slower, and the actions are carried out on a smaller scale. Although the workers strike for unionization and the poor suffer in their overcrowded tenements as they do in the larger northern cities, a central concern in *The Chosen People* is the welfare of Baltimore as a single community, an urban attitude seldom evident in the city novels written by Nyburg's Jewish contemporaries. Individual characters from different milieus are more aware of each other in Baltimore and of the relations among them as community members than is ordinarily the case in the work of, say, Cahan and Yezierska, for example, both of whom used New York settings for their fiction. But the idealism of Nyburg's young rabbi is squelched as effectively in Baltimore as it might have been elsewhere, and by the end of the novel, Rabbi Graetz seems ready to continue guiding his hypocritical uptown congregation largely in their ethical terms rather than his own.

A more implacable idealist of the period is portrayed in James Oppenheim's *Doctor Rast* (1909), less a novel than a series of episodes that center on the life of a dedicated doctor barely earning a living in the tenement district of New York's lower East Side. Oppenheim seems to have been strongly influenced both critically and thematically by William Dean Howells in his manner of weaving social problems, graphically realistic description of urban squalor, and philanthropic idealism into the fabric of his novel, but his own attachment to Judaism adds a crucial strand to his narrative that Howells only touched upon. In one episode, Doctor Rast travels a full moral circle from socialistic commitment to the tenement-bound Jewish poor, to despair over his frustrated efforts to improve their lot, to the idea of settling more comfortably and securely into a home and practice outside the city, and finally to re-identifying with the Jewish community.

This occurs when a ''Jew-jammed'' excursion boat ironically named *Old Glory* catches fire on the East River and burns for thirty hours, injuring and killing thousands of poor from the tenements who had boarded her for a ride up the river. Dr. Rast has grown so discouraged by the endless scenes of poverty among the tenements that he is ready to accept an offer to practice in a quiet small-town environment, but when the accident necessitates his aid for the injured, he realizes that love and brotherhood govern his life, and that his job is among the poor where he can help bring God ''down into the dust of things, . . . the commonplace,'' where He can be seen in each living being.

One of the more enduring authors of Cahan's generation notably exemplifies this point in both her life and work. Like Cahan, Anzia Yezierska arrived in America late in the nineteenth century from the Pale and, still a child, settled with her family on the lower East Side. Unable to endure the Old World tyranny of her father, a talmudic scholar who left to the women such practical concerns as providing a living and taking care of the family, Yezierska ran away from home before she was twenty in order to take advantage of the liberty that she believed America offered to all of its citizens. She committed herself early to realizing the intrinsic possibilities of the American Dream. Living through a period of abject poverty, she nevertheless managed to acquire a university education and published her first story in 1915. A number of others that appeared over the next few years were collected in her first volume of tales, *Hungry Hearts* (1920), many of which reflect her own ambivalence between her awakened sense of freedom to live independently and the compelling attraction of familial mores she had left behind in the ghetto. Paradoxically, the ghetto had become a part of herself, and through it—like the unnamed narrator of her early short story "America and I"—she "found America" and "began to build a bridge of understanding" between native citizens and immigrants like herself. This "bridge" helped her to answer the questions that had been plaguing her: "Who am I? What am I? What do I want with my life? Where is America? Is there an America? What is this wilderness in which I am lost?"[3] America for her became a land of both possibility and disillusion, one in which she never fully found the identity she sought.

Like most of her heroines, the leading figure of Yezierska's best novel, *Bread Givers* (1925), is partly autobiographical; Sara Smolinsky from Hester Street flees home, struggles through night school while working long, wearying hours in a laundry, and at last enters college. Yet after a while she discovers that happiness has not come and that she cannot leave Hester Street behind: "Even in college I had not escaped from the ghetto," she tearfully laments. After graduating with an estimable prize won in an essay contest, Sara returns to the ghetto as a teacher but still cannot find happiness because she recognizes that her non-conformist assertion of independence as both a woman and a Jew has created a barrier that isolates her from nearly everyone. Indeed, she begins to fear that her father may have been right, after all, in his patriarchal condescension toward women: "Maybe after all my puffing myself up that I was smarter, more self-sufficient than the rest of the world—wasn't Father right? He always preached, a woman alone couldn't enter Heaven. 'It says in the Torah: *A woman without a man is less than nothing.* No life on earth, no hope of Heaven.'"[4] Eventually Sara finds happiness by marrying the principal of her school and restoring relations with her father.

Unfortunately for the verisimilitude of her novel, however, Reb Moishe Smolinsky is not simply a tyrant as Yezierska'a own father might have been, but a *luftmensch* with a memory only for Torah and Talmud, a ludicrous Dickensian composite of unmitigated vanity and arrogance. The extremes to which Yezierska goes in all of her portraits lead her to create caricatures rather than characters; her heroines are either rhapsodic over their idealism or in a state of nearly total despair; her male figures (one is hard put to call them heroes) are with occasional exception coarse, materialistic, vain, or exploitive of women—often all of these. In *Arrogant Beggar* (1927) the heroine is again an isolated figure alternating between exhilaration and despair, a young woman forced by circumstances to become a domestic in the home of a hypocritical wealthy philanthropist, also a woman. In this novel it is not exploitive men but institutionalized charity that undermines true American democracy among the poor, who are treated more as serfs than as citizens in Mrs. Hellman's Home for Working Girls. Adele Lindner finds internationalized chaos in effect when she enters the Home. Eventually she succeeds in becoming independent, but as with Sara in *Bread Givers,* she cannot do it outside the ghetto among educated people like herself; instead, "Right here—in the heart of the tenements, where everything is so ugly and alike, this was the place to start something with Muhmenkeh's spirit in it" (Muhmenkeh is the name of a poor, saintly old woman who has recently died).[5] In Yezierska's fiction money is important chiefly because it provides for independence and freedom, not power, as it does in *Levinsky.*

Although Yezierska acquired a great deal of money fast when Hollywood offered her a contract for *Hungry Hearts,* the pull of the ghetto was too strong for her; following a short stay in California, where she could not be comfortable, she returned to New York and continued writing, but in the early 1930's her output diminished and her reputation waned until a recent revival of interest in her work revitalized it. According to Alice Kessler-Harris,

Yezierska ended her life convinced that her obsession to lift herself out of material poverty had resulted in poverty of the soul. . . . She had rejected family life and violated cherished Jewish tradition. In what may be a tribute to the power of cultural heritage, as well as to the folly of chasing after the American dream, she acknowledged finally the truth of her father's conviction that fire and water would not mix. "Hell," she wrote, "is trying to do what you can't, trying to be what you're not."[6]

As this statement suggests, Yezierska's basic problem was a matter of identity in a free America.

In one sense, of course, her success as a female author during her own day made her a writer ahead of her time rather than one of the last of a Jewish immigrant generation, and thematically she occasionally sounds chords that later authors, too, employ, apart even from issues related to feminism. Her pejoratively phrased image of the melting pot in *Arrogant Beggar,* for example, anticipated Michael Gold's description of his neighborhood in *Jews Without Money* (1930), though by a matter of only three years: "Negroes, Chinese, Gypsies, Turks, Germans, Irish, Jews—and there was even an American on our street."[7] Whereas in Yezierska's family her father was the ultra-Orthodox observer of Hebrew tradition, in Gold's family it was his mother, but in both, the religious home was oppressive. Yezierska turned away from it to secular education but was ultimately distraught in her ambivalence; Gold (born Irwin Granich), charged with idealism, turned to socialism as a young man, following what appears to have been a sudden awakening to new possibilities described only on the final page of *Jews Without Money,* a fictionalized account of his childhood on the East Side.

For Gold's narrator as a boy, school is a jail, a punishment for youth, and despite his precocity, he refuses to continue his education after graduating from elementary school. His most important and influential lesson comes from his father: "It's better to be dead in this country than not to have money."[8] In *Jews*

Without Money, Gold portrays an America governed by corruption, intimidated by violence, and humiliated by the givers of charity. "America is so rich and fat," he writes, "because it has eaten the tragedy of millions of immigrants," and "The East Side, for children, was a world plunged in eternal war."[9] There is nothing beautiful in the street-and-tenement life described in Gold's narrative, no charm of worship, no inspiring glow of sabbath candles beside a meager table made sufficient by the warmth of family love and Hebrew tradition. According to Michael Harrington, Gold purposely minimized this quality of ghetto life at the turn of the century, this "resilience and strength which was [*sic*] nurtured even in the midst of hunger," but unfortunately, Harrington does not explain why.[10] He does indicate, however, that the book is "faithful to the actual experiences of [Gold's] childhood," which suggests that the author's understating of familial and communal inner strength in the ghetto was done to heighten the contrast between the dehumanizing alienation caused by poverty and the humanizing warmth of brotherhood possible through a radical change to communism.[11]

Gold's naturalistic description of the ghetto simultaneously recalls the Bowery life of Stephen Crane's *Maggie* (1893) and anticipates the radical novels that were to follow during the next decade. Whereas Crane had emphasized man's animalistic nature on the lowest level of society, Gold never loses sight of the economic injustice that underlies the existence of abject poverty in a nation of plenty. If Crane's Bowery is a place of derelicts, saloons, punks, and streetwalkers, Gold's lower East Side is largely a world of moneyless families striving for sustenance. He, too, includes the punks and prostitutes in his panorama of ghetto life, but his focus is on deprivation as a consequence of the unjust distribution of wealth rather than upon man's innately carnal nature.

In this respect, he might also be contrasted with Samuel Ornitz, whose anonymous *Haunch Paunch and Jowl* (1923) had been published seven years earlier. In Ornitz's novel, the narrator is Meyer Hirsch, who stands largely as the author's persona. Like Gold's narrative, *Haunch Paunch and Jowl* is in part the story of growing up in the ghetto, but Ornitz carries his hero all the way to the top; Hirsch's account is a *Bildungsroman* in which he exposes his passage through a series of stages from boyhood gangland to corrupt jurisprudence as his wealth, prestige, and power accumulate along the way. Ambition governs his life, and it must be satisfied at any cost. From a shrewd, manipulative child he becomes a lecherous adult, taking advantage of any women who fall within his sphere. In his hands, money reproduces itself quickly; it buys him ever-increasing influence, and as his power expands, so does his physical bulk. By the conclusion of his narrative he waddles from one room to another altogether preoccupied with creature comforts. Hirsch's philosophy is cynical and pragmatic: "money works and money talks in America," and "idealism is the refuge of the incompetent."[12] He becomes "a Professional Jew" in emulation of the successful "Professional Irishman," capitalizing on his religion, not his faith, and promoting obligations for advancement.[13] In America, one's religion or profession readily becomes one's identity tag, and Hirsch takes exploitive advantage of it. In personality and character, Hirsch is akin to Levinsky, motivated by a combination of vanity, lust, self-aggrandizement, and greed, though he does not suffer from the torment of loneliness that plagues Cahan's millionaire industrialist. In commencing his "autobiography," Hirsch informs us immediately that he is a pathological liar and leaves it up to us to distinguish truth when it appears; clearly, Ornitz intends that we find his narrator obnoxious from the outset.[14] Through his shrewdness, Hirsch insinuates himself into the American legal and political infrastructure, which enables him to exert his influence by taking advantage of the very systems that were devised to protect the popular interests.

Hirsch's illicit exploitation of American possibilities has led Sam B. Girgus to identify Ornitz as one of several novelists for whom he finds no place in what he calls a "New Covenant" of American-Jewish authors. In *The New Covenant: Jewish Writers and the American Idea* (1984), Girgus proposes that most notable American-Jewish writers of the past century have subscribed to a set of values which upholds "the American Way" and gives substance to the possibilities inherent in "the American Dream." The authors sharing in "the New Covenant" accentuate such ideals as equality, democracy, individualism, justice, and freedom, though he acknowledges that as these ideals are represented by the various writers, they are often beshadowed and tarnished by the realities of American life.

Interpreting Henry Roth's *Call It Sleep* (1934) as an initiation novel in which David Schearl struggles into rebirth and restoration to his Jewish faith, Girgus sees Roth clearly among the mainstream authors of "the New Covenant." He says that "*Call It Sleep* constitutes a major step toward establishing the tradition of the New Covenant between Jewish writers and intellectuals and the American idea."[15] He is aware that with this interpretation he is contradicting some of Roth's own statements on what he had in mind when drafting the novel, but those statements were made in interviews long after the work was published, and Girgus reasonably but politely overrules them. Roth said that the dynamic climax in which young David is saved from accidental electrocution was not meant to represent either spiritual or creative regeneration, nor did it matter whether David and his family were Jewish or some other ethnic group; he made them Jews, he said, because he was more familiar with the Jewish life than any other, "but they might have been almost anything."[16] Yes, of course, but the very facts that Roth did know Jewish life best, specifically described that life in New York at the turn of the century, and illuminated it chiefly from a psychological perspective are precisely what make *Call It Sleep* a thematically Jewish novel. Basically it is a poetic account of the growth of a child's mind in terms of both knowledge and self-awareness amid a chaos of imposing, often conflicting, forces, values, objects, and people in the tenement district. To describe it effectively required a new kind of fiction, and Roth drew heavily from an author whose methods had become highly influential in recent years, James Joyce and *Ulysses,* in devising a compelling new literary approach of his own.[17] Despite the detailed pictures that Roth provides of neighborhood scenes—tenement flats, stores and cellars, tumultuous streets, family squabbles, *cheder* classes (elementary Hebrew school), all with the smells and sights and sounds of uninsulated, densely populated ghetto life—*Call It Sleep* is essentially the psychological portrait of one perceptive child's observations and responses. Girgus correctly assesses it as "more concerned with the ghetto as a state of mind than with the physical environment," though he possibly over-emphasizes its significance "in expressing a revivified form of the myth and ideology of America," for both the Jewish and psychological themes are more central than the nationalistic one.[18]

By the time that Roth had published his only novel, in 1934, Meyer Levin already had brought out four novels and a collection of *Hasidic* tales, and he would continue publishing through the decades to 1981, when *Architect,* based on the life of Frank Lloyd Wright, marked the end of his long career. In his autobiographical *In Search* (1950) Levin described himself as constantly self-conscious of being both Jew and American. His earliest fiction picks up where that of the first American-Jewish authors left off; in addition to the nostalgic, longing souls of the lonely immigrants in the New World is the presence of a new generation, their offspring, who could not feel the loss of what they never knew and who became quickly acclimated to their American surroundings—including the English language. One of Levin's first stories, "A Seder" (1924), reflects the dilemma of the immigrant who sees his American children moving away from him and becomes bitter, alienated both from them and the Old World Judaism he had left behind.

In his first novel, *Reporter* (1929), Levin's self-consciousness as a Jewish newspaperman in an essentially gentile American milieu tainted with subtle—when not overt—anti-Semitism is evident in retrospect through the portrait of his unnamed central figure, a reporter who is not identified as a Jew until the story is nearly half told. All of the Jewish characters in *Reporter* are basically insecure in America, which undoubtedly reflects the author's own feeling of vulnerability at the time. Another novel, *The New Bridge* (1933), published four years later, is generally comparable with much proletarian writing of the Depression era, but unlike the corresponding fiction of Steinbeck, Gold, Wright, and others, there is no socialist or communist panacea offered at the end—only an incredible coincidence which completely undermines its verisimilitude. It also differs markedly from other proletarian fiction in that it is one of the rare novels that depict the working class as stupid—almost as though ignorance were a virtue.

A more probing and yet more sweeping portrait of American society appears in *The Old Bunch* (1937). One of Levin's two or three most important novels, it deals with a group of young Jews in their teens and twenties who form a club after their high school graduation on Chicago's West Side. Levin treats the group as an "organism," as he explains in *In Search,* describing a multitude of characters both individually and collectively, tracing them through the late 1920's and into the Depression as they mix and split, work, yearn, argue, make love, and leave home. Although these are all Jewish youths, the issues that bind and separate them are for the most part secular and universal among young people. *The Old Bunch* displays the effects of a social process on a group from which the individual members largely draw their identity; as earlier they had identified with their families, so in the bunch they see themselves in relation to each other. In some cases the strengthened sense of self that comes with their new association creates an unbridgeable chasm between Old World parent and New World child— as it does when Estelle Green (née Greenstein) has her hair cut short in the new style, something her mother had warned her not to do, and she consequently brings upon the group as well as herself embarrassment in the clubhouse with enduring repercussions. Eventually, the bunch disperses, and its members are assimilated into diverse segments of society—politics, college, medicine, bicycle racing, mechanics, business, law, drifting—some finding themselves and others not. *The Old Bunch* is a long novel of 964 pages in keeping with its subject, with numerous figures moving off from a radiant center individually or in pairs and occasionally, temporarily, coming across each other again as the group becomes more diffuse.

Not surprisingly, Levin had trouble publishing *The Old Bunch* at first because of its Jewish nucleus. He refused to revise the manuscript and portray the members of the bunch as heterogeneous in ethnic background when asked to do so by Reynad and Hitchcock, his original publisher, who had given him an advance on the novel before it was written. When it was finally published by Viking, the American features were emphasized in the publicity at the expense of the Jewish ones. Again not unexpectedly, a similar problem occurred over the publication of his next major novel, *Citizens* (1940).

One of the few characters Levin carried over from *The Old Bunch* into that novel is Mitch Wilner, who has become a doctor, but *Citizens* is not a sequel to the earlier work. Based on a historic steelworkers' strike in Chicago three years before its publication, Memorial Day 1937 (which Levin shifted for ironic purposes to Independence Day of the same year), it was dedicated to the ten men killed by police called to break up the strike. Almost by accident Mitch finds himself drawn into the fracas when medical help is needed, and day by day, despite some reluctance to jeopardize his secure post in a local hospital, his role in support of the workers is enlarged. His idealism, combined with both his obsession to learn the truth behind the massacre by police and the anti-Semitic barbs to which he becomes subject, leads him to frustration over realizing how isolated a figure he is in his quest for social justice in industrialized America. The novel ends with a memorial parade for the dead strikers and the workers' anticipation of revolution—''a complete war.''

Despite the insight into social movements and issues apparent in both *The Old Bunch* and *Citizens,* Levin's most popular and thus most financially successful book was *Compulsion* (1956). Like the best of his earlier novels, it was also based on a historical incident, the so-called Crime of the Century in which Nathan Leopold and Richard Loeb murdered Bobby Franks on the South Side of Chicago in 1924. But it testifies as well to an important change that had occurred in Levin's perspective as a direct consequence of the Second World War. One of the first reporters to enter the Nazi death camps early in 1945, he was appalled, devastated, over what he saw had been done to the Jews during the Holocaust. His experiences from that period proved traumatic, and by the time he returned from Europe his Jewish consciousness had been more strongly activated than ever before. This led him to profound "self-examination," he wrote, undoubtedly sparked by the scenes he had witnessed in and around Buchenwald, Bergen-Belsen, Dachau, and other camps in the heart of Nazi Germany. His introspection generated within him a new commitment both to his Judaism as an American and shortly afterward to Israel. His revitalized sense of Jewish awareness is evident in *Compulsion,* an account in which the Judaism of its central figures provides a subtle thematic undertone with ominous social implications throughout.

Although the murdered boy was Jewish by heritage, as were Leopold and Loeb (whose father only was a Jew), he and his family had become Christian Scientists; nevertheless, he was regarded as Jewish by those who discussed the killing.[19] Franks was slain arbitrarily by two brilliant, self-hating, psychopathic teenagers. *Compulsion* exposes subtle currents in American society, most notably the basic insecurity of Jewish citizens in a large American city at the time. Levin indicates in the novel and later in his autobiography that the Jews in Chicago often expressed general relief that the Jewish murderers had selected a Jewish victim.

This recognition of vulnerability reflects Levin's earlier self-consciousness as a Jewish journalist in Chicago during the mid–1920's as revealed in *Reporter.* Levin had begun working as a reporter on one of the city newspapers the year after Franks was killed.[20] In writing *Citizens* and particularly *Compulsion,* Levin anticipated the weaving of fact and fiction into a quasi-historical narrative on the order of more recent work by Truman Capote (*In Cold Blood*) and Norman Mailer (*The Executioner's Song*). In an epilogue to *Citizens,* "A Note on Method," he explained the rationale for this fictionalizing of history: "I believe modern writers are impelled to this method by a sense that the inner human truths of motive and compulsion can be found by examining experiences of reality. By using only actual, attested events as materials, the writer reduces the possibility of arriving at false conclusions."[21]

As is clear from his second autobiographical volume, *The Obsession* (1973), he transformed in a similar manner a traumatic episode from his own life into a novel published a decade earlier, *The Fanatic* (1964). There is no question but that Levin's view of American letters and justice was dramatically altered as a result of what he regarded as a conspiracy against him by the New York literati and publishers. As the first American writer to gain access to the diary of Anne Frank, he had adapted it to the stage and found a producer for the play. Eventually, however, a different play based on the diary was produced; parts of it resemble his work, though whereas Levin emphasized that the Frank family's

Judaism led to their plight and death in the Holocaust, the play finally staged on Broadway and everywhere else, by Albert and Frances Hackett, universalized the tragedy by minimizing the specifically anti-Semitic nature of the Nazi atrocities. Embittered over what he saw as a watering down of the anti-Semitic theme for the sake of commercial success, and enraged over being completely removed from any share or role in the stage production, Levin revealed his side of the distasteful story in *The Fanatic*. This distressing episode of Levin's career affected him to the point of obsession for the remainder of his life.[22]

THE POST-WAR YEARS

Meyer Levin's death marked the end of an earlier generation of American-Jewish novelists, those of the 1920's and 1930's whose lives were shaped by an expanding culture beyond the ghettos and whose careers were deeply marked by the Great Depression. In the 1940's and 1950's another generation emerged, the most notable of whom, with a few exceptions, are still actively publishing and developing their art today. Apart from Edward Lewis Wallant, who died in 1962, all of them but J. D. Salinger have published a new novel or collection of stories at least every few years, and, remarkably, their works show evidence of the authors' continuing attempts to advance their art theoretically and individualistically through imaginative though not always successful experimentation. Whereas during the preceding half century, American-Jewish authors as individuals remained relatively consistent in their methodological approaches to writing fiction, in the post-war period one finds it all but impossible to anticipate what technical innovation may be employed for the first time in a novel or series of stories in progress. Who could predict, for example, the form and structure of *The Adventures of Augie March* (1953) from reading *Dangling Man* (1944), or *The Tenants* (1971) from reading *The Natural* (1952), or *Portnoy's Complaint* (1969) from reading *Goodbye, Columbus* (1959), or *The Book of Daniel* (1971) from reading *Welcome to Hard Times* (1960)?

In all of these comparisons the later work, though often close in time of publication, is so vastly different in nearly every respect from the earlier that one would be hard put to identify the two as having been drafted by the same hand. Comparing these radical changes with the early and late fiction of, say, Cahan, Yezierska, and even Levin will make it clear that the first two generations of American-Jewish authors were a world apart from most of our current writers in their whole concept of what fiction should be and should do. Nonetheless, the one common theme that may be singled out to relate them again hinges on identity, though in this more recent work, the questions regarding identity are no longer the same. With a few notable exceptions such as Chaim Potok, Cynthia Ozick, and Jay Neugeboren (especially in his *The Stolen Jew*, 1981), the principal aim of the author-seeker is no longer to confirm an ethnic, religious, or national identity in a society partially closed to him, but a psychological, intellectual, and perhaps even metaphysical one in an open, heterogeneous, American culture. This seems to have become the novelist's goal.

The basis for these changes is easy to fathom. First, except for Bellow, who came to Chicago as a child from Montreal, all of these writers were born, reared, and educated in the United States; consequently, they never had the experience of living as aliens in a foreign land as their predecessors did. They had no need to "find themselves" as Americans, for they were Americans at the beginning. Second, by the time they had begun to write fiction, overt anti-Semitism and discrimination against Jews were rapidly fading in this country, a trend further hastened when knowledge of the Holocaust was broadcast. Recent studies by Stephen J. Whitfield (*Voices of Jacob, Hands of Esau: Jews in American Life and Thought,* 1984) and Charles E. Silberman (*A Certain People: American Jews and Their Lives Today,* 1985) testify to this unprecedented change in the gentile public's attitude toward Jews. In a discussion of Silberman's study, Whitfield states that "the case for the openness of American society is the less controversial" of that book's two claims (the other being that Judaism in America is not dying). After reading Whitfield's own study, one cannot understand how he would find Silberman's first point controversial at all, and, indeed, a few lines later in his commentary on *A Certain People,* he refers to "the ease with which recent generations that have known no other standard but American pluralism can take their Jewishness for granted."[23] Silberman makes the point explicitly:

a profound change . . . has occurred in the position of Jews in American society since the end of World War II, and especially since 1960—a change that makes the environment of American Jewish life today wholly unlike anything that any Jewish community has ever encountered before. Change has been so rapid, in fact, that American Jews in their twenties and thirties inhabit a completely different world from that in which their parents grew up.

The essence of the change is that American society has broken open to Jews . . . in ways that were not expected—indeed, in ways that could not even have been imagined a generation ago.

But, he continues, this transformation in attitudes has generated a paradox of its own with respect to the question of Jewish identity: "In short, the position of Jews in American society has changed so dramatically, and with such bewildering speed, that American Jews are confused about who they are and anxious about how they fit into the society."[24]

Unfortunately, in this valuable study of contemporary American Judaism, Silberman's only reference in fiction to such confusion as he has observed is a glance at *Portnoy's Complaint,* now more than fifteen years old. Why no reference to Roth's more recent novels? And why no reference at all to the work of Bellow, Malamud, Doctorow, and other American-Jewish authors whose explorations into the self in their writing of the past decade are at times so revealing? True enough, had Silberman considered the work of these authors with his other sources, he would have found on the one hand confirmation of his two major theses but on the other relatively little confusion in this current fiction over the torturous ambivalence between Jewish and American identity that pervaded the novels written before the war.

On a deep psychological level this confusion does occur in Saul Bellow's second novel, *The Victim* (1947), but that was published shortly after the war, and it manifests the dilemma in which American Jews often found themselves once they had begun to move into the mainstream American culture, especially but not only its commercial life. Able to live and work amid the secular tumult of New York City, Asa Leventhal is nevertheless so self-conscious of his Judaism that he becomes paranoid over believing himself a constant object of anti-Semitic persecution. Eventually, when he learns to assume the responsibility and blame for his actions as they adversely affect others, he is restored from a neurotic preoccupation with himself to a mature awareness of human complicity. But *The Victim,* like the earlier *Dangling Man,* deals more with a state of mind than with the question of identity as American or Jew; Leventhal must come to terms with himself before he can do the same with the rest of the world.

In contrast, *The Adventures of Augie March* (1953) is Bellow's most "American" novel, a vast panoramic work in which the eponymous hero is Jewish without question, but he is not self-consciously so. Instead, it is with archetypal American figures that he is most readily identified, with Huck Finn and Walt Whitman, for example, and by the end of the novel he sees himself as a "sort of Columbus," a Columbus from Chicago, one might add, because, as Daniel Fuchs points out, there is a good deal of Bellow himself in his peripatetic hero.[25] Robert R. Dutton suggests that Bellow wrote *Augie March* in part as "a fictional history of American literature; it serves as an evaluation of a literary attitude, whose existence is reflected in the experiences of the protagonist and his reactions to those experiences."[26] He finds support for this interpretation in Bellow's acceptance speech on receiving the National Book Award in 1964, when the novelist complained about the detachment among contemporary writers between the common culture and themselves. If such estrangement has brought into existence "some masterpieces," Bellow said, it has also "enfeebled literature. ... Without the common world the novelist is nothing but a curiosity."[27] If Dutton is correct in his reading, and he makes a telling case for it, Bellow seems to have provided a corrective for the dreary state of American literature in mid-century as he saw it. He sends Augie all over the country from Chicago, north to Canada and southwest to Mexico, before the penultimate chapter, where he is seated in a lifeboat drifting in the Atlantic. But for much of the novel he has been drifting on land assuming an active but temporary and noncommittal role in the lives of a multitude of people, rich and poor, egocentric and generous, male and female, conniving and honest. Fuchs characterizes him as "the singer of the more recent song of myself," and by the time that one completes the novel, Augie does indeed seem to be a modern Whitman, embracing all things and all people with exuberance and the joy of full life.[28] Although Bellow's novel has been criticized for seeming to promote a meaningless, undisciplined course of existence, *The Adventures of Augie March* should be read more as a song of exultation over the fullness of life that America offers than as a pattern by which we should be expected to determine our own values and guide our own behavior. Moreover, it provided Bellow with a means by which he could transform the commotion and distractiveness that pervade modern American life into a source of sustaining energy from which Augie can draw for a continuous awakening to new experience.

In this respect, one might compare that novel of 1953 with another that Bellow brought out nearly two decades later, *Mr. Sammler's Planet* (1970), in which his aging hero, Artur Sammler, is overwhelmed by the moral, physical, intellectual, and psychological chaos surrounding him in New York City. Good fortune alone has enabled him to evade death at the hands of the Nazis and come to the United States, but once here, this gentle and benign intellectual quickly discovers that he is an alien in a frenzied and incomprehensible culture, as out of place in violent metropolitan New York as the Shakespeare-quoting savage is in Aldous Huxley's dystopian *Brave New World*. Bellow at the time seems to have felt that this ubiquitous, ceaseless turmoil had America tottering on the edge of madness, but in *Humboldt's Gift* (1975), in which he presents perhaps his best portrait of Chicago, much of the earlier good humor returns. (His picture of the city's South Side in "Looking for Mr. Green" [1951] is also brilliant but less encompassing.) In a sharply critical late novel, however, *The Dean's December* (1982), that sense of despair is again recognizable; Bellow contrasts American democracy with the totalitarian government of Rumania, using Chicago and Bucharest as his focal cities. The loss of authority and breakdown of moral order evident in *Mr. Sammler's Planet* are to some extent blurred by the sheer zaniness of much of its action and dialogue, but in *The Dean's December* the tone throughout is somber. For Albert Corde, the Dean, Chicago "is the contempt center of the U.S.A.," partly because of the way that politics and the media undermine both moral authority and the law, and he publishes articles in *Harper's* expressing his position on the city in decay. His conservative bias, which certainly reflects Bellow's own view on such matters, draws charges of racism against him, especially when he becomes involved in attempting to bring two young blacks to justice for murdering a white student, a case in which he becomes implicated by virtue of his being an administrator at the college. Near the end of the novel, Corde succinctly expresses his opinion of contemporary America itself as:

a pleasure society which likes to think of itself as a tenderness society. A tender liberal society has to find soft ways to institutionalize harshness and smooth it over compatibly with progress, buoyancy. So that . . . when people are merciless, when they kill, we explain that it's because they're disadvantaged, or have lead poisoning, or come from a backward section of the country, or need psychological treatment.[29]

Whereas in Russia such people have been considered expendable since the Revolution, he continues, in the United States there are now only explanations and excuses for erratic, anti-social behavior and an unwillingness to distinguish between virtue and vice. The two blacks are found guilty and sentenced to prison, after all, and Corde is pleased over that result because he feels that justice of a sort has been carried out. But he knows, too, that it might have gone the other way and that the basic problems he identified in his articles will not have changed. The novel ends with Corde and his wife at Mount Palomar; looking through the telescope he has a semi-mystical revelation that enables him to sense the tie between "the real being" underlying all the cosmos and his own. "The living heavens looked as if they would take [him] in." After that experience, despite the cold, he is reluctant to descend.[30]

Although much of Bellow's fiction implies the presence of a Jewish consciousness behind it, as time passed he seems to have made a special effort to avoid the limitations that the designation "American-Jewish novel" would ordinarily suggest. In the later work especially, Judaism is underplayed, and some of his best characters—Henderson and Hattie ("Leaving the Yellow House," 1957), for example—are not Jewish at all. Rather it is an American theme that is often emphasized. Like Bellow's, Bernard Malamud's early fiction—apart from *The Natural* (1952), of course—is more decidedly Jewish than his more recent work, though he seldom universalizes to the extent that Bellow does. His first stories, those of *The Magic Barrel* (1958) and *Idiots First* (1963), are still the most often anthologized and consequently those by which he is best known. Similarly, his second novel, *The Assistant* (1957), is probably still his most popular. In all of that early fiction, Malamud's depiction of the New York tenement area corresponds to the romanticized views of the *shtetl* in Sholom Aleichem's and Isaac Bashevis Singer's work. In all three cases the atmosphere is redolent of an Old World life that never really existed as the authors present it; the stories are often more on the order of parables than realistic fiction, and the characters are seldom developed beyond two-dimensional types. Nevertheless, they are highly effective because of the poignant suffering that comes through them to Jewish readers in particular, who are drawn to identify nostalgically with the plight of the characters. Jews are born to suffer, Morris Bober, the ailing grocer, tells his assistant, Frank Alpine; having committed his own crimes and acquired a burden of guilt in consequence, the assistant converts to Judaism and becomes the grocer himself after Bober's death. Bober's burden then becomes his own. Malamud has said, "All men are Jews."[31] Allen Guttmann finds this absurd because it broadens "the definition of 'Jew' to the point of meaninglessness."[32] But surely Guttmann is taking Malamud too literally, for the novelist was implying only that as humans we are all born to suffer alike, alienated in the midst of society. Again implicitly, of course, Malamud makes this point in those several stories that focus on interracial relations between blacks and Jews; these include some of his best early tales, such as "Angel Levine" and "The Jewbird" from *The Magic Barrel*, and "Black Is My Favorite

Color'' from *Idiots First*. Of the last two, one ends in death and the other in persistent suffering; two of the stories identify a Jew with blackness. In these stories Malamud shows little optimism for harmonious racial relations in the future—and it should be remembered that they were written in the 1950's. By 1971, when he published *The Tenants,* he apparently could anticipate only a violent, self-defeating climax in which the two minorities—blacks and Jews— would kill each other off in a final struggle for the dregs of a fundamentally divided American culture. In his work written during the decade before his death in 1986, he seems to have peered inward and found a division in himself that he represents in *Dubin's Lives* (1979) as a hopeless breach between the author-professor as scholar, writer, and seer on the one hand and as prurient lecher and adulterer on the other. His fiction was more successful when he turned his attention away from himself as his subject toward the outside world around him.

Although Malamud's earliest stories center almost entirely on Jewish figures, his first novel has nothing to do with Jews at all. Instead it is a baseball novel, which suggests his anxiety at the outset of his career to appeal not to a narrowly Jewish audience but to a broadly American one. Surely, no fiction other than a Western can be more American than a baseball story. Critics have attempted without much success to identify a Jewish theme in *The Natural*. It is simply an American novel, and they seem to have found it anomalous that a Jewish author would write a serious fiction about baseball without some ulterior religious motive. It is less extraordinary, however, when seen in the context of other Jewish writers who have done the same. Jay Neugeboren, for example, included baseball (and basketball) in his fiction before turning his major attention to more traditional Jewish materials. Mark Harris's *The Southpaw* (1953) is another example, and the long opening section of Chaim Potok's first novel, *The Chosen* (1967), describes a baseball game that brings the two central characters together and establishes the nature of the conflict that dramatizes the fiction throughout. Not only for gentiles is baseball ''the great American pastime.''

Philip Roth is also an admirer of baseball, and he, too, wrote a novel, a hilarious one, in which that is its ostensible subject, *The Great American Novel* (1973). It begins with literary parody and soon moves into barbed thrusts at politics, the armed forces, American chauvinism, and other vulnerable targets with particular jabs at Joe McCarthy, Richard Nixon, and the anti-Communist witch-hunt of the 1950's, all developed amid data that testify to Roth's broad, deep familiarity with baseball history. He acknowledges having gained a greater

feel for the American landscape . . . less from what [he] learned in the classroom about Lewis and Clark than from following the major-league clubs on their road trips and reading about the minor leagues in the back pages of *The Sporting News*. . . . And however much we might be told by teacher about the stockyards and the Haymarket riot, Chicago only began to exist for me as a real place, and to matter in American history, when I became fearful (as a Dodger fan) of the bat of Phil Cavaretta, first baseman for the Chicago Cubs.[33]

Although the novel is satirical, Roth's purpose, he said, was not to demythologize America's national sport but America itself by dramatizing through baseball "the *struggle* between the benign national myth of itself that a great power prefers to perpetuate, and the relentlessly insidious, very nearly demonic reality (like the kind we had known in the sixties) that will not give an inch in behalf of that idealized mythology."[34]

Perhaps the same idea may be applied to his writing about the middle-class American-Jewish culture from which he emerged as a major public figure in the 1950's, especially at the end of the decade with the publication of "Goodbye, Columbus" and a handful of his best stories. Roth's ambivalence as an American and a Jew is evident in his work from the beginning, where it is most overt. In "Eli the Fanatic," Eli is pulled in two directions, from outside by the assimilated life-style he has known for years and from within back toward the roots of his Judaism through the *Hasidic* group that suddenly appears in the community and activates his Jewish conscience to the extent that it alienates him from his family and friends. In "Defender of the Faith" a Jewish army sergeant is imposed upon by a new Jewish recruit who insidiously requests special favors as a *landsman*; eventually, in a manner of teaching the crass youth a lesson by acting as a sergeant and a disciplinarian rather than as a fellow Jew, he sends the private overseas though it is within his prerogatives to ship someone else out in his place. In "Savior of the People" Roth portrays a suicidal boy's determination to expose the hypocrisy he perceives behind the doctrines and dogmas of conventional Judaism, and he makes a spectacle of himself in doing it.

Roth refuses to develop his Jewish characters according to the stereotypes; he criticized Malamud's early fiction with this idea in mind, asserting that the urban Jews in the stories and *The Assistant* are neither real nor related to major issues facing contemporary Judaism; instead, he said, they live in a timeless world of the lower East Side—unlike the wealthy, partly assimilated Jews in the broader American culture. In contrast, Roth reveals Jews to themselves with all of their human shortcomings, distasteful though they may be, and in consequence he has generated considerable hostility toward himself from Jewish readers—rabbis, organization leaders, and other individuals—who complain that they have enough difficulties instigated by gentiles with which to contend. Why should they have to put up with such vile portraiture from one of their own? Abraham Cahan had to cope with similar jibes from critics, Jews and gentiles alike, but he responded differently. Whereas Cahan sought what he called "the *thrill of truth*" by ridding his fiction of artifice and sentimentality in order to reveal human nature as it really is, Roth exposes the human "condition" by permitting his fictional characters to act in a manner that ordinary inhibitions and moral restrictions preclude among the readers themselves, especially in America, despite its celebrated sense of individualism. What Henry James did in his novels with unlimited wealth for selected characters, Roth attempts to do with unlimited sexual freedom; in the work of both authors the characters are free to act as they wish, unrestrained in James's fiction by a lack of sufficient funds and in Roth's by moral scruples. In the writing of all three authors, however—Cahan, James, and Roth—the concern is to probe beneath often deceptive surfaces to reveal essential truths of human character. Roth takes the idea a step further when he says that we are often not aware of the extent of our own feelings "*until* we have come into contact with the work of fiction. . . . [Then] not only are we judging with the aid of new feelings but without the necessity of having to act upon judgment." This is true, he points out, not only of a reader reading fiction but also of the author writing it: "I often feel that I don't really know what I'm talking about until I've stopped *talking* about it and sent everything down through the blades of the fiction-making machine, to be ground into something else."[35]

Simply put, like Malamud in his recent work, Roth is writing chiefly about himself as a novelist. In the first part of his career, from the early stories to *Portnoy's Complaint* (1969), he was pulled strongly toward the two sides of his being, and it shows clearly in the fiction; although "Goodbye, Columbus" is basically a realistic portrait of middle-class (especially upper-middle-class) Jewish family life in New Jersey after the war, with no attempt to hide the blemishes, it is not difficult to see the tie between two stories of the same period—"Savior of the People" and "Eli the Fanatic"—and *Portnoy's Complaint*. In the late 1960's he became politicized, the result of which may be noted in such publications as *Our Gang* (1971), a heavy-handed satire on Nixon; and *The Great American Novel* (1973), with its attempt to expose the difference between current policies of the United States and the American myth. Between those two works, however, came *The Breast* (1972), a psychological fiction on the order of Kafka, whose work has long been influential on Roth; it was followed by *The Professor of Desire* (1978) and a trilogy, *Zuckerman Bound,* completed with an epilogue in 1985. Apart from the political fiction, his later novels are both reflective of his inward turn and characterized by continuing bouts of sexual activity, often of a perverse kind. In *Portnoy's Complaint* the sexuality is novel and funny; in the later fiction, however, it seems to have become a major preoccupation that undermines more serious central themes. The problem is that Roth's subjectivity has become his chief subject, and his fiction as result becomes both the record of a quest for psychological identity and an intimate confession of the feelings evoked by that quest. His questions are no longer: "Who am I in relation to my community? or to my heritage? or to my family? or to my faith?" but rather, "Who am I?" And he looks within to find out. More than a decade ago he recognized that one of his "continuing problems as a writer has been to find the means to be true to these seemingly inimical realms of experience that I am strongly attached to by temperament and training—the aggressive, the crude, and the obscene, at one extreme, and something of a good deal more subtle and, in every sense, refined, at the other."[36] Perhaps he will be able to integrate them more effectively in the future or at least to rechannel most of his inclination toward "the aggressive, the crude, and the obscene" into a more meaningful and productive though not necessarily less imaginative realm of experience.

In 1960 Roth observed that J. D. Salinger's reputation made him the major writer of his day. By that time Salinger had published *The Catcher in the Rye* (1951) and a number of stories about the Glass family. Although the stories are admirable individually and still better as part of a series, it was from *The Catcher in the Rye* that Salinger gained his reputation, nor had he written anything to surpass that work by the time he stopped publishing fiction in the 1960's. Thematically, the novel is a simple one about a boy who learns that the world is not what it appears to be. Holden Caulfield, the young hero, discovers this first at Pencey, the prep school where he is a student, and rediscovers it on a larger field when he leaves the school in disgust and wanders around New York. At once lonely and filled with love, he finds it difficult to overcome the death of his brother and has an intense desire to become a savior. As a child, Holden is an idealist, constantly frustrated over not finding people and things the way he believes they ought to be. In this respect he is very outspoken, and Salinger has given Holden Caulfield an idiolect that caught on quickly among students in the fifties to the extent that many of them began to imitate his peculiar form of repetitiousness and diction. Holden is not Jewish, and there seems to be nothing noticeably Jewish about the novel thematically unless one might say that it reflects the sense of alienation that many Jews feel when they first venture on their own into a gentile American world. Though often done, it is too easy and presumptuous to identify such universal feelings as fundamentally Jewish simply because the fiction in which they appear prominently was written by a Jewish author. (Salinger's father was Jewish, but his mother, like the mother of the Glass children, was Catholic.)

The same is less true of the stories, however, and it is chiefly because of them that Salinger's work holds a place in the mainstream of American-Jewish fiction. The Glass family is close-knit; the children are precocious; the mother dotes on them. Because of these traits and others, Jewish readers find it easy to identify with them, though Bessie Glass holds firmly to her Catholicism, and the children share in no Jewish ceremonies or festivities. Nevertheless, they marry into Jewish families, and their lives do seem largely to be shaped and governed by a Jewish consciousness, especially those of Seymour and Zooey who, like Holden Caulfield, are often in worlds of their own. Many of the stories are filled with flashbacks, and the siblings are described at various stages of their lives. For the most part we learn about their earlier years in retrospect, through letters, as in "Zooey" (1957), and monologues, as in *Seymour: An Introduction* (1959). The overall picture Salinger conveys of America itself in the Glass stories is a variegated one, but there is nothing striking or unusual about it. Franny's date for a college football game and the silly vanity of the collegians in "Franny" (1955) are part of the same world that Roth depicts in "Goodbye, Columbus"; Boo Boo Tannenbaum's (née Glass) house in the country ("Down at the Dinghy"), the creature comforts of the Miami Beach hotel where Seymour shoots himself while his wife lies sleeping beside him ("A Perfect Day for Bananafish"), and the New York scenes that constitute the setting for Seymour's delayed marriage to Muriel (*Raise High the Roof Beam, Carpenters*, 1963), among others, all present a view of mid-century America that suggests too great an emphasis on surfaces and particulars. This, doubtlessly, was America as Salinger himself saw it and, dissatisfied, he gave more of his attention to Zen in order either to go beyond them or to make them meaningful in a way that had thus far escaped him. Unfortunately, Salinger's critics did not make this tie; they treated the Zen motif as an oddball aberration of eccentric characters rather than as a personal reaction to shallow American values. If Buddy Glass is his persona in "Zooey," as he surely is in *Seymour: An Introduction,* Salinger seems to have accomplished both. In bringing Franny out of her quasi-religious depression and withdrawal, Buddy counsels her to strive for perfection in her art (acting) according to her own standards and to play it out for every individual, even the most ridiculous-seeming of them (Seymour's "Fat Lady"), because each person is Christ himself. Buddy is saying, then, that divinity can be found in the particular and that even the most earthbound person or thing offers redemption. To the regret of many readers, Salinger has apparently not followed his own counsel, for he stopped playing it out years ago.

In the last published novel of Edward Lewis Wallant, *The Children at the Gate* (1964), which came out posthumously, a reawakening similar to Franny's occurs, but it is more dramatic and emotionally charged. The hero of that novel is not Jewish but Roman Catholic from an Italian family, though his awakening is inspired by the self-sacrifice of an older Jew who is at once comic and profound, earthy and prophetic. As Franny must find her Truth in Seymour's Fat Lady, so is Angelo in Wallant's novel encouraged to find the meaning of his life through love and universal human kinship. He learns this at the hospital where his mentor, Sammy Kahan, works as an orderly. Sammy tells him to look at the patients lying in the ward, many of them hopeless and in terrible pain. What do we see in the dim room filled with bedded patients, Sammy asks him:

Concrete, wood, glass, paint, metal, cotton, wool, plastic. Oh, but there—see those tiny little soft things sticking out the ends of clothes? You know what they are? They're *faces*! And even some of them are hidden by glasses and masks and like that [*sic*]. And what do those creatures have inside—love? . . . How dark it gets! And when we're all in the dark—what then?—Nothing? Never mind, never mind, Sammy will kiss it, make it all better.[37]

His point, of course, is that life must be lived for the present, not for some future world, and it can be lived with fulfillment only through love: "You can touch me and I can touch you. . . . Love me, O *kinder*!" This universal love and desire for physical contact that Sammy advocates—a moral view that relates him to Salinger's Glass siblings and strongly echoes Whitman's remarks as a poet-sage and prophet—contrast sharply with the technological descriptions of the hospital and all of its scientific paraphernalia. Wallant recognized the usefulness and importance of such advances, but he feared that technology was rapidly becoming an end in itself and was commensurately dehumanizing man in the process.

Nowhere does he make this point more effectively than in his second novel, *The Pawnbroker* (1961), in which Sol Nazerman has eluded death in the Holocaust, that efficient mechanism for genocide and slave labor, but not before he passed through a living death while in the hands of the Nazis. He recalls in a series of horrifying flashbacks how the Nazis had destroyed his family and nearly did the same to him by subjecting him to excruciating physical abuse as a guinea pig for their barbaric "medical" experiments. Living in New York with his sister's demanding middle-class family after the war, Sol is completely alienated from them and everyone with whom he impersonally associates in his business as a pawnbroker. His moral sense has become warped because he believes that his suffering and experience are beyond the comprehension of other human beings. Ultimately, when a young Puerto Rican employee sacrifices his life for Sol, the pawnbroker undergoes a sudden hysterical release and an epiphany that reawakens him to love, brings new meaning into his life, and consequently ends his long period of alienation. Paradoxically, he finds salvation as a man and particularly as a Jew in the American melting pot.

All four of Wallant's novels—the other two are *The Human Season* (1960) and *The Tenants of Moonbloom* (1963)—are thematically similar, and his setting in all four is the city. Although each of his central figures is essentially isolated though residing or working in the midst of a populous city—like Poe's man of the crowd—Wallant does not focus narrowly on him (all of his protagonists are men) but gives detailed if brief glimpses of the many characters on the periphery with whom he interacts. In this way, we gain insight not only into the sense of loneliness, frustration, and despair that often infect the lives of others, but also into the alienating and at times overwhelming forces of contemporary civilization as represented by large American cities on the East Coast. As a comparison, in *Catch-22* (1961) Joseph Heller manifests a similar concern, but he treats the bureaucratic technocracy of the armed forces as apparently beyond hope; his satire is sharp and his tone cynical in that novel; like Roth in *The Great American Novel,* he comments upon all aspects of American society. Wallant, on the other hand, though recognizing the danger of over-extending ourselves in terms of technology and systems, concludes all four of his novels on an upbeat with the feeling that reawakened compassion and love for one's fellow beings have overcome the despair and consequently ended the alienation of the heroes.

Although Wallant's novels deal with the movement of a single figure from isolation into community, and the stories of Grace Paley explore loosely knit neighborhood relations, both writers emphasize the high value gained through social interaction in the city. Paley's first collection of stories, *The Little Disturbances of Man* (1959), introduces New Yorkers who reappear in later ones, including *Enormous Changes at the Last Minute* (1974) and *Later the Same Day* (1985). She presents a microcosmic view of America with her assortment of neighborhood New Yorkers, black and white, Jewish and gentile, whom she shows in the midst of ordinary activities—at home, in the park, at school, on the street, and in the subway. Paley's characters may well be Moonbloom's tenants in Wallant's third novel; the resemblance at times is quite close. Conversations carry her stories forward through a vocal amalgam of recollection, chatter, and gossip, all of which, however, constitute the social threads that hold a community together. In her ability to catch and reproduce the sounds of common speech, Paley seems to echo the racy diction of Damon Runyon in her earlier stories, and that combines in the later ones with the repetitive voices of Gertrude Stein's women in *Three Lives* (1910), voices Stein learned to capture through her early experience in Baltimore. In Paley's stories, however, the characters are more emotionally involved in their talk than Stein's, and Paley herself does not show Stein's detachment from them. Her women in particular are often outspoken, independent, capable of confronting their day-to-day problems and coming to terms with even the most trying of them, problems over parents, children, lovers. "As for you, fellow independent thinker of the Western Bloc, if you have anything sensible to say, don't wait. Shout it out loud right this minute," the narrator says in the opening of "Faith in the Afternoon," a story in her second collection, comprising a series of conversations in which serious matters of family relations are hidden beneath trivial patter before a final outburst exposes the grief and despair of an aging parent.[38] Faith, often the narrator herself, is a writer like Paley, and she speaks for the author: "Don't you wish you could rise powerfully above your time and name?" she asks someone in a more recent tale, while waiting in a butcher shop for her meat to be wrapped; "I'm sure we all try, but here we are, always slipping and falling down into them, speaking their narrow language, though the subject, which is how to save the world—and quickly—is immense."[39] Some of Paley's stories are only a few pages long, but they sparkle with suggestion and wit as a portrait does when only the striking characteristics of a face or figure are depicted and the rest of the features are left for the viewer to fill in with imagination.

Altogether different from both the clear moral intent that lies behind Wallant's fiction and the community orientation of Paley's are the experimentalism and diversity of E. L. Doctorow's novels. From his earliest work, *Welcome to Hard Times* (1960), which is briefly discussed later with reference to the western setting, Doctorow's fiction shows a continuing preoccupation with narrative form, particularly with manipulation of point of view, in order to reveal multiple perspectives from which a given experience may be understood. In this way, what has "actually happened" is impossible to distinguish because the actuality differs according to the point of view which perceives it. To complicate the ambiguities further, Doctorow interpolates specific historical facts and personalities among the fictional characters, thus endowing the latter and the attendant circumstances with historical veracity. History and biography, then, become for Doctorow elements of fiction as the imagined elements of fiction assume the garb of truth generally associated in the reader's mind with history and biography, although these, too, are always in part subjective. Only once has this imaginative integration been fused with the necessary genius in his fiction to engender a truly compelling novel; that occurred in *The Book of Daniel* (1971), which is based heavily on circumstances related to the arrest, trial, and execution of Julius and Ethel Rosenberg in the early 1950's for allegedly revealing atomic secrets to the Soviets. This is Doctorow's most powerful novel largely because the experimental form corresponds brilliantly with the shifting states of mind and points of view of the characters, who themselves come both physically and psychologically to life in the whirl of historical people and events that pull the two innocent Isaacson children into its vortex. It is a novel of total engagement. *Ragtime* (1975), a thematically less complex work, is filled with major historical personages manipulated in an incredible and often amusing plot, but the engagement of the reader is considerably more tenuous than in the earlier novel; dealing more with surfaces than their underlying significance, it is an extravagant entertainment, a fictionalized historical spectacle, but seldom more than that.

Surely, Doctorow's most authentic portrait of the American scene, especially as witnessed by a Jewish boy moving through early childhood into adolescence, appears in his latest novel, *World's Fair* (1985). Perhaps much of the authenticity is attributable to the extensive autobiographical data that Doctorow incorporates into the family life of Edgar, his central figure and voice. His account of growing up in a lower-middle-class Jewish family in the Bronx during the 1930's will revitalize memories of many readers who were reared in large American cities at that time, for the specifics are profuse and accurate as he describes life along the streets, school days, the persistent shortage of money, trolley rides, the variety of little devices that attract children to spend their pennies, and many other such things. Because a child's recollection is being presented in all but a few chapters narrated by other family voices, the descriptions comprise abundant details of color and shape. Edgar is very perceptive; what he sees registers immediately with him though he often does not understand its implications, and the reader must recognize for himself the irony in a Jewish boy's observing a city of the future's being grandly displayed in America as the Holocaust is being prepared for the Jews in Europe. Through Edgar's close-to-home observations we gain no sense of this bipolar view, but it is chiefly through his consciousness that the reader becomes acquainted with his family and realizes the love that binds them despite obvious conflicts that have generated problems over the years.

"In fact, love was what it was all about," Edgar recalls in a line thematically more characteristic of Wallant's fiction than Doctorow's. Yet if this love keeps the family together, that is to say, the entire family, including the eccentric members and the wealthy conservative ones, the parts of the novel do not mesh well enough to constitute an effectively unified piece of fiction on the order of *The Book of Daniel*; Edgar himself is too detached from what he describes, more a thinker than a doer, and the polished adult language in which he tells his story makes that detachment all the more apparent. Although *World's Fair* offers a superb representation of New York Jewish family life in the 1930's, it lacks the kind of moral and emotional commitment needed to bring its characters out of the realm of a child's consciousness into factuality. In a book published a year earlier, *Lives of the Poets* (1984), Doctorow illustrates the creative process of the novelist as he lays out the materials with which he works, a group of seemingly unrelated stories, and assimilates them into a single piece of fiction in the last segment of the volume. As illustrative of a process, *Lives of the Poets* provides an interesting and instructive glimpse into the writer's method of *com-pos*-ition, i.e., putting things together, and the real subject of that work is the method in itself. Like most of Doctorow's other fiction, however, *World's Fair* too often suffers from inadequate cohesion among the various elements as well as a discomfitting distance between narrator and events, though the events themselves and the settings in which they occur are graphically depicted.

This is an especially unfortunate shortcoming in Doctorow's work because the author himself acknowledges the need for contemporary American fiction that shows greater concern for "the social value of art"; fiction today, he says, has "reduced authority" in the minds of both readers and, paradoxically, the writers themselves, authority that needs to be regained. We need books "with less polish and self-consciousness, but about the way power works in our society [*sic*], who has it, and how it is making history." But in the same essay, written shortly before *World's Fair* was published, he pointed out:

Narrative is the art closest to the ordinary daily operation of the human mind. People find the meaning of their lives in the idea of sequence, in conflict, in metaphor and in moral. People think and make judgments from the confidence of narrative; anyone at any age is able to tell the story of his or her life with authority. . . . Everyone all the time is in the act of composition, our experience is an ongoing narrative within each of us.[40]

The problem is not in the observation but, especially in his first novel and his most recent, the lack of vitality in the finished product. Edgar tells us long afterward, in the language of a highly literate adult, about his life as a child, but he communicates little emotional involvement in these early experiences— only selected facts and perceptions but few deeply felt emotional responses. It is unexpected, then, to learn that Doctorow assesses his own "novels as part of the tradition of the social novel by such masters as Dickens, Hugo, Dreiser, Jack London." Indeed, though society may be his ostensible subject as it is theirs, his deeper subject is the way the story is told, the narrative method; consequently, his fiction lacks the vigor and power, the sheer driving energy of theirs because of the distance that so often exists between teller and tale.[41]

Nevertheless, he effectively conveys a picture of America that varies considerably from one novel to the next. In *Welcome to Hard Times* he offers a satirical version of the mid-to-late nineteenth-century American West as it exists in the popular imagination; in *The Book of Daniel* we see a violent America characterized by exploitation, hypocrisy, and fear; in *Ragtime* the setting is an America of the absurd; *Loon Lake* (1980) depicts a grotesque America preoccupied with sexuality and self-gratification; and in *World's Fair,* America is simultaneously a toy in both the Fair builders' and the novelist's hands as well as a spectacle described by the young narrator and the other voices, the diverse views combining in Edgar's climactic first visit to the World's Fair of 1939–1940.

The difference between Doctorow's America and that of Chaim Potok is immediately apparent from a brief look at the most recent novel of each, *World's Fair* and *Davita's Harp,* which was also published in 1985. Like *World's Fair,* Potok's novel is narrated by a Jewish child in a New York home, though whereas Edgar's father inclines towards socialism, Davita's parents are committed communists, and only her mother is Jewish. Though no sequel to any of his earlier novels, *Davita's Harp* may nevertheless be seen as thematically related to them in that from first to latest Potok has portrayed his central figures as moving in relation to the heart of Orthodox Judaism (and one of the earlier protagonists is mentioned as Davita's schoolmate). *Davita's Harp* differs from Potok's previous fiction in two important respects, however. First, whereas in the five prior novels the protagonist begins at the center and moves outward toward the periphery, in *Davita's Harp* the movement is in the opposite direction; that is, Davita begins as a small child in a secularized communist home and finds herself drawn back to the Judaic center that her mother had left when she married a gentile. Second, Davita is Potok's first female protagonist.

Unlike Doctorow, Potok sees himself as a novelist with a mission. He intentionally conveys a sense of moral truth in his fiction and wishes it to serve as a means of guiding his readers, especially American Jews, toward developing some form of meaningful commitment in their lives. His own commitment is evident in his background as an ordained rabbi with a doctorate in philosophy. Nevertheless, although the moral content of his novels is clear through both the intellectual dialogues that constitute a substantial portion of each and the self-doubt with which the central characters wrestle, Potok creates dramatic tension in all of them through the art of fiction, not argument or polemic. He recognizes the attractions that secular America holds out to the educated young Jew with strong intellectual predilections. For his heroes, including Davita, it is not a matter of material desires, popular esteem, or self-indulgence in sensuous delights that serve as temptations, but the increased knowledge that comes with uninhibited rational inquiry, and for the zealous *Hasidim* whom he depicts in his fiction, such knowledge and inquiry are anathema. Potok believes that he can mediate between his Hebrew and secular worlds by maintaining his own faith and addressing the conflicts in his fiction.

His first two novels, *The Chosen* (1967) and *The Promise* (1969), illustrate the way confrontation occurs among Jewish communities in New York: the *Hasidic* sect of which Reb Saunders is the *tzaddik,* or ruling sage, and the Orthodox, Conservative, even Reform congregations. For the *Hasidim* there can be no compromise. Yet by the end of the second novel (which is a sequel to the first) the oldest son of the Reb, a brilliant youth who was to have been chosen *tzaddik* for the sect, has entered the secular field of psychology instead and become a psychiatrist. His former schoolmate, Reuven Malter, has been ordained, but he, too, has had serious problems over his desire to employ new approaches to talmudic scholarship in his theological studies; eventually, both take major steps from the unpliable center of their immediate Jewish backgrounds, one from family rigidity and the other from an ultra-conservative educational institution. In *My Name Is Asher Lev* (1972), Potok's third novel, Asher is an artistic genius, but his father, a dedicated Jew highly successful in his efforts to rebuild European Jewish communities after the Holocaust, regards the boy's artwork as a waste of time. Ultimately, Asher acquires a background of art theory, history, and technique and becomes a renowned master, alienated from his family though not from his faith. Potok's fourth novel, *In the Beginning* (1975), portrays the son of a zealous Orthodox father who attempts to force the brilliant child to follow the narrow course of his own orthodoxy, including his distrust of gentiles, but like Reuven Malter, the boy acquires a knowledge of new critical methods and enters the field of biblical studies as professor in a large secular university. Always the field of study is dilating. In *The Book of Lights* (1981), Potok's most complex novel thus far in terms of the relation of form to content, a young rabbi must serve overseas in Korea during the occupation in order to receive ordination upon completing his studies at the *yeshiva*; his experience enlightens him to community needs as being no less a part of his rabbinate than his own intellectual and spiritual aspirations, and by the conclusion he is prepared to accept his role as both scholar and communal guide. Finally, the eponymous heroine of *Davita's Harp* is attracted to Judaism without understanding exactly how, and as her devotion deepens, she draws her mother back into it as well.

It should be clear from the foregoing that Potok's commitment to the value of secular learning in conjunction with a steadfast adherence to his faith is absolute. In the role of what Daniel Walden calls a *Zwischenmensch* (an "in-between person"), he advocates the value of each as a complement to the other in contemporary American life and simultaneously points to the folly of over-zealous extremism as self-defeating.[42] Danny Saunders can be at once a psychiatrist and a *Hasid*; Reuven Malter can be an enlightened rabbi bringing new historical methods to traditional scholarship; and the same is true of David Lurie who steps even further from the center as a teacher of biblical studies in a secular sphere. Asher Lev retains his commitment to both the *yeshiva* (Jewish parochial school) and his painting; Gershon Loran's experience of the outside world, especially in Korea, enables him, like Potok himself (who also served in Korea), to mediate between the extremes and strive for fulfillment through community as well as through the esoteric study of Kabbalah. And Davita illustrates Potok's commitment to the modernization of Judaism with her entry into the advanced study of Hebrew theology, heretofore restricted to men.

The overall change that occurred in American-Jewish fiction between World War II and the present is far greater than that of the earlier period, from the 1890's to the war years. America for Jewish authors is no longer a land of golden promise but a nation in which that promise has been realized for many Jews whose families have merged with the mainstream of American culture. For assimilated third- and fourth-generation Jews in the United States, as the fiction by authors of the past four decades has revealed, the original problem of identification as Jew or American, either or both, is no longer crucial. Instead the question of identity has to a great extent become secularized, and the quest for self-knowledge has generated new attempts to understand one's life in terms of universal relations and, among the authors themselves, of their art. This is true not only of such novelists as Roth, Malamud, Bellow, and Doctorow, who deal broadly with the American culture, but also of Potok, with his detailed portraits of unassimilated Jews living ritualistically on its margins.

THE WEST

Like many, indeed, most, of the American-Jewish authors, Chaim Potok has largely restricted himself to writing fiction set in the northeastern part of the United States, especially New York. Only in *The Book of Lights* does he refer on several occasions to the Far West, and those references come through brief flashbacks that do little to advance the story though they are of signal importance to the theme. The recollections pertain to frightful experiences at Los Alamos, where the father of Gershon's friend Arthur was helping to develop the atom bomb. Arthur cannot escape the memory that after the bomb was dropped in a nuclear test there, "it rained dead birds [nearby]. . . . They smelled charred. . . . Their eyes were burned out. . . . [W]e'll probably kill ourselves. We're a terrible species."[43] Although this western image of death is a singularly terrifying one, it is not altogether uncharacteristic of the West as envisioned by American-Jewish novelists.

For reasons that are difficult to fathom—perhaps because of its alien vastness for authors whose experience in this country has been limited chiefly to cities of the eastern seaboard and the mid-West—Jewish novelists seldom emphasize the natural grandeur of the western landscape with its open ranges, deserts, and mountains, but expose the trans-Mississippi American culture instead as basically provincial, hypocritical, and destructive. Characteristically they focus on people and give nature relatively little attention. All across the West, the land and its people are described as alienating. Most of the American-Jewish authors include in their work a composite theme of individualism and alienation, the first of which is often generated and fostered by the second. Their attitudes toward the West and the ways they are revealed in the fiction vary, to be sure, but from the novels and stories one may identify at least two important common themes. First is the unexpected idea that deception of one kind or another—hypocrisy, illusion, self-deception, sham, purposeful evasion, misleading statements, outright lies, and others—characterizes much of western life, not only or especially among the newcomers but among the long-term inhabitants as well. And second, a view intimately related to the first, is that the West may and should be taken as representative of the United States as a whole in broad social, economic, and political terms.

Both themes are unmistakably present, for example, in Saul Bellow's short story "Leaving the Yellow House," which opens his collection *Mosby's Memoirs and Other Stories* (1968). Hattie Simmons Waggoner, a blowsy, unhealthy divorcée of seventy-two years, lives in a state of intermittent drunkenness beside Sego Desert Lake in Utah. As a girl, she attended finishing schools in the East and during part of her childless marriage to a vain Philadelphia socialite lived in Europe. After her divorce she came west and settled in one of the only three real houses in the vicinity; another of them is owned by a rich eastern couple who often gives her neighborly assistance, and the third belongs to a man named Pace, "a genuine cowboy . . . who had grown up in the saddle" and converted his property into a dude ranch. Pace, one of the few original Westerners in the story, is a sharp who uses Hattie sexually, cheats her at cards, and attempts to swindle her out of her home, a rundown yellow house she inherited from an English woman, also whisky-dependent, with whom she had moved in after the divorce. Hattie's mind has become a roiling confluence of memories, hopes, and fears; vestiges of a cultivated life in the East until she was past fifty have merged with the sonorous regularity of her present irresponsible semi-conscious existence in the desert. Now her state has been made still more trying by a broken arm she recently suffered in an accident. All but five of her neighbors are Mexicans, blacks, and Indians with shacks or boxcars for homes. Twenty mile away a gold miner's ancient widow lives in a flimsy building she calls Fort Walters, after her own name. A totally self-reliant western woman, she raises the American flag outside her door every morning. When Hattie needs aid, the widow expresses a willingness to help her if Hattie will leave her the yellow house when she dies, but she refuses in return to will Fort Walters to Hattie because even after twenty years in the desert, still "Hattie is a city woman" to her. Feeling completely alone and knowing that her remaining years of life are few, Hattie allows her yellow house to merge with her aging body in her bourbon-fogged stream of thought, and the story concludes with her decision to will the yellow house to herself upon her death rather than to someone she believes has neglected or betrayed her.

The West appears as a major setting in only two of Bellow's other works of fiction, and in both cases it is Mexico rather than the United States, though only in the second is character significantly affected by environment and circumstance.

"The Mexican General" (1942) offers a good example of Bellow's early method. The story derives from his Mexican stay in 1940, the year of Leon Trotsky's assassination in a town near Mexico City. "The Mexican General" deals not with the assassination itself, which has already occurred when the story opens, but with its exploitation for self-aggrandizement by a vain, pompous, immoral Mexican general who had been in charge of protecting the Russian exile. Traveling with an entourage that includes three attractive young concubines at his immediate call and two lieutenants as lackeys—Citron and Paco—the general himself is at the constant service of his own image. He is a hollow man, a gilded eggshell, who has instinctively the appropriate words for any given occasion, and the same instinct enables him to use Trotsky's assassination to further his own interests through the massive publicity it has generated. In contrast to the general is Lieutenant Citron, a constant observer who comments ironically on his commander's activities. His remarks enable us to regard the general's attitude and behavior from an enlightened perspective, and the story in consequence is one in which nothing really happens; instead, as is true of all of Bellow's fiction to follow, it is a character portrait—two portraits really, because Citron's self-revelation is also substantial.

Apart from the emphasis on character, however, the story contains little that is readily identifiable with Bellow's later writing. Noting in it "an uneasy balance between originality and influence," Daniel Fuchs recognizes the strong impact of Hemingway's method and style on the young author, specifically the ironic understatement in the dialogue and the shifting of action from the center to the penumbra.[44] Perhaps he is being generous to Bellow in assessing the story in terms of a "balance" at all because the Hemingway influence is so clear and pervasive; nevertheless, it is a well-written piece that indicates how effectively the young author could manipulate a momentous historic incident soon after its occurrence so as to serve as little more than a prop for the revelation of character. Whereas in "Leaving the Yellow House" and much of his later fiction character would interact with environment, in "The Mexican General" no such interaction takes place. The general is what he is before the story begins, and the circumstances of Trotsky's assassination have no telling effect on him other than to illuminate a stage on which he may present an enhanced and inflated image of himself.

Bellow returned to a Mexican setting several years later in *The Adventures of Augie March* (1953) where Augie accompanies Thea, his wealthy sweetheart, on a hunt for giant mountain-dwelling iguanas, using a trained eagle named Caligula. But the eagle's training adversely affects its behavior; no longer a wild creature governed by the instinct to survive, Caligula refuses to battle an animal that defends itself. Its fierce appearance belies its cowardice, and consequently the long-planned Mexican hunt becomes a fiasco. Bellow's descriptions of the West in this novel draw heavily upon both convention and myth, convention in the sense that Augie is rigged up in western clothing for his grand experience, and the romantic western aura largely governs Thea's anticipation of success. Bellow's mythic references deepen Augie's response to his western environment and universalize it; moreover, an allusion to Homer, together with the imagery of death and infernal barrenness in this episode, conveys an epic suggestiveness in keeping with the mid-century panorama of American life presented in the whole of the novel. But in more specific terms the cowardice of the eagle during the hunt, completely unanticipated because of his fierce appearance and noble bearing, an eagle trained on the arms of western-garbed Easterners in Mexico, also suggests the vast difference between the West as it actually exists and as it appears to those who cannot or will not see beneath the surface.

Unlike Bellow, whose description of the West presents a real sense of place, E. L. Doctorow, in *Welcome to Hard Times,* uses the region as both a subject of satire and a vehicle for narrative experimentation. He makes no attempt to treat the West seriously as a historical reality, and to criticize the novel for its lack of authenticity misses the point. Similarly, it is difficult if not impossible to find an altogether satisfactory allegorical interpretation of the novel because of its seemingly irresolvable inconsistencies, though a number of attempts have been made. Doctorow's figures are stereotypes exaggerated into grotesques, and in *Welcome to Hard Times,* which merely exploits the West, he developed techniques and devices that enabled him to achieve greater sophistication in his literary methods in the novels that followed, but only in the conclusion of *The Book of Daniel* did he return to the West as a major setting, and then it was not until the final segment. In that complex novel he depicts Disneyland as an *ersatz,* womb-like reduction of American cultural myths, an illusory escape from life's realities, and Southern California's coastal region is seen as a land stripped of natural life in favor of rapidly expanding commercial enterprises and the structures that house them. William Goldman, in his whimsical screenplay for "Butch Cassidy and the Sundance Kid" (1969), likewise hints at the way that romantic individualism of the nineteenth century succumbed to irresistible twentieth-century mechanization and large-scale commercial interests.

In contrast to both Bellow and Doctorow, Edna Ferber has been called a regional novelist of the West because several of her best-sellers have dealt with specific areas west of the Mississippi, though that may not be an appropriate designation. Never a devout Jew, Ferber yet understood and experienced the effect of anti-Semitic prejudice in her own life, and consequently it is not surprising to find her dwelling on that theme in some of her most enduring novels. In *Cimarron* (1930), a novel of the Oklahoma land rush and its aftermath, the popular prejudice is directed chiefly against the nearby Osage Indians until they become wealthy through the discovery of oil on their reservation, whereupon they are suddenly regarded as attractive objects of commercial exploitation. In this novel, too, a Jewish merchant is ridiculed during his early years in Oklahoma, and although he accumulates great wealth through shrewd investment, he remains an alien figure in the community as well as an undeveloped one in terms of literary character.

In *Great Son* (1945), set partly in Alaska during the Gold Rush but predominantly in Seattle, Ferber again shows her sensitivity to ethnic prejudice, particularly against Jews and Orientals, but it is in *Giant* (1952), a sprawling novel of Texas during the first half of the twentieth century, that she makes that theme most pronounced. The historic antipathy of the Texas ranchers toward the impoverished Mexican Americans laboring for them is portrayed with acid candor throughout the novel, and, as in *Cimarron* regarding the Indians, this prejudice constitutes a source of conflict between the leading figures, Bick and Leslie Benedict, a conflict serious enough to endanger their marriage at times. But it was not Ferber's explicit revelation of western prejudice alone that led many Oklahomans and Texans to react strongly against her novels. Rather it was the way she perceived characteristics of their tastes and behavior and depicted them in an unfavorable light, often ridiculing them through exaggeration and presenting them in such a way that they seem to undermine the very ideals and standards that the residents of those states professed as benevolent community-oriented American citizens—such ideals as nobility, honor, democracy, and fairness.

The understandable regional resentment toward such apparent mockery, however, overlooked the national implications of Ferber's western portraits in that although she focuses on limited geographical areas, she often dilates the scope of her critiques to attack hypocritical national attitudes toward celebrated American values. Even in *Giant,* where she repeatedly jabs at the sense of uniqueness she recognized among Texans with respect to size, wealth, food, coffee, hospitality, and other features of their lives, large and small, she draws correspondences between East and West which universalize the criticism that seems to those in the center of her picture an almost personal denunciation. "Here in Texas," Bick tells his young wife, both of them having recently arrived at their quarter-million-acre ranch from her family home in the East, "The cotton rich always snooted the cattle rich. And now if this oil keeps coming into Texas the old cattle crowd will look down their noses at the oil upstarts. You know, like the old New York De Peysters snooting the Vanderbilts and the Vanderbilts cutting the Astors." Later he tells her, "I heard that Neiman-Marcus dresses the cotton crowd up in Dallas now and the new oil rich. They say they've got stuff there makes Bergdorf and Saks in New York look like Indian trading posts."[45] Through such comparisons the East appears no less foolish and trivial in its values than Texas, for the vanity behind them is equally apparent in both, but the Texans, of course, felt the sting most severely.

Whereas Ferber's representations of prejudice and exploitation are thematically important, they constitute but parts of a larger pattern in each novel, a pattern dominated by the lives and conflicts of the major characters and their social milieu. As a contrast, in Tillie Olsen's work the theme of exploitation itself is central. Born in Nebraska to Russian immigrants, Olsen, née Lerner, whose mother was not Jewish assumed her father's socialist perspective and held a variety of jobs in the West and mid-West before she was twenty-one. Her early writings, including two stories in the opening volume of the *Partisan Review* (1934), reflect her socialist outlook at that time, and the first of these, "The Iron Throat," became part of an unfinished novel composed from pieces written during the 1930's. It remained unpublished until 1974, when it appeared under the title *Yonnondio,* an Iroquois word used by Whitman in his poem of that name, signifying "lament for the aborigines." Olsen adapted it to suggest the ephemerality of existence at the bottom of the socioeconomic ladder. She cites the last four lines of the poem as her epigraph:

> Yonnondio! Yonnondio!—unlimn'd they disappear;
> To-day gives place, and fades—the cities, farms, factories fade;
> A muffled sonorous sound, a wailing word is borne through the air for a
>   moment,
> Then blank and gone and still, and utterly lost.

Although *Yonnondio,* like most of Olsen's fiction, does not deal explicitly with Jewish characters, the use of this particular Iroquois word for her title discloses the author's own subtle ethnic sensitivity; as a Jew in a gentile world, she senses the effacement of another persecuted race. More overtly, of course, *Yonnondio* reveals the strong awareness of social injustice that preoccupied many Jewish radicals and reformers during the Depression. Like much proletarian fiction of the period, it conveys a graphic picture of poverty yet offers no prescriptions for improvement. The family whose lives she traces manages to survive from year to year but more on hope than bread. The Holbrooks flee from the dangers and inadequate pay of the Wyoming coal mines to tenant farming in Dakota, dreaming of a normal life in their own home surrounded by their own productive land: "Everyone's eyes were shiny with wonder and promise." But like Hamlin Garland's farmers and John Steinbeck's, their labor brings only increased debt, and again they flee with dreams of a better life, this time east to the stockyards and slaughterhouses in Kansas City, where they are forced to subsist with the other bottom dogs in "a human dump heap." Anna becomes ill, and her husband finds another dangerous but slightly higher-paying job digging under the city streets. Though still struggling for survival, he immediately spends a sizable portion of his wages for fireworks on the Fourth of July. Anna complains, and he replies that it is Independence Day—"Grand and glorious. We got to celebrate." When she asks, "What independence *we* got to celebrate?," he answers, "Independent of property," and Olsen's heavy irony is readily apparent in that Anna's "cumulative vision of overwhelming, hostile forces surrounding [the family] . . . never left her."[46] In the words of James Russell Lowell, Anna Holbrook perceives all of America as "The Land of Broken Promise" for people like herself and her family.[47]

Whereas Olsen's figures in *Yonnondio* are economic aliens, the central characters in the college fiction of Bernard Malamud and Leslie A. Fiedler are simply isolated Jews in Oregon and Montana respectively. Although Malamud does not emphasize the Jewish theme in *A New Life* (1961), he never loses sight of it, either, in that Sy Levin is clearly a New York Jew in utterly foreign territory. "My first night in the Northwest," he muses and asks himself, "who could guess I would ever in my life come so far out?" When he tells the lone scholar of the English department that he has come so far west for the change, he is told in return, "It's more than a change, it's transmogrification."[48] Despite his initial disorientation, however, Levin becomes acclimated to his new surroundings before long, though by the end of the novel he is headed in a state of semi-bewilderment toward an altogether different and unexpected kind of life. Partly assimilated, at once pathetic and sympathetic, he is left straddling the two worlds of his New York Jewish background and his adoptive western, predominantly gentile environs.

In contrast to Levin, Fiedler's central character in "The Last Jew in America" (1966) becomes more alienated from his western surroundings as time passes. Initially one of three Russian Jews in Lewis and Clark City—"tucked away between Montana and Idaho, the cold wastes of Canada immediately to the north and a vast semi-desert to the south,'' site of Lewis and Clark College where he works in the biology department—Jacob had attempted to push his socialist views across the West, but everywhere people had regarded him as a stranger, a Jewish alien in their gentile world. A small Jewish community exists in Lewis and Clark City, but it is a very tenuous one because most of its members have become detached from the beliefs and practices of their faith. All but Jacob and the dying Louie have been taken into the social and economic life of the city, absorbed by it, but Jacob can find no fulfilling existence for himself despite the many years he has lived there. Ultimately, he elects to become for his assimilated co-religionists in Lewis and Clark ''a kind of portable [Jewish] grandfather, a door-to-door link with the past. . . . he could be for the descendants of vanished, incredible Jews a Jew in real life, a terrible fact,'' but whether he assumes this prophetic role or only intends to is left an open question.[49]

Fiedler's vision of the twentieth-century West is not as broadly presented in the title story, however, as in a less successful piece in the same volume—''The First Spade in the West''—where he describes a circus-like funeral at the end in the comic-satiric terms of a western costume party—pure sham. Ned, the black anti-hero, thinks it might be taken as a joke ''that the four of them should be standing there [on stage beside a coffin] dressed like cowpokes: a beatnik from the East, a little sheeny with a shoe-clerk's moustache, a big fat queer who'd struck it rich, and a spade. Well, he didn't know about the rest of them, Ned told himself, but *he* had a right, goddam it, he had every right in the world.''[50] It is a coarse but uproarious surrealistic vision, comic-book theater, in which the western setting reflects broader American values and shortcomings through costumes and cardboard stage settings. Like that of Doctorow and the Hollywood authors, Nathanael West and Budd Schulberg, Fiedler's West is largely a world of make-believe.

Also in the work of all three authors, it is a destructive world, for behind the facades and beneath the surfaces are tensions seeking release. Whereas the surreal dimension is only occasionally present in Fiedler, however, it is apparent continuously in West's *The Day of the Locust* (1939) and Schulberg's *What Makes Sammy Run?* (1941). Among several other characters, West's drugstore cowboy, Earle Shoop, who has come to Hollywood from a small town in Arizona, represents the *ersatz,* violent pattern of behavior that characterizes the unpredictable day-to-day life in Film City. Lacking money, talent, and brains, derided as ''a fugitive from the Western Costume Company'' by an outspoken Jewish dwarf, Shoop presents an image of the Hollywood cowboy and stands or roams aimlessly on the fringes of the film culture. In West's Hollywood, marginal figures like Shoop; Abe Kusich, the temperamental dwarf; Miguel, the cock-fighting entrepreneur; and Homer Simpson, the ultimate fear-ridden naif, constitute a loose, fragmentary layer of society. It lies below that of the relatively few people who have already achieved success through films or are on their way toward doing so, and it lies above the level of economically if not psychologically stable retirees, those frustrated souls whose dreams of California had been generated over the years by countless pictures of sunshine and oranges, but whose severe disappointment over the ordinary dullness of Southern California life has embittered them: "Once there, they discover that sunshine isn't enough. They get tired of oranges. . . . Their boredom becomes more and more terrible" until it is no longer mere boredom but a seething rage that can easily be triggered into violence by any jarring break in the routine.[51] In West's Hollywood, little is real but the emotions, and tightly pent up over a period of time, they are more often than not released as frenzy or hysteria.

West focuses on several characters in *The Day of the Locust,* but in Schulberg's contribution to the genre, *What Makes Sammy Run?,* published only two years later, Sammy Glick alone holds the center of interest. Born to the Orthodox Jewish family of Max Glickstein and reared in a dilapidated tenement between a synagogue and a fish market on New York's lower East Side, Sammy shortens his name to Glick and moves to Hollywood. There, in accordance with his initial aim, he becomes immensely wealthy and influential, a major force in the film industry, but it is all accomplished through chicanery, exploitation, and extraordinary gall; he is a Hollywood version of Ornitz's Meyer Hirsch two decades later. Although Sammy is what he is already, long before he sets off for California, the blatantly commercial and egotistical standards on which Hollywood values are based provide an arena for his manipulative energies. At whatever he attempts he succeeds but always at the cost of someone else. His running with ever more expensive shoes into ever more expensive homes through ever higher salaries and commissions is defensive, a means of his proving to himself as well as to everyone else that he is "no *loser."* At once successful, obnoxious, and pathetic, Sammy is not simply one little New York Jew who has made it to the top in Hollywood through unmitigated *chutzpah,* but as Schulberg indicates, his defensive cry "begins to take on a patriotic ring, like the opening stanza of 'The Star-Spangled Banner.' No longer the immigrant American, Sammy runs into the twenty-first century."[52] The Sammy who makes it big in Hollywood represents the quintessential American spirit of individual enterprise without the ethical control that sociability necessarily engenders. At the end of the novel, he is wealthy, self-deceiving, alienated, unhappy—and he is still running.

Though not so extreme, most of the central figures in American-Jewish fiction set in the West are in a similar plight. The narrative may be in the form of a picaresque adventure novel or a satire, an episodic proletarian work with a naturalistic thesis or a historically oriented family saga, a college novel or a surrealistic vision of Hollywood, but whatever the subject and approach, thematically there is an element of deception in much of the life represented. Probably this may be attributed in part to a sense of alienation among Jewish authors in the West where Jewish communities of more than a handful of people are simply not present except in some of the larger cities. A Jew in the West lacks the kind of relation to the land traditionally enjoyed by gentile Americans who settled there, often generations ago, to ranch or farm, and all of the authors who portray significant Jewish characters in their fiction represent them as outsiders. The West for them appears to be fundamentally unreceptive, at times hostile, and the lack of support from a sympathetic Jewish community heightens the sense of isolation they feel. It is as if they are being rejected by the ideals of the American Dream held dear in the trans-Mississippi West. Indeed, the trying situations in which the fictional characters of these Jewish writers find themselves are often the result of some kind of betrayal, actual or assumed, from the character's own perspective or the author's, and sometimes, as in Olsen and West, from both. Significantly, however, regardless of the western settings, most of the problems generated have not peculiarly regional roots or causes but national ones, as the authors suggest through symbols and pointed comparisons. In consequence, the seemingly western vision of our American-Jewish authors assumes the dimensions of our nation as a whole.

CONCLUSION

From the 1890's, then, to the years of the Second World War, Jewish writers of fiction in the United States represented America as a possible source of economic well-being and opportunity for aspiring Jews but also as a lure away from their faith and heritage. Among the first generation of these authors, that is to say, among the immigrants themselves such as Cahan, Bernstein, Oppenheim, and Yezierska, their fiction transforms the noxious statement that one can take the Jew out of the ghetto but not the ghetto out of the Jew into an expression that confirms the strong bond of peoplehood among Jews that is tightened by a largely homogeneous urban community. The suffering over alienation from a vital Jewish milieu is evident in the "autobiography" of David Levinsky and many figures in Cahan's stories, those frustrated immigrants enduring loneliness in the land that enables them to earn a materially successful living but offers nothing to replace the *shtetl* kinship they have lost. So it is, also, with Yezierska and her semi-autobiographical figures who temporarily leave the ghetto for outside success and return to it, not as a renewed source of faith, however, but as a throbbing, organic community without which they cannot be truly themselves.

Judaism lost its hold among the next generation of writers, whose proletarian sentiments reacted against what America appeared to have become in the hands of big business and machine politics—a source of exploitation. Michael Gold was lured into communism from what he regarded as a besmirched American promise, and Samuel Ornitz portrayed the type of legal grafter who had helped to sully that promise by employing it as a means of gaining access to wealth, power, and an appointed judicial bench. Meyer Levin, too, in the 1930's, though he did not turn away from Judaism, conveyed a clear picture of the way that many people did as they drifted from adolescence and family into a secular, violent, and largely anti-Semitic America. In the tradition of Sinclair, Steinbeck, and others, he implied that exploitation of the workingman would lead to a class war.

It may well be that the immediate onset of World War II kept his implication from becoming prophecy in that national defense quickly assumed the burden of the economy, and after the war, of course, socioeconomic problems were no longer the same. The changes are reflected in the fiction published from the mid–1940's to the present. Whereas the earlier authors had dealt chiefly with the Jews' finding a place for themselves in a secular America, often at the cost of their heritage, for most of the post-war writers assimilation had become a way of life by the time they began to publish. There was no longer a need for Jews to mask their Judaism in public if they intended to take advantage of the opportunities toward social and vocational success that America offered, but it was impossible for many of them to avoid self-consciousness of their Judaism nevertheless. This occurs not because of the vital, tightly bound Jewish community life they themselves had once known and left but because of their parents or grandparents who had left it before them and inculcated the ghetto lessons into their consciousness as a part of their childhood training. Generally educated in secular American schools and universities, the contemporary Jew is portrayed as respecting his heritage but only nominally sharing the faith, a faith traditionally based on love of God through obedience to the Hebraic law and devotion to the community of Israel, meaning the Jewish people as a whole.

With some exceptions, of course, most notably today in the novels of Chaim Potok, obedience to the Judaic laws that governed the manner of worship and pattern of behavior in toto is all but neglected in contemporary American-Jewish fiction, as is a true rather than symbolic devotion to the community of Israel. The neglect of these traditional obligations has led to guilt, and the universal reminders of Jewish suffering through the biblical periods and the diaspora—including the emphatic reverberations from the Holocaust—exacerbate that guilt to the extent that it endangers the mental stability of the American Jew who remains sensitive to what his people have had to endure for *him*, as he sees it. Many post-war Jewish authors employ this guilt and its psychological ramifications as major themes in their fiction. It is clear, for example, in Bellow's *The Victim,* Roth's *Portnoy's Complaint* and *The Breast,* Malamud's early stories and *The Assistant,* most of Salinger's stories of the Glass family, the last three of Wallant's four novels, Doctorow's *The Book of Daniel,* and in all of Potok's novels, among many more works by the same authors and others.

It is this idea of guilt that gives the identity theme its special poignance among Jewish authors writing of American Jews both before and after World War II. Before the war both the authors and their characters turned away from themselves toward American social, cultural, and economic possibilities for answers to questions about their own lives and values. Not long after the war, in contrast, the responses to similar queries asked under vastly different circumstances were of another kind entirely as both authors and characters turned inward. Early in the 1970's Philip Roth briefly engaged in sharp social and political satire, but by then his fiction had already begun reflecting a decidedly inward turn. This tendency toward introspection, often to an extreme degree, has led some of the best contemporary American-Jewish authors away from the world around them into a distressing preoccupation with their own motives and aims as novelists. They represent America as an often-violent moral muddle while they represent themselves as acutely aware of being simultaneously intellectuals writing works of the imagination on a high theoretical plane and animal creatures with carnal urges persistently endeavoring to assume control—a constant conflict between high ideals and over-exposed low lusts. For clear examples of this thematic internal struggle a reader need only turn to some of the more popular novels of the past decade by Roth, Malamud, Doctorow, Mailer, and others.

One cannot help but believe that it is time now for the novelists to end the conflict by resolving it in terms of a complementarity that will reveal the American Jew to himself and herself not in a torturous state of psychological warfare over guilt and lust or in a perceptual sphere detached from the surrounding milieu, but in a diversified American culture of which he or she is a complex, functioning individual, perhaps even a morally committed one. Then, like Bellow's Augie March or Potok's Gershon Loran—two American-Jewish characters from opposite ends of the gamut of commitment—the individual can take up his or her life from there. With all of its variety, the America they represent will be a truer one than we have seen from some of our best Jewish novelists for a good many years.

NOTES

1. Herman Bernstein, *In the Gates of Israel*, pp. 292. 294.
2. Stanley F. Chyet, Introduction, p. 6.
3. Anzia Yezierska, "America and I," in *The Open Cage*, pp. 25–26, 33.
4. Anzia Yezierska, *Bread Givers*, p. 270.
5. Anzia Yezierska, *Arrogant Beggar*, p. 226.
6. Alice Kessler-Harris, Introduction to *The Open Cage*, by Anzia Yezierska, pp. 11–12.
7. Michael Gold, *Jews Without Money*, p. 127.
8. Ibid., pp. 218–219.
9. Ibid., pp. 26–27.
10. Michael Harrington, Afterword to *Jews Without Money* by Michael Gold, p. 232.
11. Ibid., p. 230.
12. Samuel Ornitz, *Haunch Paunch and Jowl*, pp. 85, 122.
13. Ibid., p. 183.
14. Ibid., p. 13.
15. Sam B. Girgus, *The New Covenant*, p. 196.
16. Roth quoted by Bonnie Lyons and William Freedman. See Lyons, "An Interview with Henry Roth," p. 63; and Freedman, "A Conversation with Henry Roth," pp. 152–155.
17. Lyons, p. 61.
18. Girgus, p. 96.

19. Hal Higdon, *The Crime of the Century: The Leopold and Loeb Case*, p. 33.

20. Gary Bossin, "The Literary Achievement of Meyer Levin," p. 46.

21. Meyer Levin, *Citizens*, p. 650.

22. Bossin, chapter 5.

23. Stephen J. Whitfield, Review of *A Certain People*, p. 3.

24. Charles E. Silberman, *A Certain People*, pp. 22, 24.

25. Daniel Fuchs, *Saul Bellow*, p. 18.

26. Robert R. Dutton, *Saul Bellow*, p. 52.

27. Quoted by Dutton, p. 65.

28. Fuchs, p. 59.

29. Saul Bellow, *The Dean's December*, p. 275.

30. Ibid., pp. 311–312.

31. Quoted by Irving Malin, *Jews and Americans*, p. 176.

32. Allen Guttmann, *The Jewish Writer in America*, p. 118.

33. Philip Roth, *Reading Myself and Others*, pp. 181–182.

34. Ibid., pp. 89–90.

35. Ibid., pp. 151, 72.

36. Ibid., p. 82.

37. Edward Lewis Wallant, *The Children at the Gate*, p. 172.

38. Grace Paley, *Enormous Changes at the Last Minute*, p. 49.

39. Grace Paley, *Later the Same Day*, p. 140.

40. E. L. Doctorow, "The Passion of Our Calling," pp. 1, 21–23.

41. Herbert Mitgang quoting Doctorow in "Finding the Right Voice," p. 36.

42. Daniel Walden, "Chaim Potok, A Zwischenmensch . . . ," p. 19.

43. Chaim Potok, *The Book of Lights*, p. 279.

44. Fuchs, p. 282.

45. Edna Ferber, *Giant*, pp. 116, 138.

46. Tillie Olsen, *Yonnondio*, pp. 38, 69, 151.

47. See discussion of the phrase in context in William Dean Howells, *Literary Friends and Acquaintance* (New York: Harper and Brothers, 1900), p. 219.

48. Bernard Malamud, *A New Life*, pp. 11, 72.

49. Leslie A. Fiedler, *The Last Jew in America*, pp. 29, 48.

50. Ibid., p. 191.

51. Nathanael West, *The Day of the Locust*, pp. 150, 178.

52. Budd Schulberg, Afterword to *What Makes Sammy Run?*, p. 252.

BIBLIOGRAPHY

Bellow, Saul. *The Dean's December*. New York: Harper and Row, 1982.

Bernstein, Herman. *In the Gates of Israel: Stories of the Jews*. New York: J. F. Taylor, 1902.

Bossin, Gary. "The Literary Achievement of Meyer Levin." Ph.D. diss., Kent State University, 1980.

Chyet, Stanley F., ed. Introduction to *Forgotten Fiction: American Jewish Life, 1890–1920. American Jewish Archives*. 37.1. (April 1985).

Doctorow, E. L. "The Passion of Our Calling." *New York Times Book Review*. (August 25, 1985), pp. 1, 21–23.

Dutton, Robert R. *Saul Bellow*. New York: Twayne, 1971.

Ferber, Edna. *Giant*. New York: Doubleday, 1952.

Fiedler, Leslie A. *The Last Jew in America*. New York: Stein and Day, 1966.

Freedman, William. "A Conversation with Henry Roth." *Literary Review*. 18.2. (Winter 1975), pp. 149–157.

Fuchs, Daniel. *Saul Bellow: Vision and Revision*. Durham, North Carolina: Duke University Press, 1984.

Girgus, Sam B. *The New Covenant: Jewish Writers and the American Idea*. Chapel Hill: University of North Carolina Press, 1984.

Gold, Michael. *Jews Without Money*. Afterword by Michael Harrington. New York: Avon, 1965.

Guttmann, Allen. *The Jewish Writer in America: Assimilation and the Crisis of Identity*. New York: Oxford University Press, 1971.

Higdon, Hal. *The Crime of the Century: The Leopold and Loeb Case*. New York: G. P. Putnam's Sons, 1975.

Howells, William Dean. *Literary Friends and Acquaintance*. New York. Harper and Brothers, 1900.

Levin, Meyer. *Citizens*. New York: Viking Press, 1940.

Lyons, Bonnie. "An Interview with Henry Roth." *Shenandoah*. 25.1. (Fall, 1973), pp. 48–71.

Malamud, Bernard. *A New Life*. New York: Farrar, Straus & Cudahy, 1961.

Malin, Irving. *Jews and Americans*. Carbondale and Edwardsville: Southern Illinois University Press, 1965.

Mitgang, Herbert. "Finding the Right Voice." *New York Times Book Review*. (November 11, 1984), p. 36.

Olsen, Tillie. *Yonnondio: From the Thirties*. n.p.: Delacorte Press/Seymour Lawrence, 1974.

Oppenheim, James. *Doctor Rast*. New York: Macmillan, 1909.

[Ornitz, Samuel.] *Haunch Paunch and Jowl: An Anonymous Autobiography*. New York: Boni and Liveright, 1923.

Paley, Grace. *Enormous Changes at the Last Minute*. New York: Farrar, Straus & Giroux, 1974.

———. *Later the Same Day*. New York: Farrar, Straus & Giroux, 1985.

Potok, Chaim. *The Book of Lights*. New York: Alfred A. Knopf, 1981.

Roth, Philip. *Reading Myself and Others*. New York: Farrar, Straus & Giroux, 1975.

Silberman, Charles E. *A Certain People: American Jews and Their Lives Today*. New York: Summit Books, 1985.

Walden, Daniel. "Chaim Potok, A Zwischenmensch ('between-person') Adrift in the Cultures." *Studies in American Jewish Literature*. 4. (1985), pp. 19–25. Special Chaim Potok issue.

Wallant, Edward Lewis. *The Children at the Gate*. New York: Harcourt, Brace and World, 1964.

Whitfield, Stephen J. Review of *A Certain People: American Jews and Their Lives Today*, by Charles E. Silberman. [American Jewish] *Congress Monthly*. (January, 1986), pp. 3–5.

Yezierska, Anzia. *The Open Cage: An Anzia Yezierska Collection*, ed. Alice Kessler-Harris. New York: Persea, 1979.

13

Eastern Europe in American-Jewish Writing

Asher Z. Milbauer

I

When contemplating this essay, I intuitively reached out for a recently published collection of short stories, *The Yiddish Speaking Parrot* (1982), written by Efraim Sevela, a Russian-Jewish author, who, after a fierce confrontation with the Soviet authorities, was allowed to repatriate to Israel in 1972. The experience of re-reading Sevela not only prompted me to see American-Jewish writing in a different light but also made me aware of the close thematic and philosophical affinities between the works of Eastern-European Jewish writers and their American counterparts.

Upon his arrival in Israel, Sevela was among the few Russian émigré writers to successfully absorb the rich texture of Israel's reality, making it the source of his creative imagination as well as the subject matter of his post-Russia stories and novels. However, there is hardly anything he writes that does not convey an anguishing sense of loss generated by the abandonment of a country he once called his own. But what makes it possible for him to transcend this often crippling sensation is the overpowering feeling of responsibility for those left behind, a feeling that endows every line he creates with the fruitful alliance of moral conviction and artistic mastery. Whether he takes his readers to the vast deserts of Sinai or the mystery-filled streets of Safed, to the fertile meadows of Galilee or the dusty construction sites in Migdal Haemek, another presence is always in close proximity: Russia and her Jews. The haunting memory of the two casts a dark shadow upon fresh literary adventures, thereby creating an acute tension between the desire to forget and the inability to do so. It is precisely this friction that inspires Sevela's best work.

Of the stories, "The Sabbath Candleholders" stands out as an extremely intense personal narrative which transforms unique fates of ordinary Russian Jews into a collective and paradigmatic history of the Jewish people in Russia.

Sevela not only creates an image of Eastern Europe that is shared by the majority of Jewish writers, regardless of their place of birth, but he also outlines the duties and responsibilities these authors face by virtue of their nationality.

"'Since when have you become a Jew?'" a retired army Colonel and a member of the Communist party asks his son when the latter informs him of his intention to leave Russia for Israel.[1] To answer the colonel's shocking question our protagonist invites us to join him in his journey back to childhood to experience a Russian Jew's odyssey from namelessness to a well-defined identity. For a Jew to relate his past experiences means to relate the experiences of his ancestors. Grandmother Roza was born into a family of well-off merchants who were allowed to reside beyond the notorious Pale, because the Tsar and his court derived many financial benefits from their managerial abilities and business credibility. The Bolshevik Revolution, however, destroyed the family's fortune, and those members who survived the bloody ordeal were scattered all over Russia.

At the time of our narrator's birth, Grandmother Roza resides in a damp basement apartment, acutely experiencing the consequences of the new ideology, which considers terror and persecution as justifiable means to redistribute wealth and build a society based upon equality and brotherhood. The loss of her worldly possessions does not hurt Roza as much as the loss of her four sons, who fall prey to Marxist-Leninist teachings, and in pursuit of their careers renounce their Jewishness. Three move to different cities, where they think they can easily hide their background; and to seal their "triumphant" march toward total assimilation they marry non-Jewish women. The fourth son, the narrator's father, chooses a military career. He would have also liked to distance himself from his mother, but as chance has it, he is stationed in his native town. Careful not to be compromised, he nevertheless tolerates her weekly visits.

Although hurt, Roza takes their betrayal in good stride, finding solace in her faith and memories, which, together with her beautiful Yiddish, she tries to impart to her grandson. On Friday nights, the little boy assists her in lighting the Sabbath candles. He helps her place the candles into the two heavy silver candleholders, a family heirloom for many generations and a source of both unspeakable joy and deadly trouble.

Jewish "success stories" are short-lived in Russia. In spite of their denial of their Jewishness, Roza's sons are sought out and arrested during the purges. Their gentile wives, rejected by their own parents and relatives, turn now to the only person they know will accept them and bring their children to Roza's to wait out the trouble under the watchful guidance of a woman they ignored for a long time. In a masterfully realized scene, Sevela gathers the women and the children around the Sabbath table. They watch spellbound as Grandmother kindles the Sabbath candles and prays for her sons' deliverance. The flicker of the candles indicates that the communion has been received. Two hard years have to pass before the mother can embrace her four tortured sons and the wives and children can be reunited with their husbands and fathers. Yet during the Second

World War when the Nazi hordes overrun Roza's native town, the Jews become their first victims. Before being murdered, the Grandmother decides to take care of her most precious possession: she leaves her candleholders with her gentile neighbor. This becomes her last heroic act. Rather than destroying the heirloom, and giving into cynicism and bitterness, Roza shares her priceless gift with another human being.

With the candlesticks now gone, orphaned indeed, it seems as if the evil spirit has finally succeeded in destroying a tradition and violating a continuity upon which the survival of the Jewish people so heavily depended. Roza's heroic determination cannot so easily be reduced to ashes. Her faithful and patient devotion bears fruit. Having survived the war, her grandson experiences a subconscious urge to return to his hometown, a place which, with his Grandmother dead, he knows will be desolate and meaningless. He finds her former neighbor who quietly and with dignity removes the candleholders, wraps them in a newspaper with Stalin's picture, and returns them to someone she assumes is their rightful owner. Now, he fully understands: he came to rescue the symbol of faith, continuity, tradition, the only light of hope to the despised, oppressed, enslaved and haunted subjects of "the land of Pharaoh." Grandma Roza's labors have again paid off.

Stalin's picture foreshadows a grim future for the narrator and his people. The demise of Hitler brings no respite. Stalin initiates new pogroms in Russia. Yiddish writers are sentenced to death; Jewish doctors are accused of conspiring to kill Stalin; thousands of Jews are swallowed up by the gluttonous Archipelag Gulag. Though Krushchev's de-Stalinization later halts the indiscriminate slaughter, the price exacted from the surviving Jews is assimilation. During the Six Day War many Soviet Jews are again subjected to virulent anti-Semitism and are asked to disassociate themselves from their brethren in Israel, who dare to fight not only for their rights but also for the rights of an entire people. Many Jews, our narrator among them, realize that to preserve their identity, they have to leave Russia. The candleholders must come out of hiding.

Toward the end of the story we find the protagonist at the Sheremetyevo airport in Moscow, bidding good-bye to his still-bewildered father before going through the customs to be cleared for his passage to Israel. When he presents his luggage for inspection, the customs official ignores the meager contents of the suitcase and singles out the two beautiful candleholders for closer scrutiny. The official allows only one candlestick, since two would weigh more than the fixed weight of silver one is allowed to remove from the country.

Forgetting his pride, the narrator pleads with the unyielding official, trying to explain the unity of the pair which symbolizes the wholeness of Sabbath and the oneness of the Jewish people. His father, the decorated army officer and a member of the Communist party, upon witnessing the humiliation of his departing son, steps forward and with a trembling hand gets hold of one of the candleholders. He accepts it for safekeeping until it can again be reunited with its lonely mate. The retired Jewish colonel will never again ask his son the question, "Since when have you become a Jew?" Now he knows that no one ever stops being one.

II

Some time ago I sent a letter to a renowned American writer, requesting her assistance in illuminating certain biographical aspects of her brilliant short stories. Her prompt reply expressed a warm welcome on the occasion of my transplantation from "the land of Pharaoh"—Russia, that is—advising me, at the same time, that it was smarter and safer, to write about deceased authors, advice I later learned to respect albeit not always to follow.

I did not pay close attention to her reference to Russia as "the land of Pharaoh." The immediate experiences of leaving the country where I was born, reared, and educated and the new impressions generated by a rapid sequence of the most divergent events following my exodus, created an intellectual and emotional barrier that prevented me from turning my memories of Russia into a metaphor, a neatly packaged image to be used as a password in establishing continuity and affinity between Jews separated by fenced borders and rigid ideologies.

Only now have I begun to understand that this reference to Russia as the land of bondage, slavery, oppression, and tyranny constitutes a powerful and unchangeable image of Eastern Europe shared by many American-Jewish artists and thinkers. Whether one reads Emma Lazarus's poetry or Mary Antin's memoirs, Anzia Yezierska's short stories or Abraham Cahan's novels, Waldo Frank's travelogues or Irving Howe's treatises, Susan Fromberg Schaeffer's or Bernard Malamud's fictional histories, or Philip Roth's and Saul Bellow's romans à clef, one never fails to wonder at the strong and haunting hold the Old Country exercises upon the imagination of these writers and scholars. Representing the collective soul of an Eastern-European Jew who is restlessly roaming the "land of ice and darkness," Chaim Potok's "mythic ancestor" frequently violates the peace of an American-Jewish artist, making him listen breathlessly to the cries of the past and the anguish of dispersion. American-Jewish writers find it extremely difficult, even impossible, to ignore the treatment of their personal and the collective Jewish pasts. Their relationship with their past defines who they are and gives substance to their work.

Born years and miles apart, raised on radically different ideologies, products of diametrically opposite cultures, can Sevela and Emma Lazarus share a kinship that usually binds authors of the same age, culture, tradition, and background? Yes. The two Jewish writers are united by the vision inherited from Ezekiel. Like the prophet in the Valley of Dry Bones, they hope to "revive the scattered bones and cause them to join into a living, vigorous body."[2] In the 1880's Emma Lazarus dreamed that the Jews of Eastern Europe would be able to escape their bondage and join their brethren in the land of freedom, be it America or Palestine.

In the 1980's Sevela dreams of a reunion between the two forcibly separated candleholders.

Emma Lazarus (1849–1887) was born in New York to a prosperous Sephardic family. She was brought up on the finest traditions of European culture. She was only eighteen when, drawing on her diverse intellectual background supplemented by her familiarity with French and German, she published *Poems and Translations* (1866), renderings of poems by Heine and Hugo among others. In 1874 she issued her first novel, *Alide,* based on an incident in Goethe's life. Because she had no financial responsibilities, Lazarus could devote much time to widening her cultural horizons and writings for such publications as *Scribner's Magazine* and the *American Hebrew*. Although by no means disclaiming her Jewishness, the poet did not attribute much significance to her heritage for the first thirty years of her short life. "Her work," writes Louis Harap, "up to the late 1870's dealt with conventional themes. . . . The total effect is one of remoteness from living reality."[3] During the last years both her personal and artistic lives drastically changed directions. Lazarus came to recognize a truth with which many Jewish intellectuals sooner or later must come to terms: if one is born a Jew one will find it extremely difficult to remove oneself from the "living reality," a notion best expressed by one of I. B. Singer's characters: "We are running away and Mount Sinai runs after us."[4] Lazarus, during a time of crisis faced by Russian Jews in the late nineteenth century, became aware that she had no choice but active involvement in the destiny of her brethren in Eastern Europe. She lived up to her responsibility both in deed and art.

In the early 1880's the American people were shocked to find out that while they were busy implementing American notions of justice, emancipation, and republicanism, in other parts of the world, and most notably in Russia, anti-Semites were perpetrating atrocities on a massive scale upon the Jewish people. As a result of the assassination of Alexander II on March 1, 1881, pogroms swept through Russia. Newspapers overtly accused the Jews not only of the assassination but also of active involvement in and the organization of radical revolutionary movements. Indeed, the Jews were blamed for absolutely everything that went wrong in Russia, and these insinuations were to be frequently repeated. Whenever the authorities conceived of one or a series of pogroms, it took them no time and little effort to incite the peasants and workers against the Jews. On April 15, 1881, for example, a pogrom which began in Yelisavetgrad snowballed into an avalanche of destruction "that continued well into 1882, affecting some 225 communities. About 20,000 Jews were made homeless, 100,000 ruined, Jewish property valued at 80 million dollars was destroyed." No one made an effort to help. "Both liberal Russia and radical Russia," writes Lucy S. Dawidowicz, "remained silent".[5]

One of the consequences of the Russian pogroms was a surge in the number of immigrants to America. The American people became privy to numerous eyewitness accounts of atrocious events in Russia. When in 1882 "Representative Samuel Cox of New York City . . . listed 167 places where had been riots,

burnings, pillagings, rapes, and murders,'' many Americans, along with demanding action to prevent this violence, took a harder look at their attitude
toward Russia; others clung to a view of Russia based on distorted facts or
predicated on what they simply wanted to be true of that enigmatic country.[6]

When in 1775 Thomas Paine was reflecting on the importance of Russia to
the young republic, he concluded that this ''vast empire . . . almost shut out from
the sea'' could mean little to the formation of the New World.[7] This reluctance
to take Russia seriously has for many years impaired the American people's
ability to perceive this country in a realistic and methodical manner.[8] The lack
of urgency as well as curiosity to penetrate Russian realities led to a perception
of Russia based on myth, absence of verifiable information, misinterpretation
of historical events, and a strong desire to create an image one would have liked
to exist rather than to try to understand a system of perceptions based on fact.
In the history of American-Russian relationships, American responses to events
invariably ''rested on images, fictions, and legends rather than on facts.''[9] Because the American image of Russia was based on shaky grounds, it has undergone frequent changes, from friendly to hostile and then back again, depending
upon political circumstances and the degree of ignorance applied to their
interpretation.

In the 1880's major changes were taking place in America's perception of
Russia. Representative Cox's accounts of the horrors of the Russian pogroms,
coupled with George Kennan's testimony about the cruelties of the Russian police
state, first in his book *The Tent Life in Russia* and later in his reports to *Century
Magazine,* began to erode the Russian legend. Up until the present, however,
the tendency to substitute fiction for facts, not for malicious reasons but from
innocence and naivete, has not been totally uprooted.

The changeable popular American image of Russia, however, does not hold
true for the majority of the American Jews or American-Jewish writers. Since
the mass exodus of Russian Jews that started in the early 1880's, the pendulum
that charted the image of Russia for the American Jews stopped swinging: Russia
has become analogous to ''the land of Pharaoh,'' an image that translates into
bondage, tyranny, and obliteration of identity. The exodus from Egypt ''was so
effectively impressed on all subsequent generations,'' writes William W. Hallo,
''that it covered every subsequent crisis in the national experience. Every oppression was somehow regarded as another 'Egypt,' every liberation as a triumph
over Pharaoh.''[10] Hallo's rule has held true even when some Jewish intellectuals
tried to reshape Russia's image after the October Revolution. Subsequent crises,
however, made the rewriting of the story impossible. The living reality, as
evidenced by Sevela's accounts, comes marching in, and the story of ''Egypt''
starts all over again.

Whereas Walt Whitman, apparently oblivious to (or possibly uninterested in)
the oppressive nature of Russia's internal affairs, wrote to his Russian translator
of *Leaves of Grass* on December 20, 1881, about his discovery that the Russian
and American people had surprisingly many characteristics in common and

shared with him his dream of "an internationality of poems and poets," his contemporary, Emma Lazarus, gravely touched by the numerous accounts of suffering among the Russian Jews, underwent a spiritual and artistic conversion.[11] Not able to embrace Judaism in its totality, she nevertheless did not shy away from responsibilities to her people and her heritage.

Some of the German and Sephardic Jewish community perceived the arrival in America of the quaint-looking, impoverished masses of Eastern-European Jews as a threat to their own security as well as a spark that might fuel anti-Semitism in their adopted country. Emma Lazarus, however, contemptuously brushed aside these anxieties and immersed herself in activities that alleviated the hardships of transplantation. She was frequently meeting the new arrivals, comforting children, and supplying them with provisions and clothes. Although she saw this physical involvement as an integral part of her responsibilities, Lazarus became increasingly aware that her contribution to the plight of im-migrants could be more significant if she wrote about it.

Harap writes of a curious coincidence that was a spur to Lazarus's rising national consciousness which in turn helped transform her writing. In April, 1882, the *Century Magazine* included an article by Lazarus in which she discussed the question of Jewish national character in Emersonian terms and in the required detached tone. In the same issue Madame Z. Ragozin, a Russian journalist, bluntly blamed the Jews for the pogroms in Russia:

The Jews are disliked, nay, hated in those parts of East Europe and Russia not because they believe and pray differently, but because they are a parasitic race who, producing nothing, fasten on the produce and the land and labor and live on it, choking the life out of commerce and industry as sure as the creeper throttles the tree that holds it.[12]

Upon reading this defamation, Lazarus turned her prose into a strong vehicle for refuting anti-Semitic charges, and her poetry, from then on, was inspired by a profound love for her abused people.

This *ahavat Israel,* love for the people of Israel, permeates the whole of *Songs of a Semite,* a slim volume of poems published in 1882. In addition to "The Dance to Death," a play Lazarus dedicated to George Eliot in appreciation of the positive contribution of *Daniel Deronda* to the Jewish cause, the collection includes poems that reflect an artistic maturity informed and inspired by strong moral convictions.

When confronted with the news of the pogroms, Lazarus vents her rage at the eternal injustice in "The Crowing of the Red Cock," a poem that interprets the current crisis as an integral part of the morbidly repetitious sequence of suffering since the Jewish people gave up polytheism for monotheism. She writes:

> Once more the clarion cock crowed
> > Once more the sword of Christ is drawn
> A million burning rooftrees light
> The world-wide path of Israel's flight.[13]

Since their exodus from Egypt, Lazarus implies, the Jewish people, except for short periods of respite and peace, have been subjected to nearly constant displacement. Deprived of a homeland, they wander from country to country, always at the mercy of their new masters, who after exploiting them to the fullest, give them up to "the lust of mobs, the greed of priest, the tyranny of kings," whose only aim is "to root his seed from earth again."[14] Since there is hardly any place the Jew can run to or hardly anyone's protection he can solicit, it is time, intimates Lazarus, that he should start to fend for himself and "turn the wrath sublime, With blood for blood and crime for crime."[15]

This initially timid call for action gains strength in "The Banner of the Jew." The poetess recalls the Maccabean times, when after the death of Alexander the Great and the division of Greece into four parts, the Jews find themselves under the rule of Antiochus IV, nicknamed by his enemies Epimanes, "the mad man." In his efforts to impose Hellenism on the Jews, Antiochus IV considers all means fair in achieving his goal. He forbids circumcision, defiles the altar in the Jerusalem Temple by sacrificing on it pigs to Zeus, and slaughters those who refuse to wage war on the Sabbath. Mattathias and his five sons can no longer tolerate the injustice and atrocities the tyrant levels against their people and calmly observe how

> Jerusalem's empty streets, her shrine
> Laid waste, when Greeks profaned the Law,
> With idol and with pagan sign.
> Mourners in tattered black were there,
> With ashes sprinkled on their hair.[16]

Grieved and outraged by this awesome vision of destruction, "the Maccabean clan" and thousands of its followers descend upon its enemies in a decisive effort to free themselves of the shackles of oppression and redeem their dignity and faith. Lazarus celebrates this outburst of courage and desire of independence by comparing it to Ezra's valiant attempts to revive the spirit of Judaism and revitalize the religious and national enthusiasm after the initial joy of restoring the Temple in Jerusalem in 516 B.C.:

> Oh deem not dead that martial fire,
>   Say not the mystic flame is spent!
> With Moses' law and David's lyre,
>   Your ancient strength remains unbent.
> Let but an Ezra rise anew,
>   To lift the *Banner of the Jew!*[17]

Bearing in mind the fact that Lazarus writes this poem as a result of the Russian pogroms, it is easy to discern the parallel she draws between the times of Antiochus IV and those following the assassination of Alexander II in 1881. Upon his succession to the throne, Alexander III reverses all the relatively progressive gains achieved during his father's rule, and refuses to see the explosive nature of the Russian reality. Incited by his advisor Constantine Pobedonostsev, Over-Procurator of the Holy Synod, he blames the Jews for the recent disturbances. "To protect" the Russian people from the subversive enemy, he initiates the "May Laws," which "forbade Jews to settle in villages; gave villages the right to drive out the Jews already living in them; expelled many Jews from such cities as St. Petersburg, Moscow, and Kiev; limited the number of Jews in secondary schools and universities; prohibited the Jews from entering the legal profession and participating in local government."[18] These laws clearly indicate that the Tsar and his court are decisively set to solve the Jewish problem. As a result, they put into motion Pobedonostsev's grand plan to rid Russia of her Jews by having one-third of them die, another third convert to Christianity, and the rest emigrate, thus restoring "Nicholas I's principles of nationality, Orthodoxy, and autocracy."[19]

Even a superficial comparison of events during the reign of Antiochus IV and those happening thousands of years later in Russia clarifies Lazarus's perception of Jewish history as "one cry of pain" and explains her acute sense of urgency in saving the Russian Jews from the present-day Pharaoh. While preoccupied with their fate, she is also thinking about the question of a Jewish homeland, trying to answer her own query posed in "The Crowing of the Red Cock": "Where is the Hebrew's fatherland?" Palestine, she thinks, would be the best place to provide a secure asylum for the fleeing Eastern-European Jews. She believes, however, that any country, and most notably America, can indeed become a secure haven for her co-religionists as long as it guarantees their freedom and equality. In fact, Lazarus's views in regard to a Jewish homeland resemble closely those of Ahad ha'Am, [lit. "One of the People"; Asher Ginzberg, 1856–1927] who thought of Palestine not only as a safe haven but also as a spiritual center concerned with the preservation of Judaism. What the scholar and the poet indeed strove for was a set of circumstances that would provide the Jew with a choice, a notion Emma Lazarus very eloquently expressed in her poem "New Year":

> In two divided streams the exiles part,
>   One rolling homeward to its ancient source,
> One rushing sunward with fresh will, new heart.
>   By each the truth is spread, the law unfurled,
> Each separate soul contains the nation's force,
>   And both embrace the world.[20]

Another poem, "In Exile," once again reaffirms these ideas. She was so impressed by a letter written by a Russian Jew from Texas addressed to his people in Russia that she decided to use an extract from it as an epigraph to her poem. "Since that day till now our life is one unbroken paradise," writes the immigrant. "We live a true brotherly life. Every evening after supper we take

a seat under the mighty oak and sing our songs."[21] The biblical echoes of the
Promised Land's serenity, quiet, and peace find their way into the refugee's
missive and are then channeled into her poem. Texas becomes the land of Canaan;
by inference, Russia turns into Egypt. For the sake of emphasis, rather than
describing Russia as "the land of the Pharaoh" in detail, Lazarus chooses to
depict the paradisical atmosphere of the vast Texas prairies where

> The hounded stag that has escaped the pack,
>   And pants at ease within the thick-leaved dell,
> The unimprisoned bird that finds the track
>   Through sun-bathed space, to where his fellows dwell;
> The martyr, granted respite from the rack,
>   The death-doomed victim pardoned from his cell,—
> Such only know the joy these exiles gain,—
> Life's sharpest rapture is surcease of pain.[22]

By presenting America as the place of "Freedom to live the law that Moses
brought, / To sing the songs of David and, to think / The thoughts Gabriel to
Spinoza taught," and by shrouding, at the same time, Russia into silence, Lazarus
employs a device used in the biblical narrative when describing Egypt.[23] The
biblical rendition of Egypt is very economical, sparse, and thereby more expressive and eloquent in conveying the hardships of slavery and oppression. The
economy of expression reinforces the image of Russia as "the land of Pharaoh"
and reaffirms her views of America as "the Promised Land." Many future
American-Jewish writers came to share with Emma Lazarus her conviction that
America was indeed founded on the principles of justice, emancipation, and
independence propagated by both the Torah and the Talmud and readily adopted
by the Pilgrims, who perceived themselves as ancient Israelites fleeing into the
wilderness from oppression and tyranny. And if this is so, the poet, as well as
other American-Jewish writers, sees no difficulty in perceiving Russia as "the
land of Pharaoh" and endowing America with the biblical attributes of the land
promised to the Jews and pictured as the Mother of Exiles, crying out "with
silent lips":

> . . . "Give me your tired, your poor,
> Your huddled masses yearning to breathe free,
> The wretched refuse of your teeming shore.
> Send these, the homeless, tempest-tost to me,
> I lift my lamp beside the golden door!"[24]

As we have seen, 1881 was the year that the shocking information of the
pogroms reached American shores and forced American Jews to notice the plight
of their co-religionists in Eastern Europe. It was also the year of the birth of
Mary Antin, a Russian-American-Jewish writer, who through an eyewitness

account would substantiate Emma Lazarus's vision of Russia and reaffirm her perception of America.

Born in Plotzk, a town not unlike many other towns scattered throughout the vast Pale of Settlement, Mary Antin had learned from early childhood about the precariousness of the Jewish lot in Russia, which she later defined as a nearly schizophrenic state of insecurity. Every Jew felt that each day could also be his last, and precisely this gnawing threat of both physical and spiritual destruction encouraged Mary's suddenly impoverished father to make his way to Boston in 1891 and try his fortune. Failing to strike it rich in America, Antin never thought of returning; three years after his arrival, he borrowed money to pay for his family's passage, hoping that his reunification with wife and children would change his luck. The Antins' subsequent moves to Revere Beach, then to Chelsea, and finally to Boston's South End were not marked by financial success, but their gains proved as valuable as those measured by money and social status. What her family appropriated, Mary would later write, was "everything that makes life beautiful and gives one an aim and an end—freedom, progress, knowledge, light and truth, with their glorious host of followers."[25]

Antin experienced the urge to bear witness when she was in her early teens. Always a diligent student and a voracious reader, she nevertheless found time to address the needs of her numerous relatives left behind in Russia. She felt that her freedom entailed the obligation always to remember her less fortunate brethren and to remind the world of the bitterness generated by separation. Shortly after her arrival in America, she wrote a series of letters in Yiddish to her uncle in Plotzk, relating in detail her land trip from Russia to Germany and the ocean voyage from Germany to America. A few years later, when she showed her own English translations of the letters to Hattie L. Hecht, an influential figure in the Boston Jewish Community, the latter recruited Philip Cowen of the *American Hebrew* and the British novelist Israel Zangwill to help publish Mary's letters.

Hecht's efforts paid off handsomely. In 1889, W. B. Clarke & Company published *From Plotzk to Boston,* no mean accomplishment for a teenager. To top off her success, Zangwill agreed to contribute a "Foreword" outlining its importance. Mary Antin's "vivid description of all she and her dear ones went through," explained the novelist, "enables us to see almost with our own eyes how the invasion of America appears to the impecunious invader. It is thus a 'human document' of considerable value, as well as a promissory note of future performance."[26]

Zangwill saw still another benefit readers would derive from Mary's first book of memories. "Despite the great wave of Russian immigration into the United States," wrote Zangwill, "and despite the noble spirit in which the Jews of America have grappled with the invasion," the hosts knew "too little of the inner feelings" of the newcomers.[27] Indeed, great as Emma Lazarus's contribution to the solution of the Russian-Jewish dilemma was, her readers could hardly discern individual voices in that "one cry of pain" that accompanied Jewish destiny. And although Antin never surpassed Lazarus's artistic mastery, she made the individual voices come alive. Under the amateurish yet skillful pen of the young transplanted author, the history of the Russian Jews, their lives in and exodus from Russia, turned not into still another painfully familiar account of crisis and relief. It was an account anchored in specific and recognizable locales inhabited by characters who speak, eat, love, study, fight, dream, hope. They are flesh and blood. They resemble each other; they differ from one another. They are bound, however, by a common fate, which they share with their young creator.

From Plotzk to Boston foreshadows Mary Antin's development as a writer. Already at an early age she knew how to sustain narrative and to employ metaphor so that her account could be streamlined into a powerful and coherent unity. When she shrouds Plotzk and Berlin in heavy fog upon her family's departure and makes the sun shine brightly when they arrive in Boston, one marvels at the ease and discretion with which this thirteen-year-old employs natural phenomena to convey meaning. More significant is that Mary, like Emma Lazarus before her, employs the easily recognizable symbols of Exodus and Passover to relate the passage of her family "from tyranny to democracy, from darkness to light, from bondage and persecution to freedom, justice and equality."[28]

Had Antin limited her literary career to just this slim volume, she would, at best, be remembered as a child prodigy. Fortunately, Antin was well aware that *From Plotzk to Boston* should be seen as the first step on the way of making the American public more aware of Jewish life in Eastern Europe. To fulfill the Jewish writer's obligation to remember the plight of her people and help to bring about the reunion of the dispersed and persecuted, she would need to create a larger canvas of which *From Plotzk to Boston* would be but one part. Eleven years were to pass, however, before Mary Antin completed the task she commenced with her first little book in 1899.

Mary Antin's insatiable search for knowledge and education led her to Boston's Society of Natural History, where she met William Grabau, a man ten years her senior and a decendant of Lutheran pastors. The two fell in love and, in spite of the great difference in their background, became man and wife. When Grabau won an appointment at Columbia University shortly after their marriage, they moved to New York in 1901. Although their liaison would not prove to be a success, Mary's transplanting to New York and Columbia benefited her writing career.

It was in New York that she met Josephine Lazarus, Emma's younger sister, who introduced her to Transcendentalism, a philosophy which was to influence Mary's entire body of writing, especially her memoir, *The Promised Land* (1912). Following Josephine, she came to apply Emerson's teachings to her attempts to reconcile the differences between woman and man, between Jew and gentile. If everyone admitted the oneness of all truth and all spirit, then there would exist a strong possibility for all, regardless of race, ethnicity, age, and gender, to live in spirit and truth, sharing in Emerson's pantheistic oneness. If this were possible, the Jew, relying on his intelligence and will, could transcend his separateness.

This, Mary Antin agreed, could be done only under conditions of freedom, equality, and justice, in a country like America. It was easy to bring Transcendentalism in line with her obligations to and sense of responsibility for the fate of the Jews in Eastern Europe. They needed to be reunited with their brethren in America and able to share in the benefits this "Promised Land" provides.

Now, whether Mary Antin succeeded in her memoirs in qualifying America as "the Promised Land" is not as important as her making good on the promissory note to re-create both the inner and the outer worlds of the Russian Jews. In comparison with Russia, any world providing the "poor," the "tired," and the "huddled masses" with an opportunity for "earning their bread and worshipping their God in peace" would seem to be the land of biblical promise.

Antin's decision to write her memoir was well-timed. Professor Oscar Handlin, in his "Foreword" to a later edition of *The Promised Land,* points to an alarming attitude toward immigration from Eastern Europe at the end of the first decade of the twentieth century. The mood in the country differed drastically from that of the 1880's. Immigrants were perceived as a threat to what was considered an established and accomplished social order. "An active drive was underway to change the national policy." The Dillingham Commission Report presented to Congress in 1911 claimed that "immigrants then entering the country from Eastern and Southern Europe were different from, and inferior to, their predecessors from North and West. The danger was imminent and prompt action was necessary to guard the gates."[29] Always politically conscious and a great admirer of the Lazarus sisters, Antin couldn't remain passive when Pobedonostsev's solution to the Jewish problem was being slowly implemented in Russia and when America was in danger of disqualifying herself as the "Promised Land." In other words, she could not agree to the separation of the two candleholders, to use Sevela's image; neither could she consent to the desecration of American freedom.

While Emma Lazarus's efforts on behalf of the Russian Jews were informed by a learned sense of history and an experience acquired through mediators, Mary Antin's *The Promised Land* is an offering of lived and felt experiences. "It is because I understand my history, in its larger outlines, to be typical of many, that I consider it worth recording," wrote Antin in her introduction to *The Promised Land.*[30] Since she pictured herself as "strands of the cable that binds the Old World to the New," she was well qualified to lead the reader from the Middle Ages, where she "began her life," into the twentieth century, whose latest thoughts she was "thrilled" to absorb.[31] What Mary Antin desired her countrymen to understand is what she wanted her gentile neighbors back in Plotzk to know about the Jews. In her memoir she recalls an incident that happened when she was a little girl, who, like any other child, longed for companionship with her neighborhood peers. Each time she would go out to play in the street or run errands for her parents, Vanka, the gentile boy, would hit her, spit at her, pull her by the hair, call her names, in short, abuse the girl any way he could. Each time this happened little Mary would ask herself the same question: "why—why?" The only answer she could provide to this puzzle was that "Vanka abused me because *he did not understand*." He did not understand what it meant to be a Jew in Russia. "If he could feel with my heart, if he could be a little Jewish boy for one day," the child prays, " . . . he would know—he would know."[32]

The little girl's wish to make Vanka feel what a Jewish child feels informs the mature author's purpose in writing her memoir. She wants the world to be Jewish for at least the time the reading of her book will take and to enter a world which in the child's mind is invariably associated with trouble: "Why, in Russia lived the Czar, and a great many cruel people; and in Russia were the dreadful prisons from which people never came back."[33] It is indeed terrifying to imagine the mental anguish and intellectual bewilderment the little girl experiences while growing up under conditions of hatred and intolerance. From early childhood she comes to recognize the simple yet frightening fact that the only reason for her isolation and suffering is her heritage—she made the mistake of being born Jewish. Although this truth is being constantly drilled into the child's mind, Mary nevertheless has a hard time accepting it without yet again questioning its validity. She is trying to understand how and why people are so brutal to each other, and, most important, how they can be so ignorant about one another. It is beyond her imagination how to "worship the cross and to torment a Jew," how actions apparently contradictory in their nature can find harmonious co-existence in her gentile neighbors' minds.[34]

The ignorance in the adult world never ceases to shock the child. Aware of the accusations of ritual murder leveled at the Jews each Passover season, Mary often wonders how it is possible that grown-up gentiles are not able to see how false these allegations are if she, merely a child, can so easily recognize a blatant lie. She is constantly surprised that seemingly serious and mature people can blindly accept their priests' teachings, which never fail to point at a Jew as the Christ-killer. It is beyond her understanding how a myth, upon a moment's notice, can give rise to a bloody pogrom.

Instead of decreasing, the paradoxes Mary encounters mount in number and complexity. She discovers that the world of her home stands in direct contradiction to the world of the street. She has a hard time reconciling the feelings of joy her parents try to impart to their children when Passover is approaching with the awesome fear she experiences when through the crack of the kitchen window she observes the bloodthirsty mobs, inseparable companions of the Passover season, roaming the street in the never ceasing search for Christ-killers. This time of the year, Mary recalls, "when we celebrated our deliverance from the land of Egypt, and felt so good and thankful, as if it only just happened, our Gentile neighbors chose to remind us that Russia was another Egypt."[35]

This duality in the Jewish-Russian existence leads to the discovery of other dichotomies, not less perplexing. Mary often muses that the Russians would like the Jews to assimilate, melt into the landscape; on the other hand, though, by isolating their Jewish subjects and creating a wall of hostility around them, the

Russians make the Jews put up a wall of their own: "This wall within the wall is the religious integrity of the Jews, a fortress erected by the prisoners of the Pale, in defiance of their jailers; a stronghold built on the ruins of their pillaged homes, cemented with the blood of their murdered children."[36]

Deprived of true justice, unable to obtain a genuine education, threatened with desecration of their faith, the Jews create a network of judicial, educational, and religious institutions which administer justice to both rich and poor, leave no one without at least an elementary education, and protect Judaism from continuing assaults. This tightly knit buffer zone that separates the two worlds is based solely on trust, charity, and goodwill. No officials stall decisions, no clerks take bribes, and no prisons threaten. The network, Mary states, protects the Jews from the Russian officialdom, the police, and often from forced conscription. Everyone—the *rav,* the *dayan,* the *hazzan,* the *shohat,* the *melamed*—strives for one thing only: the preservation of Jewish identity. No wonder, then, that what little Mary fears the most is not even pogroms but, rather, baptism. Although the physical assaults induce nightmares, the horrifying dreams disappear by daytime, allaying her anxieties at least temporarily. When she thinks of baptism, however, she becomes hysterical: "I was only a little girl, and not very brave: little pains made me ill, and I cried. But there was no pain I would not bear— no, none—rather than submit to baptism."[37]

In most cases, conversion, writes Mary, takes place when Jewish boys are forced to join the Tsar's military or enroll in government-run schools where Christianity is propagated. Parents use any means available to them to avoid their sons' conscription or mandatory schooling. Frequently they resort to bribing the officials with big sums of money collected from relatives, friends, and charitable strangers. When money fails to help, maiming comes to assistance. The little girl tells us of numerous stories she had heard repeated in almost every Jewish household, of young men inflicting upon themselves sometimes fatal bodily injuries, so that they could avoid joining the enemy's ranks. Such happenings give rise to yet another paradox that Mary is grappling to comprehend. When in the street, she cannot help overhear her neighbors' constant prattle about proverbial Jewish avarice and cowardice. It is beyond her understanding how such malicious accusations can be leveled against her people. After all, she muses, it is the gentiles who are constantly "relieving" the Jews of their money, either through unbearable taxes or outright bribes. Money, then, becomes the only protection the Jews have against the greed of the outside world. Similarly, reckons Mary, if a Jew were a coward, would he voluntarily subject himself to physical pain to avoid forced conscription?

Mary's parents, like other Jewish mothers and fathers, know that they do not have the answers and recognize that the only solution to their survival is the continuation of the journey commenced thousands of years ago and the move to places where they can freeely earn their bread and worship their God. They finally have to recognize that Russia has always been "the land of Pharaoh," with no prospects of change. This image little Mary carries with her when she makes her way to America—"the Promised Land." It is this image that she shares with her readers twenty years later while fulfilling the duties and responsibilities of an American-Jewish writer:

I knew that Polotsk was not my country. It was *goluth*—exile. On many occasions in the year we prayed to God to lead us out of exile. The beautiful Passover service closed with the words, "Next year, may we be in Jerusalem." On childish lips, indeed, those words were no conscious aspiration; we repeated the Hebrew syllables after our elders, but without their hope and longing. Still not a child among us was too young to feel in his own flesh the lash of the oppressor. We knew what it was to be Jews in exile, from the spiteful treatment we suffered at the hands of the smallest urchin who crossed himself; and thence we knew that Israel had good reason to pray for deliverance.[38]

Indeed it had. For hundreds of years the Eastern-European Jews lived in hope that one day they would "earn" the privilege to call their adopted countries a real home. Each time, however, when they thought that day was finally within reach, this cherished dream was again drowned in their own blood. Chmielnitsky's massacres were followed by those of Gonta, Gonta's by Zheleznyak's, Zheleznyak's by the Tsar's bloodthirsty mobs and the Black Hundreds, and on and on. So large was their despair that the Jews, usually portrayed as stubborn and unwilling to compromise their religion, went as far as accepting self-proclaimed Messiahs, such as Shabbatai Zevi and Jacob Frank, knowing in advance the futility of their actions.

Both the hostility of the outside world and the internal communal circumstances were forcing traditional Judaism to undergo reforms so that it could be of greater help to its besieged people. Although the ways of rabbinic Judaism, *Hasidism,* and the *Haskalah* (Enlightenment), the three most prominent movements that emerged in the eighteenth century, often stood in opposition to one another, they nevertheless converged in their efforts to alleviate Jewish suffering. Whether they preached the individual's unconditional submission to tradition and the Torah, whether they called for a more creative and personal, rather than mechanical and collective approach to Judaism, whether they wanted the masses to embrace Enlightenment so that they could establish an intimate relationship with the world beyond the ghetto and the *shtetl,* the followers of the Vilna Gaon, Baal Shem Tov, and Moses Mendelssohn acknowledged through their diverse strivings the unbearable situation of the Eastern-European Jews. None of these movements could bring a permanent relief to a people living in "the land of Pharaoh."

Under conditions of tyranny any attempt to assert one's freedoms is short-lived. Even when the Russian Jews attempted to join the radical revolutionary organizations and make their own aspirations inseparable from those of the peasants and workers, their political actions were as futile as those of their predecessors who embraced the false messiahs. Thus, when the Jewish members of *Narodnaya Volya,* the organization responsible for the assassination of Alexander II in 1881, appealed to its Executive Committee to help stop the pogroms following the Tsar's execution, many of its members refused to intercede, since they considered the atrocious actions of the mob a "prelude to a revolution."[39] In other words, if the road to progress needed to be paved by dead Jewish bodies, so be it—ends, after all, justify the means. Consequently, many young Jewish men and women, disappointed by their comrades, decided to join the exodus of their co-religionists to America, where diversity and pluralism were part of national life. Among them was Abraham Cahan.

Born in 1860 in a small town near Vilna, Cahan had realized at age twenty-two that neither his experiences as a *yeshiva* student nor the knowledge acquired at the Vilna Teacher's Institute (where the language of instruction was Russian), nor his short-lived infatuation with the Russian revolutionary movement, were sufficient to help him live in dignity or even survive as a Jew in Russia. Fearing an imminent arrest, Cahan decided to make his way to America, where he arrived in 1882. By a charming Nabokovian coincidence, among the members of the Welcoming Committee at Ward's Island was also Emma Lazarus, whose devotion to the people of Israel and whose literary efforts on behalf of Eastern-European Jews Cahan was to share.

The history of Cahan's journalistic and literary career mirrors the history of the American Jews in the first half of the twentieth century. Hardly any facet of Jewish life in this country was not touched and influenced by him. The two achievements, however, for which he will be remembered with gratitude and love are his editorship (1902–1946) of the Yiddish daily *Forward* and his novel *The Rise of David Levinsky* (1917), a classic study of financial success and moral failure. Different as they are, both express a deep concern for the fate of the Jewish people.

Like Mary Antin, Cahan re-creates the Old World; like her, he bears witness to the nefarious policies of the Russian oppressors, reaffirming once again the image of Russia as "the land of Pharaoh." His writings lead to two inevitable conclusions. One, the Jews, having tried everything possible to survive in Russia and preserve their identity, have to leave that country for good before they fall victims to Pobedonostsev's solution. The *White Terror and the Red: A Novel of Revolutionary Russia* (1905), a work of moderate literary distinction, reinforces this conclusion and supplements it with yet another thesis: as long as the Jew can be of help he is tolerated; when his usefulness is exhausted he turns into just another superfluous man. Cahan's second inevitable conclusion was that if one forgets those left behind one commits a sin; neither is one redeemed if he remembers them but does nothing to alleviate their lot. Prosper as they may in America, the American Jews will never achieve fulfillment and harmony if they submit to forgetfulness and passivity. This powerful warning against legitimizing separation permeates *The Rise of David Levinsky,* a novel based upon Cahan's semi-fictional "The Autobiography of an American Jew" commissioned by

McClure's in 1913 and published in its novelistic form in 1917. *The Rise of David Levinsky* is Cahan's crowning achievement in synthesizing his journalistic and literary efforts on behalf of the Russian and American Jew.

Cahan had already touched upon the theme of separation and its consequences in earlier works, especially in *Yekl* (1896), a novel inspired by Howells.[40] Its protagonist, a young Russian Jew, Yekl, comes to this country to build a better life for himself and pave the way for his wife and son's future arrival. In his efforts to out-America America, Yekl neglects his family duties and does little to end the separation. When, against all odds, Gitl and the boy do make it to America, Yekl and Gitl's marriage does not survive. After the divorce, instead of feeling relieved and joyful, Yekl is overcome by a sense of loss and defeat. To be sure, his wish to rid himself of the past comes true; his hope, however, of being able to replace it with a better present and a brighter future remains unfulfilled. The real winner is Gitl and her new husband, a man who even in America manages to preserve a deep devotion to the two institutions that symbolize unity, continuity, and transcendence of adversity: the study of the Torah and Talmud, and marriage.

The Rise of David Levinsky takes up the theme of separation and forgetting once again, yet does so in a more sophisticated manner and on a number of different levels. On the novel's first page, David Levinsky, the narrator, sets out to explain why his "inner identity" has remained the "same as it was thirty or forty years ago" in Russia and why the riches and power he has amassed in America "seem to be devoid of significance."[41] By making the Jewish Horatio Alger admit his failure to parallel his financial growth with spiritual elevation, Cahan triggers the reader's curiosity to find out the reasons for David Levinsky's arrested spiritual development.

The first eighty pages of the novel introduce the audience to the life of a typical Russian town in the Pale, which is divided by an invisible, yet strictly adhered to, line into the Jewish ghetto and the rest of the world. We listen to the noises in the streets, observe the hustle and bustle of the marketplace, join the celebration of the Sabbath or other holidays, eavesdrop on blasphemous conversations of soon-to-be-former *yeshiva* students, and enter the households of both poor and well-to-do Jews. However, what permeates these masterful descriptions of everyday routines is a sense of fear and insecurity. To exemplify the precariousness of Jewish existence in Russia, Cahan has David recall the circumstances of his mother's death. Indeed, this sad event informs and overshadows all that takes place in the four chapters that re-create the narrator's past.

While crossing the market square, on the seventh day of Passover, David is confronted by hoodlums who first ridicule his garb and sidelocks, then throw Easter eggs at him, and, finally, beat him up. When he arrives home with a bloody nose and a split lip, his mother, against the admonitions of her neighbors and friends, rushes out of the house, pledging to avenge her fatherless son who she hopes will one day become a great talmudic scholar. "Fifteen minutes later," recalls David, "she was carried into our basement unconscious. Her face was bruised and swollen and the back of her head was broken. She died the same evening.''[42] Similar to other Jewish writers, Cahan uses Passover to link the Jewish past and the Jewish present, revealing thus the paradoxical nature of Jewish existence: while the Russian Jews are celebrating the holiday of deliverance they are acutely aware that they are still in exile. During this day of celebration, David Levinsky becomes an orphan at eighteen.

Penniless and homeless, David now totally depends upon the charity and mercy of the Jewish community, which, regardless of its internal differences and ideological divisions, sees its duty to support any Jewish child, and especially an orphan, in his scholarly endeavors. David's scholarly career, however, does not last long. After a period of an all-consuming devotion to Judaism and a short-lived infatuation with Matilda, an enlightened divorcée from a wealthy Jewish family, he realizes that the pogroms of the early 1880's have left him and millions of his co-religionist with little choice but flight to America. The Russian Jews have finally to admit that ''their birthplace was not their home.''[43]

Before his departure, David is blessed by Reb Sender, his teacher, who admonishes him to be ''a good Jew and a good man,'' an admonition which at first sight seems to be deceptively simple: the old man wants David to remember his people and not to forsake his God.[44] Mr. Even, David's first American benefactor, makes a similar request: ''There is only one thing I want you to promise me. Don't neglect your religion nor your Talmud.''[45] David's separation from his native town, his teacher, his mother's grave will soon be compounded by his separation from the promises he made to Reb Sender and Mr. Even. In pursuit of worldliness and riches, the young man is taking slow but irreversible steps that create an ever-widening gap between him and his people. He begins to miss services, which makes it easier for him to shave his beard and trim his sidelocks. Spencer and Darwin replace the Torah, Dickens and Thackeray the Talmud. He separates himself from the Jewish tradition, although he is well aware of the magical qualities of the Jewish teachings that helped the dispersed feel united for thousands of years. And while he admits that studying the Torah and Talmud can ''bring my heart in touch with my old home, with dear old Reb Sender, with the grave of my poor mother,'' he neglects the equilibrium between the past and present, between tradition and modernity, a balance that might have helped him to keep his promises.[46] As his riches increase, he pretends to remember his people by establishing the Antomir society and contributing to charities, but primarily to enhance his own position among the wealthy instead of helping those left behind. He pays lip service to the love he feels toward his friend Naphtali and his teacher Reb Sender, yet does nothing to help them escape from Russia. Passivity thus breeds hypocrisy and unjustifiable self-pity, which in turn aggravates his loneliness.

Levinsky knows that there is still another institution, marriage, long considered sacred by the Jews, that he can resort to in order to ease his loneliness and transcend his yearnings. Marriage, like the Talmud, creates a unity that defies separation. David constantly talks and broods over marriage, yet he always chooses to court women he knows in advance he will never marry, thus, deceiving, not only himself but his possible partners. Invariably something separates him from the women he admires: first religion and later revolutionary zeal separate him from Matilda; a husband from Dvora; cowardice, hypocrisy, indecision from Fanny; American pragmatism from Gussie; culture and education from Anna. In the final count, David Levinsky chooses to be lonely and unaffiliated. In spite of deceitful lamentations to the contrary, he *desires* separation from the Talmud and the Jewish people. He might indulge in reminiscences but his remembering is passive and, therefore, Cahan intimates, unbecoming of a Jew, whose duty it is to turn memory into action and to inform his talents with moral convictions. Instead, he "becomes the great Levinsky, a grotesque perversion of the American dream whose enormous economic success leaves him feeling homeless."[47]

Not only does Levinsky betray his tradition and people, but he also betrays his adopted country. While America can offer unlimited opportunities, it can also play tricks upon one's memory and sight. It can swallow one's identity, thus, obliterating, its own justification for being— to give everyone the chance to preserve his individuality, to be himself. David throws away his choice and falls. Abraham Cahan, however, after running away from a choiceless society, grasps at the newly afforded opportunities and rises to the needs of both his people and America. Like Jeremiah, he warns his people against forgetting and amnesia which can lead to complacency and, finally, to falsification of historical evidence and attempts to rewrite the story of the Jewish people, a story far from completion.

To illustrate the grave consequences of separation, Cahan introduces Mr. Tevkin, a transplanted Hebrew poet, who attributes his failure as an artist in America to his abandonment of Russia some twenty years ago. "'Russia is a better country than America,'" states Tevkin, "'even if it is oppressed by a Tzar'":

"It's a free country too—for the spirit at least. There is more poetry there, more music, more feeling, even if our people do suffer appalling persecution. The Russian people are really a warm-hearted people.... If my younger children were not so attached to this country and did not love it so, and if I could make a living in Russia now, I should be ready to go back at once."[48]

Needless to say, Tevkin does not return to his appalling yet so spiritual Russia. As his contradictory and self-exclusionary descriptions of Russia testify, his separation from common sense and his people is not final yet. While condemning materialistic America for imprisoning his poetic soul, Tevkin clings to tradition and bemoans the alienation of his children from their past. He insists that every member of his family attend the annual Passover *seder* which, as years pass by, he takes more and more seriously. His political and literary affinities do not preclude his acceptance of the meaning of Passover shared by most Jewish people and best expressed by Martin Buber:

Since the night of Exodus it has become a history feast, and indeed *the* history feast par excellence of the world; not a feast of pious remembrance, but of the ever-current contemporaneousness of that which once befell. Every celebrating generation becomes united with the first generation and with all those that have followed.[49]

By introducing Tevkin into his novel, Cahan foreshadows the ambiguous and marginal existence of the Jewish intellectual, both transplanted and native-born, who, in the twenties and thirties, because of a combination of circumstances, felt more and more alienated not only from Judaism but from mainstream America as well. There is more to Tevkin's character, however: his insistence on celebrating Passover, Cahan intimates, points to the fact that a Jewish artist's estrangement from his roots is never really complete. More often than not, it is but a temporary phenomenon. How shrewd and prophetic Cahan was becomes clear when one follows the development of American-Jewish literature, and especially its treatment of Russia, since the publication of *The Rise of David Levinsky*.

Upon coming to America many Jewish immigrants had to endure enormous hardships while adapting to the circumstances imposed upon them by the journey from the Middle Ages to a modern society. To get a good feeling of what an immigrant experienced, one only needs to read "A Bintel Brief" (A Bundle of Letters), a daily feature introduced by the *Forward* in 1906, which consisted of letters to the editor mostly written by Eastern-European Jews, who share with the paper's readers their nostalgia for the coherence of the *shtetl*, express the anguish of separation from those left behind, and reflect on the poor living conditions and the meager pay their sweatshop jobs yield. Some feel guilty for abandoning their comrades and the revolutionary movement, others for losing their children to worldliness. Yet hardly anyone wishes to go back to Russia, let alone see their children return. The majority share the sentiments of Anzia Yezierska, a Russian-American-Jewish author, who, before embarking on a literary career, earned her living in sweatshops. "There is no going back to the Old World for anyone who breathed the invigorating air of America," writes Yezierska after a visit to Europe.

I return to America with the new realization that in no other country would a nobody from nowhere—one of the millions of lonely immigrants that pour through Ellis Island— a dumb thing with nothing but hunger and desire—get the chance to become articulate that America has given me.[50]

While Yezierska was emphatically expressing this enthusiasm, the myth of America was being slowly undermined. Although neither economic hardships experienced by many immigrants, not the ever-widening gap between them and their American-born and educated children, nor the bitterness over the failure to find political solutions to prevent the atrocities of World War I should be regarded lightly, the erosion of the American myth was generated primarily by external factors, most notably by the establishment of a new social order in Russia. In the October Revolution in 1917, the Bolsheviks toppled the monarchy and committed themselves to build a "Communist Paradise" based on equality and justice for all. And if Russia made good on its commitments, reckoned some Western sympathizers, America's claim to exclusivity as "the Promised Land" would be invalidated.

This view did not draw any substantive support from the Jewish novelists of the socialist persuasion, Cahan among them. Although they considered the socialist system superior to the capitalist order, their commitment to Jewish concerns as their novels' subject matter remained intact and prevented them from using their talent to radicalize the American society. Neither were they ready to submit to quick changes of heart about Russia. In the late twenties and thirties, however, when America's economic problems mounted and finally reached a disastrous climax with the collapse of the stock market, a number of novelists of Jewish origin openly touted communism as the panacea for all ills, and held up the young Soviet republic as the social model to be faithfully imitated. The proletarian novelists, as they were now called, shied away from Jewish subjects as too narrow for intellectuals preoccupied with changing the destiny of all peoples. Instead, by using the "Socialist Realism" literary method, they addressed themselves to problems of ideology, revolution, class struggle—creating stock characters and predictable plots to further the cause of "Progress." Among the proletarian writers in general there were twice as many Jews as among the socialist writers, yet but a few are still remembered today.[51] Henry Roth has recently enjoyed a considerable revival; some of Meyer Levin's novels are in print; and Waldo Frank is often mentioned along with Koestler, Silone, and Orwell—writers who once enthusiastically embraced Marxism but gave it up upon a closer look at its practitioners, the Russian communists. One could also assume that because the Jewish proletarian writers identified Russia with the successful implementation of Marxist theories, they would be able to change the perception of Russia among their co-religionists. Yet, when even one of the best of the proletarian writers, Waldo Frank, traveled to Russia, he was hard put to convince himself, let alone his readers, that a meaningful transformation was taking place.

"When the revolutionists took Russia and set up Kerensky as premier," writes Waldo Frank in his memoirs, "I turned for my accolade not to economics but to poetry, publishing 'Holy Russia' in the *Seven Arts*."[52] In 1931, fourteen years after composing his poem, Frank set out for Russia to ascertain that his praises did indeed fall on fertile soil.

Three and a half months later, having visited Moscow, Leningrad, and Novgorod, he returned to New York and recorded his impressions of Soviet Russia in a well-written and, at times, moving travelogue, *Dawn in Russia* (1932). The entire book can be prefaced by Tevkin's earlier quoted desire to present his native country in a way that defied the knowledge he derived from living there. Regardless of how much he wanted to fashion Russia as the seat of "poetry . . .

music . . . [and] . . . feeling,'' and despite his claim that Russia was a country of spiritual "freedom," he could not but admit that Russia was oppressed by the Tsar and "our people suffer appalling persecution.''

Upon reading *Dawn in Russia,* one can easily observe how close Frank's desires are to those of Cahan's Tevkin. Frank's honesty, sincerity, and sympathies are beyond doubt; what is surprising, though, is his naivete, generated by ignorance rather than viciousness, when he tries to explain a country whose image conceived from afar stubbornly refuses to coincide with the reality he has witnessed in person. Paradoxically, the reader learns more about Russia than the writer does—Frank is so busy trying to make the hand fit the glove, he is so eager to explain away the shortcomings of Russia's present system that, to use the words of Marx, his one-time idol, he throws the baby out with the bath water.

As an honest man and an American writer who takes free speech for granted, Frank is appalled to find out about the numerous limitations imposed upon the citizens' rights to express themselves freely and openly. Yet, true to his desire to explain away the discrepancies between theory and practice, he does not hesitate to justify the absence of free speech: "If there is no freedom of speech to-day, the reason is that a people is not revolutionized in fifteen years, even by the profoundest of revolutions.''[53]

If one can justify the absence of free speech, one can justify any crime perpetrated in the name of revolution. When visiting Dr. and Mrs. Z., an impoverished older couple who once belonged to the Russian upper-middle-class, Frank discovers that his visit may endanger their well-being. The GPU, the political (and not-so-secret) police, he is told, keeps a watchful eye on the former jurist's family and may accuse them of having suspicious ties with foreigners. Frank clearly abhors this encroachment on citizens' private lives. He insists, however, that the GPU's actions are necessary:

Everywhere in the Soviet ranks there remains a lust of privilege, greed of power, even love of money. That is why the dictatorship is afraid of men like Dr. Z., who although starved are yet strong with the heritage of millenial culture and with the inward unity that comes from their acceptance of personal power as a normal value.[54]

In other words, ends justify the means.

This rule applies not only to the norms of everyday life but to art as well. While attending a well-orchestrated meeting of Soviet authors, Frank, an innovator in his own writing, finds himself in agreement with the proponents of "Socialist Realism," a method that forces the artist to create according to guidelines. Given this approach, literature and arts in general must serve the need of the hour, even if this need entails sacrificing human rights, thus putting the state's interest over those of its citizens.

The Russian citizens are of great concern to Waldo Frank. Carried away by his enthusiasm for the young Soviet state, he claims that he can communicate with the Russians without knowing Russian. Their faces express beauty and truth, he states. He has a hard time explaining how people with such beautiful and open faces can perform rather distasteful acts, like trampling each other to death in an attempt to board a barge, for example. He has to admit finally that he will never be able to understand fully the Russian people:

I feel, and am never to cease feeling, the paradox of Russia—its integral, pregnant contradiction. For these people are beasts; and yet a human pity, exquisite in grace, luminous in understanding, shines within them. These are men and women: yet their deeds do nothing to lift them above their cattle.[55]

After reading this harsh and rather perplexing description of the Russian people, one is surprised by Frank's statement that he feels at home in Russia:

I am at home in Russia, as much at home as I was in 1917 under the Bronx "L." Russia has become a theatre of the spirit: a place where human will, human values, are incarnate. . . . Russia with its chaos and its tragic search for human wholeness is a symbol. . . . It is a symbol so immediate to my modern mind that in this town on the Volga, where I and my blood have never been, I feel at home.[56]

The paradoxical yet very revealing nature of this statement is easy to recognize. In fact, it mirrors the kind of thinking that led to the philosophy of ends justifying the means, of the whole taking precedence over the particular. If "Russia is a symbol so profound that all the vast Russian lands . . . are insignificant within it," one should not be surprised that the people who populate this "symbol" are too insignificant, at least for the immediate now, to enjoy human rights, freedom of speech, and the right to privacy. It is also not surprising, then, that Waldo Frank, a descendant of immigrant German Jews, a Yale-educated intellectual, a man who "felt himself in his own words a Jew without Judaism and an American without America," finds no need to mention the plight of millions of Russian Jews who like Sevela's Grandmother Roza are deprived of their religious and political freedom or like her sons have to obliterate their identity to survive.[57]

Willing away the Jews and Jewish problems does not, however, will away the pharaonic nature of the land. When after his return from Russia, Frank decided to write his travelogue, he felt that its subject matter required a new presentation. "Unlike my other books," writes Frank, "I resolved not to work on this one: not to organize its materials, not to essentialize its form. I would let the book write itself."[58] Inadvertently, Frank gives his audience the clue to a proper understanding of his book: to comprehend fully his composition the readers must believe the tale rather than the teller. If they do, they can't help admitting that Frank's tale of Russia is not different from that of Lazarus, Antin, Cahan, Yezierska, and Sevela. His tale tells of the same land but a different Pharaoh, a Pharaoh who makes all of his citizens feel at least partially like Jews.

Indeed he did. The excesses of the cultural revolution and the processes of industrialization and collectivization claimed the lives of millions of innocent citizens. The arranged murder of Sergey Kirov, the head of the Leningrad Communist party, was used to trigger a widespread purge among party members, culminating in the notorious trials of Zinoviev, Kamenev, and Bucharin, top-ranking party functionaries accused of treason and subversion. One after another, the best representatives of Russian literature, the Jewish Mandelshtam, Babel, Pilnyak among them, fell prey to "Socialist Realism," a system of aesthetics which according to the Nobel Prize winner Czeslaw Milosz, "is directly responsible for the deaths of millions of men and women, for it is based on the glorification of the state by the writer and artist whose task it is to portray the power of the state as the greatest good, and to scorn the suffering of the individual."[59]

By the end of the thirties, not even a few timid calls of protest voiced by Western left-wing intellectuals could stop Stalin and his colleagues from establishing a frighteningly tyrannical dictatorship, let alone prevent him from signing a disgraceful peace treaty with Nazi Germany or engaging in dubious practices in the Spanish Civil War.

As Russia entered the Second World War, Stalin had somewhat relaxed his iron grip that kept the Soviet intellectuals in stride. He needed them to provide his soldiers with patriotic inspiration as well as help him win the financial support of America. Achmatova and Zoschenko, in disfavor for many years, were allowed to publish again. A Jewish delegation, headed by actor-director Michoels and Yiddish poet Feffer, was dispatched to New York to raise funds. After the war, however, to dispell any false hopes of liberalization generated by the wartime temporary relaxation, Stalin initiated a new wave of terror. Quietly and methodically he was filling the vast Archipelag Gulag with the very soldiers who helped him win the war. Not so quietly, but equally methodically, he started a vicious campaign against the Jewish people, resorting to the old and so familiar tactic of searching out a scapegoat for all the ills of his country. A team of Jewish doctors was accused of a conspiracy to poison the "Great Leader." About thirty Jewish writers were executed for crimes they never perpetrated. Another 500 Jewish artists were sent to concentration camps, many of them never to return.

As these crimes mounted, more left-wing Western intellectuals, many Jews among them, felt compelled to take and pass Orwell's test of intellectual honesty—they were willing to criticize Russia and take the communists to task. Along with Waldo Frank, they came to agree that although they strongly desired "to be ravished by a community" other than their own, the "communists would not do."[60] They had to admit that Russia, as long as it held its people in bondage, would remain "the land of Pharaoh."

Frank's failure to portray Russia as an emerging paradise, compounded by Stalin's efforts to complete Hitler's work of destroying the Jewish people, left the post-World War American-Jewish writers with no other choice but to pass on the story of Russia they inherited from their predecessors. Since Russia continued to be the land of bondage, it remained their responsibility to address the problems of Russian Jews and make sure that America endured as "the Promised Land."

Hardly any major American-Jewish writer has ignored the dispersion of the Jews or failed to explore the role of the Jewish artist in the post-Holocaust era. Many of their works are paradigmatic fictional studies of the problems an American-Jewish artist must face when confronted by the burdens of the past and the urgency of his immediate needs. Chaim Potok's *My Name Is Asher Lev* (1972) is a prime example.

In this first-person narrative, Potok has his artist-protagonist, Asher Lev, look back at his beginnings and define the forces that shaped his artistic sensibilities, sensibilities that made him expropriate Christianity's main symbol, the Crucifixion, and use it as his own aesthetic reference in portraying Jewish suffering.

Born in Brooklyn, in 1943, into a family of Ladover *Hasidim,* Asher has observed from an early age his parents' relentless efforts to save the Jews of Russia trapped behind the Iron Curtain and rebuild the centers of European *Hasidic* learning destroyed in the Holocaust. As a child, he is made aware that his father, as the Ladover Rebbe's emissary, is completing the work of his grandfather who was murdered by a Russian peasant on "the night before Easter" while making plans to "travel to the Ukraine to start underground yeshivos."[61] He is also told by his father that his grandfather believed that "All the Jewish people are one body and one soul. . . . If part of the body hurts, the entire body hurts—and the entire body must come to the help of the part that hurts."[62] As an observant and sensitive child, Asher feels acutely the pain his mother endures while grieving over the loss of her brother who sacrificed his life for the sake of the Russian Jews. Her pain, he knows, is exacerbated by her husband's long absences from home, during which he often sees her standing transfixed by the front window, looking out for Aryeh Lev to return home safely from either a clandestine mission to Russia or a tiresome trip from the war-ravished capitals of Europe. If she is not by the window, Asher sees her sitting at the kitchen table, poring over books in Russian history, literature, and international affairs, subjecting, thus, even her scholarly pursuits to the common cause. So permeated is their household by the significance of their mission that Asher begins to be haunted by a vision of a "man of mythic dimensions" who appears in his dreams as someone "tall, dark-bearded, powerful of mind and body; a brilliant entrepreneur; a beneficent supporter of academies of learning; a legendary traveler, and author of the Hebrew work *Journeys to Distant Lands.*"[63]

This dream image of a Ladover *Hasid,* a cumulative portrait of the Rebbe, his father and Grandfather, finally transforms itself into the figure of the "mythic ancestor," a "weary Jew traveling to balance the world," who turns up time and again at the most crucial junctures of Asher's life, usually during the Passover season.[64] He demands to know one thing only: "And what are you doing with your time, my Asher Lev?"

What Asher does with his time is not exactly what his parents would like him to do. They expect him to study hard and prepare himself to take over their mission to "make passageways to our people in Russia," and help reunite the hurting parts of the Jewish nation into one healthy body.[65] Although Asher does not repudiate the importance of his parents' good deeds, he chooses a different way to respond to Jewish concerns. To the dismay of those who love him, he picks art, painting, a gentile vocation, as a medium to convey his people's suffering. Admonished by the *yeshiva* principal that an artistic career is against the teachings of the Torah, berated by his father for the shame he brings upon his family, warned by the Rebbe of estrangement from his people, Asher in his dreams is often accused by his mythic ancestor of betraying the memory of those who call for help.

At times Asher doubts his artistic career. He loves his father, and their estrangement causes him much pain. He is well aware that he often forces his mother to take sides between her husband and son, in fact, between the moral code of Judaism and the aesthetics of Western civilization. Yet he persists in creating art, since he believes that he is also pursuing his parents' goals: he wants to master the intricacies of art to "draw the land of ice and darkness," and remind his audience of the part of the body that hurts. His separation from traditional Ladover *Hasidism,* he insists, does not mean abandonment of the cause of achieving unity between the Russian Jews deprived of their religious freedoms and those of America who enjoy the liberties of "the Promised Land." He knows of their anguish, and constantly searches for an appropriate symbol to convey it.

The symbol Asher Lev, a descendant of a glorious dynasty dating back to the Middle Ages, finds to make the Christian world see clearly the plight of his people is the very image the Christians have been using to convey suffering and deliverance. It is also the very symbol whose meaning has been totally misinterpreted, sometimes intentionally and sometimes out of ignorance, that inspired a continuous victimization of Asher's people. Asher paints the "Brooklyn Crucifixion" with his parents' living-room window serving as the cross on which his mother is crucified by the realities that force her to be torn between her loyalties to both son and husband. "Standing between two different ways of giving meaning to the world," comments Asher, "and at the same time pressed by her own fears and memories, she had moved now toward me, now toward my father, keeping both worlds of meaning alive, nourishing with her tiny being, and despite her torments, both me and my father."[66]

Having his mother's figure suspended between the two worlds, Asher has done more than express the private grief of the Jewish woman. His painting creates the image of the Jewish people caught in "the land of Pharaoh" and yearning for deliverance. His artwork conveys the torments of a Jewish artist who uses a non-Jewish medium to convey Jewish concerns, as well as his struggle to inform his art with deeply felt moral convictions. And yet in the traditional Jewish context Asher has sinned: he has painted the Crucifixion.

The consequence of Jewish transgression is usually banishment. Asher's lot is no different—he is exiled from the Ladover community. Potok hints, however, that Asher's separation can never be complete. When asked about his future plans, Asher says: "'I may go to Russia. . . . I need new faces. And there is the Hermitage in Leningrad and the Matisses in Moscow.'"[67] As an American-Jewish writer, Potok knows that once his artist-protagonist re-enters the land of his ancestors he will never be content with just the pure joys of seeking artistic perfection. The realities of that place will force him to become a "weary Jew traveling to balance the world."

Another fictional artist discovers this truth when he journeys to Russia. Although written a few years prior to *My Name Is Asher Lev,* Bernard Malamud's novella "Man in the Drawer" (1968) picks up where Potok's novel stops.

Malamud's protagonist, an assimilated American-Jewish writer named Harvitz, after a personal crisis decides to take his vacation in the Soviet Union, so that he can take his mind off his private problems and visit the shrines of Russia's great literary figures, Chekhov among them. He gets more than he bargained for. His first Moscow cabdriver greets him with a "soft shalom" and identifies himself as a "marginal Jew" of mixed parentage: his father is Jewish, his mother Russian.[68] Driving a cab is not his real profession, he makes it known. He is a Soviet writer forced to write for the drawer. Because of their themes and the identity of his characters (they are by and large Jewish), his stories fail to pass the strict standards of official censorship. "Like Isaac Babel," he muses, "I am master of the genre of silence."[69] Although he is a loyal Soviet citizen, he would like, however, to have his collection of eighteen stories published abroad. Therefore, he wants the American writer to read his work and tell him honestly his opinion of it. Against Harvitz's protests, Levitansky makes him accept the manuscript.

In one of the stories, a son, after becoming a party official, neglects and abandons his father. In another, an old Jewish man is ready to suffer deprivation and risk his liberty in order to obtain *matzos* for Passover only to have them stolen on his way home. The most impressive, and obviously autobiographical, piece is about an author who has his stories rejected by the publisher because he writes about Jews. In a fit of despondency, he decides to burn his artwork in the kitchen sink. "'Papa, what are you burning in the sink?'" asks his frightened son. "'I am burning my integrity. . . . My talent. My heritage,'" replies the father.[70]

Although Harvitz is shaken up by the cabdriver's work, he is too scared to smuggle the stories out of Russia. He does not want to be involved; his purpose in visiting Russia is different, he claims: "Nobody in his right mind can expect a complete stranger visiting the Soviet Union to pull his chestnuts out of the fire," he shouts at Levitansky. "It's your country that's hindering you as a writer, not me or the United States of America, and since you live here what can you do but live with it?"[71]

The fictional American-Jewish writer cannot, however, withstand the authorial intentions of his creator. For an American Jew, a visit to Russia, Malamud intimates, can hardly be a mere pleasure trip—it is a journey of self-discovery, of facing the truth. As an American and a Jew, Harvitz has no right to be indifferent and uninvolved when there is a danger that the Russian Jews of silence, to use Elie Wiesei's phrase, may become a lost tribe. Levitansky's stories are a warning that the Russian Jews may permanently be separated from their counterparts in the free world, just as his fictional father and son are. They are even being deprived of the very symbol of their deliverance, *matzos*. Their talent, identity, and heritage are being violated. Consequently, an American-Jewish writer cannot afford the luxurious role of Eliot's Prufrock. He must dare to act both for the sake of his art and for his people. "We are members of mankind," says Levitansky to Harvitz. "If I am drowning you must assist to save me."[72]

While Malamud's Harvitz succeeds in smuggling out Levitansky's collection of stories, Philip Roth's Nathan Zuckerman fails to salvage the manuscripts of a Czech-Yiddish writer, Sisovsky, who perished in the Holocaust. Zuckerman's failure is not a negative reflection on his character; it is a warning, rather, that the time to take action on behalf of thc Eastern-European Jews might be running out.

In his latest novella, "The Prague Orgy" (1985), Roth has Nathan Zuckerman approached by Sisovsky's son, himself an artist, who admonishes his American colleague to travel to Prague and retrieve his father's manuscripts, held now by his former wife, Olga. His father, he tells Zuckerman, was "not only a Jew, but like you, writing about Jews; like you, Semite-obsessed all his life. He wrote hundreds of stories about Jews, and he did not publish one."[73] According to his son, the Yiddish writer was killed during the Nazi occupation in 1941 as a result of a grudge one German officer bore against another. Jewish life, it seems, had very little value even before the mass deportation of Czech Jews to concentration camps began.

Zuckerman arrives in Prague in the winter of 1976, that is, eight years after the Russian invasion. In his pursuit of Olga, he finds himself at a party of Prague intellectuals. What Nathan sees at this gathering is a sad commentary upon the life of a city that had once been the center of European culture—it has turned now into a place of degradation and spiritual void. Olga's response to his request to relinquish Sisovsky's manuscripts further reflects the devastating influence Czechoslovakia's current state of affairs has upon a formerly famous Czech writer. Not only does Olga refuse to return the manuscript, but she also informs Nathan of a totally different version of Sisovsky's death. The story Nathan heard in New York, she claims, happened to another writer who "didn't cven write in Yiddish."[74] According to Olga, Sisovsky's father spent the entire war in the bathroom of a gentile friend who supplied him with cigarettes and whores. He was not even murdered; he died in a bus accident, she maintains.

Whose version of the story is correct is not of real importance. What is significant is what implications changing a story might have for the destiny of an entire people. In Potok's novel the American Jews are concerned with a religious survival of their Eastern-European brethren. By the time Malamud has Harvitz visit Russia, in the sixties, that is, if there is anything left to salvage it is the cultural identity the Russian Jews so stubbornly attempt to retain. What Roth is worried about is that Jewish history is being falsified, that the Jewish past is being stolen. Like Kundera, Kis, and Konrad (the Eastern-European writers he publishes in his series, "Writers from the Other Europe,"), he maintains that the history of Eastern Europe is being rewritten and altered, that the peoples under the Soviet sphere of influence, including the Russian people, are losing their past, their heritage. As a result, their hope of controlling their present is quickly slipping away. They may have no future.

Although Olga finally releases the manuscripts to Nathan, they are confiscated by the secret police. The fictional writer's failure to retrieve the murdered Yiddish author's manuscripts translates, paradoxically enough, into a victory for contemporary American-Jewish artists over the forces of oblivion: as long as there are manuscripts to retrieve they will keep sending their emissaries to save them. Like their predecessors, they remember the plight of those left behind in "the land of Pharaoh." Because of the persistent artistic efforts of the American-Jewish writer, there is hope that Grandmother Roza's candleholders will be reunited again.

NOTES

1. Efraim Sevela, "The Sabbath Candleholders," p. 76.
2. Meyer Waxman, *A History of Jewish Literature*, vol. 4, p. 990.
3. Louis Harap, *The Image of the Jew in American Literature*, p. 287.
4. I. B. Singer, *Shosha*, p. 255.
5. Lucy S. Dawidowicz, ed., *The Golden Tradition: Jewish Life and Thought in Eastern Europe*, p. 17.
6. John G. Stoessinger, *Nations in Darkness: China, Russia, and America*, p. 106.
7. Thomas Paine, quoted in Eugene Anschel, ed., *The American Image of Russia: 1775–1917*, p. 1.
8. This view can easily be sustained by reading Anschel's anthology, *The American Image of Russia: 1775–1917*. Many of the selections point to the following: when the authors of these selections are confronted by realities that do not yield themselves to an easy interpretation through the application of accepted norms of analysis, they frequently launch into unscrupulous speculations based upon their own biases.
9. Stoessinger, p. 95.
10. William W. Hallo, "Exodus and Ancient Near Eastern Literature," p. 372.
11. Walt Whitman, "So Unlike and Yet so Similar," p. 156.
12. Ragozin quoted by Harap, p. 290.
13. Emma Lazarus, "The Crowing of the Red Cock," *Songs of a Semite*, p. 52.
14. Ibid.
15. Ibid.
16. Emma Lazarus, "The Banner of the Jew," p. 56.
17. Ibid.

18. Abraham J. Karp, ed., *Golden Door to America: The Jewish Immigrant Experience*, p. 8.

19. Dawidowicz, p. 46.

20. Emma Lazarus, "New Year," p. 51.

21. Emma Lazarus, "Exile," p. 53.

22. Ibid.

23. Ibid.

24. Emma Lazarus, "The New Colossus," *The Poems of Emma Lazarus*, p. 85.

25. Mary Antin, *From Plotzk to Boston*, p. 15.

26. Israel Zangwill, Foreword to *From Plotzk to Boston*, p. 8.

27. Ibid.

28. Antin, *From Plotzk to Boston*, p. 11.

29. Oscar Handlin, Foreword to *The Promised Land*, p. 11.

30. Mary Antin, Introduction to *The Promised Land*, p. xxi.

31. Ibid.

32. Mary Antin, *The Promised Land*, p. 17.

33. Ibid., p. 3.

34. Ibid., p. 7.

35. Ibid.

36. Ibid., p. 29.

37. Ibid., pp. 9–10.

38. Ibid., pp. 226–227.

39. Ronald Sanders, *The Downtown Jews*, p. 14.

40. Abraham Cahan, *Yekl: A Tale of the New York Ghetto*.

41. Abraham Cahan, *The Rise of David Levinsky*, p. 3.

42. Ibid., p. 52.

43. Ibid., pp. 61–62.

44. Ibid., p. 81.

45. Ibid., p. 102.

46. Ibid., p. 109.

47. Sam B. Girgus, *The New Covenant: Jewish Writers and the American Idea*, p. 79.

48. Cahan, *The Rise of David Levinsky*, p. 459.

49. Martin Buber, quoted in *The Torah: A Modern Commentary*, p. 467.

50. Anzia Yezierska, *Children of Loneliness*, pp. 269–270.

51. Walter B. Rideout, "O Workers' Revolution . . . The True Messiah," p. 166.

52. Waldo Frank, *Memoirs of Waldo Frank*, p. 183.

53. Waldo Frank, *Dawn in Russia*, p. 163.

54. Ibid., p. 65.

55. Ibid., p. 83.

56. Ibid., pp. 117–118.

57. Lewis Mumford, Introduction to *Memoirs of Waldo Frank*, p. xxvi.

58. Frank, *Dawn in Russia*, p. 3.

59. Czeslaw Milosz, Introduction to *The Trial Begins and On Socialist Realism*, p. 134.

60. Frank, *Memoirs*, p. 196.

61. Chaim Potok, *My Name Is Asher Lev*, p. 117.

62. Ibid., p. 132.

63. Ibid., p. 4.
64. Ibid., p. 326.
65. Ibid., p. 110.
66. Ibid., p. 328.
67. Ibid., p. 372.
68. Bernard Malamud, "Man in the Drawer," in *Rembrandt's Hat*, p. 37.
69. Ibid., p. 48.
70. Ibid., p. 95.
71. Ibid., p. 69.
72. Ibid., p. 71.
73. Philip Roth, "Epilogue: The Prague Orgy," in *Zuckerman Bound*, p. 716.
74. Ibid., p. 757.

BIBLIOGRAPHY

Anschel, Eugene, ed. *The American Image of Russia: 1775–1917*. New York: Frederick Ungar, 1974.

Antin, Mary. *From Plotzk to Boston*. Boston: W. B. Clarke, 1899.

———. *The Promised Land*. Boston: Houghton Mifflin, 1969.

Cahan, Abraham. *Yekl: A Tale of the New York Ghetto*. New York: D. Appleton, 1896.

———. *The Rise of David Levinsky*. New York: Harper & Row, 1960.

Dawidowicz, Lucy S., ed. *The Golden Tradition: Jewish Life and Thought in Eastern Europe*. Philadelphia: Jewish Publication Society of America, 1974.

Frank, Waldo. *Dawn in Russia*. New York: Charles Scribner's Sons, 1932.

Frank, Waldo. *Memoirs of Waldo Frank*, ed. Alan Trachtenberg. Amherst: University of Massachusetts Press, 1973.

Girgus, Sam. B. *The New Covenant: Jewish Writers and the American Idea*. Chapel Hill: University of North Carolina Press, 1984.

Hallo, William W. "Exodus and Ancient Near Eastern Literature." In *The Torah: A Modern Commentary*. New York: Union of American Hebrew Congregations, 1981.

Handlin, Oscar. Foreword. In *The Promised Land*, by Mary Antin. Boston: Houghton Mifflin, 1969.

Harap, Louis. *The Image of the Jew in American Literature: From the Early Republic to Mass Immigration*. Philadelphia: Jewish Publication Society, 1974.

Karp, J. Abraham, ed. *Golden Door to America: The Jewish Immigrant Experience*. New York: Viking Press, 1976.

Lazarus, Emma. *The Poems of Emma Lazarus*. Boston and New York: Houghton Mifflin, 1889.

———. *Songs of a Semite*. 1882; rpt. Upper Saddle River, New Jersey: Literature House, 1970.

Malamud, Bernard. *Rembrandt's Hat*. New York: Farrar, Straus and Giroux, 1973.

Milosz, Czeslaw. Introduction. In *The Trial Begins and On Socialist Realism*, by A. Tertz. New York: Vintage Books, 1960.

Mumford, Lewis. Introduction. In *Memoirs of Waldo Frank*, ed. Alan Trachtenberg. Amherst: University of Massachusetts Press, 1973.

Potok, Chaim. *My Name is Asher Lev*. New York: Alfred Knopf, 1972.

Rideout, Walter. B. "O Workers' Revolution . . . The True Messiah." *American Jewish Archives*. 11. (October, 1959), pp. 157–175.

Roth, Philip. *Zuckerman Bound*. New York: Farrar, Straus and Giroux, 1985.

Sanders, Ronald. *The Downtown Jews*. New York: Harper & Row, 1969.

Sevela, Efraim. *Popugai Govoryaschiy Na Idish* [The Yiddish Speaking Parrot, my translation]. Jerusalem: Stav, 1982.

Singer, I. B. *Shosha*. New York: Farrar, Straus and Giroux, 1978.

Stoessinger, John. G. *Nations in Darkness: China, Russia, and America*. New York: Random House, 1971.

The Torah: A Modern Commentary, ed. W. Gunther Plaut. New York: Union of American Hebrew Congregations, 1981.

Waxman, Meyer. *A History of Jewish Literature*. vol. 4. New York: Thomas Yoseloff Publisher, 1941.

Whitman, Walt. "So Unlike and Yet So Similar." In *The American Image of Russia: 1775–1917*, ed. by Eugene Anschel. New York: Frederick Ungar, 1971.

Yezierska, Anzia. *Children of Loneliness*. New York: Funk and Wagnalls, 1923.

Zangwill, Israel. Foreword. In *From Plotzk to Boston*, by Mary Antin. Upper Saddle River, New Jersey: Literature House, 1970.

14

Shadows of Identity: German-Jewish and American-Jewish Literature—A Comparative Study

Gershon Shaked (Translated by Jeffrey Green)

I

What is Jewish literature in non-Jewish languages? Is it literature in those languages written by Europeans, Americans, or other nationals who happen to be of Jewish origin? Until what generation? Shall we define the writers according to Jewish law, by racial laws of various nations, or is the genetic definition valueless and meaningless, and can any person of any religious or ethnic origins whatsoever be an author whose one and only literary loyalty is to the language which he uses?[1]

Another approach to the question is to present a definition of Jewish thematics and then ascertain whether and to what degree that a priori definition is manifest or implied by the works under discussion: arguing that those nearest these thematics are Jewish writers, and those distant are outside the walls.

Another alternative, a semiotic definition, claims that Jewish literature is any literature in which a portion of the existential rites to which it refers are connected to forms of behavior which may be described by semiotic criteria derived from the Jewish social group.

II

One way or another, definitions and their refutations prove to be of little practical import, for there is an empirical reality in which a group of people define themselves as having a dual identity. The organs of that group are publications with dual identities, and their addressees expect to find materials, subjects and forms in them and in the works associated with them that respond to their needs in all the areas mentioned above: origins, thematics, and semiotics. By presenting examples of those binational publications which embody the contrast between linguistic identity and social identity, we can demonstrate the implicit self-consciousness of those groups of writers and the readers. For example, the German-Jewish periodical *Sulamit* was published in German between 1806 and 1833, the heir, as it were, of the Hebrew *Hameassef* (1783–1811), and a contemporary of *Bikurey Haetim* (1821–1831). After *Sulamit* many German-Jewish periodicals came out, from the *Allgemeine Zeitung des Judentums* (1837–1888) to the Zionist *Der Jude* (1916–1924; edited by Martin Buber, and which Franz Kafka was once asked to edit). In Russia there were publications such as *Razsvet* (1860–1861) and the *Voskhod* (1881–1906), along with a vast number of Hebrew and Yiddish periodicals.

In the United States, Jewish magazines were published in English from the mid-nineteenth century. The *Asmonean* came out in New York in 1849, and the *Hebrew Leader* lasted from 1856 to 1882. Since then a number of American-Jewish magazines have been published, the best known of them being *Commentary* and *Midstream*. Those magazines are, of course, far better known and more widely distributed than both Hebrew magazines such as *Hadoar* and *Bitsaron,* which have led a precarious existence since their establishment, and Yiddish newspapers such as the *Forward* (1897-present), the only one which still exists. At its peak it had a circulation of 200,000. Another major Yiddish paper was *Der Morgen Journal* (1901–1971), which had a peak circulation of 111,000.[2]

What emerges from this brief survey is that a culture with a dual identity is no theoretical concept (for which Professor Dov Sadan proposed a theoretical foundation), created by diligent historians of literature, but rather a real entity of which everyone has long been aware.[3] It is a culture endowed with its own organs, its own establishment, and a community of writers and readers. Literature is a kind of superstructure, a highly complex and well worked-out embodiment of that phenomenon.

III

Men of letters recognized this dual-identity literature of German Jewry. Thus Gustav Krojanker, one of its important critics, published a collection of articles as long ago as 1922, in which Jewish literary critics discuss such German-Jewish writers as Franz Werfel, Franz Kafka, Albert Ehrenstein, Jakob Wassermann, Otto Weininger, Martin Buber, Else Lasker-Schuler, Peter Altenberg, Arnold Zweig, Arthur Schnitzler, Carl Sternheim, and Max Brod, among others.[4] Since then many have written about this body of literature: some, like Harry Zohn, have limited their research to Viennese writers.[5] Others, such as Hans Tramer, have discussed the problems of Jewish and German identity in selected poets.[6]

In the United States various approaches have been taken to the subject. Some writers have tried to free themselves from the stigma of dual identity, others have approached the problem sarcastically and critically, and some have provided us with literary meditations.[7]

A number of Jews—American by birth or choice—have tried to define Jewish literature for themselves, and those definitions are often provocative. Three examples—those of Ludwig Lewisohn, Max Schulz, and Cynthia Ozick—indicate the stretch of the problem.

For one, Ludwig Lewisohn, one of the founding fathers of American-Jewish literature, addressed the question, "What is this Jewish heritage?"[8] He contended that a Jewish book is one written by someone who is well aware that he is Jewish, and that Jewish literature is composed of all the works written in every age and language, whose creators knew they were *Judische Menschen* (in Wassermann's words), or *homines judaici*. To use the phrase of Sir Philip Sydney, they looked in their hearts and wrote.

For another, Max Schulz, in *Radical Sophistication*, writes: "The Jewish imagination similarly has been stirred by the aesthetic possibilities of a radical sophistication, which simultaneously entertains contrary intellectual systems: the secular view of man alienated in an absurd universe and the religious view of man enthroned by divine fiat in God's earthly kingdom."[9]

I am not certain whether this definition fits the Jewish paradox or whether those "contrary" visions characterize American-Jewish literature. Nevertheless, Schulz's remarks, like those of Leslie A. Fiedler, who charges that literature, with the task of giving "some sense of the settling down of Jews in our steam-heated, well-furnished *Galut*—or to struggle against it, if such a struggle is still possible," certainly indicates concern with the character and function of that literature.[10]

Cynthia Ozick takes an original approach to this issue. Her essay, first presented as a lecture at the Weizmann Institute in Rehovot, Israel, in 1970, is called "Towards a New Yiddish," and seeks to justify the author's identity and that of Jewish-Americans in the golden exile.[11] I think her deep need to justify her identity is—again—indisputable evidence of the desire to come to grips with a dual identity.

She formulates a new world-view: American Jewry is like a latter-day Yavneh which will create a new, exilic Jewish culture like that created by the Babylonian rabbis of the talmudic period or the authors of the Golden Age of Spain. She writes: "Gentile readers, should this essay invite any, may or may not be surprised at this self-portrait of a third-generation American Jew (though the first to have been native-born) perfectly at home and yet perfectly insecure, perfectly acculturated and yet perfectly marginal."[12]

She argues that the aesthetics of the Jewish novel (or one close to Judaism) is different from the aesthetics of many contemporary American novels. She views the new trend in the American novel as idol worship (the idols of art) which tries to ignore human reality. Recent "modern" literature, as it were, is close to the Christian drug culture; Judaism (as a *Weltanschauung*), as she puts it, "passionately wallows in human reality."

Moreover, she claims that only those writers in every disapora who wrote as Jews will be remembered as Jews by Jews. Others, who attempted to be universalistic in their own place and time, will be quickly forgotten. "The fact is

that nothing thought or written in Diaspora has ever been able to last unless it
has been centrally Jewish. If it is centrally Jewish it will last for Jews."[13]

Her conclusion is that American Jewry must create a culture and language of
its own (the English of the Jews as a new Yiddish), a sort of new Yavneh which
will deal with a new form of Talmud: imaginative literature. She concludes that
"From being envious apes we can become masters of our own civilization—
and let those who want to call this 're-ghettoization,' or similar pejoratives, look
to their own destiny."[14]

I am not certain that her basic assumption is either correct or persuasive. The
idea that Jewish literature "passionately wallows in human reality" in contrast
to non-Jewish literature, which does not thus wallow, seems peculiar; it permits
one to designate as "Jewish" any writer working in that direction (be he as
gentile as you please, he is "Jewish" in spirit), and as "non-Jewish," Jews
whose work tends to the opposite direction. The hope for a "new Yavneh" is
more wishful thinking than reality.

Yet a convincing message emerges from Ozick's essay. She turns a shortcoming into an advantage, an undefinable situation into a defined one. A large
number of the writers in the two non-Jewish cultures and languages with which
I am familiar, German and American-Jewish writing, grappled with that experience in their works, so much so that *the issue of identity itself might be said to
have become the most important distinguishing feature of those authors with
dual identities,* struggling in their lives with the problem of identity.

IV

Although this discussion deals with the problem of identity in Jewish literature
written in non-Jewish languages, I shall begin by quoting a passage from a
Hebrew story by Micha Joseph Berdyczewski. This passage expresses the problem intensely, a problem with which both domestic (Hebrew and Yiddish) writers
and foreign writers (those using non-Jewish languages) wrestled on various levels
and in various forms. The passage comes from "The Stranger," a story first
published in 1908.

He left his people! What did he leave? Shattered bodies, shadows, just shadows. What
do you see in the Jews except shadows? But those shadows dwell in his spirit, in his
essence, and in everything within him. They say, "The seed of Abraham has passed
away," but they have not passed away. The individual is finished, but they are stronger
than the individual. You and your thoughts will wither away in inactivity, and they will
not die out. They will mock and deride you.[15]

What is characteristic of this passage is the feeling that the protagonist wishes
to rid himself of his Jewish heritage, but he understands very well that he is
pursued by it. What appears to be a shadow is stronger than the light of reason.
The irrational powers of the shadow overcome the rational forces of light in the
souls of his characters.

In Hebrew literature, and often in Yiddish literature, that formulation expresses the consciousness of the authors and their heroes rather than their actual existential situation. They were completely identified with what they called the *shadow powers*. The Jewish language itself is a shadow spreading over them. They took refuge from Jewish culture in it! Those who wrote in Hebrew (and to some extent in Yiddish) chose their identity. They could perhaps struggle against it, criticize and hate it, but they did so from within. Moreover, they maintained it by means of their struggle against it. They expanded and deepened it with every expression of love, envy, and hatred.

That is not the case with a writer who chose another language. It would seem he had chosen "spirit and light" (to use Chaim Nakhman Bialik's phrase), but the shadow remains hidden somewhere between the lines, and the work itself is an expression of the struggle against the shadow by means of (what appear to be) the linguistic "powers of light." What character did that struggle assume? What changes took place within it when it passed from a hostile cultural environment in Germany, one which did not open its arms to greet the alien Jews trying to penetrate it, to a pluralistic cultural environment which took the Jews to its heart? Those are the questions I want to address.

Let us begin with an author who occupied an intermediary place between linguistic cultures and ideological positions: Ludwig Lewisohn (1882–1955). He was born in Berlin, emigrated to the United States with his parents in 1890, assimilated rather thoroughly, and then returned to Judaism (in the national sense) so much so that in the 1920's he became a declared Zionist.

The Island Within (1928) is a kind of novel of repentance. We need not go into detail regarding this novel, which describes the relations between an assimilated Jew (Arthur) and a gentile woman and the world she represents. The upshot of those relations is that Arthur returns to his Jewish roots. This book by a Jew from Germany, written in English in the United States, is quite typical of a substantial portion of German-Jewish fiction (struggling with the problem of identity) and also of some American-Jewish fiction. The point of departure for such works is that the problem of identity for those German- or American-Jews (and their creators) derives mainly from a struggle against the outside world which is unwilling to accept the Jew as completely German or American. Therefore, he is obliged either to take that dreadful disadvantage, Jewish identity, upon himself as a tragic destiny or to turn the liability into an advantage.

Jewish literature in German sought to adjust itself to the tension between a minority with a dual identity and a majority with a single one. The problem for the minority is that the majority stigmatizes it. Worse, in general, the minority internalizes that stigma.[16] German-Jewish writers frequently believed that Jews lived in a foreign and alienating environment by sufferance, not by right. Thus they frequently believed that they and their characters had some of the negative traits attributed to them by the majority, and that it was incumbent upon them, as authors, to demonstrate that this stigma did or did not fit.

It is not my present task to explain either the source of the stigma or the reason some German Jews internalized it. That internalization frequently took on pathological proportions, as in the case of Otto Weininger. In his theoretical work, *Race and Character* (1903), he presented the most extreme expression of the *existential condition of persecution* of someone who has internalized external pursuers and justified his own fate as the victim.[17]

That existential condition produces various implicit features in the works, and may give the experience its literary form. Many works are based on a plot like that of *The Island Within*, in which the protagonist confronts his identity after encountering barriers to erotic (or other) self-realization in the foreign world which attracts him with its charms and repels him with its hatred. In a large number of the writers of the generation of 1900–1940, the problem of identity was repressed and appears in various forms.

While overt treatments of the problems of Jewish identity, with manifest use of Jewish semiotics (generally from Eastern Europe), are quite frequent, they are not quite the highest order of writing. An example of this, similar to Lewisohn's novel, depicting a Jew's path from assimilation to Zionism, is the trivial, in a literary sense, novel by Max Brod, *Reubeni, Prince of Jews* (1925).[18] The book tells the story of David Lemel of Prague, who, with the assistance of an assimilated Jew, rebels against his father, falls in love with a gentile woman, and runs away from home with her. After she leaves him, he returns, repentant, to his people and becomes a "false" Messiah, David Reubeni.

According to that novel's views, the Jews must become a nation like all others by returning to their ancient homeland. Nationalism must replace assimilation. Hence, this is a historical novel dealing with the relation between the national, messianic idea and the Jewish people, who refuse to be redeemed.[19] It has Zionist underpinnings and aims its barbs at those who are unable to absorb and implement the ideals of an exalted leader. The first parts of the book, describing the erotic attractions of the alien world, and giving ideological justification to the abandonment of family, tribe, and religion, are actually closest to most German-Jewish literature. The main crisis of the first part, which describes Lemel-Reubeni's rejection by the world which leads him to repent, is also rather conventional. Reubeni's Zionist-messianic ideology, which seeks to liberate the Jews from dependence on the world, distinguishes Brod from most of his contemporaries. The entire work is characterized by a simplistic and rather overt approach to the topic of identity: the yearning for a dual identity, disappointment with it, and the attempt to create a new identity for the Jews.

This approach also characterizes the "Jewish" works of Arthur Schnitzler: *Professor Bernhardi* (1912) and *Der Weg ins Freie* (1908). The former is an apologetic play about a Jew who seeks to defend himself against intolerance, and the irrational hatred of the anti-Semites (a response to a small-scale blood libel). The latter work is a novel about an assimilated Jew, Heinrich Behrman, who struggles with the problem of identity, and another Jew, Leo Golenski, seeking an ideological-Zionist escape from a dead end. These works by Brod and Schnitzler treat the problem of identity solely from without.

V

The works in which the problem of identity is not presented overtly but rather implicitly are much more significant. Moreover, among some of the writers in whose works this theme is depicted, there is a gap between their direct expressions in journals, essays, and letters, and their literary expressions, motivated by more primary processes.

I intend to present examples of the implicit and profound depiction of the experience of Jewish identity and its problems from the works of three very different writers; the common denominator among them is that they all wrote in German and were aware of their Jewish identity. The first is Joseph Roth (born in 1894 near Brody, in Galicia; died in 1939 in Paris). The second is Franz Kafka (born in 1883 in Prague; died in 1924 in Prague). And the third, the eldest of the trio, is Jakob Wassermann (born in 1873 in Fürth; died in 1934 in Alt-Aussee, Austria). Roth was born into an Eastern-European family, and after leaving his home, he became an assimilated Jew. The other two writers, however, belonged to the second generation of assimilated Jews. As noted, all three were quite concerned with their identity.[20]

Roth tried to create a fictional life for himself. Although he was born of Jewish parents, he claimed that his father was an Austrian officer and that he was the product of his mother's illicit romance. In the late 1920's he became a Hapsburg monarchist mainly because the welter of nations in that empire appeared to be a kind of international ideal for him, a pluralistic, universalistic paradise in which Jews could find a safe haven, without being handicapped by their identity. In his imagination he fabricated a tolerant Hapsburg empire: one which never existed, his own subjective utopia. He lavished praise on pluralistic universalism both in his imaginative works such as *Die Büste des Kaisers* (1935), and in his essays and travel writing, *Juden auf Wanderschaft* (1927), in which he described various Jewish centers.[21] There he reserves special praise for the Jews because they have no homeland: "They have no fatherland, the Jews, but every country where they dwell and pay taxes demands patriotism and a heroic death from them and reproaches them for not being pleased to die. In that situation Zionism is really the only way out: as long as there must be patriotism, it might as well be for one's own country."[22]

One must not conclude that Joseph Roth was a Zionist. He was as far as could be from that. Moreover, in a letter to Stefan Zweig in 1935, he was, to my knowledge, the first to make a comparison between Zionism and Nazism.[23] He considered that all narrow nationalism had no hope for man. Only deracinated supranationalism, one universalistic and "as free as a bird" from all national obligations, should exist. He tried to give "positive deracination" a political dimension—an idealized incarnation of that supranationalism was the defunct Hapsburg empire.

That issue concerned Roth in his writing throughout his life. His works do not express the *joy* of the universalist existential situation but rather the dreadful misery of someone who *reached* that existential situation. His novella *Die Flucht ohne Ende* (1927) is a splendid expression of the existential status of a fully deracinated person. The main protagonist, Tunda, is half-Jewish. He fights in World War I and wanders, following his imprisonment by the Russians, across landscapes and ideologies. He leaves his cosseted, bourgeois home (and his conventional fiancée) in Vienna, goes through Soviet Russia (his mistress is a communist commisar), reaching Germany in the post-World War I period. From there he goes on to the supposedly universalist Paris. Yet the deracinated hero finds himself at home everywhere and nowhere. He is always marginal, exceptional, and expelled. When he finds himself in new surroundings, the pattern repeats itself. The novel finishes with the following description:

It was August 27, 1926, four p.m., the shops were full, in the department stores women shoved, in high fashion boutiques models spun about, in the patisseries idlers chattered, in the factories wheels whirled, on the banks of the Seine beggars picked at their lice, in the Bois de Boulogne couples kissed each other, in the parks children rode on the carousel. It was at this hour. There stood my friend Tunda, 32 years old, healthy and chipper, a strong young man with all sorts of talents, in the Place de la Madeleine, in the middle of the capital of the world, and he didn't know what to do. He had no profession, no love, no desire, no hope, no ambition, and not even any egotism. No one on earth was more superfluous than he.[24]

This marvelous description contends that a person cannot live in the abstract: without place, time, and identity. The fictional creation reveals what the lips dared not utter: the obverse of the abstract universal, pluralistic ideal. It turns out that one must pay a dreadful price to live without a shadow. The effort to flee any identity leads one to a *cul-de-sac*. Here, the primary, unconscious psychological processes do not take the conscious yearning for "universal" existence literally. They lay bare the tragedy of identity.

Kafka gave that problem metaphysical and metapsychological significance. It is not by chance that while his protagonists have appellations similar to that of their creator (K. and Joseph K., for example), most of them lack an identity. Instead, we have letters standing for humans who are mere ciphers symbolizing universal man. Of all the novels, only *Amerika* (1927) is populated with characters from the Austro-Hungarian empire. Most of Kafka's protagonists are, thus, universal, and the author need not bother explaining their deracination. They were born in emptiness. They have neither historic time nor geographic space.

This contrasts with Kafka's documentary writings which are full of Jewish materials and doubts. From his journals and letters we learn that he was concerned with his Jewish identity. He was interested in Jewish history (he read Heinrich Graetz's *History of the Jews*), in Yiddish literature (he read Meyer Isser Pines's *The History of Yiddish Literature*), in Yiddish theatre (the actor Isaac Loewy), and in the customs and ways of Eastern-European Jewry (ritual baths, circumcision, *Hasidic* courts).[25] Such material was not included in his literary works.

Like Roth, Kafka was all too familiar with the inner life of people without identity. In a letter to Max Brod, he defined their character, and of course himself as one of them, in stark terms:

To get away from Judaism, generally with the unclear approval of the fathers (that unclarity was the most offensive of all) is what most of those who started to write in German wanted; they wanted it, but with their little rear paws they still clung to the father's Judaism, and with their little forepaws they found no new solid ground. Their desperation in that situation was their inspiration.[26]

Kafka's works are the most complex internalization in Jewish fiction in foreign languages of the *feeling* of persecution experienced by characters whose identity is determined by their *being persecuted*. They live in an undefined place outside any historical time, accused of a sin they did not commit and yet justifying the verdict (*The Trial*, 1925). They are expelled from their society, which does not recognize their identity (*The Castle*, 1926). Their identity gives them permission to dwell nowhere (the ambiguity here is intentional), and their lives as marginal subtenants exposes them to false accusations.

Kafka's protagonists are not pursued by external forces nor accused by courts of real jurisdiction. They internalize a social situation which assumed both a psychological and existential dimension. Since the universal Jew has no identity, is persecuted, and lacks a place in space and time, his predicament typifies the "human condition" (to the degree that modern man feels that). The Jewish plot takes on the dimensions of a universal human *metaplot*.

Let us go on to our final example in German: the works of Jakob Wassermann. *Die Juden aus Zirndorf* was published in 1897, and it is a *Bildungsroman* like many Hebrew novels of the *Haskalah* (Jewish Enlightenment) period and like Brod's novel, *Reubeni*. While it is not of great literary importance, the metamorphoses of the topics of identity, persecution, and guilt were given splendid expression in *Der Fall Maurizius* (first published in 1928), which does not treat a specifically Jewish subject.

Like Roth and Kafka, Wassermann frequently dealt in his journalistic and documentary writing with the question of his *identity*: the tension between his Jewishness and his Germany. As with those two writers, he preferred the authentic Jew, whom he called "Oriental" (referring to Eastern Europe), to the assimilated Jew (Roth, too, in *Juden auf Wanderschaft,* lavished praise upon the practicing Jews of Eastern Europe). It is no surprise that these three assimilated Jews, who were ashamed of their identity or viewed their dual identity as tragic, admired groups of Jews who, rather than concealing their identity, exhibited it conspicuously.

Wassermann expressed his admiration, as someone with a problematic identity, for people with a single, clear identity. In the following remarks taken from a letter to Martin Buber, Wasserman writes:

The Jew, in contrast, whom I call Oriental—is naturally a symbolic figure; I might have called him the fulfilled or the legitimate heir . . . since a noble consciousness, a blood consciousness links him with the past, and an enormous responsibility obligates him to the future; and he cannot betray himself for he is a revealed essence. . . . He knows his sources, and he lives with the matriarchs, he reposes and he creates; they are ever wandering people who cannot be changed.[27]

What is revealing is that he relates to them with terms taken from a lexicon typical of German romantic nationalism: *"ein edles Bewusstsein, Blutbewusstsein"* ("a noble consciousness, a blood consciousness"), as well as *"wohnt bei dem Müttern"* ("lives with the matriarchs"). It seems to me that he views them as true members of *the nation,* in contrast to himself and those like him, who have no nationality.

That authentic Jew is worthy of admiration because he is almost "non-Jewish," for he contrasts with the Judaism of Wassermann, Kafka, and Roth, which Wassermann defines in the same letter:

We know them, my dear friend, we know them very well, and we suffer on account of them, and because of the thousands who are called "modern Jews," who chip away at all the foundations, since they themselves have no foundations, discarding everything they achieved yesterday, and fouling today what they loved the day before; they, who take pleasure in treachery, who make a kind of ornament of baseness, and for whom negation is an aim.[28]

Just as in one part of the letter we find exaggerated admiration for authentic Jews, here we have radical rejection of German Jews (such as Wassermann himself) vacillating between two identities. The most pathetic expression of that vacillation is found in Wassermann's *Mein Weg als Deutscher und Jude* (1921), a kind of dismal monologue by a jilted lover, blaming his failure in love upon his identity. A sentence like, "You may try in vain to die and live for them [the Germans], they will always say, 'He's a Jew,'" one of the concluding sentences of that book, expresses Wassermann's predicament as a Jew very well: someone who tried to be completely German all his life and failed abjectly. Like Roth's character, Tunda, he is left at the spiritual crossroads of his life, with no idea where to turn. Toward the end of his life Wassermann planned a novel to be called *Ahasuer.* The main protagonist of that was to be the wandering Jew.[29]

The problem of identity could well be the main one afflicting Waremme-Warschauer, one of the central characters in *Der Fall Maurizius.* Waremme-Warschauer is reminiscent of Judas Iscariot and Ahasuerus. By his perjurious testimony he brings about the unjust condemnation of his friend Maurizius. Ever since that condemnation, Waremme-Warschauer has been wandering through Europe and the United States.

He offers a rather strange definition of his Jewishness:

I was born to Jewish parents living in the second generation of civil liberty. My father was not entirely aware that the situation of apparent equality was basically merely sufference. People like my father, in other respects an excellent man, religiously and socially speaking, were suspended in mid-air. They no longer retained their old belief, and they refused to accept a new one, that is, Christianity, sometimes for good reasons, sometimes for bad ones. A Jew wants to be a Jew. What is a Jew? No one can give an entirely satisfactory answer. My father was proud of the emancipation, a cunning invention to deprive the downtrodden of any pretext for complaining.[30]

He first pretends to be only a German nationalist. He tries to hide traces of his past. But at the end of his life he acknowledges that the blurring of his identity was a failure. What remains to him after the end of all his Germanic illusions is his miserable Jewish identity—which he tries to reinforce. He wishes to convert his handicap into an advantage and travel to Eastern Europe, to his daughter and the *Hasidim*: a positive response that emphasizes one-half of his dual identity.

Incidentally, that attempt to return to Jewish identity provided a spark of hope to all the writers considered here, although none of them went wholly through with it on either the fictional or biographical level without ambivalence. For example, Roth opened strange gates to repentance before his Eastern-European protagonists. In *Hiob* (1930), a novel, the main character emigrates to America. He is in despair after the death of his wife and the loss of his children but finally acquires a new, startling life. Roth's novella, *Der Leviathan* (1940), tells the story of Nissen Piczenik, a coral merchant, who sinned by selling artificial corals and repents by plunging into the sea to seek the Leviathan, the father of all corals, finding his own death in the ocean. At the end of *his* life in Paris, Roth formed a close friendship with a Jewish rabbinical scholar, Joseph Gottfarstein, but his funeral was a grotesque mélange of identities: attending were a rabbinical scholar, a rabbi, a Catholic priest, and a deputation of the Hapsburg royalist party.[31] It is worth noting the opposition between Roth and Kafka. In Kafka's work one finds no optimistic Jewish message at all. Yet unlike Roth, he sought to form a significant bond with the Jewish world. In addition to his study of Judaica, he contemplated a visit to Palestine, and at the end of his life a Zionist, Jewish woman named Dora Diamant cared for him.[32]

Wassermann was the most ambivalent of the three in his life (though he remained a member of the Jewish community of Gratz until his death).[33] In his latter years he became extremely sensitive to the fate of the Jews, and he planned, as noted, to write a novel about the fate of the wandering Jew, Ahasuerus. According to one of Wassermann's letters to his publisher, that work was to encompass the history of the Jewish people over two thousand years in the form of tableaux and conversations.[34] Most of the turning points in history, Wassermann said, would be illustrated in dialogues, some of which he had already written. There would be conversations with Saint Paul, Julian the Apostate, Charlemagne, Pope Innocent, Isabella the queen of Spain, Spinoza, Richelieu, Cromwell, Catherine II of Russia, Frederick the Great, Maria Theresa, Napoleon,

Karl Marx, Bismarck, Lenin, and Hitler. Along with that he promised scenes of persecution and expulsion, of *yeshivot* and the formation of religious sects.

Thus we see that before his premature death, he wished to write what he thought was *the* Jewish book of his generation. That project is a convincing expression of what the wandering Jew underwent: in the wake of events in Germany, Wassermann had to take up *his* wanderer's staff.

Generally speaking, German-Jewish literature was a literature of flight from identity. It suffered from the burden of its heritage and sought to struggle with an identity which was imposed and then internalized. The protagonists of German-Jewish literature are persecuted because of their identity, and usually the plot cannot resolve their crises. The conflict between identities as well as the loss of an identity made the experience of dual identity negative and destructive.

VI

There is probably no great disparity between American-Jewish literature and German-Jewish literature. However, it must be emphasized that today American-Jewish literature is prouder of its dual identity than any other Jewish literature with this characteristic. In his anthology *On Being Jewish* (1974), Daniel Walden sought to document three stages in the literary embodiment of the American-Jewish experience: (1) immigration; (2) Americanization; and, finally, (3) Jewish-Americans and American-Jews.[35]

I want to look—albeit briefly and by example—at the problem of Jewish identity in America in light of these stages, not only to test the heuristic nature of this thesis, but also to enrich it. Among the books belonging to the first stage (though in fact Walden places it in the second stage) is Henry Roth's novel, *Call It Sleep* (1934), doubtless the most interesting of them all.[36]

This work is permeated by the world of the *shtetl,* and it gives some description of the transplanting of *shtetl* life from Eastern Europe to the United States. Henry Roth describes the inner disintegration of the community (the collapse of paternal, divine, and communal authority), only after which does the problem of the individual's identity and his relations with the external world arise. *Call It Sleep* is close in its materials, its semiotics, and its thematics to Hebrew, and to Yiddish literature of Eastern Europe. In many respects it is closer to Sholom Aleichem's *Motl ben Peysi Hakhazan* (the story, from the point of view of a child, of the immigration to America of an Eastern-European Jewish family) than to many American and Jewish-American novels of its generation.

Roth's book tells the story of an immigrant family, most specifically of David, a young boy, who discovers his human identity through the riddle of his family. The "original sin" of the family was committed in its country of origin. Genya, the mother, was seduced by a gentile lover and married her Jewish husband as a last resort. Her past overshadows her present, determining her fate and that of her son. She submits (with deep feelings of guilt) to all her husband's caprices, whereas the boy is rejected by his father, who regards him as a stumbling block from their first encounter.

The characters have authentic linguistic and behavioral identities within the family circle. The author represents their Yiddish speech among themselves with correct English, whereas outside the family circle they have no linguistic identity (as indicated by broken English).

The loss of paternal authority and the Oedipal tension between fathers and sons, the opposition between an erotic sin (the hidden secret that motivated the family relations) and the norms of family existence, the opposition between the house as a shelter and the external world as a primal forest arousing fears— these are subjects and motifs typical of Hebrew literature (Micha Joseph Ber-dyczewski, Joseph Hayim Brenner, Isaac Dov Berkowitz) and Yiddish writing (Hayim Grade, Isaac Bashevis Singer). *Call It Sleep* is thus a Hebrew or Yiddish novel written in English, in which English tries to imitate Yiddish, just as the Yiddish and Hebrew in works set in America and written in those languages attempt to find an equivalent for English.[37] This phenomenon is far from unique. Hebrew novels such as *Married Life* (1929–1930) by David Fogel or *Shaul and Johanna* (1956–1967) by Naomi Frankl are, in that sense, German novels written in Hebrew. Similarly, *Vengeance of the Fathers* (1928) by Isaac Shami is an Arabic novella written in Hebrew, and Isaac Bashevis Singer's *Enemies, a Love Story* (1972) is a novel whose linguistic materials are Yiddish, Polish, and American, and which was written in Yiddish (but which has a literary existence only in English).

Call It Sleep, like Joseph Roth's *Hiob* (1930), is a Yiddish novel in its language, in its behavioral norms, and in the identification of the protagonists. Although it was written in English, the characters have no doubt about their identities, although, as in the Hebrew and Yiddish novels of the twentieth century, one can already discern the first stages of the collapse of identity which led to the works of "American-Jewish" writers.

Chaim Potok's *The Chosen* (1967), written some thirty years after Henry Roth's novel, is close to it in several respects. It, too, is based on the language and semiotics of the American-Jewish *shtetl* society. In the American context it raises issues of the conflicts among Enlightened Jews, *Hasidim,* and Zionists which had been quite familiar to readers in Hebrew and Yiddish. Potok's two main protagonists, Danny Sanders, the son of a *Hasidic rebbe* who yearns for secular education, and Reuben Malter, the son of a traditionalist Zionist intel-lectual who seeks the light within Judaism, are immersed in their Jewish heritage. They have no doubts about their identities despite their conflicting ambitions. Like *Call It Sleep,* this work is closer to the Hebrew and Yiddish literature of the turn of the last century than to German or American-Jewish literature of this century, for it depicts problems of identity within a milieu with a decided identity, which, in the end, is unambiguous (despite its yearnings for spirit and light), not a dual identity doubtful of the ambiguous meaning of its existence.

When American Jews become assimilated, as with their European fathers and brethren, the problem of identity arises with its full import. Surprisingly, although they have ended up in a host society different in its pluralistic character from European societies in general and German society in particular, subjects, motifs, and conflicts appear in American-Jewish literature which had been common in German-Jewish literature. These topics reappear, however, in rather strange guise in this literature. For example, American-Jewish literature, too, presents the figure of a paranoid fleeing from himself and from his environment because of external pressures exerted upon him. In some of their works, however, American-Jewish writers, unlike their German predecessors, hint that the pressure is merely apparent, and that the situation being described is a mere parody of the former one which had inner justification in a dissimilar situation.

A parody of the experience of anxiety and flight can be found in Bruce Jay Friedman's novella, *Stern* (1962). It is the story of the existential fear of a Jewish anti-hero who cannot stand his own identity and tries to escape it, to get away from people who seek to impose this burden upon him. For example, Stern, drafted into the Air Force, attributes his not being a pilot to his Jewishness: "Somehow Stern connected his non-flying status with his Jewishness, as though flying were a golden, crew-cut, Gentile thing while Jewishness was a cautious and scholarly quality that crept into engines and prevented planes from lurching off the ground with recklessness."[38] He hates his Jewish identity, which contrasts with the positive standards he created for himself from the attractive image of the true American (of which a true Israeli, according to Friedman, is the positive incarnation).

Apparently this is merely a parody of self-hatred: the internalization (here too) of an anti-Semitic doctrine, the Jew as anti-warrior. Friedman's protagonist flees because one of his neighbors insulted his family with the word "kike." That flight (like the stigma) is unjustified. The European anxiety of the hero persists, although it has lost, in Friedman's opinion, any justification in fact. Paranoia has become a psychosis with no empirical basis.[39]

We can say from this example that American-Jewish literature partakes of the legacy of German-Jewish literature. The societies have changed, but the state of having a dual identity is unaltered. More than anything else, the outer pressure changed: at first slightly, then greatly. There are works by Bernard Malamud, Philip Roth, and Saul Bellow which are far closer to their German-Jewish kinsmen than one might first imagine.

I shall illustrate the foregoing with "Eli the Fanatic" (1959) by Philip Roth, the story of a man who has been asked by his community to prevent recently arrived European-Jewish refugees from flaunting their identity so that their brethren need not be embarrassed by them. In the end Eli astonishes the members of his community because the refugees seem more authentic to him than the people he represents, and he puts on traditional Jewish costume.

It is not surprising that Philip Roth, like Joseph Roth and Jakob Wasserman, uses the "Jewish" image of Eastern-European ultra-orthodox Jews as an example of authentic Judaism as opposed to the assimilated, shallow Jewry of the American suburbs.

The traditional costume of the *Hasidim* of Eastern Europe, the Yiddish language, and their customs become worthy of being maintained. The community which tries to make them disappear by fitting them into the American scene is rejected by the author. This is a strange nostalgia for a world which is no longer, based on the feeling that the world which has taken its place is far worse.[40] In this respect we find that Philip Roth has an affinity with the German writers we have mentioned, who consciously and unconsciously chose the Jewish world of yesterday, with its single identity, as opposed to today's world with its dual identity.

Cynthia Ozick offers an ambivalent and ironic thesis about that subject. As noted, in her programmatic essay she called for the creation of a "new Yiddish." She claimed that the world of American Jewry, with its dual identity and single language, is an autonomous cultural realm. Drawbacks must be converted into advantages, and American-Jewish literature in English, which, by its very nature, has a dual identity, must be justified. That (perhaps?) is because the other, Hebrew and Yiddish culture, also lost its singleness of identity. It no longer exists as a unitary culture and no longer pretends to its own cultural identity.

The converse of the conscious assertion of the Jewish legitimacy of a dual identity can be found in Ozick's story, "Envy; or, Yiddish in America" (collected in *The Pagan Rabbi and Other Stories,* 1971).[41] This story tells of the envy felt by the Yiddish poets Edelshtein and Baumzweig towards the Yiddish novelist Ostrover. They write poems in Yiddish and remain within the pathetic, moribund confines of a backward language; he writes stories which are translated into English and have become treasured possessions of American literature. It is no startling revelation to assert that the prototype for Ostrover evidently seems to be Isaac Bashevis Singer.

What is important in this story is not so much the acute description of the prototype or the sarcastic portrayal of the wretched Yiddish poets, but rather the implicit assumption that *shtetl* culture has no possible future in America, that this injustice cannot choose a language, such as Yiddish, and that any writer in that language can come to life only if he is translated from the idiom of the *shtetl* to that of the city and suburb. Ozick, who attacked "universalism" with such vehemence, comes out against the wretched "localism" of the representatives of Yiddish culture who seek to break through the walls of the ghetto. Not only has Yiddish "culture" no chance at all, it does not aspire to life but, rather, hopes to break through the borders and put on local, American clothing.

Loyalty to European sources and refugees might be more attractive and moral than the American Jews' demand that those refugees assimilate, but in fact the refugees assimilate to stay alive. They are as eager to fit in as the culture is open to accommodate them. It is only a dual linguistic identity which can give a Jew like Isaac Bashevis Singer real existence, and only that readership of strangers, who are also related to him, that can give him any sort of identity. Cynthia Ozick senses the depths of the conflict of the cultural refugees, who, in contrast to mere physical refugees, are liable to swear themselves to silence because they have lost their natural environment, unless they succeed in passing from their original language to that of their potential readership. Ozick makes it clear that there is no room for nostalgia: *the one and only possible identity in the American-Jewish world appears to be dual identity*. The implicit assumption of her lecture (and her story) is that the best the Jews can hope for is that their authors not ignore their duality of identity in their deep ambition to flee their Jewish origins and become uniquely American in identity.

The relation between the source identity and the target identity is, as noted, a subject which has preoccupied American-Jewish literature, although it has apparently been freed of pressure from without, far more than one might first suspect. It could almost be said that, as with German-Jewish literature, that topic defines the Jewishness of the literature.[42]

The issue of an identity forced upon a person against his will is the main theme of Malamud's *The Fixer* (1966) and some short stories. This purports to be a historical novel, and the case of Yakov Bok is a reflection of the Beilis affair, one of the most notorious blood libels in Russia. This historical novel about Czarist Russia was written in the 1960's in the United States, some twenty years after the greatest blood libel in history. To the post-Holocaust American-Jewish addressee, the Russian crime seems like a small-scale dress rehearsal for the horrifying spectacle to come. What the novel implies is that a person's identity is something decreed against his will, and he must accept the destiny he has not chosen, whether he likes it or not. Yakov Bok sees his identity as a cruel fate: "From birth a black horse had followed him, a Jewish nightmare. What was being a Jew but an everlasting curse? He was sick of their history, destiny, blood guilt."[43]

In Malamud's "The Last Mohican" (collected in *Pictures of Fidelman*, 1969), Fidelman, the artist with a dual identity, tries to escape the curse of Ziskind, an "authentic" Jew who appears this time as a miserable *shnorrer* (leech) who arouses guilt in Fidelman's heart. The two figures are bound to each other and no man can sunder them—the alter ego and the ego are conjoined like Siamese twins. In "The German Refugee," or the pathetic, allegorical "The Jewbird" (see *The Stories of Bernard Malamud*, 1983), Jewish identity is conceived as something imposed; powerful impersonal forces place it upon individuals and in the end they submit.

The issue of the character of Jewish identity and its status in American society is also, to some extent, the subject of Saul Bellow's *The Victim* (1947). It must be remembered that this novel came out just two years after the Second World War, and one may not ignore its place in human and Jewish history. In 1947 even the meaning of the title was laden with more significance than it would have had ten years earlier (or later).[44]

This book presents an anti-Semitic figure, a kind of small-scale blood libel, and a Jewish protagonist (Asa Leventhal), falsely accused. The protagonist assumes indirect responsibility for the firing of his friend, Allbee, and for his nephew's death, although he is guilty of neither. Here we have a transfer of the experience of guilt and persecution typical of a writer such as Kafka from the general metaphysical and existential realm to the narrower area of human society. Now, the experience of guilt is reduced in dimension (almost parodically) and made more concrete. What is important is that the transition from a closed non-Jewish society (Germany), in which the Jews occupied a rather central place in the culture although they remained marginal socially, to an open and pluralistic non-Jewish society, where Jews occupy a central position culturally and a more comfortable position socially, does not alter the subjective experience of the main protagonist. Leventhal's antagonist, Allbee, makes the sort of anti-Semitic statements which had been common in Germany: the Jews pollute the culture (when a Jewish author writes about Emerson); they are children of Caliban; they seek to destroy the foundations of the American upper class. In fact, this is anti-Semitism from the point of view of the B'nai B'rith and Anti-Defamation League rather than the ingrained anti-Semitism of the society in which the Jews live. The model for persecution has independent existence as a supra-personal entity embodied in various trivial events, and is not connected with the changes which took place in the host country.

VII

Although several German-Jewish literary models (character, plot, subject) regarding identity recur in strange fashion in American-Jewish literature, without doubt a great change has taken place in the depiction of the Jew as a man with a dual identity. Philip Roth formulated the difficulty of the new Jewish identity in literature written by Jews for Jews in the following remarks:

Jews are people who are not what anti-Semites say they are. That was once a statement out of which a man might begin to construct an identity for himself; now it does not work so well, for it is difficult to act counter to the ways people expect you to act when fewer and fewer people define you by such expectations. The success of the struggle against the defamation of Jewish character in this country has itself made more pressing the need for a Jewish self-consciousness that is relevant to this time and place.[45]

Roth goes on to argue that it is ridiculous to pretend to be a victim in a country where no one forces you to be one if you choose to live otherwise.

The three major writers of American-Jewish literature, Bellow, Malamud, and Roth, struggled with the identity problems of an *unpersecuted minority* which is nevertheless persecuted by its own identity. The question of what is the "Jewish identity" of one who is not persecuted, yet who feels persecuted, is implicit for example in Malamud's *The Assistant* (1957), in Bellow's *Herzog* (1964), and, of course, in Roth's *Portnoy's Complaint* (1969).

In his eulogy for Morris Bober in *The Assistant,* a rabbi asks who is a Jew and in what way Morris Bober was Jewish. The rabbi's answer, more or less that a Jew is a good person, is not particularly convincing; however, that is secondary. In the novel's plot the protagonists do not flee their Jewish identity, but, in fact, the Jew and the gentile (Frank Alpine) both assume that identity. Malamud indicates that this identity is a positive one, contrasting favorably with the American-Jewish way of life. According to Malamud, a Jew is anyone who rejects the achievement orientation of the middle class (both Jewish and non-Jewish) by not acceding to the values of materialism. He is a positive failure, gaining in the spiritual realm what he loses in the everyday world.[46]

Malamud converts defeat in the battle of existence into a moral victory. He translates the historical failure of the Jews as a persecuted minority into the merely economic failure of an other-minded minority. It would seem that Bober does not wish to leave the confines of the local *shtetl,* nor does he fit into the American way of life (economically and socially); thus he remains an authentic Jew. That maintenance of the positive aspect of his identity is an attractive feature of the protagonist. By means of economic failure the character preserves his identity; conversely, economic success entails losing it.

The overall structure of the work implies that the author, through his characters, values the existence of some kind of Jewish identity in pluralistic American society. That view contrasts with German-Jewish writers, whose characters wished to rid themselves of their identity. Their creators believed that was a hopeless struggle, and therefore they frequently took a negative view of their own protagonists.

In *Herzog,* Bellow approaches this issue in more complex fashion. He removes the problematics from the area of relations between Jews and non-Jews. The structure of relations he describes in *Herzog* is mainly intra-Jewish. The two main characters of the novel are both Jews: Herzog, the refined, aristocratic intellectual, on the one hand, and the plebeian, vulgar Gersbach, on the other. Bellow presents the struggle between these characters as that of two faces of a new generation of Jews, who had taken an important position in American society as creators and purveyors of the spirit. The purveyors outdo the creators as the two men vie for the same woman; they represent a struggle for the "world."

Herzog is *not* a "classic" *shlemiel*—women are fond of him; he has a position in the academic establishment, but he takes Madeleine's (his wife's) betrayal as an absolute treachery, isolating him and making all his activities in the world seem unreal. Instead of political action or working to influence the development of the human spirit, he composes political and philosophical epistles which take the place of deeds. He lives too often within his imagination and enjoys his situation as a tortured romantic, in contrast to his friend and his divorced wife, who take pleasure in the vanity of this world.

Bellow ambivalently views the romantic in a mass society. Herzog struggles for his identity against a society which blurs identities, and he enjoys (to a great extent) being trapped in the romantic's plight of weakness and isolation. He has been separated from the one social group which might have protected him: the Jewish family as a group with an identity, persisting within, and in spite of, the American melting pot. Having left the family circle, he is exposed to the ravages of American society. In this instance we do not have the survival of the fittest in economic life but rather his survival in cultural life, the area in which intellectuals strive for achievement. The Jew, uprooted from his family, endures the struggle of all against all, and when overwhelmed, the family (his brother and sister) steps in and rescues him.

Like Malamud, Bellow also has a nostalgia for another identity; let us say, for that primary matrix, the family, where one is welcomed because of blood ties, without having to take part in an erotic and pseudo-intellectual war in which the talented and vulgar survive. The hero does revel in his suffering (like all romantic heroes), but his redemption lies in the past or in a far distant future. Yesterday, the world of his forefathers, is a safe haven for him. In "modern" society his identity is uprooted and he must constantly prove himself anew. Only in the world of his past does his identity exist as an unshakable wholeness, accepted by the family as it is.

In *Portnoy's Complaint*, Roth presents the problem of a Jew whose identity is not defined with the "assistance" of outside pressure. Roth's protagonist, like those of German-Jewish writers, gets no pleasure from his Jewish identity. The mother in *Portnoy's Complaint,* who represents the family and the tribe, stifles the young hero and his father in the embrace of her love. She demands complete identification with her values. One might say that she binds herself to her son more than he is bound to her. He is expected to remain an infant all his life and also a substitute for his impotent father. Alex Portnoy is called upon to open the gates to the non-Jewish world which were closed to his father, and yet to remain loyal to his mother and family.

Lying on his psychoanalyst's couch, Portnoy is well aware of his predicament but his awareness does not alter the experience. He enjoys the situation: he flees from his mother to strange women; however, he never takes the decisive step and marries one. He enjoys the ambivalent situation of dual identity, hatred for the mother's tribal Jewish identity on the one hand, and on the other hand, revulsion for gentile women and their families. That ambivalence is also, of course, a source of suffering, but the hero enjoys using the rhetoric of a patient and describes his parents' world and that of his women with pleasure. The story tickles Portnoy. He fills it with jokes and puns and is amused by his memories. As he tells about his experiences, he relives every moment with warmth, as it were (whether it is his father's constipation or his own lovemaking with the "monkey"); and the *story* implies that its setting, the analyst's couch, gives great pleasure to the teller.

The tale finishes without offering a solution. The conclusion of the story is its beginning, and the end is left entirely open; in response to the protagonist's monologue, the analyst proposes that they begin! Thus the author signals that this is merely the start of a process, not its termination. The rhetorical process of the "complaint" will go on and on, and just as the hero has enjoyed his own cleverness up to now, so the enjoyment will endure; just as he enjoyed reviling his controlling mother and his weak father, so he will also continue to make ironic fun of the WASPs, whose every "good morning" is a reference to absolute goodness. He finds his family's weakness repulsive, but he also is revolted by the qualities of his gentile "hosts," who stand for the good, the marvelous, and the enlightened everywhere and at all times.

Portnoy's Complaint speaks on behalf of abnormality and sings its praises. Rather than "Lucky me, I'm an orphan" (as Sholom Aleichem wrote), he says, "Lucky me, I'm neurotic, lucky me, I suffer from a dual identity." When he encounters a Jewish woman with a single identity in Israel, he becomes impotent.

One could almost say that Malamud and Bellow's characters take pleasure in their peculiar identity as self-persecutors, and Roth's Portnoy enjoys the neurosis of a character who wants to have his (Jewish) cake and eat it too, resorting to professional help because he prefers the situation of a man with a complaint being analyzed to any other situation.

However, the German-Jewish authors I have discussed took their identity as thrust upon them, a cruel fate against which they all sought to rebel. Nonetheless, they viewed those who rejected it with contempt, as miserable anti-heroes, hopeless and pitiful. American-Jewish writers place less emphasis on pressure from the outside and emphasize the positive-negative bond between the characters and their identity. They choose it even though all gates seem to be open before them in their pluralistic country: Frank Alpine converts; Moses Herzog flees to the bosom of his family in his hour of need; Alex Portnoy does not marry a gentile woman, and he enjoys his ambivalent monologue on the psychoanalyst's couch. It is possible to offer universal (psychological and philosophical) interpretations for the pleasure taken in ambivalent situations or in pain and suffering. *American-Jewish literature of the 1960's formulated those explanations in openly tribal and ethnic terms, whereas in the German-Jewish literature the tribal and ethnic terms were implicit.*

European-Jewish culture was almost completely destroyed during the Holocaust. The society which produced German-Jewish authors has been wiped off the face of the earth; either the authors were murdered or they died without leaving a usable legacy. In post-war Europe no "European"-Jewish literature as extensive or on such a high level has yet developed. If European-Jewish literature in general and German-Jewish writing in particular have any heirs, they are on the other side of the Atlantic. The culture with its dual identity has passed from one place of exile to another and been modified. The identity of its Jewish readership has changed, as have the authors. Yet the problem of Jewish identity plagues Jewish writers, their characters, and their readers as much as ever.

NOTES

1. For a definition of Jews and Judaism in literature, see Hans Mayer's *Aussenseiter* (Frankfurt am Main, 1977), especially *"Genosse Shylock"* (Comrade Shylock) about Leon Trotsky, and the essay on the literary portrayal of Jews in the bourgeois civil novel, *"Jüdische Kunstfiguren im bürgerlichen Roman."*

2. See the article on the (Jewish) Press in the *Encyclopaedia Judaica,* pp. 1023–1056.

3. Dov Sadan, "Introductory Essay" (Hebrew), *Avney Bedek,* especially pp. 16–25.

4. *Juden in der deutschen Literatur,* ed. Gustav Krojanker. Arnold Zweig's *Bilanz der deutschen Judenheit* is particularly useful, especially pp. 238–263.

5. Harry Zohn, *Wiener Juden in der deutschen Literatur.*

6. See Hans Tramer's discussion of identity in the poetry of Karl Wolfskehl and several other poets in *"Über deutsch-jüdisches Dichtertum, zur Morphologie des judischen Bekenntnisses,"* pp. 88–103.

7. See the essays by Philip Roth, "Some New Jewish Stereotypes," "Writing about Jews," and "Imagining Jews," in *Reading Myself and Others.*

8. Ludwig Lewisohn, *What Is This Jewish Heritage?,* pp. 81–83.

9. Max F. Schulz, *Radical Sophistication, Studies in Contemporary Jewish/American Novelists,* p. 26.

10. Leslie A. Fiedler, *To the Gentiles,* p. 99.

11. Cynthia Ozick, "Towards a New Yiddish," *Art & Ardor,* pp. 154–177.

12. Ibid., p. 152.

13. Ibid., pp. 168–169.

14. Ibid., pp. 177–181.

15. Micha Joseph Berdyczewski, "The Stranger" (Hebrew), *Collected Stories,* p. 67.

16. The term "self-hatred," coined by Theodor Lessing in *Der jüdische Selbsthass,* is appropriate here. Hans Mayer, op. cit., p. 420, accounts for the connection between self-hatred and Jewish identity: "Jewish integration in Europe proceeded in such a way that the Jewish language and history was sacrificed, as Moses Mendelssohn had taught: that here would be no Jewish territory, consequently no Jewish nation. Everything should be "taken over" from the host nation: language, culture, territory. That miscarried."

17. See Hans Kohn, *Karl Kraus, Arthur Schnitzler, Otto Weininger; Aus dem jüdischen Wien der Jahrhundertwende,* esp. pp. 34–37. A Hebrew author, David Fogel, wrote a novel, *Married Life,* based on Weininger's doctrine.

18. Max Brod, *Reubeni, Fürst der Juden; Ein Renaissanceroman.*

19. Brod's Reubeni is similar to Haim Hazaz's depiction of Juspa in *The End of Days* (translated by Dalya Bilu). See Gershon Shaked, *"The End of Days* and the Expressionist Play," ibid., pp. 131–158.

20. David Bronsen, *Joseph Roth, eine Biographie.*

21. Joseph Roth, *Die Büste des Kaisers,* in *Werke,* vol. 3, p. 192.

22. Joseph Roth, *Juden auf Wanderschaft,* in *Werke,* vol. 3, p. 304.

23. Joseph Roth, *Briefe 1911–1939,* pp. 419–422. I refer to the letter dated August 8, 1935, in which deranged remarks are made about Zionism, such as: *"Ein Zionist ist ein Nationalsozialist, ein Nazi ist ein Zionist"* (A Zionist is a National Socialist, a Nazi is a Zionist), p. 420. He goes on to say:

Therefore I cannot fathom how it is that you wish to start the fight against Hitler, who is merely an imbecilic brother of the Zionist, using a brother of the National Socialist, i.e., a Zionist, even the most ingenious of them. Perhaps you can protect Jewry in that way. But I wish to protect both Europe and mankind from Nazis *and also* from Hitler-Zionists. I don't wish to protect the Jews, except as the most endangered vanguard of all mankind. (p. 421)

In these remarks, addressed to another assimilated Jew, Stefan Zweig, pathological universalism reaches its apogee.

24. Joseph Roth, *Die Flucht ohne Ende,* in *Werke,* vol. 1, p. 421.

25. See Gershon Shaked, "The Kafka Syndrome," esp. pp. 64–67.

26. Franz Kafka, *Briefe 1902–1924.* Letter to Max Brod, June 1921, p. 337.

27. Jakob Wassermann, *Lebensdienst,* p. 277.

28. Ibid., p. 276.

29. I have examined Wassermann's handwritten notes taken from Heinrich Graetz's *History of the Jews* and other sources he used in preparation for his novel. The manuscripts are in the National Archive for German Literature in Marbach am Neckar, and I am grateful to have been given permission to examine that material.

30. Jakob Wassermann, *Der Fall Maurizius,* pp. 247–248.

31. Bronsen, pp. 598–608.

32. See above, n. 27.

33. Two of his letters are highly instructive about Wassermann's ambivalent attitude towards his dual identity. One is to the Jewish community of Gratz dated May 15, 1933, in which he informs them that he cannot pay the amount demanded of him for membership in the community, because his books are no longer sold in Germany (on the one hand he is bound to the community, but on the other hand he slips away from it). The second letter, a rather pathetic one, is dated August 1, 1933, addressed to the Association of German Writers in which he retracts his letter of resignation from that organization. He claims that he left the organization because he had seen an announcement in the press stating that any non-Aryan author would be expelled, and because he did not wish to be expelled, he submitted his resignation first. In the meanwhile, he says, he has learned from his German friends that the announcement in the newspaper was erroneous, and only new non-Aryan members would be rejected. Therefore, he withdraws his resignation and encloses his membership dues: "*Indessen haben mich deutsche Freunde belehrt, das jene Notiz auf einer falschen Voraussetzung beruht und nur Neuaufnahmen nach jenem Prinzip nicht mehr stattfinden. Ich ersuche also die Austrittserklärung als ungeschehen zu betrachten und mir mitzuteilen, an welche Stelle ich den rückständigen Mitgliedsbeitrag von 35 Mark einzuzahlen habe.*" That letter is in the possession of the Schiller German National Archives in Marbach am Neckar. The quotation taken from that letter shows the humiliating self-abnegation to which Wassermann brought himself in order to belong to the institutions of the German people.

34. The précis is given in a letter dated August 25, 1933, to Klement, apparently the intended American publisher of the proposed book. That letter is also in the archive at Marbach.

35. Daniel Walden, ed., *On Being Jewish; American Jewish Writers from Cahan to Bellow.*

36. Henry Roth, *Call It Sleep,* rpt. 1967.

37. I refer to the novels and stories about Jewish migration to American in Hebrew by writers such as Reuven Wallenrod, *For the Day Is Ended; With No Generation*; Sh. Halkin, *Yekhiel the Hagarite; Till Breakdown*; Sh. L. Blank, *Mister Kunis*; *On American Soil,* and the Yiddish novels of Joseph Opatoshu, *Lost People*; and *The Dancer.*

38. Bruce Jay Friedman, *Stern*, p. 54.

39. It appears to me that the interpretations offered by Schulz about Friedman's novel and Edward Lewis Wallant's *The Pawnbroker* are no less symptomatic than the works themselves. Schulz almost ignores the problem raised and even disregards the fact that the writer, Friedman, intended to parody Jewish fears. See Schulz, op. cit., pp. 186–194.

40. Roth himself presents a series of letters to the editor protesting the "anti-Semitic" character of his works (the writers refer to stories such as "Defender of the Faith"). Philip Roth, *Reading Myself and Others*, p. 159.

41. Cynthia Ozick, "Envy; or, Yiddish in America," *The Pagan Rabbi*, pp. 41–100.

42. I believe that the struggle for identity and doubts about it are part of that desperate striving for historical continuity which is typical of contemporary secular Jewish culture. Here is Robert Alter's formulation: "I would suggest that Jewish life since the entrance of the Jews into modern culture may be usefully viewed as a precarious, though stubborn, experiment in the possibilities of historical continuity, when most of the grounds for continuity have been cut away." Robert Alter, "Preface," *After the Tradition; Essays on Modern Jewish Writing*, pp. 10–11.

43. Bernard Malamud, *The Fixer*, p. 187.

44. See, for example, John H. Clayton, "The Victim," pp. 31–51 in *Saul Bellow*, ed. Rovit. See pp. 34–37 in particular.

45. Philip Roth, "Writing about Jews," in *Reading Myself and Others*, p. 165.

46. Robert Alter links the figure of Bober to the *shlemiel* (as does Ruth Wisse in her book *The Schlemiel as Modern Hero*). In Alter's opinion, the main image in *The Assistant* is that of the prison which "is Malamud's way of suggesting that to be fully a man is to accept the most painful limitations. . . . " R. Alter, "Bernard Malamud: Jewishness as Metaphor," op. cit., p. 122.

BIBLIOGRAPHY

Alter, Robert. *After the Tradition; Essays on Modern Jewish Writing*. New York: E. P. Dutton, 1969.

Bellow, Saul. *Herzog*. Greenwich, Conn.: Fawcett Crest, 1965.

———. *The Victim*. New York: New American Library, 1965.

Berdyczewski, Micha Joseph. *Collected Stories*. Tel Aviv: Am Oved, 1951. [Hebrew]

Blank, Shmuel Leyb. *Mister Kunis*. Tel Aviv: Stiebel, 1934. [Hebrew]

———. *On American Soil*. Tel Aviv: A. Zioni, 1958. [Hebrew]

Bradbury, Malcolm, ed. *Saul Bellow*. London and New York: Methuen, 1982.

Brod, Max. *Reubeni, Fürst der Juden*. München: Kurt Wolff, 1925.

Bronsen, David. *Joseph Roth, eine Biographie*. München: D.T.V., 1981.

Fiedler, Leslie A. *The Last Jew in America*. New York: Stein & Day, 1972.

———. *To the Gentiles*. New York: Stein & Day, 1972.

Friedman, Bruce Jay. *Stern*. New York: New American Library, 1967.

Halkin, Simeon. *Till Breakdown*. Tel Aviv: Am Oved, 1945. [Hebrew]

———. *Yekhiel the Hagarite*. Berlin: Stiebel, 1929. [Hebrew]

Hazaz, Haim. *The End of Days*, trans. by Dalya Bilu. Tel Aviv: Institute for the Translation of Hebrew Literature, 1982.

Kafka, Franz. *Briefe 1902–1924*. Frankfurt am Main: Fischer, 1975.

————. *Die Romane Amerika, Der Prozess, Das Schloss*. Frankfurt am Main: Fischer, 1966.

Kohn, Hans. *Karl Kraus, Arthur Schnitzler, Otto Weininger*. Tübingen: J.C.B. Mohr, 1962.

Krojanker, Gustav, ed. *Juden in der deutschen Literatur*. Berlin: Welt Verlag, 1922.

Lessing, Theodore. *Der jüdische Selbsthass*. Berlin: Jüdischer Verlag, 1930.

Lewisohn, Ludwig. *The Island Within*. 1928; rpt. Philadelphia: Jewish Publication Society, 1968.

————. *What Is This Jewish Heritage?* New York: B'nai Brith Hillel Foundation, 1954.

Malamud, Bernard. *The Assistant*. Harmondsworth, England: Penguin, 1967.

————. *Idiots First*. 1963; rpt. New York: Dell, 1967.

————. *The Fixer*. 1966; rpt. New York: Dell, 1968.

Mayer, Hans. *Aussenseiter*. Frankfurt am Main: Suhrkamp, 1977.

Opatoshu, Joseph. *The Dancer; Around Grand Street. Collected Works*, vol. 11. Vilna: Kletzkin, 1930. [Yiddish]

————. *Lost People*. Berlin: Yiddisher Literarisher Verlag, 1922. [Yiddish]

Ozick, Cynthia. *Art & Ardor*. New York: Alfred A. Knopf, 1983.

————. *The Pagan Rabbi*. 1971; rpt. London: Secker & Warburg, 1972.

Potok, Chaim. *The Chosen*. 1967; rpt. Hartford: Fawcett Crest, 1968.

Roth, Henry. *Call It Sleep*. 1934; rpt. London: Mayflower-Dell, 1967.

Roth, Joseph. *Briefe 1911–1939*. Köln-Berlin: Kiepenheuer & Witsch, 1970.

————. *Werke*, ed. Hermann Kesten. 4 vols. Köln-Berlin: Kiepenheuer & Witsch, 1975–1976.

Roth, Philip. *Goodbye, Columbus and Five Short Stories*. 1960; rpt. New York: Bantam, 1963.

————. *Portnoy's Complaint*. 1969; rpt. London: Corgibook, 1971.

————. *Reading Myself and Others*. New York: Farrar, Straus and Giroux, 1976.

Rovit, Earl, ed. *Saul Bellow; A Collection of Critical Essays*. Englewood Cliffs, New Jersey: Prentice-Hall, 1975.

Sadan, Dov. *Avney Bedek*. Tel Aviv: Hakibbutz Hameuhad Publishing House, 1962. [Hebrew]

Schulz, Max F. *Radical Sophistication, Studies in Contemporary Jewish/American Novelists*. Athens: Ohio University Press, 1969.

Shaked, Gershon. "The Kafka Syndrome." *Jerusalem Quarterly*. 33. (Fall, 1984), pp. 64–78.

Tramer, Hans. "*Uber deutsch-judisches Dichtertum, Zur Morphologie des judischen Bekentnisses*." *Bulletin des Leo Baeck Institut*. 2. (1957), pp. 88–103.

Walden, Daniel, ed. *On Being Jewish; American Jewish Writers from Cahan to Bellow*. Greenwich, Connecticut: Fawcett, 1974.

Wallenrod, Reuven. *For the Day Is Ended*. Tel Aviv: Newman, 1964. [Hebrew]

Wassermann, Jakob. *Der Fall Maurizius*. 1928; rpt. Frankfurt am Main: Fischer, 1964.

————. *Lebensdienst*. Leipzig: Grethlein, 1928.

————. *My Life as German and Jew*. London: G. Allen & Unwin, 1934.

————. *Mein Weg als Deutscher und Jude*. Berlin: Fischer, 1921.

Wisse, Ruth. *The Schlemiel as Modern Hero*. Chicago: University of Chicago Press, 1971.

Zohn, Harry. *Wiener Juden in der deutschen Literatur*. Tel Aviv: Edition Olamenu, 1964.

Zweig, Arnold. *Bilanz der deutschen Judenheit*. 1933; rpt. Köln: Joseph Melzer Verlag, 1961.

15

Fiction of the Holocaust

Dorothy Seidman Bilik

In 1948, four years after the revelation of Auschwitz, Isaac Rosenfeld wrote:

We still don't understand what happened to the Jews of Europe, and perhaps we never will. There have been books, magazine and newspaper articles, eyewitness accounts, letters, diaries, documents certified by the highest authorities on the life in ghettos and concentration camps, slave factories and extermination centers under the Germans. By now we know all there is to know. But it hasn't helped; we still don't understand. . . . there is no response great enough to equal the facts that provoke it.[1]

Today, forty years after, there are mountains of books, masses of information and visual evidence, the results of decades of research that confront us, sometimes daily, in newspapers and journals and on the big and little screens. We are now epistemologically more cautious than Rosenfeld was in 1948. We know that we are not destined to "know all there is to know" about the Holocaust, nor is all knowable.

Rosenfeld, one of the first American-Jewish writers to articulate the themes that were to become pervasive in the literature of the Holocaust, continues with self-reproach: "There is nothing but numbness, and in the respect of numbness we, the innocent and the indignant . . . are no different from the murderers who went ahead and did their business and paid no attention to the screams."[2] Rosenfeld indicts the world for its indifference to the victims' screams *during* the Holocaust and calls "the prophets and inheritors of the present world" to witness, for "It is impossible to live, to think, to create without bearing witness against the terror. But once we do so—behold our great theme and occupation, our role, our language, our tone, and our audience—for what else is worth hearing today?"[3]

The American-Jewish literature that flourished in the fifties did not, however, include Rosenfeld's "great theme." Rosenfeld expressed in eloquent essays what

American novelists, dramatists, and poets were as yet reluctant to represent. Numbness, horror, shock, shame, guilt, and outrage do not comport with the creation of fictional worlds and the renderings of personal relations and emotions. The resources of the imagination have been irrevocably altered by the unbelievable *actualities* of Auschwitz. We, of the post-Holocaust world, *know* of terrors never imagined by previous generations.

And in the light of such knowledge critics such as T. W. Adorno, A. Alvarez, Alfred Kazin, and George Steiner questioned in the sixties whether the power of the imagination could or even should transform this particular darkness into "art." In the face of radical evil of such magnitude, it was argued, imaginative literature is irrelevant. Silence, it was argued eloquently, was the appropriate response.

The contrast of the silence of the bystanders and the screams of the victims that Rosenfeld adumbrated in the late forties manifests itself less graphically in the tension between language and silence that has marked much commentary about the Holocaust. It is not uncommon to find strained paradoxes and metaphors of voicelessness in the literary criticism: sheer opaqueness (1966); numbed exaltation (1981); muted tactfulness; numb agitation; mute refusal (1986). The tropes illustrate the deeply felt disproportion and inadequacy of language and literature to what are conventionally referred to as the unspeakable, unutterable events of "the Holocaust."

Despite the patina of inapplicable Greco-Roman and biblical associations with religious sacrifice, the word "Holocaust" in its present sense is a neologism first used by the French to describe the devastation after the First World War and recycled to designate the horrendous desolation of the Second. That the word "Holocaust" has been compromised by egregious analogizing and diluted by too many meanings does not negate its usefulness as general signifier. Ironically, the original Nazi euphemism *Endlösung der Judenfrage*, "the final solution to the Jewish question," is more concrete as is Lucy Dawidowicz's telling title *The War Against the Jews*, since both these phrases make clear that the primary victims of Hitler's vast technology of extermination were the Jews of Europe.

Through centuries of persecution, Jewish communities have commemorated their martyrs, preserved communal memory and beseeched God in a lamentation literature of response to collective catastrophe. From biblical times to now, elegiac poetry and exemplary narratives that chronicled a past event could be evoked and interpreted as models for present and future persecutions. By drawing upon the lamentation tradition, Hebrew and Yiddish writers in Europe and in Palestine could, in the thirties, seem to predict the totality of the coming destruction. At the same time some Hebrew and Yiddish writers acknowledged the abyss that separated the Holocaust from earlier Jewish catastrophes by inverting the tradition. The Hebrew and Yiddish poet Aaron Zeitlin parodied Jeremiah's Book of Lamentations to indicate the difference in "Yisroyel's ashn" (Israel's ashes):

If Jeremiah were to sit
On Israel's ashes
He would not cry out
His book of Lamentations
Nor would he wash the ruins
With any tears
For his tears could not be released
By the Almighty Himself.
Together with the burned millions
He would maintain
The deepest silence.
For
Even an outcry
Is now a lie
Even tears are
Mere literature
Even prayers are false. (1945)[4]

Nobel Peace laureate Elie Wiesel is the modern exemplar of the lamentation tradition. He is the scribe of and quintessential witness to the Holocaust. He is challenged not only to retell the untellable to an indifferent and disbelieving world but also to interpret the disjuncture of the Holocaust in the context of Jewish history. Because he is deeply rooted in Eastern-European Jewish religious culture he can from within that tradition probe the theological void of the idea of the death of God. Wiesel, it should be remembered, is also a French writer in the manner of Sartre and Camus, and a journalist. Given the magnitude of Wiesel's tasks and the extraordinary range of his writings, it is not surprising that the melding of Hebraic, French, and journalistic modes sometimes strains the resources of fiction. Wiesel's body of work is of unparalleled significance.

The questions of theodicy so often raised by Wiesel are also eloquently presented by the Vilna-born Yiddish writer Chaim Grade in "My Quarrel with Hersh Rasseyner" (1951). Firmly placed within the talmudic tradition, the dialogue relentlessly probes the philosophical and theological arguments that separate secular from orthodox Jews in the post-Auschwitz universe. Both the teller, a secularist Yiddish writer, and his orthodox opponent were trained in the Mussarist *yeshive* with its rigorous commitment to an ascetic, ethical way of life. To oversimplify, the "quarrel" between Hersh and Chaim is a *midrash* (revelatory commentary) on the paradox: "How can one believe in God after the Holocaust?" "How can one not?" The opposed polarities of this complex and impassioned debate are faith in humanity and the world and faith in God and the Law. Hersh's intense piety and his scrupulous adherence to Jewish ritual sustained him through the horrors of the death-camp and left him more devout than ever:

I know that the reckoning is not yet over. . . . And I have never thought for one moment that anyone in the world besides the jealous and vengeful God would avenge the helpless little ones that the Gestapo stuffed into the trains for Treblinka. . . . That is why I don't have the slightest shadow of a doubt that the great and terrible day, behold it comes! . . . I know that there is another set of books kept in fire and blood. There's no use asking me whether I want it that way or not; that's the way it has to be! And that's what sustains me as I try to go in tranquility about the work of the Creator.[5]

Hersh's speech is one of the most forceful arguments for theodicy in all of Holocaust literature. In place of Hersh's total certainty, Chaim offers doubts and open questions. Yet Grade has structured the story toward the secularist point of view and not just by giving Chaim the last word. For Hersh, though fervent and admirable, has been adjudged as narrowly exclusionist by reserving redemption for pious Jews like himself and excluding other Jews judged unworthy along with the "righteous gentiles." These exemplify Chaim's humanistic faith. Hersh's selectivity is a bitterly ironic counterpoint to the Nazi *selektsia* which included *all* Jews. The dialogue, is, of course, one of self and soul, for Hersh is a part of Chaim.

I include Grade under our American-Jewish rubric because although "My Quarrel with Hersh Rasseyner" (like the works of Wiesel and Isaac Bashevis Singer) was not originally written in English, Grade's story is widely available in English.

Out of humiliation, pain, rage, and at considerable emotional cost, death camp survivors like Wiesel and Primo Levi selected and ordered even these unspeakable events and created memorable works of art.

Yiddish writers like Grade, I. B. Singer, Jacob Glatstein (Yankev Glatshteyn), and others could say with Hersh Rasseyner that it was not a third of the House of Israel that was destroyed but a third of each Jew's body and soul. For not only were their families destroyed, their audience was destroyed, and the impact of the loss on Yiddish writers is not to be measured.

Without the resources of Jewish language and a traditional literature of response to collective destruction, American-born Jewish writers with their ironic vision, their wariness of public poetry and love of ambiguity were not engaged with the Holocaust for some time. Yet the need to bear witness in some manner persisted and remains a significant preoccupation in the literature of the seventies and eighties. In the 1940's, however, the most tragic decade in Jewish experience, the Jew was universalized and mythologized as a symbol of twentieth-century man, a homeless victim in an indifferent universe.[6]

At the same time, fear of American anti-Semitism and horror at the more virulent German strain combined to foster a bland American-Jewish "problem novel" of anti-Semitism with non-Jewish protagonists, i.e., Laura Hobson's 1947 best-seller *Gentleman's Agreement* and Arthur Miller's *Focus* (1945). Miller explained his literary trompe l'oeil in 1947: "I think I gave up the Jews as literary material because I was afraid that even an innocent allusion to individual wrongdoing of an individual Jew would be inflamed by the atmosphere, ignited by the hatred I was suddenly aware of, and my love would be twisted into a weapon of persecution against the Jews."[7]

The most gifted of American novelists, Saul Bellow, may have felt similarly constrained in his first novel, *Dangling Man* (1944). While awaiting induction into the army, the apparently Jewish protagonist has "bare and ominous" dreams which reveal his awareness of the massacres in Europe and his detachment from these events. Perhaps as apologia, Bellow has Joseph muse "that our senses and our imaginations are somehow inadequate. . . . " In *The Victim* (1947), however, Bellow richly imagines the symbiotic relationship of a Jew and his paranoid anti-Semitic *Doppelgänger* who blames all his troubles on the Jew. The irony of the title is patent: the anti-Semite feels that he has been the victim of a Jewish plot, while the Jewish protagonist feels quite rightly that he is being tormented yet cannot refrain from feeling the guilt of the scapegoat.

Bellow's friend Isaac Rosenfeld died in 1956 at thirty-eight. As his essays show, he was haunted by the Jewish tragedy. He left behind a number of allusive Kafka-like tales that are aptly characterized by Sidra DeKoven Ezrahi as "allegories of terror" and "parables of the closed society."[8] The beginnings of an incipient post-Holocaust consciousness can thus be sensed if not delineated in Bellow, Rosenfeld, and in some early short stories of Bernard Malamud.

In *The Magic Barrel* (1958), survivors of the Holocaust began appearing as fictional characters. In "The Lady of the Lake," one of Malamud's false questers attempts to free himself of his Jewish past by changing his name from Levin to Freeman. In Italy, Levin falls in love with a beautiful Italian girl who represents to him all of Western-European civilization. Levin-Freeman lies about his Jewishness and receives his ironic comeuppance since Isabella, a survivor of Buchenwald, rejects him as he rejected his history. She retains her blue tattoo since she treasures what she suffered for. Like Levin, Fidelman, the protagonist of "The Last Mohican," runs away from his Jewish past to Italy where he encounters the title character who has survived the death camps and is a "refugee" from Israel. The survivor, Susskind, leads the unwilling Fidelman through a thousand years of Jewish history that culminates in the ancient Roman Jewish cemetery with its memorial to Auschwitz.

Philip Roth's "Eli, the Fanatic" (1958), like Malamud's short stories, also includes a Holocaust survivor who acts as moral teacher to an initially flawed quester. Eli is a young lawyer designated by the parvenu Jewish inhabitants of a formerly exclusively gentile suburb to get rid of a newly established *Hasidic yeshive*. That the men and boys are Holocaust survivors is irrelevant to the embarrassed Jews of the community who are dismayed to be identified with such oddly dressed "fanatics." Eli and the head of the *yeshive* engage in quasi-talmudic dialogues with the teacher upholding the *Law* while Eli argues about zoning laws. The story ends in a moral conversion of sorts when Eli exchanges his Brooks Brothers outfit for the musty black garb of the *Hasid*. That Eli is unstable (he has had a history of breakdowns) does not invalidate Roth's espousal of orthodox values at the decided expense of the boorish modern Jews.

Malamud's and Roth's stories are important as indicators of renewed interest in the particulars of Jewish life as part of a generally favorable literary climate for ethnic specificity. The survivors portrayed in these stories and elsewhere are often modern equivalents of the *tsadik* (pious, saintly man) of traditional Hebrew and Yiddish literature, who acts as teacher and moral example. The reissue of two classics of earlier immigrant fiction, Abraham Cahan's *The Rise of David Levinsky* (1917; reissued 1960) and Henry Roth's *Call It Sleep* (1934; reissued 1964) also attests to the increasing attention to the Jewish past that is the mark of a growing post-Holocaust consciousness.

One cannot fault Susan Sontag's statement that "the supreme tragic event of modern times is the murder of the six million Jews." One may not necessarily agree with her corollary that "the most interesting and moving work of art of the past ten years is the trial of Adolph Eichmann in Jerusalem in 1961."[9] Nevertheless, the trial with its harrowing testimonies proved a decisive turning point in the consciousness of many American-Jewish and Israeli writers who were moved to bear witness to the Jewish catastrophe.

In place of the invaluable immediate experience of the personal witness, the writer who is not a survivor must use knowledge, imagination, and the strategies of distance and memory. The results may be trivial, simplistic, or meretricious. However, the Holocaust cannot be declared off-limits to the critical intelligence or the imagination. Further, the value and effectiveness of imaginative literature are not the by-products of a writer's geographical origins or biographical credentials. That the Holocaust is in the public domain challenges a writer's mind and imagination all the more. For belletristic renderings of Holocaust themes must be judged against rigorous standards of truth and probability.

Norma Rosen in a 1974 essay describes the proper stance for the American-Jewish novelist as that of a "witness through the imagination," a "documenter of those who have (merely) heard the terrible news."[10] Practicing the distance and displacement she advocates, Rosen centers her novel, *Touching Evil* (1969), on the reactions of American non-Jews to the televised proceedings of the Eichmann trial. The central character then describes her responses and those of other characters to her absent lover in letters. Jean Lamb's struggle to extract "private symbols of horror from the welter of horror symbols," though admirable, serves to expose once again the immense disproportion between the terrible events recounted on the screen and everyday events in America.

The literary tact that motivated Norma Rosen to avoid Jewish characters except as apprehended by non-Jewish viewers is markedly different from the deliberate confusion of Jerzy Kosinski's *The Painted Bird* (1965), where neither the reader nor the Polish peasants nor the child-protagonist is certain whether the boy is a Jew or a Gypsy.

Kosinski's appalling and compelling work is one of the rare "testimonial" novels by European-born American citizens who, like Wiesel, miraculously survived the horrors of the war against the Jews. Other semi-autobiographical novels include Zdena Berger's *Tell Me Another Morning* (1961), Elzbieta Ettinger's *Kindergarten* (1970), Ilona Karmel's *An Estate of Memory* (1969), and the translated fiction of writer and filmmaker Arnost Lustig. These works differ from those of most mainstream American-Jewish Holocaust fiction writers in their European settings and in the actual or metaphoric concentrationary universe that is the core of what is portrayed.

Kosinski's Polish landscape, surrounded by the death camps and traversed by the death trains, constitutes a metaphoric Auschwitz wherein the unimaginable horrors of the gas chambers and crematoria are symbolized by the rendering of "situations equally gruesome, reported with remorseless exactitude." What is most appalling is that the relentless reporter of atrocity upon atrocity is a young child. The horrified reader is drawn into the moral chaos as the child tries without success to make sense of the horrific events he silently observes. *The Painted Bird* contains little dialogue, and few direct quotations. Says Kosinski, in his introduction to the German edition of *The Painted Bird*, "in the attempt to recall the primitive, the symbols are sought more pertinently and immediately than through the superficial process of speech and dialogue."[11]

Deprived of communication, the alien child is likewise deprived of participation and community and in his alienation is contaminated by the pervasive bestiality and evil of the menaced and menacing peasant culture. The boy's many fruitless attempts to gain some mastery over his nightmare world leads to frenetic travesties of Catholic religious rituals and culminates in his being flung in a pit of manure by the enraged congregation of superstitious peasants. From this, one of many descents into the pit that punctuate the novel, the boy emerges with "slime-obscured eyes"—mute.

The reader participates in the atrocities and collaborates when the boy's desire for revenge causes the death of many innocent people. The effect of the novel may be compared to one of its many bestial scenes where the protagonist is forced to strip the skin of a supposedly dead rabbit. Kosinski's prose flays the skin of language and lays bare the hidden terror of European culture of the mid-twentieth century. Because of the child-narrator, the novel resembles a perverted fairy tale or contaminated fable where witches' magic doesn't work, beasts are tortured to death, and hopes of rescue are continually destroyed by cruelly arbitrary and indifferent powers. That the boy regains his voice arbitrarily is symptomatic of the disjuncture between cause and effect that has marked the entire novel. For "it mattered little if one was mute; people did not understand one another." Although Kosinski has only written one novel that directly confronts the Holocaust universe, much of his considerable later fiction is informed by his experience.

Unlike Norma Rosen, who achieves distance by using non-Jewish television viewers, and Kosinski, who annihilates distance between reader and horror, Malamud bases his survivor novel, *The Fixer* (1966), on past history. Malamud says that the story of Mendl Beilis, the history upon which the novel was based, was paradigmatic for him: "Somewhere along the line, what had happened in Nazi Germany began to be important to me . . . and that too is part of Yakov's story.''[12] To include the Jewish catastrophe, Malamud confronts it indirectly: in microcosm, in the past. Malamud avails himself of the reader's knowledge of the contemporary Jewish tragedy to illuminate both past and recent Jewish history. Yakov comes to realize that "being born a Jew meant being vulnerable to history including its worst errors." The future of Jews in Europe is succinctly expressed by the fixer's lawyer: "Rich or poor, those of our brethren who can run out of here are running. Some who can't are already mourning. They sniff at the air and it stinks of pogrom.''[13]

The fixer, Yakov Bok, a typical Malamud *schlemiel* protagonist, leaves the *shtetl*, doffs his Jewish identity and rises economically for a short time to find himself unjustly accused of ritual murder. His imprisonment and its accompanying torture, cruelty, and humiliation are the concrete manifestations of a virulent and irrational anti-Semitism. In a perception unique in the Malamud canon, Yakov endorses revolution and political action: "One thing I've learned," he thought, "there's no such thing as an unpolitical man, especially a Jew. You can't be one without the other, that's clear enough. You can't sit still and see yourself destroyed.''[14]

The ending of *The Fixer*, Malamud's most consciously political book, is ambiguous. If the reader wishes to take comfort from the historic fact that the historic Mendl Beilis was finally released from prison, the comfort lies well outside the bounds of the novel.

Malamud said of his widely publicized statement "all men are Jews," that it was "an understandable statement and a metaphoric way of indicating how history, sooner or later, treats all men.''[15] Such abstract universalizing does not negate the concrete unassimilated, linguistic, ethical, and historical Jewish particulars of Malamud's fiction. Malamud's Jewish personae have been faulted for being spectral.[16] But in their very insubstantiality, Malamud's immigrants, refugees, and survivors are examples of post-Holocaust consciousness and commemorations of a vanished culture.

More direct expressions of post-Holocaust consciousness are embodied in the immigrant-survivor protagonists of Edward Lewis Wallant's *The Pawnbroker* (1961); Saul Bellow's *Mr. Sammler's Planet* (1970); Isaac Bashevis Singer's *Enemies* (1972); Susan Fromberg Schaeffer's *Anya* (1974); Cynthia Ozick's "The Shawl" (1980) and "Rosa" (1983). The title character of Arthur Cohen's *In the Days of Simon Stern* (1973) is a first-generation American but the teller of the tale and most of the personae are immigrant-survivors.

Immigrant-survivors address the problem of how one lives in contemporary America after experiencing near death and qualified rebirth—experiences that separate them from other Americans. Yet the relative openness and anonymity of American society allow not only for the survival of these human remnants but also for the survival of parts of the traditional culture, history, and religion they embody.

With distance and time the immigrant-survivor explores some of the moral and intellectual dimensions of his suffering. Through memory and reflection the victim who was deprived of his power of action by oppressors is frequently able to achieve self-perception by exploring an individual past and the collective Jewish past. The pain and anguish of the quest and the historic magnitude of the context endow the survivor with the modern equivalent of tragic stature. For the most part the tragedy lies outside the individual's power and responsibility in the enormity of the catastrophe. Within this context the protagonists may perform heroic actions or they may not. Bellow's Artur Sammler was a hero partisan; Singer's Herman Broder was hidden in a cellar throughout the war. But far more important in post-Holocaust literature is the action that takes place in the characters' minds. Those who have undergone death and experienced unimaginable but historic hell are expected to emerge with uncommon insight and wisdom. Not all fictional survivors meet the challenge. Those who do undertake the painful quest for comprehension, however incomplete, mitigate the pathos of their undeserved misfortune with heroic efforts of mind.

The fictional presentation of memory is of major importance in works with survivor protagonists. Wallant, Singer, Schaeffer, and Bellow attempt to integrate unprecedented past experiences into the ongoing present of their central characters. The survivor-protagonist contains the bloody past that obsesses him, and he is, in turn, surrounded by other survivors who are also obsessed to varying degrees. Some continually ruminate upon the past; some attempt unsuccessfully to suppress memory.

Wallant's pawnbroker rigidly attempts to keep his past repressed and unremembered. Like some real-life survivors, Sol Nazerman hates his survival. But his brutal past experiences must be reckoned with, for, as the "anniversary" of the annihilation of his family approaches, Sol's horrendous dreams create in vivid and unbearable detail his death-camp experiences. Wallant presents these searing memories in chronological order, moving from the bestiality of the cattle cars to the grisly pile of corpses. The dreams are naturalistic, recounted by an omniscient narrator who presents them like a sequence of film. Such "objective" reportage gives an impression of completeness, verisimilitude, and order that is undreamlike and unlike survivor dreams in the literature of atrocity.[17] More than the presentation of horrors is called for—they need to have happened to someone. Sol does not confront his experiences nor does he reflect on them. *Thought* is missing, a disturbing lack in an erstwhile philosopher reliving his past with spatial and temporal distance.

Sol's dreams include some of the most loathsome examples of anti-Jewish atrocity, but the novel is apologetic and ambivalent toward its Jewish personae and the Jewish past. Wallant simplistically associates the pawnbroker's lack of feeling for his victimized Harlem customers with Nazi barbarism; thus, Nazerman is both "Nazerene" and "Nazi-man." In the formulaic dénouement, the stonelike pawnbroker is redeemed through the sacrifice of Jesus Ortíz, Sol's Puerto Rican assistant. Jesus dies violently for Sol, and the pawnbroker is reborn through love and compassion. But Wallant has withheld compassion from his Jewish characters, whose suffering he has exploited, and has sentimentalized his Black, Puerto Rican, and even Mafia characters.

Only two of Wallant's four novels were published in his brief lifetime. *The Pawnbroker* is one of the earliest Holocaust novels in American-Jewish literature. Later novels reflecting greater awareness of the continuing effects of the catastrophe have more ambiguous endings. Wallant's novel with its realistic form and its absence of intellectual exploration evades the aesthetic and philosophical challenge that the use of such tragic historical material demands.

Susan Fromberg Schaeffer is a poet and a scholar, and her historical romance, *Anya* (1974), is marked by impressive research and poetic sensibility. Schaeffer uses the form of the family novel, rich with details of worldly European-Jewish life in pre-war Vilna. Anya is at once accurate recorder and the heroine of a fairy tale populated by wondrous beings of almost mythic stature. Anya's parents and servants are gifted storytellers who enjoy sharing superstitions, tales, fables, and parables. The fairy-tale world contains grotesque and sinister elements: Hitler's *Mein Kampf* is dismissed as a "fairy tale." But grim historical reality invades the kingdom. The particulars of the slaughter of the innocents in the Vilna ghetto are verified in historical accounts but the manner of death transcends verisimilitude. Thus Anya's intellectual, cultivated father, an omnivorous reader, is shot by the Nazis on his way to get a book to ease his confinement. Anya's gentle sister chooses to die with the man she loves. Anya's saintly mother—the apotheosis of survival—hides and allows herself to be selected for death in order that Anya and her baby may live. In this fictional world random murder becomes meaningful death.

Imaginary cruelties collected by the Brothers Grimm comport with the day-to-day Nazi terror and slaughter. People are hidden in walls, in ovens, in made-up beds. Treasure is buried in jars of preserves. People in the ghetto read *The Three Musketeers* and *The Scarlet Pimpernel*. Says Emanuel Ringelblum, the historian and archivist who perished in the ghetto, "being unable to take revenge on the enemy in reality, we are seeking it in fantasy, in literature."[18]

Like other American-Jewish writers, Schaeffer does not directly portray a Nazi death camp but she does include a displaced and metaphoric equivalent of the crematoria in the burning of the barracks next to Anya's. Anya fears she will be burned to death: "This is the most terrible way to die; dear God . . . let me die any other way. . . . And the flames came to a stop at our barracks."[19] In the documented but unbelievable world of the camps such "miraculous" survivals did indeed occur. But probability is suspended with the inclusion of a bizarre "fairy godmother" in the person of a Nazi soldier who is a disguised Jew. He gives Anya a "magic Thing," a cross that helps her pose as a gentile. The work contains other disguise motifs, heroic actions, hairbreadth escapes, remarkable coincidences—the literary conventions common to romance. Anya and her daughter are exceptionally beautiful. The baby is protected by a "righteous gentile" who is murdered because he sheltered her. The novel contains extraordinary people who sacrifice much and who are more courageous than possible against a background of Nazi horror that is implacable and inhumanely brutal.

The fairy-tale elements point to what life in extremis ought to have been, filtered through Anya's vivid though partly flawed imagination. Radical evil is uglier and more inexplicable in a fictional context where so many admirable characters are wantonly destroyed. For all its vividness and authenticity, the overall effect of *Anya* is elegiac. The novel begins with memorial candles commemorating the unburied dead and ends in a lament for the prematurely destroyed people and their slaughtered world. *Anya* is Schaeffer's unique contribution to American-Jewish Holocaust literature. Schaeffer's other works do not focus on the Jewish catastrophe.

Cynthia Ozick's brilliant novella, "Envy; or, Yiddish in America" (1969), was written, she says, as "a lamentation, a celebration, because six million Yiddish tongues were under the earth of Europe."[20] From her earliest Jamesian novel *Trust* (1966) to the intricately anatomical *The Cannibal Galaxy* (1983) and in many short stories as well as in her provocative essays, Ozick explores what it means to be Jewish (authentically) in the post-Holocaust world. "Stories," says Ozick, "ought to judge and interpret the world."[21] Following the rabbinic tradition of *midrash*, Ozick reinterprets existing stories that she has judged wanting. She has reshaped Roth's "Eli, the Fanatic" in her novella "Bloodshed" in which the community of Holocaust survivors practices a rigorous *Hasidism* far more demanding than Eli's quixotically donned orthodox costume. In "The Shawl" and "Rosa" Ozick wrenches some of Anya's life out of Schaeffer's romance into far more agonized terrain. Ozick boldly recreates the death-camp world with striking enomomy in the two harrowing pages of "The Shawl." Like Anya, Rosa desperately struggles to keep her baby alive during forced marches and death-camp torment by means of a "magic" shawl that sustains and conceals the child. This magic does not suffice and the baby is flung onto the electrified fence. The Christian "magic" of the cross is more powerful than the Jewish "magic" of the prayer shawl.

Even with the background of the collective Jewish tragedy, the individual tragedy of surviving one's child proves as devastating for the fictional Rosa as it has been for real-life survivors. Rosa, in today's Miami Beach, is "a madwoman and a scavenger" who denies her daughter's death by writing copiously to her in elegant Polish. Ozick, with customary rigor, does not make Rosa a sympathetic figure, for along with fantasies of her daughter's contemporary lives, Rosa cherishes her own assimilationist, snobbish, pre-Holocaust Warsaw background. Ozick mocks Rosa's pretensions to "an aristocratic sensibility" as Rosa's family mocked ghetto Jews. Nevertheless, Rosa embodies the anguish and isolation of the witness-survivor who goes mad because she cannot reach "deaf" and indifferent Americans with her horrific testimony. Rosa rejects the academic parasitism of the "bloodsuckers" who use survivor testimony as subjects for research, analogously to how the Nazis used Jews.

Ozick succinctly captures the paradoxically vital atmosphere created by elderly immigrant Jews who retire to a decaying Miami Beach to die. Ironically, it is to one such older immigrant that Rosa ultimately chooses to tell her story—one of those Yiddish-speaking ghetto Jews formerly looked down upon by her family.

Far more satirical is Ozick's deft portrayal of West Side would-be glitterati in "Levitation" (1979). Lucy Feingold, a convert, somewhat resembles the parasitical professor of "Rosa" but Lucy only nibbles at Jewish experience. Both Lucy and her husband belong to the "secondary level" literary world. Feingold's writing is saturated with Jewish history and martyrology, while Lucy is "lapidary." The shallowness of Lucy's conversion is exposed at their unsuccessful party when Lucy finds herself the only non-Jew in a "chamber of Jews." They are listening to the compelling voice of a refugee who has come to bear witness and who casts a spell on the Jews. As they listen intently, the living room ascends, leaving Lucy below as "the black floor moved higher and higher." She tries unsuccessfully to rise with the levitating Jews by means of Christian visions and pagan myths. Ozick thus decisively distinguishes between those at the party "who can still smile" and the levitating Jews who are participating in the ceremony of listening to the "terrible news" and the "miracle" of the ascension.[22]

Lucy, in contrast, can barely hear the voices:

but she knows which word it is they mainly use. How long can they go on about it? How long? A morbid cud-chewing. Death and death and death. The word is less a human word than an animal's cry; a crow's Caw caw. It belongs to storms, floods, avalanches. Acts of God. "Holocaust" someone caws dimly from above; she knows it must be Feingold. He always says this word over and over and over. . . . Lucy decides it is possible to become jaded by atrocity. She is bored by the shootings and the gas and the camps, she is not ashamed to admit this. They are as tiresome as prayer.[23]

The lack of shame is most shameful and the simile is most apt. But Lucy is not entirely condemned. As she listens to the refugee's "noble" voice, Lucy's mind, bored by many atrocity films and photographs, makes images of hillsides full of crucifixions: "otherwise it was only a movie . . . —if there had been a camera at the Crucifixion Christianity would collapse, no one would ever feel anything about it. Cruelty came out of the imagination, and had to be witnessed by the imagination."[24] Ozick has often expressed her own struggle between the Hebraic distrust of image-making and the "idolatrous" art of making stories and here Lucy is the unlikely Ozick surrogate.

The "miracle" of the ascending Jews is one of those suspect magical components that Ozick prefers to regard as "conditioned probabilities." The Jews in the levitating chamber have been chosen or have chosen to listen to the Jehovah-like voice (Lucy's allusion) of the survivor. Because the Jews have witnessed with their imaginations and renewed the Covenant, they float above and apart from the Jewish and gentile "humanists and humorists" who remain far below with Lucy. Though Lucy's imagination may be flawed, the ascension is her perception and she identifies the levitating Jews with their slaughtered brethren: "All the Jews are in the air."

In Ozick's fiction and in many of her thought-provoking essays, the place of Jewish memory, especially survivor testimony, is hallowed. Ozick's fiction and essays on the Holocaust are among the most compelling in American-Jewish literature.

Like Cynthia Ozick, Isaac Bashevis Singer expresses an ambivalent attitude toward belles lettres in his fiction. The irony is that Ozick squirms as she writes eloquently about the existential difficulty of writing in a Christian language— English, while Singer in countless fictions abjures the pernicious effects of novels and other secular literature—in Yiddish.

"Although I did not have the privilege of going through the Hitler holocaust, I have lived for years in New York with refugees from this ordeal."[25] Singer's note to *Enemies* (1972) conveys his characteristically wary and apologetic approach to the Holocaust. Singer says in an interview that even if he had been present he would not write about the destruction of European Jewry because fiction deals with the individual, with the unique character and not with the masses. There is no need, says Singer, for novels about the Holocaust since memoir literature of actual survivors is more significant and authentic than any imaginary re-creation.[26]

Singer, who left Poland in 1935, is the product of the destroyed Jewish community of Eastern Europe and the best-known contemporary chronicler of the Jewish past. The central catastrophe of that past, the destruction of European Jewry is (as Singer's comments make clear), never directly presented in his work. Nevertheless, a pervasive post-Holocaust consciousness manifests itself throughout Singer's fiction. It can be discerned in his historical works and those works which transcend history, in his fictions in European settings and in his few works that are set in contemporary America and Israel. Singer's careful delineation of the world from which he draws emotional, spiritual and literary sustenance is clearly shaped by his having escaped from that world before it was totally destroyed. Withal Singer sees the European-Jewish past whole and with considerable restraint refrains from idealizing or sentimentalizing Jewish life. He does present two distinct visions of life in Europe before 1939—one firmly rooted in the catastrophic history of the Jews in Eastern Europe, the other just as determinedly ahistorical. Through the stories set in a timeless fictional milieu, Singer preserves a world which endured for centuries and was destroyed in a historical instant.

"The purpose of literature," says one of Singer's fictional spokesmen, "is to keep time from vanishing."[27] And Singer's work demonstrates his commitment to such a purpose. Most of Singer's fictions are set in Europe before 1939 and are commemorations of the destroyed Jewish past. Not until Singer had been in the United States for thirty years did he attempt an American post-Holocaust setting (*Enemies*). Singer's fictional time line ends in 1939 as the bombs fall on Warsaw in *The Family Moskat* (1950), when Jewish life as Singer knew it ceased to be. None of his works directly presents events in Europe from 1939 to 1945. Instead, Singer writes in the seventies of life among refugees and survivors in the fifties and sixties. Removed by time and distance Singer's survivors recall, in disconnected fragments, the terrible events of their European pasts.

In one story, however, "The Last Demon" (1964), the timeless and the apocalyptically historical are combined. The story is unique in the Singer canon since it bears the imprint of the Holocaust and is also set in a destroyed *shtetl*. In the monologue the demon-narrator laments the destruction of the Jewish world, yet so rooted is the story in the details of traditional Jewish life that the catastrophe might have been a Cossack pogrom rather than the Nazi annihilation. While the cultural milieu that is conveyed is indeed timeless and no twentieth-century details obtrude, the absence of living Jews brands the story as twentieth century.

The devil-narrator is a Singer surrogate, who, like Singer, subsists on Yiddish letters and has no way to go but back into the past. The bitter paradox is that the demon's only post-Holocaust nourishment is a modern, worldly Yiddish book that the demon condemns as heretical. No matter how debased and profane, however, the Yiddish letters preserve the Jewish past. The story is thus elegy, lament, and ironic apologia.

No apologia is needed or offered for the many particulars of Jewish life that make up the essence of Singer's fiction. Yiddish words are neither glossed nor italicized. He does not condescend by annotating references to *midrashic* texts. He casually mentions obscure holidays and customs with the insouciance of an author writing for an audience of Jews well versed in law, lore, and custom. This is the underlying Singerian fiction that fortifies the elegiac and particularist shape of his work. The assumption is that the reader knows as much as he has to in order to experience the ficitonal world.

The post-Holocaust American and Israeli settings of *Enemies* and *The Penitent* (1984) allow for a range of immigrants and survivors through whom Singer tells the survivor story in infinite variety based on the recognition "that the whole truth would never be learned from those who had survived the concentration camps or the wandering through Russia—not because they lied but because it was impossible for them to tell it all!"[28]

Singer does not ennoble his personae, just as their experience of suffering has not necessarily ennobled them. He does, however, revere his subject: "The vandals who murdered millions of these people have destroyed a treasure of individuality that no literature dare try to bring back."[29] Singer is the chronicler of the butchered Jewish past and the keeper of the memories of those few who survived its destruction.

Although Singer's works are imbued with contrasting Jewish religious traditions, his skepticism and his cyclical view of history form a sensibility quite different from the theological consciousness conveyed in the works of Ozick, the late Arthur Cohen, and Hugh Nissenson.

As novelist and theologian, Cohen uses "fiction to smuggle Jewish ideas into the general culture."[30] *In the Days of Simon Stern* shatters the boundaries of conventional fiction with its deliberate anachronisms, legends, excerpts from doctoral dissertations, talmudic commentary, cabalistic references, parallel versions of the creation myth, epilogues, and appendices. Cohen himself refers to it as a "ragbag" but it is more an anatomy or *aggada*, an encyclopedia of prose forms. There are few works in English, other than Bashevis Singer in translation, that make so little concession to an audience ignorant of the particulars of traditional Jewish life. Cohen's novel, like his characters, is unassimilated.

The narrator of the novel is Nathan Gaza, a Holocaust survivor who was blinded in a Nazi death camp. Nathan is writing a hagiography of the modern messiah, Simon Stern.[31] Halfway through the war, when two million Jews have already been murdered, Simon vows that he will devote himself and his huge fortune to the rescue of a "remnant whose strength shall be in mutual love and helpfulness and disdainful removal and estrangement from all others."[32] To accomplish his high purpose, Simon builds a fortress-like survivors' compound on the lower East Side that is elaborately disguised to resemble its decrepit surroundings. American affluence is thus used to create a modern Jewish ghetto. Simon's fortress is an analogue to the Puritan concept of "a city on a hill" with America as a haven for religious particularists and social experimenters.

All the major characters are immigrant-survivors who embody much of the European-Jewish experience: Eastern, Western, Spanish Marrano, secular and sacred, assimilated and traditional, *Hasidic* and revolutionary. Simon and his parents exemplify the American immigrant experience. Cohen's novel exhorts, preaches, and, above all, urges retention and transmission of the Jewish past. Nathan, like a Hebrew prophet, sets forth the continuing task of the survivor as an ongoing war "of explication, the inculpation of the innocent and the exculpation of the guilty, the torment of broken hearts, moans in the night, visits to the cemetery of remembrance."[33] The work boldly explores diasporal salvation and the Jewish moral function in an unredeemed world. The universalism of Malamud's argument that all men are Jews is rejected by Cohen. Simon Stern instead expresses moral authority and insists on the survival of Jewish particularity. Cohen's novel, like his expository prose on the Holocaust and other Jewish themes, teems with ideas and vitality.

Hugh Nissenson's writings are deeply imbued with Jewish knowledge and the religious sensibility noted in Ozick and Cohen.[34] He is also one of the few American-Jewish writers to draw attention to the complexities of survivor life in Israel. Nissenson has set stories in Israel in *A Pile of Stones* (1965) and *In the Reign of Peace* (1972). His *Notes from the Frontier* (1968) describes his long sojourn in Israel. In "The Law" (1965) Nissenson graphically and economically explores both the struggle of speech and silence that pervades so much Holocaust literature and the meaning of the Jewish assumption of the yoke of the Torah. More ambiguous is his novel *My Own Ground* (1976), a travesty of an immigrant novel set in 1912 but dated 1965 to include the violence, sadism, and obscenity of a post-Holocaust perspective.

As general editor of the Penguin series "Writers from the Other Europe," Philip

Roth has helped to make important Eastern-European Holocaust literature available to a wide public. The series has included Tadeusz Borowski's *This Way to the Gas, Ladies and Gentlemen* (1976) and the remarkable works of Bruno Schulz, a Polish Jew. In his fiction, Roth directs his manic, biting satire at affluent suburban American Jews whose ''experience'' of the Holocaust is limited to seeing the Broadway production of *The Diary of Anne Frank*. But in *The Ghost Writer* (1979), Roth creates a fictional past for an enigmatic young woman with a (fake) foreign accent. She is Anne Frank, resurrected in the writer's imagination as having miraculously survived the gas chamber. Roth's imaginary ghost of the historic Anne Frank is placed in a fictional world that contains the ghost of his former self and other literary ghosts. Unlike the literary ghosts whose fictional lives are probable and indeed recognizable, the Anne Frank episode is a poignant impossibility, a product of the surrogate author's wishful imagination. The tribute to the memory of Anne Frank is counterposed to those early stories of Roth's that caused such discomfort in the Jewish community. In *The Ghost Writer* he obliquely commemorates the Holocaust and with some irony offers an apologia, thereby enabling him to lay a number of his own ghosts to rest.

In ''Epilogue: The Prague Orgy,'' part of *Zuckerman Bound* (1985), the trilogy that includes *The Ghost Writer*, Roth weaves a comparable conceit. The historic inspiration for Roth's imaginative flight is the tragedy of Bruno Schulz, who wrote haunting Kafka-like stories in Polish and who was shot in 1942 by a Gestapo officer who had a grudge against another Nazi. In Roth's sardonic variations, the young writer of *The Ghost Writer*, now a world-famous novelist, is in Prague on a literary junket and a wild, doomed quest for a manuscript written in the ''Yiddish of Flaubert'' by a Czech Jew who was allegedly shot by a Nazi officer for fictional ''reasons'' as absurd and arbitrary as the Nazi ''logic'' that murdered Schulz and millions of others in ''real'' life. Amid the descriptions of frenetic and blackly humorous ''orgies'' among Prague's dissident artists and intellectuals, and insights into the bureaucratic repression that pervades Kafka's bleakly beautiful city, the true or false story of the improbable Yiddish manuscript evokes the pain and the sense of irretrievable loss that is characteristic of Holocaust literature.

Saul Bellow's *Mr. Sammler's Planet* (1970) is the most intellectually rich and challenging of the American survivor novels because of the extraordinary range and quality of the protagonist's mind—a mind much like Bellow's own. Yet both Sammler's encyclopedic mind and his devastating past experience are differentiated from the author's by the use of a third-person point of view. Intimacy and intensity are maintained by focusing on what Sammler, with his ''relentlessly ironic vision,'' is thinking.

Although the primary action of the novel takes place in Sammler's head, other dramas occur among the denizens of Sammler's frenzied Manhattan. A significant part of the novel is centered on the death of Sammler's nephew and benefactor, Dr. Elya Gruner. The novel's three days' duration also centers on two rather bizarre criminals. One is Sammler's daughter Shula (another survivor), who has stolen a manuscript from a Dr. Lal on the colonization of the moon. The other is an elegant black pickpocket whom Sammler observes as the pickpocket practices his craft on Manhattan buses. These "events" are opportunities for the septuagenarian Sammler to reflect on the meaning of life, death, and morality. Sammler characteristically distinguishes between what is peripheral and what is central, between the "civilian" and desperate matters of life and death. For Sammler's credo is that it is necessary to live with all combinations of facts and that "all postures are mocked by their opposites." These tenets are particularly embodied in Sammler's reflections of his Holocaust experience.

In Poland, in 1939, a Nazi rifle butt knocked out Sammler's left eye just before he and his wife were forced to dig the communal grave in which his wife lies buried. Sammler's experience has endowed him with special insights, but in Bellow's hands the usual metaphors of sight and insight transcend the conventional. The difference between Bellow's and Wallant's treatment of the same material is instructive. Nazerman finds his tinted spectacles in a pile of corpses and they exemplify his embittered view of the world. In America, after Nazerman's rebirth, the spectacles are cleansed with redemptive tears. In Bellow's baroque variation, Sammler is a one-eyed man who was the erstwhile follower of H. G. Wells. Sammler, in the wisdom of his experience, specifically describes Wells's "The Country of the Blind" where proverbially the one-eyed man is king as "not a good story." Bellow playfully refers to Sammler's "different looking eyes"—not only do the eyes appear different, but each looks in a different direction. One looks primarily outward and to the present, while the eye socket looks inward to the past. Sammler's smoked glasses not only protect his one good eye and his sensitive "nerve spaghetti" from the outside world but also protect the world from his disfigurement.

Sammler's one-eyed state and his intensified inner vision are the result of the historical reality of being a Polish Jew in 1939. His descent to the kingdom of the dead is not the metaphoric journey of the epic hero but the grisly historic actuality of burial in a mass grave. He does not retell the tale with the art and artifice of a narrator. Instead he experiences in involuntary memory the constant mental confrontation of self and soul. The most crucial memory is Sammler's killing of an unarmed German soldier.

Sammler at the time of the killing had been living with Polish partisans as a partisan until they reverted to the old-fashioned desire for a "Jewless Poland." Then Sammler, starving, naked, frozen, "the dead eye like a ball of ice in his head" derives rich Dostoyevskian warmth from the killing of the German straggler for his shoes, his bread, and his socks. Nearly thirty years later Sammler painfully attempts to evaluate his behavior and concludes that "he was then not entirely human." What distinguishes the human in Sammler's perception is the recognition that life is sacred and the taking of life a sin. Sammler's murder for need and perhaps revenge is an action that will always haunt him and make him aware of the limitations of his individual humanity.

Sammler characteristically distinguishes even among various ways of death and murder. In recalling the mass grave Sammler muses in a bitterly ironic parenthesis "that over a similar new grave Eichmann had testified that he had walked, and the fresh blood welling up at his shoes had sickened him. For a day or two, he had to lie in bed."[35] Sammler offers no comment on Eichmann's testimony, but it is clear that Eichmann wanted to demonstrate his humanity by testifying to his revulsion. Eichmann protected his consciousness from guilt or responsibility for the millions who were murdered and protected himself from recognizing the gruesome consequences of his exercise of power. Bellow rejects Hannah Arendt's thesis of "the banality of evil" by asserting that the Germans had "an idea of genius" in making "the century's great crime look dull." Sammler argues, "What better way to get the curse out of murder than by making it look ordinary, boring, or trite."[36]

The implicit comparison of the fictional Sammler with the historic Eichmann is balanced by the juxtaposition of Eichmann with another historic figure, Mordechai Chaim Rumkowski, the mad "king" of the Lodz ghetto. This occurs late in the novel when Sammler is induced to speak aloud what he has been thinking in the communion of a shared meal with his daughter, his niece, and his new friend Dr. Lal. The Rumkowski vignette is equivalent to one of those short views that Sammler prefers to summary or explanation. Rumkowski is, in Sammler's words, "a parody of the thing—a mad Jewish King presiding over the death of half a million people."[37] At this place in Sammler's discourse he offers commentary on *Job*. It is a daring association, but he clarifies the comparison by directly posing the question: "What is the true stature of a human being?" Sammler contends that modern man, like Job, is subject to too great a demand upon human consciousness and human capacities. "I am not speaking only of moral demand, but also of the demand upon the imagination to produce a human figure of adequate stature."[38] Here Bellow not only points to the challenge to the imagination of *creating* a protagonist of sufficient stature to convincingly embody the experience of the Holocaust, but he also indicates the immense difficulty of transmitting even the contours of such a complex *historical* figure as Rumkowski. Even Sammler, who has been ruminating on the subject for many pages, can do no more than tell the Rumkowski story and incompletely comment on it: "This . . . was what I meant by speaking of the killers' delight in abasement in parody—in Rumkowski, King of rags and shit . . . ruler of corpses . . . though the man was perhaps crazy from the start; perhaps shock even made him saner; in any case, at the end, he voluntarily stepped into the train for Auschwitz."[39]

Implicit in the juxtaposition of Eichmann and Rumkowski is the contrast in their horrendous "moments of honor." The powerful Eichmann offers an example of his "humanity" by demonstrating distasteful sentimentality and craven self-protection in his "sensitivity" to the horror for which he was responsible. The powerless and revolting Rumkowski exhibits courage in his ghastly role, and his final action imbues his death with uncharacteristic dignity.[40]

"All postures are mocked by their opposites": thus complex distinctions are made between historical Holocaust figures and comparisons suggested between Sammler and Job. Sammler's life, like Job's, is marked by disproportionate suffering and tentative, painful movements toward faith. Sammler finds theories and explanations pernicious as early in the novel he abjures "the roots of this, the causes of the other . . . the reasons why."[41] Much of *Mr. Sammler's Planet* is commentary on the plethora of explanations that resists obstreperous facts and ignores meaningful distinctions. Sammler, the most intellectually gifted of the fictional survivors, presents qualified and partial conclusions and judgments. And his "short views" are further refracted by time, distance, and, above all, memory. Sammler's most important reflections are of his experience of unprecedented evil and the possible wisdom that he may be able to extract and transmit to others. Bellow's is the most successful of American-Jewish Holocaust novels.

In one of his "short views" Sammler describes Rumkowski as "a parody of the thing—a mad Jewish king." In *King of the Jews* (1979) Leslie Epstein treats the tragedy of the Lodz ghetto as a parody or travesty. In a manic atmosphere of strained slapstick, animals and people cavort wildly, stand-up comedians perform frenetically and, as deportations deplete the suffering population of the ghetto, characters behave like personae in a Jonsonian comedy of humors. Of course, there is a place for humor in the literature of the Holocaust, as Bellow, Cohen, and Singer have effectively demonstrated in their engaging survivor-clowns. Such mordant gallows humor accentuates grim survivor memory. But the vaudeville ambiance of *King of the Jews* seems little more than a bizarre failure of literary tact.

Another distressing component of the novel derives, paradoxically, from Epstein's use of authentic historical documents. Under constant threat of discovery and death, Ringelblum used ironic cryptic names and collected ghetto jokes. Readers familiar with his precious and painfully written notes and the other historical and fictional materials that Epstein freely appropriates, will experience the most dismaying *déjà vu* again and again. This is Epstein's "raw material" and it remains raw, untransformed by the shaping power of the imagination.

The narrative stance is also problematic. The teller of Epstein's tale is an ambiguous chronicler of the destruction of a ghetto much like Lodz who is describing the mock epic rise and fall of a leader much like Rumkowski. In this desperate context, narrative ambiguities do not enrich, they irritate.

Richard Elman's tendentious trilogy suffers from documentary overkill of another kind. The reader cannot believe that the letters written in *The 28th Day of Elul* (1967), the diary of *Lilo's Diary* (1968), and the ledgers kept in *The Reckoning* (1969) are written by fictionally credible people, not to speak of survivors. The novels of Elman and Epstein lack authenticity, a central issue in the literature of the Holocaust.

Alvin Rosenfeld poses three critical questions about Holocaust literature in general: "What kind of story is it? Who is its rightful teller? And how much should we trust him? . . . For if we do not recognize the story for what it is, or the storyteller for what he is, it becomes impossible to give credence to his tale.''[42]

How have American-Jewish writers established their admittedly derived authority? As we have noted, the most successful have created, with great care, centers of consciousness, who, while occasionally flawed (Ozick's Rosa and Lucy, Singer's Herman Broder, Schaeffer's Anya) are, nonetheless, reliable recorders of experience. Further, the American setting allows for temporal and spatial distance that contributes to the authenticity of survivor memories. Whether with deliberate or involuntary memory like Singer's characters; with dogged recollection like Anya and Rosa; in archaic imitation, like Nathan Gaza; or in ever-present fragments, like Sammler, the survivor contains and is committed to his Holocaust past. Such varied strategies of memory together with the distance afforded by the American context have enabled many American-Jewish writers to write about the Holocaust with authority and rectitude.

Distance makes it possible for the American-Jewish writer to omit, or only touch peripherally on, *l'univers concentrationnaire*, which is the central experience in European-Holocaust literature. Ozick's ''The Shawl'' is an outstanding exception and may indeed point the way to other representations of the death-camp experience. That her horrendous story is two pages long and that its sequel is set in America indicates the difficulties of sustained treatment of the theme. The empirical evidence is that with the exception of Ozick's story, American-born writers have not yet succeeded in presenting credible portrayals of ghettos and camps *in situ*.[43]

Given the prominence of the theme, speculation about the future of American Holocaust literature is problematic. However, it is well to remember that American writers did not respond to Isaac Rosenfeld's ''great theme'' until the mid-sixties. Since then American-Jewish writers have contributed a remarkable body of fiction to Holocaust literature and have thereby enriched world literature.

NOTES

1. Isaac Rosenfeld, ''Terror Beyond Evil,'' in *An Age of Enormity*, p. 197
2. Ibid.
3. Isaac Rosenfeld, ''The Meaning of Terror,'' in *An Age of Enormity*, p. 209.
4. Aaron Zeitlin, *''Lider fun khurbm un lider fun gloybn''* in *Poems of the Holocaust and Poems of Faith*, p. 59. The translation from the Yiddish is mine. The lamentation tradition in Jewish literature is the subject of Sidra DeKoven Ezrahi's *By Words Alone*; Alan Mintz's *Hurban*; and David G. Roskies's *Against the Apocalypse*.
5. Chaim Grade, ''My Quarrel with Hersh Rasseyner,'' p. 598.
6. W. H. Auden, ''The Wandering Jew,'' pp. 185–186.
7. Arthur Miller, cited by Abraham Chapman, ed., in *Jewish-American Literature*, p. xxvii.
8. Ezrahi, *By Words Alone*, p. 198.
9. Susan Sontag, ''Reflections on *The Deputy*,'' in *Against Interpretation*, p. 125.

10. Norma Rosen, "The Holocaust and the American-Jewish Novelist," p. 57.

11. Lawrence Langer, *The Holocaust and the Literary Imagination*, pp. 166, 169. Kosinski quoted by Langer on p. 169.

12. Haskel Frankel, "An Interview with Bernard Malamud," p. 39.

13. Bernard Malamud, *The Fixer*, p. 247.

14. Ibid., p. 271.

15. Leslie and Joyce Field, "An Interview with Bernard Malamud," p. 11.

16. Robert Alter, *After the Tradition*, p. 117; Alfred Kazin, *Contemporaries*, p. 306.

17. Langer, p. 51.

18. Emanuel Ringelblum, *Notes from the Warsaw Ghetto*, p. 300.

19. Susan Fromberg Schaeffer, *Anya*, p. 234.

20. Cynthia Ozick, "A Bintel Brief for Jacob Glatstein," p. 60.

21. Cynthia Ozick, *Bloodshed*, p. 4.

22. Cynthia Ozick and Norma Rosen have written *midrashim* on Bertolt Brecht's pronouncement "he who can still smile has not yet heard the terrible news."

23. Cynthia Ozick, "Levitation," *Levitation*, p. 19.

24. Ibid.

25. Isaac Bashevis Singer, "Author's Note," *Enemies, A Love Story*, n.p.

26. Isaac Bashevis Singer on "The Dick Cavett Show," February 5, 1980.

27. Isaac Bashevis Singer, *Shosha*, p. 16.

28. Isaac Bashevis Singer, *Enemies, A Love Story*, p. 70.

29. Isaac Bashevis Singer, *A Crown of Feathers*, p. 9.

30. See "Arthur A. Cohen," *Dictionary of American Biography*, vol. 28, p. 38.

31. The original Nathan of Gaza (c. 1643–1680) was a cabalist and a learned man who was the *discipulus primus* of Shabbatai Zevi (c. 1626–1676) the "false" Messiah who converted to Islam in 1665.

32. Arthur A. Cohen, *In the Days of Simon Stern*, p. 198.

33. Ibid., p. 227.

34. Nissenson describes himself as "a classic religious personality" and "a militant atheist," a not uncommon Jewish paradox. See Diane Cole's "A Conversation with Hugh Nissenson," *National Jewish Monthly*, 92. (September, 1977), pp. 8–16.

35. Saul Bellow, *Mr. Sammler's Planet*, p. 137.

36. Ibid., p. 18.

37. Ibid., p. 231.

38. Ibid., p. 232.

39. Ibid., pp. 232–233.

40. The conflicting versions of Rumkowski's death only reinforce Sammler's point of view. See Solomon Bloom, "Dictator of the Lodz Ghetto," *Commentary*, 7. (February 1949), pp. 111–122; Michael Checinski, "How Rumkowski Died," *Commentary*, 68. (May, 1979), pp. 63–64.

41. Bellow, *Mr. Sammler's Planet*, p. 3.

42. Alvin Rosenfeld, "The Problematics of Holocaust Literature," p. 25.

43. William Styron's *Sophie's Choice* and John Hersey's *The Wall* are *not* exceptions.

BIBLIOGRAPHY

Alter, Robert. *After the Tradition: Essays on Modern Jewish Writing*. New York: E. P. Dutton, 1969.

Auden, W. H. "The Wandering Jew." *New Republic*. 104. (February 10, 1941), pp. 185–186.

Bloom, Solomon, "Dictator of the Lodz Ghetto." *Commentary*. 7. (February 1949), pp. 111–122.

Chapman, Abraham, ed. *Jewish-American Literature: An Anthology of Fiction, Poetry, Autobiography, and Criticism*. New York: New American Library, 1974.

Checinski, Michael. "How Rumkowski Died." *Commentary*. 68. (May, 1979), pp. 63–64.

Cohen, Arthur. *In the Days of Simon Stern*. New York: Random House, 1973.

Cole, Diane. "A Conversation with Hugh Nissenson." *National Jewish Monthly*. 92. (September 1977), pp. 8–16.

Ezrahi, Sidra DeKoven. *By Words Alone: The Holocaust in Literature*. Chicago: University of Chicago Press, 1980.

Field, Leslie and Joyce Field. "An Interview with Bernard Malamud." *Twentieth-Century Views: A Collection of Critical Essays*. Englewood Cliffs, N.J.: Prentice-Hall, 1975.

Frankel, Haskel. "An Interview with Bernard Malamud." *Saturday Review*. 149. (September 10, 1966), pp. 39–40.

Grade, Chaim. "My Quarrel with Hersh Rasseyner." *A Treasury of Yiddish Stories*, ed. Irving Howe and Eliezer Greenberg. New York: Schocken Books, 1973.

Hersey, John. *The Wall*. New York: Alfred A. Knopf, 1950.

Kazin, Alfred. *Contemporaries*. Boston: Little, Brown, 1962.

Langer, Lawrence. *The Holocaust and the Literary Imagination*. New Haven: Yale University Press, 1975.

Mintz, Alan. *Hurban: Responses to Catastrophe*. New York: Columbia University Press, 1984.

Ozick, Cynthia. "A Bintel Brief for Jacob Glatstein." *Jewish Heritage*. 14. (September 1972), p. 60.

———. *Bloodshed and Three Novellas*. New York: Alfred A. Knopf, 1976.

———. *Levitation*. New York: E. P. Dutton, 1983.

Ringelblum, Emanuel. *Notes from the Warsaw Ghetto*, trans. Jacob Sloan. New York: McGraw-Hill, 1958.

Rosen, Norma. "The Holocaust and the American-Jewish Novelist." *Midstream*. 20. (October 1974), pp. 54–62.

Rosenfeld, Alvin. "The Problematics of Holocaust Literature." *Confronting the Holocaust: The Impact of Elie Wiesel*, ed. Alvin Rosenfeld and Irving Greenberg. Bloomington: Indiana University Press, 1978.

Rosenfeld, Isaac. *An Age of Enormity: Life and Writing in the Forties and Fifties*. Cleveland: World, 1962.

Roskies, David. *Against the Apocalypse: Responses to Catastrophe in Modern Jewish Culture*. Cambridge: Harvard University Press, 1984.

Schaeffer, Susan Fromberg. *Anya*. New York: Macmillan, 1974.

Singer, Isaac Bashevis. *A Crown of Feathers and Other Stories*. 1973; rpt. New York: Fawcett, Crest, 1974.

———. *Enemies, A Love Story*, trans. A. Shevrin and E. Shub. 1972; rpt. Greenwich, Connecticut: Fawcett, Crest, 1973.

———. *Shosha*, trans. I. B. Singer and Joseph Singer. New York: Farrar, Straus & Giroux, 1977.

Sontag, Susan. "Reflections on *The Deputy.*" *Against Interpretation*. New York: Farrar, Straus & Giroux, 1966.

Styron, William. *Sophie's Choice*. New York: Random House, 1976.

Zeitlin, Aaron. *Lider fun khurbm un lider fun gloybn* [Poems of the Holocaust and Poems of Faith]. New York and Tel Aviv: Bergen Belsen Memorial Press, 1967.

FOR FURTHER READING

Fiction

Bellow, Saul. *Dangling Man*. New York: Vanguard, 1944; rpt. New American Library, 1965.

———. *The Victim*. New York: New American Library, 1947.

———. *Mr. Sammler's Planet*. New York: Viking, 1970.

Berger, Zdena. *Tell Me Another Morning*. New York: Harper, 1961.

Elman, Richard. *Lilo's Diary*. New York: Scribner, 1968.

———. *The Reckoning: The Daily Ledgers of Newman Yagodah Advokat and Factor*. New York: Scribner, 1969.

———. *The 28th Day of Elul*. New York: Scribner, 1967.

Epstein, Leslie. *King of the Jews*. New York: Coward, McCann & Geoghehan, 1979.

Ettinger, Elzbieta. *Kindergarten*. Boston: Houghton Mifflin, 1970.

Karmel, Ilona. *An Estate of Memory*. Boston: Houghton Mifflin, 1969.

Klein, Edward. *The Parachutists*. New York: Doubleday, 1982.

Kosinski, Jerzy. *The Painted Bird*. New York: Pocket Books, 1965.

Kotlowitz, Robert. *The Boardwalk*. New York: Alfred A. Knopf, 1976.

Levin, Meyer. *Eva*. New York: Simon & Schuster, 1959.

Lustig, Arnost. *Darkness Casts No Shadow*, trans. by Jeanne Nemcova. Washington, D.C.: Inscape Publishers, 1976.

———. *Diamonds of the Night*, trans. Jeanne Nemcova. Washington, D.C.: Inscape Publishers, 1978. Rpt. Evanston, Illinois: Northwestern University Press, 1986.

———. *Night and Hope*, trans. George Theiner. Washington, D.C.: Inscape Publishers, 1978.

———. *A Prayer for Katerina Horovitova*, trans. Jeanne Nemcova. New York: Harper & Row, 1973.

Malamud, Bernard. *The Fixer*. New York: Farrar, Straus & Giroux, 1966.

———. "The German Refugee." *Idiots First*. New York: Farrar, Straus, & Company, 1963.

———. *The Magic Barrel*. New York: Farrar, Straus & Cudahy, 1958.

Nissenson, Hugh. *In the Reign of Peace*. New York: Farrar, Straus & Giroux, 1968.

———. *My Own Ground*. New York: Farrar, Straus & Giroux, 1976.

———. *A Pile of Stones*. New York: Scribner, 1965.

Ozick, Cynthia. *The Cannibal Galaxy*. New York: Alfred A. Knopf, 1983.

———. *The Pagan Rabbi and Other Stories*. New York: Alfred A. Knopf, 1971.

———. "Rosa." *New Yorker*. 59. (March 21, 1983), pp. 38–71.

———. "The Shawl." *New Yorker*. 56. (May 26, 1980), pp. 33–34.

Rosen, Norma. *Touching Evil*. New York: Curtis Books, 1969.

Roth, Philip. "Eli, the Fanatic." *Goodbye, Columbus and Five Short Stories*. 1959; rpt.
    New York: Bantam, 1974.
———. "Epilogue: The Prague Orgy." *Zuckerman Bound*. New York: Farrar, Straus
    & Giroux, 1985.
———. *The Ghost Writer*. New York: Farrar, Straus & Giroux, 1979.
Singer, Isaac Bashevis. "The Last Demon." *Short Friday and Other Stories*. New York:
    Fawcett, Crest, 1964.
Singer, Israel Joshua. *The Family Carnovsky*, trans. Joseph Singer. New York: Vanguard
    Press, 1969.
Steiner, George. *The Portage to San Cristobal of A.H*. New York: Simon & Schuster,
    1981.
Stern, Daniel. *Who Shall Live, Who Shall Die*. New York: Crown Publishers, 1963.
Wallant, Edward Lewis. *The Pawnbroker*. New York: Manor Books, 1962.
Wiesel, Elie. *The Accident*, trans. Anne Borchardt. New York: Hill and Wang, 1962.
———. *Dawn*, trans. Anne Borchardt. New York: Hill and Wang, 1961.
———. *The Fifth Son*, trans. Marian Wiesel. New York: Summit Books, 1985.
———. *The Gates of the Forest*, trans. Frances Frenaye. New York: Holt, Rinehart &
    Winston, 1966.
———. *Night*, trans. Stella Rodway. New York: Hill and Wang, 1960.
———. *The Town Beyond the Wall*, trans. Stephen Becker. New Yorker: Holt, Rinehart
    & Winston, 1967.

Poetry

Cohen, Leonard. "All There is to Know about Adolph Eichmann." *Poems, 1956–1968*.
    London: Jonathan Cape, 1969.
Feldman, Irving. *The Pripet Marshes and Other Poems*. New York: Viking, 1965.
Hecht, Anthony. *The Hard Hours*. New York: Atheneum, 1967.
Levertov, Denise. "During the Eichmann Trial." *The Jacob's Ladder*. New York: New
    Directions, 1958.
Reznikoff, Charles. *Holocaust*. Los Angeles: Black Sparrow Press, 1975.
Sklarew, Myra. *From the Backyard of the Diaspora*. Washington, D.C.: Dryad Press,
    1976.
Taube, Herman. *Between the Shadows*. Washington, D.C.: Dryad Press, 1985.
———. *A Chain of Images*. New York: Shulsinger Brothers, 1979.
———. *Questions*. Washington, D.C.: Yiddish of Greater Washington, 1982.

Drama

Goodrich, Frances and Albert Hackett. *The Diary of Anne Frank*. New York: Random
    House, 1956.
Lieberman, Harold and Edith Lieberman. "Throne of Straw." *The Theatre of the Hol-
    ocaust*, ed. and introd. Robert Skloot. Madison: University of Wisconsin Press,
    1982.
Miller, Arthur. "After the Fall." *Arthur Miller's Collected Plays*, vol. 2. New York:
    Viking, 1981, first performed in 1964.
———. "Incident at Vichy." *Arthur Miller's Collected Plays*, vol. 2. New York: Viking,
    1981, first performed 1964.

————. "Playing for Time." *Arthur Miller's Collected Plays*, vol. 2. New York: Viking, 1981, screenplay, 1980, based on the book by Fania Fénélon.

Skloot, Robert, ed. *The Theatre of the Holocaust: Four Plays*. Madison: University of Wisconsin Press, 1982.

Wincelberg, Shimon. "Resort 76." *The Theatre of the Holocaust: Four Plays*, ed. and introd. Robert Skloot. Madison: University of Wisconsin Press, 1982.

Anthologies and Collections

Eliach, Yaffa, ed. *Hasidic Tales of the Holocaust*. New York: Avon, 1982.

Friedlander, Albert, ed. *Out of the Whirlwind: A Reader of Holocaust Literature*. New York: Doubleday, 1968.

Glatstein, Jacob, Israel Knox, and Samuel Margoshes, eds. *Anthology of Holocaust Literature*. Philadelphia: Jewish Publication Society, 1968.

Howe, Irving and Eliezer Greenberg, eds. *A Treasury of Yiddish Stories*. New York: Schocken, 1973.

Schwartz, Howard and Anthony Rudolph, eds. *Voices Within the Ark: The Modern Jewish Poets*. New York: Avon, 1980.

Literary Criticism

Adorno, T. W. "Engagement." *Noten zur Literatur*. Frankfurt am Main: Suhrkamp Verlag, 1965.

Alexander, Edward. *The Resonance of Dust: Essays on Holocaust Literature and Jewish Fate*. Columbus: Ohio State University Press, 1979.

Alvarez, A. *Beyond All This Fiddle*. New York: Random House, 1969.

Berenbaum, Michael. *Vision of the Void: Theological Reflections on the Works of Elie Wiesel*. Middletown, Connecticut: Wesleyan University Press, 1978.

Berger, Alan. *Crisis and Covenant: The Holocaust in American-Jewish Fiction*. Albany: State University of New York Press, 1985.

Bilik, Dorothy Seidman. *Immigrant-Survivors: Post-Holocaust Consciousness in Recent Jewish American Fiction*. Middletown, Connecticut: Wesleyan University Press, 1981.

Des Pres, Terrence. *The Survivor: An Anatomy of Life in the Death Camps*. New York: Oxford University Press, 1976.

Fine, Ellen S. *Legacy of Night: The Literary Universe of Eli Wiesel*. Albany: State University of New York Press, 1985.

Halperin, Irving. *Messengers from the Dead: Literature of the Holocaust*. Philadelphia: Westminster Press, 1970.

Insdorf, Annette. *Indelible Shadows: Film and the Holocaust*. New York: Vintage, 1983.

Kazin, Alfred. "Living with the Holocaust." *Midstream*. 16. (June-July, 1970), pp. 3–7.

Mintz, Alan. *Hurban: Responses to Catastrophe in Hebrew Literature*. New York: Columbia University Press, 1984.

Murdoch, Brian. "Transformation of the Holocaust: Auschwitz in Modern Lyric Poetry." *Comparative Literature Studies*. 2. (1974), pp. 123–150.

Rosenfeld, Alvin S. *A Double Dying: Reflections on Holocaust Literature*. Bloomington: Indiana University Press, 1980.

———. *Imagining Hitler*. Bloomington: Indiana University Press, 1985.

Steiner, George. *Language and Silence*. New York: Atheneum, 1967.

Young, James E. "Holocaust Literary Criticism." *Midstream*. 30. (June-July, 1984), pp. 39–41.

Other References

Dawidowicz, Lucy. *The War Against the Jews, 1933–1945*. New York: Holt, Rinehart & Winston, 1975.

———. ed. *A Holocaust Reader*. New York: Behrman House, 1976.

Walden, Daniel, ed. *Twentieth-Century American-Jewish Fiction Writers*. Vol. 28 of *Dictionary of Literary Biography*. Detroit: Gale Research, 1984.

16

The Holocaust and Its Historiography: The Major Texts

Saul Friedman

Since Jacob Robinson and Philip Friedman attempted their massive, yet inchoate, *Guide to Jewish History under Nazi Impact* (1960), a veritable industry has developed purporting to shed insight into lessons of the Holocaust. Not even the Library of Congress is able to estimate the number of publications which relate to the Nazi murder scheme of World War II, but it is clear that the flowering of Holocaust studies is attributable to several factors: (1) a heightened sense of Jewish identity brought on by fears for Israel's security during the June War of 1967; (2) the proliferation of Jewish studies programs, derived in part from the atmosphere of ethnicity associated with the Civil Rights movement of the 1960's and a recognition that major historical archives in Europe no longer existed; (3) the slow but constant stream of translated documents from Eastern Europe; (4) notoriety surrounding maneuvers of escaped war criminals who reside in the West; (5) the tolling of Simon Wiesenthal's biological clock, which has forced once laconic survivors to confront their own mortality; and (6) what may be the most important reason, the innate morbidity which pervades the nature of man.[1]

Despite preachments of goodness which undergird the ethics of every civilization, man is a voyeuristic creature, preoccupied with pain, evil, and suffering. Many Holocaust dramas and histories play to this base instinct, serving to titillate rather than educate. It has almost become a cliché to suggest that such pieces—like Vanessa Redgrave's limp performance in *Playing for Time* (1980) or George Steiner's awkward portrayal of an aged Adolf Hitler in *The Portage to San Cristobal of A.H.* (1981)—trivialize and profane the memory of those who made what Emil Fackenheim terms that "unique descent into Hell."[2]

If a book or play is inaccurate, clumsily written, or superficial, it reinforces the growing number of critics who argue that the world has been saturated with tales of exclusively Jewish suffering. Shoddy methodology supplies all the needed evidence for revanchist anti-Semites of the Institute for Historical Review, who claim that the Holocaust was a Zionist invention, that there were no gas chambers, and that no more than 600,000 Jews perished of disease in German "detention camps."[3] Fortunately, there are a number of serious works available to scholars and students of the Holocaust to combat such canards. These may be separated into three categories:

1. Historical Texts Covering the Entire Nazi Period

Basically, there are six of these: Yehuda Bauer's *A History of the Holocaust* (1982); Lucy Dawidowicz's *The War Against the Jews, 1933–1945* (1975); Raul Hilberg's *The Destruction of the European Jews* (1961); Nora Levin's *The Holocaust* (1968); Leon Poliakov's *Harvest of Hate* (1954); and Gerald Reitlinger's *The Final Solution* (1953). The list is compelling for several reasons: first, because a subject of such great interest has evoked only a handful of texts; second, periodically some historian feels compelled to issue another "definitive" study; and third, three of the authors mentioned (Reitlinger, Poliakov, and Bauer) are not American. They are included in this survey because their works have been used extensively throughout the United States. No understanding of Nazi genocide may be undertaken without familiarity with these standard works, about which a comparative analysis is provided below.[4]

2. Specialized Works

At the secondary level is that profusion of books focusing upon narrower aspects of the Holocaust. A non-exhaustive listing of books in English and English translation includes:

A. *The treatment of Jews in specific areas:*

Randolph Braham's two volume *The Politics of Genocide* (1981); Lucjan Dobroszycki's *Chronicle of the Lodz Ghetto, 1941–1944* (1984); Julius Fisher's *Transnistria* (1969); Philip Hallie's *Lest Innocent Blood Be Shed* (1979); Celia Heller's *On the Edge of Destruction* (1977); Paula Hyman's *From Dreyfus to Vichy* (1979); Ezra Mendelsohn's *The Jews of East Central Europe between the World Wars* (1983); Jacob Presser's *The Destruction of the Dutch Jews* (1969); David Weinberg's *A Community on Trial: The Jews of Paris in the 1930s* (1977); and the American Jewish Committee's reprint of *The Jewish Communities of Nazi Occupied Europe* (1982).

B. *The Allies' response to the plight of Europe's Jews:*

Henry Feingold's *The Politics of Rescue* (1970); Walter Laquer's *The Terrible Secret* (1980); Arthur Morse's *While Six Million Died* (1968); Monty Penkower's *The Jews Were Expendable* (1983); David Wyman's *Paper Walls* (1968) and *The Abandonment of the Jews* (1984); and Saul Friedman's *No Haven for the Oppressed* (1973).

C. Memoirs and diaries:

Josef Bor's *The Terezin Requiem* (1963); Elie Cohen's *The Abyss* (1973); Alexander Donat's *The Holocaust Kingdom* (1965); Judith Strick Dribben's *A Girl Called Judith Strick* (1970); Charlotte Delbo's *None of Us Will Return* (1968); Anne Frank's *The Diary of a Young Girl* (1952); Bernard Goldstein's *The Stars Bear Witness* (1959); Janus Korczak's *Ghetto Diary* (1978); Luba Krugman Gurdus's *The Death Train* (1978); The Warsaw Diary of Chaim Kaplan (1973); Primo Levi's *Survival in Auschwitz* (1961); Isabella Leitner's *Fragments of Isabella: A Memoir of Auschwitz* (1978); Sala Pawlowicz's *I Will Survive* (1962, 1964); Oskar Pinkus's *The House of Ashes* (1964); Emanuel Ringelblum's *Notes from the Warsaw Ghetto* (1958); *Hannah Senesh: Her Life and Diary* (1973); Leon Wells's *The Janowska Road* (1963); Elie Wiesel's *Night* (1960).

D. Oral histories:

Azriel Eisenberg's *Witness to the Holocaust* (1981); Yaffa Eliach's *Hasidic Tales of the Holocaust* (1982); Helen Epstein's *Children of the Holocaust* (1979); Dorothy Rabinowitz's *New Lives: Survivors of the Holocaust Living in America* (1976); Lucy Steinitz and David Szonyi's *Living after the Holocaust* (1976); Isaiah Trunk's *Jewish Responses to Nazi Persecution* (1979); and Saul S. Friedman's *Amcha: An Oral Testament of the Holocaust* (1978).

E. General anthologies and supplements:

Roselle Chartock's *The Holocaust Years: Society on Trial* (1978); Lucy Dawidowicz's *A Holocaust Reader* (1976); Albert Friedlander's *Out of the Whirlwind* (1968); Philip Friedman's *Martyrs and Fighters* (1954); Jacob Glatstein et al., *Anthology of Holocaust Literature* (1969); Raul Hilberg's *Documents of Destruction* (1971); Milton Meltzer's *Never to Forget* (1976); Albert Nirenstein's *A Tower from the Enemy* (1959).

F. Jewish resistance:

Reuben Ainsztein's *Jewish Resistance in Nazi Occupied Eastern Europe* (1974); Alexander Donat's *Jewish Resistance* (1964); Yuri Suhl's *They Fought Back* (1967); Marie Syrkin's *Blessed Is the Match* (1948); Joseph Tenenbaum's *Underground* (1952); Isaiah Trunk's *Judenrat* (1972); Leonard Tushnet's *To Die with Honor* (1965).

G. Psycho-social and religious analyses:

Hannah Arendt's *Eichmann in Jerusalem* (1964); Bruno Bettelheim's *The Informed Heart* (1960); Terrence Des Pres's *The Survivor* (1976); Emil Fackenheim's *God's Presence in History* (1970); Helen Fein's *Accounting for Genocide* (1979); Viktor Frankl's *Man's Search for Meaning* (1963); Abraham Heschel's *Man Is Not Alone* (1951); George Kren and Leon Rappoport's *The Holocaust and the Crisis of Human Behavior* (1980); Stanley Milgram's *Obedience to Authority* (1974); Richard Rubenstein's *After Auschwitz* (1966).

3. Fiction

Finally, there are the works of fiction or quasi-fiction which many teachers employ in their classrooms. Lamentably, they may be the only books which people read about the Holocaust. As with all published materials, fiction may range from the very good (Hans Habe's *The Mission*, 1966; John Hersey's *The Wall*, 1950; Anatoly Kuznetsov's *Babi Yar*, 1967; Robert Lewis's *Michel, Michel*, 1967; Andre Schwarz-Bart's *The Last of the Just*, 1960) through the pedestrian (Frederick Forsyth's *The Odessa File*, 1972; Ira Levin's *The Boys from Brazil*, 1976; Leon Uris's *Mila 18*, 1961) to the overrated (Leslie Epstein's *King of the Jews*, 1979; Bernard Kops's *Yes from No-Man's Land*, 1965; Jerzy Kosinski's *The Painted Bird*, 1970; Arthur Miller's *Incident at Vichy*, 1965; Steiner's *The Portage to San Cristobal of A.H.*, 1981).

Because some readers believe what they read (merely because it appears in print), selection of novels requires caution. Authors of mediocre literature may, on rare occasions, succeed in touching the emotions of their readers. Others rely upon pure sensationalism bordering on necrophilia. Passages of explicit brutality and sex may seem obligatory to some, but serve only to degrade the victims of Nazism. If the purpose of fiction is, as John Hersey once remarked, to make the reader feel that he himself took part in the great or despicable events of the story and "make anyone who reads it better able to meet life in his generation," then invented violence or sexuality is gratuitous.[5]

COMMON PROBLEMS IN HOLOCAUST HISTORIOGRAPHY

No one has ever claimed history to be an exact science. The best that any historian can do is to attempt a reconstruction of past events, as fairly as possible, based on available sources. Recognizing the limitations of his own profession, Livy once remarked cynically: "There is really no limit to historians' lies."[6] Although such warning may be overstated, numerous problems do exist within the body of Holocaust literature.

1. Hyperephania

In most academic fields, there exists a spirit of healthy competition. Not so in the study of Holocaust. Where one ought to expect cooperation, there is rancor. Perhaps it is because the phenomenon is so recent that some scholars are eager to proclaim themselves the "first" to develop curricula in schools or universities, the "first" to guide study missions to concentration camps or hold conferences among survivors, the "first" to obtain source materials or tape interviews. Still worse is the egoism of scholars who denigrate the work of any who disagree with them, without any supporting evidence. Such individuals are guilty of what the ancient Greeks once called *hyperephania*, in Yiddish *Besser-*

wissen, an arrogant sense of superiority. They attempt to foreclose new attitudes or interpretations.

2. The Curse of Polemic

In their quest for objectivity, historians are instructed to keep their emotions under check, avoid hortatory phrasing, and refrain from polemic. What the latter means is unclear. If, as it has been suggested, history is so imprecise that one man's history is another man's lie, then it must also be true that one man's polemic is another man's history. All manner of polemics have been acknowledged as having vital importance in history, from Josephus's ancient apologetics to Heinrich Graetz's monumental *History of the Jews*. In our own day, Simon Wiesenthal and Emil Fackenheim engage only in "controversial argument." The same is true of every journal with a particular editorial viewpoint.

There are instances in history where circumstances cry out for condemnation. The question then is not whether historians should make a judgment, but how the judgment is phrased. If the language employed is deemed too inflammatory, too emotional, too ethnocentric, if the individual's personal past is distasteful, his work may be dismissed as "purple" polemic. In urging cautious evaluation of cultural differences, even to the point of rationalizing brutality, some Jewish scholars have sacrificed judgment to equivocation.

3. Banalities from the Ivory Tower

Oftentimes, when Holocaust scholars venture forth with judgments, they are so badly phrased, so bromidic or inaccurate that they weaken their own case. George Santayana's famed dictum on the lessons of history is an example. Cited ad nauseam, it lacks the impact of variants offered either by Emil Fackenheim ("those who do not appreciate the significance of the first Auschwitz cannot comprehend the threat of the second Auschwitz") or Alexander Donat ("to insist upon reminding the world of what happened, to insist upon sensitizing the conscience of mankind, is the only guarantee that the Holocaust will not happen again").[7] Other conclusions appear with such regularity—"the Jews went to their deaths like sheep," "concentration camps were Hell on earth," "American Jews were powerless to help their European brethren"—that they have become clichés, whether they are true or not.

More disturbing is the concerted effort on the part of some social scientists to make comparisons between the death camps and Hiroshima, Dresden, American internment camps for Japanese, the Soviets' Siberian network, and American behavior in Vietnam.

Granted, whoever is wrongly detained enters what Terrence Des Pres calls "the victim world." But it is an exercise in the reductio ad absurdum to equate Auschwitz with any of the aforementioned. Loathsome as Manzinar may have been, it was not an extermination center. Deadly as the bomb dropped on Hiroshima was, it was not a device intended to celebrate war or prolong torture. Terrible as the destruction of Dresden may have been, it was designed as retaliation for those who actively embraced a system of racism and expansionism. Kurt Vonnegut may not have welcomed the firebombing of this classic city, but survivors of death marches housed in Dresden arms factories did.[8] Notwithstanding Alexander Solzhenitsyn's vivid images of hunger, cold, and cruelty, inmates of Russian labor camps are not the same as those sent to their deaths in Auschwitz or Maidanek. To suggest that all so-called labor camps, including those in Russia or even Buchenwald, are death camps because prisoners "died every day," is to obscure the unique nature of the Holocaust.[9]

Whether one agrees with Elie Wiesel that Holocaust studies should focus primarily upon the six million or with Simon Wiesenthal that the subject encompasses eleven or twelve million innocents slaughtered by the Nazis, there was something unique about Hitler's treatment of Jews. Not every Pole or priest or Russian or Social Democrat or Communist was to be arrested, dehumanized, and executed. That distinction was reserved for Jews and Gypsies and should be emphasized in any discussion of inhumanity.

4. Mellow Maunderings

In Anatole France's *Penguin Island*, the protagonist Pyrot is accused of stealing 500 sheaves of grain. His many relatives (700 in all) are described as being "at first crushed by the blow struck at one of their family." They "shut themselves in their houses, covered themselves with ashes, and blessing the hand that punished them, maintained a strict fast for forty days." Subsequently, they abandoned their timidity and set out to prove Pyrot's innocence.[10]

How different from some contemporary historians who, in an effort to avoid the pitfall of emotionalism, soften their judgments. The result of such diffidence may weaken what was intended. Cagey maunderings obscure issues. One such example may be found in Bernard Wasserstein's *Britain and the Jews of Europe* (1979). The author conclusively demonstrates the feasibility of aerial bombardment of the death camps, but like another British scholar, Martin Gilbert in *Auschwitz and the Allies* (1981), shifts much of the blame for inaction to personnel in the U.S. government.[11] Wasserstein also feels compelled to end an otherwise sound study with a challenge and a platitude. "It may be objected," he writes, "that if Britain's record on the Jewish question during the war was unimpressive, that of other countries was often far worse." Then, noting the low priority for rescue of the Jews, he compares the actions of the British with the passerby Good Samaritan in the New Testament: "And so they came and looked and passed by on the other side."[12]

The *Penguin Island* mentality is more evident among scholars who address the subject of American culpability during the Holocaust. Here, the tendency has been to muffle rather than reveal apathy and lethargy. For nearly twenty years, until the publication of Arthur Morse's *While Six Million Died*, it was argued that "we didn't know" what was happening in Europe. If the Jews of France, Greece, and Hungary did not appreciate the threat of extermination, how could any American diplomat, politician, or housewife? It has taken nearly a decade to dispel this myth. Americans were informed about mass murder, from articles not merely in the Yiddish press, but in the mass media. The *New York Times*, the Cleveland *Plain Dealer*, and *Collier's* detailed events in the Warsaw Ghetto and Bucharest long before 1945. A striking example was the two-page pictorial essay titled "Germans Impose Mass Death on Red Prisoners and Poles," which appeared in *Life* magazine, a journal with the nation's second largest subscription list (six million readers). This photographic essay showed Russian POWs, prone on the ground after forced marches, strung on electrified barbed wire, whole stacks of starved victims gathered for burial. A second collection of photos revealed the bony carcasses of Jews in Warsaw being counted and buried in common graves. Some were children, their bellies bloated with edema common to the children of Cambodia and Ethiopia. One especially grotesque picture was of a man holding by the throat what appeared at first glance to be a chicken. In reality, the victim of "slow starvation" was a Jewish infant. The date on *Life's* feature was February 23, 1942, one month after the determination of the Final Solution at the Wannsee Conference, three full years before the concentration camps were shut down.

From "we didn't know," some Americans retreated for a time to a second line of rationalization: the U.S. government was unable to help. This too has been proven by a number of researchers—David Wyman, Seymour Finger, Elie Matzovsky—to be untrue. Before the war, the United States could have reformed its immigration laws, welcoming more than a paltry 30,000 refugees each year. We could have pressed for temporary havens in Australia, Canada, Alaska. Before Hitler declared war against the United States in 1941, we could have increased amounts of food and medical supplies shipped to ghettoized populations in Europe. Later, troop ships which carried 400,000 Axis POWs to American ports could have been used to rescue Jews and other victims of Nazism. Allied governments which negotiated the exchange of small numbers of civilians on a dozen occasions could have utilized blocked bank accounts to arrange additional ransoms. North Africa, in American possession after 1942, could have been opened to refugees fleeing Spain, Italy, or Southern France. British authorities in Palestine, so desperate for manpower when Rommel's tanks were slashing toward El Alamein, could have been pressed to admit refugees who could walk to the Holy Land from the Balkans. Arms could have been dropped to the desperate Jewish partisan groups that paid premium prices to anti-Semitic nationalist elements for weapons that backfired. Rail lines leading to the death camps and the camps themselves could have been bombed. Failing that, the Allied governments could have issued a strong statement acknowledging the existence of genocide and promising retribution, beyond the one brief reference to the destruction of "the Jewish race" dating from President Roosevelt's statement of December 17, 1942, and buried in Volume 5 of *Documents of American Foreign Relations*.

For those willing to grant the feasibility of at least some of these actions, Arthur Morse's book provided a third retreat: the U.S. government, particularly the State Department, misled the Jews of America. Again not so. What Morse and others like Henry Feingold, David Wyman, and Melvin Urofsky have noted is that the Roosevelt Administration manipulated the Jews, played upon their fears and gullibility. American Jewish leaders knew early on, as early as the summer of 1942, what was happening in Eastern Europe and supposedly could do nothing because they were powerless.

The concept of powerlessness is justified by reference to public opinion polls, Jewish unemployment during the Depression, lack of economic and political clout, and insecurity in a new land. At the same time, it justifies a lack of boldness in both contemporary Jews and their predecessors. In 1984, however, the concept of powerlessness was challenged by the American Jewish Commission on the Holocaust. Comprised of more than thirty luminaries (including Justice Arthur Goldberg, Abraham Ribicoff, Bruno Bettelheim, Judge Simon Rifkind, Philip Klutznick, Martin Peretz, Irving Howe, Stella Adler, Rabbi Marc Tanenbaum, Jacob Javits, Elizabeth Holtzman, Leon Wells, and the Presidents of the Jewish National Fund, B'nai B'rith, Hadassah, and the Synagogue Council of America), the Commission came under attack long before its final report was issued.[13] Ten months before the Commission issued its findings, Lucy Dawidowicz, writing for *Commentary*, lacerated its mandate, methodology, and conclusions. Of course, nobody had read the report; it was not written yet. When the mammoth document finally appeared in the spring of 1984, a spokesman for the Anti-Defamation League scored the Commission, labeling its findings wrongly timed, counterproductive, and, forty years after the Holocaust, "premature." An even more intemperate and inaccurate assessment of the "Goldberg Report" found its way into the pages of *Midstream* in February, 1985.[14]

The "Goldberg Report" is critical of American-Jewish behavior during the Holocaust. Taking into account all the economic and social factors of the time, it nevertheless rebukes Jewish leaders for not setting aside personal differences and presenting a united agenda to the White House. Reactions to the report reveal a major inconsistency in those who allegedly cleave to rigid standards of objectivity and impartiality. Gone are the mellow words in favor of bitter invective and ad hominem attacks. Critics of American Jewry, like myself, have been labeled Revisionists (the same term applied to isolationist historians of the interwar period, "right-wing" Zionists, and those anti-Semites who deny the historicity of the Holocaust). In professional forums their findings are misquoted to suggest that American Jews did "nothing" to succor their brethren in Europe or that the failure of American Jewry was a "major" factor in the success of Nazi genocide. None of those who questioned the role of American Jews during the Holocaust have ever said this, but such irrational responses underscore the need to assess all Holocaust literature, especially that which is placid about American-Jewish responsibility.

5. Inadvertent Innuendo

This ranges from platitudes about universalism uttered by Arthur Miller's characters in both *Incident at Vichy* (1964) and *Playing for Time* (1980), to the oft-cited banality that the Jews went to their deaths like sheep. No one questions Miller's commitment to the downtrodden, but the practical result of his labor is to minimize the uniqueness of the Holocaust and demean the character of those who endured the camps. In his drama *Incident at Vichy*, the French doctor Leduc warns: "Each man has his Jew; it is the other. And the Jews have their Jews. And now, now above all, you must see that you have yours—the man whose death leaves you relieved that you are not him, despite your decency. And that is why there is nothing and will be nothing—until you face your own complicity with this—your own humanity."[15]

During the war, Fania Fénélon was dumped into Auschwitz not because she was a woman, but because she was a Jew. In the docudrama based on her life (*Playing for Time*), the traditional melody "Josef, Josef" plays as Jews qua Jews are beaten from cattle car to gas chamber. Vanessa Redgrave stitches back the upper triangle of her badge. Yet repeatedly Miller makes her speak not for Jews, but for "humanity." She exclaims how sick she is of Jews and gentiles, Germans and Frenchmen: "I'm a woman, not a tribe, and I have been humiliated. That's all I know." Later, Redgrave and others are reproached by the one truly repulsive member of the orchestra (a Zionist) for finding something "human" in Shirley Knight's *Lagerführer*. As the camp is bombarded, Redgrave laments it may be "too late for the human race." In a dialogue with Jane Alexander, she declares, "Who knows what's in the human heart?" In another dispute with the Zionist Giselle, she adds, "We know a little more about the human race, and it is not good." When the camp is finally liberated, Redgrave feebly, but defiantly, sings, not "*Hatikvah*," which was the chant of survivors at Belsen, but the internationalist anthem "*Le Marseillaise*."

Miller's effort to subsume the Holocaust under a general heading of human tragedy, like relativist disclaimers noted above, is incorrect. It is doubtful that Miller intended for his writings to erode respect for the victims of Nazism, but they could serve the purposes of those who, given the opportunity, would replicate Hitler's feats against the survivors.

In like manner, Lucy Dawidowicz never meant for any of her writings to be cited by spokesmen for the Palestine Liberation Organization (PLO), but just as in Miller's works, Zionists emerge as villains. The reader of *The War Against the Jews* may observe that Hitler had little inclination for a Jewish state. Nevertheless, there is substantial discussion of pre-war collaboration between Zionists and Nazis. Quoting the SS publication *Das Schwarze Korps*, Dawidowicz states, "The Zionists adhere to a strict racial position and by emigrating to Palestine they are helping to build their own Jewish state."[16] Later, we read of Reinhard Heydrich's favorable attitude toward Zionist youth activity which "lies in the interest of the National Socialist state's leadership." And again, Zionists believed that "the Gestapo favored them over the non-Zionists."[17] Such passages convey the improper impression that the Zionists' highest priority was creating a state, not saving lives. They are exactly the proofs needed to sustain charges of Jewish collaboration made in a recent PLO documentary narrated, coincidentally, by Vanessa Redgrave. Vigorously phrased caveats are meaningless to propagandists who see more evil in the survivors than the victims of Nazism. Miller and Dawidowicz did not foresee that their writings could be appropriated.

Scholars have tried to explain the utter despair which robbed Jews of the thought of existence during the Holocaust—a two thousand-year tradition of pacifism, devout belief in the intervention of God, faith in the twentieth century and the decency of German civilization, the impact of starvation and disease, the lack of weapons or support from Christian countrymen, concern for families, the invention of a language of deception, and the success of Nazi terror tactics— but unfortunately many people remember only that Jews went to their deaths like sheep. Thus while Bruno Bettelheim mentions that active resistance was suicidal, a more lasting, negative impression of Jewish passivity comes from such statements of his as: " . . . prisoners knew they were destined to die and still made almost no effort to revolt"; " . . . people submitted to extermination because SS methods had forced them to see it not as a way out, but as the only way to put an end to conditions in which they could no longer live as human beings"; "It may have been Jewish acceptance, without fight, of ever harsher discrimination and degradation that first gave the SS the idea that they could be gotten to the point where they would walk to the gas chambers on their own"; "Millions could have marched as free men against the SS rather than to first grovel, then wait to be rounded up for their own extermination and finally walk themselves to the gas chambers"; and "Why then did millions walk quietly without resistance to their death?" Bettelheim displays more understanding of citizens of Dachau and Weimar who psychologically blocked out knowledge of the nearby camps than the "antlike creatures" who "dug their own graves and laid themselves into them or walked on their own to the gas chambers."[18]

Another scholar accused of likening Jews to animals drawn to the slaughter was Hannah Arendt. Her *Eichmann in Jerusalem* (1963) was intended to be a critique of what some regarded as an unworthy show trial for and by Israelis. In her analysis, Arendt noted that diaspora Jews "had degenerated until they went to their death like sheep."[19] Arendt intended this to be the view of the Ben-Gurion government which wanted to contrast the activist strength of Israel with the submissive meekness or ghetto mentality of European Jews. Correctly, she pointed out that no non-Jewish group succeeded before the SS system.[20] In a bitter postscript to the first edition, Arendt found it necessary to defend herself against charges that she was guilty of self-hatred or had suggested Jewish victims facilitated genocide with a collective death wish.[21]

Arendt recognized the danger of inadvertent innuendo, the propensity of readers to project into writings what they wanted to believe. Every author runs the risk of having his words taken out of context. All the more reason that anyone who engages in Holocaust studies should be aware of his supreme obligation to exactitude and specificity. The survivor who relies upon personal recall for his information, the European who may not yet have acquired a dexterity with the English language may be excused; not so those American scholars who stumble in the manner noted.

Few, if any, of these writers thought they were tarnishing the memory of the six million. Their affection for Zionism may be another thing. The Jews who perished in the Holocaust and their surviving brethren possess no special aura of sainthood. Neither, however, do they merit censure.

THE SIX MAJOR TEXTS

Students of the Holocaust should be wary of bias, condescension, tendentiousness, banality, limited source materials, accidental error, deliberate misstatement of fact, cynicism, and *argumentum ad horrendum*. As a rule, the six principal texts authored by Reitlinger, Poliakov, Hilberg, Levin, Dawidowicz, and Bauer avoid most of these editorial pitfalls. Each has been commended in its time as "painstaking research," "masterful," "extraordinary," or "rounded narrative," and acclaimed "likely to become the standard work."[22]

However, a random comparison of the treatment of several fundamentally important topics reveals major discrepancies in historiography among the six books. The subjects examined included Auschwitz and other killing centers, the "paradise ghetto" of Terezin, Vilna Jewry, and Jews in Vichy France.

1. Death Camps

Whether the author has used the title "The Annihilation Camps: Kingdom of Death," "Gas Chambers," "Industry of Death," "The Final Solution," "Concentration and Death Camps," or "Killing Center Operations," each author invariably devotes a chapter of twenty to thirty pages to the major extermination centers.[23] The most comprehensive study offered is that of Hilberg, which tracks the development of the Nazi concentration camp system from the days when Theodor Eicke served as the first commandant of Dachau through the liberation of Belsen. In the process, Hilberg supplies his readers with bureaucratic charts ("the conveyer belt"), neologisms which cloaked Nazi mass murder, glimpses of camp life (enfeebling diet, forced labor at I. G. Farben plants and coal mines, fear which prevented inmates from turning on their guards, the vain self-deception that governed actions of the *Sonderkommandos*), statistics on clothes and other confiscated property shipped back to Germany for Winter Relief, a brutal, yet necessary, listing of medical experiments conducted by Drs. Mengele, Wirth, Clauberg, Kremer, and others, and the legend of soap-making factories. Like

Reitlinger, Poliakov, Levin, and Bauer, Hilberg explains how the Nazis explored a number of techniques before deciding upon gas as the most efficient solution to Europe's Jewish Question.

The only work which may be labeled inadequate in this respect is Dawidowicz's. For whatever reason, the author devotes more space to the conflict about extermination or retention of Jewish slave labor than to the operations of Auschwitz, Belzec, Maidanek, Treblinka, Chelmno, and Sobibor. The reader of *The War Against the Jews* is taken to the gates of the killing centers but, with the exception of a two-page excerpt, is left to his own resources.[24] As for what happened in Belsen, there are two undeveloped references.[25]

2. Terezin

Nora Levin's *Holocaust* contains a superb section on the transit camp outside Prague which processed 140,000 Jews in World War II.[26] The reader learns how the Germans converted this eighteenth-century Austrian fortress (dubbed *Schlamperei*) to their needs. In controlled but gripping prose Levin tells the story of 15,000 children who left drawings, poetry, and diaries expressing "what was gone, what they could no longer have." She tells of the courage of artists Bedrich "Fritta" Taussig, Karel Fleischmann, and Otto Ungar, of musical performances in attics that doubled as cafes, of visits by representatives of the International Red Cross to Hitler's model ghetto. We learn how Dr. Leo Baeck, once Germany's leading rabbi, realized in 1942 where the trains were going and declined to inform his comrades because "living in the expectation of death by gassing would only be the harder."[27] Reitlinger, Hilberg, and Bauer also find the Terezin story compelling, Poliakov less so.[28] For Dawidowicz, however, a single paragraph dismissing the ghetto as a "Potemkin village" suffices.[29]

3. Vilna

Here, Dawidowicz's book is more complete than others. Whereas Reitlinger, Poliakov, and Hilberg accord the Vilna ghetto no special treatment, Dawidowicz is extremely thorough.[30] She gives both population and dimensions, telling of the brutality of *Einsatz* groups at Ponary and the subsequent travesty of different colored work permits, condemning the mendacity of *Judenrat* chairman Jacob Gens, linking Vilna's *yeshivot*, *mikvehs*, and orchestras with cultural efforts in Warsaw, and telling of resistance spearheaded by Itzik Wittenberg.[31] The problem with Dawidowicz's approach, like that of Yehuda Bauer, is that it takes the form of a scatter gun, leaving the novice with confusing, unconnected bits of information which are not necessarily in chronological sequence.[32] Far preferable is Nora Levin's evaluation of Vilna, which details what happened at the slaughterground of Ponary, gives us a more substantial glimpse of resistance operations of the Bielsky brothers, *Nekomah* (Vengeance), and Wittenberg's United Partisan Organization, and does so in eight compact pages.[33]

4. Vichy France

Finally, there is the matter of Vichy France. With the exception of Dawidowicz, there is methodological agreement among the principal Holocaust scholars. The subject deserves and receives a full chapter of analysis ranging from Bauer's scant ten pages to more than thirty in Hilberg's *Destruction of the European Jews*.[34] Each of these scholars drew from a common pool of sources—Zosa Szajkowski, George Wellers, the International Military Tribunal, the *Centre de Documentation Juive Contemporaine*—adding (in the case of Hilberg) reports of the German General Staff, documents of the U.S. State Department, a memoir by onetime Chief Rabbi of France Jacob Kaplan, and, in the case of Levin, works by Donald Lowrie, Pierre Laval, Philip Friedman, Zamuel Diamant, and David Knout. Hilberg's study of French Jews contains 133 citations, that of Reitlinger, 85. How different from Dawidowicz, who offers no chapter, merely a five-page précis in an appendix.[35] Her bibliography for "The Fate of the Jews in Hitler's Europe by Country" consists of fifteen works, only three of which bear directly on France. Her summary of France contains not a single footnote.

More complete citation may seem unnecessary to one who disdains specifying references to *Mein Kampf* "because of the extensive use of this book and also Hitler's *Secret Book*," but it is poor methodology.[36] *The War Against the Jews* received the greatest acclaim of any of the six texts, and was written from a calm perspective of thirty years when records were available, but it proves to be the least satisfactory. It might be argued that such a conclusion is premature, that the lapses noted are anomalous, and that four different topics (Teutomania, the structure of the SS, the world's indifference to Jewish refugees, the saga of Denmark) might yield different results. Yet these findings are sustained by analysis of each of the major texts on their own merits.

The Final Solution

Reitlinger's *The Final Solution* departs from the normal outline favored by the others in that it offers practically no historical background on the causes of anti-Semitism. Following a superficial examination of the Nuremberg Laws and *Kristallnacht*, the reader is taken with invading German armies into Poland in September, 1939.[37] Thereafter, Reitlinger combines a chronological-conceptual approach which is relatively easy to follow.

The major weakness of the original work was its age. When Reitlinger wrote, the whereabouts of Adolf Eichmann and *Einsatzgruppe A* leader Herbert Cukurs (both since executed) were unknown. Otto Skorzeny (dead in 1982), Hitler's favorite giant storm trooper, was in Spain, bragging about his wartime feats; Erich Koch, Gauleiter of East Prussia, was awaiting trial, and there was only a brief mention of "SS Lt. Doctor Mengele." A stickler for semantics, Reitlinger stumbled when he referred to Herschel Grynszpan as a youth who had "brought such misfortune on his race."[38] He also waged a losing battle in favor of the term *Vernichtung* (annihilation) instead of the "hybrid" genocide which "says nothing which cannot be conveyed in plain speech."[39]

These are small problems. Overall, Reitlinger established standards which others emulated. His character analyses of Heinrich Himmler; Reinhard Heydrich, "the real engineer of the Final Solution"; Hans Frank, the schizophrenic Catholic Nazi who ruled Poland's Government General; and Adolf Eichmann, "the painstaking bureaucrat . . . absorbed in his work and getting no glory from it," may have inspired Nora Levin's character sketches in *The Holocaust.*[40] Long before Hannah Arendt developed her thesis on the banality of evil, Reitlinger was speaking of bureaucrats who, though "no more cruel and callous than the human race as a whole," found it necessary to "invent a mumbo-jumbo language . . . to hide from themselves what they were doing."[41] His portrayal of Goering's opposition to *Kristallnacht* (for fear of what the pogrom might mean to German trade), his belief that the Nazis intended to ship Jews off to Madagascar before the invasion of Russia made such plans obsolete, accord with the idea posed by Karl Schluenes that the Nazi road zigzagged to the death camp.[42] Raul Hilberg followed his pattern of listing war criminals at large, and Lucy Dawidowicz may have modelled her country-by-country appendix after a similar one found in Reitlinger.[43]

Unlike Dawidowicz, however, Reitlinger devotes major portions of his text to subjects which are little more than asides in *The War Against the Jews*. The reader of Reitlinger's thirty-year-old book can learn in depth what happened in France, Holland, Denmark, Norway, Italy, Croatia, Slovakia. Reitlinger was among the first to acknowledge the importance of Raul Wallenberg, the Swedish diplomat "of immense courage" who rescued Jews in Budapest in 1944–1945. Reitlinger distinguishes between Jewish councils in Galicia which expedited the deportations and the UGIF in France which resisted. Reitlinger attempts to reconcile those who regarded the Warsaw Ghetto uprising of 1943 as the first Jewish resistance since Bar Kochba with others who likened it to a limited anti-partisan action. No frontline troops were diverted, he notes, and no Polish populace rose to stop the massacre of the Jews. Yet he shows that the Nazis were genuinely surprised by the fight waged by the Jews, so much so that casualties reported may have been deliberately understated "to please Himmler."[44]

Reitlinger also addresses a warning to those with limited memories. From Beckley, Sussex, in November, 1952, he wrote: "Time has been the friend of the war criminal, for the public sense of fair play is offended by charges which it takes years to produce."[45] Recent controversies swirling about the alleged "persecution" of accused war criminals residing in the West have shown Reitlinger to be correct in this and may other respects.

Harvest of Hate

Leon Poliakov's *Harvest of Hate* is so similar in style and structure to *The Final Solution* that it is difficult to separate them. The two appeared about the same time, Poliakov's French version, *Brevaire de la haine*, antedating Reitlinger by two years.[46] Both are terse on pre-war antecedents of Nazism (Poliakov hastening to "the crucial month of November, 1938" in the first fifteen pages of text). This is all the more surprising since Poliakov, one of the founders of the Jewish Documentation Center in Paris, has published a four-volume study on the root causes of anti-Semitism. His *Aryan Myth* (1971) is one of the best expositions of pseudo-scientific racism.[47] Lamentably, little of this appears in the first chapters of *Harvest of Hate*.

Like Reitlinger, Poliakov takes Nazi discussions of the mass transfer of Jews to Madagascar seriously.[48] Like Reitlinger, he assesses the personality of Heinrich Himmler. Only his analysis of "the model inquisitor" is more extensive, with glimpses of Himmler's curiosity about the Rosicrucian brotherhood and the Irish harp, his interest in new sterilization techniques, whether by x-ray or the Brazilian plant *Caladium senguinum*.[49] Again, like Reitlinger, Poliakov traces at length the Warsaw Ghetto rebellion and concludes its importance was chiefly symbolic. Though scholars continue to debate how many German troops lost their lives or were wounded in this struggle, Poliakov states this is of secondary importance. "The epic of the Warsaw ghetto," he writes, "will not live in the memory of man just because of the number of German losses."[50]

Two scholars working in different languages in separate lands yielding similar results may be less a marvel than a testimony to sound scholarship. This is not to suggest that Reitlinger and Poliakov merely duplicate one another. There are places where Poliakov is more complete than Reitlinger. Much like Nora Levin, he incorporates major portions of reports, diaries, and other documents into the narrative.

In a dramatic chapter, titled "Responsibility," Poliakov assesses the behavior of the German people, 90 percent of whom he says were indifferent to Hitler's racial policies, but most of whom were swept up in "morbid rationalization and nationalistic exaltation."[51] He contrasts the attitudes of peoples in Eastern and Western Europe, arguing that with rare exceptions, like the Ukrainian Metropolitan Szepticki, Eastern Europeans generally supported the Nazis' policies toward the Jews. Such an attitude was especially ironic, for Poliakov demonstrates that the Nazis intended to continue "purifying" Europe through kidnapping, sterilization, shooting, and the use of *Zyklon B* against Gypsies, Poles, Slavs, and Russians until all such "inferior" people were either enslaved or exterminated.[52] *Harvest of Hate* is especially useful, for it explodes the myth that the Holocaust is solely a Jewish problem. At the same time, it emphasizes the centrality of Israel in the destiny of the Jewish people.

The Destruction of the European Jews

Of the six major Holocaust texts, the one that has elicited the greatest outcry is Raul Hilberg's *The Destruction of the European Jews*. A revised edition has been published in 1985, but for the sake of this analysis all references are to the version which has been in print for the past quarter-century.[53]

Just as Reitlinger and Poliakov, Hilberg tells the story of the final days of the Warsaw Ghetto, but in a manner that infuriates some of his critics.[54] Where Reitlinger qualified German losses, which were probably higher than sixteen dead and some ninety wounded (and nowhere near the thousands estimated by the American Council of Warsaw Jews), Hilberg recites Jurgen Stroop's figures as fact. Where Albert Nirenstein, Philip Friedman, and others estimated the number of active Jewish fighters at no more than several hundred pitted against several thousand *Waffen* SS and auxiliaries, Hilberg maintains the *ZOB* (Jewish Fighting Organization) numbered 1,500, a fair challenge to 2,000–3,000 lightly armed training and replacement batallions.[55]

For Hilberg, "the documentary evidence of Jewish resistance, overt or submerged, is very slight."[56] When Jews were being ghettoized, "the system induced [them] to be even more docile, more responsive to command than before."[57] According to documents from the Reich's Main Security Office, with few exceptions "Jews allowed themselves to be shot without resistance" during the operations of the mobile killing squads in 1941.[58] Later, after Jews had been deported to death camps, SS General Erich von dem Bach-Zelewsky would declare that "millions" could have been saved had they been forewarned, better organized, or determined to abandon their homes and businesses and flee eastward across the Bug River. Instead, dulled by a Jewish administrative machine which operated as a tool for destruction, they "walked back to their undoing."[59]

For its overreliance upon German sources and tone evocative of the "Jewish sheep" canard, *The Destruction of the European Jews* has been lacerated by Nathan Eck as bordering on slander.[60] Such judgment is too harsh. Hilberg's work may be faulted for several things (ponderous prose, a confusing list of principals, even its cavalier treatment of Jewish resistance), but it is an extremely useful document, thorough almost to the point of punctiliousness. Just as Reitlinger and Poliakov, Hilberg was an innovator. His discussion of Holocaust antecedents (comparing medieval church decrees with Nazi legislation, the teachings of Martin Luther or Karl Ahlwardt with twentieth-century Nazis) may be brief, but established a model for Levin, Dawidowicz, and Bauer to follow.[61] Hilberg was among the first to point out the low priority which the Allies placed upon rescue of captive populations. We may read of the wire issued by World Jewish Congress representative Gerhart Riegner in August 1942, advising Stephen Wise of the Nazi extermination plan, of Treasury Secretary Henry Morgenthau's pressure for the creation of a War Refugee Board, Joel Brand's futile negotiations with Eichmann to exchange Hungarian Jews for trucks, British concern over Jewish immigration into Palestine, and UNRRA discrimination against Jewish displaced persons.[62] Hilberg also revealed how denazification had become a sham by 1950, what with the Cold War, escapes managed by comrades of accused war criminals, and the disinclination of peacetime soldiers to prosecute what appeared to be friendly peoples.[63]

Above all, Hilberg attempts to understand the killing process, both through the actions of the killers and the responses of the victims. German troops were instructed that Jews were criminals whose property belonged to the Reich. To reinforce the legality of their operations, "unauthorized" killings were prohibited. So, too, any criticism or discussion of the mass murders. Like Arendt and Stanley Milgram, Hilberg noted that the Nazis were forced to invent a new, sanitary language to distance themselves from their deeds. Bureaucrats functioned out of duty, not malice, "shifting blame to the next level." Their actions were justified by the knowledge that others were doing the same task, still others doing more.[64]

Most illuminating is Hilberg's "Jewish reaction pattern," a continuum outlining potential responses to force. Not once, but twice, does he discuss the options available to ghettoized Jews.[65] These consisted of alleviaiton (attemps to reason with an irrational foe), evasion (running away to woods, joining partisans, going to the Aryan side of a city), compliance (including anticipatory compliance, not unlike Bettelheim's "childlike behavior"), paralysis (seen in many ghetto residents who simply abandoned hope and volunteered themselves at deportation staging centers), and resistance. Though he may have characterized the amount of Jewish resistance as "very slight," Hilberg was not as crass as some of his critics would have been. When he wrote his book, much of the evidence of Jewish partisan activity in Minsk, Lachwa, Horodenka, Czestochowa, Kolyczewo, Sobibor, and Auschwitz was being withheld behind the Iron Curtain. Nevertheless, Hilberg attempted to account for what he perceived to be a dearth of Jewish militancy by listing a number of factors: 2,000 years of persecution where Jews "deliberately unlearned the art of revolt," German exploitation of Jewish wishful thinking and ignorance about the deportations, the impact of whips and beatings upon families with babes, and nakedness which benumbed the thought of resistance.[66]

In retrospect and in fairness, *The Destruction of the European Jews* is a much better book than some critics will allow. In its original form, it may be used with discretion. Hilberg's current, three-volume revision includes materials unavailable in the late 1950's (some of his in-depth studies of the workings of the railroads in the killing process, declassified American and British government files, recent trials of war criminals) and reflects the high level of scholarship manifest throughout his first edition.

The War Against the Jews

"The most complete, the most authoritative, the most nearly definitive" book ever written on the subject of the destruction of the Jews is how the jacket proclaims Lucy Dawidowicz's *The War Against the Jews*, and indeed, no book on the Holocaust has elicited more acclaim. Yet there are weaknesses that demand our attention.

First, there are omissions and slightings, of a kind noted previously—the glancing references to Terezin or Jews of France. In its simplest form, an omission may read: "The man who succeeded [Adam] Czerniakow was nothing more than a faceless tool of the Germans."[67] The reader is left without any reference to Marek Lichtenbaum, who presided over the Warsaw *Judenrat* in its last days, apparently because the author felt such information was trivial. In another form of omission, Dawidowicz notes how Baltic-born Alfred Rosenberg elaborated the Nazi ideology, but offers little background on Tsarist policies which paved the way for Eastern-European anti-Semitism other than a brief mention of the *Protocols of the Elders of Zion*.[68] Dawidowicz merits commendation for raising the spectres of Ernst Arndt, Johann Fichte, Friedrich Jahn, Friedrich Rühs, Paul de LaGarde, Wilhelm Marr, Heinrich Treitschke, Arthur de Gobineau, and Richard Wagner.[69] There is no citation in her survey of nineteenth-century racists, however, and of important critical works of Peter Viereck, Peter Pulzer, and Leon Poliakov.[70]

On occasion, Dawidowicz repeats herself. There is little difference, save in length, between her initial treatment of the Nuremberg racial laws and a later, page-long discussion of the same edicts.[71] In like manner, the reader is twice told how Hitler warned on January 30, 1939, that the outbreak of war would result not in the Bolshevization of the world but "the destruction of the Jewish race in Europe."[72]

Dawidowicz's work is marred by structural faults and lengthy asides which intrude upon the narrative. Not until chapter 4, after study of Hitler's seizure of power, beatings and boycotts administered by the Brownshirts, the purge of Ernst Rohm and the SA, and enactment of the racial laws, is there discussion of the SS, Gestapo, and concentration camp system.[73] Later, following the incomplete chapter on the death camps, and before her analysis of life in the ghettos, Dawidowicz interjects a philosophical section ("A Retrospective View") which contains the distasteful and illegitimate title of the book.[74] It is an unnecessary and awkward presentation.

Dawidowicz's apodictic statements make her vulnerable to criticism. With certainty, she posits *Kristallnacht* as "Goebbels' pogrom."[75] Rita Thalmann and Emmanuel Feinermann allocate responsibility among Himmler, Heydrich, Muller, and Goebbels, all of whom were responding to Hitler's desire to give the SA a last fling before the onset of war.[76] The efforts of famed Austrian surgeon Heinrich Neumann to convince delegates at the Evian Refugee Conference in June 1983 to ransom Jews at $250 a head are dismissed as "pure fantasy," though recounted by several credible authorities.[77] The Madagascar scheme, too, is sloughed off. While Wiesenthal, Reitlinger, Poliakov, Hilberg, and others concede it was a momentary plan, Dawidowicz writes, "everything we know of National Socialist ideology precludes our accepting the idea of a Jewish reservation as the last stage of the Final Solution."[78]

This brings us to one of the major problems with *The War Against the Jews*— its inability to countenance another point of view. The purpose of the misplaced chapter, "A Retrospective View," is to drive home the point that genocide was not merely a tenet of Nazism, but the *essential* tenet of Nazism. When, following the Reichstag Fire of February 1933, the Enabling Act gave dictatorial powers to Hitler, "the question uppermost in his mind concerned the Jews."[79] Other scholars allow that the period known as the *Gleichschaltung* was taken up with the suppression of Communists, Social Democrats, labor leaders, intellectuals, the churches, the SA; that for five years at least the Nazis were committed primarily to the ouster of Jews from the *Lebensgebiete* (economic life) or *Lebensraum* (living space) of Germany; that even during wartime there was no absolute commitment to extermination given the prospects for an armistice with or victory over Britain in 1940–1941. Not so Dawidowicz. For her, there was no twisted road to Auschwitz. When Hitler spoke in 1919 of the *Entfernung* (removal) of Jews, he really meant massacre as "the destruction of Jews was not just a matter of words."[80] At the center of *Mein Kampf* is "the war against the Jews," a strange and perverted conflict where the Jewish participants, unarmed and helpless, did not even know they were belligerents.

Usually when one finishes a book on the Holocaust, there is a feeling of despair mixed with sympathy. *The War Against the Jews* does not answer a number of nagging questions. What was the role of the aged President Hindenburg during the initial persecution of Jews? What difficulties did the Nazis encounter in defining Jewish businesses in 1933? What prompted thousands of Jews to *return* to Germany in 1934? Why were Jews so disorganized, disunited in adversity? Why were spokesmen for the socialist *Bund*, rabbis, and historians, so naive about what might happen to Jews assembled in the ghettos? What prevented leaders from seeking better communication with other ghettos, sending individuals out sooner to discover the truth about the camps? Why did people who managed hand-to-hand resistance in 1940 wait until the summer of 1942 to secure firearms? Dawidowicz barely addresses any of these questions or one she phrases herself: "How was it possible for the world to stand by without halting this destruction?"[81]

One question which *The War Against the Jews* tries to answer is "How was it possible for a whole people to allow itself to be destroyed?"[82] Like the title of the book, the very framing of the question—"allow itself"—is perplexing. Still, Dawidowicz does attempt an answer in a concluding chapter titled "Jewish Behavior in Crisis and Extremity." Patterned after Raul Hilberg's summary, this chapter lacks Hilberg's sensitivity, perception, and clarity. It offers such truisms as "The Final Solution was a new phenomenon in human history" and "all are guilty, or perhaps more truly, all are innocent and holy."[83] It invokes suppositional history, suggesting that the Holocaust might not have happened had Hitler died or been assassinated.[84] It offers the metaphor of a lifeboat which cannot hold all the passengers of a sinking ship.[85] It waxes profound about "existential guilt."[86] Then, without taking us into the concentration camps, without satisfactory answers to any of the three major moral and passionate questions raised at the beginning of the essay, the text abruptly ends. In short, *The War Against the Jews* is old ground, plowed poorly.

A History of the Holocaust

Yehuda Bauer's *A History of the Holocaust* also is problematic. Its organization is sound (tracing the origins of the Jewish people and anti-Semitism through the now familiar evolution of Nazi genocide). Bauer makes extensive use of Martin Gilbert's maps, probes various aspects of rescue and resistance, and discusses Holocaust theodicy. These, however, are more than outweighed by lacunae and instances of faulty reasoning. Like Dawidowicz (whom he cites frequently), Bauer does not feel compelled to inform readers about all of his sources. Speaking of the massive pogroms which occurred in the Ukraine between 1919 and 1921, Bauer estimates 70–100,000 Jewish dead (the actual count was closer to 150,000), but offers no citation.[87] We learn that there are several theories concerning the origin of the Reichstag Fire, but again obtain no reference to this scholarship.[88] Isaiah Trunk's monumental work on the Jewish Councils of Eastern Europe is listed in the bibliography, but while Bauer cites Hilberg, Yisrael Gutman, Aharon Weiss, and himself, there is no mention of Trunk in sections titled "The Jewish Councils—the *Judenraete*," "Life in the Ghettos," or anywhere else in the text.[89]

Many of Bauer's assessments are debatable or puzzling. It is curious to learn that Henri Michel is "perhaps the most important contemporary historian of anti-Nazi resistance."[90] Discerning readers may be befuddled by a selective writing process which devotes as much space to the rescue of Bulgarian Jews as to the intricacies of pre-war American society.[91] Bauer also manages to place himself on all sides of an issue. At one point, he declares, "Nazism was an anti-Christian movement," and supports this contention with reference to the actions of Pope Pius, Cardinal Faulhaber, Pastors Niemoeller and Bonhoeffer.[92] Immediately after, however, he grants that the German churches "never publicly recognized defense of the Jews [as] a Christian duty" and "did not oppose Nazi anti-Semitic policy."[93]

Bauer has been among the most outspoken critics of the Goldberg Commission, dismissing notions of assistance or rescue proffered by members of the Commission. Yet in his own *A History of the Holocaust* he states, "There were, apparently, alternatives," and goes on to suggest that "by negotiation, by bombing, and other means" some Jews and others could have been saved.[94] The "other means" of rescue are not specified.

The most vexatious aspect of Bauer's work is his passage dealing with Holocaust theodicy (where was God? where was man?). Following single-line references to the teachings of Rabbi Joseph Soloveitchik, Rabbi Eliezer Berkovits, Elie Wiesel, Emil Fackenheim, Richard Rubenstein, and Alexander Donat, he calls for "an early warning system" to detect in Western democracies "the signs of totalitarianism, intolerance, and prejudice that breed genocide."[95] Bauer does not explain that such a system may encompass any society which has violent groups committed to paramilitary training, racial animosity, and a "new prioritization of history"; groups which may be organized in secret cells and embrace archaic symbols; those who wear uniforms in public and foster a generation gap; and those who deceive or confuse public opinion by infiltration or subversion of public institutions—in short, practically any free society.[96] Moreover, Bauer and others who subscribe to the notion of such a theoretical grid ignore the basic fact that for the past forty years, the greatest threat of mass murder and totalitarianism has come not from nations which subscribe to free enterprise or right-wing ideologies, but from those of the so-called left.

A History of the Holocaust probably owes much to Bauer's lectures at the Hebrew University in Jerusalem. It is easily readable but offers few new insights and is superfluous as long as Nora Levin's excellent study is available.

The Holocaust

From its opening poetry of death camp survivor Nelly Sachs to its closing images of Jewish DPs huddled at La Spezia, Italy, bent on fulfilling the prophecy of Ezekiel 37, Nora Levin's The Holocaust has its readers galvanized. It is literate and complete, the perfect admixture of fact and reminiscence.

Where else do we obtain in-depth studies of Dr. Wilhelm Filderman and Gisi Fleischmann, who labored tirelessly to save Jews in Rumania and Slovakia?[97] Where, other than in specialized biographies, do we come to understand Hannah Senesh, Emmanuel Ringelblum, Tobias Bielski, Joop Westerweel, or the tormented SS leader Kurt Gerstein, who appealed to the Vatican to intervene on behalf of Europe's doomed Jews?[98] Levin reveals the inept nature of the French general staff, so riddled with the creaky antiquarians Maurice Gamelin, Maxime Weygand, and Henri Petain, that defeatism seemed appealing.[99] Like Hannah Arendt, she provides insight into the character of Adolf Eichmann showing how his celebrated negotiations with Joel Brand were an extension of earlier bribes accepted to spare Austrian Jews' deportation to Dachau.[100] But Levin goes beyond Arendt, Poliakov, or Reitlinger in her portrayal of Nazi leadership. Only in this book does the reader learn of the private motivations of Einsatzgruppe leaders Otto Ohlendorf, Artur Nebe, Otto Rasch, and Ernst Biberstein.[101] Only here do we learn that the 600,000 Serbs who perished in World War II may have been victims of Hitler's violent hatred derived from his youth in Austria.[102] Only here do we learn of Himmler's erratic behavior as the war wound down in the spring of 1945. The SS commander who fantasized he might negotiate an armistice with the Western Allies is portrayed as storming about his headquarters in a gray greatcoat, furious that the same Allies were not grateful to him for "allowing" them to liberate the Belsen and Buchenwald concentration camps.[103]

Levin does not shrink from volatile issues. She makes note of the indifference and hostility of the world to Jewish suffering before, during, and after the Holocaust. In chapters titled "The Year 1938" and "The Struggle to Leave Europe," she discusses the efforts of Jewish self-help organizations like the Hilfsverein der Deutschen Juden (German Jewish Relief Association), the American Joint Distribution Committee, and Aliyah Bet Mossad (Committee for Illegal

Immigration to Palestine) in the face of hypocritical international meetings, whittling away of the Palestine Mandate, and, ultimately, British assaults upon desperate refugee ships like the *Lizel, Dora, Tiger Hill, Pencho, Atlantic,* and *Patricia.*[104]

In her chapter dealing with the Nazi ghetto in Warsaw, she quotes Emanuel Ringelblum's lament: "Does the world know about our suffering, and if it knows, why is it silent?"[105] Subsequently, she notes that "the BBC maintained a complete radio silence" about the deportations of 1942, and adds Shmuel Zygelboim's eloquent suicide letter in which the former *Bund* leader protests against "the passivity with which the world is looking on and permitting the extermination of the Jewish people."[106]

In chapter after chapter, Levin points out how the hostility of different nationalities facilitated the Nazi killing process. Poles, whose society was even more anti-Semitic than pre-Hitler Germany, refused to give much support to the ghetto resistance. France, Bulgaria, Rumania, and Hungary all gave up "foreign" Jews, refugees, or those unfortunate enough to reside in territories acquired through alliance with Germany. What was said of Polish fields and forests, that they were vast and open yet "each bush, each inch of earth, each human heart, would be closed," might be said of all Europe.[107]

Alone among the six major authors, Levin clearly demonstrates that a stupid Marshal Stalin (who deluded himself that he might share in the spoils of Hitler's 1940 triumphs) not only muffled word of Nazi atrocities against Jews, but extended Hitler's anti-Semitic policies in Eastern Europe after the war ended.[108] The Western Allies earn their share of rebuke for dilatory actions on behalf of Jews and Gypsies, as do humanitarian agencies like the International Red Cross and the Vatican.[109] Levin confirms Rolf Hochhuth's sensational drama, *The Deputy,* noting that the Vatican assured Vichy officials in 1942 it had no intention of interfering with anti-Semitic legislation in France, noting moreover that the Vatican was primarily concerned with the treatment of converts in Slovakia and Hungary. Although the Vatican possessed vast amounts of information on the killing process in the spring of 1943, it remained mute, even when the Nazis attempted a roundup of 8,000 Jews in Rome in November, 1943. Levin contrasts the silence of Pope Pius on gassing with earlier condemnations of Germany's attack on the Low Countries and Russia's attack on Finland and asks rhetorically whether a John XXIII or Pius VI would have remained silent.[110]

Early on, Levin devotes a lengthy section to the Gestapo, *Sicherheitsdienst,* and SS, the primary forces in "the apparatus of terror."[111] At the same time, she does not ignore the role of the *Waffen* SS and *Wehrmacht* in the killing process. Whereas veterans of thirty combat SS divisions (which allegedly fought on the battlefields of Eastern Europe) have been partially successful in rehabilitating their post-war reputations, few have ever questioned the behavior of the regular German army.[112] When President Ronald Reagan visited Bitburg in the spring of 1985, he and General Matthew Ridgway were accompanied by former

Wehrmacht General Johannes Steinhoff. Levin not only documents atrocities committed by SS killing squads during the *Blizpogrom*, she also reminds us that the *Wehrmacht* enthusiastically suppported Hitler's invasion of Poland, "did not, apparently, oppose the wiping out of Jews and certain classes of Poles, but wanted to avoid blame," and participated in the destruction of the Warsaw Ghetto during the spring of 1943.[113]

What happened in Poland was typical of the *Wehrmacht's* performance everywhere. In France, the military commander Heinrich von Stulpnagel, lionized for his role in the 1944 assassination plot against Hitler, was "a great believer in the deterrent power of shooting hostages and executed thousands."[114] His kinsman, General Otto von Stulpnagel, instituted Aryanization of Jewish businesses, imposed a billion franc fine against the Jewish community in 1941, and was responsible for the deportation of the first 1,000 Jews to Auschwitz in March, 1942.[115] Some 60,000 Jews were deported from Athens, Salonika, Corfu, and Rhodes during World War II. Only a handful returned. The military commander for the Aegean, Lieutenant General Ulrich Kleeman, banned any discussion of such movements, while the *Wehrmacht* made temporary use of Jewish slave labor in Greece.[116] When the Nazis struck into Yugoslavia in the summer of 1941, they instituted the principle of shooting 50–100 civilians for every soldier slain by partisans. When a troop convoy was attacked in October, 1941, 2,100 Jews and Gypsies were murdered in retaliation. In several instances, executions took the form of public lynchings. Although *Einsatzgruppe* units screened the victims, Professor Levin adds that "the shooting was done by Army troops."[117]

The Holocaust is an emotionally draining book which cannot be read in great passages. It is impossible to read the chapter dealing with Heydrich's order of September 21, 1939, which created the *Judenräte* without agonizing with those deportees who were shunted in subzero temperatures to regions where, the Nazis taunted, there were no houses, no water, only "cholera, dysentery, and typhoid."[118] Equally moving is the chapter on Rumanian Jews, detailing the butchery perpetrated by Iron Guardists in Bucharest and Jassy in 1940–1941, the operations of camps like Bogdanovka (which Levin terms the most appalling in Europe), the cruel disaster of the *SS Struma* (turned away from freedom only to sink with 760 passengers in the Black Sea in February, 1942), Ion Antonescu's half-hearted negotiations with Ira Hirschmann to save Jews that Antonescu really detested, and the irony of Russian soldiers pogromizing Jewish survivors in Transnistria as the war came to an end.[119]

The book's scope is large—Germany's pre-war psyche; the failure of Weimar; Adolf Hitler's family history; testimony of Zindel Grynszpan at the Eichmann trial; the Madagascar Plan; diaries of ghetto survivors and the dead telling of "snatchers and catchers"; partisan resistance; Jan Karski's meeting with the doomed leaders of Warsaw; factors in mitigation of armed resistance; the transition from euthanasia centers to death camps; rescue in Denmark; the mockery that was the Bermuda Refugee Conference of 1943; seventy pages telling of

Hungarian Jewry through the regimes of Bela Kun, Paul Telecki, Nicholas Kallay and the Arrow Cross; and the performance by a handful of survivors in Berlin in 1945 of Gotthold Lessing's "Nathan the Wise."

CONCLUSION

More than seventy years ago, the great Yiddish writer I. L. Peretz declared: "Our program is education. We want to educate our people. We want to transform fools into sages, fanatics into enlightened human beings, idlers into useful, decent workers, who live by labor and thereby benefit the entire community."[120]

Holocaust history should at least fulfill John Hersey's criteria for what constitutes edifying literature—a search for understanding, a desire for communication, controlled anger which stems from social protest, and a will for world citizenship.[121] These are also the goals of legitimate history.

Though some would have it otherwise, the field of Holocaust studies is in its infancy. Despite the flow of an inestimable number of publications, much remains to be done. Ukrainian and Baltic participation in the killing process, Russian collaboration, Arab complicity, and Latin American disinterest remain to be investigated. Long after the last inmate of Auschwitz has gone, scholars and propagandists will be drawing their own inferences from what happened in Europe between 1933 and 1945. Some of these, as noted above, will be inaccurate, redundant, clumsily drawn, or superficial. All the more reason that writers, reviewers, and educators concern themselves with content and not reputation. Judicious use of some of the books mentioned may help achieve the goals of history. Otherwise, we shall witness more instances of the Holocaust tragedy being manipulated against the victims.

NOTES

1. The Library of Congress's computerized catalogue, in place since 1968, is of little help in determining the number of Holocaust publications. According to one reference librarian polled June 13, 1985, the Library lists only thirty-nine titles under "Holocaust." It is all the more remarkable since Jacob Robinson, Mrs. Philip Friedman, and others have compiled eleven additional volumes of Holocaust bibliography since 1960.

2. Emil Fackenheim, *The Jewish Return into History*, p. 27.

3. Based in Torrance, California, the Institute for Historical Review (IHR) publishes a specious journal and holds periodic conferences where individuals with suspect credentials denounce the veracity of the Holocaust. When the IHR, which is rooted in the old anti-Semitic right, first appeared in 1980, the American Historical Association was in the forefront of its critics.

4. What constitutes a text may be a subjective decision. The only other books which might fall into this category are Judah Pilch's *Jewish Catastrophe in Europe* (1968) and Paul Massing's *Rehearsal for Destruction* (1949). To the best of my knowledge, neither is used extensively in classrooms.

5. John Hersey, "The Novel of Contemporary History," pp. 25–27.

6. Livy, *The War with Hannibal*, p. 419.

7. Emil Fackenheim, "*Yom ha-Shoah* Memorial Speech", Youngstown, May 3, 1981, and Alexander Donat, "Like Sheep to the Slaughter," p. 67, respectively.

8. Sam and Nadja Eilenberg were among 500 Lodzer Jews who came to Dresden under the care of Hans Biebow in the last days of the war. Forced to work in supposedly non-existent arms factories, they were denied access to bomb shelters during the fire-bombing and cheered as the city was destroyed. See Saul S. Friedman, *Amcha*, pp. 121–123.

9. Terrence Des Pres, *The Survivor*, p. 114.

10. Anatole France, *Penguin Island*, p. 157.

11. Bernard Wasserstein, *Britain and the Jews of Europe*, pp. 306–320.

12. Ibid., p. 357.

13. *American Jewry during the Holocaust*, ed. Arthur Goldberg and Seymour Finger.

14. See Lucy Dawidowicz, "Indicting American Jews," pp. 41–44; and Yehuda Bauer, "The Goldberg Report," pp. 25–28.

15. Arthur Miller, *Incident at Vichy*, p. 105.

16. Lucy Dawidowicz, *The War Against the Jews*, p. 84.

17. Ibid., pp. 191–192.

18. Bruno Bettelheim, *The Informed Heart*, pp. 243, 245–246, 253, 257, 258, 291, respectively.

19. Hannah Arendt, *Eichmann in Jerusalem*, p. 10.

20. Ibid., pp. 11 and 283.

21. Ibid., pp. 283–284.

22. Hugh Trevor-Roper labeled Hilberg's work "a massive, important study," a judgment echoed by Jabob Robinson and the *Christian Science Monitor*. Henry Friedlander called Poliakov's *Harvest of Hate* "undoubtedly the best introductory text" on the Holocaust. Robert Alter, Rena Fowler, and Dorothy Rabinowitz all saluted Dawidowicz's *The War Against the Jews*, with Irving Howe going so far as to tell readers of the *New York Times* that her "severely controlled narrative" supplied the first, full account of the Holocaust. Subsequently, *Choice* praised Bauer's "masterful" treatment and *Christianity Today* predicted that it would replace "the standard work" (Dawidowicz). Far more legitimate was L. L. Snyder's evaluation of Levin's *Holocaust*. Writing for *The Saturday Review*, 50 (March 9, 1968), Snyder declared, "This is the way history should be written—carefully planned, painstakingly researched, skillfully organized, written with clarity, and documented."

23. Gerald Reitlinger, *The Final Solution*, pp. 123–154; Leon Poliakov, *Harvest of Hate*, pp. 182–223; Raul Hilberg, *The Destruction of the European Jews*, pp. 555–635; Nora Levin, *The Holocaust*, pp. 290–316; Dawidowicz, *The War Against the Jews*, pp. 129–149; and Yehuda Bauer, *A History of the Holocaust*, pp. 207–226.

24. Dawidowicz, *The War Against the Jews*, pp. 148–149.

25. Ibid., p. 340.

26. Levin, *The Holocaust*, pp. 476–493.

27. Ibid., p. 486.

28. Reitlinger, *The Final Solution*, pp. 165–173; Poliakov, *Harvest of Hate*, pp. 106–107; Hilberg, *The Destruction of the European Jews*, pp. 277–284; and Bauer, *A History of the Holocaust*, pp. 189–191.

29. Dawidowicz, *The War Against the Jews*, p. 137.

30. Reitlinger, *The Final Solution*, pp. 54, 65, 131, 214–216, 289–290; Poliakov,

Harvest of Hate, pp. 106 and 231; and Hilberg, *The Destruction of the European Jews*, pp. 252–254, 668.

31. Dawidowicz, *The War Against the Jews*, pp. 128, 140, 198, 201, 207–208, 237–241, 249–251, 253–259, 279, 285–289, 295, 326–327, 348, 427.

32. Bauer, *A History of the Holocaust*, pp. 160–163, 178–180, 183, 198, 200, 250, 270, 303, 326, 340.

33. Levin, *The Holocaust*, pp. 372–380.

34. Reitlinger, *The Final Solution*, pp. 305–326; Poliakov, *Harvest of Hate*, pp. 168–181; Hilberg *The Destruction of the European Jews*, pp. 389–421; Levin, *The Holocaust*, pp. 423–458; and Bauer, *A History of the Holocaust*, pp. 227–236.

35. Dawidowicz, *The War Against the Jews*, pp. 359–363.

36. Ibid., p. 405.

37. Reitlinger, *The Final Solution*, pp. 3–22.

38. Ibid., p. 31.

39. Ibid., p. 8.

40. For these character analyses of Himmler, Heydrich, Frank, and Eichmann, see pp. 5–6, 13, 22–31, 38, and 25–27 in *The Final Solution*.

41. Ibid., pp. 485–486.

42. Ibid., pp. 11, 76–79; and Karl Schleunes, *The Twisted Road to Auschwitz*.

43. Compare Reitlinger's *The Final Solution*, pp. 505–517, with Hilberg's *The Destruction of the European Jews*, pp. 704–715; compare Reitlinger's *The Final Solution*, pp. 489–500, with Dawidowicz's *The War Against the Jews*, pp. 357–401.

44. Reitlinger, *The Final Solution*, pp. 272–281.

45. Ibid., p. 504.

46. Poliakov's book was not published in this country until 1954 by Syracuse University Press. Technically, therefore, Reitlinger's study was the oldest for an English-speaking audience.

47. See Poliakov, *The Aryan Myth*, especially pp. 255–325.

48. Poliakov, *Harvest of Hate*, pp. 43–46.

49. Ibid., pp. 245–262.

50. Ibid., pp. 235–236. For the entire Warsaw uprising, see pp. 229–236.

51. Ibid., pp. 281–307.

52. Ibid., pp. 263–280.

53. The revised edition was published by Holmes and Meier in 1985.

54. Hilberg, *The Destruction of the European Jews*, pp. 318–327.

55. Ibid., p. 324.

56. Ibid., p. 662.

57. Ibid., p. 121.

58. Ibid., p. 209.

59. Ibid., pp. 662–663 and 122.

60. Nathan Eck, ''Historical Research or Slander,'' pp. 385–430.

61. Hilberg, *The Destruction of the European Jews*, pp. 1–17.

62. Ibid., pp. 715–738.

63. Ibid., pp. 684–715.

64. Ibid., pp. 647–662.

65. Ibid., pp. 14–17 and 662–669.

66. Ibid., pp. 624–628.

67. Dawidowicz, *The War Against the Jews*, p. 302.

68. Ibid., pp. 15–16.

69. Ibid., pp. 26–32.

70. See Peter Viereck, *Metapolitics*; Peter Pulzer, *The Rise of Political Anti-Semitism in Germany and Austria*; and George Mosse, *Toward the Final Solution*.

71. Dawidowicz, *The War Against the Jews*, pp. 64–69, 159.

72. Ibid., pp. 106 and 161.

73. Ibid., pp. 70–87.

74. Ibid., p. 157.

75. Ibid., p. 102.

76. Rita Thalmann and Emmanuel Feinermann, *Crystal Night*, pp. 58–62 and 93–116.

77. Dawidowicz, *The War Against the Jews*, p. 190; G. E. R. Gedye, *Betrayal in Central Europe*, p. 293; Levin, *The Holocaust*, p. 77; and Habe, *The Mission*, pp. 305–306.

78. Dawidowicz, *The War Against the Jews*, pp. 118–119.

79. Ibid., p. 52.

80. Ibid., p. 154.

81. Ibid., p. xiii.

82. Ibid.

83. Ibid., pp. 341 and 353.

84. Ibid., p.346.

85. Ibid., p.352.

86. Ibid., p. 353.

87. Bauer, *A History of the Holocaust*, p. 57. For a discussion of the number slain in 1919, see Saul S. Friedman, *Pogromchik*, pp. 24–25.

88. Bauer, *A History of the Holocaust*, pp. 93–94.

89. Ibid., pp. 155–167 and 69–191 respectively.

90. Ibid., p. 246.

91. Ibid., pp. 289–290 and 296–297.

92. Ibid., p. 133.

93. Ibid., p. 136.

94. Ibid., pp. 329–330.

95. Ibid., pp. 333–334.

96. The concept originated with Temple University theologian Franklin Littell, who explained it to scholars convened at a conference on genocide in Tel Aviv in June 1982.

97. Levin, *The Holocaust*, pp. 564–571 and 535.

98. For characterizations of Senesh, Ringelblum, Bielski, and Gerstein, see pp. 679–681, 209–211, 372–373, and 306–313 respectively in *The Holocaust*.

99. Ibid., pp. 424–425.

100. Ibid., pp. 103–112.

101. Ibid., pp. 242–251.

102. Ibid., p. 511.

103. Ibid., pp. 705–706.

104. Ibid., pp. 74–94 and 124–146.

105. Ibid., p. 232.

106. Ibid., pp. 320 and 354 respectively.

107. Ibid., p. 385.

108. Ibid., pp. 268–386.

109. Ibid., pp. 667–681 and 685–693 respectively.
110. Ibid., pp. 685–688.
111. Ibid., pp. 45–58.
112. See Charles Sydnor's *Soldiers of Destruction: The SS Death's Head Division, 1933–1945*, pp. 318–319.
113. Levin, *The Holocaust*, p. 153.
114. Ibid., p. 430.
115. Ibid., p. 441.
116. Ibid., pp. 519–524.
117. Ibid., p. 511.
118. Ibid., pp. 164–184.
119. Ibid., pp. 561–596.
120. Peretz, *Peretz*, p. 328.
121. Hersey, "The Novel of Contemporary History," pp. 28–29.

SELECTIVE BIBLIOGRAPHY

[This bibliography includes, in addition to works cited in the end-notes, selected works mentioned in the essay.]

Arendt, Hannah. *Eichmann in Jerusalem*. New York: Viking, 1963.
Bauer, Yehuda. "The Goldberg Report." *Midstream*. 31. (February, 1985), pp. 25–28.
———. *A History of the Holocaust*. New York: Franklin Watts, 1982.
Bettelheim, Bruno. *The Informed Heart*. New York: Free Press, 1960.
Dawidowicz, Lucy. "Indicting American Jews." *Commentary*. 75. (June, 1983), pp. 36–44.
———. *The War Against the Jews, 1933–1945*. New York: Holt, Rinehart, & Winston, 1975.
Des Pres, Terrence. *The Survivor: An Anatomy of Life in the Death Camps*. New York: Oxford University Press, 1976.
Donat, Alexander. "Like Sheep to the Slaughter." *Out of the Whirlwind*, ed. Albert Friedlander. New York: Union of American Hebrew Congregations, 1968, pp. 50–67.
Eck, Nathan. "Historical Research or Slander." *Yad Vashem Studies*. 6. (Jerusalem, 1967), pp. 385–430.
Fackenheim, Emil. *The Jewish Return into History*. New York: Schocken, 1978.
———. *"Yom ha-shoah* Memorial Speech." Youngstown, Ohio, May 3, 1981.
France, Anatole. *Penguin Island*, trans. Belle N. Burke. New York: New American Library, 1968.
Friedman, Saul S. *Amcha: An Oral Testament of the Holocaust*. Washington, D. C.: University Press of America, 1979.
———. "Judaism: Enter the Psychohistorians." *Congress Monthly*. 46. (September-October, 1979), pp. 8–11.
———. *Pogromchik: The Assassination of Simon Petlura*. New York: Hart, 1976.
Gedye, G. E. R. *Betrayal in Central Europe*. New York: Harper, 1939.
Goldberg, Arthur and Seymour Finger, eds. *American Jewry during the Holocaust*. 1984; rpt. New York: Holmes and Meier, 1985.
Habe, Hans. *The Mission*. New York: Coward-McCann, 1965.

Hersey, John. "The Novel of Contemporary History." *The Writer's Book*, ed. Helen Hull. New York: Barnes and Noble, 1956, pp. 25–29.

Hilberg, Raul. *The Destruction of the European Jews*. Chicago: Quadrangle, 1961.

Levin, Nora. *The Holocaust*. New York: Crowell, 1968.

Livy. *The War with Hannibal*, trans. Aubrey de Selincourt. Baltimore: Penguin, 1965.

Milgram, Stanley. *Obedience to Authority*. New York: Harper and Row, 1974.

Mosse, George. *Toward the Final Solution*. New York: Harper's, 1968.

Peretz, I. L. *Peretz*, trans. Sol Liptzin. New York: YIVO, 1947.

Poliakov, Leon. *The Aryan Myth*. New York: Basic Books, 1971.

———. *Harvest of Hate*. Syracuse: Syracuse University Press, 1954.

Pulzer, Peter. *The Rise of Political Anti-Semitism in Germany and Austria*. New York: Wiley, 1964.

Reitlinger, Gerald. *The Final Solution*. New York: Beechurst Press, 1953.

Schleunes, Karl. *The Twisted Road to Auschwitz*. Urbana: University of Illinois, 1970.

Sydnor, Charles. *Soldiers of Destruction: The SS Death's Head Division*. Princeton, New Jersey: Princeton University Press, 1977.

Thalmann, Rita and Emmanuel Feinermann. *Crystal Night*. New York: Coward, McCann and Geoghegan, 1974.

Viereck, Peter. *Metapolitics: The Roots of the Nazi Mind*. New York: Knopf, 1941.

Wasserstein, Bernard. *Britain and the Jews of Europe*. New York: Oxford University Press, 1979.

FOR FURTHER READING

Dawidowicz, Lucy. *The Holocaust and the Historians*. Cambridge, Mass.: Harvard University Press, 1981.

Fleming, Gerald. *Hitler and the Final Solution*. Berkeley: University of California Press, 1984.

Mendelsohn, John, ed. *The Holocaust: Selected Documents in Eighteen Volumes*. New York: Garland, 1982.

Prince, Robert. *The Legacy of the Holocaust: Psychohistorical Themes in the Second Generation*. Ann Arbor: UMI Research Press, 1985.

Szonyi, David. *The Holocaust: An Annotated Bibliography and Resource Guide*. Hoboken, New Jersey: KTAV, 1985.

17

American-Jewish Fiction: The Germanic Reception

Sepp L. Tiefenthaler

An investigation of the reception of American-Jewish fiction outside the United States appears particularly instructive with regard to Germanic countries because a historical survey of the critical response in these countries reflects to a certain degree general trends in the attitude of scholars, publishers, and the readership toward Jewishness and Jewish writers.[1] This inquiry covers the spectrum from extreme anti-Semitism during the Nazi regime, followed by a period of tabooing and suppression in view of the Holocaust, superseded by a gradual process of coming to terms with the horrors of the historical past and feelings of guilt, to a steadily growing interest in many aspects of Jewish life, tradition, and history, including literature created by writers with a Jewish background.

This bibliographical survey attempts to suggest the range and development of the Germanic reception of American-Jewish fiction from the 1910's to the present. The term "Germanic" is used to refer to the German-language countries: Germany, including the Federal Republic of Germany and the German Democratic Republic, both established in 1949; Austria, and Switzerland. Above all, the essay focuses on the academic reception of American-Jewish fiction in these countries; to a lesser extent it takes into account German translations of American-Jewish novels and stories. A discussion of reviews in the daily and weekly press and in other media is not within the scope of this essay.

Between approximately 1910 and 1933, the year the Nazi regime gained complete control over Germany, a considerable number of works by American-Jewish writers appeared in German translation.[2] A German version of Mary Antin's *The Promised Land* (1912) was published as early as 1914; Edna Ferber's novel *Dawn O'Hara* (1911) appeared in German in 1916, followed by another six of her novels until 1933. Ludwig Lewisohn's *Up Stream* (1922) was issued in German in 1924 while translations of *The Case of Mr. Crump* (1926)—prefaced by the famous German novelist Thomas Mann, *The Island Within* (1928) and *The Last Days of Shylock* (1931) appeared in 1928, 1929, and 1931 respectively.

Myron Brinig's *Singermann* (1929) was published in German in 1930, and Michael Gold's *Jews Without Money* (1930) in 1931. During these years German translations also included novels by Nathan Asch, Lester Cohen, and Fannie Hurst. Some of the outstanding examples of American-Jewish fiction of this period like Abraham Cahan's stories or Anzia Yezierska's works have so far remained untranslated, while Cahan's masterpiece, *The Rise of David Levinsky* (1917), was not published in German until 1962 and Henry Roth's *Call It Sleep* (1934) not until 1970.

The academic reception of American-Jewish fiction in Germany in the pre-Nazi period was on the whole negligible. However, in one of the very few historical surveys of American literature written in German before World War II, *Die englische Literatur der Vereinigten Staaten von Nordamerika* (English Literature in the United States of America; 1929), Walther Fischer briefly discusses the writings of Jewish immigrants such as Marcus E. Ravage, Elias Tobenkin, and Ludwig Lewisohn, and makes some mention of Edna Ferber, Ben Hecht, and of the American-Jewish poets Emma Lazarus, James Oppenheim, Alter Brody, Louis Untermeyer, and Babette Deutsch.

The twelve years of the Nazi regime (1933–1945) affected the literary and intellectual life in Germany in a devastating way. In the auto-da-fé of books in most German university towns on May 10, 1933, not only the works of Jewish writers but also those of Marxists, pacifists, republicans, social democrats, antifascists, humanitarians, and liberals were burned. The cultural and educational policy of the Nazi regime aimed at a complete intellectual isolation of the German population and the elimination of "subversive," "un-German," and Jewish writings produced by the "enemies of the German people."

The literary policy of the Third Reich was administered by section 8 of Goebbels's "*Reichsministerium für Volksaufklärung und Propaganda*," an authority that was responsible for surveillance and censorship, and by the "*Reichsschrifttumskammer*," an institution which directed all literary activities, issued blacklists of "undesirable" authors, and passed on instructions for public libraries, publishers, and the book trade. These compulsory measures also determined the fate of many books by non-German authors. The works of American-Jewish writers were no longer translated and published; some new German translations of American-Jewish books were published abroad—for example, Nathan Asch's *The Valley* (1935) came out in a German translation in Budapest in 1935—but such publications were not allowed to be publicized. During the war practically all books from countries with which Germany was at war were completely banned. A list of books of British and American writers, *Verzeichnis englischer und nordamerikanischer Schriftsteller* (1942), was published by the "*Reichsministerium für Volksaufklärung und Propaganda, Abteilung Schrifttum*" for librarians, with the instruction to remove books by these authors from public libraries. The names of American-Jewish writers included Mary Antin, Nathan Asch, Myron Brinig, Lester Cohen, John Cournos, Edna Ferber, Joseph Gollomb, Fannie Hurst, Ludwig Lewisohn, and Irving Stone.

A far more comprehensive list of more than one thousand British and American writers of Jewish descent, *Index der anglo-jüdischen Literatur* (Index to Anglo-Jewish Literature, 2 volumes; 1938–1939), also included the names of writers whose works had not been translated into German as well as authors of scientific and other non-literary publications; it was compiled and annotated "for informative purposes" by Karl Arns, at that time professor at the University of Bochum. In the preface to the second volume of his *Index*, Arns remarks: "Our own literature has now become national again. The degree of foreign infiltration of English and especially of American literature makes evident how judaized the two Anglo-Saxon countries still are. It is this 'still' on which our great hope rests!"[3]

The fate of books written by Jewish authors during the Nazi regime, the systematic elimination of German-Jewish authors, publishers, and booksellers as well as the crucial role of Salman Schocken's publishing house in Berlin have been subjected to detailed analysis and painstakingly documented in two extensive articles by Volker Dahm, *"Das jüdische Buch im Dritten Reich"* (The Jewish Book in the Third Reich): *"I. Die Ausschaltung der jüdischen Autoren, Verleger und Buchhändler"* (The Elimination of Jewish Authors, Publishers, and Booksellers; 1979) and *"II. Salman Schocken und sein Verlag"* (Salman Schocken and His Publishing House; 1981).

During the period immediately following the fall of the Nazi regime the conditions for the reception of American literature were exceptionally favorable in Germany and Austria. As has been argued by several German literary historians, a large number of circumstances contributed to this unprecedented interest in American writers: an eagerness to make up for the intellectual deficit in information between the years 1933 (1938 for Austria) and 1945, in particular a curiosity about America and the American novel as a source of information; educational aspects like the gradual recognition of American literature in schools and universities, the installing of chairs in American studies, the teaching activities of American guest lecturers; mediating factors like the rise of the paperback industry and the need for new books to refill public and private library shelves which had been decimated by Nazi raids, destroyed through city-bombing, or left behind by refugees.[4] Above all, of course, this new interest in all aspects of American life, including literature, was the result of the political situation: essential parts of Germany and Austria were occupied by American forces, and one of the major political concerns of the Allies was denazification, reorientation, and re-education—the attempt to purge the Germans and Austrians of their Nazi past and to convert them into democrats.

The media played a role of paramount importance in the endeavor to counteract the twelve (for Austria seven) years of Nazi influence and to re-establish the prestige of American culture. One of the measures to achieve this aim was the attempt to put literature at the service of politics by way of a controlled export of works written by American authors. This phase of American cultural and educational policy has been investigated with regard to Germany in Hansjörg

Gehring's book *Amerikanische Literaturpolitik in Deutschland 1945–1953. Ein Aspekt des Re-Education-Programms* (American Literary Policy: Germany 1945–1953. An Aspect of the Re-Education Program; 1976) and in Hans Borchers and Klaus W. Vowe's study *Die zarte Pflanze Demokratie. Amerikanische Re-education in Deutschland im Spiegel ausgewählter politischer und literarischer Zeitschriften (1945–1949)* (The Fragile Plant Democracy. American Re-Education in Germany as Reflected in Selective Political and Literary Magazines (1945–1949); 1979).[5] With regard to Austria, see Alfred Hiller's doctoral dissertation, "*Amerikanische Medien- und Schulpolitik in Österreich (1945–1950)*" (American Educational and Media Policy in Austria (1945–1950); 1974).

In Germany and Austria, America houses were established to make American literature, but also works by German and especially German-Jewish authors, which had not been available for a long period, accessible to a larger public. In cooperation with German and Austrian publishing houses, the U.S. occupation forces provided the reading public with translations of American political and scientific literature; translations of poetry, drama, and fiction; and several scientific and cultural magazines. The role that American-Jewish fiction writers played within the framework of these cultural measures seems to have been quite marginal.[6] The large number of new translations of American novels and stories which appeared on the German and Austrian market between 1945 and 1949 included only a few books by American-Jewish writers, among them novels by Howard Fast, Albert Maltz, Robert Nathan, and Irwin Shaw; during the same years publishers in neutral Switzerland, which had not been affected by the Nazi regime, brought out translations of novels by Edna Ferber, Fannie Hurst, Ludwig Lewisohn, and Maurice Samuel. Out of the four important novels dealing with anti-Semitism, published in the United States between 1945 and 1948, Arthur Miller's *Focus* (1945), Saul Bellow's *The Victim* (1947), Laura Z. Hobson's *Gentleman's Agreement* (1947), and Irwin Shaw's *The Young Lions* (1948), only the last one appeared in Germany as early as 1948. Shaw's novel, however, gained a German readership not because of its thematic concern with anti-Semitism but as one of several examples of the popular American war novel. It seems symptomatic that Arthur Miller's novel *Focus*, which appeared in German translation in Switzerland in 1950, was not published in Germany until 1955, and Saul Bellow's novel *The Victim*, not until 1966. Laura Z. Hobson's *Gentleman's Agreement* has not been translated into German so far. It may be assumed that these three novels by Miller, Bellow, and Hobson, which deal with the presence of anti-Semitism in America, were not sponsored by the U.S. occupation forces because the Information Control Division believed that no books could be disseminated which disparaged the United States in any way or presented a negative image of U.S. civilization and therefore did not qualify for the literary re-education program. On the other hand, American novels dealing with the fate of Jews under the Nazi regime, like John Hersey's story of the destruction of the Jews in the Warsaw ghetto, *The Wall* (1951), appeared in German in 1951, soon after the original publication.

During the 1950's the number of translated works of American-Jewish fiction increased steadily, including novels and stories by Saul Bellow, Vera Caspary, Edna Ferber, Laura Z. Hobson, Aben Kandel, Norman Mailer, Arthur Miller, J. D. Salinger, Budd Schulberg, Jerome Weidman, and Herman Wouk. With the exception of Norman Mailer, whose German version of *The Naked and the Dead* became an extremely successful best-seller in 1950, these and many other younger American novelists were put in the shade by the work of Ernest Hemingway, who gained more popularity among the German-language readership than any other American twentieth-century author. It has been argued that the retarded reception of Hemingway and some of his contemporaries, including William Faulkner, delayed the Germanic reception of the following generation of American writers, like Saul Bellow and J. D. Salinger.[7] In how far the belated Germanic reception of Saul Bellow, Bernard Malamud, and other American-Jewish writers (both with regard to translation and to scholarly analysis) was at least partly due to a slow process of coming to terms with some of the darkest sides of recent German and Austrian history can only be conjectured. It seems rather symptomatic that most of the early post-World War II studies dealing with American-Jewish writers published in Germany were authored by American scholars who either taught as guest-lecturers at German and Austrian universities or functioned as cultural correspondents. In one of the first articles on the American novel after World War II published in the German Federal Republic, *"Der Nachkriegsroman in Amerika. Eine Bestandsaufnahme um die Jahrhundertmitte"* (The Post-War Novel in America. Stock-Taking in the Mid-Century; 1951), Irving Howe includes brief discussions of Irwin Shaw, Norman Mailer, Saul Bellow, Delmore Schwartz, and Isaac Rosenfeld, while John O. McCormick deals with Lionel Trilling and Saul Bellow in his article "The Novel and Society" (1956), published in the first volume of *Jahrbuch für Amerikastudien*.[8]

One of the first important German evaluations of the American novel after World War II was Ursula Brumm's article *"Die Kritik des American Way of Life im Roman der Gegenwart"* (Criticism of the American Way of Life in the Contemporary Novel; 1964), which incorporates a discussion of novels by Norman Mailer, J. D. Salinger, Saul Bellow, and Bernard Malamud. Brumm claims that in contrast to several novelists of the 1930's the writers of the post-war period no longer attempt to change society in a revolutionary way. Nevertheless, these novelists point out the shortcomings of contemporary American society and probe the influence which society exerts on the individual.

The same issue of *Jahrbuch für Amerikastudien* which contains Brumm's article also includes Jules Chametzky's essay "Notes on the Assimilation of the American-Jewish Writer: Abraham Cahan to Saul Bellow" (1964). This article, which illustrates the process of acculturation over three generations in the works of Abraham Cahan, Michael Gold, Clifford Odets, and Saul Bellow, deserves special mention as the first study published in a German periodical investigating American-Jewish writers as a literary ethnic group and pointing out important stages of the tradition of American-Jewish writing to a German readership.

In an early reaction to views held by the chroniclers of a Jewish breakthrough in the American novel, Wolfgang Bernard Fleischmann calls into doubt the validity of the term "Jewish novel" in his programmatic essay "The Contemporary 'Jewish Novel' in America" in the *Jahrbuch* for 1967. Basing his argumentation on a critical survey of research in the field of the American-Jewish novel, he claims that so far neither a historical approach to the "Jewish novel" nor attempts to create a stylistic, formal, structural, or thematic uniqueness for the American-Jewish novel have succeeded in establishing a genre by that name. He maintains that the Jewish milieu in works by J. D. Salinger, Saul Bellow, Philip Roth, and Bernard Malamud possesses only an exemplary status; in his view the books by these writers could contain the same plots but with different ethnic groups and perspectives.

The most significant contribution to the study of American-Jewish fiction by a German-speaking scholar so far is Kurt Dittmar's comprehensive and highly informative volume *Assimilation und Dissimilation: Erscheinungsformen der Marginalitätsthematik bei jüdisch-amerikanischen Erzählern (1900–1970)* (Assimilation and Dissimilation: Manifestations of the Theme of Marginality in American-Jewish Fiction Writers: 1900–1970), published in 1978. In over five hundred pages the book deals with more than three hundred works of primary literature, mainly novels, but also short story collections, autobiographies, and anthologies. In his introduction Dittmar offers a critical review of the major studies of the subject; on the crucial questions of definitions and typologies he draws the conclusion that the history of American-Jewish literature should be understood primarily as the genesis of the creative self-consciousness of the Jewish writer. The first part of the book is concerned with the relationship between social reality and literary convention and examines the sociocultural and historical conditions of the Jews in America and their literature. It provides a survey of American-Jewish history as well as a historical outline of American-Jewish prose. In a brief section concentrating on the concepts of marginality and alienation, Dittmar aims at de-ideologizing literary criticism. In the second part, the author employs a binary model entailing the two key concepts of assimilation and dissimilation for his investigation of American-Jewish prose. In his view Jewish writers in America have dealt with assimilation from two points of view. The first, an objective sociological approach, has produced two typical forms of Americanization, represented by the figure of the Jew as "culture hero" and by the character of the Jewish "allrightnik"; the second, a subjective psychological component of Americanization, views assimilation as a crisis of identity. The term "dissimilation" is basically used as a literary topos subsuming various self-conscious gestures of resistance to assimilation to American society and its values as well as a return to Jewish roots and a re-identification with Jewishness. The phenomenon of dissimilation is examined in prose texts which deal with the Jew as a non-conformist, as a character whose Jewishness is an affirmation of protest and self-imposed exile or of traditional Jewish culture and morality. In a concluding section Dittmar evaluates the prospects of American-Jewish literature at a time when the marginal status of Jews in America has come to an end. The erudition of Dittmar's critical analysis is equally reflected in his extensive bibliography, which includes several entries not listed in other standard books on American-Jewish writing.

The first important phase of American-Jewish literature is thoroughly investigated in Kurt Dittmar's *"Jüdische Gettoliteratur: Die Lower East Side, 1890–1924"* (Jewish Ghetto Literature: The Lower East Side, 1890–1924), one of ten articles on the literatures of ethnic, oppressed, and marginal groups in America, collected in *Amerikanische Gettoliteratur* (1983), edited by Berndt Ostendorf. After a survey of historical, sociological, and cultural aspects of this period of American-Jewish life, Dittmar charts the emergence of American-Jewish literature against the conflicts of cultural, social, and aesthetic loyalty. He concentrates on Jewish ghetto literature as "local color writing," with examples from Isaac K. Friedman, Herman Bernstein, Bruno Lessing, and James Oppenheim; on the autobiographies of Mary Antin, Marcus Eli Ravage, Elizabeth G. Stern, Rose Gallup Cohen, Elizabeth Hasanovitz, and Marie Ganz; on tendentious Jewish literature, exemplified by some novels by Edward A. Steiner, Elias Tobenkin, Albert Edwards, and Ezra R. Brudno, and in two long sections on the most original American-Jewish writers of the period, Anzia Yezierska and Abraham Cahan. In his informative *"Einleitung,"* the introductory essay to *Amerikanische Gettoliteratur*, editor Berndt Ostendorf investigates some of the general features that characterize hyphenated literatures produced in the United States and pays special attention to the literature of the Jewish group.

Cahan's major novel has also been analyzed in Peter Freese's article "From Talmud Scholar to Millionaire, or a Jewish Variant of 'Making It' in America: Abraham Cahan's *The Rise of David Levinsky* as a Comment on the Myth of Success in the U.S.A." (1985). Freese argues that the broad spectrum of themes dealt with in this novel warrants a reading of this work—at least in excerpts— in courses on immigration, ethnicity, the American dream, and American Jewry for German students. An interpretation of Abraham Cahan's short novel *Yekl* is rendered in Berndt Ostendorf's article "Marginal Men: *Jüdische und schwarze Autoren in Amerika*" (Marginal Men: Jewish and Black Writers in America; 1979), in which the development of American-Jewish literature is discussed in conjunction with the evolution of black American writing. On the basis of Marcus Lee Hansen's three-generation theory, Ostendorf argues that the literatures of these two minorities could emerge fully only after their members had achieved a high degree of assimilation. The fact that *Yekl*, first published in 1896, was rediscovered in the 1960's and adapted for the screen in 1974 corroborates Ostendorf's thesis that American-Jewish literature as a full-blown ethnic literature could only emerge in a process of renaissance and recollection.

While no works dealing exclusively with American-Jewish writers as a literary ethnic group between the two World Wars have appeared so far, most of the major figures of this period have been covered in several German studies devoted to an investigation of American literature and literary criticism in the 1920's and

1930's. Henry Roth's novel *Call It Sleep* is analyzed as one of four examples of proletarian prose in *Der proletarische Roman in den Vereinigten Staaten von Amerika (1930–1935)* (The Proletarian Novel in the United States of America, 1930–1935; 1977) by Dieter Buttjes; the author reconsiders the novel and evaluates its artistic message against the background of social history and literary tradition. In *Die "Rote Dekade". Studien zur Literaturkritik und Romanliteratur der dreissiger Jahre in den USA* (The "Red Decade." A Study of Literary Criticism and the Novel in the USA in the Thirties; 1980), Rolf Meyn includes critical discussions of a wider range of works by American-Jewish novelists, among them Edward Dahlberg, Howard Fast, Waldo Frank, Michael Gold, Albert Halper, Meyer Levin, Isidor Schneider, Lionel Trilling, and Nathanael West. Michael Gold figures again in Olaf Hansen's book *Bewusstseinsformen literarischer Intelligenz: Randolph Bourne, Herbert Croly, Max Eastman, V. F. Calverton und Michael Gold* (The Concept and Function of the Literary Intellectual: Randolph Bourne, Herbert Croly, Max Eastman, V. F. Calverton, and Michael Gold; 1977), which aims at a critique of the literary intelligentsia with regard to its interpretation of social reality. The chapter on Gold as literary critic and theoretician examines the relationship between aesthetic consciousness and utopia. The important role of American-Jewish critics in the realm of Marxist literary theory and criticism is amply documented in *Marxistische Literaturkritik in Amerika* (Marxist Literary Criticism in America; 1982), edited by Martin Christadler and Olaf Hansen, who have assembled almost fifty relevant sources ranging from literary manifestos, polemic reviews and articles, and theoretical statements to retrospective views. These texts, which first appeared between 1921 and 1952, are reprinted in their original English version and include pieces by Michael Gold, Isidor Schneider, Philip Rahv, and many other critics.

American-Jewish fiction after World War II is surveyed in Kurt Dittmar's concise essay *"Die jüdische 'Renaissance' in der Literatur der USA nach 1945"* (The Jewish "Renaissance" in U.S. Literature after 1945; 1985). Dittmar briefly explores the thematic, stylistic, and formal spectra of contemporary American-Jewish fiction, comments on the literary tradition of American Jews since the end of the nineteenth century, and then concentrates on the major exponents, Saul Bellow, Bernard Malamud, and Philip Roth, evaluating the literary presentation of the Holocaust in the works of these writers. An appendix also includes an annotated list of more than three dozen works by American-Jewish fiction writers and a selected bibliography of secondary sources. Dittmar's study is part of a collection of fifteen essays, *Juden und Judentum in der Literatur* (Jews and Jewishness in Literature; 1985), edited by Herbert A. Strauss and Christhard Hoffmann, which focuses on various aspects of the image of the Jew in German, Austrian, English, French, Russian, and American literature.

In another general study of contemporary American-Jewish fiction, " 'All men are Jews.' *Der Jude als Mythos in der jüdisch-amerikanischen Erzählliteratur der Gegenwart"* ("All men are Jews." The Jew as a Myth in Contemporary American-Jewish Prose Fiction; 1983), Manfred Markus pleads for the necessity of a historical approach to an interpretation of contemporary American-Jewish authors. Markus maintains that in present-day America the Jewish writer can define himself as a Jew only by mythologizing the Jew.

Some of the major trends in the recent development of American-Jewish prose fiction have been analyzed in Kurt Dittmar's authoritative article *"Partikularistische Gestaltungstendenzen in der zeitgenössischen jüdisch-amerikanischen Prosaliteratur"* (Particularistic Trends in Contemporary American-Jewish Prose; 1980), which introduced several less familiar American-Jewish writers to a German readership. Dittmar concurs with the argument of several critics that the American-Jewish novel has exhausted its traditional subject matter, the social and spiritual problems of marginality. However, he points out that there are certain thematic innovations which seem to disprove all speculations about the inevitable decline of American-Jewish literature. Dittmar elucidates the new group of Jewish writers in America who repudiate the humanistic generalizations about Jewish existence and strive instead to rediscover the specific ethnocultural and theological determinants of Jewish identity. This shift to a religious ethnocentricity is exemplified by the work of Arthur A. Cohen, Hugh Nissenson, Cynthia Ozick (whose fictional and theoretical writings Dittmar closely examines without neglecting the concomitant creative difficulties), and Chaim Potok in the realm of the popular novel. A similar trend is traced in the genre of the autobiography represented by Herbert Gold, Ronald Sanders, and Mark Jay Mirsky.

The subject of the Holocaust in American-Jewish literature has been approached by several German-speaking critics in various articles which examine individual works by Bellow, Malamud, and others. A detailed and judicious analysis of the literary representation of the Holocaust in American-Jewish literature is given in Kurt Dittmar's article *"Der Holocaust in der jüdisch-amerikanischen Literatur"* (The Holocaust in American-Jewish Literature; 1982). Excluding such genuine survivor literature as Elie Wiesel's novels from his analysis, Dittmar distinguishes several trends in interpreting the Holocaust experience. The humanistic, universalizing trend characterizing the American-Jewish literature of the 1950's and 1960's brought forth two versions of a universalist interpretation of the Holocaust: a version shaped by existentialist ideas, represented by Malamud's literary treatment of the Holocaust, and an interpretation based on concepts of social and cultural criticism, exemplified by Bellow, who— according to Dittmar—considers the Holocaust not a singular event but an exemplary manifestation of a radical destructiveness comparable to Hiroshima and Dresden. Dittmar suggests that the Holocaust experience is approached in a satirical vein by Philip Roth, who caricatures the re-identification of American Jews with their Jewishness as a consequence of their secondhand knowledge of the Holocaust. The group of particularistic American-Jewish writers, on the other hand, attempts to understand the Holocaust from an ethnocentric perspective as a part of the continuity of Jewish history; these writers have created a wide stylistic spectrum of novels dealing with the Holocaust, ranging from experimental actualizations of Jewish mythology (Arthur A. Cohen) to meticulously realistic historical novels (Susan Fromberg Schaeffer). A further development that runs counter to this attempt to view the Holocaust in its specific historicity is apparent in the works of gentile authors who have developed a universal concept of the Holocaust, which is turned into a metaphor and an allegory of extreme human suffering. A final step in the appropriation of the Holocaust by the dominant American culture is its commercialization in novels by non-Jewish writers like William Styron's *Sophie's Choice* (1979) and by the mass media, as in the case of the "Holocaust" television series. The literary treatment of the Holocaust in Styron's novel is subjected to a critical analysis in David Galloway's essay "Holocaust as Metaphor: William Styron and *Sophie's Choice*" (1981); Galloway suggests that in his novel Styron attempts to represent the Holocaust both as a unique instance of evil and as a complex, universal metaphor for the condition of man in a universe stripped of value.

As was true for many other contemporary American fiction writers, the Germanic reception of Saul Bellow was greatly delayed with regard to both translation of his work and its scholarly analysis. The first Bellow novel in German translation was *The Adventures of Augie March* published in 1956; *Henderson the Rain King* appeared in German in 1960, followed by *Seize the Day* in 1962. However, Bellow did not reach full recognition with German readers and critics until *Herzog* appeared on the German market in 1965. Since then Bellow has gained a firm position in the German-speaking literary world, which encouraged Bellow's German publisher to bring out translations of his first two novels: *The Victim* appeared in 1966, nineteen years after original publication, while *Dangling Man* became available in German in 1969, a full quarter century after the date of publication of the original. Since the late 1960's, German translations of Bellow's books have appeared soon after the English-language publication.

The steadily growing body of critical responses has been the subject of scholarly investigation. For example, Stephan E. Gramley's doctoral dissertation, "*Saul Bellows deutsche Rezeption. Eine Untersuchung zur deutschen Romankritik*" (Saul Bellow's Germanic Reception. An Analysis of German Criticism of Novels; 1973), deals with the process of reception of Bellow's novels by the German language press and radio and covers the period between 1956 and 1969. One of the instructive results of Gramley's study is his discussion of the treatment of Bellow's Jewishness and the Jewish elements in his novels. The reviews of the first three translated novels still seem to have been subjected to the taboo of dealing with Jewishness and generally avoided any mention of it; moreover, the blurbs of these books omitted any reference to the Jewish identity of the author and his protagonists. It was not until the German publication of *Herzog* and the novels published later on that the theme of Jewishness started to figure prominently in many reviews. It seems reasonable to assume that by the mid–1960's critics from Germanic countries slowly began to free themselves from this taboo. The response of the German press to Bellow's Nobel Prize lecture, to Bellow's oeuvre in general, and to his novel *Humboldt's Gift* in particular is explored in Manfred

Markus's article *"Bellows Vermächtnis: Zur Rezeption eines Nobelpreisträgers in der Bundesrepublik Deutschland"* (Bellow's Gift: On the Reception of a Nobel Prize Winner in the Federal Republic of Germany; 1978). Markus doubts whether Bellow's work has been read and understood adequately by German reviewers and tries to correct some of the misreadings and misunderstandings.

In one of the first German articles exclusively devoted to Saul Bellow, a review of *Herzog*, published in the magazine *Neue Rundschau* (1965), Ursula Brumm emphasizes the innovative aspect of the novel within the tradition of the American novel, the use of the intellectual as a hero, and the novel as a medium of coping intellectually with the world. Brumm does not consider *Herzog* a philosphical novel although it ranks as Bellow's intellectually most demanding novel, which, however, suffers from stylistic imperfections and fails to give adequate literary form to the theme of the struggle between the sexes with which the novel is preoccupied. *Herzog* is also the subject of Brigitte Scheer-Schäzler's study *A Taste for Metaphors. Die Bildersprache als Interpretationsgrundlage des modernen Romans, dargestellt an Saul Bellows "Herzog"* (A Taste for Metaphors. Some Aspects of Style as a Basis for the Interpretation of the Modern Novel, Demonstrated by the Example of Saul Bellow's *Herzog*; 1968). Scheer-Schäzler demonstrates how an investigation of metaphors and related stylistic features can contribute to an understanding of the content, characterization, and structure of the modern novel. The most detailed analysis of *Herzog* by a German-speaking scholar so far is the doctoral dissertation *"Die Figur des 'Helden' in Saul Bellows Roman 'Herzog' "* (The Hero in Saul Bellow's Novel *Herzog*; 1970) by Heiner Bus, who provides a systematic study of the possibilities of characterization in this work.

In another early essay on Bellow, *"Die Farbe als dichterisches Gestaltungsmittel in den Romanen Saul Bellows"* (Color as a Literary Device in Saul Bellow's Novels; 1971), Brigitte Scheer-Schäzler suggests that in Bellow's novels color is employed as a literary device which can function as a structuring instrument, a means of characterization and intensification, and a tool for signaling transcendence and ambivalence. Scheer-Schäzler also made an important contribution to the study of Bellow's oeuvre by German-speaking scholars with her monograph *Saul Bellow* (1972). Written in English and published in the Modern Literature Monographs series in New York, it offers a perceptive introduction to Bellow's writings from *Dangling Man* to *Mr. Sammler's Planet*, including analyses of his work as a dramatist and short fiction writer.

Peter Bischoff's *Saul Bellows Romane: Entfremdung und Suche* (Saul Bellow's Novels: Alienation and Quest; 1975) was the first published German-language monograph on Bellow's novels. Bischoff analyzes Bellow's first seven novels in the light of the alienation motif and explores the contemporary cultural and political milieu that influenced Bellow's work. He then concentrates on the forces that counteract alienation in Bellow's novels and are reflected in several motifs: the search for identity, the question of what is human, the American dream, and chivalric romance. Bischoff reasons that in his quest Bellow's hero does not find a solution to his troubles but arrives at an axiomatic metaphysical statement which points to a new beginning for him. Throughout his book, and in particular in his discussion of *Herzog*, Bischoff comments on the Jewishness of Bellow's work.

A comprehensive German monograph of Bellow's oeuvre designed for a wider readership rather than for a primarily academic audience was written by Walter Hasenclever, who has also provided competent German translations of many works by Bellow. His book *Saul Bellow: Eine Monographie* (Saul Bellow: A Monograph; 1978) offers many perceptive insights into Bellow's universe and presents the reader with a novel-by-novel analysis, with discussions of Bellow's short stories as well as his play *The Last Analysis*.

In her essay "Epistemology as Narrative Device in the Works of Saul Bellow" (1979), Brigitte Scheer-Schäzler maintains that in his novels Bellow undertakes an investigation of the origin and the nature of knowledge and develops a theory of the nature of knowledge, making the novel his instrument of investigation. An important thesis advanced in the article places Bellow's attempt to discover the universal in the particular in the tradition of American Transcendentalism and transcendentalist ways of thinking. The role which the extensive reflections play in Bellow's novels is also the subject of Hubert Zapf's book *Der Roman als Medium der Reflexion. Eine Untersuchung am Beispiel dreier Romane von Saul Bellow ("Augie March", "Herzog", "Humboldt's Gift")* (The Novel as Medium of Reflection. A Study of Three Novels by Saul Bellow; 1981). Zapf argues that the reflections are inextricably related to the structure of Bellow's fictional world and the experience of modern subjectivity. Zapf contends that the break between modern consciousness and modern society is at the center of Bellow's novels and is the epistemological basis of their reflective structure. He discusses three Bellow novels as examples of the novel of reflection dealing with different variations of the central break between inner and outer world, personal consciousness, and impersonal reality: the problem of broken identity (*Augie March*), broken intersubjectivity (*Herzog*), and broken interaction (*Humboldt's Gift*).

Five Bellow novels are analyzed in the context of the genre of the picaresque novel in Heidrun Knop-Buhrmann's *Die Romane Saul Bellows: Neue Dimensionen des Pikaroromans* (The Novels of Saul Bellow: New Dimensions of the Picaresque Novel; 1980). Knop-Buhrmann claims that Bellow in some of his early novels adhered closely to the figure of the traditional picaro, but in his later works he surpassed and extended these modes, thus opening up new possibilities for the neo-picaro to explore intellectual experience.

In her study of the female characters in Saul Bellow's novels, *Die Idee der Liebe: Die Frau in Saul Bellows Romanen* (The Idea of Love: The Woman in Saul Bellow's Novels; 1984), Christiane Maurer demonstrates the different functions of Bellow's fictional women in relation to the male protagonists. She maintains that Bellow's women typify certain modes of behavior and characteristics and distinguishes five essential types of women: (1) the obedient bourgeois woman, (2) the domineering woman, (3) the enchantress/seductress, (4) the decadent/eccentric woman, and (5) the (Great) Mother. Although the woman is restricted to the subordinate rank of the *sexus sequior*, she often provides a mirror for the protagonist: As a negative alter ego she functions as a passive screen on which the hero can project his own incapacities; as active, she reflects and exposes the protagonist's character and shortcomings and thereby instigates his process of cognition.

Saul Bellow's use of comedy is highlighted in "Saul Bellow's Humor and Saul Bellow's Critical Reception" (1984), in which Brigitte Scheer-Schäzler comments on some stages of the critical controversy on whether Bellow is a predominantly serious novelist of ideas or a humorous, comic writer and applies some of the deduced answers and observations to an analysis of *Humboldt's Gift* and *The Dean's December*.

The academic Germanic reception of Bernard Malamud's work happened as late as 1968 with Peter Freese's article *"Parzival als Baseballstar: Bernard Malamuds 'The Natural' "* (Parzival as a Baseball Star: Bernard Malamud's *The Natural*), in which Freese points out the numerous parallels between the career of the protagonist and characters and episodes from the real world of American baseball. He unravels a network of associations and references to the medieval legend of the Holy Grail, concluding that, through the analogies to the legendary quest, Roy Hobbs becomes a new Parzival and his story appears in turn as a timeless formulation of the theme of man's search for his identity and for self-realization. Freese also provides a first critical survey of research on Malamud's novel *The Assistant* in his article *"Bernard Malamuds 'The Assistant' "* (1972) and offers an interpretation of this work in the context of the myth of the American dream in his essay *"Ökonomisches Scheitern und moralischer Erfolg: Bernard Malamuds 'The Assistant' als Kritik am amerikanischenTraum"* (Economic Failure and Moral Success: Bernard Malamud's *The Assistant* as Criticism of the American Dream; 1984).

The first book-length study in German of Malamud's work, *Die Bedeutung der Bibel im Romanwerk Bernard Malamuds* (The Function of the Bible in the Novels of Bernard Malamud; 1977) by Ernst Engelbert, explores the function of the Bible in Malamud's novels. Engelbert provides six detailed analyses of Malamud's novels from *The Natural* through *The Tenants* focusing on biblical references and their functions within the contexts of the novels. Engelbert holds the view that Malamud uses the Bible as a major source in his novels because he is convinced that the biblical message supports his intention of keeping civilization from destroying itself. The comprehensive bibliography which lists about 350 titles functions as an authoritative guide to Malamud criticism up to June 1975.

Malamud's novels are approached from a different, motif-oriented, thematic angle in Tobias Hergt's book *Das Motiv der Hochschule im Romanwerk von Bernard Malamud und John Barth* (The Motif of the University in the Novels of Bernard Malamud and John Barth; 1978), which compares Malamud's works with three novels by Barth as examples of the college novel. Hergt concludes that in Malamud's novels the fictional college and its characters remain closely linked to empirical reality although a technique of satirical distortion may have been employed; references to university life and to the idea of social rise through education make Malamud's fictional world sociologically, historically, and morally credible.

Malamud's short stories have been covered in detail in Peter Freese's book on the contemporary American short story, *Die amerikanische Kurzgeschichte nach 1945: Salinger, Malamud, Baldwin, Purdy, Barth* (The American Short Story since 1945: Salinger, Malamud, Baldwin, Purdy, Barth; 1974). In the section on Malamud, Freese distinguishes several groups of stories: naturalistic stories set in the milieu of poor immigrants, allegorical parables and surrealistic collages, stories set in the world of the American college, and the group of Italian stories in which an American Jew is confronted with a European past or in which the artist functions as the protagonist. Freese maintains that two central themes are predominant in Malamud's stories: the emphasis on suffering as a necessary precondition for compassion and human maturity, and the insistence on the meaningfulness of the past which must be acknowledged and mastered before the present life can become worth living. One of the most original contributions to an evaluation of Malamud's short fiction is made in Renate Schmidt-von Bardeleben's article *"Bernard Malamuds 'The Lady of the Lake': Jüdisch-amerikanische Selbstdarstellung und britisch-englische Literaturtradition"* (Bernard Malamud's "The Lady of the Lake": American-Jewish Self-Portrayal and British Literary Tradition; 1981). The story is analyzed as a surprise story dealing with the self-awareness of the American Jew and as one of several Malamud stories addressing the experience of Holocaust survivors. Moreover, in an examination of literary influences, Schmidt-von Bardeleben explores the genesis of Malamud's story and demonstrates how Malamud employed the subject matter, themes, motifs, and structure of Sir Walter Scott's narrative poem "The Lady of the Lake" (1810) in his own story of the same title.

A significant aspect of Malamud's Germanic reception is the fact that more than any other American-Jewish writer Malamud has increasingly gained the status of an author whose oeuvre is considered particularly useful for English classes in high school and whose rank as an author of classic set texts for the English classroom may, before too long, match that of long-term favorites like Hemingway, Orwell, Huxley, and Golding. His novel *The Assistant* and more than a dozen of his stories have been edited and annotated in various collections designed for the German-speaking high school and college student of English.[9] The edition of the unabridged text of *The Assistant* has been well annotated by Peter Freese (1982) and is illustrated with stills from the Sender Freies Berlin television production of *"Der Gehilfe"* (The Assistant) broadcast in 1978. In a second volume of almost 400 pages, *Bernard Malamud. The Assistant: Interpretations and Suggestions for Teaching* (1983), Freese has provided a comprehensive companion to this novel and to Malamud's works in the context of

American-Jewish literature. It contains a survey of Malamud's oeuvre and a meticulous interpretation of *The Assistant*; moreover, Freese presents the most comprehensive Malamud bibliography that exists today, and in a bibliographical essay annotates lists of additional American-Jewish novels and short stories as well as significant books and articles on Jewish life in America. The fact that Freese has selected a novel that deals with essential aspects of Jewish life and culture as a model for interpreting a novel in the classroom seems of momentous significance since a reading of this work is bound to confront the young German reader with his own history.

Of the several readers and anthologies dealing with Jewish culture, literature, and society in America, aimed at German-speaking students of English, two publications deserve special mention. The booklet *Jewish Americans* (1980), edited by Siegfried Singer, contains twenty-four annotated fictional and non-fictional texts arranged under the four headings of "Immigration and Adjustment," "Religion and Society," "The Holocaust," and "The American Jew and Israel" and includes poems by Emma Lazarus, Allen Ginsberg, Muriel Rukeyser, and Karl Shapiro as well as excerpts from stories and novels by Anzia Yezierska, Philip Roth, Bernard Malamud, Saul Bellow, Harry Kemelman, Gerald Green, and I. B. Singer. A second anthology, *America, the Melting Pot: Fact and Fiction* (1978), edited by Peter Bischoff, incorporates several texts by Jewish authors like Emma Lazarus, Israel Zangwill, Elmer Rice, Michael Gold, and Henry Roth. The accompanying "Teacher's Book" by Peter Bischoff (1978) provides additional material relating to the subjects of immigration, assimilation, acculturation, and a special section on American-Jewish writers.

The Germanic reception of J. D. Salinger's work started relatively late and reached its climax in the late 1960's and the 1970's. Although a first—and rather poor—German translation of *The Catcher in the Rye* appeared in 1954, the novel did not catch on with the German-language reader until a revised translation by the late Nobel Prize laureate Heinrich Böll was published in 1962. Since then Salinger has become one of the most popular contemporary American writers for the German-speaking readership.[10] The academic response to Salinger commenced in 1960 with Hans Bungert's article *"J. D. Salingers 'The Catcher in the Rye': Isolation und Kommunikationsversuche des Jugendlichen"* (Isolation and Search for Communication of the Adolescent; 1960), which analyzes the alienation of an individual from society and the reasons for Holden's failed attempts at communication. Peter Freese offers a survey of critical opinions on this novel in his essay "J. D. Salinger: *The Catcher in the Rye*" (1968), provides a perceptive interpretation of Salinger's short fiction in his article *"J. D. Salingers 'Nine Stories': Eine Deutung der frühen Glass-Geschichten"* (An Interpretation of the Early Glass-Stories; 1968), and includes an extensive analysis of *The Catcher in the Rye* in his book *Die Initiationsreise. Studien zum jugendlichen Helden im modernen amerikanischen Roman, mit einer exemplarischen Analyse von J. D. Salingers "The Catcher in the Rye"* (The Journey of Initiation. The Adolescent Hero in the Modern American Novel, with a Special Study of

J. D. Salinger's *The Catcher in the Rye*; 1971), which also deals with novels and stories by other American-Jewish authors like Bellow, Mailer, Malamud, Budd Schulberg, Henry Roth, and Philip Roth.

Since the late 1960's numerous articles and several book-length studies on various aspects of Salinger's work have been written, including Renate Stepf's book *Die Entwicklung von J. D. Salingers Short Stories und Novelettes* (The Development of J. D. Salinger's Short Stories and Novelettes; 1975) and Karl Ortseifen's study *Kritische Rezeption und stilistische Interpretation von J. D. Salingers Erzählprosa. Studien zum Stil der frühen Kurzgeschichten und zu seinem Fortwirken im späteren Werk* (Critical Reception and Stylistic Interpretation of J. D. Salinger's Narrative Prose. Studies on the Style of His Early Short Stories and Its Continuity in the Later Works; 1979). Moreover, many readers and anthologies designed for use in the classroom include stories by Salinger and provide interpretations of his writings.

Isaac Bashevis Singer's work has been widely reviewed in the press and other media ever since the first German translation of one of his novels, *The Slave*, appeared on the market in 1965. By now most of his works, including his autobiographical volumes and some of his children's books, have become available in German. The Nobel Prize award, the film version of his story "Yentl the Yeshiva Boy," and a steadily growing interest in Eastern European Jewry have contributed to Singer's great popularity with the German-language readership. The scholarly reception of his work, however, has so far been relatively marginal compared to the non-academic reception of his writings. This regrettable fact possibly results from the small number of scholars specializing in Yiddish literature and from the reluctance of scholars of American literature to study translated versions of texts originally written in Yiddish.

Claudio Magris, a philologist equally fluent in Italian and German, has provided analyses of Singer's novels and stories in several essays, such as *"Isaac Bashevis Singer, der lebende Klassiker der jiddischen Literatur. Das Gesetz und das Leben"* (Isaac Bashevis Singer, the Living Classic of Yiddish Literature. Life and the Law; 1977), *"Randbemerkungen zum heutigen Sinn der jiddischen Literatur"* (Marginal Notes on the Contemporary Meaning of Yiddish Literature; 1979–1980), and *"Kein Unglück, ein Gespenst zu sein. Isaac Bashevis Singer zwischen Erzählung und Roman"* (No Misfortune to Be a Ghost. Isaac Bashevis Singer Between Story and Novel; 1981). In these articles Magris explores Singer's work against the sociocultural tradition of Yiddish literature and emphasizes the contemporary relevance of Singer as a writer not only of Jewish exile but of exile in an all-encompassing way. Moreover, Magris investigates Singer's work in his monograph on the Austrian-Jewish writer Joseph Roth, *Weit von wo. Verlorene Welt des Ostjudentums* (Far from Where. The Lost World of East European Jewry; 1974), first published in Italian under the title *Lontano da dove* in 1971, in which he also contributes important insights on several other American-Jewish fiction writers.

As already mentioned, Norman Mailer's first novel, *The Naked and the Dead*, gained a large readership immediately upon publication of the translation in 1950. His subsequent novels, although made available in translation often within months after the publication of the English original, have had a much slighter impact on German-language readers with the possible exception of *The Armies of the Night*. Armin Paul Frank's article *"Literarische Strukturbegriffe und Norman Mailers 'The Armies of the Night'* " (Concepts of Literary Structure and Norman Mailer's *The Armies of the Night*; 1972) deals with various concepts of literary structure and demonstrates how these can be applied to an analysis of Mailer's non-fiction novel.

The relationship between fact and fiction and the merging of these two realms have been the subject of several German studies, which invariably analyze Norman Mailer's works as one of the prime examples of the documentary novel. These studies include Dietmar Haack's essay "Faction: *Tendenzen zu einer kritischen Faktographie in den USA*" (Faction: Trends toward a Critical Factography in the USA; 1971), Erwin J. Haeberle's contribution *"Norman Mailers Reportagen (The Armies of the Night; Miami and the Siege of Chicago)"* (Norman Mailer's Reports; 1975), and Peter Bruck's article "Fictitious Nonfiction: *Fiktionalisierungs- und Erzählstrategien in der zeitgenössischen amerikanischen Dokumentarprosa*" (Fictitious Nonfiction: Fictionalizing and Narrative Strategies in Contemporary American Documentary Prose; 1977). The process of the initiation rite in two novels by Mailer is examined in Rainer A. Zwick's book *Rites de Passage in den Romanen "Why Are We in Vietnam?" und "An American Dream" von Norman Mailer* (Rites of Passage in the Novels *Why Are We in Vietnam?* and *An American Dream* by Norman Mailer; 1984), in which this phenomenon is studied along anthropological lines.

Several American-Jewish authors have so far been less explored by critics, but their writings have nevertheless been the subject of Germanic scholarship. Stanley Elkin's fiction, which has for a long time received extensive reviews in the United States, was first introduced to a German-speaking readership by Kurt Dittmar's interpretation of one of his short stories, "Stanley Elkin, 'I Look Out for Ed Wolfe' " (1976), and was given detailed attention in the first book-length study, *The Fiction of Stanley Elkin* by Doris G. Bargen (1980). She provides a biographical sketch of Elkin, attempts to place the author in the context of several contemporary American literary groups, and devotes four theme-oriented chapters to the relevance of his fiction for an understanding of man in modern American society: "Modern Man in Consumer Culture," "From Jewish Peddler to American Franchiser," "The Problem of Communication between the Hero and His Audience," and "Modern Man in Search for the Primitive." The book also includes an extensive interview with Elkin and a useful bibliography incorporating a checklist of reviews of his fiction.

Two novels by Raymond Federman, *Double or Nothing* and *Take It Or Leave It*, have been subjected to a critical investigation in Joseph C. Schöpp's article "Multiple 'Pretexts': *Raymond Federmans zerrüttete Autobiographie*" (Multiple "Pretexts": Raymond Federman's Disrupted Autobiography; 1981). The two books are understood as texts attempting to build a solid "house of fiction," yet at the same time failing in their attempt. One of Schöpp's theses relates to Federman's Jewish background; his novels are "pretexts" in the sense that they try to cover up the horrors of the Holocaust. The failed attempt explains, in Schöpp's view, the "unconcentrated" appearance of these texts.

Since the 1960's and especially during the 1970's several collections of essays on various aspects of American literature were published in Germany which in general incorporate critical discussions of American-Jewish writers. For example, *Die amerikanische Kurzgeschichte* (The American Short Story; 1972), edited by Karl Heinz Göller and Gerhard Hoffmann, includes interpretations of J. D. Salinger's "The Laughing Man" by Armin Geraths and Bernard Malamud's "Angel Levine" by Rudolf Haas, who comments on the religious-mythological references to the *Book of Job* made in the story and points out interesting similarities between the work of the writer Malamud and the painter Marc Chagall. A comprehensive handbook, *Amerikanische Literatur der Gegenwart in Einzeldarstellungen* (Contemporary American Literature in Single Presentations; 1973), edited by Martin Christadler, surveys the panorama of contemporary American literature. The Jewish novel and story is discussed in the essays on J. D. Salinger by Peter Freese, Saul Bellow by Wolfgang Peter Rothermel, Bernard Malamud by Peter Freese, Philip Roth by Gottfried Krieger, Norman Mailer by Olaf Hansen, and Joseph Heller by Walter J. Kühnel. American-Jewish writing is equally well represented in *Amerikanische Erzählliteratur 1950–1970* (American Prose Fiction 1950–1970; 1975), edited by Frieder Busch and Renate Schmidt-von Bardeleben, with interpretations of Norman Mailer's *The Deer Park* by Jürgen Koepsel, Joseph Heller's *Catch–22* by Frieder Busch, Saul Bellow's *Mr. Sammler's Planet* by Heiner Bus, J. D. Salinger's "De Daumier-Smith's Blue Period" by Karl Ortseifen, and two articles on Malamud: Hans Helmcke deals with "Take Pity," while Renate Schmidt-von Bardeleben attempts a re-evaluation of *The Assistant* by tracing the impact of the literary and Christian tradition. A wide range of works by American-Jewish writers has also been selected for *Die amerikanische Short Story der Gegenwart. Interpretationen* (The Contemporary American Short Story. Interpretations; 1976), edited by Peter Freese. This collection includes detailed analyses of J. D. Salinger's "Uncle Wiggily in Connecticut" (Horst Groene), Saul Bellow's "The Gonzaga Manuscripts" (David Galloway), Bernard Malamud's "The Last Mohican" (Peter Freese), Philip Roth's "Eli, the Fanatic" (Martin Hellweg), Irvin Faust's "Jake Bluffstein and Adolph Hitler" (Hans-Werner Wilz), and Stanley Elkin's "I Look Out for Ed Wolfe" (Kurt Dittmar).

Moreover, since the mid–1960's several studies by West German and Austrian scholars have included American-Jewish writers without necessarily considering them in the context of their Jewishness. In his book *Odyssee zum Selbst. Zur Gestaltung jugendlicher Identitätssuche im neueren amerikanischen Roman* (The Odyssey toward the Self. The Theme of the Adolescent's Search for Identity in the Contemporary American Novel; 1973) Arno Heller devotes one chapter each to Saul Bellow's *The Adventures of Augie March* and to J. D. Salinger's *The Catcher in the Rye*. Two articles concerned with the image of Germany in American literature, Marian E. Musgrave's *"Deutsche und Deutschland in der schwarzen und weissen amerikanischen Literatur des zwanzigsten Jahrhunderts"* (Germans and Germany in 20th Century U.S. Literature by Black and White Writers; 1976) and Anne Halley's *"Der 'väterliche Deutsche': Ein Stereotyp des Ausländers im Werk amerikanischer Schriftstellerinnen"* (The "Fatherly German": A Stereotype of the Foreigner in the Writings of Female American Authors; 1976), address the delicate relationship between American-Jewish writers and their views of Germany. Musgrave makes works by Saul Bellow, Ben Hecht, and Irwin Shaw part of her study, while Halley gives consideration to works by Lillian Hellman, Hortense Calisher, and Erica Jong.

Most of the more recent genre-oriented studies dealing with the twentieth-century American novel usually incorporate selected works by American-Jewish writers. The American-Jewish novel is particularly well represented in Brigitte Scheer-Schäzler's book *Konstruktion als Gestaltung: Interpretationen zum zeitgenössischen amerikanischen Roman* (Construction as Creation: Interpretations of Contemporary American Novels; 1975); chapters on novels by Philip Roth, Nathanael West, Bernard Malamud, Saul Bellow, and Norman Mailer investigate the analogous relationship between the concept of construction and the process of literary and intellectual creation in novels by these and some other writers. Dieter Meindl's investigation of the evolution of the American novel, *Der amerikanische Roman zwischen Naturalismus und Postmoderne, 1930–1960. Eine Entwicklungsstudie auf diskurstheoretischer Grundlage* (The American Novel from Naturalism to Post-modernism, 1930–1960. A Developmental Analysis Based on a Model of Narrative Discourse; 1983), provides important insights into Henry Roth's *Call It Sleep* and Lionel Trilling's *The Middle of the Journey* as well as several novels by Saul Bellow and Norman Mailer.

Since the proclamation of the German Democratic Republic (GDR) in the Soviet Zone in October 1949, GDR scholars have studied and reappraised American literature from the point of view of Marxist-Leninist theories of culture and society. At the same time the decision of GDR publishing houses to bring out books from Western countries is determined by criteria entirely different from those governing the private enterprise book market of non-communist countries. According to Karl-Heinz Schönfelder's essay of 1959, in periods of transition the major task of literature consists in ideologically re-educating its readers, in eliminating the remains of capitalist thinking, in strengthening the socialist or communist consciousness of readers, and in turning them into useful members of the new social order.[11] The major concerns and the development of American studies in the GDR are documented in numerous articles in the major GDR periodical concentrating on English and American literature, *Zeitschrift für Anglistik und Amerikanistik (ZAA)* (Journal of English and American Studies), founded as early as 1953.

As Karl-Heinz Schönfelder points out in his review essay *"Strömungen der*

neueren US-amerikanischen Literatur im Urteil von Amerikanisten der DDR"
(Trends in Recent U.S. Literature as Viewed by American Studies Scholars in
the GDR; 1984), scholars in the GDR concentrated in the 1950's and 1960's on
the intellectual and cultural achievements of the progressive forces in the USA.
The major concerns during this period included the investigation of the development of critical realism in U.S. literature and the critical analysis of the
proletarian-revolutionary writings of the Red Decade, of leftist and Marxist-
American authors and critics, of elements of socialist realism and of literature
of anti-imperialist protest. Several studies dealing with these issues also focus
on some American-Jewish authors like Howard Fast and Albert Maltz, who,
however, have never been analyzed in the GDR, in the context of their ethnic
background.

During the first years of the existence of the GDR Howard Fast was the best-
known American writer in the country; a large number of his novels were made
available in German translation and gained enormous popularity. Fast was read,
studied, and celebrated in the GDR as a representative of the other America, for
example in Hans W. K. Kopka's article *"Howard Fasts Entwicklung als Mensch
und Schriftsteller"* (Howard Fast's Development as Man and Writer; 1954). Fast
himself contributed essays on "The Literary Scene in America," published in
Zeitschrift für Anglistik und Amerikanistik (1955, 1956). Since 1957, when Fast
(who was awarded the Stalin International Peace Prize in 1954) left the Communist party in protest against the Soviet action in Hungary and against the
Russian attitude toward Israel, his works have no longer been published or
reviewed in the GDR.

Another American-Jewish writer in high favor with GDR readers and critics
in the 1950's was Albert Maltz, who is studied as an American working-class
writer in Eberhard Brüning's monograph *Albert Maltz. Ein amerikanischer Arbeiterschriftsteller* (Albert Maltz. An American Working-Class Writer; 1957),
which also includes a chapter on the proletarian drama of the 1930's, a subject
that Brüning covers extensively in his pioneer study *Das amerikanische Drama
der dreissiger Jahre* (American Drama in the Thirties; 1966). Translations of
Maltz's novels published in the GDR include *The Cross and the Arrow* (1948),
The Underground Stream (1949), and *A Tale of One January* (1965), an anti-
fascist novel dealing with the escape of six prisoners from Auschwitz.

Since the mid–1960's the range of reception of American literature in the
GDR has widened gradually. Eberhard Brüning distinguishes three major trends
and concerns for the period since 1965.[12] He sees, first, a continuation of the
critical analysis of classic American authors of bourgeois-humanist provenance
with special emphasis on revolutionary, proletarian, and socialist writers; second,
an increased attention to modern American writers, including authors of the post-
World War II period; third, a catching up with writers who had been neglected
until then. Moreover, the growing interest in contemporary American literature
benefited from the fact that the U.S. government extended complete formal

recognition to the GDR in 1974, which brought about an intensification of cultural exchange.

Several studies published in the GDR since 1965 dealing with the progressive tradition in American literature incorporate critical discussions of American-Jewish writers, like Michael Gold, Isidor Schneider, and others, including Eberhard Brüning's booklet *Die Entwicklung progressiver und sozialistischer Literatur in den USA* (The Development of Progressive and Socialist Literature in the USA; 1974) and Erich Leitel's analysis of the magazine *New Masses*, *"Die kulturpolitische Zeitschrift 'New Masses' und die Entwicklung einer proletarisch-revolutionären Literatur in den USA"* (The Politico-Cultural Magazine *New Masses* and the Development of a Proletarian Revolutionary Literature in the USA; 1976).

The beginnings of the greatly delayed reception of contemporary American fiction, including works by American-Jewish authors, in the GDR are marked by the GDR publication of J. D. Salinger's *The Catcher in the Rye* in 1965 and the anthology *Moderne amerikanische Prosa* (Modern American Prose Fiction; 1967), edited by Hans Petersen, which contains among many other texts short fiction by Norman Mailer, Arthur Miller, Bernard Malamud, Saul Bellow, and Philip Roth. In his afterword, Petersen points out that in contrast to the progressive U.S. literature of the 1930's these contemporary stories are no longer manifestations of a political commitment. In his view, the themes of the stories reflect the atmosphere in which the American writer lives: loneliness, fear of life, racial segregation, the destruction of human relationships, alienation, isolation, the stigma of failure, and the influence of money. However, Petersen argues that as critical observers of the American dream these authors have retained their position as moralists.

Since 1966 several novels and collections of stories by American-Jewish writers have been published in translation in the GDR. Saul Bellow's first novel to appear in the GDR was *Henderson the Rain King* in 1966; his second novel was *Herzog* in 1975. Malamud's novels began to become available on the GDR book market in 1970 with a translation of *A New Life*, followed by *The Fixer* in 1971 and *The Assistant* in 1974, while Philip Roth's *Goodbye, Columbus* was not in print in the GDR until 1977. Norman Mailer's *The Naked and the Dead* and Joseph Heller's *Catch–22*, which appeared in the GDR in 1967 and 1973 respectively, were introduced as contemporary American anti-war novels and highly praised for their humanist, anti-militaristic, and anti-fascist messages.

Most of the GDR studies analyzing contemporary American-Jewish writers focus on the relationship between the individual and society as well as on the projection of the image of man and the image of America presented in these works. Hardly any of these investigations, however, address the issue of ethnicity in American-Jewish writing since this question seems irrelevant to Marxist critics unless a specific ethnic group constitutes an underprivileged, oppressed class of society as in the case of American blacks, whose writings have been subjected to extensive scrutiny in the GDR. The prevailing tenor characterizing GDR analyses of contemporary American fiction relates to the criticism of American life and society inherent to these works.

The first academic analyses of contemporary American fiction in the GDR including works by American-Jewish writers were provided by Karl-Heinz Wirzberger in his article *"Der impotente Retter. Das Dilemma des bürgerlichen amerikanischen Romans der Gegenwart"* (The Impotent Savior. The Dilemma of the Bourgeois Contemporary American Novel; 1966) and in his essay " 'Great Tradition' *oder Episode? Nonkonformismus, Protest und Engagement in der amerikanischen Gegenwartsliteratur"* (Great Tradition or Episode? Non-conformity, Protest, and Commitment in Contemporary American Literature; 1968). Wirzberger evaluates works by Saul Bellow, Bernard Malamud, Edward Lewis Wallant, J. D. Salinger, Joseph Heller, and Norman Mailer against the tradition of non-conformity and protest in U.S. literature and diagnoses the psychological state of the hero in contemporary American fiction as one of isolation from society. The novels dealing with attempts to overcome man's isolation and alienation and with issues which confront the individual with society (e.g., *The Assistant*) are viewed more favorably than works in which the hero cuts himself off from the world and withdraws into a state of introspection (e.g., *Dangling Man*). The nature of the protagonist in contemporary American novels is the subject of Eberhard Brüning's critical essay *"Tendenzen der Persönlichkeitsgestaltung im amerikanischen Gegenwartsroman"* (Trends of Character Presentation in the Contemporary American Novel; 1968). Brüning argues that the protagonists in novels by Saul Bellow, J. D. Salinger, Bernard Malamud, and other writers are characterized by their experience of alienation; this manifests itself as lack of communication, isolation, and loneliness. Their protagonists sever their ties with society because they believe that only by retiring from their meaningless environment can they be guaranteed the genuine existence of individuals striving for a life determined by liberal, enlightened, and humanist principles. At the most these "non-heroes," after a long process of suffering or introspection, reach a new beginning in their lives, which, however, is never portrayed in these novels. In contrast to such novels, the protagonists in the novels by contemporary American writers in the tradition of progressive literature, such as Albert Maltz, are characterized by optimism, faith, and trust in their fellowmen, a feeling of solidarity as well as the striving for a meaningful existence for all men. These protagonists are primarily interested in comprehending the social, economic, and political conditions which should be changed to achieve these goals.

During the late 1960's and early 1970's, the first analyses of individual American-Jewish writers began to appear in the GDR. Norman Mailer is approached as a bourgeois author personifying the questionable opportunities of the late bourgeois development of art in Heinz Wüstenhagen's article *"Instinkt kontra Vernunft: Norman Mailers ideologische und ästhetische Konfusion"* (Instinct versus Reason: Norman Mailer's Ideological and Aesthetic Confusion; 1968).

Although Wüstenhagen acknowledges Mailer's criticism of war and of fascist tendencies in the American army in *The Naked and the Dead*, he observes a gradual loss of both a critical, realistic viewpoint and a progressive, humanist orientation in Mailer's later works. Wüstenhagen extends his critical comments on Mailer in the chapter *"Norman Mailer: Zwischen gesellschaftlichem Engagement und ideologisch-ästhetischer Konfusion"* (Norman Mailer: Between Social Commitment and Ideological-Aesthetic Confusion) in his book *Krisenbewusstsein und Kunstanspruch. Roman und Essay in den USA seit 1945* (Awareness of Crises and Artistic Demands. The Novel and Essay in the USA since 1945; 1981).

The first detailed analysis of a work by Saul Bellow published in the GDR was Dudley Flamm's article "Herzog—Victim and Hero" (1969), which claims that in *Herzog* a fusion of the concepts of victim and hero takes place and that Bellow's own vision necessitates an exploration of the world of the Jew who is not fully assimilated to his surrounding culture. Flamm's theses have been contradicted in the essay *"Herzog—Modell der acceptance. Eine Erwiderung"* (Herzog—A Model of Acceptance. A Rejoinder; 1969) by Peter Lucko, who argues that Flamm's interpretation is one-sided because it does not take into account the dialectical relationship between the general and the particular in a work of art. Lucko maintains that the most general constellation of any work of art is the relationship between the individual and his social environment and that in the case of *Herzog*, the central problem is Herzog's confrontation with the reality that surrounds him. Analyzing this novel merely in terms of the Jewish experience, i.e., explaining the cause of Herzog's condition as a result of the incompatibility of two different cultures, precludes the necessity of making the bourgeois society responsible for the alienation of all members of such a system and implies an apology for the existent capitalistic conditions.

A more comprehensive investigation of Bellow's fiction has been provided in Eva Manske's article *"Das Menschenbild im Prosaschaffen Saul Bellows—Anspruch und Wirklichkeit"* (The Portrayal of Man in Saul Bellow's Prose Fiction—Intention and Reality; 1973), which discusses Bellow's novels in chronological order from *Dangling Man* through *Mr. Sammler's Planet*. Manske suggests that Bellow's fiction is characterized by a discrepancy between his critical and humanist intentions and the effect of his writings within American society. These contradictions, which are most evident in Bellow's portrayal of man and his environment, demonstrate the dilemma of the late bourgeois, non-conformist writer who lacks a scientific world-view. Such a writer cannot understand the processes governing the world, nor can he envision the possibility of the individual exerting a shaping influence on the development of society. Manske argues that in the end Bellow merely resorts to an interiorized protest and a retreat to the self as a result of intellectual activity and moral self-contemplation, whereas a close alliance with the progressive forces of society appears as the necessary prerequisite for man's proving himself a humanist.

Two Malamud novels are the subject of Utz Riese's article *"Das 'neue Leben'*

ohne Neues. Zum Menschenbild in Bernard Malamuds Romanen 'The Natural'
und 'The Assistant' '' (The "New Life" without Anything New. On the Portrayal
of Man in Bernard Malamud's Novels *The Natural* and *The Assistant*; 1973), in
which it is stated that Malamud's characters are completely subject to the limitations of the imperialist social system and therefore have no prospects of self-
realization. Their retreat from socially relevant activities forces them into a state
of passivity, which brings about an increased alertness of their inner lives. Riese
argues that the endings of Malamud's novels demonstrate that the suffering of
the characters does not facilitate a genuinely new life; it merely confirms the
uselessness of a passive attitude toward a hostile social organization.

The work of Bernard Malamud, J. D. Salinger, and Saul Bellow is analyzed
in a broader context in Utz Riese's book *Zwischen Verinnerlichung und Protest:*
McCullers—Salinger—Malamud—Bellow—Capote (Between Inwardness and
Protest: McCullers—Salinger—Malamud—Bellow—Capote; 1982). One of
Riese's theses is that the writings of these authors form part of an independent
literary trend that began in the 1940's and is defined by Riese as the literature
of an inwardly turned humanity. Riese's study aims at historicizing this literature,
which in his view is characterized by a basically humanist position, a critical
distance towards the monopolistic social system, a rejection of the values of the
establishment, its search for alternatives, and a tendency to interiorize and
contemplate.

An even larger number of American-Jewish writers are explored in several of
ten essays in *Studien zum amerikanischen Roman der Gegenwart* (Studies on
the Contemporary American Novel; 1983) by Eberhard Brüning, Heinz Förster,
and Eva Manske. In his essay *"Der 'moderne Held' der siebziger Jahre"* (The
"Modern Hero" of the Seventies) Brüning includes discussions of works by
E. L. Doctorow, Erica Jong, Saul Bellow, Joseph Heller, and Philip Roth. He
concedes that many of the heroes in these novels are valuable human beings
whose suffering and mental torment demonstrate the stage of decay of their
environment but they belong to a class which no longer understands that it has
a historical mission or perspective; therefore, they accept social reality as it is.
In Brüning's view the ideological guideline followed at least subconsciously by
most of the humanist novelists is Albert Camus's concept of a tragic humanism
in an absurd world. Heinz Förster's article *"Der anti-McCarthyistische Roman*
in der Ära des McCarthyismus" (The Anti-McCarthy Novel in the McCarthy
Era) incorporates analyses of works by Norman Mailer, Arthur Miller, and Albert
Maltz, while Eva Manske completes her critical exploration of Saul Bellow, first
published in 1973, with a study of *Humboldt's Gift* in her essay, *"Das Prosa-*
schaffen Saul Bellows—Anspruch und Wirklichkeit" (Saul Bellow's Prose Fiction—Intention and Reality).

Out of the numerous GDR studies exploring American war novels, including
those by American-Jewish authors, Sigmar Pfeil's article *"Bemerkungen zu*
einigen bedeutenden amerikanischen Kriegsromanen über den 2. Weltkrieg"
(Notes on Some Important American Novels on World War II; 1965) deserves

special mention since the treatment of anti-Semitism in the war novels by Norman Mailer and Irwin Shaw figures prominently in his analysis.

The post-World War II Germanic academic reception of American-Jewish fiction, which slowly started around the mid–1960's in the Federal Republic of Germany and in Austria and in the late 1960's and early 1970's in the German Democratic Republic, has by now become an established field for the scholars of American literature in these countries as the still increasing number of studies dealing with American-Jewish writers, conferences on American-Jewish literature, and courses on American-Jewish writers offered at universities testifies. This growing concern is also demonstrated in the large number of German translations of American-Jewish writers which by now include not only almost all works by the major representatives of American-Jewish fiction, like Saul Bellow, Bernard Malamud, Philip Roth, I. B. Singer, but also the writings of many other authors, like Harry Kemelman, Grace Paley, Tillie Olsen, E. L. Doctorow, Leslie Epstein, and Cynthia Ozick. This interest in American-Jewish fiction is to be viewed as part of a growing general interest in and genuine curiosity about Judaism and the manifold aspects of Jewishness, demonstrated in the response to television films like "Holocaust," and in the enormous number of reprints and new publications on various aspects of Jewish history, culture, and literature available on the German-language book market.[13]

NOTES

[*ZAA* is *Zeitschrift für Anglistik und Amerikanistik*; *JA* is *Jahrbuch für Amerikastudien* for articles published prior to 1974, and *Amst, Amerikastudien/American Studies* thereafter.]

1. The "Guide to European Bibliography" which follows this essay includes some important works on American-Jewish fiction published in France, Italy, the Netherlands, Belgium, the Scandinavian countries, and Great Britain.

2. For the reception of American literature in Germany until 1944, see Erich Leitel, *Die Aufnahme der amerikanischen Literatur in Deutschland: Übersetzungen der Jahre 1914–1944. Mit einer Bibliographie.*

3. *Index der anglo-jüdischen Literatur*, 2 vols. My translation.

4. E.g., Rudolf Haas, "*Über die Rezeption amerikanischer Romane in der Bundesrepublik 1945–1965*"; Hans Bungert, "*Zur Rezeption zeitgenössischer amerikanischer Erzählliteratur in der Bundesrepublik.*"

5. A comprehensive collection of bibliographical material and contemporary documents dealing with the American cultural and educational policy relating to Germany between 1942 and 1949 was compiled by Michael Hoenisch, Klaus Kämpfe, and Karl-Heinz Pütz in their book *USA und Deutschland: amerikanische Kulturpolitik 1942–1949. Bibliographie—Materialien—Dokumente.*

6. The role of American-Jewish playwrights was more prominent; American plays translated into German between 1945 and 1951 include plays by S. N. Behrman, Lillian Hellman, Arthur Miller, Clifford Odets, and Elmer Rice.

7. Bungert, "*Zur Rezeption,*" p. 255.

8. This first West German periodical exclusively devoted to American studies, pub-

lished by the German Association for American Studies, changed its title from *Jahrbuch für Amerikastudien (JA)* to *Amerikastudien/American Studies (Amst)* in 1974.

9. E.g., Tobias Hergt, ed., *Four Short Stories*, by Bernard Malamud; Willi Real, ed., *"Idiots First" and Other Stories*, by Bernard Malamud.

10. The Germanic reception of Salinger has been documented in Hans Bungert, *"Zur Rezeption,"* pp. 258–259.

11. Karl-Heinz Schönfelder, *"Amerikanische Literatur in Europa. Methodologisches zu geschmacksgeschichtlichen Überlegungen,"* pp. 54–55.

12. Eberhard Brüning, *"US-amerikanische Literatur in der DDR seit 1965,"* pp. 294–295.

13. The television series "Holocaust" was shown in the Federal Republic of Germany in 1979 and later on in many other European countries; the response has been documented in a large number of books and articles; see Yizhak Ahren et al., *Das Lehrstück "Holocaust". Zur Wirkungspsychologie eines Medienereignisses. Literatur zum Judentum*, ed. Rachel Salamander (München: Literatur zum Judentum Handel und Verlag, 1983), lists 7,000 titles of German books in print on all aspects of Jewish culture, history, and literature.

BIBLIOGRAPHY

Ahren, Yizhak, et al. *Das Lehrstück "Holocaust". Zur Wirkungspsychologie eines Medienereignisses*. Opladen: Westdeutscher Verlag, 1982.

Arns, Karl. *Index der anglo-jüdischen Literatur*. 2 vols. Bochum: Pöppinghaus, 1938–1939.

Bargen, Doris G. *The Fiction of Stanley Elkin*. Frankfurt am Main: P. Lang, 1980.

Bischoff, Peter. *America, the Melting Pot: Fact and Fiction. Interpretations and Suggestions for Teaching*. Paderborn: Schöningh, 1978.

———. *Saul Bellows Romane: Entfremdung und Suche*. Bonn: Bouvier, 1975.

———,ed. *America, the Melting Pot: Fact and Fiction*. Paderborn: Schöningh, 1978.

Borchers, Hans and Klaus W. Vowe. *Die zarte Pflanze Demokratie. Amerikanische Reeducation in Deutschland im Spiegel ausgewählter politischer und literarischer Zeitschriften (1945–1949)*. Tübingen: Narr, 1979.

Bruck, Peter. *"Fictitious Nonfiction: Fiktionalisierungs- und Erzählstrategien in der zeitgenössischen amerikanischen Dokumentarprosa." Amst*. 22. (1977), pp. 123–136.

Brumm, Ursula. *"Die Kritik des American Way of Life im Roman der Gegenwart." JA*. 9. (1964), pp. 23–35.

———. *"Saul Bellow: Herzog." Neue Rundschau*. 76. (1965), pp. 693–698.

Brüning, Eberhard. *Albert Maltz. Ein amerikanischer Arbeiterschriftsteller*. Halle: Niemeyer, 1957.

———. *Das amerikanische Drama der dreissiger Jahre*. Berlin: Rütten & Loening, 1966.

———. *Die Entwicklung progressiver und sozialistischer Literatur in den USA*. Berlin: Akademie-Verlag, 1974.

———. *"Tendenzen der Persönlichkeitsgestaltung im amerikanischen Gegenwartsroman." ZAA*. 16. (1968), pp. 390–401.

———. *"US-amerikanische Literatur in der DDR seit 1965." ZAA*. 28. (1980), pp. 293–319.

Brüning, Eberhard, Heinz Förster, and Eva Manske. *Studien zum amerikanischen Roman der Gegenwart*. Berlin: Rütten & Loening, 1983.

Bungert, Hans. *"J. D. Salingers 'The Catcher in the Rye': Isolation und Kommunikationsversuche des Jugendlichen."* Die Neueren Sprachen. n.s. 9. (1960), pp. 208–217.

―――. *"Zur Rezeption zeitgenössischer amerikanischer Erzählliteratur in der Bundesrepublik."* Die amerikanische Literatur der Gegenwart: Aspekte und Tendenzen, ed. Hans Bungert. Stuttgart: Reclam, 1977, pp. 252–262.

Bus, Heiner. *"Die Figur des 'Helden' in Saul Bellows Roman 'Herzog'."* Ph.D.diss., Mainz, 1970.

Busch, Frieder and Renate Schmidt-von Bardeleben, eds. *Amerikanische Erzählliteratur 1950–1970*. München: Fink, 1975.

Buttjes, Dieter. *Der proletarische Roman in den Vereinigten Staaten von Amerika (1930–1935)*. Meisenheim am Glan: A. Hain Verlag, 1977.

Chametzky, Jules. *"Notes on the Assimilation of the American-Jewish Writer: Abraham Cahan to Saul Bellow."* JA. 9. (1964), pp. 173–180.

Christadler, Martin, ed. *Amerikanische Literatur der Gegenwart in Einzeldarstellungen*. Stuttgart: Kröner, 1973.

Christadler, Martin and Olaf Hansen, eds. *Marxistische Literaturkritik in Amerika*. Darmstadt: Wissenschaftliche Buchgesellschaft, 1982.

Dahm, Volker. *"Das jüdische Buch im Dritten Reich. I. Die Ausschaltung der jüdischen Autoren, Verleger und Buchhändler."* Archiv für die Geschichte des Buchwesens. 20. (1979), pp. 1–300.

―――. *"Das jüdische Buch im Dritten Reich. II. Salman Schocken und sein Verlag."* Archiv für die Geschichte des Buchwesens. 22. (1981), pp. 301–916.

Dittmar, Kurt. *Assimilation und Dissimilation: Erscheinungsformen der Marginalitätsthematik bei jüdisch-amerikanischen Erzählern 1900–1970*. Frankfurt: P. Lang, 1978.

―――. *"Der Holocaust in der jüdisch-amerikanischen Literatur."* Die amerikanische Literatur in der Weltliteratur. Themen und Aspekte, ed. Claus Uhlig and Volker Bischoff. Berlin: E. Schmidt, 1982, pp. 392–414.

―――. *"Jüdische Gettoliteratur: Die Lower East Side, 1890–1924."* Amerikanische Gettoliteratur, ed. Berndt Ostendorf. Darmstadt: Wissenschaftliche Buchgesellschaft, 1983, pp. 50–112.

―――. *"Die jüdische 'Renaissance' in der Literatur der USA nach 1945."* Juden und Judentum in der Literatur, ed. Herbert A. Strauss and Christhard Hoffmann. München: Deutscher Taschenbuch Verlag, 1985, pp. 367–391, 420–426.

―――. *"Partikularistische Gestaltungstendenzen in der zeitgenössischen jüdisch-amerikanischen Prosaliteratur."* Amst. 25. (1980), pp. 7–46.

―――. *"Stanley Elkin, 'I Look Out for Ed Wolfe.'"* Die amerikanische Short Story der Gegenwart. Interpretationen, ed. Peter Freese. Berlin: E. Schmidt, 1976, pp. 252–261.

Engelbert, Ernst. *Die Bedeutung der Bibel im Romanwerk Bernard Malamuds*. Frankfurt: P. Lang, 1977.

Fast, Howard. *"The Literary Scene in America, 1–3."* ZAA. 3. (1955), pp. 175–184.

―――. *"The Literary Scene in America, 4–5."* ZAA. 4. (1956), pp. 64–72.

Fischer, Walther. *Die englische Literatur der Vereinigten Staaten von Nordamerika*. Wildpark-Potsdam: Akademische Verlagsgesellschaft Athenaion, 1929.

Flamm, Dudley. "Herzog—Victim and Hero." *ZAA*. 17. (1969), pp. 174–188.

Fleischmann, Wolfgang Bernard. "The Contemporary 'Jewish Novel' in America." *JA*. 12. (1967), pp. 159–166.

Frank, Armin Paul. *"Literarische Strukturbegriffe und Norman Mailers 'The Armies of the Night'."* *JA*. 17. (1972), pp. 73–99.

Freese, Peter. *Die amerikanische Kurzgeschichte nach 1945: Salinger, Malamud, Baldwin, Purdy, Barth.* Frankfurt am Main: Athenäum, 1974.

———. *Bernard Malamud. 'The Assistant': Interpretations and Suggestions for Teaching.* Paderborn: Schöningh, 1983.

———. *"Bernard Malamuds 'The Assistant'."* *Literatur in Wissenschaft und Unterricht.* 5. (1972), pp. 247–260.

———. "From Talmud Scholar to Millionaire, or a Jewish Variant of 'Making It' in America: Abraham Cahan's *The Rise of David Levinsky* as a Comment on the Myth of Success in the U.S.A." *Das Verstehenlehren einer paradoxen Epoche in Schule und Hochschule: The American 1920s*, ed. Lothar Bredella. Bochum: Kamp, 1985, pp. 114–134.

———. *Die Initiationsreise. Studien zum jugendlichen Helden im modernen amerikanischen Roman, mit einer exemplarischen Analyse von J. D. Salingers "The Catcher in the Rye."* Neumünster: Wachholtz, 1971.

———. "J. D. Salinger: *The Catcher in the Rye.*" *Literatur in Wissenschaft und Unterricht.* 1. (1968), pp. 123–152.

———. *"J. D. Salingers 'Nine Stories': Eine Deutung der frühen Glass-Geschichten."* *Amerikanische Erzählungen von Hawthorne bis Salinger. Interpretationen*, ed. Paul G. Buchloh. Neumünster: Wachholtz, 1968, pp. 242–283.

———. "Ökonomisches Scheitern und moralischer Erfolg: Bernard Malamuds 'The Assistant' als Kritik am amerikanischen Traum." *Die USA in Unterricht und Forschung*, ed. Lothar Bredella. Bochum: Kamp, 1984, pp. 190–201.

———. *"Parzival als Baseballstar: Bernard Malamuds 'The Natural'."* *JA*. 13. (1968), pp. 143–157.

———, ed. *Die amerikanische Short Story der Gegenwart. Interpretationen.* Berlin: E. Schmidt, 1976.

———, ed. *The Assistant.* By Bernard Malamud. Paderborn: Schöningh, 1982.

Galloway, David. "Holocaust as Metaphor: William Styron and *Sophie's Choice.*" *Zeitgenössische amerikanische Literatur*, ed. Hans-Jürgen Diller et al. Trier: Wissenschaftlicher Verlag Trier, 1981, pp. 57–69.

Gehring, Hansjörg. *Amerikanische Literaturpolitik in Deutschland 1945–53. Ein Aspekt des Re-Education-Programms.* Stuttgart: Deutsche Verlagsanstalt, 1976.

Göller, Karl Heinz, and Gerhard Hoffmann, eds. *Die amerikanische Kurzgeschichte.* Düsseldorf: Bagel, 1972.

Gramley, Stephan E. *"Saul Bellows deutsche Rezeption. Eine Untersuchung zur deutschen Romankritik."* Ph.D. diss., Konstanz, 1973.

Haack, Dietmar. "Faction: *Tendenzen zu einer kritischen Faktographie in den USA.*" *Amerikanische Literatur im 20. Jahrhundert*, ed. Alfred Weber and Dietmar Haack. Göttingen: Vandenhoeck & Ruprecht, 1971, pp. 127–146.

Haas, Rudolf. *"Über die Rezeption amerikanischer Romane in der Bundesrepublik 1945–1965."* *Nordamerikanische Literatur im deutschen Sprachraum seit 1945. Beiträge zu ihrer Rezeption*, ed. Horst Frenz and Hans-Joachim Lang. München: Winkler, 1973, pp. 20–46.

Haeberle, Erwin J. *"Norman Mailers Reportagen ('The Armies of the Night'; 'Miami and the Siege of Chicago')."* *Geschichte und Gesellschaft in der amerikanischen Literatur,* ed. Karl Schubert and Ursula Müller-Richter. Heidelberg: Quelle & Meyer, 1975, pp. 232–251.

Halley, Anne. *"Der 'väterliche Deutsche': Ein Stereotyp des Ausländers im Werk amerikanischer Schriftstellerinnen."* *Die USA und Deutschland. Wechselseitige Spiegelungen in der Literatur der Gegenwart,* ed. Wolfgang Paulsen. Bern: Francke, 1976, pp. 138–151.

Hansen, Olaf. *Bewusstseinsformen literarischer Intelligenz: Randolph Bourne, Herbert Croly, Max Eastman, V. F. Calverton und Michael Gold.* Stuttgart: Metzlersche Verlagsbuchhandlung, 1977.

Hasenclever, Walter. *Saul Bellow: Eine Monographie.* Köln: Kiepenheuer & Witsch, 1978.

Heller, Arno. *Odyssee zum Selbst. Zur Gestaltung jugendlicher Identitätssuche im neueren amerikanischen Roman.* Innsbruck: Institut für Sprachwissenschaft der Universität Innsbruck, 1973.

Hergt, Tobias. *Das Motiv der Hochschule im Romanwerk von Bernard Malamud und John Barth.* Frankfurt am Main: P. Lang, 1978.

———, ed. *Four Short Stories.* By Bernard Malamud. Frankfurt am Main: Diesterweg, 1977.

Hiller, Alfred. *"Amerikanische Medien- und Schulpolitik in Österreich (1945–1950)."* Ph.D. diss., Wien, 1974.

Hoenisch, Michael, Klaus Kämpfe, and Karl-Heinz Pütz. *USA und Deutschland: amerikanische Kulturpolitik 1942–1949. Bibliographie—Materialien—Dokumente.* Materialien 15. Berlin: John F. Kennedy Institut für Nordamerikastudien Freie Universität Berlin, 1980.

Howe, Irving. *"Der Nachkriegsroman in Amerika. Eine Bestandsaufnahme um die Jahrhundertmitte."* *Universitas.* 6. (1951), pp. 1199–1208.

Knop-Buhrmann, Heidrun. *Die Romane Saul Bellows: Neue Dimensionen des Pikaroromans.* Frankfurt am Main: P. Lang, 1980.

Kopka, Hans W. K. *"Howard Fasts Entwicklung als Mensch und Schriftsteller."* *ZAA.* 2. (1954), pp. 275–294.

Leitel, Erich. *"Die Aufnahme der amerikanischen Literatur in Deutschland: Übersetzungen der Jahre 1914–1944. Mit einer Bibliographie.* Ph.D. diss., Jena, 1958.

———. *"Die kulturpolitische Zeitschrift 'New Masses' und die Entwicklung einer proletarisch-revolutionären Literatur in den USA."* *ZAA.* 24. (1976), pp. 213–225.

Lucko, Peter. *"Herzog—Modell der acceptance. Eine Erwiderung."* *ZAA.* 17. (1969), pp. 189–195.

McCormick, John O. *"The Novel and Society."* *JA.* 1. (1956), pp. 70–75.

Magris, Claudio. *"Isaac Bashevis Singer, der lebende Klassiker der jiddischen Literatur. Das Gesetz und das Leben."* *Studien zur Literatur der Juden in Osteuropa,* ed. Jacob Allerhand and Claudio Magris. Studia Judaica Austriaca 4. Eisenstadt: Edition Roetzer, 1977, pp. 83–94.

———. *"Kein Unglück, ein Gespenst zu sein. Isaac Bashevis Singer zwischen Erzählung und Roman."* *Merkur.* 35. (1981), pp. 1130–1143.

———. *"Randbemerkungen zum heutigen Sinn der jiddischen Literatur."* *Neohelicon.* 7.2. (1979–1980), pp. 203–211.

500 Sepp L. Tiefenthaler

————. *Weit von wo. Verlorene Welt des Ostjudentums*. Wien: Europaverlag, 1974. (*Lontano da dove*. Torino: Einaudi, 1971.)

Manske, Eva. "*Das Menschenbild im Prosaschaffen Saul Bellows—Anspruch und Wirklichkeit*." ZAA. 21. (1973), pp. 270–288, 360–383.

Markus, Manfred. " 'All men are Jews.' *Der Jude als Mythos in der jüdisch-amerikanischen Erzählliteratur der Gegenwart*." Zeitschrift für Kulturaustausch. 33.2. (1983), pp. 191–199.

————. "*Bellows Vermächtnis: Zur Rezeption eines Nobelpreisträgers in der Bundesrepublik Deutschland*." Zeitschrift für Kulturaustausch. 28.4. (1978), pp. 101–109.

Maurer, Christiane. *Die Idee der Liebe: Die Frau in Saul Bellows Romanen*. Frankfurt am Main: P. Lang, 1984.

Meindl, Dieter. *Der amerikanische Roman zwischen Naturalismus und Postmoderne, 1930–1960. Eine Entwicklungsstudie auf diskurstheoretischer Grundlage*. München: Fink, 1983.

Meyn, Rolf. *Die "Rote Dekade". Studien zur Literaturkritik und Romanliteratur der dreissiger Jahre in den USA*. Hamburg: Hamburger Buchagentur, 1980.

Musgrave, Marian E. "*Deutsche und Deutschland in der schwarzen und weissen amerikanischen Literatur des zwanzigsten Jahrhunderts*." Die USA und Deutschland. *Wechselseitige Spiegelungen in der Literatur der Gegenwart*, ed. Wolfgang Paulsen. Bern: Francke, 1976, pp. 119–137.

Ortseifen, Karl. *Kritische Rezeption und stilistische Interpretation von J. D. Salingers Erzählprosa. Studien zum Stil der frühen Kurzgeschichten und zu seinem Fortwirken im späteren Werk*. Bern: P. Lang, 1979.

Ostendorf, Berndt. "*Marginal Men: Jüdische und schwarze Autoren in Amerika*." Einführung in die Amerikanische Literaturgeschichte, ed. Jakob J. Köllhofer. Heidelberg: Deutsch-Amerikanisches Institut, 1979, pp. 211–245.

————, ed. *Amerikanische Gettoliteratur: Zur Literatur ethnischer, marginaler und unterdrückter Gruppen in Amerika*. Darmstadt: Wissenschaftliche Buchgesellschaft, 1983.

Petersen, Hans, ed. *Moderne amerikanische Prosa*. Berlin: Verlag Volk und Welt, 1967.

Pfeil, Sigmar. "*Bemerkungen zu einigen bedeutenden amerikanischen Kriegsromanen über den 2. Weltkrieg*." ZAA. 13. (1965), pp. 61–74.

Real, Willi, ed. "*Idiots First*" and Other Stories, by Bernard Malamud. Paderborn: Schöningh, 1981.

Riese, Utz. "*Das 'neue Leben' ohne Neues. Zum Menschenbild in Bernard Malamuds Romanen 'The Natural' und 'The Assistant'*." ZAA. 21. (1973), pp. 11–33.

————. *Zwischen Verinnerlichung und Protest: McCullers—Salinger—Malamud—Bellow—Capote*. Berlin: Akademie-Verlag, 1982.

Salamander, Rachel, ed. *Literatur zum Judentum*. München: Literatur zum Judentum Handel und Verlag, 1983.

Scheer-Schäzler, Brigitte. "Epistemology as Narrative Device in the Works of Saul Bellow." *Forms of the American Imagination. Beiträge zur neueren amerikanischen Literatur*, ed. Sonja Bahn et al. Innsbruck: Institut für Sprachwissenschaft, 1979, pp. 99–110.

————. "*Die Farbe als dichterisches Gestaltungsmittel in den Romanen Saul Bellows*." Sprachkunst. 2. (1971), pp. 243–264.

————. *Konstruktion als Gestaltung: Interpretationen zum zeitgenössischen amerikanischen Roman.* Wien: W. Braumüller, 1975.

————. *Saul Bellow.* New York: Ungar, 1972.

————. "Saul Bellow's Humor and Saul Bellow's Critical Reception." *Delta*, No. 19 (October, 1984), pp. 47–65.

————. *A Taste for Metaphors. Die Bildersprache als Interpretationsgrundlage des modernen Romans, dargestellt an Saul Bellows "Herzog".* Moderne Sprachen, Schriftenreihe 11. Wien: Verband der österreichischen Neuphilologen, 1968.

Schmidt-von Bardeleben, Renate. "*Bernard Malamuds 'The Lady of the Lake': Jüdisch-amerikanische Selbstdarstellung und britisch-englische Literaturtradition.*" *Geschichtlichkeit und Neuanfang im sprachlichen Kunstwerk*, ed. Peter Erlebach et al. Tübingen: Narr, 1981, pp. 257–271.

Schönfelder, Karl-Heinz. "*Amerikanische Literatur in Europa. Methodologisches zu geschmacksgeschichtlichen Überlegungen.*" *ZAA.* 7. (1959), pp. 35–57.

————. "*Strömungen der neueren US-amerikanischen Literatur im Urteil von Amerikanisten der DDR.*" *ZAA.* 32. (1984), pp. 247–256.

Schöpp, Joseph C. "*Multiple 'Pretexts': Raymond Federmans zerrüttete Autobiographie.*" *Arbeiten aus Anglistik und Amerikanistik.* 6. (1981), pp. 41–55.

Singer, Siegfried, ed. *Jewish Americans.* Stuttgart: Klett, 1980.

Stepf, Renate. *Die Entwicklung von J. D. Salingers Short Stories und Novelettes.* Bern: P. Lang, 1975.

Verzeichnis englischer und nordamerikanischer Schriftsteller, ed. Reichsministerium für Volksaufklärung und Propaganda, Abteilung Schrifttum. Leipzig: Verlag des Börsenvereins der Deutschen Buchhändler, 1942.

Wirzberger, Karl-Heinz. "*'Great Tradition' oder Episode? Nonkonformismus, Protest und Engagement in der amerikanischen Gegenwartsliteratur.*" *ZAA.* 16. (1968), pp. 5–24.

————. "*Der impotente Retter. Das Dilemma des bürgerlichen amerikanischen Romans der Gegenwart.*" *Sinn und Form.* 18. (1966), pp. 987–996.

Wüstenhagen, Heinz. "*Instinkt kontra Vernunft: Norman Mailers ideologische und ästhetische Konfusion.*" *ZAA.* 16. (1968), pp. 362–389.

————. *Krisenbewusstsein und Kunstanspruch. Roman und Essay in den USA seit 1945.* Berlin: Akademie-Verlag, 1981.

Zapf, Hubert. *Der Roman als Medium der Reflexion. Eine Untersuchung am Beispiel dreier Romane von Saul Bellow ("Augie March", "Herzog", "Humboldt's Gift").* Frankfurt am Main: P. Lang, 1981.

Zwick, Rainer A. *Rites de Passage in den Romanen "Why Are We in Vietnam?" und "An American Dream" von Norman Mailer.* Tübingen: Narr, 1984.

LIST OF GERMAN TRANSLATIONS OF THE PRIMARY WORKS MENTIONED IN THE TEXT

(The bibliographical data refer to the first edition.)

Antin, Mary. *Vom Ghetto ins Land der Verheissung*, trans. M. and U. Steindorff. Stuttgart: Lutz, 1914 (*The Promised Land*).

Asch, Nathan. *Das Tal.* Budapest: Biblos, 1935 (*The Valley*).

Bellow, Saul. *Die Abenteuer des Augie March*, trans. Alexander Koval. Köln: Kiepenheuer & Witsch, 1956 (*The Adventures of Augie March*).

———. *Der Dezember des Dekans*, trans. Walter Hasenclever. Köln: Kiepenheuer & Witsch, 1982 (*The Dean's December*).

———. *Das Geschäft des Lebens*, trans. Walter Hasenclever. Köln and Berlin: Kiepenheuer & Witsch, 1962 (*Seize the Day*).

———. *Herzog*, trans. Walter Hasenclever. Köln and Berlin: Kiepenheuer & Witsch, 1965 (*Herzog*).

———. *Humboldts Vermächtnis*, trans. Walter Hasenclever. Köln: Kiepenheuer & Witsch, 1976 (*Humboldt's Gift*).

———. *Die letzte Analyse*, trans. Walter Hasenclever. Köln and Berlin: Kiepenheuer & Witsch, 1968 (*The Last Analysis*).

———. *Mann in der Schwebe*, trans. Walter Hasenclever. Köln and Berlin: Kiepenheuer & Witsch, 1969 (*Dangling Man*).

———. *Mr. Sammlers Planet*, trans. Walter Hasenclever. Köln: Kiepenheuer & Witsch, 1971 (*Mr. Sammler's Planet*).

———. *Das Opfer*, trans. Walter Hasenclever. Köln and Berlin: Kiepenheuer & Witsch, 1966 (*The Victim*).

———. *Der Regenkönig*, trans. Herbert A. Frenzel. Köln: Kiepenheuer & Witsch, 1960 (*Henderson the Rain King*).

Brinig, Myron. *Die Singermanns*, trans. Lisa H. Löns. Hannover: Sponholtz, 1930 (*Singermann*).

Cahan, Abraham. *David Levinsky. Ein Aufstieg in New York. Roman aus den Anfängen der Konfektion*, trans. Gisela Breiting-Wolfsholz. Frankfurt am Main: Lorch, 1962 (*The Rise of David Levinsky*).

Ferber, Edna. *Lachen unter Tränen*, trans. Julia Gräfin Baudissin. Stuttgart: Engelhorn, 1916 (*Dawn O'Hara*).

Gold, Michael. *Juden ohne Geld*, trans. Paul Baudisch. Berlin: Neuer Deutscher Verlag, 1931 (*Jews Without Money*).

Heller, Joseph. *Der IKS-Haken*, trans. Irene and Günther Danehl. Frankfurt am Main: S. Fischer, 1964 (*Catch–22*).

Hersey, John. *Die Mauer*, trans. Ernst Bucher and Edwin Maria Landau. Zürich: Diana-Verlag, 1951 (*The Wall*).

Lewisohn, Ludwig. *Das Erbe im Blut*, trans. Gustav Meyrink. Leipzig: Paul List, 1929 (*The Island Within*).

———. *Der Fall Herbert Crump*, trans. Anna Kellner. München: Drei Masken-Verlag, 1928 (*The Case of Mr. Crump*).

———. *Gegen den Strom*, trans. T. Wolf. Frankfurt am Main: Frankfurter Societäts-Druckerei, 1924 (*Up Stream*).

———. *Scheilocks letzte Tage*, trans. Magda Kahn. Leipzig: Paul List, 1931 (*The Last Days of Shylock*).

Mailer, Norman. *Der Alptraum*, trans. Paul Baudisch. München and Zürich: Droemer/Knaur, 1965 (*An American Dream*).

———. *Am Beispiel einer Bärenjagd*, trans. Matthias Büttner. München: Droemer/Knaur, 1970 (*Why Are We in Vietnam?*).

———. *Heere aus der Nacht*, trans. Matthias Büttner. München: Droemer/Knaur, 1968 (*The Armies of the Night*).

————. *Der Hirschpark*, trans. Johanna Thomson and Walter Kahnert. Berlin: Herbig, 1955 (*The Deer Park*).

————. *Die Nackten und die Toten*, trans. Walter Kahnert. Berlin: Herbig, 1950 (*The Naked and the Dead*).

————. *Nixon in Miami und die Belagerung von Chicago*, trans. Hubert Deymann. Reinbek bei Hamburg: Rowohlt, 1969 (*Miami and the Siege of Chicago*).

Malamud, Bernard. *Der Fixer*, trans. Herta Haas. Köln: Kiepenheuer & Witsch, 1968 (*The Fixer*).

————. *Der Gehilfe*, trans. Annemarie and Heinrich Böll. Köln: Kiepenheuer & Witsch, 1960 (*The Assistant*).

————. *Die Mieter*, trans. Annemarie Böll. Köln: Kiepenheuer & Witsch, 1973 (*The Tenants*).

————. *Ein neues Leben*, trans. Herta Haas. Köln: Kiepenheuer & Witsch, 1964 (*A New Life*).

————. *Der Unbeugsame*, trans. Walter Hasenclever. München: Deutscher Taschenbuch Verlag, 1984 (*The Natural*).

————. *Das Zauberfass und andere Geschichten*, trans. Annemarie Böll. Köln and Berlin: Kiepenheuer & Witsch, 1962 (*The Magic Barrel*).

Maltz, Albert. *Geschichte eines Januar*, trans. Eberhard Brüning. Berlin and Weimar: Aufbau-Verlag, 1965 (*A Tale of One January*).

————. *Das Kreuz und der Pfeil*, trans. Kurt Wagenseil. Berlin: Dietz, 1948 (*The Cross and the Arrow*).

————. *Der unterirdische Strom*, trans. Kurt Wagenseil. Berlin: Dietz, 1949 (*The Underground Stream*).

Miller, Arthur. *Focus*, trans. Doris Brehm. Zürich: Universum Verlag, 1950. Republished under the title *Brennpunkt*. Reinbek bei Hamburg: Rowohlt, 1955 (*Focus*).

Roth, Henry. *Nenne es Schlaf*, trans. Curt Meyer-Clason. Berlin: Kiepenheuer & Witsch, 1970 (*Call It Sleep*).

Roth, Philip. *Goodbye, Columbus*, trans. Herta Haas. Reinbek bei Hamburg; Rowohlt, 1962 (*Goodbye, Columbus*).

Salinger, J. D. *Der Mann im Roggen*, trans. Irene Muehlon. Stuttgart and Konstanz: Diana Verlag, 1954. Republished under the title *Der Fänger im Roggen*, rev. trans. Heinrich Böll. Köln and Berlin: Kiepenheuer & Witsch, 1962 (*The Catcher in the Rye*).

————. *Neun Erzählungen*, trans. Heinrich Böll and Elisabeth Schnack. Köln: Kiepenheuer & Witsch, 1966 (*Nine Stories*).

Shaw, Irwin. *Die jungen Löwen*, trans. Egon Strohm. Stuttgart and Hamburg: Scherz & Goverts, 1948 (*The Young Lions*).

Singer, Isaac Bashevis. *Jakob der Knecht*, trans. Wolfgang von Einsiedel. Reinbek bei Hamburg: Rowohlt, 1965 (*The Slave*).

FOR FURTHER READING

Bock, Hedwig and Albert Wertheim, eds. *Essays on the Contemporary American Novel*. München: Max Hueber, 1986.

Link, Franz, ed. *Jewish Life and Suffering as Mirrored in English and American Lit-

*erature. Jüdisches Leben und Leiden im Spiegel der englischen und amerikan-
ischen Literatur.* [sic] Paderborn: Schöningh, 1987.
Trabert, Michael T. *Das religiöse Erbe im Frühwerk Philip Roths: "Goodbye, Columbus."* Frankfurt am Main, Bern, and New York: Peter Lang, 1985.

18

Guide to European Bibliography

Sepp L. Tiefenthaler

Apart from some additional Germanic studies, this list includes selected works on American-Jewish fiction published in France, Italy, the Netherlands, Belgium, the Scandinavian countries, and Great Britain.

Abramson, Edward A. *The Immigrant Experience in American Literature*. BAAS Pamphlets in American Studies 10. Durham: British Association for American Studies, 1982.

Ahokas, Pirjo. "Two Immigrations: Singer's 'The Joke' and Malamud's 'The German Refugee.' " *American Studies in Scandinavia*. 11.2. (1979), pp. 49–60.

Bailey, Jennifer. *Norman Mailer: Quick-Change Artist*. London: Macmillan, 1979.

Best, Otto F. *Mameloschen: Jiddisch—Eine Sprache und ihre Literatur*. Frankfurt am Main: Insel Verlag, 1973.

Bischoff, Peter. "*Protagonist und Umwelt in Saul Bellows Romanen: ein Forschungsbericht*." *Literatur in Wissenschaft und Unterricht*. 8. (1975), pp. 257–276.

Boelhower, William. "The *Fabulae Mundorum* of Jewish American Autobiography." *In Their Own Words*. 1. (Summer 1983), pp. 29–45.

Bradbury, Malcolm. *The Modern American Novel*. Oxford: Oxford University Press, 1983.

———. *Saul Bellow*. London: Methuen, 1982.

———. "Saul Bellow and the Nobel Prize." *Journal of American Studies*. 11. (1977), pp. 3–12.

Chénetier, Marc, ed. *Stanley Elkin*. Delta. 20. (February 1985). Montpellier: Université Paul Valéry, 1985.

Cohen, Sandy. *Bernard Malamud and the Trial by Love*. Amsterdam: Rodopi N. V., 1974.

Corona, Mario. "Norman Mailer." *Studi Americani*. 11. (1965), pp. 359–407.

Dommergues, Pierre. *L'aliénation dans le roman américain contemporain*. 2 vols. Paris: Union Générale d'Editions, 1976–1977.

———. *Les U.S.A. à la recherche de leur identité. Rencontres avec 40 écrivains américains*. Paris: Editions Bernard Grasset, 1967.

———, ed. *Saul Bellow*. Paris: Grasset, 1967.

Ducharme, Robert. *Art and Idea in the Novels of Bernard Malamud. Toward "The Fixer."* The Hague: Mouton, 1974.

Elbaz, André E. *Les romanciers juifs américains et les mariages mixtes.* Paris: Jean Grassin, 1972.

Ertel, Rachel. *Le roman juif américain. Une écriture minoritaire.* Paris: Payot, 1980.

Galinsky, Hans. *Amerikanisch-deutsche Sprach- und Literaturbeziehungen. Systematische Übersicht und Forschungsbericht 1945–1970.* Frankfurt am Main: Athenäum, 1972.

Gallino, Luciano. *"Lionel Trilling: critica e narrativa." Studi Americani.* 2. (1956), pp. 248–259.

Hermans, Rob. "The Mystical Element in Saul Bellow's *Herzog." Dutch Quarterly Review of Anglo-American Letters.* 11. (1981), pp. 104–117.

Hoffmann, Gerhard. "Social Criticism and the Deformation of Man: Satire, the Grotesque and Comic Nihilism in the Modern and Postmodern American Novel." *Amst.* 28. (1983), pp. 141–203.

Högel, Rolf. *"Gegenwart und Vergangenheit—ihre synchrone Darstellung in Saul Bellows Roman 'Herzog'." Literatur in Wissenschaft und Unterricht.* 14. (1981), pp. 103–115.

Holm, Astrid. "Existentialism and Saul Bellow's *Henderson the Rain King." American Studies in Scandinavia.* 10.2. (1978), pp. 93–109.

Hulley, Kathleen, ed. *Grace Paley. Delta.* 14. (May 1982). Montpellier: Université Paul Valéry, 1982.

Kritisches Lexikon zur fremdsprachigen Gegenwartsliteratur, ed. Heinz Ludwig Arnold. München: edition text + kritik, 1983–

Kroes, Rob, ed. *The American Identity: Fusion and Fragmentation.* Amsterdam: Amerika Instituut Universiteit van Amsterdam, 1980.

———, ed. *American Immigration: Its Variety and Lasting Imprint.* Amsterdam: Amerika Instituut Universiteit van Amsterdam, 1979.

———, ed. *The Intellectual in America.* Amsterdam: Amerika Instituut Universiteit van Amsterdam, 1979.

Kuna, F. M. "The European Culture Game: Mr. Bellow's Planet." *English Studies.* 53. (1972), pp. 531–544.

Lee, Hermione. *Philip Roth.* London: Methuen, 1982.

Lercangée, Francine. *Saul Bellow. A Bibliography of Secondary Sources.* Brussels: Center for American Studies, 1977.

Levine, Paul. "The Conspiracy of History: E. L. Doctorow's *The Book of Daniel." Dutch Quarterly Review of Anglo-American Letters.* 11. (1981), pp. 82–96.

———. *E. L. Doctorow.* London: Methuen, 1985.

———, ed. *The Jewish-American Novel.* Kopenhagen: Skoleradioen: Danmarks Radio, 1980.

Lévy, Claude. *Les romans de Saul Bellow. Tactiques narratives et stratégies oedipiennes.* Paris: Klincksieck, 1983.

———, ed. *Saul Bellow. Delta.* 19. (October 1984). Montpellier: Université Paul Valéry, 1984.

Lindberg-Seyersted, Brita. "A Reading of Bernard Malamud's *The Tenants." Journal of American Studies.* 9. (1975), pp. 85–102.

Lombardo, Agostino. *"La narrativa di Saul Bellow." Studi Americani.* 11. (1965), pp. 309–344.

Materassi, Mario, ed. *Rothiana: Henry Roth nella critica italiana*. Firenze: Giuntina, 1985.

Michel, Pierre. "Philip Roth's *The Breast*: Reality Adulterated and the Plight of the Writer." *Dutch Quarterly Review of Anglo-American Letters*. 5. (1975), pp. 245–252.

———. "*Portnoy's Complaint* and Philip Roth's Complexities." *Dutch Quarterly Review of Anglo-American Letters*. 4. (1974), pp. 1–10.

Miller, Letizia Ciotti. "*L'arte di Bernard Malamud*." *Studi Americani*. 7. (1961), pp. 261–297.

Mortara, Eléna. "*L'arte di Henry Roth*." *Studi Americani*. 12. (1966), pp. 231–257.

Mortara di Veroli, Eléna. "*Dal Vecchio al Nuovo Mondo: Isaac Bashevis Singer*." *Studi Americani*. 17. (1971), pp. 289–341.

Mowat, John. "*Humboldt's Gift*: Bellow's 'Dejection' Ode." *Dutch Quarterly Review of Anglo-American Letters*. 8. (1978), pp. 184–201.

Newman, Judie. "*Mr. Sammler's Planet*: Wells, Hitler and the World State." *Dutch Quarterly Review of Anglo-American Letters*. 13. (1983), pp. 55–71.

———. *Saul Bellow and History*. London: Macmillan, 1984.

Nilsen, Helge Normann. "Bellow and Transcendentalism: From *The Victim* to *Herzog*." *Dutch Quarterly Review of Anglo-American Letters*. 14. (1984), pp. 125–139.

———. "Jewish Nationalism: A Reading of Ludwig Lewisohn's *The Island Within*." *American Studies in Scandinavia* 15.2. (1983), pp. 59–68.

———. "Rebellion Against Jewishness: *Portnoy's Complaint*." *English Studies*. 65. (1984), pp. 495–503.

———. "Saul Bellow and Wilhelm Reich." *American Studies in Scandinavia*. 10.2. (1978), pp. 81–91.

———. "The Status of Waldo Frank in American Letters." *American Studies in Scandinavia*. 12.1–2. (1980), pp. 27–32.

———. "A Study of the Protagonist in *Call It Sleep*." *Dutch Quarterly Review of Anglo-American Letters*. 13. (1983), pp. 28–41.

———. "Trends in Jewish-American Prose. A Short Historical Survey." *English Studies*. 64. (1983), pp. 507–517.

Oppel, Horst. *Die Suche nach Gott in der amerikanischen Literatur der Gegenwart*. Wiesbaden: Franz Steiner Verlag, 1972.

Riese, Utz. "*Bernard Malamud: 'Die Mieter'*." *Weimarer Beiträge*. 23.4. (1977), pp. 141–155.

Rubin, Derek. "Philip Roth and Nathan Zuckerman: Offences of the Imagination." *Dutch Quarterly Review of Anglo-American Letters*. 13. (1983), pp. 42–54.

Sanavio, Piero. "Il romanzo di *Saul Bellow*." *Studi Americani*. 2. (1956), pp. 261–283.

Savona, Jeannette Laillou. *Le juif dans le roman américain contemporain*. Ottawa: Marcel Didier, 1974.

Schmitt-Kaufhold, Angelika. "The American Jew." *Nordamerikanische Literatur im deutschen Sprachraum nach 1945: Positionen der Kritik und Kriterien der Urteilsbildung*. Frankfurt am Main: H. Lang, 1977, pp. 39–46.

Schraepen, Edmond, "America in Saul Bellow's Novels." *Revue des Langues Vivantes. Tijdschrift voor levende talen*. Brussels: Didier, U.S. Bicentennial Issue (1976), pp. 263–271.

———. "Comedy in Saul Bellow's Work." Ph.D. diss., Liège, 1975.

————, ed. *Saul Bellow and His Work*. Brussels: Centrum voor Taal- en Literatuurwetenschap Vrije Universiteit Brussel, 1978.

Schroeter, James. "Saul Bellow and Individualism." *Études de Lettres* (Université de Lausanne). Series 4.1. (January-March, 1978), pp. 3–28.

Smith, Stan. *A Sadly Contracted Hero: The Comic Self in Post-War American Fiction*. BAAS Pamphlets in American Studies 5. Durham: British Association for American Studies, 1981.

Stemberger, Günter. *Geschichte der jüdischen Literatur: Eine Einführung*. München: C. H. Beck, 1977.

Stora, Judith. "*Paroles de Shlemil ... L'humour juif dans la littérature américaine*." *Revue francaise d'études américaines*. No. 4. (October, 1977), pp. 81–90.

Strano, Mario. "*La visione entropica di Norman Mailer*." *Studi Americani*. 21–22. (1975–1976), pp. 309–345.

Stringher, Bonalda. "*Edward Dahlberg e la ricerca del mito*." *Studi Americani*. 14. (1968), pp. 309–338.

Tanner, Tony. *City of Words. American Fiction 1950–1970*. London: Jonathan Cape, 1971.

————. *Saul Bellow*. Edinburgh: Oliver and Boyd, 1965.

Thomas, Claudine. "*À propos de Norman Mailer: Autobiographie et prise de parole*." *Revue francaise d'études américaines*. No. 14. (May, 1982), pp. 257–268.

Unali, Lina Garegnani. "*Introduzione a Edward Dahlberg*." *Studi Americani*. 11. (1965), pp. 271–308.

Vincent, Bernard. *Paul Goodman et la reconquête du présent*. Paris: Seuil, 1976.

Weiand, Hermann J., ed. *Insight V: Analyses of Twentieth-Century British and American Fiction*. Frankfurt am Main: Hirschgraben, 1981.

Winther, Per. "Joseph Heller on *Something Happened*: An Interview." *American Studies in Scandinavia*. 8.1. (1976), pp. 17–31.

Wüstenhagen, Heinz. "Edgar L. Doctorows 'Ragtime'. Geschichte als Roman." *Weimarer Beiträge*. 31. (1985), pp. 452–465.

Yudkin, Leon Israel. *Jewish Writing and Identity in the Twentieth Century*. London: Croom Helm, 1982.

Zapponi, Niccolò. "*J. D. Salinger e l'estetica dell' innocenza*." *Studi Americani*. 16. (1970), pp. 393–405.

Selected Reference Materials and Resources

JOURNALS AND MAGAZINES

American Jewish Archives. 1948–; bi-annually. Cincinnati: Hebrew Union College. Essays exploring American-Jewish life.

American Jewish History (formerly *American Jewish Historical Quarterly*, 1961; formerly *Publications of the American Jewish Historical Society*, 1892). 1978–; quarterly. Waltham, Massachusetts: American Jewish Historical Society. Of special interest is "Judaica Americana," a bibliography published bi-annually of journals and articles sent to the American Jewish Historical Society's library.

American Sephardi. 1966–; irregularly. New York: Yeshiva University. Contains material about American-Sephardic history and culture.

Commentary. 1945–; monthly. New York: American Jewish Committee. Issues pertinent to Jewish political and cultural life.

Conservative Judaism. 1945–; quarterly. New York: Rabbinical Assembly and Jewish Theological Seminary. The major journal of American Conservative Jewish theology.

Ethnic Forum. 1980–; bi-annually. Kent, Ohio: Center for the Study of Ethnic Publications at Kent State University. Reviews of ethnic bibliographic material including works about American Jewry.

In Their Own Words. 1983–; bi-annually. Venice, Italy: Institute of Anglo-American Literature, Universita degli Studi di Venezia. Studies on multi-cultural aspects of American and Canadian ethnic literatures, including American-Jewish literature.

Journal of Reform Judaism (formerly *CCAR Journal*, 1953). 1978–; quarterly. New York: Central Conference of American Rabbis. The journal of American Reform theology.

Judaism. 1952–; quarterly. New York: American Jewish Congress. Aspects of Jewish thought and tradition.

MELUS. 1974–; quarterly. Los Angeles: Society for the Study of Multi-Ethnic Literature of the United States. American ethnic literatures including American-Jewish literature.

The Menorah Journal. 1915–1962; bi-monthly during academic year, 1915–1927; bi-monthly, irregularly, 1928–1930; quarterly, irregularly, 1931–1952; twice a year, some issues combined, 1953–1962. Harrisburg, Pennsylvania: Intercollegiate Menorah Association. Discussions of Jewish theology, literature, history, and politics.

Midstream. 1955–; monthly, New York: Theodor Herzl Foundation. Israeli and American political culture.

Modern Judaism. 1981–; tri-annually. Baltimore: Johns Hopkins University Press. Jewish life and thought since the Enlightenment.

Prooftexts. 1981–; tri-annually. Baltimore: Johns Hopkins University Press. Contains articles about or pertinent to American-Jewish literary culture.

Reconstructionist. 1935–; eight issues a year. New York: Federation of Reconstructionist Congregations. The journal of American-Jewish Reconstructionist thought.

Sh'ma. 1970–; bi-weekly. Post Washington, New York: Eugene Borowitz. Explorations of Jewish traditions and contemporary problems.

Studies in American Jewish Literature. 1975–; semi-annually 1975–1979; annually 1980–. Kent State University. American-Jewish literature and literary culture.

Tradition. 1958–; quarterly. New York: Rabbinical Council of America. The journal of Orthodox thought.

Yiddish. 1974–; quarterly (irregularly). New York: Queens College. Yiddish literature, and the culture of Yiddish-speaking peoples. There is a combined annual issue with *Studies in American Jewish Literature.*

SERIALS

American Jewish Year Book. 1899–. Philadelphia: American Jewish Committee/Jewish Publication Society. Essays on American-Jewish political culture and problems of world Jewry.

ARBA. 1970–; yearly. Littleton, Colorado: Libraries Unlimited. Reviews of American reference books; section on Judaica.

Index to Jewish Periodicals. 1963–; semi-annually. Cleveland Heights, Ohio: Index to Jewish Periodicals. Index of selected English-language journals. Lists academic and general-interest journals.

Jewish Book Annual. 1942–. New York: Jewish Book Council of America. Emphasis on bibliographies. Deals with work in English and non-English languages.

BIBLIOGRAPHIES AND REFERENCE WORKS

Brickman, William W. *The Jewish Community in America: An Annotated and Classified Bibliographic Guide.* New York: Burt Franklin, 1977.

Bunis, David. *Sephardic Studies: A Research Bibliography Incorporating Judezmo Language, Literature and Folklore, and Historical Background.* New York: Garland, 1981.

Fox, Stuart, comp. *Jewish Films in the United States: A Comprehensive Survey and Descriptive Filmography.* Boston: G. K. Hall, 1976.

Gurock, Jeffrey. *American Jewish History: A Bibliographical Guide.* New York: Anti-Defamation League of B'nai B'rith, 1983.

Lubetski, Edith and Meir Lubetski. *Building a Judaica Library Collection.* Littleton, Colorado: Libraries Unlimited, 1983.

Mason, Philip P., ed. *Directory of Jewish Archival Institutions*. Detroit: Wayne State University Press for National Foundation for Jewish Culture, 1975.

Nadel, Ira. *Jewish Writers of North America*. Detroit: Gale Research, 1981.

Rischin, Moses. *An Inventory of American Jewish History*. Cambridge, Massachusetts: Harvard University Press, 1954.

Rosen, Oded, ed. *The Encyclopedia of Jewish Institutions: United States & Canada*. New York: Mosadot Publications, 1983.

Rosenbach, Abraham Simon Wolf. *An American Jewish Bibliography, Being A List of Books and Pamphlets by Jews, or Relating to Them, Printed in the United States from the Establishment of the Press in the Colonies until 1850*. Baltimore: American Jewish Historical Society, 1926. This work has been augmented by—among others—Jacob Marcus's *Jewish Americana* (Cincinnati: American Jewish Archives, 1954) and Edwin Wolf's "Some Unrecorded American Judaica Printed Before 1851" (*Essays in American Jewish History*, Cincinnati: American Jewish Archives, 1958).

Roth, Cecil, et al., eds. *Encyclopaedia Judaica*. 16 vols. Jerusalem: Keter, 1972.

Segall, Aryeh, ed. *Guide to Jewish Archives (preliminary edition)*. Jerusalem and New York: World Council on Jewish Archives, 1981.

Shunami, Shlomo. *Bibliography of Jewish Bibliographies*. Jerusalem: Magnes Press, 1936; 2d enl. ed., 1965; with corrections, 1969; supplement, 2d ed., 1975.

Singerman, Robert. *Jewish Serials of the World: A Research Bibliography of Secondary Sources*. Westport, Connecticut: Greenwood Press, 1986.

Szonyi, David, ed. *The Holocaust: An Annotated Bibliography and Resource Guide*. Hoboken, New Jersey: KTAV, 1985.

Walden, Daniel, ed. *Twentieth Century American-Jewish Fiction Writers*. Vol. 28 of *Dictionary of Literary Biography*. Detroit: Gale Research, 1984.

Wynar, Lubomyr and Anna T. Wynar. *Encyclopedic Directory of Ethnic Newspapers and Periodicals in the United States*. 2d ed. Littleton, Colorado: Libraries Unlimited, 1976.

LIBRARIES AND OTHER SOURCES OF INFORMATION

American Jewish Archives. 3101 Clifton Avenue, Cincinnati, OH 45220. Holdings in American-Jewish religious, political, and literary life, notably the Henry Hurwitz Menorah Association Memorial Collection; the Horace Kallen Collection; the Jacob Schiff Collection; the Isaac M. Wise Collection; and the Stephen S. Wise Collection.

American Jewish Historical Society. 2 Thornton Road, Waltham, MA 02154. Holdings in the broad range of American-Jewish history, notably the papers of Bernard Felsenthal, Rebecca Gratz, Emma Lazarus, and Isaac Leeser; and the records of the Baron de Hirsch Fund.

Association of Jewish Libraries. National Foundation for Jewish Culture. 122 East 42nd St., New York, NY 10017. Helps to disseminate information relevant to Jewish librarianship and to encourage publication of work pertinent to this career.

Jewish Division, New York Public Library. Fifth Avenue and 42nd St., New York, NY 10018. Holdings of Hebrew and Yiddish journals and newspapers including some printed in America; has the complete set of *La Vara* and *La America*, American-

Ladino newspapers. Also, holdings of Yiddish manuscripts, notably the Boris Thomashefsky collection.

Library of the Jewish Theological Seminary. 3080 Broadway, New York, NY 10027. Holdings in theology, American-Jewish community life, Yiddish writers, and American-Jewish history, notably the papers of Louis Ginzberg, of the Jewish Information Bureau of Greater New York, and of N. Minkoff.

William E. Wiener Oral History Library. American Jewish Committe. Institute of Human Relations. 165 East 56th St. New York, NY 10022. Material in modern American-Jewish life, notably oral histories of Holocaust survivors; American civil rights struggles; and Eastern-European Jewish communities. Among the figures in the collection are Otto Bettman, Arthur Miller, Alfred Kazin, and Theodore Reik.

YIVO Institute for Jewish Research. 1048 Fifth Avenue, New York, NY 10028. The major American archive for Yiddish language and literature. Holdings in European and American-Yiddish literature and letters, notably various papers of S. Niger, M. L. Halpern, A. Glantz-Leyeles (Glantz, Glanz), Morris Rosenfeld, and Morris Winchevsky (Vinchevski).

Index

Contributors and Advisors

CONTRIBUTORS

DOROTHY SEIDMAN BILIK is an Associate Professor of Yiddish language and literature in the University of Maryland's Department of Germanic and Slavic Literatures. The author of *Immigrant-Survivors: Post-Holocaust Consciousness in Recent Jewish American Fiction*, she is currently working on a study of the image of the German in Yiddish literature.

DAVID MARTIN FINE is Professor of English and American Studies at California State University, Long Beach. He has written *The City, the Immigrant and American Fiction* as well as essays on the tenement tale and the immigrant-Jewish literary imagination.

HANNAH BERLINER FISCHTHAL teaches English composition and literature at Hofstra University. She has written bibliographies of Yiddish literature in English translation and a study of I. J. Singer and has served as assistant editor of *Yiddish* and *Modern Jewish Studies Annual*.

LEWIS FRIED is an Associate Professor of English at Kent State University. He has written essays on the significance of the Jew for nineteenth-century writers; on the brothers Singer; and, with Sanford Marovitz, a bibliography of Abraham Cahan.

SAUL S. FRIEDMAN is a Professor in the Department of History at Youngstown State University. He is the author of *No Haven for the Oppressed*; *Pogromchik*; *Amcha: An Oral History of the Holocaust*; and *The Oberammergau Passion*

Play. He has also been a producer-writer for three Holocaust television documentaries.

R. BARBARA GITENSTEIN is Chairperson of the Department of English at the State University of New York at Oswego. She has written essays on Bellow, Malamud, Ozick, and other American-Jewish writers. Her most recent work is *Apocalyptic Messianism and Contemporary Jewish-American Poetry*.

KATHRYN HELLERSTEIN is a post-doctoral Research Fellow in the Department of Germanic Languages at the University of Pennsylvania. She translated, edited, and wrote the "Introduction" to *In New York: A Selection* (Yiddish poems by Moyshe Leyb Halpern). She is currently writing a book on women Yiddish poets.

JOSEPH C. LANDIS is Professor Emeritus (English) at Queens College, CUNY. He is a founding editor of *Yiddish* and an editor of *Die Zukunft*. He has translated and edited *Great Jewish Plays* and edited *Memoirs of the Yiddish Stage* and *Aspects of I. B. Singer*.

BONNIE K. LYONS is an Associate Professor in the Department of English, University of Texas at San Antonio. She has written essays on Bellow, Olsen, Ozick, Isaac Rosenfeld, Henry Roth, Delmore Schwartz, and other American-Jewish writers and is the author of *Henry Roth: The Man and His Work*.

SANFORD MAROVITZ is Professor of English at Kent State University. He has written studies of Abraham Cahan, Chaim Potok, Edward Lewis Wallant, and with Lewis Fried, a bibliography of Cahan. He is Associate Editor of *Studies in American Jewish Literature*.

ASHER Z. MILBAUER is an Associate Professor in the Department of English, Florida International University. He has written *Transcending Exile: Conrad, Nabokov, I. B. Singer*. He is co-editor of a collection of essays entitled *Reading Philip Roth*.

RABBI DAVID POLISH was past president of the Central Conference of American Rabbis, and is the founding rabbi of *Beth Emet*, the Free Synagogue in Evanston, Illinois. He is the author of *Israel, Nation and People; Renew Our Days*; and *The Higher Freedom*. He has written essays on post-Holocaust Zionism and the Reform rabbinate.

STEVEN J. RUBIN is Professor of English at the University of South Florida. He is the author of *Meyer Levin* and has written essays on Mary Antin, Bernard

Malamud, Philip Roth, and I. B. Singer. He is completing an anthology of American-Jewish autobiographies.

ELLEN SCHIFF is Professor of French and Comparative Literature at North Adams State College. She has written *From Stereotype to Metaphor: The Jew in Contemporary Drama* as well as essays on Jews and the theatre.

GERSHON SHAKED is Professor of German and Comparative Literature at the Hebrew University in Jerusalem. His most recent book is *Die Macht der Identitat: Essays uber judische Schriftsteller*. Currently he is a visiting professor at the Jewish Theological Seminary and Columbia University.

SEPP TIEFENTHALER is *Universitatsassistent* in the Department of American Studies, University of Innsbruck. He is the author of *Jerzy Kosinski: Eine Einfuhrung in sein Werk* and has co-edited a collection of essays on American thought and literature, *Forms of the American Imagination: Beitrage zur neueren amerikanischen Literatur*. At present, he is completing a book on the history of American-Jewish literature.

RABBI ARNOLD JACOB WOLF is affiliated with KAM Isaiah Israel Congregation in Chicago. He has written *Challenge to Confirmands*; *Rediscovering Judaism* and *What Is Man?* He has taught at Yale University and Hebrew Union College and now teaches at the University of Chicago Divinity School.

ADVISORY EDITORS

GENE BROWN was an editor at Arno Press, and is an Associate Editor with Morningside Editorial Associates. He is the author of six books and has collaborated on several others.

JULES CHAMETZKY is a Professor of English and Director of the Institute for Advanced Study in the Humanities at the University of Massachusetts (Amherst). He is the author of *From the Ghetto: The Fiction of Abraham Cahan* and *Our Decentralized Literature*. He has co-edited *Black and White in American Culture*.

LOUIS HARAP is an editor of *Jewish Currents*. He is the author of *Social Roots of the Arts*; *The Image of the Jew in American Literature: From Early Republic to Mass Immigration*; *Creative Awakening: The Jewish Presence in Twentieth-Century American Literature, 1900–1940; In the Mainstream: The Jewish Presence in Twentieth-Century American Literature, 1950s–1980s*; and *Dramatic Encounters: The Jewish Presence in Twentieth-Century American Drama, Poetry, and Humor and the Black-Jewish Literary Relationship* (Greenwood Press, 1987).